Thomas R. Nevin, associate professor of classical languages at John Carroll University, is author of *Irving Babbitt: An Intellectual Study.*

SIMONE WEIL

Thomas R. Nevin

The University of North Carolina Press

Chapel Hill and London

SIMONE WEIL

Portrait of a Self-Exiled Jew

Library of Congress Cataloging-in-Publication Data

Nevin, Thomas R., 1944–

Simone Weil : portrait of a self-exiled Jew / by Thomas R. Nevin.

p. cm.

Includes bibliographical references and index.

ISBN 0-8078-1999-9 (cloth : alk. paper)

1. Weil, Simone, 1909–1943. 2. Weil, Simone, 1909–1943—Religion. 3. Philosophers—France—Biography. I. Title.

B2430.W474N48 1991

194—dc20

[B] 91-9784

CIP

The paper in this book meets the guidelines for permanence and durability of the Committee on Production Guidelines for Book Longevity of the Council on Library Resources.

Design by April Leidig-Higgins

Manufactured in the United States of America

95 94 93 92 91 5 4 3 2 1

Frontis illustration of Simone Weil by Richard A. Masters

For Austin, Toby, Elodie, and Miranda

CONTENTS

PREFACE

> Comprendre un auteur, c'est, non pas l'exposer, le développer en surface, mais le construire suivant la proportion vraie des parties qu'il contient. C'est mettre à la base celles qui supportent les autres et qui portent en elles, dans leur idée, tout l'édifice, tandis que les parties les plus en vue, celles qu'on regarde plus souvent que les autres parce qu'elles représentent les questions ou les points de vue les plus familiers, et d'après lesquelles on essaie de caractériser l'ensemble, n'ont pas de sens en elles-mêmes, et, par suite, comportent les interprétations les plus contraires.
>
> JULES LAGNEAU, "Quelques notes sur Spinoza"

The challenge in Lagneau's remarks proves imposing but indispensable to any study of Simone Weil. Nearly fifty years after her death she continues to be generally regarded—one cannot say known—according to "les questions ou les points de vue les plus familiers." These views, or to use a term that in Weil's lexicon was negative, these perspectives have arisen chiefly from caricatured facts about her life and from two of her works which have exerted a disproportionate influence in shaping her reputation: *La pesanteur et la grâce* and *Attente de Dieu*, both of them edited by enthusiastic and not disinterested friends. The two standard French biographies, both competent, inclusive, and generously documented, are not wholly free of hagiographic language. In consequence, primary and secondary literature alike have contributed to the formation of unreflected and useless tags, whatever their positive or negative ring: mystic, heretic, gnostic, saint.

How, then, can one attain "la proportion vraie," in Lagneau's words, or, in Matthew Arnold's, "the rounded estimate?" Quite helpfully, Weil herself in reviewing a biography of Marx identified the Scylla and Charybdis awaiting the presumptuous. She commends the author, Otto Rühle, for having escaped "one of the dangers which menace all biographers of great men . . . the danger of writing something too much like a saint's life." But Rühle fell victim, she thought, to the opposing hazard, stressing Marx's personal faults and thus effacing all that was of singular merit and superiority in his subject. As to the truly great, "it is in their work that they have put the best of themselves."

Weil wished to be assessed not for her life (she said it was of no importance) but for the worth of the ideas she propounded and for which she felt herself to be a mere cipher. Although a kind of topography of her mind, this study does not pay heed to her wish. Her thought is inextricably bound to her life and her dramatic times. I believe that it is necessary to weather not only the severity of her thoughts, her opinions, and her prejudices but to examine the basis of her entertaining them, and that requires historical focus.

Accordingly, in concession to Charles-Augustin Sainte-Beuve, I have attempted to indicate something of the milieux in which Weil lived and worked and wrote. Nothing could be more disastrous than the abstraction of her ideas from the times in which she conceived and developed them, especially given her own relentless dedication to experience as the home base of thought. Her "Journal d'usine," the daily record of her months in factory work, is only the most vivid example of a compelling but easily forgotten fact about all of Weil's writings, that they are commentaries on her time. Take, for example, one of her better-known essays, "L'*Iliade* ou le poème de la force." It is not about Homer's Troy but about what war in the twentieth century should teach us. Its true context is not to be found at Ilium but at Compiègne in June 1940. Or take so vast a topic as her theology. Is it incidental that all of her writing on God, religion, and the Christian church issued from the Vichy years? What can that consistently ignored fact tell us?

These remarks do not mean, of course, that Weil's writings are merely commentaries on the age. A milieu, intellectual or otherwise, may provide the mode of a philosophy, but it will not furnish all of its substance. Both are necessary objects of study, and a biography of the mind loses nothing in being as well a biography of a time. That truism holds special value in reference to Weil's generation, for which the Spanish civil war, the Popular Front, the ascendance of Hitlerism, and the Vichy years were not mere backdrops but definitive events.

This study addresses Weil's writings—many of them not yet published or translated—in the hope of presenting her thinking, to use Sartre's words, "in situation." That thinking is not without flaws (some of them profound), but such flaws do not detract from her stature; rather, they serve as credible and necessary dimensions of it. Her many virtues will speak for themselves, but one deserves notice here: her absolute intellectual integrity. This quality abides in all her work. It is made transparent by the almost ingenuous limpidity of her prose. It would be difficult to number many thinkers of this century who while demanding a great deal of reflection from the reader invite that reader so straightforwardly to the effort.

Finally, *caveat lector*, this study is not about an *anima naturaliter christiana*, a Christian or Christian manqué. From first to last I have been concerned with Weil as a Jew. It is the fact that she was a Jew which provides much of the discussion, in Lagneau's phrase, "à la base." It is true that she did not consider herself a Jew, did not want to be one, and placed herself with considerable advertisement in the Christian "inspiration." Yet a Jew she was, not in any racial sense (which we have learned to regard as spurious) or in a religious sense (Judaism is more than a religion, and her upbringing was nonobservant) but in a historical sense. Like Henri Bergson, Kurt Tucholsky, Walter Benjamin, Jean Améry, Primo Levi, and countless others who were nonobservant or freethinking, she became a "catastrophe Jew." The term is Améry's and denotes the Jew astray from Judaism or forgetful of it, to whom fate gave a harsh awakening. In Weil's story that awakening proved an unbearable lesson.

Having been born a Jew, a Jew by ancestral destiny, she did not have the freedom to choose to be a Jew. Apparently she resented and rejected that constraint, and yet, as I hope the following pages will demonstrate, much that is most positive in both her life and her writing suggests an *anima naturaliter judaica*.

This view may not be welcome to some readers, but then Weil herself has never been able to please everyone. What she does do is excite people one way or another. To judge from the hundreds of essays and reviews on Weil and her works, it would seem impossible for anyone to be left indifferent toward her. In the nearly fifty years since her death she has continued to be an object of contempt and adoration, of indulgence and scorn. Charles de Gaulle's dismissal, "Elle est folle!" is well known. Pope Paul VI claimed her as one of the three definitive influences on his life. T. S. Eliot considered her a genius, and Graham Greene saw in her an impetuous adolescent. George Steiner has found her "perverse," and Malcolm Muggeridge has written of her as one of "the lights in our darkness." She has been mentioned in countless inspirational tracts and in a long, impassioned book she has been compared to Hitler. Such reactions, judgments, and impressions could be documented indefinitely; indeed, the mass of literature about her threatens to get out of hand.

All of this signifies that a history of Weil's reputation, a *Rezeptionsgeschichte*, would amount to a lengthy, ever-lengthening book, one that would rival René Etiemble's study of the Rimbaud legend. It is a book that deserves to be written. The bibliographical annotations I have provided at the end of this volume will perhaps encourage someone to climb the mountain of that effort.

Although this study is not a biography, it charts roughly a chronological progression. After a brief overview of Weil's life, I address what I have called her education through the 1930s. It began with Emile Chartier, known by his nom de plume, Alain, her teacher at Lycée Henri IV and the definitive influence on her thinking. Subsequently, it included her schooling in the harsh curriculum of experience: her rapid political involvement with French trade unions, her activism in the brief life of the Popular Front, and her initially pacifist response to the emergent menace of Hitler's Germany.

The 1930s shaped her politics but also informed her philosophical views. Some of their richest formulations she wrote during World War II, but because many of her papers cannot be dated precisely, it would be arbitrary to presume that the war marks a decisive division between her formative and her mature thinking. I have concentrated on four philosophical topics: Weil's metaphysics, her aesthetics, her views on friendship, and her philosophy of science. These were not her exclusive concerns, but they were predominant ones.

In contrast to her philosophical positions, her religious attitudes and beliefs were substantially the product of the wartime. The Vichy years precipitated what I have called her spiritual crises: her rejection of Judaism and her effort to embrace Christianity by recasting it into her own heterodox mold. This is the Weil of legend, renown, and notoriety.

Her politics, her philosophy, and her spirituality tended toward an almost feverish cohesion in the last eight months of her life. It would be gratuitous to assume that all she wrote in 1943 she meant as a summing up, but the forceful, apodictic tone of her late writing to some degree warrants what I have called resolutions of issues she had long been weighing.

My concluding chapter, although reiterating some essential points about her, attempts to leave Weil free of final judgment so that she may remain an open challenge for each reader to pursue. Although I believe that, taken as a saint or "religious genius," Weil is disastrous, even the evidence I afford may not deter some from embracing her in a hallowing manner. Taken with caution, Weil is an excellent teacher.

Unless otherwise indicated, all the translations, both of published and archival materials, are my own. I have chosen this route not only for the sake of consistency; some English translations of Weil's works are not entirely faithful, and some are long out of print. Also, many of Weil's essays, including those long in print in France, have never been translated. Much of my work involves translation from archival writings which have not yet appeared to the French public. All of the known titles of Weil's works or those assigned by her archivist I have kept in the original. They can then be easily located on the completion of Gallimard's *Oeuvres complètes*.

In the composition of this book I have become heavily indebted to many helpful people. Foremost of these is André Weil, who kindly gave me permission to consult the microfilm copies of the Simone Weil Archives at the Institute for Advanced Study in Princeton and to quote brief passages from the papers. I am also grateful to him for receiving me into his home in Paris and for graciously putting up with my importunate questions. On behalf of all people interested in Simone Weil I would like to express my regret that the person uniquely qualified to write about her has, whether in humility or by the caution and reserve of his formidable intellect, chosen not to do so for nearly fifty years.

I am also indebted to the efficient staffs at the Widener Library, Harvard University, the Hatcher Library at the University of Michigan, the Firestone Library of Princeton University, the Cambridge University Library, and the couriers of the Bibliothèque Nationale's manuscripts, periodicals, and microfilms divisions. I owe particular thanks to Florence de Lussy, the archivist in charge of Weil's papers at the Nationale. For an especially enjoyable summer at the Institute for Advanced Study, Princeton, I wish to thank Elliot Shore, Librarian of the Historical Studies and Social Science Library, and his invaluable assistants, Faridah Kassim, Ellen Riordan, and Barbara de Meritt.

André-A. deVaux, former president of l'Association pour l'étude de la pensée de Simone Weil, has been unflagging in his help and enthusiasm for my efforts.

I have benefited substantially from several readers. I wish to thank Louis

Feldman for his criticisms, insights, and abundance of suggestions regarding the chapter entitled "A Stranger unto Her People." Alain's definitive biographer, André Sernin, kindly read and provided helpful remarks on the chapter "Le Maître." Rabbi Nicholas de Lange took precious time to read and discuss with me the biographical overview. Allan Megill gave a generously thorough reading to the manuscript in its second draft and offered many helpful comments. I owe the greatest debt to Germaine Brée, who patiently read all of the chapters in their initial drafts and provided me with lengthy critical responses. Whatever the strengths of this book, they are on several counts owing to her attention and to her encouragement.

I wish to thank John Carroll University for granting me academic leaves in 1985 and 1988, and I am most grateful to the George E. Grauel Foundation for a research grant that allowed me to complete the manuscript of this work during the academic year 1988–89.

For their patient assistance in helping me put the manuscript on a computer, I wish to thank Alex Bartsch, Chip Freund, and Elizabeth Zitnik.

The Lucius N. Littauer Foundation generously provided financial assistance toward the publication of this book. I am profoundly grateful to the foundation and to its president, William Frost.

Once again, I am deeply obliged to the editorial staff of the University of North Carolina Press and particularly to Sandra Eisdorfer for all the confident, thorough, and professional attention given to my work.

Finally, I wish to thank my wife and children for putting up with me in my years of servitude to a difficult task and an extraordinarily difficult person.

SIMONE WEIL

J'ai le droit, j'ai le devoir, dans l'exercise de ma puissance, de renoncer parfois au plaisir, d'affronter parfois la douleur, de risquer parfois ma santé et ma vie. Je n'ai pas le droit d'abdiquer.

SIMONE WEIL, "Réflexions concernant le service civil"

ONE

A Short Biography

Notes on an Itinerant Slave

Childhood and Education

Simone Weil was born in Paris on February 3, 1909. Her father, Dr. Bernard Weil, was Alsatian; her mother, Mme Selma Weil, came from Russia. Both parents were freethinking Jews who did not instruct Simone or her brother, André, three years her senior, about their Jewish origins or the ambiguous roles Jews played in the daily life of predominantly Catholic France. The family's position, in short, was equivocal: it was well entrenched in the professional bourgeois class and remained tacitly on the outside of the Jewish community. Because Dr. and Mme Weil had come of age in the fin de siècle, the time of Edouard Drumont and Alfred Dreyfus, they could hardly have been ignorant of anti-Semitism's virulence in French society, but their children grew up when racist antagonisms were relatively quiescent.

The Weil family was close knit. When Dr. Weil was called up to medical service in the Great War he went to the unusual length of taking his family, including his mother-in-law, to the towns where he was stationed: Neufchâteau, Mayenne, Chartres, Laval. The family took these disruptions in stride, and the children learned some of the fundamental lessons history has enforced upon European Jews, that security is an illusion, that home must be centered on packed bags.[1]

As siblings, André and Simone led apparently happy lives. They played and fought with each other like most children. She had a tenacious will and, with her brother, knew how to wheedle and cajole their indulgent parents. Both could cry forced tears to get their way. Both were exceptionally bookish. Their parents gave them no toys so books were a means of escape from the child's inevitable sense of being hostage to fortune. André taught his sister how to read. They memorized Edmond Rostand's *Cyrano de Bergerac*, exchanged parts, and declaimed before their parents. It was in reading Balzac during childhood that Simone learned that "Jew" meant usurer.

The primacy the Weils gave to education and cultivation of intellect was typical of a Jewish home. Before he was ten, André had developed a keen ability in solving mathematical puzzles. Although not an exceptionally accomplished student, Simone showed facility in Latin and Greek. She learned English by listening to her brother's tutor, and both children learned German by overhearing their parents.

Throughout her schooling Weil seems to have suffered from the sense that she was intellectually inferior to her brother, and her family, presuming him a genius, did not comfort her. In an autobiographical letter she wrote toward the end of her life, she claims that at fourteen she despaired of living because, given "the mediocrity of my natural faculties," she felt closed off from the "transcendent realm where the authentically great men alone enter and where truth dwells."[2] After months of agony, she goes on, she suddenly realized that anyone could enter truth's realm if only the desire for it could be sustained.[3] What is so striking here is not only her ascription of this exalting notion of desire to her early adolescence—the pertinent fact is not that she suffered but that she recalls that she suffered—as that she clothed her recollection in language suggesting a fairy tale.

With her emulous but disadvantaged position toward her brother as background, the language of her account announces a veritable holiday for Freudian clichés. She came to regard sexual metaphors as the legitimate property of mystical experience and would perhaps admit some truth even in the prurient hypotheses of psychoanalysis. Interpretations of her life tell us far less about her, of course, than her own interpretations. In her last years she read extensively in fairy stories and myths from diverse cultures, convinced that they were a repository of spiritual truths common to all peoples, but her fascination with them began early in her childhood.

When she was only three, her mother told her a Grimm fairy tale about "Marie in gold and Marie in tar." The heroine is sent by her stepmother into a forest, comes to a house, and is asked whether she wants to enter it through a door of gold or one of tar. She answers that the tar will do, and she is showered with gold. The stepmother's own daughter answers the same question by choosing the gold, with predictable results. According to Weil's biographer, Simone Pétrement, "Simone later said that this story had had an influence on her whole life."[4] We should like to know when "later" was, what the influence amounted to, why her entire life. That one who asks for bread will not be given a stone was a gospel truth Weil says she embraced fervently in her adolescent despair, long before she had read the Bible. It is the desire-as-salvation motif again, but how can we reconcile it with the lesson of the two Maries, where scruples win out? It may be best to leave them unreconciled. A tension between the affirmative acceptance of life and a desire to attain something infinitely precious and hidden within it was to inform Weil's character and thought to the end.

Weil remembered that she heard the *conte* of the Maries while recuperating from an operation for appendicitis. Throughout her life illness played a role far more substantial than has usually been credited. A physician's daughter, she would have acquired an awareness of disease and pathological conditions, but her own subjection to illness and physical debility taught her more.

When she was only six months old, her mother had to be hospitalized for appendicitis. Mme Weil tried to nurse Simone during her recovery, but she steadily weakened, and the transition to solid foods was difficult. Pétrement records Weil's belief that she had been poisoned in her infancy. "That is why," she would say, "I am so bungled [*ratée*]."[5]

At nine, she suffered a prolonged bout of whooping cough; it forced her absence from a school ceremony at which she was to be awarded a best-in-the-class prize. For the entire school year of 1920–21 her parents, convinced that she was too weak to attend school, had her tutored at home by instructors from the Lycée Fénelon. She had never enjoyed a strong constitution and was continually a prey to exhaustion and disease, but she was also a victim of her parents' acute sensitivity to sickness. They instilled in their children a dread of contamination—the effect, in part, of their war experiences in medical treatment—and Simone conjoined to the family's fussy hygienic rituals an acute aversion to physical contact: "She did not want to be hugged, or to eat certain things, or to touch certain things. Sometimes she did not want to touch something that had been touched by other people. She spoke of her 'disgustingness' [*dégoûtation*]. She would say, when it was a question of doing this or that, 'I can't, because of my disgustingness.' "[6] Though we might presume to find here transmuted, scarcely conscious forms of Hebraic taboos about uncleanness, it is also tempting to find in Weil's childhood experience of debility and repulsion the adumbration of two beliefs that would dominate her mature years: distance is the position one must occupy in the experience of precious things, and only in weakness can one attempt to imitate God.

Debility and repulsion, the conviction of enforced or desired apartness, might also figure in Weil's early protestations against the social order, a precocity to which both of her French biographers have given attention. Weil herself made the point in a letter to Georges Bernanos in 1938. She states that the Versailles Treaty and "the will to humiliate the conquered enemy" struck her at age ten in "a manner so repugnant" that she was cured forever of "naive patriotism." Similarly, "While still a child, in everything that I read or heard described, I have always put myself instinctively, due to indignation rather than pity, in the place of all those who suffered constraint."[7]

Just as in the dramatic turnaround of the story of her rescue from intellectual mediocrity (another species of weakness) Weil as an adult made sense of her earlier life, so in her recollections to Bernanos she gave a coherence to it by hyperbole: "in everything . . . always . . . all those. . . ." It is gratuitous to assume the hyperbole was either facile or disingenuous, but it is not mere charity to assume that Weil from childhood had a keen sense of justice and injustice. One must look to a beginning somewhere. "The seed is in the furrow," writes Jacques Cabaud, "and will bear its fruit in time,"[8] but we can antedate even his timing: her passionate, exigent view of justice is altogether Jewish. It came with her mother's milk.

For the academic year 1924–25, while completing her baccalaureate, Weil elected to attend the Lycée Victor Duruy so as to hear lectures from René Le Senne, whose *Introduction à la philosophie* appeared the following year.[9] She also formed some close relationships, including one with Edwige Copeau, who discussed religion with her. Copeau was a practicing Catholic (she shortly entered the order of Benedictine Sisters) and Weil was "antitala" (student slang for nonbeliever) so their friendship seems to have thriven on contrariety. Their exchanges were an early instance of what became typical in some of Weil's later friendships: perhaps the deepest were those in which she felt a profound challenge to her intellect and her will, a sort of test put to her entire sensibility. She did not flinch before these contrarities. Indeed, they were as much internal as external. Copeau, discussing St. Paul and Thomas Aquinas with her, had the impression that Weil was far better informed about them. She also believed Weil intimidated people "by the profundity of subjects she touched."[10]

In October 1925 she entered the Lycée Henri IV, one of the most prestigious preparatory schools for students intending to go on to the Ecole Normale Supérieure. There, for the next three years, she read, wrote, and thought under the aegis of Alain, perhaps the most influential figure in her life. "Le maître," as his students knew him, deserves a lengthy discussion separate from this narrative.

To one lasting friendship Weil formed in those years, that of Simone Pétrement, we owe her definitive biography. Pétrement provides a lengthy, invaluable characterization of Weil in her Henri IV years. Despite its hagiographic tendencies, notable in remarks such as "she was already well above the common level, owing to the purity of her feelings and the force of her personality even more than of her intellect,"[11] it makes clear in a refreshing way that the woman whom cultists have seized upon, this "pilgrim of the absolute," would likely have driven them off had they known her in the flesh.

Pétrement dwells on one aspect of Weil's personality and behavior that might explain why some fellow students found her not only odd but off-putting, even monstrous. That is her seemingly cultivated masculinity. It was not, says Pétrement, an affectation but a calculated expression of will bent upon minimizing what Weil regarded as the handicaps of being a woman, the socially obligatory shows of deference, charm, frailty, and a general purposelessness. To her resolute will she added a sartorial vanity in reverse, "clothes with a masculine cut, always the same outfit (a kind of suit with a very wide skirt and a long, narrow jacket), and always flat-heeled shoes."[12] Once, when her mother invited her to the Opéra, she dressed not in an evening gown but in a tuxedo of black skirt and jacket. Pétrement suggests that her unconventional clothing suited Weil's already leftist scorn of bourgeois proprieties, that she even took a mischievous delight in offending people. But these motivations seem superficial when we consider that for years at home she set herself in a competitive but hopeless way with her brother: he was older, he seemed much brighter, and he was he. Pétrement recalls that Weil at Henri IV signed letters to her parents with "your respectful son," part of a family joke involving her efforts to be considered a boy. In letters to her brother years later, she would sometimes refer to "your parents," a poignant emblem of estrangement from her own family. Mme Weil played along by calling her "Simon" and early in her daughter's life confessed that she herself did her utmost "to encourage in Simone not the charms [*grâces*] of a little girl but the uprightness of a boy, even if it had to look like bluntness."[13]

No statement could better suggest the peculiar tensions at work in Weil from her earliest years: the need to overcome the accident of birth, her femaleness, by sheer exertion of will. The obvious absurdity of this enterprise should not conceal the vast store of energy that went into it. Weil's occasional remarks in her correspondence about her inadequacy or mediocrity serve as a concession to the fact that she is a woman, and it may fairly be wondered whether a pivotal idea in her mature thinking, the decreation or willed annihilation of the ego, the self of personality, would have come to her independent of this private wretchedness. Her intellectual rigor, apparent from her first writings for Alain, her relentless, never concessive way of arguing a position, her quest for the pure—all such exertions, already evident at Henri IV (Alain called her "the Martian" in token of her otherness) worked as mechanisms for distancing her from herself as others might see her, as a woman.

It is as though for her, to be recognized as female was tantamount to being reduced, to being only female. Neither her will nor her intellect could overcome an acute vulnerability in this regard, just as neither could defend her against that other primordial fact of her birth, that she was a Jew. At some level of awareness Weil must have known or felt that she was always living at risk, that she could at any time be made to accept herself on the most degrading terms, despite all her efforts toward autonomy. Offbeat clothing was armor for confronting the world and for concealing herself from it.

Unlike Pétrement, André Weil believes his sister was neither calculated nor even conscious of her scandalizing way of dress.[14] This is to say that what outwardly set her apart from others she assumed naturally as part of an identity well formed before her late adolescence. Likewise, her aggressive, willful intellectuality did not perhaps bring with it any sense of how she was affecting other people, which was often negatively, even among friends. Pétrement generalizes of her sensibility: "In reality, it was a strange mixture of coldness and passion; on the one hand, something reasonable, rigorous, calm, slow, on the other, there were lively, sometimes clumsy, sometimes naive and charming impulses, a blaze of enthusiasm, and violent shows of indignation."[15]

While in school she expressed the sense of having a vocation. She wanted, as she told Pétrement, "to do something for the good of humanity."[16] At that time, however grandiose Weil's intent, this vocation was surely vague. It may be doubted, given her later uneven record as a teacher, whether she ever envisioned the classroom as the place to carry out her mission. It may also be wondered whether she was aware that in her studies with Alain she was already developing her true strength and calling as a writer.

Alain's trimestrial evaluations of her over three years are important. From the first term he recognized her analytical powers, yet he noted a discrepancy between her style and her ideas, as though her pen could not keep up with her thoughts. He complained of her penchant for tortuous constructions, her "overly crowded meditations expressed in an almost impenetrable language."[17] He believed that she cultivated these subtleties in the spirit of a game. If so, Alain might be credited with sobering and directing her writing, for her subsequent work bears the hallmarks of the best classical French style: it is lucid, direct, and, though abundant in abstractions, never marred by jargon or abstruse language. These merits are not altogether concealed in the topos or short essays she wrote for Alain from 1925 to 1927.

By June 1927, Weil had passed the four licensing examinations that qualified her for teaching philosophy, but in that month she failed the entrance examination for the Ecole Normale. She had fared poorly in the history test, a not surprising result for a student of Alain's because he disdained historical studies. She continued to attend his lectures even after she was admitted to the Normale in July 1928. That was not untypical of Henri IV graduates who had gone on to the Sorbonne. In each graduated class Alain had a coterie of disciples (a word not wholly appropriate when applied to Weil) and, besides, attendance at Sorbonne lectures was not required. There was even, in Cabaud's phrase, "a boundless impertinence toward professors," to which Weil, with her maverick comportment, openly contributed.[18] Contempt of the instructor was almost de rigeur among *normaliens*. They were, after all, assured of a future in France's professional elite and could afford to be obstreperous and defiant in a way that only the brightest youth can be.

During her *normalien* years, 1928–31, she earned some tags that stuck to her long afterward. For her uncompromising belief that ideas must be acted upon, she came to be known as "the categorical imperative in skirts."[19] She once remarked to Pétrement "à propos of those who do not live in conformity with their principles, 'What I can't put up with is that people compromise.' In those days she would make a horizontal, cutting gesture with her hand that seemed to be the very expression of her intransigence."[20] No wonder that she had few friends in those years. She seems to have struck most of her fellow students as a gorgon of intellectuality, and a moralizing one to boot. Few could have responded to what seems to have lain behind her intransigence, that profound disappointment, that exasperation with human weakness which weighed upon Plato and Kant, the two minds she embraced early, under Alain, and never forsook.

She also earned the title of "red virgin," an appellation from one of the Normale's directors who had no fondness for her militant left-wing positions. Now that she was coming of age, she lost no time in showing her sympathies openly. Her attitude toward working people was not an abstract indulgence at a convenient distance from daily realities. At the Sorbonne she raised funds for the unemployed, pressing teachers as well as students for contributions. She joined the League for the Rights of Man and campaigned with the pacifists of its membership for disarmament and obligatory arbitration of international disputes. As she already perceived, these were working-class issues no less than they were matters of foreign policy because they determined the relationship of the overweening and powerful state to the people it was supposed to serve. Her first tilts against *étatisme* date from her twentieth year.

Despite her involvement in social issues and her demonstrated support for working people, she did not then nor subsequently join the French Communist party. She likely recoiled from membership for fear of losing the indispensable freedom to think for herself.[21] Unlike her later entertainment of membership in the Christian church, there remains no record of her having wrestled at any length with herself or anyone else about becoming a party member. Her reticence did not, of course, diminish her acutely sympathetic understanding of Marx, whose place in her intellectual maturation has been generally underestimated.

Her temperament isolated and so defined her politics far better than any programmatic differences with fellow activists. She could argue issues well, but what she responded to from her innermost self was the conditions from which they arose, and these she grasped with a lively sense. Three anecdotes make the point.

In her memoirs, Simone de Beauvoir recollects once meeting Weil at the Sorbonne. They quickly got into an argument in which Weil contended that "only one thing mattered on earth today: the Revolution which would feed the world."[22] The cause of that effusion was a newspaper report on a famine that was devastating China. When Weil read the account, she wept. On another occasion, fellow student Raymond Aron saw her extremely dejected because strikers in Shanghai had been shot. And she once grabbed another student by the coat while they walked in the Luxembourg Gardens, asking, "How can you laugh when there are children suffering in China?"[23]

This peculiar, telescopic sensitivity made her wretchedly indignant: she could envision horrors over the distance of time and space but could do nothing about them. Her outbursts over China—"words of sainthood," gushes Cabaud[24]—indicate a tension she had apparent difficulty in controlling. Isolated in and by her temperament, her insistent moralizing, and her exacting intellect, she suffered. Fierce headaches began during 1930–31 when she was preparing her agrégation in philosophy, the French government's competitive test for admission to teaching positions in lycées and universities. These headaches went on unabated for nearly a decade before her father secured a specialist who diagnosed her condition as larval sinusitis and gave her opium as an analgesic. To some degree, these pains were perhaps the effect of Weil's intensely driven intellectual energy. The sheer volume of what she wrote in her slow, precise hand would have exhausted someone of a stronger physique, and this is not to mention the staggering amount of what, under heavy lenses, she read. Her indifference to eating well and her diet of cigarettes also contributed. The dense multivolume edition of her *Oeuvres complètes* from Gallimard suggests what a mere fifteen years must have cost her. (One thinks of other brief yet abundantly creative lives, Schubert's and Nietzsche's, in which blinding headaches took a similar toll.)

Perhaps not incidentally her headaches began in her last year as a student, immediately before her entry into the world of work. Adolescence had ended; she was now twenty-one. In what was probably an agrégation exercise, "Fonctions morales de la profession," she characterized youth as a golden age, "the moment of virtue apart, of pure, interior freedom; it is a moment which is to humanity what Greek civilization is in human history. All labor is performed for the child, and all that is asked is self-development, or, as it is well put, self-cultivation. One lives in complete leisure."[25] Such is that blessed life of leisure which Aristotle made the aim of the state; it was the life Weil had enjoyed with her brother at home. Now the mind's idyll was at an end.

To assume a profession, she wrote, one must enter a caste system and become a mere instrument of production. In the occupational strata of needs, the adolescent must learn to put aside intellectual and moral scruples: "In each profession there are questions that are not posed, they are resolved in advance; regarding such questions, conscience is suppressed and one is blind."[26] People become conscripts to the complex of needs insofar as society makes them tools of production rather than true producers. That is, they serve as slaves in the social convention, cut off from the very object of their work, which is nature.

Weil was already developing, in addition to this Marxist view of capitalist labor, a philosophy of work with a more classical base, specifically a Baconian view that the natural world becomes ours only by our obedience to it, by our acceptance of matter as an obstacle to thought that liberates the will.[27] Precisely there lay the moral function of every profession, with needs converted into objects of action rather than its shackles.

Reality obliged her to admit that the caste system was still intact, that exchange rather than cooperation served as the medium of human relations. Transformation of the economy from a system of needs to one of products would require professional groups like the labor unions. They alone could ensure both the individual freedom to confront objects of one's will and one's equality with others in doing so. The moral function of the professions would be identical to their social function. Concluding her argument, Weil adds: "And the more the professions have a material object, the better they fulfill this role. Also, it is not enough to say that the emancipation of the proletarians will be the work of the proletarians themselves; it is necessary to say that the emancipation of every citizen whomever depends upon them."[28]

Looking beyond Weil's Marxist presumption about the working class and observing all cautions owed to conjecture, we might perceive a good deal of unease, if not dissatisfaction, about the teaching career she was about to enter. Was it worth the effort? More accurately, would the object of her will, the obstacle posed as a challenge and thus an occasion of work, suffice? "The professions which do not consist of changing something deserve the name only by analogy with material labor, as consisting in its material control as well."[29] Although she recognizes that a professor of philosophy is a worker by analogy in correcting the errors of students' writings, there remains some concern about the "métier mal défini" for which one's thought must be substituted because a material object is lacking. One may suspect that Weil regarded pedagogy as an ill-defined métier. What was the work object? One is bound to others by material activity or thought, she says, but to be tied to a social order in the latter sense is to be a slave; even those who work by their wits rather than their hands play the master's part. The truly servile professions are those without a real object.

It is a peculiar argument but one altogether typical of Weil's virtuosity in cultivating paradoxes. It shows how she could take up a well-established ideological assumption (here Marxist but with debts to Pierre-Joseph Proudhon) and inform it with her particular insight. At the same time, she had almost nothing to say about the morality of teaching itself, as though Alain could not have furnished her with optimal standards of expectation. Implicit in her essay was the conviction of her own imminent servitude as a teacher, society's intruder into youth's golden age.

The Careers of an Outsider

Pétrement observes that Weil had for some time planned to become a factory worker upon receiving her diploma and was dissuaded only because the

Depression was beginning to cause a great deal of unemployment.[30] In the event, upon her first teaching assignment, at Le Puy, she joined the proletariat.

At the girls' lycée she taught philosophy, Greek, and the history of art. Later she added Latin and an optional free course in the history of mathematics. A few of her lecture notes have survived. They show that with Alain's Cartesian dogmas she was already working out a conception of necessity, a linchpin in all her mature thought, the reality we must choose to undergo or to seize. One can know the world only by seizing it, she observes. Her assertive, voluntarist accents, the legacy of Henri IV, are evident in the definition of necessity as "the ensemble of conditions for a free action."[31] Contrary to fatality, in which only lawless sensations succeed one another, necessity is governed by the intermediary of time. Weil gives two examples of necessity encountered as real and abstract: laboring all day in a field and mathematically calculating the total work accomplished.

It might be assumed that with her view of world as obstacle she would have prepared students to face the hurdles of their qualifying tests. In fact, she was indifferent to their fears or ambitions in this regard; she did not train them up in the conventional way. Undoubtedly she drew great stimulation from the task of having to present the very difficult business of thinking to young minds. From biographers' evidence, her students seem to have responded warmly to her. Her own awkwardness put them at ease. One day, for example, she came to class with her sweater on backward. How could she help but endear herself to them after that?

Her greater devotion, the goal of her energy and most of her time away from class she invested in associations quickly formed with regional labor movements, particularly with the miners' union of the Confédération générale du travail unifiée (CGTU). She prepared lecture courses for the miners at the Workers' College at Saint-Etienne (three hours by train from Le Puy), organized meetings to promote syndicalist unity between the communist and noncommunist unions, participated in a *cercle d'études* that discussed Marx's writings, and wrote articles on syndical life for *L'effort*, a Lyons newspaper.

These articles provide invaluable indexes of Weil's commitment to a workers' revolution and the basically Marxist perspective she kept in her first few years of union activity, a matter easily obscured by her subsequent criticisms of Marx. In her first writing for *L'effort*, published less than two months after she began teaching, she reviewed a meeting of all the local trade unions, commended their show of unity despite partisan differences, but remarked on the failure of the socialist and communist unions to unite at the top. "This seemingly insoluble problem the working class must resolve or condemn itself to disappear as a revolutionary force."[32]

Nowhere is her debt to Marx more apparent than in her iteration of his point that revolution works chiefly to restore the unity of intellectual and manual labor which capitalism had destroyed. Revolution did not mean the rejection of an inherited culture but its reappropriation. "This taking possession is the Revolution itself." The workers' education projects to which Weil gave so abundantly would, she hoped, help them to acquire the power of understanding language and so displace "these word gatherers, priests, and intellectuals" who traditionally served the exploiters against the true producers. Workers needed to be made aware of the rapport between work and all varieties of theoretical knowledge. A study of politics and economics "and Marxist doctrine in particular" would enable them to understand their present place in society.[33]

Put more succinctly, revolution, according to Weil in early 1932, differs from revolt in that it understands oppression and so is able to transform it. The proletariat must know the modes of capitalist exploitation "so as to realize what a hold [*prise*] it offers to the action of oppressed people who want to deliver themselves from it."[34]

Marx had taught her, as Alain could not, that one must understand history in order to comprehend the relation between modes of production and modes of exploitation. Productive modes never stop changing. History is the record of their intensification, with each generation leaving a greater sum of products than it received. Concurrently, she observed, exploitation has been refined by the divisions of labor, which are pushed to an extreme when each worker assumes only one task. In this *machinisme*, intelligence and all an artisan's skills belong to inert devices, so the worker is left only with his "animal strength." The central revolutionary problem was to "reestablish the laborer's domination over work conditions without destroying the collective form which capitalism has imposed upon production."[35]

Syndical cohesion, workers' education, restoration of an *artisanat* within the productive system matured under capitalism—such were the desiderata for which Weil worked from the first and never abandoned. These criteria reveal how essentially conservative her Marxist assumptions were. They also indicate that she ignored the revisionism of Marx, which had predominated for over a generation in French leftist ideology. The insights of Georges Sorel and Henrik de Man have no place in her analysis. She belonged rather to the old-school socialism of Jean Jaurès and Léon Blum. Though hoping the USSR would serve as a beacon light for the international proletariat, she urged that "the working class's sincere defenders in the capitalist nations avoid putting the revolutionary movement into the hands of the Russian bureaucracy."[36]

Stalin was even more objectionable to her for having publicly commended the methods of Frederick Winslow Taylor in American industry. The cult of efficiency in production, with the worker's slightest gesture "determined by specialists with a view to the best possible result," seemed healthy to the Soviet dictator. He must have forgotten Marx's contention that capitalism imposed only unhealthy attitudes. "The fact that Stalin, on this question which is central to the conflict between capital and labor, has abandoned Marx's point of view, and has let himself be seduced by the capitalist system in its most perfect form, demonstrates that the USSR is still far from possessing the foundations of a workers' culture. . . . It must be hoped that the same is not true of the Russian workers themselves."[37] Weil's attitude toward Soviet Russia seems virtually identical to her attitude toward the French trade unions: suspicion of leadership, open contempt for organizational hierarchy, and fond expectations of the rank and file.

Her labor activities brought notoriety. When participating in demonstrations by unemployed municipal workers at Le Puy, she was singled out by local newspapers as a communist agitator. The presence of an instructor from a girls' school in the demonstrations and in workers' meetings with the city council was good press. Local police identified the pointed, sardonic language of the protest committee's communiqués as Weil's own work, as in fact they were. When a school official urged her to apply for a transfer, implying that she might be fired, she is alleged to have replied that she had always considered dismissal the high point of her career.

Unions as far away as Saint-Etienne passed resolutions and sent protests in her favor. Her lycée colleagues signed a letter of support, and her students on their own initiative enlisted their parents to request that she not be dismissed. Nothing could be officially charged against her, and the school authorities were forced to ride out the storm. The accusation from a Paris weekly that she was "a militant of Moscow"[38] seems ludicrous in light of Weil's later remarks on the Le Puy demonstrations: "During all that, the local communists kept telling me that they considered me, in relation to them, on the other side of the barricades, and they occasionally treated me as such; at the same time, they were very happy to see me exposed to repression instead of them, since I was suspected of being one of them."[39]

Given this invaluable lesson in political decorum, she had no need to become disillusioned with the Communist party's machinations during the years of the Popular Front and the Moscow trials. Often with them, she was never of them, and unlike many French leftists of the 1930s (not to mention the postwar years) she offered no allegiance whatever to Stalinism.

Though she was often with working people, she was never of them either. But there is a profound difference between her associations with political activists and with "proletarians." From labor militants she demanded consistency of principle and clarity of doctrine and seldom found either to her satisfaction. With working people she sought out a deeper, psychological rapport, and she was perhaps no less frustrated. An anecdote that found its way into neither of the standard biographies opens a window, however small, onto one of her difficulties. It comes from a fellow teacher and labor activist, Jean Duperray.

In the winter of 1932 she participated in a miners' demonstration at Saint-Etienne, where she had close ties with unionists. After street marching, banner waving (Weil carried the red flag), and a few rounds of the "Carmagnole" and the "Internationale," the protesters retired to a bistro. Weil made sure she was seated next to a veteran miner and former convict, François Chapuis, known as Le Boul. While he rambled, she took notes. She asked him how solidarity was organized against the bosses where he worked. Le Boul did not understand her initially, then said everyone was ranked by his "caid" (an Arab term for magistrate). "In the evening there's a fight in the shack [*goubi*] to see who's the more cunning. After that, there's only one caid." Weil answered, "What? You're under the thumb of a brutal authority and you imitate it among yourselves?" Le Boul rejoined, "Well, there just has to be a leader." Duperray concludes: "Simone had imagined a brotherhood. She discovered a transference of the oppressive system to the rowers' galley."[40] Disconcerted, she gave up her inquiries and put her head in her hands. It seems almost symbolically appropriate that when Le Boul later asked her to dance with him, she could not manage any of the most common steps.

One of the most substantial lessons Weil learned about workers came during a trip to Berlin and Hamburg in the summer of 1932. She had intended to observe German fascism at first hand, but the articles she wrote for *L'école emancipée*, the journal of the national teachers' union, concentrated on the sad spectacle of the German trade union movement as a house divided, much like France's own. She castigated the German Communist party for its failure to match the Nazis' activism, and she exposed as blind and preoccupied its antagonism toward the reformist Social Democrats. Weil needed no acuity of vision to realize that Hitler was profiting from leftist differences.

The clichéd rhetoric of revolution sufficed to keep the communists impassive and inert in the face of an obvious menace. It was in Germany, surely, that Weil came to believe, as one of her later, most quoted *boutades* puts it, that revolution is the opiate of the people. History does not take care of itself, nor is revolution made inevitable by dialectic: such were the first lessons by which she came to question the soundness of Marxist dogma.

During her visit, Weil acted as go-between for French and German syndicalists and Trotskyists, carrying messages and documents both ways. She became acquainted with Trotsky's son, who had been deported with his father. After Hitler became chancellor and political repression mounted, she helped German refugees by furnishing contacts and even the hospitality of her parents' home in Paris. Trotsky himself called there incognito in December 1933.

Transferred, she resumed her teaching at a lycée in Auxerre, less than fifty miles southeast of Paris. She enjoyed proximity to the capital and its libraries, and the school year 1932–33 passed without incident, but she was not popular with the school administration, and the students' mediocrity did not inspire her. Cabaud quotes from Weil's dossier at the Ministry of National Education an inspector's report on one of Weil's lectures. Her presentation on the notion of error in Plato, Descartes, Spinoza, Kant, and Hegel seemed unorganized and inconclusive, her remarks "a constant scattering of thought" that forced students to take notes they could not understand.[41] Perhaps dogged by a vague hopelessness, as some teachers are when faced with indifference, she was conversing with the texts alone.

For 1933–34 she was again assigned to the Loire district, this time to Roanne, not far from the syndicalist beehives of Lyons and Saint-Etienne. This year has been memorialized by notes which one of Weil's students, Anne Reynaud-Guérithault, took from her lectures. In contrast to the Auxerre rector's observations, the presentation at Roanne ranges coherently over many philosophical questions, including political issues Weil was dealing with in union meetings. More than a primer, though they might serve as such, these *Leçons de philosophie* mirror her efforts to survey theory and method, to comprehend them as preliminaries to the chief effort of all, that consciousness of reality which neither theory nor method can foresee.

That endeavor seems to have figured largely in her decision to take a year's leave from teaching in 1934 and go to work in a factory. But her motivation was not only epistemological and experimental, it was ethical. Her Roanne lectures are the prolegomena to what followed because they repeatedly enforce upon their reader a sense of obligation to come to terms with oneself and the world.

Here are two brief but exemplary passages. Discussing Freudian notions of the unconscious, Weil says repression must be dealt with socratically, that we are as responsible for our evil thoughts as for our good ones: "We are completely responsible for the degree of clarity there is in our own thoughts; we do not always make the necessary effort to become fully aware of them, but we always have the ability to become so." Consciousness, in short, is not only a psychological state, it is a moral one as well. Then, reviewing political theory and economic practice, the dire facts of statism, industrial organization, and oppression by collectivity, she concludes: "If one stops oneself from thinking of all this, one makes oneself an accomplice of what is happening. One has to do something quite different: take one's place in this system of things and do something about it."[42] Vague in direction, the injunction shows clear intent. To think lucidly, to act resolutely: these simple, far from easy imperatives, hallmarks of Kant's influence on Weil, carried for her a burden that was psychological, moral, and political.

The school inspector's report in November 1933 observed that the Roanne girls "have the feeling that Mlle Weil is pulling them from scholastic exercises so as to take them into real life and, naturally, this feeling delights them."[43] Now, with perhaps the academician's faint prejudice that school is not part of real life, Weil was ready to follow her students out the door.

Her third year of teaching had been her best. There was little friction with school factotums; her students "everywhere had loved her," says Pétrement,[44] and she was thoroughly at home in the company of workers whose respect and friendship her devotions had earned. Pétrement has shrewdly suggested that the very absence of difficulties might have helped her decide to leave Roanne. With her very Protestant sense of individual obligation went a no less Protestant horror of comfort. She chose to assume the daily life her worker friends had to live. There also lay in this adventure a vagabondage not unknown to someone of Jewish background.

It is too easy to point out, as some have, Weil's penchant for undertaking tasks for which she was not fit. Her decision to take up factory work is the capital instance. She was posing for herself an almost impossible physical exertion, one sure to intensify her headaches and sap her refractory energy. That is what happened. Yet there was nothing disingenuous in her statement requesting academic leave "for personal studies."[45] The factories were to provide a kind of schooling even as they were occasions for testing at the most elementary level her capacity to maintain thought and action in effective cohesion. A dutiful pupil, Weil carefully registered her successes (few) and her failures (many) in that testing. In the factory, she was the only student, and she was the bourgeoise who could and did walk away.

Her months at Alsthom, Carnaud, and Renault could only have reinforced in her the tension between being called and being cut off, between exclusivity affirmed and exclusivity imposed. She might well have intuited that it would be so before she arranged, by connections with Alsthom's director, Auguste Detoeuf, to get herself hired. She wanted to find out if factory work could be carried out without oppressing the worker, without, that is, taxing unduly one's mental and physical powers in cooperation. As Pétrement observes, Weil thought she might find a way out of proletarian misery by plunging into it.[46] But that intent, though possible or even likely, rings as too intellectual and rationalized to be a complete explanation. The assumption of isolation, the playing out of inadequacy and failure, might also be reckoned.

To suggest as much seems condescending, even gratuitous, but there is warrant for it in the long essay she completed just before her leave took effect. "Réflexions sur les causes de l'oppression et la liberté" form a cogent, somber discourse on the sophisticated means, ideological and technological, by which humankind's natural and creative freedoms have been more and more constrained. Her essay reads like a postmortem to the Renaissance belief in human worth and individual dignity. She called it her magnum opus, and nothing she wrote later surpasses it in taut argument or luminous insight. It surveys the terrain where totalitarianism alone can thrive. Most important to the context of her entering working-class life, it profiles a modern industrial organization in which human labor has been debased to drudgery. How could she reasonably expect to find a way out, a key to restore the precapitalist integrity of work within the very structures that had destroyed it? Her "reflections" allowed (or forced) her to anticipate intuitively the conclusion she arrived at eight months later, that she had become a slave, branded for life. The factories helped to ratify her sense of her own miserable limitation, the burden of personal inconsequence she had carried from adolescence.

They also reminded her of how vulnerable she was as a woman. Although feminists cannot claim Weil because she does not show a generic consciousness that would set women against men, it might be argued that she was a victim of sexist attitudes. Her mother's praise of boyish assertiveness and contempt for girlish coyness inspired her pathetic game of playing the second son. At Henri IV and the Normale, she had been in a conspicuous minority, for then as now it was very difficult for young women to advance with young men. That milieu, however, was one of privilege, and intellectual promise safeguarded everyone. Vigor and dedication had won her parity with men in syndical circles, causing some apprehension and resentment among their wives.[47] Finally, in her three years of teaching, she had enjoyed a good deal of autonomy in a predominantly female environment. In exchanging the lycée for the factory, she was yielding relative mastery for total subjection.

Her remarks on female co-workers are occasional but instructive. She noted that women were paid even less than men and were the butt of obscene jokes. As Le Boul had told her, even the lowly must have their hierarchy, but Weil did not protest this most obvious degradation even to herself in her daily journal. Following Spinoza's injunction neither to deride nor to fume but only to understand, she registered her observations on situations that would perhaps have challenged even Spinoza's equanimity.[48] For example, she mentions seeing a group of factory women standing in a downpour one morning, waiting for the signal that would allow them to pass through an already open door into shelter. They were well conditioned to servitude. We would like to know where Weil herself was situated when she observed this wretched tableau. It is enough to note that she seems to have remained an outsider even to the lowliest.

The same distance occurs in another scene-painting shortly after Weil quit factory work for the last time, in August 1935. She had gone with her parents on a trip along the Iberian coasts. Near the Portuguese fishing village of Póvoa do Varzim, she watched a procession of women as they sang "what certainly must be very ancient hymns of a heartrending sadness."[49] It was the festival day of the village's patron saint, and what Weil heard was probably of a genre known as the *fado*, which typically carries a plaintive melody.[50] *Fado* is a stepchild of the Latin *fatum*, meaning fate or destiny, not inappropriate here because the experience was Weil's first of what she later called her "three contacts with Christianity that have really counted." She had read Scripture and argued theology at school. Now, feeling ill in a place she describes as miserable, "the conviction was suddenly borne upon me that Christianity is preeminently the religion of slaves, that slaves cannot help belonging to it, and I among others."[51] The conjunction of Christianity with slavery sounds much like Nietzsche's in *Der Antichrist*, but Weil meant something quite different from what Nietzsche calls *ressentiment*. Of course, in no descriptive sense could it be true that she was "a slave among others." She was a well-educated bourgeoise on vacation, about to resume teaching. Her statement was true, however, as an affirmation or declaration of allegiance to Christianity, even though she wrote that slaves "cannot help belonging" to it. What is most striking in her description of the scene is what is most obvious: the distance. She was neither "among others" nor of these fishermen's wives any more than she was of the workshop women at Renault. She alerts us to the obliquity of her position in the first words: it was a "contact," not a communion or conversion, and even "contact" suggests something immediate and with a potential intimacy to which nothing in this aesthetic experience corresponds.

But there is more. "The affliction of others entered into my flesh and my soul. . . . There I received forever the mark of slavery." Pétrement relates these words to the Portuguese "contact": "Having experienced slavery, she recognized from then on the religion of slaves."[52] She showed nothing of Charles Péguy's indignation that the Christian church had sided with propertied classes and abandoned the workers. If the proletariat belonged to Christianity, it was well hidden; that it did not belong to the church had been evident from the Revolution, and one has only to read labor journals to which Weil contributed to find the animus of anticlericalism still strong in the 1930s.

The academic year 1935–36 found her simultaneously occupying several fronts. She began to attend church services; she worked occasionally on a farm; she taught; she became acquainted with the director of a foundry at Bourges, tried without success to get hired there, and immersed herself in projects for factory reform. For all the violence she had suffered in body and spirit during her own factory work, Weil retained a feeling of joy in its performance, and from this time to her life's end she gave much of her intellectual energy to the problem of how the dignity of work could be rescued from its degradation. That problem's resolution had been her one revolutionary agendum before she went to Alsthom, but now it was informed with experience. Oddly, though her "reflections" on oppression had ended in a *huis clos*, her personal experience of it left her, if not sanguine, at least pragmatically aware of possible ways to its alleviation. Alain, having commended her analytical skill in the "Réflexions," had warned her that indignation unchecked would lead to misanthropy. The factory year enabled her to temper indignation with a good deal of savvy.

Neither she nor anyone else could have anticipated the sit-in strikes that swept the Parisian metal industries through May and June of 1936. Following election of the first Popular Front administration under Léon Blum, the strikes gave the new regime a dramatic occasion for enacting legislation that would permanently benefit labor. Weil supported the Popular Front with reservations: she backed wholeheartedly the need for unity among reform socialists, communists, and anarchists in resisting fascism, which had been exerting considerable appeal in young intellectual circles. But she feared the statism that could overtake a government of benign intent and beneficial programs. She rejoiced over the strikes, especially because they had been the spontaneous expression of the rank and file rather than orchestrations directed by labor militants, and they were mercifully nonviolent. Yet she also knew the dreamlike euphoria could not last. The industrial bosses, however needlessly fearful in their reaction, would continue to be bosses.

In the event, foreign winds dissipated the unreal joy of that summer. The civil war in Spain, begun July 17, became an international crisis by month's end. As though she had felt cheated in missing the strikes (she was obliged to continue teaching at Bourges into July), she lost no time in going to Spain. Unable to dissuade her, her fretful, ever-protective parents followed shortly after. By mid-August she had joined the Spanish anarcho-syndicalists' Confederación nacional del trabajo (CNT) at the front and enlisted with a ragtag group of non-Spanish volunteers. Too familiar with Communist party chicaneries and unwaveringly hostile to Moscow, she could not have supported the Loyalist mainstream. Her place, if indeed she felt she had any, could only be with the Left's dissidents, with those who preferred, like the communards of 1871, a quixotic revolution in the midst of war rather than waiting for battle's end.

Sporting a rifle—her comrades kept clear of her—Weil was in the ranks only a few days when she stepped into a campfire pot of boiling oil. It had been set in the ground over burning coals to conceal the fire from enemy observation. She was admitted to a military hospital in Sitgès but was given inadequate care. Her parents found her and persuaded her to return to France to save her leg from infection.

During her brief convalescence in Spain, she heard of numerous atrocities committed on both sides. She had been present when anarchists were about to shoot a priest. She remembered an incident she never witnessed, the execution of a fifteen-year-old phalangist after he refused to be converted to anarchism. It is not surprising that her interrogation of factory workers and campesinos did not result in any newspaper stories: her journal records would not have flattered the intensely partisan prejudices of the Parisian presses, especially since she continued to identify herself as a supporter of the CNT. What little she learned in her few weeks in Spain gave her no cause to be hopeful about a triumph for dissidents, whom, in spite of their crimes, she continued to support in public meetings after her return to France.

Two photographs of Weil in Barcelona deserve remarking. In each she wears the mechanic's dungarees that served as the CNT's military uniform. In each she has donned the militia cap. One shows her impishly grinning, a carbine strapped over her shoulder. In the other, without her glasses, she looks off with a dreamy smile as though to a distant landscape upon which her astigmatism refuses to focus, a gaze evocative of a passage in her "Réflexions," that an ideal is what we can never realize and cannot live without.

Her support of Spanish anarchists was not nominal. At CGTU meetings she wore their black and red scarf as though in defiance of the communist majority (anarcho-syndicalism in France virtually dissolved itself during the Popular Front) and she refused to stand when the "Internationale" was played. The grounds of her support are easily determined: the anarchists, having no organizing hierarchy, no bureaucracy, and no tendency to *étatisme*, could rightly claim to be a popular movement. They were anachronistically dedicated to local autonomy and popular ownership of industry, and they proved gallantly impatient in trying to realize their program. They were the twentieth century's misfits, fated by the noble ineptitude of their theories to succumb before totalitarianism's inexorably moving machinery. An outsider herself, Weil felt enough sympathy with this losing side to don its uniform. That did not make her an anarchist in any binding, official way, but it showed she could entertain the possibility that the powerless need not be Christian slaves. However absurdly—and all the better so—they can fight.

She was extremely fond of the Spanish people. Her brief look at what war was doing to them should be reckoned among her unspoken motives in opposing the Popular Front's militarization of heavy industry as France drifted toward war with Germany.

Weil's leg injury won her a leave from the first academic term of 1936–37. Headaches and an anemic condition that apparently began in 1934 were also adduced, and the leave was extended through the following summer. Had she been as debilitated as all those troubles suggest, she would have been bedridden. These problems seem more like excuses for giving her the time she needed to take up positions on a two-front war: against the submergence of the trade unions under a communist-dominated Confédération générale de travail (CGT) and against "the politics of prestige" that threatened to plunge

France into war. It was also possible that France would follow Spain into civil war. Her apparent pacifism was a sensible but foredoomed struggle to preserve the trade union movement and its gains in 1936 against fascism within France and without. To her defense of working-class interests she conjoined a series of polemics against French colonial policy and its oppression of foreign labor, exposing and denouncing whatever vestiges of imperial power France could muster in the face of German and Italian dictatorships.

Years Astray

Most of her writing from 1936 through 1938 was occasional rather than theoretical. It has found little critical attention and virtually no translation. Although relegated to the side-line status of "historical interest," her essays in this period could help to overcome a common and erroneous assumption about Weil: that she abandoned political activism and became a Christian mystic.

During that time she experienced her two other "contacts" with Christianity. In the spring of 1937 she spent several weeks in Italy, attending concerts, visiting museums, and talking with young fascists. She crowded the hours. Not many tourists to Italy spend their time reading Galileo and Machiavelli. Charmed by the country's beauty and its people, she observed the peculiar hollowness of fascist war rhetoric. Fascism's "camouflaged deification of death" did not seem to comport with the elementary warmth and decency of people she talked with, fascists included.[53]

She wrote to her parents of her particular fondness for the Umbrian district. Near Assisi, a Franciscan had guided her through a mountain chapel to which, in the fifteenth century, a woman disguised as a man had been admitted. The woman's identity was not known until her death twenty years later, when she was beatified. "If I had known this story before going up, who knows if I would not have given it a new edition?[54] To have put on, as St. Paul would say, maleness and Christian piety—how attractive that story must have been to someone whose greatest burden was her Jewish and female destiny.

How her parents reacted to her remarks we can only guess. More interesting is what she did not tell them or anyone else until in her "Spiritual Autobiography" of 1942 she wrote to Joseph-Marie Perrin of her second "contact" with Christianity that at the chapel of Santa Maria degli Angeli "something stronger than I forced me for the first time in my life to get down on my knees."

Like the Portuguese *fado,* the chapel, "an incomparable marvel of purity," was an aesthetic experience, and as in Portugal, the story is left strangely incomplete.[55] Why did she keep this experience to herself for nearly five years?

Shortly after her return to France in June, the Popular Front collapsed.[56] She resumed teaching in October at a lycée in Saint Quentin, not far from Paris. By the first term's end, she requested another leave because of her headaches. It was granted, and by a series of other leaves she never taught again. As before, sickness was not so much a condition as a pretext. The tremendous productivity of her year away, especially during the spring of 1937, indicated that her true métier was writing.

The range of journals to which she contributed included two pacifist bulletins, *Feuilles libres de la quinzaine* and *Vigilance,* the latter an organ of the Committee of Vigilance of Anti-fascist Intellectuals; the CGT *Syndicats,* founded by René Belin;[57] and *Nouveaux cahiers,* the creation of Auguste Detoeuf, the enlightened industrialist who first employed her.

Nouveaux cahiers originated from a series of informal weekly meetings Detoeuf had arranged among fellow industrialists, intellectuals, and trade unionists. The participants' heterogeneity ensured substantial discussion of current industrial problems "in a shelter from collective passions."[58] Weil attended fairly regularly. She thrived in such an atmosphere. The group's journal provided résumés of the discussions. In one, late in 1937, Weil argued that Hitler's racist propaganda was perhaps meant solely for internal consumption. Just as his attempt to appear reasonable to foreign states seemed a deceit, his monstrous race dogma might well be another. Like Plato, she assumed that official lying need not catch up with its instigator, as though Hitler manipulating the collective imagination was not himself a victim of its illusions.[59]

For the Christian Holy Week of 1938, Weil went with her mother to the Benedictine abbey of Solesmes, just south of Le Mans. At the small chapel bordering its walls, she regularly attended services so as to hear Gregorian chants. (Did she join in the liturgical prayer of Good Friday *pro perfidis Judaeis*?) Although suffering more than ever from headaches, she was rapt with "a pure and perfect joy in the unheard-of beauty of chant and words." In this, her third aesthetic "contact" with Christianity, and her first in a communal, ritualized setting, she grasped "the possibility of loving the divine love through affliction." In her 1942 letter to Perrin she claimed that "the thought of the Passion" had entered her at Solesmes. While there, she had another aesthetic moment, seeing a young Englishman shine with "truly angelic éclat" after receiving the host. She later characterized him as an angel because he referred to her the metaphysical poets of seventeenth-century England. In a subsequent mantric recitation of George Herbert's "Love bade me welcome," "Christ himself descended and possessed me."[60]

She kept this mystical initiation secret for more than three years. Neither her family nor her friends nor her Christian acquaintances in the Vichy years knew of this experience. She was later reading a text of Plato with her brother and remarked on Plato's mysticism. When André, a student of the Vedas and of San Juan de la Cruz, said he could find nothing mystical in the Greek text before them, she replied that one can be a mystic without showing it. He did not realize until after her death that she had been speaking of herself.

During her last academic leave, for the entire year of 1938–39, she immersed herself in historiography, mostly Greek and Roman, and in ancient religious texts, including the Torah and the Egyptian Book of the Dead. She was pursuing not two itineraries but one: readings in history informed her understanding of Hitler's expansionism while a reading of the Bible led her to believe she had found a perverse spirituality in Judaism. The common denominator of Roman imperialism and Judaic monotheism was, she believed, their appropriation and falsification of the transcendent to serve contingent ends. Weil knew that the subjugation or massacre of one people by another was a historical commonplace; what offended her violently was any specious justification of such brutality in the name of God or *Pax Augusta*.[61] Perhaps as early as 1938–39 she had intuited the link she later made explicit between Roman and Judaic absolutism in historic Christendom. If so, that intuition would have been one factor in keeping her from conversion to Christianity after Christ's "possession" of her. It might also suggest why she remained silent about that experience, as though to keep it pure, as though divulgence would be contamination and an exposure of her own vulnerability.

Stalinists had taken over the CGT; the Popular Front had no real hope of resuscitation, and militarization of France in response to Munich seemed an evil both inevitable and futile. In that scenario Weil was foredoomed to a fruitless pacifism and to associations she later condemned more harshly than any other she had known.

She was now forced to recognize the burden of having no community, neither Jewish nor Christian, because she could not unlearn the history lesson of collectivity, that whether cryptic or overt, totalitarianism informs all organized beliefs. Indeed, it amounts to their definition. Worst of all, Weil felt herself an accomplice to evils she condemned: her awareness of France's brutality toward its colonial peoples had long angered her, but now she understood in Hitler the logical extreme of France's own chauvinistic statism. Because she was French, she felt a historical culpability in regard to Hitler.

It does not seem coincidental that her headaches became especially severe at the very time when she was free of teaching responsibilities and could enjoy, at age thirty, the sustaining comforts of her parents' home. Toward the end of 1938, fearing she had a brain tumor, she consulted a brain surgeon. Pétrement records that Weil also feared a mental collapse and that she contemplated suicide.[62] Perhaps the mystical revelation she experienced in the midst of her bouts alleviated some of her stress, for, again according to Pétrement, the headaches became less violent after 1938.[63] The connection remains tenuous and hypothetical, but Weil's characterization of her mystical event as "the presence of a love analogous to that which one reads in the smile of a beloved face" would suggest a relief, a solace or acceptance she had not been able to find in any human milieu and now needed possibly more desperately than she would have admitted.[64]

In her captivating wartime study, "L'amour de Dieu et du malheur," she remarks that "a solely physical pain is a small matter and leaves no trace in the soul," whereas a physical pain awaited or experienced as a result of "a deracination of life" affects a person "in all parts, social, psychological, physical. The social factor is essential. There is truly no affliction unless there is some form of a social forfeit [*déchéance*] or the apprehension of such a forfeit."[65] *Malheur* or affliction, in Weil's definition, is a sociogenic disaster of the soul manifested in physical pain or its anticipation. Recalling in April 1942 her headaches four years before, she wrote, "I thought my soul menaced," but she had known that menace since 1930–31, when she stepped into the slave world that was to stamp upon her an indelible identity: more than an intellectual as outsider, she was a Jew and a physical weakling. The many insights she gathered into her essay on affliction did not come solely as wartime reflections; they are the intimate product of her own gradual *déracinement* in the 1930s. *Malheur*, social, psychological, physical, is the rubric of her biography.[66]

In the spring of 1939, Weil contracted pleurisy. After her convalescence she went for a vacation with her parents to Switzerland. They were in southern France when the *drôle de guerre* began in September. Weil's pacifist hopes that Hitler could be contained by Anglo-French diplomacy capable of treading the thin line between prestige and capitulation had been confounded, and the blitzkrieg through Poland and Scandinavia exposed the pointlessness of her hope that Germany would be internally weakened by its own fascist dynamic. The hazardous game of historical analogy had misled her completely. She had presumed that Germany was a new imperial Rome content to rest on its Austrian and Czechoslovakian annexations, but ancient Rome had passed from republicanism to empire by coming to the aid of its satellites, not by using Hitler's variety of bluffs and delays to confuse its enemies. And neither was Germany, as she had hoped, like Soviet Russia, a threat to the Western democracies that became less formidable with time.

Weil's ideas when war came were even more untimely. She presumed that France and England could fight Germany effectively only if their conscience were cleansed of their own colonial iniquities. Her belief that a revision of colonial policy could be instigated under wartime conditions recalls the Spanish anarchists' program for implementing social revolution in the midst of civil war. She expected propaganda to be anomalously free of convenient lies, and she took Jean Giraudoux to task for whitewashing French colonial policy in a November 1939 broadcast: "I would want you to speak the truth always, even on the radio."[67] As though to call attention to her imprudence, she reminded Giraudoux that under a statute of May 24, 1938, her criticisms of him made her liable to imprisonment.

Whatever Weil understood, which was little, of the political and military crises of late 1939, her response was warped by a heroic futility. As a bizarre example: when she learned of the German repression of a student uprising in Prague she submitted to some politicians a proposal for parachuting troops and supplies into Czechoslovakia. She insisted upon participating in this kamikaze mission and pledged that if it was performed without her, she would throw herself under a bus.[68] It is impossible to determine whether she actually believed this scheme would benefit the hapless Czechs or whether it was primarily the expression of her restive need to submit herself to extraordinary violence. The Spanish war seems to have given her the conviction that courage, dignity, and honor find their verification only when they are destroyed; heroism must end in defeat.[69]

Another of her schemes indicates that this somber view was not exclusive. Early in 1940, when Germans and French alike presumed that the fighting would basically follow the trench lines of the Great War, Weil drew up a plan for sending nurses into combat zones to tend the wounded and dying troops. Again, she insisted on taking part and began first aid studies. Not only would the plan put women on a footing with men and boost soldiers' morale, she reasoned, it would serve as magnificent propaganda by underscoring the difference between fascism and its opponents in respect for life. In this plan she did not pre-suppose that valor must lose; she even conceded that a high number of casualties among the nurses would put an end to the effort.

She had begun to peddle her plan among some politicians when the war finally came to France. Oddly, the suddenness of the Occupation, the realization that this war would not be fought in trenches, indeed, that the war was over as far as France was concerned, did not deter her. As long as she could persist in this noble but unreal proposal (and her stubbornness was unbounded), she would be able to conceive an active part for herself in the war. Writing in English, she resumed her importunities before American officials when she arrived in the United States two years later.

In War's Crucible

On June 13, 1940, one day before the Germans' entry, Paris was declared an open city. Although earlier resolved to stay on because she had hoped the city would be defended, she immediately left with her parents (they did not even take time to pack bags) by train for the south. When she realized there would be no second front in the south (the Germans occupied the Loire valley by June 16), she initially decided to try to reach England and join her brother, who had crossed in the evacuation from Cherbourg. That recourse was dangerous, if not impossible, and she had her parents to look after. After two weeks in Nevers, the Weils passed into the unoccupied zone (ZNO) and stayed at Vichy until mid-September.

Weil felt no hatred or resentment of the Germans, but she was bitter toward those who looked forward to accommodating the new overlords. She also rejected the hopes of those who saw in the armistice the possibility of instituting some reforms. Her violent rejection of her former pacifism dates from that summer, when France's humiliation was most keenly felt, even though the uneasy peace gave France an opportunity that resistance and destruction would have precluded to maintain some semblance of its culture albeit under German hegemony. This accommodation had been acceptable to her in 1938, but her studies in 1939–40 analogizing Hitlerism and Roman imperial practices argued the obvious, that nations under totalitarian rule suffer a desiccation of spirit.

The war's coming had not angered her; even the peace was not so infuriating as the patent fact that it was generally received with relief. This very human response amounted to precisely the sort of compromise she found so morally degrading. To her credit, Weil's moral absolutism allowed her to see what many in France, the "forty million Pétainistes," refused to see: a personal culpability, that "every Frenchman, myself included, bears as much of the responsibility [for the armistice] as Pétain."[70] Two years later, in New York, she defended those same people against French exiles, who, secure in America, reviled their compatriots for collaboration. Consistently she took positions that precluded self-justification or complacency for herself, even while exposing such postures in those with whom she argued. It was not only her intransigence that offended many; her unrelenting moralism could only lower them in their own eyes. Yet her essay on Vichy (in English) is free of censure, humane and perceptive of facts (not salient qualities of writing in that time), an apologia not in the least craven, and one that is certain to elevate Weil further in the final estimate.

In August, Weil applied to the Vichy Ministry of Education for a teaching assignment abroad but received no response by October 3, when anti-Jewish legislation kept her permanently from resuming her job. She then wrote, but perhaps never sent, a letter to Jérôme Carcopino, secretary of state for public education, arguing fantastically that she was not a Jew.

Settled with her parents in Marseilles, Weil entered a period rich in creativity and acquaintances. It began with the completion of one of her best-known essays, "L'*Iliade* ou le poème de la force." It appeared in the Marseilles journal *Cahiers du Sud*, under the anagram Emile Novis. The editor, Jean Ballard, bravely ignored Vichy statutes in allowing Weil, a Jew, to publish her work there over the next eighteen months. She also attended meetings of the Société d'études philosophiques, which quickened her interest in ancient religions and Eastern philosophy. She had already studied Babylonian through the Gilgamesh epic and now took up Sanskrit and its immortal texts, the Vedas and the *Bhagavad Gita*.[71] She also wrote or revised a small number of poems, began work on a play, and translated lengthy passages from Plato and the Greek tragedians.

It attests the sophisticated intelligence of the milieux in which she was moving that her new enthusiasm for studies in Eastern religion and philosophy were encouraged by two devout Roman Catholics, Pierre and Hélène Honnorat. Mme Honnorat also cultivated Weil's interest in Christianity, hoped for her conversion, and shrewdly introduced her to a man who might help her overcome her many scruples about the church.

This was Joseph-Marie Perrin, a nearly blind Dominican priest only a few years older than she. Had Weil known that Perrin was active in promoting Christian-Jewish fellowship (not a fashionable calling at that time), she might have hesitated to meet him. A kindly and learned man, author by then of a book on Catherine of Siena, Perrin lacked to his advantage André Weil's cosmopolitan breadth of intellect and its correspondent itinerant restlessness. He had all the insouciant patience of someone born, raised, and sustained in a creed. Weil likely knew from the first meeting that he offered her in the church a warmth and security unknown to her. Possibly she felt that coming in from the cold would be tantamount to an intellectual but therefore personal betrayal of André, her parents, and herself. From her talks with Perrin, begun in June of 1941 and resumed sporadically till her departure for America the following spring, came a substantial although not exclusive development of what has been called her religious metaphysics.[72]

With the CGT driven underground by government proscription, Weil's most important labor contacts were now with Christians of the Jeunesse ouvrière chrétienne (JOC), known as *jocistes*. They did not influence but rather confirmed her shift toward a corporatist or nonrevolutionary position on labor, and they may have helped her grapple with the possibility of conversion to Christianity; theirs was one collectivity she did not fear, resent, or criticize.

Disqualified from teaching, she used her professional exile to seek agrarian work. She rationalized this effort in a letter to Gilbert Kahn, a Marseilles friend: "Lowly conditions suit me, but that's by special vocation."[73] Through Perrin she met Gustave Thibon, who owned a farm at St. Michel d'Ardèche, in the heart of the Massif Centrale.

Thibon, a supporter of Action Française, a contributor to right-wing journals, and a friend of Philippe Pétain, was reluctant to receive a leftist Jewish intellectual from Paris on any terms, but in deference to Perrin he hired Weil. As he anticipated, they disagreed about everything, but the intellectual discord was fruitful to them both. He was at first exasperated by her unyielding argumentation, but his position as a voice of the agrarian, perceptibly vanishing Catholic France, with its ancient values statically rooted in the land, contributed much to her vision of a spiritually regenerated postwar society. It says much about her regard for Thibon that to him she entrusted her notebooks and a large number of her writings when she left France in 1942.

Like her factory work, Weil's farm drudgery was experimental, save that now the exhaustion she imposed on herself had a spiritual value for her. She told Kahn she expected that fatigue would "extinguish" her mental capacities:

"Nonetheless, I regard physical work as a purification—but a purification on the order of suffering and humiliation. One also finds, at its depths, instants of profound, nourishing joy, without equivalent elsewhere."[74]

The *conte* of the tar and golden doorways now had a new meaning for her: to choose the tar meant to receive it along with the gold, or rather, the gold was in the tar, as inextricably mixed with it as the peculiar joy to be found only in lowliness and debilitation. That was how she rationalized the farm work even before she assumed it. She also wanted to discover if there was, as Plato believed, an immortal, irreducible part of the soul which nothing could destroy—a bizarre perspective to take, surely, but Weil's was not merely some exercise of a hypertrophic intellect. It had much to do with her status as a Jew.

In June 1941, the Vichy regime required all Jews in the ZNO to register. Weil refused. Jean Rabaut, an old syndicalist friend, saw her in Marseilles: "We spoke of the persecution of Jews. She judged with severity the Jews who accepted the segregation. 'I would prefer to go to prison rather than to a ghetto,' she said. The preservation of Judaism as a cultural collectivity did not interest her at all. Her revolt was prompted by a very general feeling of personal dignity."[75]

She saw, however, that the Vichy law was a form of imprisonment, that her identification as Jewish threatened her not as a Jew but as an intelligent being. If she had to submit to annihilation, she wanted to do so on her own terms: "Why should I attach a lot of value to this part of my intelligence which anyone, absolutely anyone, using whips and chains, or walls and bars, or a scrap of paper covered with certain writing, could deprive me of? If this part is everything, then I am completely a thing of almost no value, and why spare myself?"[76] Here she adumbrates negatively what she later gave a positive meaning, the decreation of self. Registration as a Jew was one form of decreation she could not accept. She believed that for slaves and outcasts, adherence to Christianity was inevitable, but when it was unmistakably clear that Jews, both native and foreign, faced exactly the Christian's humiliation, she declined to join them.

Neither did she show any solidarity with the CGT and the Christian Confédération française des travailleurs chrétiens (CFTC), outlawed by Vichy in the fall of 1940. Shortly after their dissolution, they joined together in a manifesto which "reaffirmed the signers' faith in a free trade union movement."[77] Weil's former associates of *Syndicats*, whom she once judged "the only comrades I value among the responsible militants of our syndical organizations," were now solidly *Pétainistes*.[78]

It would have been wholly foreign to her disposition to withdraw altogether from activism. She became interested in the plight of Vietnamese soldiers and civilian laborers interned by the Germans at Mazargues, in the ZNO. To these twice-over victims of France's disastrous policies she regularly brought food, clothing, and ration coupons, including those of her parents.

Among her attempts to secure better treatment for the Vietnamese and other aliens in the camps, many of them antifascist refugees, was a letter she wrote in March 1941 to William Leahy, then America's ambassador to Vichy. It is a startling document on two counts. She thanks Leahy for American relief efforts to France but urges that further aid to her country be contingent upon ending "these cruel treatments" of internees, not only for their sake but "for the sake, also, of the French men and women to whom honor is dearer than food." One can only wonder how many French people were similarly motivated. Even more extravagantly she asked that "no help given to France should be in the least harmful or dangerous to the cause of England. Many men and women in France would gladly starve if they felt that through starvation they could be useful to England."[79] She did not credit the fact that many French in the ZNO accepted, however sullenly, Pétain's "national revolution" under German hegemony.[80] The "true" France she carried in her mind and heart.

Why, then, did she not become a fighter in the Resistance and, now that opportunities abounded, implement her "most dangerous mission" fantasies that had been thwarted in the Spanish and Czech crises? In 1941 Resistance groups (the Communist party apart) were still in the inchoate stages of organization; they were mostly local and wholly unprepared for covert, paramilitary action. Besides, the defeat of Britain and a total victory for Hitler seemed likely. Russia's heavy losses after the June 1941 invasion did not brighten prospects. Seeming futility would not have deterred Weil, however. In fact, she did make a contribution.

Only after publication of the Cabaud and Pétrement biographies did the extent of her work in the Resistance come to light. She was impelled in part by her keen regret for espousing pacifism in the late 1930s, a position that proved completely inadequate and unreal in the face of Hitler's designs for war. It was also impossible for Weil to remain long on the periphery of a crisis, veteran as she was of so many, even though disillusioned many times over about political action.

Soon after arriving in Marseilles, she became acquainted with leaders of Combat, the main leftist Resistance cadre in southern France. She was arrested while distributing anti-Vichy pamphlets, taken to court and threatened with imprisonment. The judge presumed that an educated bourgeoise would be repelled by the presence of prostitutes in jail, but their company was fetching: "I've always desired to know this milieu," she informed the judge, "and I do not see any other means to know it than prison."[81] This rebarbative posture recalls her response when threatened with dismissal from teaching at Le Puy: it seemed natural and acceptable for her to be thus abused. She was perhaps disappointed when the judge dismissed her as a lunatic.

In December 1941 she met Marie-Louise David, an acquaintance of Perrin. David, ten years her junior, came from a conservative Catholic family that fully supported Pétain. Revolted by Nazism, she went to work for *Les cahiers du Témoignage chrétien* and on Perrin's recommendation enlisted Weil in circulating some three hundred of its issues.[82] The February–March 1942 edition carried the title "The Racists Self-Portrayed"; the April–May issue was titled "Antisemites." It is doubtful that Weil would have had any part in distributing these texts if she had not fully supported their antiracist arguments.[83]

She also secured false identity cards for refugees, including Jews. Knowing the risks, she advised David: "If ever you're taken by the police, put everything on my back. You're more useful than I am. I'm content to distribute, but it's you who are organizing everything."[84] The combination of naiveté and myopic nobility was wholly typical of Weil. Less so was her counsel to lie. It seems to have troubled her that her complicity in the activities of Combat and the Témoignage required continual dissembling. While accepting the necessity of a lesser evil such as forgery or theft to save a life, she recognized the evil as a crime and therefore harmful to respect for laws, bad laws though they were. To have entertained such scruples under a regime like Vichy's might seem to us now ridiculously fussy, but Weil's subsequent emphasis in *L'enracinement* on civic responsibility and obedience to law reflects in part a penance for her brief career as a criminal.

These activities did not deflect her from the intense intellectual pursuits she had begun on arriving in the ZNO. One of the effects of talks with Perrin was a project for rereading Greek texts as anticipations of Christianity.[85] This was a disastrously misconceived enterprise. Written after her farewell to Perrin, Weil's search for the "Greek source" is an apologia for a Hellenized Christianity he would have been hard put to admit, founded as it is on Weil's desire to displace Hebraic sources which inform every page of the synoptic gospels. To set aside historical texts in favor of analogized philosophical terms (as though the Johannine gospel is derived from Plato) amounts at best to a game or exercise, but for Weil it fulfilled an urgent need to establish, rather, to restore an intellectual bond between Christianity and pagan antiquity. Only by thus revealing a "pure" Christianity, free of its Jewish heritage and Roman institutions, could she accept it and disarm the Catholic dogma that had been troubling her since 1938: *extra ecclesiam nulla salus*.

On May 14, 1942, she left with her parents by steamship for Morocco; thence, on June 7, for New York. Her biographers believe she was prompted to go chiefly by her desire to become active in the Allied effort and to get her nurses plan accepted, but had she been so eager she would not have let two years pass.[86] The more likely primary motive was one that Pétrement considers secondary, her parents' safety. As Perrin has noted, the threat of German occupation of the ZNO was a lively concern, and the deportation of Jews from Paris early in 1942 quickly became common knowledge.[87] Her parents refused to leave France without her, and so she went. She profoundly loved France—her severe criticisms of it are the best proof—and she departed with a painful sense that she would never return.[88] Yet she also felt something beyond suffering, what she called a purity "common to joy and suffering and which is the love of God," the effect of her taking on as her own the cry, "My God, why have you abandoned me?"[89] She wrote those words in a camp in Casablanca, in the company of several hundred exiled Jews, including some Orthodox rabbis from Poland.

Like Marseilles, New York City, where she spent four months, brought an enforced leisure, and she used it well. She wrote to several people, including Jacques Maritain and her Henri IV schoolmate Maurice Schumann, asking help in getting her nurses plan accepted by the United States government. She also visited the French consulate and the Free French offices in hope that she could be sent to England. She told Schumann she was willing to return to France on a sabotage mission, claiming her Resistance contacts for credentials. She later wrote to him that she wanted "the amount of suffering and useful danger which will save me from being consumed by grief," and she added that "the *malheur* extended over the world obsesses me and overwhelms me to the point of annulling my faculties."[90] She was no coward, but she was tormented by the feeling that she had deserted France.[91]

In mid-July she read newspaper accounts of demonstrations at Marseilles, Lyons, and Toulouse in which two people were killed and several wounded. It is reported that Weil "had been so affected by this that she went two days without eating." Did she learn as well of the twenty-two thousand Jews arrested in Paris on July 16–17 and the Vel'd'Hiver? Did her exclamation to her mother, "I can't go on living like this," acknowledge more than she could say?[92]

Her tremendous intellectual activity, evident chiefly in her New York notebooks, indicates that her faculties, despite the psychological strain of exile, remained intact. She spent a great deal of time at the New York Public Library researching folklore, including American Indian tales. She wrote two essays on the Cathars and a lengthy letter to the Dominican Père Marie-Alain Couturier in which she amassed thirty-five points (or theses) as intellectualized objections to the church. That "Letter to a Priest" indicates how well she had armed herself against Perrin's efforts to bring her to baptism.

Yet she continued to attend Roman Catholic masses. She derived great pleasure from the liturgy, even though, not being a communicant, she could rehearse again and again her exclusion. She took on the outsider's voyeuristic role even more openly in attending a Baptist church service in Harlem, where "the faithful explode into dances like the Charleston, shouts and spirituals. That's worth seeing. . . . Authentic faith, it seems to me."[93] Her friend Louis Bercher once remarked that had she stayed in America, Weil would have become a black.[94] The only time she entered a synagogue was on a visit to the Abyssinian temple, of very ancient pedigree, in upper Manhattan.

On November 10, 1942, one day before the German occupation of Vichy France, Weil embarked for England. She had succeeded in joining the Free French staff, but when she finally reached London and the Resistance offices she was assigned, much to her disappointment, the desk job of reviewing proposals for postwar France. Nothing ever came of the nurses plan or her requests to be sent to France by parachute for espionage. From mid-December to mid-April, 1943, when she contracted tuberculosis and had to be hospitalized, she wrote prodigiously. The projects she examined undoubtedly gave her some inspiration,[95] particularly those of the reactionary Organisation civile et militaire, which threatened to impose a fascist statism, but much she was now setting down on paper she had reflected upon long before. Some of her work has the character of a summation, which raises the lurid question of whether she sensed she would not live much longer.

Rejection of her requests for service in France compounded what she called her "triple limit": a conviction of moral failure—she reproached herself for cowardice, as though she had subconsciously schemed for the security enjoyed in America and England; an intellectual restlessness, limited as she was to designs for France's spiritual rebirth while she was left in exile; and increased physical debility.[96] Each of these limits constrained the others. The astonishing energy she gave to writing could not fully expiate her remorse for leaving France. Her punitive attempts to minimize her diet eventually sapped her mental vitality. Even when hospitalized, she continued to eat little. What meager strength she had she used in writing dissembling cheerful letters to her parents and in reading Sanskrit from the *Gita,* that master text of activism.

It is alleged that someone baptized her, either in the London hospital where she was initially placed or later at the Ashford sanatorium where she died, but Pétrement makes a good case for the invalidity of this gratuitous act: there is no evidence that Weil solicited it. When she entered Ashford she asked that no religion be listed on her registration form, and she never requested a priest. She once made the ironic stipulation that she would accept baptism only if she had no mind left.

Speculation as to whether she willed her death or wanted to die seems entirely useless, not to say morbid. Without doubt she faced the imminence of death with an acceptance that sometimes disconcerts healthy onlookers. It does no violence to fact to suppose that that acceptance was her supreme gesture of *amor fati.*

Heart failure ended her life shortly after she became comatose, on August 24, 1943. She was buried in the Roman Catholic section of the New Cemetery at Ashford and continues to be the celebrity there. Even death has not rescued her from a peculiar isolation.

PART ONE

The Education of Simone Weil

T W O

Le Maître

Ce n'est pas hors d'une limite qu'on depasse
le maître, mais au dedans de sa pensée.
ALAIN, *Entretiens au bord de la mer*

Master of Those Who Doubt

When he heard she was dead, Alain said, "It isn't true. She'll come back, yes?"[1] He had not seen her since her *normalien* days when she visited the Lycée Henri IV for his lectures. His health declining, he retired in 1933. She sent him some of her writing, and after her death he read in her publications a warrant for his belief that she had been his finest student.

His influence on her can be read throughout her mature writings. A study of Simone Weil is, in a sense, a study of two extraordinary people.

Alain had occupied a central position in France's intellectual life for over a generation, and more than forty years after his death, he is still known to every student of a French lycée. He was a polemicist, an outspoken Dreyfusard, a pacifist, a member of France's Radical party of petit bourgeois reformers. He was also an outsider, proud of his Norman roots, always content despite his eminence to remain an instructor at a preparatory school.

His pedagogy was interrupted once, by the Great War, when at forty-six he enlisted and served for two and a half years as a brigadier in artillery. Those who oppose war must submit themselves to it, he felt, lest their opposition be discredited as cowardice or pusillanimity. His reflections on those years, when some of his most promising students were lost, he later gathered in *Mars ou la guerre jugée*, one of the most thorough psychological studies of war since Thucydides.

Like many truly interesting people, Alain had a fair number of contradictions and inconsistencies within him. The liberating effect of his voluntarism on young minds seems at odds with his resolute provincialism: he traveled little, may have gloried in his ignorance of foreign languages, took little interest in modern literature (Paul Valéry excepted), and lazily disdained the theoretical prime movers of twentieth-century science. Freud, he once remarked, ignored human freedom. Einstein meddled in metaphysics, a province Alain jealously reserved to philosophers. He disliked radios, telephones, politicians, and airplanes.

Some of the most striking facts about Alain concern his life with women and may not be out of place in a study of his foremost female student. His mother's failure to give him affection bred a certain misogyny in him. He was long hostile to marriage, rationalizing that domesticity might rob his mind of energy and peace. During his first years in Paris he lodged in a brothel district. Once, when visited by a school inspector, he went on, undaunted, instructing his midterm boys on one's obligations to prostitutes.

In his mid-thirties he met a young widow, Mme Monique Morre-Lambelin. For forty years she served Alain as a confidante and unstinting editor of his writings. In his many letters to her she became "mah meh," "mon jumeau," and "mon Egerie." Not long after this friendship began, he met Gabrielle Landormy, a beautiful woman who became wholly devoted to him. He did not soon relax his scruples about marriage: he married Landormy forty years after they met, when she was near sixty and he eighty. His two faithful women lie beside him at Père Lachaise.

Alain wrote prodigiously. His works (not complete) fill four volumes of Gallimard's Pléiade series, the French equivalent of immortality.[2] The well-known daily reflections called *propos*, "improvisations never retouched," live on as virtually his own genre.[3] Perhaps the best avenue to Alain is his *Histoire de mes pensées*, a leisurely, almost rambling sequence of thoughts. The tone of defensive confession, so like that of Rousseau, informs remarks such as this: "I've made my way in the company of some authentically great men, and nothing else matters to me."[4]

Of these great men one is nearly forgotten: Jules Lagneau, Alain's teacher and the only god Alain said he had ever met. It seems difficult to justify this esteem unless we credit the pedagogical example Lagneau set. He died in 1894, age forty-three, having published little, and the posthumous works serve mainly to show the sophisticated acuity of philosophical speculation Alain himself was to practice. But Lagneau is of considerable importance to the study of Weil. His writing on Spinoza provides an indispensable touchstone in the difficult task of assessing Weil's debt to the one Jew to whom she was willing to accord intellectual greatness. A quote from Lagneau, "If there were only ideas, there wouldn't be anything more," comes in some notes she took at the girls' lycée Sévigné, where Alain lectured on aesthetics. Alain added: "What belongs to ideas doesn't exist. . . . So far as one has only an idea, one has nothing that's real. . . . The great human error is to reason in place of finding out."[5] This trumpet call to certify reality for oneself took Weil far from the classroom, to Alsthom and Renault, to Germany in 1932 and Spain in 1936.

Bound to a classical humanism, Alain held little esteem for any departure from what the ancients had said, for the problems they addressed, however elementary, loom eternal. He defined this allegiance as true originality: "It's to invent in the most profound sense, since it is to continue what is human."[6] Plato was the first of Alain's intellectual progenitors. Alain said he saw nothing in Plato to correct, but in Aristotle, so helpful in "scraping the soil like a peasant," he found a mind perhaps more like his own, rooted in that life of experience without which there can be no knowledge. Alain admits that in his youth Aristotle's influence had preponderated so long that he almost forgot Plato, in strong contrast to Weil, for whom Plato was so authentic she seems scarcely to have heeded Aristotle.[7]

Alain's attitude to Stoicism reveals more. Though accepting the Stoic doctrine of necessity, so central in Weil's thought, he laments its "enervation of power." It seems absurd to him that the Stoics sought knowledge of the world without the will to know it because truth resides, he maintains, in the very tensions of the will which seeks it.[8] For Alain, will is the keystone of intellect.

This celebration of will, derived from Lagneau's prescription of its exercise toward a universal skepticism, appears to have borne no fruit in Weil. She generally hedges the will's efficacy and seems to identify it with imagination as a prime mover of illusions. Further, her own metaphysical dogma of *attente* suggests the passivity Alain censured in the Stoics. But Weil's disposition was essentially voluntarist, her thought the model of Alain's hortatory description of the will: "energetic searching is the sign of the true."[9] Weil's *attente* is Alain's will in sheep's clothing.

Of the moderns in Alain's favor, Descartes stands as the indispensable examplar of skepticism as method. It is, in fact, the only legitimate passageway to truth; it is the opposite of dogmatism and foe to the belief that everything can be explained. It is also the opposite of fanaticism, which hates doubt in oneself and in others.[10] Although no truth, however hidden, lies beyond experiential reach, it must be teased out by a thorough doubt of anything's certainty. Doubt, Alain insists, is not weakness but strength, and real genius knows how to undo even the eternal truths.[11] The atom, for example, may be a fact for fools or an idea for intellectuals; for genius, it is a mere convention. Alain ascribes to Descartes this unraveling genius of doubt and at the same time makes it normative for intelligence. Mind denies, rejects, casts all experience and ideas away. It secures everything by refusal. Descartes showed how even mathematics, rightly understood, consists of negations—"he scorned revealed truths"—as an exercise of will.[12] One must be immoderate, venturesome, excessive in seeking to comprehend even the simplest things, for truth itself is excessive. The injunction was not lost on Weil.

What, then, does experience give? This world's inertia, Alain claims, offers absolutely no hint of divine intent. Void of final causes (Alain could forget Aristotle), the world requires neither hope nor fear, neither the recourse to prayer nor the blandishments of imagination. We must accept the Lucretian chill of life's immense solitudes, the immeasurable beauties of nature, which prove, if anything, only that God is not there. Alain speaks of celestial justice, an order that Weil was to affirm in the Stoic *amor fati*. It served him as a caveat against the dogma of philosophical idealism (Bishop George Berkeley's, for instance), which would reduce the phenomenal world to unprovable appearances and substitute for it a false world of subjectivity. Alain reminds us that there is a ridiculous disproportion between the world and the self, between the enormity of what we apprehend and the idleness of our talk in trying to explain it. But that is no justification for trying to withdraw oneself from experiencing the world.[13]

Far from determinism, as any genuine humanist must be, Alain rejects its manifestations in nineteenth-century nostrums of progress, including the Marxist mystique of perpetual change. The only admissible mystique lies in a Kantian esprit, where humanity can safely take refuge because it will always be recognized there, and accordingly served, as an end. By contrast, any fatalism, however benign, employs people as a means. It is no wonder that Marxism has never developed a doctrine of freedom, or of humanity, or even of war. Hegel himself, although admirably illustrating mental progress as an "ardor to die so as to live again," must be faulted for failing to see that in the world's history the mind has reached insurpassable moments. Alain cites first-century Christianity as such a moment.[14]

Alain was insistently libertarian. By his cardinal rule, "be free," he inspired his students to win themselves free from all given opinions and conventions of bourgeois contentment so as to know good from evil as precisely as possible. His mainspring for liberty amounts to Kant's equation of it with obligation, freedom at the greatest remove from license. If one's first obligation is to believe oneself free, the greatest fault lies in a belief or rationalization that one can do nothing. The "satanic position" of determinism amounts to "bad faith" (*mauvaise foi*), a term we recognize not in Weil but borrowed subsequently by Jean-Paul Sartre.

It remains one of Alain's most commendable traits that he seemed to facilitate exercise of the intellectual freedom he prescribed. He rejected philosophical jargon, confident that truth lies in commonplace language, not in contrived systems or pretentious argot. Likewise, he admired Rousseau for his adherence to the commonness of experience. He submitted that thinkers who dogmatize by abstraction must be guilty of a bad education—a warning to any who would like to discover or impose a system upon Weil's thought. Besides, ideas must be regarded as means, not ends, as pincers with which to grasp the objects of experience.[15] One must be receptive to alien notions and learn to live with them rather than overcome or confound them: "It's a work of patience always to be begun anew." To read worthy writers without posing objections, without even the compulsion to understand them but simply to be familiar with what they say, should always suffice.[16]

Alain believed that one can best test one's ideas by denying them in a spirit of contradiction. He likened this process to shaking the tree of knowledge: the good fruits will be saved; the bad will fall useless. "Opposition is the very movement of thought and the only means of giving body to ideas."[18] Contradiction as a means of liberating oneself from a point of view may be among Alain's most important contributions to Weil's intellectual development.

If, as Lagneau had taught, the best-proved theses lose efficacy to the extent that they seem evident, then doubt may well be the true agent of enlightenment. In every case, in every word, everything must be risked. Doubt, then, does not arrest, it propels, and the way lies open for an active will's embrace of paradox and absurdity. Alain, who may otherwise be reckoned among the late, if not last, voices of Kantian rationalism, figures as a harbinger of existentialism.

Alain's advocacy of a resilient openness to experience and a concomitant horror of dogmas explains his support of the Radical party in France and his rejection of socialism. Humanism itself—and he is one of its foremost proponents in this century—belongs too much to the individual to serve, like most isms, as an ideological centrifuge.

He practiced another form of distance in the classroom, where, as he liked to say, he often held genius between his hands but was careful not to extort it.

He was not inclined to confessions and confidences. Affection must not be confounded with instruction, he said, for in that confusion an instructor would usurp the place of parents.[18] How such reserve might have affected Weil, tortured in the adolescent conviction of her intellectual mediocrity, we do not know. Was he the evangelist of his own prescription who speaks not in proofs but proclamations? "You are not damned, or wretched, or useless, or without courage. I am telling you because I know, and you, you are badly informed."[19] Perhaps it was from Alain that Weil learned to regard distance as the key to friendship. Yet one may doubt the apparent severity of Alain's reserve: almost every photograph of him shows within the patrician's aquiline profile an avuncular ease and a welcoming insouciance.

Such a portrait suggests someone at the farthest possible remove from Weil, no less in temperament than in appearance. A central incongruity must be reckoned, too, in that this friend of Plato had little of the academic about him. Shuffling about the classroom with a leg limp from a war injury, making his reading aloud from a text the sufficient, in fact exclusive, interpretation of it—he permitted no questions, this libertarian—Alain looked more peasant than professor. He was almost defiantly proud in refusing conformity to the refined, if not effete image of the *conférencier*. In his war memoirs he recounts with satisfaction his fraternity with common soldiers in preference to the officers whose company his age and education would have merited. Similarly, he must have savored some private joy in rejecting an offer from the Sorbonne to give a series of public lectures.

Alain enjoyed an unfailing self-assurance (he never corrected his manuscripts), yet he declined to use his career and the eminence it secured him as a stepping-stone into the bourgeoisie and thus escape his origins. His "soi libre" doctrine amounted in part to a class gesture. This point has relevance to Weil. Was it not possibly from him that she assumed the prejudice that learning belongs to the scions of the toiled land, perhaps far more than to occupants of salons? Whatever that possibility, her friendship with the erudite gentleman farmer Gustave Thibon (a contest of opposites) must have given that prejudice a very wide girth.

Weil did not make explicit departures from or objections to Alain's teachings, but that does not mean that he hovered over her as Lagneau had over him a generation earlier, an indispensable tutelary spirit. His pedagogy, urging total freedom of expression, must have instilled confidence and courage in her at an ungainly age. He required of her a Stoic's perseverance in casting out the phantoms of imagination so easily taken as thoughts. Ideas, once informed by experience, must claim reality by application to experience. Weil early learned to regard understanding as a geometrical tool, and so she would later tend to indulge metaphors of balance and symmetry in provocative, sometimes unlikely contexts.[20]

The acuity of skill with which she did so, and in a spirit of self-confidence at times as peremptory as Alain's, came with a practice Alain taught his students to demand of themselves: writing and writing. He made much of Stendhal's "Write every day, whether inspired or not." Even as her freethinking Jewish family had virtually imposed intellectual autonomy upon her, so Alain encouraged its expression, and both of these influences must be read in the bold, restive tone that strikes the reader in almost all of Weil's writing.

Perhaps it is to Alain especially that we owe the staggering abundance of Weil's productivity, not least in the unpublished "cahiers divers" in which she recorded Alain's obiter dicta at a length that might place him with the great maximists of the seventeenth century:

> The cult of the dead ends in a song of admiration and joy. It's the true paradise, a kind of existence where the world's weight is no longer felt. Such is the soul.
>
> Religion as imagination's game is natural to us. It has the shape of human nature, and is the least astonishing thing in the world.
>
> A question is truly posed only by passion.
>
> We do not seek the truth from biographies but our own nourishment.
>
> If there were no god, would that at all change the moral problem? There's the will of God, that he changes nothing.
>
> Plato, a jansenist without religion.[21]

These sweeping remarks with their aphoristic boldness undoubtedly informed Weil's thought and style, especially in the notebooks, her laboratory tables of reflection in which she sets down propositions in all their bracing spareness. There she carried out most faithfully the Stendhalian imperative of a daily record. There, too, thought could exercise its own economy, free from the phalanx order imposed by developed arguments. Her many essays show that Weil was fully capable of argument, but she worked best from an inspired intuition, and with a potent and comprehensive brevity aimed at essentials.

Having survived her by eight years (he died in 1951 at age eighty-two),

Alain must have rejoiced to read in her published works the unmistakable ratification of so much he had taught: the immediacy of the immortal worthies, Plato and Descartes before all; the transforming power of perception; freedom of judgment; a gospel of action that extolled the reflective potential in manual labor; and, central to all else, one's intellectual responsibility to the world.

The very breadth of topics she took up in writing, from folklore to the role of political parties, from science to life in the factories, from literary reviews to theology—all shaped by a steady insight and a judgment charged with a sense of mission—mirrors Alain's own. Alain made his students, and Weil foremost among them, slaves to freedom, to an unqualified intellectual liberty.

How did she go her own way? She seems to have passed by the explicit voluntarism that made Alain a resolute optimist, but in substituting *désir* for *volonté* she could adopt to her own uses the imperative to confer upon the mind a restless, creative life. The apparent, perhaps essential difference between master and pupil was temperamental. André Maurois has written that "Alain made us better, more contented with ourselves, happier and at home with the human race."[22] Alain could discipline Weil's considerable energies and direct them toward the illuminations of noble thinkers, but he could not alter the immediate data of her consciousness, that she was female, a Jew, and since childhood self-convicted of intellectual inferiority. Thus triply burdened, how could she presume she would ever be reconciled to the human race or content with herself?

In one of her letters to that other father, the ever-patient Père Perrin (May 15, 1942), she claims that about the age of fourteen she had such contempt for herself that suicide seemed the only way to break free, but she survived by the "certitude" that in longing for truth, her own shabbiness in mental endowment would not matter, that the longing itself for "the realm where authentically great men alone enter" would, if sustained, amount to a kind of genius.[23] Could Alain's prescribed voluntarism be plainer?

She dates this awakening to sometime in 1923, two years before her entrance into Lycée Henri IV, but though she might have found rescue in *désir* and rationalized it into an intellective faculty, the language of her testimony to Perrin argues familiarity with Alain. Memory may deceive by anachronism, especially if, as here, it reaches back nearly twenty years, but it may be an instructive exercise to read Weil's correspondence with Perrin as a tribute to Alain. Specifically, the realm of genius she portrays to Perrin contained for her Alain's Platonic verities, "beauty, virtue and every aspect of good."[24] When she claims that her desire possessed of itself "an efficacy in this domain of spiritual good under all its forms," it recalls Alain's militant view that "virtue is only efficacity, intention is nothing."[25] When she asserts that she holds an extremely rigorous view of intellectual probity to which no one she has known has ever attained, including herself, one may be inclined to some sympathy for Perrin, who must have been bemused that this inquirer into Christian faith had her own *chevaux de frise* more menacing than any church dogma. What more than this probity did Alain demand in urging her to doubt everything?

In the inventory of explanations, queries, and qualms that kept her from submitting herself to the Roman Catholic church Weil never invoked Alain, but her final and buoyant independence owed incalculably more to him than either she or anyone else has credited, and not even Christ's "possession" of her could cause her to lose it.

Weil's First Writing

Perhaps in nothing was Alain's influence on Weil so substantial as in his reflections on God, religion, and faith. One might initially presume the contrary because since Alain held no allegiance to any religion, was temperamentally averse to mystic raptures, and never stated so much as a personal credo. It is even tempting to regard him as a foil to Perrin and Thibon, to whom Weil revealed so much of her sensibility.

An essential thrust in Alain's voluntarism was the claim of subjectivity as an achieved truth, that Goethean motif of freedom through the unrelenting exertions of will. To aim toward the real, the true, without flinch of conscience, was Alain's ideal. He set himself against religion as dogma, that is, as a social force constraining or canceling individual endeavor. Inevitably, his sympathies lay with the heterodox and heretical, with the patently irreligious outsiders. Setting their dearly paid illuminations against the conventions of credulity upon which collectivized faith depends, Alain believed, in rather Hegelian fashion, that religion progresses naturally away from its forms in nature and society toward esprit. His attitude toward historical faiths was ambivalent. He accepted them all as movements, but he resisted their tendency to arrest, particularly as they hardened in confrontation with reason. To set faith against reason is to pose a false antinomy, he maintained. The genuine conflict was between religions past and future. Weil's desiderated "new religion" to supersede Christianity owes much to Alain. Similarly, her opposition to religion as a cult of natural forces (as she saw Judaism) and as an institutional power (Christendom) may be derived from Alain's opposition stated precisely in those terms.[26]

For Alain as for Weil, that new religion assumed a Christian guise. It rested primarily, however, upon the Stoics' *amor fati*: "What I wanted to call celestial justice is the very inertia of this world, which shows no trace of intention or will."[27] Like Weil subsequently, Alain regarded Christianity as Platonic rather than Hebraic, meaning that its spirit moves internally by compunctions of intellect or will rather than outwardly by social constraints, and his condemnation of idolatries of force anticipates Weil's words on the Great Beast and her equation of it with ancient Israel. He found the antidote for all such collectivity in a theological separation of spirit and power, a disjunction similar to and no less violent than the Cartesian separation of soul and body: "That which is god now is man still powerless and even always powerless, the man of the crèche and of Calvary."[28] For Weil, the backdrop of a *theologia crucis* was this darkness of a hidden God, but Alain preceded her in an enthusiasm for the Jansenist paradox of a God who "has nothing to bestow but mind . . . a god absolutely weak and absolutely proscribed."[29]

In view of Alain's athletic voluntarism, one might question how much the weakness of God represents the position of his faith and whether it does not rather express covertly a desired enfeeblement of theism in favor of a Comtean religion of Humanity. As Pétrement has observed, Alain (and Weil after him) owed much to Lagneau's Platonic idea of "a sort of religion where the supreme value was detached from existence."[30] To a temperament as assured and combative as Alain's, the nonexistence of God would construably be good news indeed, leaving to the will a world in which to bustle. Besides, Alain's unbounded confidence in the mind's potential implicitly argues the mind's divinization: "The mind is neither within nor without; it is the all of all. Beyond the known it thinks regions upon regions; it is all that is possible, and where it wishes to deny itself, there too it is. It is present at its own death." Alain claims that the mind judges all virtues, obligations, and dogmas, replacing them with a freedom that owes nothing. "If God is mind, God is free and for the free. Such is the most beautiful mystery, and undoubtedly the only mystery."[31] It is as though everything, including deity itself, must finally be addressed to this anthropocentrism. Mind is the measure of all things.

When Weil was his student, she naturally showed the influence of Alain's Protagorean devotions. In her 1926 essay "Le beau et le bien," for example, she equated God with humanity and the human spirit, a position quite foreign to her later thinking.[32] Yet sometime after she left Henri IV she was still grappling with the moral implications of the mind's autonomy. Like Alain predisposed to philosophical idealism, she set herself the task of testing and, when necessary, confounding idealist thought. That effort is revealed brilliantly in a short unpublished essay on the relation between mind and the good.

Entitled "Kant: obligation de prendre comme objet le Souverain Bien," this work is directed with Alain's prescribed dialectical vigor to a problem he recast many times, and it carries out his injunction to entertain thoughts that, however alien to one's own, impose forceful conclusions. It argues that no work is ever the fruit of a moral law because obligation (*devoir*) is a pure form, a pure negation, always ahead of us.

Weil rejects Rousseau's Stoic claim that the recompense of virtue lies only in the knowledge of it. Kant himself, she notes, knew no other paradise. It will not do, though, because all we ever know is our phenomenal happiness. We cannot savor our own acts as such. To the saintliest man, his virtue is never a fact, only what must be, and yet we must accept the existence of virtue as an object. How else could we speak of it at all? Kant, Weil submits, might be regarded as an ancestor of pragmatism in that as concerns value he places our beliefs above knowledge because they are useful, indeed necessary for action.

In Stoic fashion she supposes an identity of pure spirit in all thinking beings. When I think for myself, she asserts, I think for all minds. It is this universal aspect of every solitary mind which constitutes morality; it is the freedom we can identify in Socrates, Descartes, and Rousseau. Morality, therefore, is not a rule of conduct but an expression of it, and justice is "that which I do when I obey nothing that is foreign to me. Thus one sees that if there is a god, far from God being my judge, it is my liberty, in some fashion, which God sets up."[33]

These statements are indistinguishable from Alain's voluntarism, but Weil pushes on to its central weakness. Mind cannot be equated with will, thanks to necessity. She adverts here to Berkeley, who though a Platonist, identified will as a simple power of action within the world of matter, a world whose reality his idealism denied. Matter separates one mind from another, yet it is the means by which one mind dominates another. Like Plato, Berkeley acknowledged an opposition between the mind's essential activity and its passivity, but he did not see the danger in subordinating nature to mind. Everyone knows that nature is not subordinate to one's own mind. Worse, Weil observes that

Berkeley's idealism makes the material world into a divine caprice, an arbitrary expression of God. Weil seems to suggest through Berkeley that Alain's divine esprit has a nightmarish underside: apparently free participants in it, we may have no more real claim to it than puppets have to their strings.[34]

Weil could thus press a philosophical position to its logical extreme, even (or especially) one to which she might have wanted to give her fealty. A philosophy that denies nature's claims and limits on us sounds a siren's song; it prompts Weil to embrace a view in which necessity occupies a commanding position but without sacrifice of a divine otherness found in dualism.

This effort figures in a topos or student exercise Weil wrote for Alain, "L'existence et l'objet."[35] Its subject is a Kantian aesthetic play in the strict court of time.

She begins on a down beat: humanity cannot escape the shadows of Plato's Cave. The *Republic* includes this caveat, but Weil wants to update it. We would like to minimize the shocks of phenomenal life, she says, and so we exalt science to aid us in that effort, but science is essentially only another order of magic or divination.

At least we can acknowledge that we are slaves, and in that knowledge we can perhaps deliver ourselves: "The meditation upon the limits of human power and the invincible obstacles to human freedom is itself undoubtedly the only meditation which really gives strength and faith to the mind. One can find a very beautiful, although abstract example of it in Kant." Chief among these obstacles is time. We are forever in its flow yet it remains unintelligible. It can be limited only in works of art, which check our restless desire to break out of time, to arrest or to accelerate it. Music is fixed and eternal, yet it unfolds in time, and that paradox Weil elaborates into a hypothesis.

Let us suppose, she says, a series made up of one sound repeated many times at regular intervals. Would we then have in time a reversible series? An enthusiast of Bergson would say no, because a second sound would be apprehended not only as sound but as coming second. If we could make the repetition infinite and without counting, however, by imagination we could change the order and claim there was no change because the sounds would be alike.

Suppose now that all the changes in the universe follow a rhythm and form periods of whatever length but all identical. In a span of one hundred thousand centuries there would have to be an instant exactly identical to that in which we read these words; likewise, in two hundred thousand centuries, and so on. In that case, time would be reversible, that is, there would be no time. This metaphysical will-o'-the-wisp is instantly identifiable as the Greek notion of eternal recurrence. It enthralled Nietzsche, but Weil no sooner entertains it than she backs away, and nowhere later would she consider it as part of the fabric of necessity.

Instead, she goes back to the alluring phenomenon of music. Music gratifies the intellect by measure, but this measure, always like itself, has the form of diversity. In a sonata, for instance, a theme repeated makes us consider the relation of its second statement to its first as simultaneously one of likeness and difference. The uniformity satisfies intellect while the diversity satisfies imagination. In their accord Weil recovers Kant's definition of beauty, and her example evokes Vinteuil's magical and elusive phrase in *A la recherche du temps perdu*.

Through these thoughts on music Weil realizes why eternal recurrence has no final appeal for her. The hypothesis of divided time does not repel understanding, but it does repel experience; one can be certain that it does not conform to the truth even if that certainty amounts not to a geometrical demonstration but only to a reflection upon existence. What is essentially possible may also be experientially absurd.

Returning to her remarks on the Cave, Weil observes that Plato was more rigorous in his myths than most philosophers in their reasoning, for he perceived that though shadows depend on their objects, they nonetheless have their own nature. An existent object likewise has an essence manifested in it, yet it belongs to an order other than essence. The inspiration of this view seems to be taken from Spinoza (thought and extension, idea and thing, though united in substance are independent modes of being), but Plato's cave imagery brings home the dismal fact Weil wishes to accept, that appearances have a brute reality that will not go away.[36]

The play of freedom and necessity can be regarded concretely: just as no free act can be imagined for another which it is not, each note a musician writes can only be that note. But if external conditions were constant, a piece of music would be nothing more than an ensemble of notes. The listener could not tell in advance whether the next note to be heard would be beautiful or not but could tell what that note would have to be if it were to be beautiful. Let us say, for example (Weil gives none), that a diminished seventh chord begs for resolution. The change would not be free but contingent.

Music, in sum, proves finally irreducible to the mind that plays with it. Because it is matter, it belongs to existence and to time. Weil concludes that a sonata expresses not only humanity but the universe. In "L'existence et l'objet" we find early adumbrated a concept predominant in Weil's later metaphysics, the mediation or *metaxu* that reconciles two worlds in an equipoise of their fundamental tensions.

Thoughts Extended to Descartes and Spinoza

The fundamental intellectual distinction separating Weil from *le maître* could be, if not precisely defined, approached through their views on Descartes and Spinoza. Weil's essential tendency, one might say her affinity, lies with Spinoza, Alain's with Descartes.[37] Neither of them has left an explicit, exclusive declaration of loyalty; neither would have been disposed to do so.

Indeed, Alain wrote a lengthy summation of Spinoza's philosophy and said of his student days with Lagneau, "I was a spinozist and I am so still."[38] Nor are these simply passing affirmations, for Alain's writing in later years bears the same stamp. In a *propos* dated February 21, 1931, he referred to the predominance of a hardy joy in Spinoza and called it a sign of the heroic. To Thomas Hobbes's dictum that man exists as a wolf to man, Alain rejoined with Spinoza that man is a god for man.[39] Drawing on Spinoza's insight that we feel ourselves to be eternal, Alain joined Goethe in an enthusiastic grasp of the idea within that feeling: nothing inherent in the human personality can be contrary to it because the self could not endure at all if it bore its own destruction within. Vanity, wickedness, and folly do not belong to the human race; they simply manifest weakness in our responses to the external conditions that can destroy us.[40]

If we object that Alain suppressed the definitive term in our sense of eternity, that we feel so only in God, he might rejoin that God is nothing other than the eternal reason in which we all partake.[41] It was Spinoza who argued that in our passage, vouchsafed by reason, to a higher perfection, *tristesse* marks a step backward, and neither pity for others nor repentance is a genuine virtue.[42] Alain seems to speak for himself and Spinoza when he writes that the only way of helping others, of speaking to them as one should, is not to be concerned about them and to work out one's own salvation. However austere this philosophy, Alain hailed its courage and found in it a springboard for his own voluntarism, "the true foundation of self-esteem."[43]

All this aside, Alain was fundamentally at odds with Spinoza. Although they shared a joy in human potential, Alain departed from Spinoza at the crux. He had no use for and no need of Spinoza's mysticism and its *amor Dei intellectualis.* Knowledge that is acquiescent like love perhaps threatened him with an implicit recumbence. Alain was set willfully against this seeming surrender, and his summary essay on Spinoza not surprisingly understates God's definitive position in the *Ethics.* As Alain objected, however imposing the crystalline geometry of Spinoza's universe, the philosopher finds himself enclosed and pressed down within it like a botanical specimen: "It is to think according to God. But it is necessary in the first place to think according to the human."[44] Alain thought by the Protagorean measure first and last. He believed that the Spinozist love of God could be attained only at the too high cost of one's free will. That is, Spinoza placed everything, both matter and thought being attributes of divine substance, under necessity.[45]

As Leibnitz first observed, mysticism separated Spinoza from Descartes, but there was more. Descartes had distinguished thought as the perfection of being, matter's near opposite. The radically insufficient corporeal world can never approach divinity, but in Spinoza's view matter is no less an attribute of God than is thought. Alain heeded the philosophical prejudice that insists there can be no parity, and he backed away from the engulfing object of Spinoza's theism. His refuge in Descartes, who rescued philosophy from theology by erecting a God-subject, had been fostered by Lagneau, even though Lagneau taught Alain not to be troubled about "the no of Spinoza and the yes of Descartes," but rather to consider them both in correlation.[46]

Weil's thought approaches that correlation. Her dissertation of 1929–30 at L'Ecole Normale, "Science et perception dans Descartes," directed by Léon Brunschvicq, reflects Alain's influence transparently and must preface any assumption that Weil was essentially Spinozist.

First, however, Brunschvicq himself deserves some note. When Weil entered the Normale, he had occupied a chair in philosophy for over twenty years. He remains well-known in France for his studies of Spinoza and Pascal, and his 1897 edition of the *Penseés* still serves as a standard reference. Shortly before Weil's entrance, he had published *Le progrès de la conscience dans la philosophie occidentale* in which he propounded an idealism to supersede Kant. Brunschvicq argued against an apriorism of unchanging categories and for a progressive accommodation to new ways of examining thought and morals. Science and society, as his banner title indicates, must march on.

Brunschvicq's appreciation of philosophy's historical evolution beyond the apparently constant laws set down by canon and convention put him at odds with many students reared at Henri IV. They responded to his subtle and oblique lectures with amused contempt.[47] Alain, with his prejudice that we need only recast thoughts from antiquity, had little in common with Brunschvicq.

Neither did Weil, as her dissertation on Descartes shows. When Brunschvicq awarded it ten points out of twenty (the lowest passing mark), Alain allegedly accused him of nearly failing Weil because she was a Jew, as though Brunschvicq, also a Jew, were more assimilated or freethinking than Weil and needed to show her as much.[48]

In her introduction Weil hails the true priesthood of intellect inaugurated in Greek science and the regal part which mathematics played in it. She laments modern science's demotion of mathematics from queen to servant, as abstract reason triumphed over intuition. Her pleas for the intuitive grasp of science have a populist ring: she demands that science remain accessible to ordinary people's perceptions, that it first answer the external world before losing itself in theories. The thesis marks an attempt to go back to Descartes for a reorientation of scientific endeavor. Descartes was the first among moderns, she claims, to understand that science takes as its sole legitimate aim the measure of quantities and their interrelations determining such a measure. He was a kind of Thales; he tutored our knowledge of nature away from the domain of the senses to that of reason: "So he purified our thinking of imagination and modern scientists, who have applied analysis directly to all objects susceptible to this study, are his true successors."[49]

Weil commends Descartes's concern for the practical applications of scientific speculation, the catholicity of his perspective, and his belief in the unity of scientific knowledge. In effect, she uses him as a butt against the perhaps unhappy but inescapable fact that modern science has become so specialized that no individual can comprehend it as a whole. It seems captious, then, to plead through Descartes that science be accessible to the most commonplace lay intellect, but Weil looks confidently to the earthbound nature of Cartesian science as a trustworthy *point de repère* for such a plea. It is, she notes, a legitimately imaginative employment of geometry in forming ideas about material relations. Perception, the mind's natural geometry, is the equivalent of science as "a mental inspection."[50] It serves as the foundation for Descartes's belief in a common lay wisdom, that any intelligence at work is equal to the greatest genius—a liberating view for Weil, who had grown up with an extraordinarily gifted brother.

Descartes promoted a kind of everyman's access to science, and Weil formulates the Cartesian method in Alain's unmistakable accents: to doubt everything, to examine thoroughly, to rely solely on clear and distinct thoughts, to give credence to no authority. Crossing the caliginous terrain of doubt, she dutifully remarks the profound snares of human consciousness, the narrow circuit of its awareness, its subjection to chance, the prestige of illusion. Then she breaks through to a reformulation of the Cartesian *cogito* brilliantly à la Alain. It might be put this way: cogito, ergo possum: "To know is to know that which I can do, and I know to the degree that, for playing, suffering, feeling, imagining, I substitute acting and submitting, thus transforming illusion into certitude and chance into necessity."[51]

Had she stopped there, Weil would have been a thorough votary of Alain, but she is faithful to doubt as one's sole refuge. Thought may enjoy a compelling sovereignty, and the will can give one a sense of being God, but we must recognize that in fact we are not gods. So far as thoughts depend upon us, they are signs of the self; to the extent they do not, they are signs of another existence: "To know is to read in any thought whatever this double meaning."[52] The limit of our power shows us how God keeps us from being God.

This is no argument for theism, for by God Weil means simply the world to which we respond with our fantasies of hope and fear, but Weil's subsequent notion of attention is embryonic in this thesis because the effect of knowing as recognizing limit is precisely the effect she later associates with attention, humility. It is a submission to immobility, to the reception of ideas from without.[53]

Weil's boldness lies in her equation of this passivity with scientific method: to make oneself a scientist is to achieve self-mastery by realizing one's limits. Logic is a method for ordering knowledge, not for gaining it; mathematical proofs are not created but accepted. In Weil's constrictive view, there are only three ways of knowledge: to respond effectively to a question, to know on what terms one can do so, or to know that one cannot do so.

Has Weil's apparently Cartesian exercise not become an intellectual self-portrait? Particularly in her circumscription of logic and mathematics a violent modesty about the self seems to lie.

This impression is reinforced when Weil takes up the matter of how the *moi* interacts with the world it experiences. At times in her discussion the reader may feel transported from Descartes's world to Rousseau's, for the self now appears to be buffeted as a *jouet*, a laughingstock of its environment and at the same time a prey to its own imaginary trepidations.[54] Weil sets down her plaintiff's case against the imagination as an agent of uncertainty and error, collusive with the outer life to the harm of the inner.[55] Indeed, the imagination puts the world irremediably within the self; the world is "all which is not me within me."[56] As a haven from this storm of impressions, doubt methodically secures for the will a latitude for acting on the world: first, by apprehending that everything in the world is apart from, foreign and indifferent to everything else; second, by the unity of oneself responding to this obstacle course through "indirect action, action conformed to geometry, or to call it by its true name, work."[57]

It follows that work manifests the mind's genuine freedom. In it, the mind, using the body itself as pincers with which to grasp matter, realizes its own freedom and, simultaneously, the inadequacy of its ideas. As the geometrical application of clear and distinct ideas, work is the outward sign that perception can actively accommodate the world.

From Descartes's *Dioptric* Weil borrows an image to which she reverts repeatedly in her later writing, the blind man's cane. The cane symbolizes the sensory realm that thought uses as its intermediary for grasping the object of its work, the world as obstacle. Work in no way detracts from the exercise of doubt which forms the core of Cartesian method; rather, it feeds doubt in affording perception something to be explored, matter.

Science's role is to enable anyone to become, as it were, a tool of perception, but Weil states that the benefit of that process is strictly internal. Once we know the world as extension (matter), we know all we can know. Science serves only to make the mind master its imagination in response to the world. Here Weil lodges a caveat against notions of scientific progress. Technology gives us the illusion of power over matter, but the world no more belongs to us than to the ancients. It is easy to imagine how Brunschvicq would have bristled at such a statement and its celebration of work: "Workers know everything, but outside of working they do not know that they possess all the wisdom there is."[58]

As a cautionary script, "Science et perception dans Descartes" provides an indispensable prolegomenon to Weil's subsequent writings on the integrity of work and work's function as a sacrament of life.

THREE

Descent into the Cave

Weil's Works and Days in French Syndicalism, 1931–1936

Chercher les conditions matérielles de la pensée claire.
Combien il serait facile (et difficile!) de trouver de la joie
dans tous les contacts avec le monde.
SIMONE WEIL, *La condition ouvrière*

Historical Backgrounds

Although Weil had a sincere interest in leftist politics and the workers' movement before she passed her *agrégation* tests (July 1931), her involvement with them began in earnest during her first year as a lycée instructor of philosophy at Le Puy, seventy miles southeast of Clermont Ferrand, in the Massif Central.

The "red virgin" scandals of her year there, her activities on behalf of the unemployed through speeches, demonstrations, and confrontations with public authorities, have been sufficiently detailed in her biographies and need no iteration here. Although she joined the leftist teachers' union (Syndicat national des instituteurs), her involvement in workers' protests was from the start her own undertaking, and she was so conspicuous in their ranks that she quickly won notoriety from the local press. She immediately committed herself to the syndicalist establishment and worked steadily and critically for several years thereafter toward the order and direction for which it groped in the midst of economic and political crisis. Her writings from 1931 through the collapse of the Popular Front seven years later have enduring value not only as brilliantly reflected analyses of that acutely turbulent time but as exemplary records of how well she learned one of Alain's urgent lessons, that thought must be wedded to experience. Many of her essays, although reflecting the ad hoc quality of the issues they address, sustain an instructive forcefulness that transcends their occasions.

Weil did not single-handedly enrich the leftist proletariat with her learning. Kantian moral idealism had long been in the French leftist mainstream. But she had the gift of first scrutinizing immediate problems and then integrating them clearly and succinctly in accordance with her idealism. Unlike many leftist intellectuals, she eschewed the clichés and bromides of socialist rhetoric. Her writing remained free of hortatory platitudes and tired rhetoric. Imposing sobriety meant more to her than giving hope. Cartesian on the Left, she insisted above all on integrity of method, of skeptically refined, often disillusioning adherence to facts. Her celebrated experience of factory labor was experimental in a fully scientific way, and she learned from it a brutal fact that Alain could not have prepared her for, that experience can destroy the very capacity for thought.

The conjunction of *theoria* and *praxis* which Weil obliged herself to maintain can hardly be overstated because it has immediate relevance to one of the besetting difficulties of the French Left from its earliest days, that it so often failed to bridge the substantial gap between the bourgeois utopism of socialist thought and the daily concerns of *la vie ouvrière*. For generations, the workers' movement had to borrow much of its political ideology from middle-class thinkers and at the same time preserve its identity and integrity over and against the bourgeoisie. The history of laboring classes in France is not the history of French socialism. To understand the context in which Weil was working, it is necessary to backtrack a good way and see where the Left had come from and where it presumed to go.

One of the unimpeachable truisms about modern France is that it had been, in comparison with Britain and Germany, tardy in entering the economy of urban industry and technology. If the Revolution had endowed its politics with an unparalleled sophistication, France throughout the Third Republic preserved an increasingly outdated prerevolutionary devotion to the land as the fundament of its values.[1] That primary value occupies an important position in the history of French labor. Industrial retardation allowed labor to organize itself around the *artisanat* of skilled workers in resistance to a gradual capitalist concentration of work in the cities. *Syndicalisme*, a synonym for the trade union movement in the Third Republic, was nourished by hostility to the creeping proletarianization of work, its reduction to the unskilled cog labor of urban factories. The *syndicats* had their precedents in the locally based and exclusive workers' organizations of the early nineteenth century, the mutual aid societies (*sociétés de secours mutuels*), and the journeymen's *compagnonnages*.[2]

The political dimensions of this inchoate *ouvrièrisme* can be gauged in its response to the state, but that response had long been deeply ambivalent in the French people. The *étatisme* of the Revolution endured as a model of government to which Jules Michelet's mysterious entity "le peuple" enjoyed perhaps only illusory, direct access, but the oppressive statism of the ancien régime was no less forceful to memory and indeed returned under Louis Napoleon (who, however, tolerated the older *artisanat* forms of workers' associations): "The Empire may be credited with having forged that very special sense of internal exile, of deep class resentment combined with political frustration, which has ever since characterized the French working-class movement, even in its rare moments of optimism."[3]

The workers' movement was in a sense caught between the enticements of *politique d'abord*, as in the middle-class socialism of Louis Blanc, and the anarchist reaction, epitomized in the works of Pierre-Joseph Proudhon, against all forms of centralization which political activity presupposed. The bourgeois vanguard of theorists proved lucid enough in diagnosing the ills of labor under capitalist industrialism but could not provide coherent remedies. In consequence, *praxis* had in its two great moments, the Revolution of 1848 and the Commune of 1871, the precipitous aspect of miracle, but it suffered a sudden and disastrous aftermath. Early Third Republic *syndicalisme* was mainly an expression of disillusionment and retreat from political to strictly industrial organization, with skilled or draft workers generally preferring the localized structures known as *bourses de travail* and factory workers preferring "vertical" federation by industry. Their merger in the Confédération générale du travail (1895) did little to cement a political ideology other than the strike mystique, made gospel in the 1906 Charter of Amiens, to which both artisans and proletarians could and did subscribe.

Only with great effort did Jean Jaurès at the century's turn overcome the *syndicats*' antipathy to parliamentary (bourgeois) socialism. The Socialist party (SFIO), itself the uneasy fusion of Marxists (formerly the Parti ouvrier français, led by Jules Guesde) and republican reformers or moderates (the Parti ouvrier socialiste, first headed by Paul Brousse) could not realistically have hoped to provide French laborers with much coherence and direction. In less than a decade the Socialist party was debauched by the Great War. Like the socialist parties of other European states, it fell an all too willing accomplice to nationalist exigencies. But it underwent an even greater crisis in the immediate postwar years, when the party was split along the old divisions by the Russian Revolution's example, by a rash of strikes in 1919–20 which took

Bolshevism's success as inspiration and accordingly suffered harsh reprisals from the government, and by the party's failure to secure representation in parliament commensurate with its numbers.

Ironically, the woes of the leftists were a function of their sudden rise in party membership, from about 40,000 in 1917 to 180,000 just three years later. The influx of young, inexperienced militants helped to push the party from the reformist majority's position to a radicalism that embraced Lenin and the Third International, thus isolating the dwindled Jaurès wing. The break came formally in the 1920 party congress at Tours, which saw the birth of the modern Communist party. The Socialist party was headed by Léon Blum.

A parallel development occurred in the trade unions. Their ranks were massively enlarged by the postwar enrollment of women (not newcomers merely, for women had been an integral and indispensable part of the work force in some industries, notably textiles, throughout the previous century) and peasants in flight from the land.[4] Many in the unions were immigrants (Poles, Italians, Russians) who could not speak French but had been effectively radicalized by unemployment or oppression in their homelands or by displacement in war. The 1921 CGT congress at Lille witnessed the creation of the *moscoutaire* Confédération générale du travail Unifiée (CGTU), and thereafter the extent of labor's responsiveness to the "Moscow line" was in part a function of relations between the CGT and the CGTU.

The communists' splintering of socialism and syndicalism won for the Socialist party and the CGT a kind of old-guard respectability in the eyes of the bourgeoisie. "Neosocialists" could make common cause at election time with the petit bourgeois Radicals (Alain's party), and the CGT took into its fold the government's *fonctionnaires*, unionized in 1924. Although the CGT did not ally itself with any party, not even the Socialist, "because it intends to keep for itself the possibility of being heard by all the administrations and being supported by many parties," as one veteran commentator fondly put it,[5] it did attempt rapprochement with both the hated government and the *patronat* in establishing a labor council (1925) for cooperative decision making about the nation's economic policy.

The price of such accommodations proved high. The Socialists were exposed to communist charges of collaboration with the ancient propertied enemy, even though Socialist support of the short-lived Cartel des gauches (1924) was marginal; worse, in the early 1930s the communists branded them as fascists, even though Socialist rhetoric about nationalization of monopolies and the overthrow of capitalism had remained intact after Tours. It was the old, bitter family quarrel of the Left undergoing yet another round, but one made more intense by Moscow and, subsequently, by Berlin.

For its part, the CGT quickly learned how limited its initiatives were in the face of powerful employers' associations, and its rapport with the state depended mostly on personal ties with ministers such as Aristide Briand and Pierre Laval, old-time syndicalist sympathizers. Perhaps its greatest challenge came from the productive system itself, specifically in the war-boosted industries which imposed the American system of a calculated quantitative efficiency of production. Known after its originator as Taylorization, the plan was intended to employ unskilled (cheap) labor at piecework tasks of mass production. Oddly, this scheme was in operation at a time (the late 1920s) when the proletariat's collaboration with the *patronat* held out to the workers some hope that they might share in middle-class prosperity, indeed of delivering themselves from the ranks of labor altogether. Collective bargaining, officially recognized in 1919, aimed at achieving a forty-hour week (the average was then forty-eight) and a minimum wage and had legitimate expectations of success.

The Depression of the early 1930s, although it came to France later than to the more developed industrial and financial nations, collapsed these tenuous promises. Pressure for unification of the CGT and CGTU came from the incontestable fact that syndicalism had been robbed of its illusions on both ends: neither revolution nor respectability was within its grasp. Although the CGTU relished the opportunity to exploit class antagonisms aggravated by the crisis, while the CGT turned to America's New Deal and Belgium's Plan du travail for models of structural reform that could unite the syndical interests with those of the middle class, the common denominator of their concern was negative: the ascent of crypto-fascist leagues in France and the growing menace of Hitler's Germany.

These issues—the reunification of *syndicalisme*, its policies toward the government, the *patronat*, and the fascist threat—were only gradually coming into focus under the impact of the Depression when Weil entered the Left in 1931. Her writing from 1931 to 1938 may be classed under four headings: (1) analyses of the economic crisis and the problems it posed for *syndicalisme*; (2) reviews of the international crisis and its implications for both theory and action; (3) prescriptions, general and particular, with attention to young leftist intellectual currents (to what extent can Weil be identified with or distinguished from them?); and (4) her own experiences as a factory worker.

Because of the complexity of the issues, we cannot follow a consistently chronological sequence. Indeed, many of Weil's unpublished writings are not dated and cannot be dated on the basis of internal evidence. The thematic coherence I have attempted to give to these materials must stand in lieu of a linear, historical account.

Toil and Trouble

Within a few weeks of her arrival at Le Puy, Weil, as a member of the CGT (it included the public school teachers' union), wrote a pointed series called "Réflexions concernant la crise économique."[6] It is her earliest Marxist critique of capitalism and indicates how, at least at this time, her thinking was closer to the radical CGTU than to the reformist CGT.

Her central argument is that the working class would have to deliver itself from the blind artifice that had lulled it into collaboration with "la classe dirigeante."[7] This artifice rested on the notion that prosperity required the most intense productivity possible, in return for which workers would secure higher wages, consume more, and thereby open new avenues for production. In fact, she asserts, capitalism intends to improve the situation for labor only for the sake of increased productivity. Material comforts for workers always run secondary to profits. So, though labor's cooperation in rationalization schemes gives workers the illusion of gain without class struggle, the proletariat has in fact played the role of a trained dog rewarded with sugar. The Depression, in reducing to nothing the advantages workers felt they had won on their own, showed how ephemeral was the bond of their common interest with the *patronat*.

Weil urges labor to reject the assumption that economic crisis requires more collaboration, as though workers and bosses had common problems. The prosperity-crisis cycle of capitalism, endemic to a system in which there can be no correspondence between work and profits, marked a decomposition in the economic regime. Weil is eager to expose a predominant fallacy in an economy based on speculative finance rather than industry: overproduction does *not* signify disequilibrium between production and consumption. For needed products humanity has *not* exceeded the limits of what it can consume. The capacity for consuming luxuries is, she grants, limitless: "It is not in relation to consumption that over-production has a meaning, but in relation to the parasitic profits for which the capitalist regime functions."[8] The ever greater work rhythm of rationalization ends as an obstacle not to the venerable laws of supply and demand but to profit itself because the productive machinery is run on the basis of gain without relation to work.

Suppose, she asks, that after a period of misery, the ruling class restored prosperity by a new search for profits. Then the productive frenzy would merely begin anew until the next collapse: "One must choose. If one chooses not to give in to an indefinite (for the workers) succession of well-being paid out by exhausting labor and total misery, one must decide that there cannot be any common interest between the exploited and the exploiters."[9] Echoing the CGTU's position, she concludes that there should be no attempt to end the crisis so as to help the *patronat*. Collaboration could be justified only if it could be shown that the finance-capitalist system must go on indefinitely and if the workers' movement failed to achieve unity, organization, and clear ideas.

This essay indicates Weil's debt to Lenin. Her references to the modern replacement of industrial capital by speculative, a phase Marx did not theorize, and to the urgency of new markets for profit argues a familiarity with Lenin's *Imperialism, the Highest Stage of Capitalism* (1916).[10] More important are some questions unanswered in these "réflexions." Did Weil have a broader, historical understanding of capitalism? Having called for a united workers' struggle against capital, how did she conceive of this revolution and her own part in it?

As to the first question, it is instructive that, however well read she was in Marx and Engels, Weil did not parrot their thesis of historical materialism, that history moves according to changing modes of production and the resultant tensions between classes. She was not ignorant of history as a Marxist might interpret it, and she was capable of reading history analogically.[11] Still, she was inclined to a balanced, almost static view, an analysis by pro and contra. In a sketch entitled "Les conquêtes du régime capitaliste du point de vue de la civilisation," she enumerates capitalism's four distinct advances over nature, that (1) it has put production, "the truly human activity," at the center of social life, in conscious domination of nature; (2) it has methodically rendered work into a series of realizable movements freed from chance; (3) as opposed to medieval scholasticism, it has applied thought to its true end, nature; and (4) in collectivizing labor it has maintained social cohesion subject only to the laws of production.

Capitalism's negative aspects, however, outweigh all the positive: (1) it has subordinated people to the material conditions of their work, both by division of labor and by submission of workers to their machinery (they work for its efficiency rather than it as a tool working for their own); (2) its collective (factory) labor is blind—indeed, only individual labor can be conscious; and (3) it has alienated thought from nature. The separation of intellectual from manual labor defines oppression in all its forms by creating a class of directors distinct from producers. Historically, Weil notes, this oppression has been a precondition to all progress because productive or integral labor has hindered cultural development (modern civilization has been built on factories, not craftsmen's shops), but capitalism's methodical action on nature has by division degraded both mental and manual labor, and it has transformed the serviceable sciences into a scholasticism no one can grasp.

This last point, recalling Weil's thesis at the Normale, suggests that her perspective on revolution derived not from "classical" nineteenth-century socialists but from Descartes. Not productive forces but individual psychology must serve as the criterion for determining the well-being of society. Weil's Cartesianism accounts in part for her unique attitude toward revolutionary activity.

An insightful expression of this attitude occurs in her remarks on André Malraux's novel on the Chinese revolution, *La condition humaine* (1930), a work she praised for portraying revolutionary activity as a spiritual malaise. Her question was, Must it be so? In Malraux's depiction, the unity of the many characters lay in their attempts to escape the intolerable feeling of their own nothingness.[12] Weil observes that Pascal (she might have added Dostoevsky) believed that the only sure refuge for this *divertissement* is religion. (It is revealing that she then cites as though with approval Marx's "brilliant formula" that religion is the awareness of one who has either lost or not yet found himself.) But if revolutionary action is a drive toward loss of self-consciousness, it amounts to an attempt to escape life itself. Citing the case of Malraux's Kyo, she says that attempt leads naturally to defeat and death. But the revolutionary, she insists, must love life even though revolution confers no sense upon it. For those who seek revolution to make sense of life, success would be disaster. As Pascal says, the hunter is wretched when the beast is caught and the game is over: "If the revolution is something other than a game, it is so only to the extent that it alleviates the life-hindering weight which social conditions now impose upon each person."[13] The key words are *alleviate* and *now*. Weil foresees no utopic release or escape. The focus typifies her concern for concrete problems and possible solutions but with a scrupulous acknowledgment that solutions are seldom either easy or complete.

No less typical is her attempt to define problems from their basic psychological denominator. An illuminating example is her essay, "Après la mort du Comité des 22," which appeared in the Lyons journal *L'effort*, in January 1932.[14] The Committee of Twenty-Two, composed of CGT and CGTU delegates as well as members of the independent Fédération autonome, had met in November 1930 to discuss reunification of the workers' movement and recommended unity on the basis of strikes called for in the 1906 Amiens Charter. The entrenched union officialdom of the CGT rejected the committee's recommendation as a threat to itself; the CGTU was opposed to a merger at both the administrative and rank-and-file levels. Weil chose not to condemn the unions' leadership, an easy target, arguing instead that it was a lack of class consciousness in the workers that hindered unity.

In any society, she contends, those wanting change have grouped themselves according to their affinities but in phantom alliances and struggles that have not altered real conditions. Apart from such groups are others which, without any concern for divergence of views, have actually prevailed. The *mysterium magnum* she points to is that social order does *not* rest on a community of views. Shop workers need not agree in their opinions; they merely have to cooperate. Those associating on the first basis have no power whatever over those of the second. A slave's real bond is not with other slaves but with the master:

> Slaves have always suffered from slavery, they have always desired deliverance. Sometimes this desire has been sufficiently powerful to elevate them, to cast them in savage bands against their murderous masters; but this unanimous desire in itself has never been able to sweeten slavery. That's because slaves in fact never form a society with those sharing their desires and hopes but with their overseers who, whip in hand, direct their work.

Nineteenth-century socialists, outraged by the exploitation of laboring men, women, and children, never exercised the least action on capitalism's development. Neither common feelings nor common views suffice as a basis for common action.

Weil's conclusion could not be more pessimistic: "It's not the fact that they're exploited which makes workers a revolutionary force; otherwise, the revolution would have been a fait accompli centuries ago."

What role, then, could leftist intellectuals from the universities play in the workers' movement? To approach this question we must briefly review the articulated efforts of that intelligentsia to impose itself on social and political thought in the 1930s. Characteristically, Weil has no place in any of the identifiable groups that expressed the common *volonté révolutionnaire*, but she does share some of the tenets of each as though she might have reconciled their differences in a private synthesis.

The journals of that time profile four distinctive movements. First, *Reaction* and *Combat* carried the legacy of the neotraditionalist Action Française of Charles Maurras, which the Vatican had suppressed in 1927. Their royalist pretensions to a past somehow lost in the imputed decadence of democracy, class struggle, and individualism proclaimed the need for a social humanism submissive to monarchy and a supposedly Christian order. The static nature of its accents suggests not so much the fascism with which it has been tagged[15] as a hierarchic neofeudalism to which Weil, a friend of Plato and the *Gita*, was later to show some susceptibility, especially in her concern not to transform, in Marxist fashion, the relations of production but to spiritualize them.

A second movement, expressed in the journal *L'ordre nouveau*, rejected Western capitalism and Bolshevik totalitarianism, parliaments and dictators. In the spirit of Saint-Simon it programmed the subordination of the state to the individual. Best known among its small group of voices were its founder, Arnaud Dandieu (he died in 1933, age thirty-five), Robert Aron, and Henri Daniel-Rops. In its doctrinaire inversion of personality over institutions, the *spiritualisme* of *L'ordre nouveau* mirrors Weil's preface to *Oppression et liberté* (1933), "Allons-nous vers la révolution prolétarienne?": "Let us not forget that we wish to make the individual, not the collectivity, the supreme value."[16] Further, this group's decentralization program, with its *dichotomique* setting labor as mechanical function into service to labor as creative pursuit, seems to run in tandem with Weil's Marxist endeavor to restore the primacy of thought and invention over manual work, with both functions being combined in each worker.

Third, Emmanuel Mounier's *personalisme*, voiced in the journal *Esprit*, which he founded in October 1932, set itself against all the forces of materialism. Mounier exemplified the resistance of many young intellectuals to the tags of Right and Left. Trying to restore a metaphysical sanctity to life, he defined *personne* as "a center of freedom, meditation, creation, and love." Humanity's restoration would require "the gift of self and service," an aesthetic freed from snobbery, an economics based on decentralized collectivities.[17] His program for a wholly new social order did not signally differ from that of *L'ordre nouveau* as both hearkened back to the syndicalist will-o'-

the-wisp of localized economic control and to the antistatism of Proudhon.[18] This libertarianism sought freedom from tradition but longed for a communal face such as only tradition can give. It tended ineluctably to direct itself toward Roman Catholicism.

Weil herself, well before her mystical experience in 1938, was aware of religion (or religiosity à la Rousseau?) as a centripetal force, but she also perceived the snare of chauvinism to which even Christians might be subject. If the French trade unions' non-partisan integrity was threatened by communists within it all too ready to deliver syndicalism to the Kremlin's dictates, could Christian workers keep the movement safe from slavish collaboration with capitalism?

Finally, the mystique of technocracy found a voice in two journals, *Plans* and *L'homme nouveau*. To rationalize the economy along corporate but anticapitalist lines and to establish an elitist hierarchy at the head of a reformed state were two of their objectives, but the political ambiguity of technocratic dogma made it vulnerable and available. A government might be fully staffed with graduates of l'Ecole des Sciences politiques, but might they not all be fascists? Did not the anti-politique, the missionary zeal of the young intelligentsia, suggest that possibility? Mussolini's state corporatism provided an alluring model. (Pierre Drieu la Rochelle, a contributor to *Plans*, became a notorious convert to fascism.) Indeed, Bertrand Varages, in *L'homme nouveau* (February 1934), claimed that the youth of l'Ecole des Sciences politiques agreed on the need to replace parliamentarianism "with a regime inspired by fascism but adapted to the French mentality." They also believed, he claimed, that "The intellectuals ought to go to the masses, not only to direct them but to receive from them 'the sense of life,' that is, the taste for reality as well as the feeling for social justice."[19]

Precisely at the time Varages's article appeared, Weil was reaching a crossroads in her own politics. A letter to Pétrement reveals her despair that the country seemed to be moving rapidly toward a reactionary dictatorship, perhaps to fascism. In part this foreboding reflected a dismay over ominous trends in Germany which had totally collapsed her sanguine views on young trade unionists there; more specifically, the show of hooliganism from rightist *ligues* on February 6, 1934, when mob action nearly toppled the French government, suggested that Nazism was becoming contagious. Even Alain was stirred from retirement into open protest against extremism, and the *normaliens* prepared "to bar the route to fascism with their own breasts."[20] Weil had decided to withdraw completely from activism, not in a spirit of weary disillusion or indifference but to satisfy her need to achieve reflective distance.

Perhaps she most needed some critical distance from her own kind, all the youthful bourgeois intellectuals bent on redeeming the world. An indispensable document of this time says as much. It is her lengthy review, identified in her papers as "Sur *l'Ordre nouveau*," of an unnamed book by Aron and Dandieu (most probably *La révolution nécessaire*, published by Grasset in 1933).[21]

The Ordre nouveau, she begins, is made up of the time's ambiguities: young people with the best intentions, avowed enemies of the state and of economic oppression, Aron and Dandieu had sent Hitler an open letter expressing their approval of him. She finds their book's tone prophetic, pretentious, wholly at odds with the need for true intellectual probity by analysis. Hardly alone in this fault, Aron and Dandieu seem unaware of the limits of their own thought and the disproportion between their grasp of ideas and reality. Complex problems find cloudy formulas.

Weil takes them so severely to task because she mainly agrees with their perception of economic and political oppression and their conviction that liberation from those two forms must be *au fond* spiritual. People must stop being servants to things they have created for their own use, be it government or a factory machine—a vintage Marxist view. Aron and Dandieu believed they had found deliverance: separation of automatic or nonspecialized and creative labor, the former to be centralized by the government and carried on by young civil servants rather than the proletariat. In the decentralized, creative sphere a corporation of skilled labor would stimulate initiative and risk taking. By this scheme, production would be subordinate to consumption, the state to the corporation, the economic to the spiritual.

Weil dismisses the separation of skilled from unskilled labor as fantastic; they are inextricably united in the heart of every enterprise. The Ordre nouveau's *corporatisme* would simply recast existing hierarchies, and its civil service plan would give the government even greater economic control. By uniting political and economic powers, Aron and Dandieu would create either a totalitarian or a technocratic regime—exactly what they wished to avoid.

In response to this hell of good intentions, Weil sets down the desiderata for economic liberty: a decentralized economy, popular control of business, skilled labor, a total transformation of every structure in enterprise and technique. But could these goals be achieved? "This problem may be insoluble. In any case it certainly exceeds our present capabilities, yet it must be perceived.

That's not the case with the Ordre nouveau's young and ardent reformers and numerous kindred groups that have recently arisen. Otherwise, they wouldn't be writing so proudly, 'Let's go there.'"

These reformers, she says, must either choose to act and "realize immediately an ideal other than their own" or preserve their ideal through "an impotent fidelity." It is as though she wanted to preserve in her generation a new breed of Montagnards poised for disaster: "They are so avid to act and to play a role on history's stage that one might foresee their choice from this moment. To copy a formula of Pascal, not being able to make the revolution realize itself, they will make their realizations revolutionary." They should content themselves, she urges, with "obscure toil and an effectiveness at best remote and perhaps nil. Then they won't be sustained by the intoxication of action or by a naive faith in an ineluctable progress." Her own resolve to enter a factory may be intimated here, but she seems simply to intend a willed freedom from the delusions inherent in political programs and social planning. All confused thinking ends up "by the force of things" in service to totalitarianism.[22] Only clear ideas, she concludes, will not turn against us.

If not a call to retreat, this skepticism could hardly inspire anyone, whether in the Ordre nouveau or beyond, to action. It is the muted *volonté* of William Blake's saving particulars set against all pleas for the common good.

Weil's remarks to Pétrement indicate an acute ambivalence toward the "revolutionary will." She did not wholly preclude for herself an eventual participation in "a great spontaneous mass movement" (Sorel's fantasy), but she wanted no responsibility for pointless bloodshed, certain as she was that "one is beaten in advance."

This ambivalence finds articulation, if not resolution, in the essay that occupied her through 1934, "Réflexions sur les causes de la liberté et de l'oppression sociale." Perhaps only by projecting a "theoretical tableau of a free society" in which she could give untrammeled voice to a Goethean humanism, that the life of humankind be "a perpetual creation of itself by itself," was she able to confront the weight of her central theme, collectivity's menace to freedom of intellect and labor.[23] The tableau is set between an analysis of oppression and a "sketch of contemporary life," each of which reflects Weil's penchant for an unrelieved pessimism. Yet her closing remarks show her resilient and assertive, with what might be called a humanistic confidence in the saving power of methodical intelligence to secure for humanity the promise of its own dignity, or at least insight into why that dignity has been lost in the twentieth-century darkness.[24]

Weil saw that all of the young activist journalists shared the fundamental weakness of bourgeois reformers of earlier times: they had no direct experience of the lives of the workers they presumed to plan, to transform, to uplift. The elementary obligation to yoke ideas to experience, the lesson Lagneau and Alain passed on to Weil, enjoyed no reckoning. Of schemes and manifestos there was no end; the banners of rhetoric flew high in the wind. Weil herself had become a veteran, a vigorous partisan in words, and her activism had taught her crucial limits. The real instruction, as she had guessed even before passing the *agrégation*, could come only from taking on the full burden of the worker's life. Before the months she gave to factory work, in 1934 and 1935, she had tried to live as closely as possible to working people. She talked, drank, and smoked with them in bars, gave of her modest earnings to unemployment funds, and won from many of them respect and trust. She knew better than to talk down to them, and her slovenly appearance, a calculated assault on feminine sartorial vanity, had its own peculiar eloquence.

She thought a good deal about how young intellectuals like herself, once they left their editorial desks and meeting halls, could best serve the workers' movement. Responding to an article that posed the question of relations between workers and university graduates, Weil submitted what she called "Réflexions brutales."[25] She asked whether educated youth in the CGT were not in peril of being drowned in *syndicalisme*. With her usual arresting bravado she expressed the hope that it would be drowned. The day young intellectuals manifested influence in union ranks she would tear up her union card. The real issue, she adds, is not whether they would be understood but whether they could themselves understand. Could they put aside their leisure-baked dogmas and learn humbly about working-class life?

Pétrement overstates the case that Weil was "absolutely hostile" to the influence of intellectuals in workers' circles. What she resented was their condescension, as though their learning were a Promethean gift. In her typically original way of assessing a problem, she did not divide graduates and workers into the educated and the deprived. She saw what they had in common:

> I've lived in university and working-class milieux—I don't mean militants but the uncultivated, unorganized, uneducated working masses—and as to average intelligence I haven't found any real difference between them. Among the workers, intelligence is more or less paralyzed by daily contact with a brutal, oppressive, devastating reality; among the students,

> intelligence plays idly for want of an object. In both cases, the mind's ability to seize a concrete problem precisely is gradually diminished. But among the workers there's a much greater desire to raise themselves to a higher level, from the very fact that suffering fetters them and one always seeks deliverance from suffering.

That intellectuals might help in the alleviation Weil does not doubt. Their attempts would be "excellent" if they could simply recognize the marginal value of their degrees and assimilate themselves to the workers' esprit, rather than to theses and doctrines. Just what assimilation means, given the mentally paralytic quality of labor characterized in Weil's remarks, remains vague, nor does she make clear how, as she says, a professor paying his CGT dues must become capable of putting himself mentally into the skin of a child who by factory work has earned a birthright to CGT membership.

She closes these remarks, however, with high praise for the Institut supérieur ouvrier, "one of the most beautiful realizations of the CGT." In 1932, the CGT followed the example of syndicalism abroad and made a systematic effort to educate workers. The Institut in Paris (the provincial unions ran Collegès du travail) offered courses to workers and other employees after their regular hours. By 1939, there were about four thousand of these student laborers in France.[26] In that scheme Weil believed educators could unite with union militants. Then intellectuals would no more be drowned than fish in water. Weil herself gave many "educational" talks to workers, of which some outline notes survive among her papers. Votary of Plato as she was, she could not relinquish the expectation that education would liberate and make whole the cave dwellers of capitalism. On the eve of the May 1936 sit-in strikes, she was writing lectures on Greek tragedies—*Antigone*, *Elektra*, *Philoctetes*—expressly with a working class audience in mind, and she planned articles on Greek science in a Cartesian spirit, "comprehensible and interesting for any task."[27]

In short, not only was she far from hostile to intellectuals in trade unions, she was urging their participation. How else could she have justified her own presence among factory workers? It is true that she scornfully rejected the *normaliens*' presumption that they could be taken into union ranks by their "bookish knowledge of syndicalism," but there is a solicitude in that scorn.[28] She fears that their academic posturing will earn them the workers' ridicule. Not once, however, does she consider education, or rather her disposition toward it, as part of the bourgeois world from which the working class had long been cut off. One wonders how she might have responded to George Orwell's insight: "Working people often have a vague reverence for learning in others, but where 'education' touches their own lives they see through it and reject it by a healthy instinct."[29]

Weil never faltered in her belief that education had redemptive value for working people, not in delivering them upward to the bourgeoisie but in helping them to understand and to respond critically to their work. Toward her life's end, in *L'enracinement*, she would return to this subject in provocative detail.

She did not limit her scope to trade union efforts at education. In her draft "Sur une tentative d'education de prolétariat," she refers sympathetically to a group known as the Jeunesse ouvrières chrétiens. The *jocistes* tried to organize workers' education on two lines: first, strictly within syndicalism, for the benefit of union militants; second, more broadly for the general education of young people in labor's ranks.[30] That distinction posed the question, what should be the *syndicats*' attitude toward general education? The real issue for Weil, however, was the determination of what kind of organization the union was to be. Did it exist chiefly to perpetuate itself in power, like the churches and political parties, or was it merely a tool of popular will, like Rousseau's state? Optimally, the *syndicat* would be made up not only of militants and unionists but of the free. General education for young workers would be an imperative of the unions, "a pressing obligation to the extent it is true that education liberates the workers."[31] How it would free them, Weil did not yet presume to say.

No matter how beneficial the intellectuals' presence might be in the union, no matter how educated its workers, its bureaucratic structure remained. Weil saw this structure as perhaps the greatest problem facing the workers, one far more critical to their daily lives than issues of class struggle or collaboration. Her hostility to labor's bureaucracy is not easy to comprehend. Her vehemence seems disproportionate, even peevish, given that labor faced a powerfully organized *patronat* and enjoyed little support from government and the bourgeoisie. Her grounds, though, are more psychological than political or economic.

An unpublished fragment focuses her point.[32] She vigorously objects to unionists' lack of impartiality, blaming their adversaries in all disputes. This failure in objectivity is not a function of doctrine; it is inherent in all struggles of organizations as such. Even the CGT is subject to demagogy and lies of its own manufacture, and bureaucracy serves that corrupting process by perpetuating power and rationalizing it. The demagogy Weil was opposing almost certainly refers to the CGT's doctrinaire resistance to any cooperation with the *patronat*, a position dictated by a long-established anarchist tradition of union autonomy. Weil was not unsympathetic to this urge to independence, but she realized it could be a snare. She used as a kind of lever against CGT intransigence the proposals of the Confédération française des travailleurs chrétiens for sharing economic planning with the patrons as well as the state.

Far more cautious than the CGT about strikes, the CFTC favored social legislation to protect workers' families, but it rejected economic statism. It was strongly influenced by papal encyclicals, and thus open to the charge of playing the bosses' game. (It never joined the Popular Front). Weil willingly entertained the CFTC's collaborationism only for the sake of equality of rights and powers between the *syndicats* and the *patronat*. Collaboration must not, she admonishes, serve as a code word for abdication or passive obedience. The boss, after all, opposed cooperation because he had virtually absolute power: "Speaking of class collaboration one may wish to lie, to disguise the reality of oppression and the incontestable opposition of some interests under pious fictions. Or one may wish to effect a situation where collaboration between all those engaged in industrial production becomes a reality and not a deceit."[33]

Complementing this fragment is a long letter Weil wrote to Emmanuel Mounier. There are two drafts. Pétrement's biography includes lengthy parts of only the draft that gives Weil's favorable views on Christian morality and its role in the labor movement. There, Weil tells Mounier that the CGT's ideals and traditions are not incompatible with Christianity, that one cannot renounce without self-degradation "the Christian idea, which has its roots in Greek thought." But even Christianity must condone the workers' release from "the deadly passivity . . . the piteous resignation thanks to which they are reduced to inhuman misery."[34]

The other draft seems to be answering a point Mounier had apparently made in *Esprit*, that Christianity could deliver workers from their hatred of the bosses. She admits there may well be some in the *syndicats* who bear such hatred, but she insists that such feelings do not depend on doctrine, but rather on "elevation of mind, greatness of soul," and much suffering. "It is relatively easy not to hate when one has never felt impotently outraged to the depths of oneself." She denies that Christianity keeps its believers from hate and cites the pervasive French loathing of Germans in the Great War. Were Catholics more immune to it than freethinkers? Besides, "Hate was excusable among the inhabitants of invaded regions who felt themselves oppressed for four years. The proletariat lives all its life in an invaded region."[35]

Still, Weil commends the efforts of CFTC and *jociste* workers to mitigate rancor, hatred, and other passions that spawn demagogy. She remains wary of a neighborly love ethic that might obscure the fact that virtue presupposes "a certain ease": "So it's a primary duty to fight when necessary to wrest or to preserve this minimum of well being below which virtue itself disappears. Generosity of feeling toward an adversary is secondary to this essential struggle."[36]

Loving one's neighbor as oneself is not an injunction to put up with oppression. It really means that oppressors must be chastised.[37] There follows a refined distinction between the two kinds of collaboration she mentions in the fragment. Those who look to "a bit of reciprocal goodwill" play the game of wolf and lamb. The only alternative in worker-boss relations is one of "a relation of interests such that the suffering of some is not a condition for the success of others." The *patronat*'s obduracy would have to be broken, and class struggle was the only effective way.

Her conclusion makes three striking assertions: that this method is not contrary to Christian morality, "which, besides, is morality period"; if that statement contradicts Marx and Mikhail Bakhunin, it simply shows that the CGT owes them no inspiration; and if the workers' movement owes any debts, they belong to Proudhon. Each of these sweeping statements could be challenged. They matter little as to fact, but they say much about Weil's orientations. Her appropriation of Christian morals to the workers' movement, coming well before her mystical experience, is noteworthy.[38]

The CGT did not have to borrow Christian morality; it was already Christian. This assumption, preemptive and categorical like the patristic legerdemain which argued that everything true and good is Christian, shares with Weil's remark about herself in a letter to Père Perrin the implication that she had always been imbued with a Christian spirituality.[39] She clearly felt the same way about *syndicalisme*. That perspective tells us why she did not enlist herself in the CFTC or the JOC and remained faithful to the CGT: she could interpret trade union visions on her own heterodox terms. The issue of why Weil never entered the Christian church has occupied many readers and critics; it should first be considered within the context of her relations with the unions. Weil was even inclined to confer upon syndicalism a mystique that would somehow keep it inviolable, free from its own bureaucracy, rather as she later wanted to see the Christian church sacramentally apart from its dogmas and councils.

This inclination appears in an important unpublished essay answering a proposal of her friend Auguste Detoeuf that trade unionism overcome its political divisions and become "unique, apolitical, and obligatory."[40] She rejects Detoeuf's plan in fear that syndical unity would entail a machinery to kill, by excess of means, its own noble ends. To answer the forces of the *patronat* and the state with syndical force would require a displacement in the social mechanism. What could be worse than that the united *syndicats* emulate Bolshevism as a means and end up working for its own perpetuity? Here is yet another of Weil's caveats about revolutionary action. Unique here is her remark on how Detoeuf's unification scheme would abolish true syndicalism: "Syndicalism, especially in France, is a popular movement, as mysterious in its origins, as singular and inimitable as a popular song; it has a tradition, an esprit, an ideal, it has its heroes, martyrs, and near saints, mostly unknown; it answers to no doctrine, tactic, or particular opportunity but to the aspirations and needs of people at a certain time in history."

Detoeuf's psychological error, according to Weil, was to presume that passions could be quelled by making the *syndicats* mere interpreters of common interests. But, she lectures, passions are inevitable and never shift as interests do. (That statement comes wholesale from Alain, who used it in his analysis of war, *Mars ou la guerre jugée*.) Conflicts of interest alone are rare. To understand *syndicalisme*, one must understand the feelings that give it vitality.

Weil admits that in the generations since the Third Republic's inception, "the soul's needs" made syndical action become desperate and violent. She is concerned to examine the workers' "moral suffering," which she identifies as ennui. More than tedium or boredom, it is a deep spiritual malaise. Weil saw it as the predominant ailment of her age. Although pervading all social groups, it set one against the other because it was not a material fact; it was a malaise from which each group thought it alone suffered. Peasants in the field believed there was no ennui in the cities; workers could not imagine ennui in a bureau of engineers. Ennui in the factory's proletariat was aggravated by the monotony of tasks, multiplied indefinitely by fear of change, because any change was likely to be bad. Hence a paradox arose: the factory's interminable dreariness became the sole object of hope, a senseless iteration the worker clung to in fear of dismissal.

As Weil had observed in person, workers responded variously to this Dantesque situation: the physically or morally weak succumbed to ennui in a form of spiritual death that, if extended to the entire work force, would ensure social tranquillity—and a catastrophe, Weil adds, worse than all possible troubles. Others would try to climb up into the industrial hierarchy, but most would simply go on hating their workplace as prisoners their cells. It was to these that syndicalism offered something new and adventurous, "something which is violently opposed, by its atmosphere, its esprit, its goals and hopes, to a daily life known all too well." Whatever the workers' meager gains in wages and benefits, they needed to be encompassed "halo-like by an atmosphere of struggle and by the more or less distant and always vague perspective of a total overturning that is bound to lead in turn to a wholly new, and fresh view, wholly penetrated with enthusiasm."

It is worth stressing that that "total overturning" has more in common with the "great waves" of Socrates' proposal for a new society than with a mystique of violence à la Sorel.[41] Weil's language conjures an eschatological myth for labor, a far-off divine event toward which the proletariat had to feel itself moving. When dealing with actual social conditions, she tended toward pessimism, fearing that the centralization of state and economy was irreversible. If her response to Deteouf holds an antidote to that process, it is to be found in workers' voluntarism, a psychology that would enable them to resist despair. The unions, churchlike, would be charged with sustaining the proletarian faith.

Was her vision, then, utopist? It has sometimes been assumed that her "theoretical tableau of a free society," the hypothesized alternative to the mechanisms of oppression she analyzes in her "Réflexions," amounts to a utopia. She prefers to write of the "ideal," chief predicate of which is freedom conceived as "a relation between thought and action." But that freedom is irrevocably bound by "a tissue of necessities." The difference between servitude and freedom lies entirely in the difference between abject submission to necessity and a creative response to its limits. Alain's "soi libre" emanates from words such as these: "A completely free life would be one where all real difficulties would present themselves as kinds of problems, where all the victories would be like solutions enacted."[42] In an ideal society everyone could (and would) exercise the intellectual freedom of problem solving. Weil's scheme has been characterized as "the democratization of Plato's philosopher king,"[43] but it may also be read as a restatement of her thesis on Descartes, that science, properly understood, is everyone's work. Her "free society" might further be described as Kantian, with the phenomenal or apperceptive ego of every individual elevated to the noumenal self; it belongs to the realm of pure reason and eschews any organizational dynamic. Like Plato (in the

Republic), and Rousseau, Weil shows no interest in the details of social planning.

So far as she explicitly entertained a utopia, it was one intended solely for working people. It involved "working to strip bare of all its mystery the struggle against nature, in all its aspects (science, organization, technique), and proposing to workers another morality, not well-being, but solidarity and responsibility."[44] The stress on obligation—Kant's maxim on duty now made a principle of social organization—rather than well-being needs a gloss.

Weil regarded a modicum of comfort as indispensable to the proletariat. It must be held and preserved at all costs as an integral part of "this essential struggle." But she seemed uneasy about material benefits and concessions such as the Blum administration secured for labor in 1936: the paid, two-week vacation came like a miracle. Weil worried about the fifteenth day. Nothing could be more fatal to the worker than the sense that wage increases and other benefits served as recompense, as though toil in itself could only be an indignity, as indeed it was whenever workers became slaves to their machine or tools. The remedy was to insure that work was the union of the laborer's own thought and action: "If work naturally gives play to all one's faculties, all is well, but that is not always the case; if work gives no play to any faculties, there is compensation only beyond it, and it undergoes the worst assault upon a human being's dignity." Weil notes that it was the sorry lesson of the apparently prosperous years 1927–30, that workers let themselves be lulled by higher wages while the cadence of their productivity was accelerated. When the worldwide Depression hit France in 1931, they were caught, "bent under brutal force," their wages reduced and yet production demands accelerated.[45] Looking to America and *fordisme*, she observed that the autoworker who had bought the company car became a slave twice over because the effect of elevating the proletarian to the bourgeois status of consumer was to make him dependent upon machinery to deliver him to his noxious job.

Weil's opposition to the *patronat*'s divisive co-option of workers by material benefits and incentives went hand in hand with her syndicalist schemes of solidarity and responsibility, a practical and moral cohesion that would ideally unite the urban industrial proletariat with the agrarian: "My utopia: scattered shops—workers at once designers, regulators, operators. . . . Peasants, instructed in mechanics—simple machines in their homes for the winter months. Workers' participation in field labor, the summer months for peasants and workers to teach one another . . . school up to 20 years (half-day beginning at 10) from time to time, 6 months or a year off for advanced schooling, the *tour de France*."[46] The utopic elements are manifest: dispersed shops rather than factories and each worker at once competent to perform all required tasks, from design of products to maintenance of equipment; most noticeable, the interchange of agrarian and urban production, complementary tasks for a labor force delivered to total autonomy, free of bureaucratic or patronal overseers. If there could be trouble in this paradise, it could come perhaps only from those free months in the advanced schools. Here, instead of assimilating university intellectuals to the working movement, Weil presumes to assimilate the workers to the bourgeois school system, but she gives no heed to the possible psychological consequences. Sorel had pointed to the problem half a generation earlier: "Too often, under the fallacious pretext of ennobling the proletariat's soul by elevating it to the level of bourgeois genius, one gives the sons of laborers an aesthetic education so ridiculously grasped that it tends to make them disgusted with the work they would have performed to earn their living."[47] Every conceivable paradise has its corrupting fruit, but the apple of this workers' Eden would be found beyond it.

Being Broken:
Weil's Work in the Factories and Beyond

One of the best-known facts about Weil is that she spent somewhat less than a year working in factories. She has often been celebrated for this effort, and the experience ratifies her sincere commitment to something for which other leftist intellectuals have usually given only their rhetoric. She once took Marx and Lenin to task for not knowing, in a Cartesian sense, the life of the proletariat, the work they talked and wrote about.

In so complex a personality as hers, many motivations played when she entered a sullen, tedious world for which, as she knew, nothing could have prepared her. Surely she felt some bourgeois guilt and a desire to be not only with the workers she had championed in strikes and meetings but of them daily. She felt, too, an intellectual curiosity: some latent impulse toward self-degradation, perhaps; a need of release from the easy, predictable constraints of teaching; an attraction to physical toil, which, when she had previously attempted it, voluntarily and briefly, had exhilarated her. We can count as well a lesson she took from Lagneau, that one's ideas have no validity in themselves; they must be tested in the crucible of experience. In Descartes's terms, thought must be given extension, the world of matter. To say, then, that she undertook factory work experimentally is valid. She learned its rude lessons quickly and, despite frequent exhaustion, kept a scrupulous record of them in her invaluable *journal d'usine.*

Where was she and when?

On December 4, 1934, she entered the Alsthom factory, Sociéte de constructions mécaniques, in Paris. Her tasks included piling iron bars and loading, then removing, copper bobbins at a furnace. A week's layoff at Christmas, leave granted for an ear infection, and another layoff subtracted several weeks before she quit on April 5, 1935.

On April 11, 1935, she began work on a stamping press at an *atelier*, J. J. Carnaud et Forges at Boulogne-Billaucourt (west of Paris, just south of the Bois). She was forced to turn out a minimum of eight hundred pieces an hour, an impossible quota for her limited strength. She found herself "prey to a cold, concentrated rage."[48] Her journal contains only a few pages on this place, but they attest to her awareness of sexual discrimination within the work force. On May 7, she was fired. At last she knew firsthand the humiliation of the unemployed.

On June 6, 1935: she began work at Renault on a milling machine. She left on August 22, but why and how remain unclear. Her journal records complaints of heat, exhaustion, and headaches.

Subsequently, during her employment as a teacher in Bourges, she entertained the possibility of working at the Rosières foundry there. Apparently she also visited other shops and factories, perhaps in search of work or of contacts. One would like to know the provenance and date of the following remarks:

> I visited a little country factory, in a workshop for riveting by compressed air drills. The shop head, only a little time before that a worker and still one by appearance, radiated joy in completing a task where he had all day for invention, where he wasn't subject to any control, and could give his whole heart. Around him men, or rather shadows of men hovered at their drills in a frightful noise, their faces worn by fatigue, suffering, ennui, a total absence of interest in or hope for anything. The difference between his lot and theirs infinitely exceeded the difference in their pay.[49]

This tableau points to a tension that predominates like a leitmotif in her journal on Alsthom, Carnaud, and Renault.[50] That tension was an oscillation, irregular but distinct, between her urge to achieve a detailed understanding of her productivity relative to mechanical dynamics on one hand,[51] and, on the other, a helpless subjection to the dispiriting psychological conditions imposed by production demands. Analysis, including diagrams and unending statistics, alternates with notes on exacting foremen, her fatigue, and a sense of imposed degradation. The tone is surprisingly detached throughout. Cartesian injunctions stand heraldically on the journal's cover, urging her to perceive in labor a modification of nature—"May his own work be for each an object of contemplation"[52]—but then come phrases compacted by lassitude and anger: "Profound sense of humiliation from this void imposed upon thought"; "Deep satisfaction that the work is going badly"; "Depression, bitterness of brutalizing work, loathing."[53] It is the tension of an artisan struggling to master, or at least to survive, the drudgery.

From the start, Weil faced substantial handicaps in the factory: she had little physical stamina and was quickly debilitated; she suffered frequently from sinusitis, a poor diet, and the pressure of her often futile attempts to meet quotas. An entry at Alsthom reads, "Very violent headache, work finished while crying almost without a stop. (On return, a breakdown into endless sobbing.)" Such a collapse prompted her sense that she was becoming a slave, wholly unable to control her body's elementary responses to pain. Concomitant was a worse slavery, "the strongest temptation this life admits, that of no longer thinking."[54]

Amid fastidiously detailed notes on her daily work, Weil entered a good deal about fellow workers, their advice, their seasoned resignation, their dread of dismissal for botching a job. She did not forget that unemployment held far more terror for them than for her. When a foreman bullied her into a dangerous operation, she caught the furtive "pity and mute indignation of my neighbors." The dismal image she sketched of the provincial riveting shop recurs in a remark from her first week at Renault: "The inconvenience of a slave's situation is the temptation to regard pale shadows in a cave as really living human beings."[55] So thoroughly did she apprehend the slave in herself that she found it a bizarre gratuity to be allowed a bus ride to work; it would seem natural, she felt, were she to be ordered off the bus.[56]

Her factory journal records two kinds of closely related experiences which, almost redeeming the generally wearisome whole, deserve emphasis. One is *fraternité*. It came not in an awakened collectivity (syndicalist politics are strangely absent from the journal) but in a series of intimate miniatures, as when a welder at an Alsthom furnace smiled at her sympathetically every time she scorched herself, or when assigned a remote corner of the shop where overseers never came, she could enjoy the "free, fraternal atmosphere, with nothing more of the slavish and mean."[57] These passages are the more eloquent for their brevity; often they are no more than phrases: smiles or an exchange of jokes "more cheerful than usual—this little bit of fraternity makes my soul so joyous that for a while I no longer feel weary."[58]

She gave a willing ear to other workers, especially women, who shared with her gossip, recitations of family woes, and the history of their illnesses. No lasting companionship came from these desultory associations, but on leaving Alsthom Weil claimed a sense of "total camaraderie. For the first time in my life, in short. No barrier, either in differences of class (since it's suppressed) or sex. Miraculous." By contrast, the atmosphere at her next job, at Carnaud, was unrelievedly repellent, the women isolated by the contempt and obscene humor which their male co-workers visited upon them: "Not once have I seen a working woman raise her eyes from her work, or two of them exchange words."[59]

With *fraternité* went the intermittent experience of a peculiar satisfaction in her work when it went well, when a new task was mastered or a mistake corrected. *Joie* has generally been associated with Weil's theological affirmations, as the counter to her more developed idea of *malheur*,[60] but it can be applied here as the counter to the helplessness and woe she felt as a factory drudge. *Joie* was the spontaneous effect of work she performed with an artisan's sense of control. Such moments were few, at least by the journal's reckoning, but they must have been the more precious. They tell us that for Weil the work in itself, no matter how taxing, was not slavery; slavery lay entirely in the artificial divorce of work from control and understanding, in submission to the foreman's obtrusive demands.

In her first weeks at Alsthom she wrote of "a certain joy of muscular effort" in lifting and piling metal rods, painful and enervating though that task was. About that time, she gave to her first riveting "constant effort—not without a certain pleasure because I succeed." Having studied the way to avoid friction from a hole press, she finds the task "not too tedious, thanks to a feeling of responsibility." During one of her last days at Renault she managed to repair a cutting machine for the first time, and her delight knew no bounds: "Victory, better than speeding."[61] These fleeting moments held a strange exhilaration because of the atmosphere of dread that surrounded them: fear of damaging a machine, of spoiling too many pieces, of being bawled out by an overseer.

By any material measure, Weil's achievements in the factories were meager. She mastered no skills. Yet those few times when she became momentarily an artisan and understood work as a conscious transformation of nature made a lasting impression on her. It is likely that in those months of 1935 she gained some intimation of labor as communion, an interchange of esprit and matter, with the mind yielding up the body to nature on behalf of a union with it. One night, on leaving Alsthom, she reflected upon the curious conjunction which the factory's noise caused in her, "at once a deep moral joy and a physical pain."[62]

To understand this mixed experience, particularly the "moral" nature of joy in work, we must look to her conclusions about factory work. She noted first her slavish sense of total deprivation of will. She had no right to anything. But with that she learned to distinguish an imposed humiliation from one internalized in self-constraint. She had discovered "the capacity to suffer morally on my own . . . to taste intensely each moment of freedom or fellowship, as if it were to be eternal. A direct contact with life." These might be called social lessons, and her inferences from them are contradictory: in working life one's personal dignity, "such as it has been contrived by society," is destroyed.[63] One must create one's own sense of worth. Yet one always depends on outward signs of that worth, and the proletariat is condemned to count for nothing, ever, in anyone's eyes.

But she learned as well that the character of one's relationship to one's work is of greater psychological moment than the social standing derived from it. Work can be painful in two ways, she remarks: it can be part of a victorious struggle over matter and the self, or it can be the pain of a degrading servitude. A worker's well-being depends on an unrestricted epistemology of labor, an understanding of oneself as producer and of one's productions as an activity free of arbitrary impositions or constraints. Her utopia, we recall, had no overseer. The only admissible authority should be "the person over the thing," not one person over another.[64]

Weil did not presume to sweep away the class of *régleurs* and *chefs d'atelier*. Rather, as though to minimize their harm, she looked for ways to elevate mechanical labor to a scientific consciousness in the laborer. This consciousness would require an integration of geometry, physics, and practical mechanics, entailing "a new method of reasoning absolutely pure—both intuitive and concrete."[65] This Cartesian ideal recalls the popularization of science Weil called for in her thesis at the Normale. Now she would have every worker understand work scientifically. These two goals are identical in that geometry and mechanical work may be considered analogous; each is a succession of logically combined movements.[66] In mathematics, problems are stated by signs; in work, they are posed by nature. So among the tasks she gave herself for further investigation, she included a study of the history of signs in series through "those who create them in combinations ever more analogous to *real* conditions of human labor."[67]

Weil tried to understand labor as art, too, that is, as a union of worker and tool through a steady *régime de l'attention* distinct from both thought in itself and the servile activity common to factory work. She probably conceived of her rare successes in production at Alsthom and Renault as artful in that sense. It was attention she had noticed in the artisan at the riveting shop and its absence in those "shadows of men" around him. What counts in life, she concluded, are not the events that dominate years, months, or even days, but the way one moment succeeds another and what that succession takes from one's body, heart, and soul. She could never have attained this orientation to work had she not submitted herself to the drill press and the furnace. And the notion of attention to which her later *cahiers* are often devoted has its genesis in the reflections she drew daily from the factory.

June 1936

No account of Weil's thoughts on labor and the workers' movement can ignore the momentous significance of the sit-in strikes of June 1936. They came like a cannon shot proclaiming a revolution, and indeed they seemed to many at the time an augur of what might be expected of the Popular Front and the newly elected Blum administration. Weil's detailed responses to the strikes and their aftermath provide an insider's profile of one of the pivotal events in France in the troubled 1930s.

She had resumed teaching, assigned in the fall of 1935 to a lycée at Bourges, but she continued to think about her factory experiences. She wrote of them to Victor Bernard, father of one of her pupils and chief engineer at the Rosières foundry. She even addressed a lengthy and extraordinarily naive appeal to Rosières workers to submit anonymous accounts of their hardships at work so as to enlighten their bosses: "Often bosses who are good men at heart show themselves harsh simply because they don't understand. That's the way human nature is. People never know how to put themselves in others' places."[68] Characteristically, she looked to education as a means to redress problems that her own analysis found virtually irresolvable. On one hand, the debasement of factory work would be mitigated "when we realize the mechanism of necessities which cause it." On the other, as she told Bernard, she had taken from her own experience the "most bitter and unexpected" lesson that oppression begets not revolt but an almost ineluctable susceptibility to complete submission. To be made to feel one is nothing entails soon enough the inner conviction that one indeed is nothing.[69] What, then, did she presume a worker would write for her complaint box?

Bernard, priding himself on a paternalistic attitude to his workers (the foundry had a superb safety record), was nonetheless wary of Weil's attempted rapprochement. He grew more wary when, contrary to her earlier words on the effects of oppression, she observed that some workers do try to educate themselves, either to rise on the social scale or to prepare for revolution. She argued that short of revolution or a return to the chimerical prosperity of the previous decade, there was no way to ameliorate working conditions without a collaboration between labor and the *patronat*. Her difficulty with Bernard lay in her expectation that he take the initiative toward collective bargaining because "generally the French working class's capacity for action is nearly zero. I believe that only the bourgeoisie has any illusions about this matter." Yet, in the same letter (March 3, 1936), she concluded that the workers' humiliation and moral suffering ran so deep that "a boss's goodness or brutality can't change anything."[70] With him lay all the decision making and power—more that of a god, she told him candidly, than of a man—and she hoped that he, Prometheus-like, would bestow something of them upon his workers. As he realized, Bernard faced an opponent (so he now saw her) of unusual sophistication. She expressly rejected revolution in favor of an enlightening interchange that would transform submission to "unavoidable physical and moral suffering" into an acceptance of them.[71]

Most salient in her plan was its conservatism. Overseers would continue to give orders but by cultivating the workers' responsive participation they would enlist "the virtues of courage, will, awareness, and intelligence which define human value."[72] For Weil, Alain's student, the readiness was not all. To recognize the mind's dignity meant to engage it. All she asked of Bernard was that he help make his workers cooperatively obedient. This was not a tall order, but it was a subtle one, and he recoiled from it.[73]

The letters to Bernard show Weil's willingness to adopt benign corporatism in lieu of the strict syndical apartness she had supported until 1935. This corporatism was not a guise for the *patronat*'s domination of labor. Under the pretense of common interests over and against the meddling state, bosses in the 1930s did try to manipulate unions, but nothing could have been further from Weil's intent. Her corporatism was a bourgeois show of enlightened goodwill.

Ironically, her correspondence with Bernard suddenly ended when its guiding assumptions were confounded by the sit-in strikes. They had begun in the provinces in May, then swept the metalworkers' factories of Paris. Two features of the strike had for Weil a miraculous aspect: first, the nonviolent sit-in was a new way of striking; second, the strike was entirely unforeseen; both the bosses and the union leadership were taken by surprise.[74] Weil had told Bernard the French working class was virtually incapable of revolutionary action. Now it had shown itself capable of spontaneous revolt against the oppression which, according to her, rendered workers mute and helpless.

She immediately wrote an essay for one of her favorite journals, *La révolution proletarienne* (it appeared on June 10), titled "La vie et la grève des ouvrières métallos." She prefaced her thoughts on the strike with vivid recollections from her factory journal: the pay which seemed like alms, the constant obligation to comply in silence, the humiliating reprimands one had to endure in abject deference. She then passed to a dithyrambic celebration of the strikers' *joie* (she uses the word a dozen times in two pages), joy that they could at last stand straight: "Joy in living, amid the silent machines, in the rhythm of human life—the rhythm of respiration, heartbeats, natural movements of the human body—and not according to the cadence imposed by the chronometer."[75] But she lost no time in retreating to a skeptical distance from the event, as though the strike, dreamlike, might vanish.

Her cautions and prescriptions came in an unpublished essay entitled "La victoire des métallos."[76] It quickly assumes the sobering tone of the problems she began to foresee in consequence of the strike's precipitous nature. She feared above all that the workers' feeling of victory, their *joie,* would prove disastrously disproportionate to any concrete gains they could exact from a now intimidated *patronat.*

The events of June 1936 should be likened, she said, to the taking of the Bastille, a legendary moment around which the élan and camaraderie of the workers could be centered. It could help determine what had been lacking in their work: feelings of pride, dignity, freedom, "discipline voluntarily accepted."[77] But the hazards were many. Politicians and bosses reckoned by weeks and months, whereas exhaustion forced workers to reckon by the day. How could they become daily aware of what was happening and not yield to the militants' leadership? Would wage hikes and the new eight-hour day suffice as bases for effective and lasting improvements of working conditions? To what degree were these changes compatible with capitalism's industrial functions? If they were not compatible, what transformations did the successful strike presuppose? After years of silent complicity before the bosses' brutish constraints, how could workers be brought to examine such issues?

Weil carefully conjoined the material claims of collective bargaining with the moral benefits they might entail. A guaranteed minimum wage, for example, would relieve the demoralizing concern for speed and quantity of production. Inevitable interruptions in work—waiting on overseers for tools and material—would possibly no longer cause the anxiety attending a pay-by-the-piece system. The resulting slowdown in production, however, would lead to a new and even more cruel constraint—the threat of being fired. So workers would continue to face "a moral suicide of every moment."[78] Further, the overseers' arbitrary control of a contractually set, "normal" work pace could open the door to Stakhanov notions of productivity.

Concerned either that the *patronat* might co-opt shop delegates in negotiations or that they might become partisan (communist) tools, Weil urged that delegates be kept in permanent contact with their fellow workers through *syndicat*-sponsored study circles. There, militants and union regulars could meet and draw upon the advice of industrial technicians in shaping reforms. Analogous study groups could be opened to the public for airing any issues or grievances—a public forum version of the Rosières complaint box.

For Weil the guiding issue was psychological. Workers buoyed by vague expectations in June 1936 gradually slipped back into their ages-old torpor, "where the day is passed waiting for the hour to leave, and the evening is passed trying to forget there's a tomorrow."[79] The greatest danger was that, their hopes cheated, the workers' movement, lacking clearly defined direction and objectives, would contribute to the desperate atmosphere upon which fascism was feeding.

Weil was convinced that the penalty for muddleheadedness is that its victims become accomplices of their despotic foes. Her unease about the well-being of labor after the June strikes proved all too well founded. Labor's sudden advances and the establishment of the Popular Front not only energized the professional rightists but panicked many in the petite and haute bourgeoisie into support of the Right's reactionary or crypto-fascist associations. Jacques Doriot's Parti populaire français, for instance, founded in the month of the strikes, had a hundred thousand members within a year. Would Blum and the Red-ridden *syndicats* deliver France to Moscow? For the sake of stability and order, the alternative being civil war, would it not be best to embrace the totalitarian model of Mussolini's Italy? Should France bow to the apparently inevitable and allow Hitler to unite Europe under Germany?[80]

At more than fifty years' distance, these questions, which many entertained in the late 1930s, attest to the collective nervous breakdown France was beginning to undergo. They reveal how foreign and domestic issues were forming a crisis of national identity.[81] Labor had emerged suddenly as a major player in the national drama, but it was also establishing an identity for itself internationally. Weil's keen attention to the course of syndicalism abroad is in fact integral to her involvement at home.

On the International Crisis of Labor

She traveled to Berlin in August 1932. According to Pétrement,[82] she had resolved to find out firsthand precisely in what the ascendant strength of Nazism consisted. She was also exercising her predilection for being in the midst of action. Most of her writings on Germany from that time through March 1933 do not address national socialism but rather the astounding debility of the German Left that was contributing to Hitler's rise.[83]

The first of these she wrote in July, before her departure. She reviews Trotsky's assessment of contemporary Germany. In everything she had read by him, including his text on permanent revolution, the Third International, and his history of the Russian Revolution (which she considered his best work), Weil consistently commended "the penetration, the marvelous lucidity" of his analyses.[84] This quality impressed her the more that a man officially vilified by Moscow and hounded throughout Europe by Stalin's agents could maintain objectivity in an international struggle in which he continued to be a central participant. Still, she perceived shortcomings in Trotsky's arguments and failures in the premises themselves.[85] She rejected, for instance, his Leninist belief that revolution in the West would recapitulate the essential features of the Russian Revolution. But she rejoiced in the light Trotsky's historiography cast on the relations of organizations to masses in times of crisis. As he recounted, the Bolsheviks in August 1914 had let themselves be lulled just like other socialist parties; they, too, gave way before the nationalist war-making fervor. The populace woke up first; the party that had been preparing for revolution for over fifteen years did not recognize it when it happened. The party let itself be carried along, initially against its own disposition, by the irresistible élan of the people, whom it could follow only with effort. Who, then, made the revolution? Weil answers: "It was individuals, resolute, conscientious workers, who otherwise remained anonymous, undoubtedly educated in the school of the socialist movement, but judging, deciding, acting all on their own and in their own name."[86] These remarks, a splendid view of the incalculable, irrational element in politics which Trotsky was inclined to emphasize, have direct application to the June 1936 strikes, another "anonymous" and spontaneous uprising that the union militants neither wanted nor expected.

The situation in Germany was far different. There, the workers' movement was stifled by the lethargy of the Social Democrats and the Communists, those parties themselves bound respectively to the capitalist bureaucracy and to the Kremlin's dictates. Workers' committees set up to form a united front against Hitler were subordinated to an organizational deadweight, listless, unimaginative, and helpless before the Nazis' peculiar dynamism. Such were the preconceptions Weil took to Germany.

What she actually found there was more enlightening. She learned that the Weimar government had set up concentration camps where the unemployed could work voluntarily for ten pfennigs a week. Under Hitler, she notes, this *Arbeitsdienst* would become obligatory.[87]

Unemployment occupied center stage in the political crisis, specifically in the struggle between Social Democrats, most of whose supporters were employed, and Communists, who drew their strength mainly from the jobless. Weil believed the Social Democrats' chief weakness lay in their abject dependence on the capitalist state. They seemed tied to it for their very survival. The economic crisis made workers fearful of breaking away from a reform capitalism that for two generations had given them greater prosperity than their fellow workers enjoyed in any other European nation. It had not delivered them from bondage, but it did afford them some benefits and thus made them dependent on an exploitative system. The Depression intensified that dependence and made the burden of commitment to revolution more ponderous. Weil wondered whether syndical complicity would satisfy the German middle class, or whether the bourgeoisie, in terror of the Communists, would ally itself with Hitler against the unions altogether?

She found the communist workers in disarray. Unable to pose essential questions among themselves, they fell back on the clichés of party rhetoric. Their fatal illusion, that time itself would bring them to power, that they need only preach revolution without preparing for it, was sustained by their blind fealty to Moscow, even while Soviet interest in preventing any European alliances against Russia wholly eclipsed solicitude for the future of Germany's proletariat. Not surprisingly, only the Trotskyists and youths of the Socialist

Workers' party (SAP) were awake and engaged in the essential agendum of stopping Hitler.[88]

Amid Weil's somber reports on the parties and the *syndicats*, her remarks about young people in the German workers' movement have an almost startling optimism. Although youth had been hit as hard as any group by unemployment, it seemed in the main impervious to Nazi propaganda. Young people had resisted despair even though "continually aware of their tragic lot." She found them "highly cultivated," regarded at a sentimentalizing distance their "joyous bands" engaged in sports, and commended their study groups on revolutionary literature.[89]

Subsequent to the transport workers' strike in Berlin in the fall, which Communists and Nazis alike supported so as to confound the Republic, Weil acknowledged that Hitler had a substantial following among some young workers, but she rationalized that they had joined him in the conviction that the future belonged to them. To claim it, they realized they would have to "smash the system."[90] Both the Nazis and the Communists presumed to lay hold of the future, but while Marxism offered only the inevitability of revolution, Hitler seemed to unite all classes by maintaining their fuzzy dreams with promises of forceful action.

Still, Weil was reluctant to believe that German workers, especially young ones, would willingly consort with Hitler. Perhaps with some relief she accepted Ernst Günther-Gründel's explanations in *La mission de la jeune génération*, which she reviewed in 1933 for the Trotskyist journal *La critique sociale*.[91]

Günther-Gründel called for a new socialism to overthrow capitalist castes, but he argued that only through a regenerating warrior spirit, not a free association of workers, would the revolution be effected. His prescriptive language for this event, "an equilibrium of competence and obedience, responsibility and submission," sounds very much like Weil's terms for a corporatist ethic a few years later (except that submission for Weil had to be and remain voluntary), but she faults him for purveying a pure and therefore confused German romanticism that lacked theoretical substance. She concedes, however, that his book reflected the feelings of German youth exceptionally well: their new spirit born from suffering, their implacable opposition to Weimar and to the indignities of capitalism, their yearning for dignity. That such irrational factors could play a predominant role in political motivations is not stated in her conclusion of this review, but it is strongly implied.

Much of Weil's apparent pessimism, as in her writings on Germany and her essay on oppression and freedom, derives from an insistence upon seeing problems from a vantage that minimizes illusions about their easy resolution. Weil herself seemed subject to hopes or expectations she knew to be vain (as her sanguine view of German youth suggests), but many problems did not admit reasonable solutions. For example, she realized obvious dangers in the German Communists' tactical alliance with the Nazis against the Social Democrats: the workers' movement was thus divided pointlessly against itself. The sole way to defeat Hitler, Weil asserted, was to provide a countervailing force to his, "that of the proletariat grouped into its own organizations."[92] Instead, as she wrote to her parents, "The Nazi ideology is astonishingly contagious, notably in the Communist Party."[93] It dismayed her that the Communists so foolishly aped the Nazis' nationalist rhetoric instead of exposing the true nature of the workers' plight, that the subordination of production to capitalist profits, not the Versailles Treaty, was their ground of misery. The painful lesson of the *union sacré* in the Great War, that the proletariat was as susceptible as any class to chauvinism in an international crisis, she did not wish to accept. Instead, she blamed the Second International and "its treason of August 1914" as though its debauch had been a cause, not a symptom, of nationalism.[94]

Weil's programmatic campaign of reason against the irrational tidal waves of events in Germany was unreal. While denouncing the self-defeating Communists for their nationalism, she urged the French federation of teachers to organize "a vast campaign through articles, tracts, brochures and meetings" to indicate to Germany's workers its sense of culpability for the aggressive policies France had carried out against Germany in the 1920s.[95] Such a campaign could help, she thought, to open the door to German laborers whom a fascist regime would soon force into emigration. It did not occur to her that a fascist government across the Rhine would not likely induce France, so given to xenophobic fits, to welcome yet another wave of immigrants, least of all Germans.

One of her most revealing works from this time comes from a series of letters simply identified in the archives as "to a syndicalist."[96] It probably dates from the winter of 1932–33 because one of its major concerns is to review strategies for dealing with Hitler. Weil admits that whenever she senses that the battle between communism and Nazism is about to be joined, she feels a deserter by staying in France, "a feeling all the less reasonable as I have no illusions at all about the likely outcome, and besides I am intensely aware that one is fighting wholly, if at all, blindly."

Three options for action seemed available: first, an insurrection like the

Paris Commune of 1871, admirable but doomed because, though the proletariat was stronger now, so was the bourgeoisie, especially when its long arm wore a black shirt; second, the October 1917 model, which if successful would only reinforce the oppressive machinery of bureaucracy, police, and army; and third, nonviolence à la Gandhi, an alternative Weil dismissed as hypocritical reformism. She shows herself impatient, not that a fourth option had yet to appear but that syndicalist militants seemed unwilling to compare the lessons of 1871 and 1917. But if those revolutions bore anything in common, it was a spontaneous reaction to a wartime crisis, an uprising not planned but thrust upon those who subsequently emerged as its leaders. Weil, looking not to the nature of these upheavals but to their disastrous effect, the crushing of trade unionism, concludes that the militants fear "demoralizing reflections." A statement of her own commitment to revolutionary struggle shows how far to the periphery her scruples had pushed her:

> For myself, I decided some time ago that, a position "above the fray" being in fact impossible, I would always choose, even in case of certain defeat, to have a part among defeated workers rather than with victorious oppressors; but as to closing my eyes in fear of weakening the belief in victory, I do not want that at any price. And I can't help being struck by the weakness with which we accept everything (even the militants most worthy of admiration among us) and repeat formulas to which we cannot attribute a precise significance.

These are hardly academic objections. Weil was intolerant of confused ideas but, as this letter shows, a deliberate contentment with clichés, a fear of exposing hackneyed arguments and putting one's own position at intellectual risk was to her a crime. She probably offended many syndicalist comrades, in France and in Germany, by her attempts to impose upon them a Cartesian attention to first principles. In her stringent reasoning, however, she failed to appreciate the emotive, cohesive appeal of slogans and partisan platitudes in mobilizing large numbers of people.

This letter also betrays an abstract, formulaic view of revolution. Weil passes quickly from specifics of the German crisis to historical references she employs as strategic emblems, serviceable to any national struggle. In fact, she regarded the struggle in Germany before Hitler's chancellorship as a test case for syndicalism elsewhere: "Our greatest hope resides in this German working class, the most mature, disciplined, and cultivated in the world, and more particularly in the youthful workers in Germany."[97]

When, as she had feared, the Nazis triumphed, she saw that disaster's immediate implications for French syndicalism. The French communists' demand for a united front and the CGT's for "syndical unity" were negative terms used to oppose each other. The calamity of the German leftists' family quarrel would be repeated in France: "This little game has lasted long enough. At this point it has become frankly criminal. The collapse of the German working class, its capitulation without combat before all the forces of barbarism, ought to instruct us that the crisis which it is thought will line up the proletariat against its oppressors, weakens and corrupts the proletariat more quickly than it does the bourgeoisie."[98]

Whatever appeal united syndicalism had in France, Weil was skeptical about it. She doubted it could be realized and maintained free of bureaucratic domination either from without or within labor's ranks. Even as the Second International had betrayed the international workers' movement in 1914, so the Third (the Comintern which Lenin inaugurated in 1919 for "the founding of an international Soviet republic"[99]) "by its absurd politics has delivered the German proletariat to fascism."[100] With the Comintern's sudden call for the Communist party to ally with other leftist parties against fascism (a strategy that helped form the Popular Fronts in Spain and France), the Soviet manipulation of European *syndicats* became all too evident. The only alternatives were anarchism (as in Spain's CNT), which hindered organized action on principle, and a bureaucratic reformism such as had co-opted Germany's Social Democrats: "The latter is, even in France, an apparatus of constraint weighing upon the proletariat much more often than it is an arm between the proletariat's hands; that's even more true in other countries, where a broad-based syndicalism is more developed." The *syndicats* were thus caught between the Kremlin's Scylla and the Charybdis of capitalist reformism. The only concrete difference between these two engines of oppression was that, as Weil wrote in another "letter to a syndicalist," "the capitalist's parasitism translates into an increase in personal consumption (luxuries), the bureaucrat's parasitism translates into an increase in the number of bureaucrats, without luxuries."[101]

These characterizations, however crude, mark one of the first salvos Weil launched against collectivity, the bugbear she later identified as the Great Beast of Plato's *Republic*. Here it is the weighty, self-perpetuating machinery of *étatisme*; later it becomes for her a despotic psychological force for conformism. Her horror of bureaucracy was much more than the average person's resentment of red-taped ineptitude; she saw bureaucracy as the ideological expression of centralization in every national economy. The issue belongs to the present discussion because she took her insights into it chiefly from Germany, where, in 1931, Ferdinand Fried's *Ende des Kapitalismus* hailed a tripartite bureaucracy of unions, industry, and the state as the key to a managed economy. In Berlin Weil saw for herself that Hitler once empowered would prove no friend to trade unions, but Fried's thesis (an anticipation of James Burnham's *Managerial Revolution*) worked for Nazism simply by putting union bureaucracy directly into the state's hands. Bureaucracy meant fascism, and she began to see it as such in various guises, as technocracy in the United States and as Stalinism in Russia.

The guiding spirit behind Weil's attacks on the state is Proudhon, the founding father of French syndicalism. (A close study of Proudhon's influence on her remains a major desideratum of Weil scholarship.)[102] Yet not even Proudhon could have foreseen that in the abolition of the state, "la Sociale," as he called it, would be transformed into a new despotism. The lesson of October 1917 was that revolutionary means become reactionary ends. Weil did not believe that the proletariat (or *artisanat*) would become oppressive; rather, she felt that it would be betrayed by the leadership required for a successful struggle against capitalism.

If she had briefly fancied that Russia could serve as an enclosed paradise for experimental socialism, events disabused her. The Kremlin's abandonment of German communists to the Nazis would have been portentous enough (Weil was verbally and physically threatened at the 1933 CGTU Congress while distributing leaflets calling for relief measures for exiled Germans),[103] but as she wrote in "Le rôle de l'U.R.S.S. dans la politique mondiale," Soviet foreign policy—precisely, the question of rapprochement with Hitler—exposed Russia as a jockeying member state of the old Order, "one power among others."[104] Addressing fellow dissidents on the French Left, her conclusion reads like the sort of heroic manifesto which some of the enduring writers of her generation (Ignazio Silone, Arthur Koestler, George Orwell) were depicting in fiction, the heroism unflinching before certain defeat, protesting for a common humanity against a faceless machinery that grinds down the old truths: "Let us not close our eyes. Let us be ready to count only upon ourselves. Our power is very small. Let us at least not abandon what little we can do into the hands of those whose interests are alien to the ideal we are defending. Let us at the least think of preserving our honor."[105]

Her noble fatalism runs through another essay of this time, "Allons-nous vers la révolution prolétarienne?" Although the anxiety Weil expresses about a dictatorship of technicians in the United States has not been fully justified by history, her equation of Stalinism with fascism as forms of state capitalism or managerial oppression deserves scrutiny. On the psychology of domination she observes: "Every human group that exercises power does so not in a way to make happy those who are subject to it but so as to increase that power. It's a question of life or death for any kind of domination whatsoever."[106]

With that dismal reality stands (or falters) the anachronistic socialist vision Weil seeks to defend: the dignity of individual manual labor and the subordination of society to the individual. Even so, recognizing with Marx that society is "a natural force, as blind as others and as dangerous if one doesn't succeed in mastering it," she no sooner asks whether the workers' movement can still exert itself upon history than she answers: "If, as is only too possible, we must perish, let us do so in such a way that we do not perish without having lived. . . . In any case the greatest misfortune for us would be to perish unable either to have succeeded or to have understood."[107]

Weil's analysis of bureaucracy as oppression inspired an attack on her by none other than Trotsky. In a pamphlet dated October 13, 1933, "La Quatrième Internationale et l'U.R.S.S.," even while admitting that *bureaucratisme* was debauching "the moral tethers of Soviet society," he lambasted her for her bourgeois solicitude "refreshed by a cheap anarchist exaltation" toward Russia's proletariat: "It would take several years to liberate her and her kind from the most reactionary petit bourgeois prejudices."[108]

Two months later, Weil asked her parents to house Trotsky, who was traveling incognito with two armed bodyguards. The seriocomic notes she has left of their exchanges (from another room her parents could hear Trotsky shouting) form a lively document. Though sympathetic to his exile, she pressed him to defend his ruthless suppression of the Kronstadt rebellion. Theatrical, imposing, masterful in debate and unyielding, Trotsky must have been caught off guard by this twenty-four-year-old upstart, his presumed hostess. He unloaded upon her a barrage of denunciatory tags. When he called her an idealist, she answered that he was the idealist in calling Soviet bureaucracy a subject class. Her skepticism exasperated him: "Why do you have doubts about everything?" He contended that though the October Revolution was analogous to a bourgeois one, he and Lenin had been preparing for the postcapitalist future. Weil in turn analogized their role to that of capitalists who "progressed" at the cost of thousands of lives.[109]

Strangely, Trotsky declined to criticize Stalin (whom he had consistently underestimated), but Weil was already in contact with a Russian exile, Boris

Souveraine, who had participated in the October Revolution and had written a history of it highly critical of Stalin. Trotsky had in fact included Souveraine in his printed attack on Weil. She hailed Souveraine's then unpublished study for some of the merits she ascribed to Trotsky's history of the same events. At least twice she asked Alain to use his influence on his old friend Gaston Gallimard to have Souveraine's manuscript published: "It's our only chance of having an interior and yet not blinded analysis of the revolutionary experience begun in October 1917; there's no one else like Souveraine, who has had very wide-ranging responsibilities in the international working movement, and who yet has broken since then with this movement's prejudices, not excepting the Marxist tradition."[110]

Weil herself had become critical of this Marxist tradition. She had never had any use for the tired orthodoxies of those whom George Orwell called polysyllable-chewing Marxists.[111] She once suggested that an ideal torture for a Marxist would be to exact from him an intelligible definition of dialectical materialism. Her time with working people brought her new insight into the validity of Lagneau's dogma: ideas are useless when left in thin air, and they cannot be born there, either. Viewing Marxism as spurious prophecy (a fault only partly attributable to Marx himself), Weil criticized its peculiar failure to attach itself to reality—the fatal mistake of Germany's Communist party. Would France suffer the same fatality?

The growing influence of communists in the French workers' movement, especially after the unification of the CGT and CGTU in the Popular Front, pushed Weil toward the sort of *corporatisme* she proposed to Bernard at Rosières.

She addressed the problem the communists were creating in "La situation actuelle dans le CGT."[112] She believed that CGT federalism's guiding principle, the final autonomy of the *syndicats*, was being usurped by the workers' shop delegates. At the Toulouse Congress in 1930, the CGT had 1 million members; by the end of 1936, it had 4 million. Most newcomers had been brought in by communists via the delegates. Infiltrating at the shop level, the communists intimidated or co-opted union militants, shaped strike proposals without consulting the rank and file, and challenged the CGT's already feeble leadership.

That neither the workers' aspirations nor their sufferings counted in the communists' eyes particularly troubled Weil. Even for the most sincere Marxists, workers were only "history's prime material." Besides, the communists were forever subject to Stalin's bidding, which generally had no bearing on

French syndical needs: "It's certain that Communist Party functionaries never hesitate, as their policy requires, to keep workers inactive when movement is necessary or to throw them into an ill-pledged strike that has no objectives." How could syndicalism or democracy itself, she asked, survive "the deception of the working masses"? The workers' increasing disaffection, aimed mostly at the CGT, and the Popular Front's decline could only encourage fascism: "I don't see how a totalitarian state can be evaded."

Despite, or because of, unification, the CGT and CGTU carried on a propaganda war, with René Belin's *Syndicats,* to which Weil contributed articles, pitched against the communists' "colonization" and *La vie ouvrière.* The division of labor and the Left over the Spanish civil war further exacerbated tensions.

Weil saw no remedy for the division, but in "La situation actuelle" she urged all noncommunists to join with the CGT, "the old house," as she called it. To oppose reds in the CGT was, she owned, a nonconformist position (the only kind she could really be comfortable with), because most workers accused the CGT of inaction: "They say, not without reason, that they no more count in the eyes of those directing their efforts than in the eyes of those directing their labor; that they're being swindled everywhere and that there's nothing to do for it." Having passed two months in Spain, she resisted firmly the possibility that the civil war there would necessitate a new *union sacré.* The struggle to restore syndical independence from the state, the bureaucracy, and the communists would suffice, she hoped, to deliver the workers from "chauvinist madness" and "the scab of nationalism." Otherwise, France's entry into a proletarian war on behalf of the Spanish Republic would have the disastrous effect of solidifying communism's ascendance in the French workers' movement, thus destroying syndicalism as only France had known it.

From the beginning of the Spanish war to September 1939 Weil's concern to preserve syndicalism in France was closely bound with the pacifism she espoused as the one legitimate way to keep France from going the dark way of Hitler's Germany and Stalin's Russia.

FOUR

Between the Bullet and the Lie

> La préparation à la guerre pèse sur nous comme un cauchemar, bouche toutes les issues, rend illusoire tout espoir de libération, et nous protège de rien. Car la course aux armements a toujours mené au massacre.
>
> SIMONE WEIL, "Il faudrait aussi un plan de la CGT pour la politique internationale"

> Et nous périrons pour n'avoir pas voulu saisir un moment marqué dans l'histoire des hommes pour fonder la liberté.
>
> ROBESPIERRE, Dernier discours, 8 Thermidor, II

It has often been written that Weil participated in the Spanish civil war under the red banner. In fact, she scarcely fought at all, and she gave no allegiance whatever to the Spanish communists. Her two months in Spain included a brief time in a column of anarchists, whose commander in chief, Buenaventura Durruti, pledged himself to the razing of churches so that the masses might build a new culture from the rubble. Weil served long enough, however, to perceive the disasters of war and to win a sobering acuity about political ideals when they are placed in the crucibles of fear, terror, and cruelty.

What prompted her to go? She told her anxious parents that she was going as a journalist.[1] By her own written admission, she believed she was a moral participant in the Spanish conflict, but that statement requires a good deal of background. Without question, she backed Léon Blum and the Popular Front on most domestic issues, but as to foreign policy she must have realized in herself something of the sharply divided feelings of Blum's administration, caught by sympathy for the beleaguered Spanish Republic on one hand, and, on the other, by a deep revulsion against war. Blum feared a French civil war would ensue if he openly supported the Loyalists with arms. Weil had no such burden of scruples, and she went.

For five years she had been a member of the national teachers' union. A mainstay of the CGT in the 1930s, this *syndicat* had helped to found, in 1934, the Comité de vigilance des intellectuels contre le fascisme in reaction to the threat of a rightist coup. (Alain himself had come out of retirement and joined the Comité.) The union helped substantially in the formation of the Popular Front, but as most of its membership was pacifist, chiefly in bitter remembrance of the Great War, it even opposed Blum's plans to send supplies to the Spanish government. Until 1939, it took a conciliatory attitude toward Hitler's menaces, including German entry into the Sudetenland. Weil remained in theoretical accord with her *syndicat*'s stringent pacifism as late as the autumn of 1938. Why, then, did she decide to enter the Spanish war less than a month after its inception, in the summer of 1936? The answer may lie in what she had learned from Alain's war experience.

A pacifist no less resolute than Jaurès, Alain had volunteered for service in 1914. He was convinced that only by submitting himself to the war's caldrons could he save his position from charges of cowardice or treason, but his participation in combat afforded him far more than a strategic ploy against the militarists. He learned a great deal about himself that perhaps only war could have taught him. It was, he found, an escape from the scholastic role he had played so well for twenty years.[2] Though he resisted the chauvinist appeal of heroism, having seen at close range its high and inglorious cost, he recognized that the war held for him a peculiar allure: "It's said we're soon returning to our old situations. I violently want this rousing job. It's stupid. Well, there's the secret of war."[3] He was not exposed to the daily hazards confronting the *fantassins*, infantrymen half his age, but he experienced the peculiarly exhilarating effects of danger. In his last assignment he was stationed near Verdun and wrote down his thanks to the gods who put him there.

He had passed a test, too. In willingly subjecting his body, he had been able to keep his mind free. Weil had used a similar experimental gambit in entering the factories, and it might also have informed her decision to go to Spain.[4]

Not long before the Spanish war began, she answered a question Alain had posed when, in the early spring of 1936, Hitler moved into the Rhineland: are those who reckon honor and dignity above life ready to commit their lives, and, if not, what esteem do we owe them? Alain had never lost a bitter contempt for flag-wavers and politicians of the Great War who had urged young men to their deaths. (He even held Raymond Poincaré personally responsible for France's entry into the war.) Weil took up his position and elaborated on her experience at the Alsthom and Renault fronts: "Those celebrated hypocritically from the rear are effectively treated like slaves. And those surviving troops who are poor, delivered from military bondage, fall back into civilian bondage, forced to endure the insolence of those who enrich themselves without risks."[5]

Following Alain's contention that the causes of war lie not in conflicts of interest (the mere occasions) but in passions, almost all of them noble,[6] Weil warned against the intellectual cowardice that fails to examine the propulsive sentiment of "wounded honor."[7] Honor must be reckoned solely in individual, not collective, terms, she maintained, because only the individual can make a decision about honor; whether, that is, it is better to die than to be despised.[8]

Weil also accorded to warfare the possibility of a chivalric or Homeric dignity: "The free resolve to put one's life at stake is the very soul of honor; it is not involved where some make decisions without risk and others die carrying them out."[9] A war without conscripts, waged solely by volunteers, would be a fortiori honorable. Constraint precludes dignity; therefore, a sense of dignity outraged precludes vengeance. Only danger frees one from shame.

Had Weil not gone to Spain, she would have been faced with *mépris de soi*, but she would never have gone under external compulsion. She enlisted as but one of many international volunteers on the Republican side. The impromptu, comic-opera aspect of the fighting owed much not only to the particular fatalism of the Spanish themselves but to the ragtag leftists from abroad, people who would likely have understood Weil's voluntarist notion of honor. It is perhaps the only modern war to which many went so willingly, as though invited by their own sense of dignity.

Weil's accident in camp removed her from a situation in which she would almost certainly and quickly have perished. The column to which she was assigned was destroyed in combat shortly after her withdrawal. She never committed her impressions to any lengthy record, but their pith and moment she passed on in an eloquent letter to the novelist Georges Bernanos, whose own account of the war, as he had witnessed it in Majorca, anticipated her conclusions. She was deeply moved by that account, and it deserves some attention here.

Les grands cimetières sous la lune, while indicting the war as "the charnelhouse of true and false principles, of good and bad intentions," reads as a death notice for European civilization.[10] Although a Christian and a royalist, Bernanos claimed he had lost any illusions about Francisco Franco, and the terms of his grievance justify the claim:

> It's not the use of force that seems to me worthy of condemnation, but its mystique, the religion of Force put in service to the totalitarian State, to the dictatorship of Public Safety, considered not as a means, but as an end.
>
> Terror seems to me inseparable from revolutionary disorder because between the forces of destruction, it is Terror which goes farthest, penetrates furthest, and gets to the soul's roots.[11]

To invoke rubrics of the French Revolution, which he as a royalist abominated, in describing a situation in which royalists were gaining victories, required intellectual honesty, a quality Weil prized highly in any writer. His scorn of "the religion of Force" and "l'Etat totalitaire" was, of course, her own.

Animated by a bitter yet vibrant quixotism, *Les grands cimetières* decries European democracy's exploitations of the ideals of justice, law, and grandeur, most especially of that sense of honor which, conceived in a fairer age as an absolute, had carried Bernanos through four years of trenches in the Great War. Now, with Christianity dead, "the emerging world suffers from an extreme shortage of spiritual values and ardently wishes to dispose of ours."[12]

Bernanos's acerbic generalities appealed to Weil; they gave her a sense of shared, unequivocal disillusionment with political enthusiasms. She wrote him that the anarcho-syndicalist Confederación nacional del trabajo was of all popularly based movements "the last that inspired in me some confidence."[13] Yet she went on to assert that she would have returned to Spain but had come to realize the combat lay primarily between Germany and Russia.

Substantially, however, her letter to Bernanos suggests that the lessons she drew were more psychological than political. She passes on tales of capricious murders of innocent people, crimes committed by anarchists no less thoroughly than by fascists, and, worse, the general acceptance of, even an indulgence in, atrocity: "I've never seen anyone express even privately any repulsion, disgust or simply disapproval regarding the pointless shedding of blood."[14]

The Thucydidean horrors of that time[15] were not the only decisive factor in her judgment. Fragments composing her "Journal d'Espagne" reveal a more complex interplay and, as in situ notes, impose themselves perhaps more convincingly than the letter to Bernanos.

On arrival in Barcelona (August 1936), she looked past the routine punctuated by "so many urchins with rifles" to a vision of the war as part of the modern revolutionary experience.[16] The year signified not merely the revolt of Spanish generals against their republic; it was the beginning of an era, like 1789, 1871, and 1917. Twice within a season, first in the sit-in strikes of June, now in Spain, she witnessed with heady delight the assumption of power by those who seemed born only for submission. Her proclamatory "Men in blue are taking over" is an explosive, oxymoronic pendant to her factory journal. So we must be cautious in assuming Pétrement's retrojected view that Weil went to Spain "without believing too much in this war, but so as not to miss it."[17]

Her first disillusionment came in the countryside, where she subjected peasants to relentless interrogation about their daily lives and their attitude toward priests, toward townspeople, and toward their own service in the ranks. As though fearful of any illusions begotten in Barcelona's buoyant atmosphere, she found in these cursory encounters with the illiterate and barefooted a way of breaking through to the cold and unhappy data which her factory experiences had taught her to identify with reality. Peasant hatred for the wealthy, for example, did not preclude hatred among the poor, the paradoxical fear of inequality emergent from a common struggle. Although their term in the military ran to only a year, they thought of nothing but returning home; they were debauched by fatigue and harsh discipline, just like the Alsthom workers who could fix their thoughts only upon the evening's *buvetier*. In her automatic deference to the lowly, Weil could read behind their listlessness and equivocation a nakedness that does not lie. Here, the anarcho-syndicalist dreams of collectivizing farms, of abolishing money, and of establishing autonomy from Madrid evaporated. Only the programmatic absurdities of murder seemed to have an assured vitality: clergy and land proprietors were being shot as "de facto fascists."[18]

In the face of such atrocity, or at least in oblique testimony to it from others, Weil could entertain no illusion about the cost of partisanship. Loyalists, including anarchists, and the dissidents of the Partido obrero de unificación marxista (POUM) had no claim to righteousness over the fascists. Accordingly, she figured that if captured, she and her comrades would deserve their certain fate before a firing squad: "Our side has spilt enough blood. I am morally an accomplice."[19]

Her acceptance of the fighting as a moral catastrophe was not the only lesson of this harsh schooling. The war seemed as well an epistemological blind. Remarking in a fragment, probably from this first year of the war, that social transformation would matter only if people could be directly and daily affected, Weil at once subscribes to and exposes the central flaw in the anarcho-syndicalist prescription for a revolution concurrent with the war.[20] The daily life of that most elusive entity, the people, seemed impenetrable, and the war itself quickly took on a mercurial complexion. In short, facts were confused, and any attempt to gain a perspective on them was confused by what Weil characterized as a mixture of constraint and spontaneity. The central fact about the war and its greatest evil, in her view, lay in the impossibility of differentiating necessity from the ideal.

Spain in its melancholy way afforded an example to substantiate for her Plato's lesson that necessity and the good are distant from one another. As yet, however, she was not articulating the inevitability of this notion; she was confronting dismally concrete politics: "It is not true that revolution automatically corresponds to a higher, more intense and clearer awareness of the social problem. The opposite is true. . . . In the torment of civil war, principles lose all common measure with realities."[21]

Not even Durruti's libertarian rhetoric—"We carry a new world in our hearts"—could mask anarchism's sullied face.[22] Of what value was a free commune in Saragossa if workers were being forced to labor overtime underpaid and under threat of a death penalty, failure to meet production requirements being considered evidence of factiousness? There had emerged no syndical authority nor even the likelihood of one when Durruti died at forty in Madrid (November 1936). Absence of a coherent leadership (save what communist regulars took from the Kremlin), absence of a Lenin, did not prevent the recurrence in Spain of the bad faith he had shown in shaping the Russian Revolution into an oppressive state machine of police, armies, and bureaucracy. Weil precipitously ends her "Réflexions pour déplaire" by projecting a similar process at work from the very beginning of the Spanish war: "Organized deceit has existed since the 19th of July."[23]

In a single sentence Weil anticipates the message of perhaps the best-known work in English on this war, George Orwell's *Homage to Catalonia*. For him, the chief casualty was not only the truth but the elementary desire to determine it as best one could. In Spain, facts were being systematically contrived; propaganda was successfully transforming itself into fact. The POUM, of which Orwell was a member, was tarred with the Trotsky-fascist brush by Moscow and accordingly calumniated by party-liners throughout western Europe: "One of the dreariest effects of this war has been to teach me that the Left-wing press is every bit as spurious and dishonest as that of the Right."[24]

What Weil adumbrates in her "remarks to displease" French Marxists might well be amplified in reference to one of the few accounts of the war that has kept its integrity, Franz Borkenau's *Spanish Cockpit*. Like Orwell and Bernanos, Borkenau, an Austrian socialist, related only a brief and limited chronicle, but unlike them he looked broadly to the conflict's dynamics in the context of past revolutions.

Borkenau argued that Spain's fundamental resistance to modernization meant that it could not follow the revolutionary models of other states—France in the eighteenth and nineteenth centuries, and Russia in the twentieth. The Spanish Right formed an ersatz fascism because it had no deep-rooted popular support, while the Left, communists and anarchists alike, was tied to textbook formulas, incapable of creating anything fresh. Consequently, Spain proved acutely susceptible to foreign intervention. Hitler's entry marked an irreversible break with all previous struggles: "Now, every revolution is likely to meet the attack of the most modern, most efficient, most ruthless machinery yet in existence. It means that the age of revolutions free to evolve according to their own laws is over."[25]

One "law" apparently working itself out, however, was the centralization of authority and control, which Borkenau described as "elements of modern life, most needed in moments of acute crisis. It is the basic weakness of the anarchists not to understand this." There, perhaps, lies the reason for Weil's bitter postmortem on the Spanish war. She understood well enough that Russian intervention came, in Borkenau's words, "not with the aim of transforming chaotic enthusiasm into disciplined enthusiasm but with the aim of substituting disciplined military and administrative action for the action of the masses and getting rid of the latter entirely."[26]

Although Weil had always been too heterodox to subscribe fully to dictates from anyone, including the deposed and peregrine Trotsky, the Spanish experience seems to have galvanized her ready suspicions against all collective endeavor aimed at political power. In Spain she beheld, as she had been unable to in Germany four years earlier, the ugliest face of the Great Beast.

Orwell's 1938 retrospection exposed the wormwood: "No one in his senses supposed that there was any hope of democracy even as we understood it in England or in France, in a country so divided and exhausted as Spain would be when the war was over. It would have to be a dictatorship, and it was clear that the chance for a working class dictatorship had passed."[27] Weil's Spanish journal shows that, as though by instinct, she sensed that the inchoate processes of that other-than-proletarian regime were in place in the war's first weeks.

That intimation, or her private need to give the situation some stamp of honor, may illuminate two incidents during her short time in Spain. When Joaquin Maurin, founder of the POUM, disappeared at the beginning of hostilities, Weil implored his successor to allow her to pass into Franco's territory and make inquiries. She was refused for the obvious reason that, though she could read Spanish without difficulty, she was not a fluent speaker. Detected straightaway, she would be shot.

Another account complements the first in exposing her hapless importunity. Michel Collinet, a Parisian acquaintance who visited her often after her accident, claims she several times tried to get the POUM leadership to send her into enemy territory so that she might rouse Spanish women against Franco. The pointlessness of such a mission was clear to everyone but herself.[28]

These schemes anteceded by nearly seven years two others remarkably similar. During World War II, she sought permission from the Free French in London to form a group of women for front-line service; she also asked to be parachuted as a reconnaissance agent into occupied France. The different circumstances and objectives of the two wars notwithstanding, Weil's rationalized impulses toward missions almost certain to entail her death seem identical. In each instance self-appointment figures as possibly the most important denominator. Her courage is repeatedly vitiated by her folly. It may have been a most admirable fatuity, but a fatuity nonetheless.

What matters is the determination of Weil's motives for conceiving these plans:

> Violent acts done to the self belong to states inferior to perfection and ought to be considered an indispensable exercise imposed by outward circumstances and inherent imperfections. The need for such actions is a measure of one's imperfections. . . . As with physical sufferings and temporal fears, one ought to taste and thereby measure the extent of one's wretchedness. Such violence is not an effect that the will produces; it is imposed by one's imperfections and by particular circumstances in which the mind perceives an obligation.[29]

Because Weil was never disposed to credit the will as an exclusively positive force, even though much in her thought seems willful in the extreme, it is no surprise that she viewed self-exposure to danger as deontological rather than voluntarist. In Spain, not only combat (of which she had no experience) but war's hazardous contingencies provided an optimal scenario for her "indispensable exercise." If in this time she had already cultivated a belief that human existence as such bears culpability, then her POUM proposals take on transparence. Perilous circumstances and risks ensuring failure would be welcomed as opportunities for atonement. In this perspective, the Spanish war's ideological dirtiness was irrelevant, and Weil's hope of going back to Spain exposes a horrific sincerity in her, an imperative not to fight but to sacrifice.

She later rationalized risk taking as an essential need of the soul; she imputed to it a value comparable to honor, intellectual freedom, and equality. It signifies, she said, a capacity to react to danger, which, if spurred by a sense of obligation, becomes the loftiest possible stimulant. She saw risk taking with Roman eyes, as a bracing discipline. A Kantian sense of duty seems to have figured, and Alain's horror of the imagination's tendency to anxiety, for which he prescribed action as a remedy, should not be discounted.[30] Spain was Weil's testing ground.

Alsthom and Renault had instructed her in degradation, contempt, and the sterile listlessness of monotony and fatigue, where her own awkwardness and physical weakness worked as shackles, but in those factories she had not found a sufficiently creative means of response. The Spanish war afforded a far more evil terrain but one in which she could glimpse penance.

Confronted with war's bizarre, dreamlike episodes, she may have plumbed Freud's insight that warfare allows some neuroses to disappear because its disastrous conditions appease one's need for punishment. But it would be unfair and capricious to give Freud the last word, especially when Weil's scruples served her so well: "Criterion: dread and the taste for killing. Avoiding both of these—how? In Spain, this seemed to me a heartbreaking effort, impossible to keep up for long. Make oneself such, then, that one is able to maintain it."[31]

All Roads Lead to Fascism

The foot injury Weil received while in Spain so incapacitated her that she had to abandon plans to return to the campaign. She had to take an extended leave from teaching and did not assume another position until October 1937. As a result, the year was extraordinarily productive in writing, most of which concerned the growing threat of war with Germany.

It must be emphasized that her resistance to the war fever which began to seize hold of France in 1936 was not based on an individualistic pacifism or a nonviolent Gandhian philosophy. She was dedicated to preserving the substantial gains and hopes the Popular Front had begun to secure for the workers' movement.

A brief review may be helpful. During the sit-in strikes, the CGT, with Léon Blum presiding, had met with the employers' Confédération générale de la production française (CPGF) and won its agreement to reforms the Left had been seeking for half a generation: collective bargaining contracts, across-the-board wage hikes, appointment of workers' delegations to management, a forty-hour week, and paid vacations.[32] Within six months, CGT membership rose from 2.5 to 5 million. Ironically, these reforms were enacted at a time when France could not afford them.

Hitler's move into the Rhineland in April, Mussolini's war in Ethiopia and his cultivation of a pact with Berlin, and the chaos in Spain all contributed a vague urgency to put France on a war economy. But such preparation was greatly hindered by the labor reforms. France's industrial weakness was accentuated in the face of Germany's buildup. To France's further detriment, less was now required of its inferior work force at the very time when more seemed imperative. Domestic opposition to union gains would have been strong even in a time of international stability, but instituting such reforms "at five minutes to twelve," in one historian's words, guaranteed an atmosphere of tension.[33]

Weil's orientation to this crisis was psychological rather than political. Diplomatic maneuvers were secondary, she felt, to the question, Would France oppose German fascism by becoming fascist herself? Would the workers' movement be sacrificed to militarism in the name of national security? Would Hitler that way win the war before the first shot? Such questions variously figured in nearly everything Weil wrote from the autumn of 1936 until the Germans entered Prague two years later.

Fascism had compelled her attention since she saw it crescent and nearly victorious in Berlin during Weimar's last year. She had identified some of its features: more than the bourgeoisie's final card, it was a demagogy of the lower middle class that forcefully resisted even capitalist control. Concentrating all economic power under a party leader, it rejected the class struggle. Its faces included Soviet statism, American technocracy, and bureaucracy everywhere. Weil claimed that fascism did not destroy free thought in Italy or Germany; rather, it arose in those countries from the lack of clear, precisely exercised thinking. For the same reason, it was enjoying furtive status in cultures outwardly opposed to it: "In our day every attempt to brutalize human beings has powerful means at its disposal."[34] Those words date from 1934, two years before the Rhineland coup, four before Munich, six before the surrender at Compiègne, but only weeks after the French government's near collapse before a rightist gang assault on the Assembly, February 6. Weil foresaw that France, like Germany, might fall victim to its own debauch.[35]

She made numerous notes on fascism.[36] She remarked on the novelty of an ultrareactionary movement that made revolutionary propaganda, that the cultural consequences of fascism's spread included the increased need for technical progress, terror, and a total stifling of the critical temper. Fascism signified the decomposition of civilization itself, and so "do not prattle about the impossibility of murdering ideas."

Weil questioned fascism's relation to capitalism. Although no economist, she read widely and well enough to identify how capitalism, instead of collapsing before the forces of modern revolutionary ideologies, Left and Right, was resiliently assuming a new life under them. Why was Taylorization so eagerly embraced by Stalin? Why were Farben and Krupp thriving under Hitler?

Under the rubric "Nouvel état du capitalisme," she enumerated for further study the limited exportation of goods; increased investments in a war economy; finance capitalism's separation from production; the maintenance of business by anonymous and irresponsible bureaucracy; monopolization of all aspects of production in some businesses; and the increased role of the state facilitated by class conflict: "The *impersonal* character of capitalist domination has never appeared so distinctly," attended by "rebellion and despair in *all* classes (save large-scale capitalism)." The effect of despair was fascism, but it would be impotent, she concluded, if it did not have some basis in production.[37]

With fascism came a "mystique of work and war (together!) and essential sadism," a peculiar, albeit pseudo-spiritual exhilaration to which she confessed herself not immune. Her antidote seems feeble—"that men take upon themselves the task of planning their own life. May they find in work itself a discipline, a culture and a means of leisure."[38] To fascism's sinister mystique of labor, she offered what had been virtually forgotten in Marxism, "the glorification of productive work, conceived as one's supreme activity; the affirmation that only a society where the act of work engages all one's faculties, where one who works is of the first rank, would realize the fullness of human nobility."[39]

How was a culture possible when, as Weil admitted, work had become useless for most people; when, "in fascism's wake," the apparent ideal to which Europe was heading could only be "a world of parasites to which the machine's masters will dispense what is necessary to life"? Capitalism now enslaved consumers through *fordisme,* while technocracy's administrators "sovereignly determine production worldwide, which is consequently oriented to the perfection of equipment and consumption."[40] But this luxuriant parasitism in which the proletariat itself became a kind of phantom bourgeoisie was secondary to the main event, capitalism's change to a war economy in time of peace.

Weil's analysis of warfare capitalism updates Lenin's. He had abandoned Marx's hope that war could be "bourgeois-progressive" and liberate the working class. In 1914 Lenin had noted how, while dividing socialists along nationalist lines, war served capitalism by a massive arms production and an intensified struggle for markets.[41] Weil saw the peacetime war economy as a logical extension of capitalism's central contradictions: its use of methodical work subordinated people to the things they made, and its collective expression turned cooperation into its opposite, competition. War was a nationalistic expression of capitalism's essential tendencies, a furtherance of internal oppression.[42]

The conjunction of profit and chaos in August 1914 posed the question, What was the workers' obligation to a nation whose economy subjected them twice over, first in factories, then in trenches? Why had socialists and trade unionists made common cause with their adversaries in a *union sacrée*? In "Quelques réflexions sur le patriotisme," Weil indicates why the *union sacrée* would continue under the dictation of war preparation.

She began by contending that good patriotism can be distinguished from bad. The Spartans at Thermopylae exemplify the good because they died fighting as free men; their true country was freedom.[43] Defending their state against internal enemies with as much ardor as they resisted foreign ones, the Athenians honored tyrannicides no less than soldiers because enslavement to anyone, foreign or domestic, was ruin to them. That lesson was resumed in 1789, when patriots were enemies of aristocrats in their own land.

Such patriotism was no longer possible because "there's no privileged terrain for liberty." The love of freedom had ceased to have any relation to national frontiers. Capitalist countries, to be nations in the Greek sense, would have to have citizens:

> Who is a citizen among the wretched soldiers whom machine guns of their own government force to risk death? Colonial slaves, shamelessly obliged to die to save so-called freedom, after they've had their own real freedom taken from them? The proletariat, work fodder before it is cannon fodder? The scoffed masses, deprived of all control over a diplomacy that risks their lives without their knowing it? Or the capitalists, who, even in wartime, are interested only in exploiting their country?[44]

Weil held that it is impossible to assume one defends freedom in warring on a foreign people because the mere fact of going to war requires a dictatorship. A modern love of country, it would seem, means only the preference of domestic masters to foreign. She did not reckon that, even granted her premises, it would be easier for a slave to serve a known master than to join hands with another but unknown slave.[45] Instead she extended good patriotism to a love of humanity. Patriotism implies preferential love of one's compatriots, but why should one love the German people, their music and poetry, their science, less than the French? Weil's conclusion, that civilized people are separated only by oppressive state machines, may be true, but it leaves no clear agenda.

If she could not follow Diogenes, the first cosmopolitan, she could invoke Socrates, who matured in an imperialized democracy, fought in its war, and died at the hands of its reactionaries. In her notes, she weighs the possibilities for individual action in a war economy. In modern society injustices are founded on necessities like national defense. What methodical means can oppose them? Goodwill, if efficacious, appeals to all available means, but freedom of mind by itself amounts to nothing. Even in prison, Socrates was able to practice both, and the brilliance of his example lay in the equilibrium he kept between the social order and his own spirit, that he could affirm the law's sovereignty even when the law condemned him: "Socrates' solution: never do anything that can destroy order, for order is an inferior requisite of thought, so always obey, but without making oneself oppression's instrument . . . never bend thought before the established order, as this order has no value apart from its relation to thought. . . . Always judge."[46]

These few lines cast so broad a light over Weil's thought, especially her corporatist ethic and her pacifism, that Plato's *Crito*, which is their reference, seems as central as the *Republic* in shaping some of her fundamental assumptions. They are important, too, in catching precisely Alain's disposition to the state, his delicate balance of obedience to its laws and a resistance, steady compliance with authority, and a voluntarist inclination to oppose it, to assert the enlightened self as final arbiter of the good, the just, and the true.

Weil's *corporatisme* was an attempted equipoise between submission to the demands of work (obedience) and informed initiative in its direction (judgment), and her pacifism prescribed for France the equivocal situation of a voluntary satellite of German domination, submission in exchange for cultural autonomy.

Late in 1936 Weil was still some distance from that dire situation, but she was already having to face problems in the unions and in French society which finally carried her to a *huis clos*. In "La Déclaration de la CGT," for example, answering a call to replace strikes with arbitration, she noted the twin dangers of agitation and abdication. The paradox was that communists, transparently supporting Moscow's interest in the Franco-Russian treaty negotiated the previous year, were joining reformers in sacrificing labor's rightful claims to those of productivity and national defense. Simultaneously, as though by reflex, they were engaging in "the most pointless and clumsy agitation." Either way, the *patronat*, chastised by the June strikes, would win out: by recovering its "insolent authority" or by provoking a backlash to communist excesses. Weil's remedy was the fond old unionist chimera, "worker control."[47]

Within days of writing this "declaration," Weil was addressing war agitation, specifically the communists' concern to expand the Spanish war. She noted that a journalist claiming to be a Marxist spoke of the politics of stiff buttocks. Her response was a question worthy of Alain: "Can any war bring into the world more justice, more liberty, more well-being?" Like Alain, she could claim immunity from the charge of cowardice. She had been to Spain. But the issue was one neither of courage nor of cowardice: "It's a matter of weighing responsibilities and not taking up one of incomparable disaster."[48] In late 1936 Weil was reflecting not only the centrist or noninvolvement sentiments of most CGT members; she was expressing as well the reluctance of most French people to risk French interests.

War could not serve leftist interests, either. Her "Réflexions pour deplaire" had pointed to the common lesson of Russia in 1917 and now Spain: revolutionary promises of abolishing the state's oppressive bureaucracy and military machinery vanished behind the war's intensification of these means, with no possibility of popular control over them. Early in 1937, Weil addressed the possibility that France's economic structure, even with labor's gains from the June strikes, might take the country into war.

From its inception the Popular Front was pledged to suppressing rightist leagues, nationalizing arms industries, and promoting reforms. Blum's economic policies followed Franklin D. Roosevelt's New Deal: higher wages for labor would encourage consumption, thus increase production, lower its costs, and make French manufactures cheaper and more competitive in world markets. The gargantuan deficit (8 billion francs in 1936) would be reduced.

But Blum's plans misfired. The propertied classes, frightened of nationalization, sent much of their wealth abroad and made it more difficult for the Socialist government to borrow money. Production lagged, and prices remained high, absorbing the workers' wage gains. Blum's recovery plan ironically included rearmament, a ready means of increasing employment and production. It was this anomaly in a scheme for higher living standards that Weil attacked.

She focused on the CGT's unwitting part in erecting this Trojan horse. Despite the unions' representation in economic planning councils, labor's interests and influence were offset by government and industry, which formed a bloc with "a half-statist, half-technocratic orientation."[49] By controlling industrial budgets, they could transform a nationalization plan directed at energy, transport, and extraction industries into reactionary ends. Interest in workers' benefits could be sacrificed to war preparation merely by changing the guard in the government apparatus. Weil feared that international politics might excuse the dissolution of workers' gains into war productivity: "From there it's but a step to making the struggle for wages an act of high treason. Just as in Germany, and for the same reasons. In short, one can reckon today that the armaments race obscures any practical difference between a directed economy and a totalitarian economy."[50]

Close upon these words came one of Weil's most vigorous attacks on the war economy, "Il faudrait aussi un plan de la C.G.T. pour la politique internationale." In her estimate, social justice was being forfeited to a hysteria gripping not only the press and public but the government itself. Complementing the capitalists' "craze for money-making contrary to all humanity" went the state's "craze for piling armaments upon armaments." In the fearful atmosphere following Hitler's anti-Comintern pact with Japan, obsession with national defense was subverting the élan of reforms; "it has even deprived the idea of revolution of all its sense."[51]

Even antimilitarist Spanish anarchists, she observed, were now proclaiming that a new Spain of their fashioning would have to be militarily strong. How disheartening their conversion, as it were, must have been for Weil can be sensed in her saying she would not deliberately sacrifice peace "even when it's a matter of saving a revolutionary people from extermination."[52] Her resolution did not mean, however, that she was advocating isolationism, as though France could carry out its experiment with the Popular Front in a vacuum. Rather, she looked on the CGT as a trans-national guardian of workers' interests, implicitly a syndicalist rival of the Comintern. The CGT would proclaim the immediate and long-range interests of workers abroad as well as in France.

Weil did not invest much hope in the longevity of Blum's administration; besides, it was a victim of the rearmaments craze. Perhaps she did not entertain high expectations of the Popular Front itself, especially as it was increasingly subject to communist pressures. So, for that matter, was the CGT, but at least traditionally it was a nonpartisan standard-bearer for trade unionism, and because the interests of workers were fundamentally the same in every country, the CGT was the voice she wanted heard above the clamors of militarizing nationalism.[53] But the CGT's own commitment to rearmament posed an obvious difficulty for her.

In April 1937 she tried to spell out "Les dangers de guerre et les conquêtes ouvrières." The June strikes had shown that a fait accompli persuades better than all arguments; nothing could replace its effectiveness in imposing something new. But the strikes' failure to address basic issues of social life was now becoming evident. Left and Right now agreed that a strong France was necessary to ensure peace, but that meant factories would have to increase production in a seventy-hour week. The old brutal and arbitrary working conditions would have to return. France, Weil concluded, had to choose between war preparation and its commitment to social justice, and "if the working class loses its rights, there's no more interest in having a strong France, indeed there would be nothing more to defend."[54]

In the same month, in "Prestige national et honneur ouvrier," she stressed that France's choice of militarism or revolution was effectively a choice between the specious claims of national pride and the substantial claims of syndicalism. Suppose, she said, the newspapers reported Hitler's sudden occupation of Tanganyika. No one would be likely to know where Tanganyika was, but such a *coup de force* would seem a national humiliation to France. But the real, tangible humiliations France had undergone occurred in its factories before June 1936. What did it matter, she asked, whether France endured all manner of mortifications from Germany now that the honor of its own working people was being reclaimed? A bloodless revolt had been carried out against true oppressors, and was the working class now to be made conscript for one imagined?

Why should anyone agree to kill lads from Berlin or Hamburg who had done France no harm, just because of a so-called humiliation that affects no one in particular? Of course, Weil was underestimating the German threat, but her criterion was the tangibility of honor, that no nation can genuinely claim it while condoning the degradation of its own people: "There is an honor that must be defended, that of those who are at the bottom of the social scale against those at the top. It must be defended by the daily social struggle, which does not imply use of cannons, tanks and aerial bombers. So-called national honor, common to oppressors and oppressed, is not worth one drop of blood."[55]

These remarks suggest why, after the Popular Front's death in 1938 and the ensuing reaction, the working class took little interest in defending France against Germany. They also show that Weil saw the war preparation program as counterrevolutionary, a Thermidor in which the Popular Front and the CGT were unwitting accomplices. Most important, it shows that the emergent crisis intensified her commitment, against all odds, to a peacetime workers' revolution.

The weapon she used most frequently against militarism was historical analogy. It is likely that in the spring of 1937, one of her extraordinarily productive periods, she wrote "Sur la guerre révolutionnaire."[56] There she compares the so-called revolutionary war of 1792 and the war to which France now seemed reconciled. The war of 1792 was no defense of the republic against monarchy; it was initially a maneuver of the courts and the Girondins to break the Revolution. Robespierre and his associates were unable to effect the social transformations that justified their authority. They could not forestall the corruption and terror war made indispensable through centralization. Weil regarded Robespierre as the dishonored prophet who, with "this astonishing lucidity which made his greatness," foresaw the disasters of military dictatorship. It is clear that she sought to resume his insight. In this essay she also cites Marx, who held that for liberty, equality, fraternity, war substitutes infantry, cavalry, artillery.

The drumbeating communists of the CGT were playing the Girondist role. They had already performed it in Spain, suppressing the anarchists' program for revolutionary changes. Were Blum, the Popular Front, and the CGT to miss the lessons of 1792? "If one admits, with Marx and Lenin, that revolution in our time means above all breaking immediately and definitively the state's machinery, war, even waged by revolutionaries to defend the revolution they have made, constitutes a counterrevolutionary factor."

Having argued that the real contest was not between France and Germany but between oppressors and oppressed, Weil compared Franco-German relations after 1918 to boss-worker conflicts before 1936.[57] French demands at Versailles were like the bourgeoisie's recourse to law in the face of the workers: in each case, "right" and "law" were functions of force. Germany's treaty violations aroused nationalistic anger in France comparable to bourgeois indignation over the strikes of 1936. Weimar Germany, pacific, disarmed, economically broken, won only contempt for its pleas that the treaty's terms be modified; Hitler having resorted to force, France was now asking for justice as the basis of negotiation. Likewise, as late as 1935, labor's piteous requests met with scorn, but when workers organized, the bosses suddenly came to terms.

Weil was not content merely to list these "striking resemblances." The hazard in the turnabout of Franco-German power relations, pitting a democratic regime against a totalitarian one, was that it made France appear to represent justice and Germany, aggression. Such a notion might bring France to accept war.

Weil's own analysis subverted her conclusion that the victory of 1918 had only to be erased from the memories of both nations so that Germany and France could build a new Europe through mutually respected treaties. Although France was far from being in the right, the character of Hitler's vengeance was hardly analogous to the workers' satisfaction in forcing their bosses to negotiation. Further, the Popular Front had already met stiff resistance from bankers and businessmen loath to support Blum, whereas Hitler was moving contemptuously from one success to another. Perhaps Weil perceived the shakiness of her argument—she did not submit the essay for publication—but the labor behind her analogies reveals her inclination to excoriate France for its cruelty and hypocrisy. It also shows her recognition that abstract notions like national prestige were intimately bound up with force.

She plumbs this theme as the mystery of the modern age, possibly the key to history in general, in "Ne recommençons pas la guerre de Troie." Unlike her other writing of early 1937, this essay transcends an ad hoc focus. France and

Germany, workers and bosses, play only passing exemplary roles in a kind of meditation. Turning to "the Greek experience," Weil displays a balance, acuity, and breadth anticipating her work on the *Iliad* three years later. The Trojan War became her metaphor for the incommensurability of force, violence, and war with the objectives their agents impute to them. The Greeks themselves acknowledged this absurdity, and Weil possibly took her cue from Herodotus, who suggested that making an issue out of the abduction of women was a fool's vengeance. The real conundrum was that Helen symbolized only an indefinable, nonexistent "stake."[58]

To struggle without an objective is to struggle without measure, proportion, or balance. A conflict's importance can then only be tangibly determined by what it costs. In the *Iliad*, Odysseus argues that the war against Troy must go on because so many have died in it. Weil saw precisely the same rationale in Poincaré's conduct during the Great War. Peacemaking, short of total military victory, would betray the dead.

The twentieth century's Helen, as it were, is every word that can muster mass passions and spill blood without anyone's comprehension of what the word corresponds to. According to Weil, such words include *nation*, *order*, *democracy*, and *communism*. They are taken as absolutes, independent of all modes of action, even though we live in a world of demonstrably changing realities: "We fight, we sacrifice, ourselves and others, because of abstractions that are crystallized, isolated, and impossible to place in relation to each other or to concrete things. Our so-called technological age knows only how to beat at windmills."[59]

The problem Weil identified might be called a crisis of language. Instead of words shifting their semantic ground, as Thucydides and Plato said they do in times of social convulsion, they were becoming frozen and static, void of meaning. Weil's typically intellectual response was to call for clarification of ideas, exposure of shibboleths, definition by precise analysis. Imperfect though language must be, she summoned up its geometrical properties, chiefly in qualifying phrases that might establish degree, proportion, or necessary condition. A nation can be called a democracy "insofar as," a communist government amounts to a dictatorship "to the extent that," and so forth.

She insists that neither democracy nor dictatorship exists absolutely. Any social mechanism can be defined only by the relations of its parts and by the conditions in which they work. However imperceptibly, those relations and conditions are always changing. Such abstractions formed the vital basis of Weil's hope that an alteration of social conditions in Germany might somehow make it less fascist. Such a change, she believed, would be far more effective in defeating Hitler than killing off those young men of Berlin and Hamburg.

Again, however, her analysis overwhelms her sanguine conclusions. By their sheer acuity her psychological perceptions defeat the claims of reason she wants to uphold. She equates German fascism and Russian communism, for instance, because in practice they are both *étatisme* carried to militaristic extremes, forced unity of thought, and one-party domination. These predicates are so bold, so apparently absolute, that it is hard to imagine what alterations in the mechanism of Hitler's Germany or Stalin's Russia would be possible. Weil argues well for the nuances required of careful speech, but their application to totalitarian realities remains tenuous, if not futile.

When she recasts her tweedledum-tweedledee argument to the political extremes of the Spanish war, it does not fare much better. Although evidence says that both leftists and royalists became savagely unjust, Weil's case that civil war, by destroying order and freedom, cost both sides more than any regime could exact, does not impose itself. The war was a violent means, an attempt at radical adjustment of the social mechanism. Would a civil war in Germany in 1933 have been worse than the dark peace of Nazism? That Weil did not ask herself this question in 1937 suggests how resolutely she was dedicated to pacifism at that time.

Her discussion moves to safer ground when she takes up the class struggle. Unlike other catchwords of hate, this term has substance, she says. It identifies a real tension between those in power and those who submit to it. The claims of social order and individual dignity both hold a legitimate place in a collective equilibrium. Whereas capitalism is a vacuous abstraction, a real complex of social and economic relations will have capitalistic elements. If capitalism is evil, in other words, it is only relatively so and change can be justified if a lesser evil is identified. Weil shows, however, that the psychological tensions of the class struggle work against the rational approach to change: the bourgeoisie, not knowing what changes might bring disorder, opposes all change, even though its resistance to new circumstances amounts in itself to a modification. The proletariat meanwhile imputes all evils to the *patronat* without asking whether management under any other property system would be less brutal. Could the causes of hardship be removed without altering the system? Such were the issues and impasses facing the Popular Front in 1936–37, as the propertied classes dug in and the CGT increasingly came under communist domination.[60]

"Ne recommençons pas la guerre de Troie" draws on Alain's maxim that interests change but passions do not. Language can determine interests and defuse passions, but Weil recognized that phantom words have people behind them and that power exists by necessity as a social function. Because all power is held more or less arbitrarily, it must be cloaked in prestige so as to sustain the illusion that it is absolute.

Maintaining this façade is costly and absurd, especially in international relations, where whole systems of prestige become competitive. Weil contended that no nation can afford to show a desire for peace because it will give an impression of weakness and thereby encourage its neighbor's aggression. Universal disarmament, she noted, would end the game but remains inconceivable.

Finally, she isolated the contradiction her argument implied. Every society requires equilibrium through an orderly distributrion of power, but its prestige, its ideological fuel, has no limits. To borrow Alain's terms once more, all interests are bound to be devoured by passions. How can we escape this Hobbesian terrain?

It is just at this point that her essay seems weakest. Peace in Europe could go on indefinitely, Weil said, but she did not attempt to explain how it might, or, conversely, why warfare is not the constant condition of prestigious nations. Rather than yield to fatalism, even to its Homeric strain, she iterated that the crisis of language can be addressed: "A problem posed with all its real données is very nearly resolved."[61] To distinguish the real (interests) from the imaginary (passions) so as to diminish the risks of war was, she granted, no small agendum, especially as "the cloud of empty entities" obscured the very perception that there was a problem. Exposing such entities was "an urgent matter of public health. It is not easy; the whole intellectual atmosphere of our time favors the flourishing and multiplication of entities."[62]

Whatever its deficiencies, this essay provides a lucid analysis of political fanaticism and propaganda and cogent statements against them. Yet it was out of joint with its time. Hitler, one of history's most successful merchants of "empty entities," was hardly a contributor to "the intellectual atmosphere of our time" who could be called to the bench of reason. Before the Munich crisis, however, many in France and Britain still hoped he could be.

That hope lingered in Weil's "Les rapports franco-allemands."[63] Although the atmosphere Weil depicts in it could not have been more inauspicious—"confusion, vagueness, incomprehension, daily anxiety"—chiefly because no one had access to or control over secret diplomacy, she supported the nebulous formula of Léon Jouhaux, the CGT's president, that peace is defended by peaceful means. Preventive war or threats of war could not be the best means of preserving peace and could not succeed against Hitler because his fascist regime depended on prestige. The Nazis would precipitate a war rather than lose prestige with their own people, Weil figured. Consequently, negotiation deserved first consideration, no matter what the adversary's internal orientation and foreign ambitions. She urged that nothing be done to make Hitler resort to intimidation. Negotiation would aim toward "a terrain of possible entente" with the awareness that "foreign nations are what they are, and not what we would like them to be." In March 1938 she signed (and perhaps co-authored) a declaration supporting Neville Chamberlain's conciliatory policy toward Germany.[64]

"Les rapports franco-allemand" demonstrates how far Weil was willing to go to relax her stringent moralism for the sake of peace. It is strange writing from someone who, in a postmortem on the Popular Front, identified as Léon Blum's major problem his failure to cultivate a "cynicism indispensable to clear-sightedness," namely a mediation of "the always unstable double perspective, of real conditions of social equilibrium and movements of collective imagination."[65] Weil believed, and said so, that Blum should have traded Marx for Machiavelli, yet she herself seems to have forgotten the author of *Il Principe* when she turned to Germany.

But not quite. When, having annexed Austria to Germany, Hitler looked to Czechoslovakia for his next prize, Weil made a case for him. Though acknowledging that rights figure in every international issue, she was willing to accept an apparently inevitable German hegemony in Europe. Czech submission to Hitler would be an obvious injustice, but so was the submission of Sudeten Germans to Czechoslovakia: "That simply proves that the right of peoples to order their own lives meets an obstacle in the nature of things, by the fact that the three maps of Europe, the physical, economic, and ethnographic, do not coincide." Because Nazism's only "universal" aspects were anticommunism and anti-Semitism, the Czechs, said Weil, could banish the Communist party and shut out Jews from important posts "without having to sacrifice their culture, their language, and their national characteristics."[66]

She made a similar case for France. If German hegemony required France simply to take measures against its communists and Jews, the price would not be too high, and most French would not refuse to pay it.[67] And could German hegemony be worse, she asked, than "the nervous, maddening tension, the siege mentality, the material and moral impoverishment that we are undergoing more and more."[68]

Weil's most ingenious (or sophistical) argument here is derived from her thesis in "Ne recommençons pas la guerre de Troie." Because no political system is free from change, Germany would possibly be weakened by its own expansion, and she urged that France assume a defensive strategy by liberating the colonies of its own hegemony. Inherently unstable because of its acute tensions, Nazism could not endure, she insisted, and its influence might eventually lead to "many possible consequences which are not all wicked."[69]

Although Weil gradually realized that even war over Czechoslovakia would be preferable to further "terrible humiliations,"[70] she foresaw the possibility that with the Popular Front dissolved, a rightist coup would impede war by carrying out Hitler's program on French soil through "a very violent explosion of anti-Semitism (signs of it are appearing everywhere), and of brutal measures against leftist parties and organizations. I would prefer this eventuality as less murderous overall for French youth."[71]

Her desperate acceptance of such a scenario shows how vigorously she clung to an anything-but-war position. Another proof is that, though she could countenance a rightist government persecuting Jews and communists, she did not want a French government of any stripe to make France an armed camp on perpetual alert. The hope of containing Germany by exerting such a counterforce would be a political and psychological disaster, the end of freedom and democracy.

That France was undergoing a psychological debauch in the months before Munich Weil saw clearly enough. The predominant quality of this muddle was, in her view, its dissolution of everyone's private life into a public one, not through the galvanizing élan of revolution but through "the harsh conditions of our existence which keep us from finding in daily life moral resources independent of the political and social situation."[72] It was cold comfort to her that France had lost the lulling illusions of security because it had so quickly traded them for a generalized fear of war propagated through the popular media.

One peculiar effect of this dread was an envy of Hitler's triumphs. The bourgeoisie seemed ready to embrace a totalitarian dictatorship. Weil perceived that one result of such emulous nationalism was that in giving way to it one sacrificed "the thoughts in whose name one defends one's interests and which ennoble those interests by giving them universal scope."[73] Indeed, interests themselves would be lost in submission to the annihilating constraints of war preparation. She remarked that the striking outcome of Munich was that war appeared to be a fact although it did not happen, while peace, although it continued, ceased to seem a fact.

If mental paralysis was the hallmark of the prewar crisis, Weil was not one of its victims. Although events successfully despoiled her rationalizations for peace, she busied herself with other alternatives. Outstanding among these are her notes on a decentralized defense, written in response to a lecture that the pacifist Henri Bouché had given in March 1938.[74] She realized that though nonviolence might serve as an individual's response to war, it could hardly suffice as a government's policy. She proposed "a complete transformation of military method" along the syndicalist line of a complete decentralization in France's political, economic, and social life.[75] An armed resistance would also be decentralized and work as a guerrilla force to harass and demoralize the Germans, break up their communications, and score small but psychologically valuable victories.[76] But Weil figured that France was too selfish and spiritually enfeebled to rise to such a concerted effort.

If freedom was dead in the soul before it was outwardly destroyed, what was the point of national defense? Yet, true to her intuition that from weakness strength might come, she suggested that France put itself to the test, live up to its libertarian tradition, and help its colonies toward independence. That course would be better than losing them by humiliating defeats at German or Japanese hands.

This argument came too late to catch much attention. The French were understandably too concerned about the safety of their nation to fret about a review of colonial policy, and the guerrilla war scheme, which could have delivered Vercingetorix and Gaul from Rome, flew in the face of France's long-sanctified Grand Armée traditions. Only events could force these issues, and they did, in 1940, in 1954, and in 1962.

In the spring and summer of 1939, the paralysis Weil described as Munich's legacy reached the scale of a "collective obsession." The anticipation of war prompted her to gather thoughts she had been developing since Spain. "Réflexions en vue d'un bilan" shows her penchant for interweaving historical analogy, political psychology, and an inspired moral vision. It argues that Germany's hypertrophic *étatisme* implied virtually "a supernatural right to colonize other peoples," that Europe was effectively forfeit to a state "at once taken by a mystical exaltation of the will to power, governed by a leader who combines the advantages of a semihysteria to those of a most acutely lucid and audacious political intelligence."[77] Hitler's aim at universal domination was not maniacal, as commonly supposed; not since the Scipios had it been possible to any other conqueror.

Weil indulges an odd sort of historical pessimism. She takes the Roman example—its annihilation of Carthage, its suffocation of Greece—as renascent in Nazi Germany. In the face of history's other oppressors, civilization had managed to hold out: the Hundred Years' War had no effect on "the development of the little florentine miracle"; Charles V and Napoleon had not destroyed "milieux and men who developed and exercised their own abilities freely."[78] It did not occur to Weil that in the time of such warlords, those free minds might well have trembled no less than her contemporaries before Hitler; or, in turn, that even in the present darkness, not all lights were going out. As she had earlier written to a former student: "On all the earth's surface, oppression and nationalism are triumphing. That's no reason to renounce one's idealism: it's already something not to give in to humbug."[79] Still, she insisted, in the play of forces, spiritual values can perish. Contrary to Orwell's fond hope, bursting bombs do shatter "the crystal spirit."[80] That Europe's democracies (rather those states tending to democracy) had been reduced to war's barest objective, survival, argued to her a catastrophe that would extend to whatever peace followed the war. Drawing on her previous analysis of prestige, she saw that "negotiation is then regarded itself as a phase of war."[81] She thus had an inkling of cold war diplomacy; Munich had become fixated in the political consciousness of contesting nations.

"Réflexions" also clarifies her understanding of pacifism and why she now rejected it. Like Alain, she never developed a private philosophy of nonviolence discrete from what she here calls a political policy of generosity through strength. She believed that had France been able to carry out Aristide Briand's initiatives after the Great War, Hitler could not have come to power: "Virtue in itself is a timeless thing, but it has to be exercised in the course of time; and when, having the power to act wisely and justly in a given situation, one abstains from exercising virtue, one is often punished by the very ruin of that power. That is what has happened to France."[82] Pacifism meant this wisely employed strength, not some turn-the-cheek or recumbent posturing.[83]

With Hitler triumphant and France virtually prostrate before him, Weil tried to rally her readers to a counteroffensive. Against the Nazi will to power she invoked "men's natural love of freedom," with France serving as freedom's "perpetually gushing source." Let all lovers of freedom be glad that France exists, she urged, yet she had to concede it was unlikely that they did. She closed on a voluntarist note: "It depends upon us that it be so hereafter."[84]

As the "phony war" entered the spring of 1940, Weil wrote to her brother, who had been imprisoned on a trumped up charge of draft evasion, that, with the Popular Front deceased, "there will never come anything like it; various political convulsions perhaps (which will be sterile), but parliamentarianism in France is, I believe, dead."[85] People were restless and discontented with everything yet "disposed to bear anything without protests or even surprise." Although it is difficult to reckon how deeply despair had affected Weil herself, these remarks indicate that for her the worst had come to France. The disposition to war had transformed the nation into a simulacrum of its enemies: "Certain specific traits of fascism are missing (one-party power, physical violence in public) but the atmosphere no longer differs much from that of Italy."

This was no hysterical ejaculation. As though her brother's imprisonment was not a sufficient sign, she offered him some disheartening facts: "All trace of the events of '36 have vanished from the factories, where the regime is once again very harsh." Her warnings three years before about the cost of war preparation now had the bitter justification of prophecy. Ten years in prison could be dealt to anyone talking so as "to injure the nation's morale." Military tribunals were being set up, and government prefects could intern political suspects in camps. In sum, everything Weil dreaded and detested in *étatisme* was coming to pass. She knew that psychologically, politically, in every sense of esprit, the real war was already lost.

PART TWO

Philosophical Problems

FIVE

On Necessity Divine and Dire

Qui sait si l'homme n'est pas un repris de justice divine? Regardez la vie de près. Elle est ainsi faite qu'on y sent partout de la punition.
VICTOR HUGO, *Les Misérables*

Jadis, les conquérants exigeaient que les députés des nations conquises parussent à genoux en leur présence. Aujourd'hui, c'est le moral de l'homme qu'on veut prosterner.
BENJAMIN CONSTANT, *De l'esprit de conquête et de usurpation*

In almost everything she wrote, Weil was a Hellenist. Among French writers of the twentieth century only Péguy rivals her in this title, and both of them would have recognized it as bestowing the highest honor. No more than he was she a philologist or classical scholar, but she was a keen reader of Greek texts and used them to arrive at her own sense of the world. She was an inspired reader and an eclectic one. Certain passages in certain Greek works took on for her the force of a gospel. They served her as intuitive flashes of genius or gnomic revelation.

One of the most important of these occurs in the *Timaeus*, Plato's treatise on cosmology, the physical elements, the human soul and the human body. This work is perhaps best known for its mythic exposition of Atlantis. For Weil, however, the *Timaeus* virtually amounts to one passage (48a): "The origin of this world came as a mixture and combination of necessity and intelligence, intelligence ruling over necessity by persuading it to bring most of the things created toward the best." Implicitly, necessity inheres in everything, and by contrast to intelligence (*nous*) it is unruly and unpredictable. Plato describes it as a "wandering cause."

Like Plato, Weil looks upon necessity with ambivalence. It is our first instructor in the way things are. It is a sovereign irrationality that seems to prevail over the material world so powerfully that human reason is daunted.

In all the brutish gratuity of nature and of life itself (who has not at some point asked, What is the point of living?), necessity's sway is evident and incontestable. But to see reality as only what necessity imposes would amount to atheistic desperation and might prompt a revolt against reason on behalf of force. Plato, of course, gave primacy to intelligence or mind as the ordering principle at work in matter, and that primacy amounts to a theistic affirmation. Necessity itself, says the *Timaeus*, is tamed (or persuaded) into a compliance with reason that ensures things work or move toward the best: ultimately and primarily, reality is intelligible. As the good, the true, and the beautiful, it is the goal of the human mind's endeavor.

What might be called Weil's Platonic doxology rests on that contention. It is epitomized in the *Symposium* (205e–206a): "It is not true to say that one cherishes what is one's own. There is no other object for human desire than the good." And from the *Laws* (716c): "God is the measure of all things"—the answer to Protagoras, to humanism and to all materialistic philosophies.[1]

Weil's theocentrism properly belongs to a subsequent discussion of her theology. In this chapter necessity appears in its two fundamental aspects: as an instrument of a higher reason and as the "wandering cause" of brute force. For Weil, the Greeks, especially the Stoics, were the foremost interpreters of the first and Hitler of the second.

For her as for Plato and the Stoics, necessity serves as a nexus binding human action and divine will. It is itself divine, a "cas de force majeure" as the French might say, because it is God's own dispensation. Indeed, the Stoic masters, Zeno and Chrysippus, equated necessity to Zeus himself,[2] but Weil does not go that far.

Her debt to Stoicism, although chiefly limited to particulars implicit in the idea of necessity, proves substantial. Fortunately, she does not entangle herself in the predestinarian problem of fate. In a passage suggesting the influence of English empiricism[3] she notes:

> There are two ideas of necessity: one rests upon the intuition of time only—that there will be a tomorrow. Unconditional necessity, but it's not truly necessary internally. Why would there have to be a tomorrow? We think of necessity only by relationship of cause and effect, but that's the idea of a conditional necessity. The other amounts to fatality.
>
> The idea of conditional necessity is inseparable from the idea of free action. The condition is necessarily that of an action. If you suppress

> every notion of free action, there is no longer necessity but fatality. But the thought of space and then of the world disappears at one blow.

Necessity also supposes

> liaisons established by our thought. . . . In fact there is no necessary condition. The result is not guaranteed in advance and cannot be. . . . The result can arrive without preparations; there is in fact no necessary succession between sensations, and we always know that.

Hence, via Kant, she arrives at David Hume's position, that "necessity cannot be found by experience, it is a relationship and we record only facts." But it is the very fact that necessity eludes epistemology which makes it the more compelling, a force at once divine and dire.

How closely, then, did Weil subscribe to the Stoics' necessity? As Plutarch objected, if Chrysippus was right in saying that necessity is set as a limit on all things, then one has no freedom of judgment or will. What would be the point of any action, what the meaning of virtue, if we are only puppets?[4] This so-called lazy argument, the *argos logos*, did not trouble the Stoics because they concerned themselves with a conformity to necessity as God's will. They were psychologically predisposed to affirm all that happens.[5] In a comparable way, Weil looks at the world not so much as a logician but as a moralist. She responds to the Stoic dogmas not with a systematic rigor but in a spirit (the word is not too labored) of voluntaristic faith. Such a disposition reveals itself in her choice of Stoic texts; she prefers, for example, the poetic simplifications in Cleanthes' Hymn to Zeus over the scholastic architecture of Chrysippus, whom she seldom mentions, even in her notes.[6]

Epictetus, one of Weil's favorite ancients (an intellectual and a onetime slave) bade his reader to acquiesce in everything even as it happened, but such advice seems a bit complacent. Alain faulted the Stoic dogma of necessity precisely because it inculcated resignation. To him it implied an enervation of will. Late in her life Weil concluded that Alain had not understood the real value of "pure" necessity—another way of saying that he was not a theist.[7] She perceived, and more shrewdly than Alain, that the Stoic position requires an immense effort of will because it prescribes one's consent as a steady imprimatur given to destiny.[8] Further, one must consent not in a spirit of grudging concession but with cheer. To the degree that one obeys God thus, one participates in fate, and such collaboration Weil considered the only freedom.[9]

Conformity to God meant for the Stoic a conformity to nature as the world's ordering principle. It would be difficult to overstate Weil's endorsement of this *Weltanschauung*. Her translation and interpretation of a Stoic apostrophe to the cosmos deserves notice:

> All that pleases you, oh world, pleases me; for me nothing is too early or too late that is timely for you. All is fruit for me in what your seasons bear, oh nature! From you [comes] everything, in you [is] everything, into you [returns] everything.
>
> The Stoic doctrine regards the universe as a city of which all rationally endowed beings are citizens and of which Zeus (or God) is founder and legislator. That's why the good citizen of the universe must cherish everything that conforms to the laws of the city, that is *everything* since nothing occurs that is not conformed to nature's laws. He who permits himself to be discontented by an event shuts himself out from the city of rational beings.[10]

However thoroughly cut off from the common circuit of unreasonable men Weil may have felt herself to be, as a Jew, as a woman, and as an intellectual (a word she disliked), she retained this invisible citizenship, this Stoic credence that would persuade itself of an ultimate order in which to participate.

That participation, however, appears to remain contemplative. Eyes it has, but where are its legs? There seems to be no incentive for acting upon a world where everything that happens is a function of divine will. The Stoics assumed nonetheless that they were not borne along by fate but keeping pace with it. If they knew where it was going, Seneca once remarked, they would get there first.[11] This effort to keep up with fate inevitably has a macabre side. In anticipation of personal misfortune, Epictetus told his reader to rehearse a range of disasters with the thought, I knew I might be exiled, imprisoned, and so forth. He even suggests, in Seneca's vein, that if the upright man knew in advance "he would cooperate in his own sickness, his own death, his own mutilation."[12] Weil herself went so far as to pray that God might give her such calamities.[13]

However dire one's personal misfortunes, Stoicism in its inveterate devotion to *logos* looked upon the world as good. Weil shares that affirmation but regards necessity as, by God's will, a blind and brutish mechanism. She begins with Stoic premises but subjects them to a twentieth-century setting, even as she reads Homer in the refractory light of the blitzkrieg. The world's order affords a terrible beauty, terrible because it includes evil.[14] Necessity has been willed by God's providence, left to play a harsh game on the face of nature while God remains hidden.[15] Invoking the Greek notion of nemesis, Weil grants that Necessity works out a rude justice that redresses the balances of power, but power itself is not and never can be canceled so long as the material world exists. Necessity cannot be divorced from human history; it cannot be suspended as an abstraction for some kind of salon theism. It must be contemplated, she insists, through the dismal record of the human will striving to break its bonds. Her Stoic cosmology inextricably involves if not a philosophy, a psychology of history.

In the approximately ten years of her mature writing Weil gave numerous formulations to her concept of necessity, but they are all strikingly coherent. What might be called her theology developed and deepened but did not alter that fundamental coherence. The Christianity she embraced (or contrived) was, she was convinced, essentially one with Stoicism.

Her 1934 essay, "Réflexions sur les causes de la liberté et de l'oppression sociale," offers her first and shrewdest examination of necessity. The picture she paints does not comfort. The power by which institutional authority oppresses people is, she maintains, derived from forces in nature. Social organization, in other words, translates the necessities which nature imposes on humanity. She discerns "a mysterious equilibrium" at work in what optimists would call progress: as far as a culture is released from nature's immediate burdens, so the mechanisms of oppression are increased. The most "advanced" society, then, one burgeoning with technological wizardry, is best equipped to overwhelm its individual members with the force of a natural cataclysm. The weight of necessity has been shifted, transmuted, but not discharged.

If this conundrum has a happy aspect, it is that all power is essentially unstable. Power, like water, seeks its level, but it remains, like water, fluid. Although oppression's designers and agents may believe otherwise, power does not belong to its wielders. Nemesis, we recall, does not punish power but power seeking when taken to obscene and deluded excess. Necessity, Weil remarks, thus exerts a kind of fatality upon all social organization, with power playing the role of worm-in-the-bud of all human harmony, corrupting and yet limiting its apparent possessors. In deference to Marx, whose insights into social mechanisms she applauds even while deploring his failure to analyze their content as forms of oppression, she recommends as "a scientific study of history . . . a study of actions and reactions perpetually produced between the organization of power and the processes of production."[16]

A study of history would be a profile of necessity set within the human drama. Weil thus commits herself to what Engels in *Anti-Dühring* and with him Marx in *The German Ideology* had dismissed, the view that history amounts to the exercise of force.[17] The locus classicus for this position is, of course, Greek but not Stoic. The so-called Melian Dialogue in Thucydides' history of the Peloponnesian War (5:87–111), a text Weil admired and cited frequently in her writing, is cast as an eristic exchange between Athenian generals and men of the small island of Melos, which Athens wanted to use in its war against Sparta. The dialogue swiftly comes to the point that neither justice nor honor nor even prudence holds up before sheer power. The gods themselves rule not by virtue but by what Thucydides calls natural necessity. It is an argument for the expediency of might that anticipates Callicles' denial of justice in Plato's *Gorgias*.[18] From the supernatural sanction of might, the Thucydidean argument passes to justice as a function only of equal contestants. Where one proves more powerful than the other, the stronger always dictates and the weak either submits or perishes.[19]

Weil's essay concentrates on the oppressive bonds in relations of labor to capital, but she looked to other instrumental forces such as propaganda and war. It is not surprising, then, that when, as though seeking a respite from these tableaux she seeks to sketch out an ideally free society, she resorts to the individual mind and a kind of Promethean grappling, not first with the circumstances necessity imposes but with the stark, irrefragable idea of necessity as a problem for methodical confrontation. Only in thought, she believes, can human individuality reside, and only in its calculation of necessity's imposed limits can a truce with matter be achieved.[20] One's life can thus be a continual creation of self by the self: "One is a limited being to whom it is not granted to be, like the theologians' God, the direct author of one's own existence, but one would possess the human equivalent of this divine power if the material conditions permitting human existence were the work of one's thought directing the effort of one's muscles. Such would be true liberty."[21]

Weil admits that what defeats this enterprise from the start is the plain fact of other people and that work—thought itself—bears ineradicably a social component. Not blinking this fact, she tends to mystify it to excess as a metaphysical horror, a tertium quid that spoils one's acceptance of nature by transforming the terms of necessity from something wondrously daunting to something cruel: "absolutely mysterious, inaccessible to sense and thought," collectivity stands between the self and nature, its "relations of oppression and servitude posing permanently the impenetrable screen of human arbitrariness."[22]

Her point is simple: necessity as nature may well confound human energy and strip bare human illusions (Weil later considered these reductions desirable), but as matter it does not and cannot reduce thought itself. Only in a collectivity can human life and thought be truly degraded. Hence her picture of a free society amounts to a minimalization of that degradation, a map, to use her image, where individual thought would exercise the greatest possible freedom for the social good and thereby "constitute the human act par excellence."[23]

Not surprisingly, this map does not finally include any really human terrain. It is faceless, and Weil abandons it for the sorry but immeasurably more gripping cartography of twentieth-century statism, in which collectivity has reached its most brutal extremes and individual thought has dwindled into insignificance before the mechanical complexities of social organization. The very notion of value, Weil claims, has virtually passed from mind to matter, and the state has taken the struggle for power which historically lay between classes and has bureaucratized it into a contest with other states. In a remarkable anticipation of Orwell's *Nineteen Eighty-Four,* she observes that the state's uncontested organization of social and economic life leads to preparedness for war, with the laboring masses docile accomplices of their own slavery.

Weil's analysis does not indict totalitarianism as a cause of enslavement. A system such as fascism is the effect, she contends, of the powerlessness of that methodical exertion of thought over action which she sketched for her impossibly free society. When irrationality informs matter, matter becomes all-powerful in a way incalculably more devastating than any it takes in its pure form as nature.[24]

For Weil, necessity translated into a social principle grimly at play in human relations makes labor and warfare almost interchangeable activities. This conjunction occurs in some notes she wrote upon reading a novel about life in mines, Pierre Hamp's *Glück Auf!*[25] His scenarios of people collectivized and made helpless in the narrow and strangely unintimate milieu of workers and overseers gave her occasion to comment on necessity in a daily context: "A half-second's hesitation in obedience gives way to more, to exhaustion, fatigue, revolt. In each case, training protects the workers against themselves—on the other hand it puts them at another's discretion. They submit to the constraints of their wages, but this habit of obedience holds them more closely." Her remarks about training (she uses the word *dressage,* denoting the discipline of animals) refer not only to the submissive miners but to their overseers as well: "It subdues to a pitiless constraint the one who gives orders just like those who obey them." This constraint must be distinguished from the sort of conditioning which Emile Zola set in relief in *Germinal*. It is neither heredity nor environment that moves the puppet strings; it is power: "It belongs to no man, no more to the commander than to the commanded. It is a relationship between him and them."[26]

Weil's enthusiasm for *Glück Auf!* complements her response to Charlie Chaplin's film *Modern Times* (1936) in which ineluctable power is embodied in assembly line mechanisms that enforce a mechanical obedience from the workers, with the dynamos looming so large as to dwarf even the harried foreman.[27] In both works she read a ratification of her own trials at Alsthom and Renault. In her notes on *Glück Auf!* she refers to Mouquet, one of her factory bosses, as an example of the compromised overseer forbidden to dwell on his moments of bad humor. Mouquet, according to Pétrement, was known at home as a jocular man, "but when he put on his factory smock, he was the boss, he did not joke."[28] Not incidentally, Weil sees a similar contrast in the *Iliad*, where the most commonplace affections pass as "moments of grace" that make the pervasive violence more keenly felt.[29]

Given the connection between labor and war which Weil established in her "Réflexions" and the *Iliad*'s brief mention in them, her notes on Hamp's novel might be taken as a link between her writings gathered in *La condition ouvrière* and one of her best-known essays, "L'*Iliade* ou la poème de la force." The common element is the indifferent nature of power: "The capacity it possesses to transform people into things is twofold and it works both ways: it petrifies differently but equally the souls of those who suffer it and of those who wield it."[30]

"La poème de la force," an essay begun in 1939 and published in 1941, might best be read for its transparent application to that time: the petrification of a people by its conquerors, their peculiar power to make living men into things, "terror, grief, exhaustion, massacres, friends destroyed"[31]—these matters seem to belong to the twentieth century's "long night of barbarism," as Winston Churchill called it, more than to the majestic horrors in Homer's epic. Surely Weil intended these timely correspondences, and they would have been obvious to her readers, yet it is necessity once more that holds sway. War may fascinate because in it power works such varied and horrible transformations, whereas the living death in labor relations holds only the static monotony of iterated tasks. But there is a fundamental identity between these two experiences that rests in their violation of the limit, the measure and equilibrium which necessity imposes upon nature itself.

If, as Weil states at the beginning of "La poème de la force," force plays the central role in the *Iliad*, it does so through a dynamic that is much greater than the actions of heroic Achaeans and Trojans, much greater even than the momentum suggested in Homer's similes likening masses of troops borne along in combat to the sweeping herds and swarming bees of animate nature. The domain of force proves unbounded; "its empire goes as far as that of nature," and farther still, one might say, because force, the hand of necessity, governs all matter. Necessity can be made horrible by abuse, but necessity punishes that abuse. The *Iliad*, barren of victories, mirrors "this chastisement of a geometric rigor."[32]

This last phrase indicates that Weil chooses not to read Homer on what might be called Homeric terms. She does not heed the Homeric warrior's code of merit, that in waging war, in killing, the warrior carries out his business, achieves and sustains his renown. In short, there is an excellence to be performed, an *arete*, and the god of war, Polemos, is not a metaphysical bogey that Sarpedon and Diomedes wring their hands over.[33] Weil's reading draws definitively on "pre-Socratic" texts, particularly the fragment of Anaximander which characterizes the alternation of phenomena as a warlike contest within the symmetries of nature: winter's cold and summer's heat run to excesses that must "pay penalty and render justice mutually according to the ordinance of time."[34] Everything proceeds as a birth from or a return to indeterminate matter "according to necessity." The passage of all things, their very being, inevitably brings about injustice, for which they must pay tribute. More positively, Plato's *Timaeus* speaks of the oscillation of all things in the cosmic equipoise of necessity and divinity.

According to Weil, Anaximander's text is "unfathomable," yet the pendular rhythms of becoming which it illuminates figure in her reading of the *Iliad*, where "there is not found a single man who is not compelled at some moment to yield under force."[35] She sees war not as an aberration or violent departure from order into chaos; rather, it is a dramatization in extremis of existence. It is not war merely that Homer shows us; it is a hideous order in reality. As though in compensation for that hideousness, war's disasters furnish what she calls "luminous moments," when feelings are wholly free of ambiguity, when courage and love attain a patent visibility, as between Hector and Andromache on the parapets of Troy. Thus in an unpublished variant to her essay, Weil remarks: "Human emotions are almost wiped out by the pitiless necessities of war, but to the extent that they subsist, precarious and threatened, they subsist pure, nowhere can one find them more pure."[36]

"La poème de la force," then, is no pacifist's tract. Written subsequent to Weil's bitter rejection of pacifism, it might even have taken inspiration from some gnomic words of Heraclitus which Weil translated: "War is the mother and queen of all things, it has revealed some as gods, others as men, some as slaves, others as free."[37] In this tableau of fateful caprice it becomes clear that all exercises of power are human attempts to arrest necessity's mechanisms, to co-opt them for one's own ends, and the effect is maddening.[38] We recall Achilles' raging vengeance taken for the death of Patrocles, where the Homeric warrior par excellence is transformed, as it were, into a natural power until he is checked by another power, the river god bloated with Trojan youths Achilles has slain. Madness ensues from the effort to exceed the limits necessity imposes through nature. That there can be no escape, no mastery, that is, of nature through reason or will is a concession every mortal must make: "Man must never fall into the error of thinking that he is lord and master of nature. . . . He will then sense that in a world where the planets and the sun follow circular trajectories, where moons revolve around planets, where force reigns everywhere and alone in mastery of weakness, which it constrains to serve it docilely or be broken, man cannot set up special laws." These are not Weil's words, but she hailed them when she read them in *Mein Kampf*.[39]

Yet the catastrophic time in which "La poème de la force" was written suggested that man *does* set up special laws, that servitude means the triumph of history as Hitler conceived it, an achievement of evil rationalized as a good; an armor, as Weil puts it, to keep suffering away from the victor's soul. In her 1938 letter to Gaston Bergery she noted that Nazi Germany's momentum was so inherently unstable that it would have to change. Now, in 1940, with virtually all of Europe under Hitler's boot, this historical fatalism appeared to have halted. That is why enslavement, a fate that descends hardly at all in the *Iliad*, occupies so much of her discussion.

In an unpublished part of her manuscript she even rationalizes the slave's abject complicity with his master: "What does it matter that he has been the cause of every evil, since life weighs too harshly to permit the soul to voyage in time?"[40] It is as though Weil were saying that human brutality can be exonerated because it reveals the way things are. Hitler as man of destiny is an instructor in the truths of necessity. At times, it would seem, human history approximates gravitational force so that adversity and every onslaught upon one's sensibility have an overwhelming effect of leveling. Oppression is the metaphysical proof that we do not live with the good, the beautiful, and the true.

In another unpublished passage (was it censored?) Weil cites Hector's taunts (8:225–34) to Greek warriors fleeing the momentarily overweening Trojans—words that would have been bitter enough to the French army in June 1940: "Shame, Argives, miserable scum, so imposing in form, where have your boasts gone when we call you brave?" Her remarks on these lines are a gloss on what happened to France after the humiliation at Compiègne:

> Once the enemy is present it is too late; to capitulate is to be massacred. It is necessary to accept (since one must suffer it) this life where thought cannot pass from one day to the next without death's evocation. The mind is then stretched as it can be only for a little while, a single day; but after that, another day comes, requiring an equal tension; and another after that, until weeks, months, years roll on. This situation is impossible for the soul, but it *is*—the soul must do itself violence to bow to it. It must void itself [*s'emputer*] of all hope, of all thought of the future, of every notion of an end near or far.[41]

These words do not describe Ilium (not Homer's anyway); they describe the soul of Europe under Hitler; they are the prophetic scenario of Le Struthof and Auschwitz. It is perhaps just as well that they do not appear in the essay's published version, which is weakened enough by tendentious remarks toward the end about grace and the gospels, that world unknown to the dark, suspirious majesty of Homer's victors and vanquished.

The passage just cited on the bleak tensions of enslavement bears directly upon another aspect of necessity as Weil reads it, the role of human illusion in response to its operation. Before nature one feels subject to inscrutable laws, but in their mysterious translation into powers of social organization, one may well feel a slave or master by nature's sanction—as though one were "predestined from all eternity" to one position or the other.[42] All social order, Weil contends, rests in varying degrees upon these complementary illusions of mastery and subjection, the lies that would usurp force from matter and reduce people to things, often with their own hapless cooperation. Conversely, every genuine good—the independence of thought, the vitality of love—works against that mechanism by a prompting that is revolutionary in the most basic sense: it would turn back to the legitimate order of things which is found in nature. There, as Anaximander had taught, excess must pay out to justice.[43]

Society, then, is necessity taken to one fatal remove from nature. Weil expressly identifies social organization as evil, but she insists that it cannot be undone any more than the courses of the stars: "The struggles between fellow citizens derive not from a lack of understanding or of goodwill; they belong to the nature of things, and cannot be appeased, but only stifled by constraint."[44] So she attacks vigorously the mainsprings of illusion in Marxism and Hitlerism alike, for both share a belief that history can be transformed, that people can take charge of nature. Hitler had betrayed his own insight into the unchanging laws of nature.[45]

All that society can achieve is a stifling coercion that operates from the state's bureaucracy, whether it be denominated fascist, communist, or capitalist. Such is Weil's somber, Hobbesian estimate of what James Burnham called "the managerial revolution" of our time.

Virtually all her references to Hitler are approbatory. She does not share the moral despair implicit in national socialism, and she does not endorse its attendant violence, but she does appreciate in Hitler its cunning architect. She sees that his view of history is one that Western culture has sanctioned since Roman times, the organization of evil as a good. It is the cult of grandeur; in Nietzschean terms, the will to power, that lust for triumphant domination which began, according to Weil, with Rome—not as history's first empire, of course, but as the first to impose a universal ideological domination of the world it knew. It found a transmogrification first in ascendant Christendom and subsequently in the modern states of Europe. Hitler's totalitarianism amounts to the latest expression of the Roman idolatry of power.

All such expressions are violent but futile assaults on the limits of necessity. They are attempts to subvert nature and convert relative good into a programmatic absolute good, conferring what can only prove a bogus spirituality upon the agencies of human will. Collectivity, the inevitable social form which that urge takes, arrogates to itself a power that menaces the intimate recesses of individual thought. It stands in a metaphysical revolt against unwritten laws to which nature itself is obedient. Human history is an attempt to refute Anaximander. From the *imperium sine fine* pledged to Vergil's Caesars, from the Church Militant and its Inquisitions to the Big Brothers of modern statism and dictator cults, the collective lie remains the same.[46] No assertion of social influence, Weil maintains, no resort to any kind of force can lay claim to true good; conversely, true good cannot find expression in any social mechanism. The fires in Plato's Cave do not come from the sun. They never shall.[47]

Weil has no difficulty documenting the atrocity of Rome's imperial sway; it is the stuff of Roman historiography, of Appian, Polybius, Julius Caesar.

Behind the war chronicles Weil perceives a Roman proto-Nazism. For example, she ascribes to the Romans "the conviction that they were a superior race and born to command"; theirs was "a calculated, methodical employment of the most pitliess cruelty, of cold treachery, of the most hypocritical propaganda," all fueled by "an unshakable resolve always to sacrifice everything to prestige."[48]

The key to Roman imperialism, she argues, was the psychology of its cruelty, for cruelty proves "an incomparable tool for domination. Being blind and deaf like the forces of nature, and yet clear-sighted and provident like human intelligence, by this monstrous alloy, it paralyzes the mind by the feeling of fatality."[49] What wreaked a mysterious pathos on Homer's warriors, war hypostasized as necessity's sharp edge, Rome appropriated as policy, a consciously directed device of collective subjugation. Two thousand years before Hitler the Romans realized that strength avails only when wedded to policy. Rome's enslavement of Greece in the second century B.C.E. (Weil slips by the fact that Greek vitality had long been atrophied) marked the end of ancient civilization.[50] Roman literary culture (the Stoics and Lucretius excepted) is almost entirely contaminated by the ulterior demands of imperial politics.

Roman statism, then, was the first successful attempt to co-opt necessity. Statism's spurious good would be exposed, Weil asserts, were we as its inheritors not blinded by our own collusion and hypocrisy. She commends Hitler for reaching out toward the Roman model of power epitomized by Sulla: "It is this grandeur which he has attained, the very same before which we all bow basely when we turn our eyes to the past. We hold ourselves in cowardly submission of spirit before it, we have not, like Hitler, tried to seize it in our hands. But in that, he is better than we are. If one recognizes something as a good, one must wish to grasp hold of it. To hold off from doing so is cowardice."[51]

If Weil's attacks on Rome are so sweeping as to suggest caricature rather than characterization, it must be noted that her hostility toward Rome derives partly from Caesarism's role in her own country. One might begin with Gaul's doom and noble Vercingetorix—Weil, like any French schoolchild, does not forget him—but her protest is not a romanticized vengeance. It is that Rome was reborn in the France of Richelieu, the author of the modern European state. Indeed, his statism, a centralized authority exacting obedience and devotion, served, Weil claims, as the modern source of Hitler's inspiration; it is the connecting link between ancient Rome and the twentieth century's official terrors. In Richelieu she recognizes a remarkably lucid rationalization of power, that the state, once rendered "the blind, anonymous machine, the creator of order," puts aside all morality so as to perpetuate itself.[52] Its people's souls will find salvation in the other world.[53]

However derivative, Hitler himself was not to be underestimated, and Weil's post-Munich characterizations almost mystify him as an incalculable force: "He commands a country stretched to the maximum, he has a consuming, tireless and pitiless will . . . an imagination that fabricates history in grandiose proportions according to a Wagnerian aesthetic, and well beyond the present; and he is a born gambler."[54]

Perhaps the greatest danger came not from Hitler or from a rearmed Germany but rather from the spiritual humiliation which Munich had exposed, "the abasement of thought before the power of fact."[55] Like the Roman scheme of teaching peace to one's neighbors, Hitlerism required the cooperation of its victims, their willingness to feel their own subjection as fated, and their master's policy as a natural law.

Weil readily admits that all peoples are capable of giving themselves, if only briefly, to the enthusiasm generated by totalitarianism. Oppression's modern machinery carries power-wielders to such excess that the necessity revealed in nature is not merely aped by them but seemingly outdone. (As Winston learns in *Nineteen Eighty-Four,* two plus two are five when the state says so.) But Weil refuses to draw the curtain at this point. Furtively confident in the final truth of Anaximander's physics, that oppression cannot permanently appropriate the harshness of necessity, she exposes some fatal weaknesses in Hitlerian despotism.

Mostly, they are psychological. The artificial enthusiasm a totalitarian regime requires makes the masses passive. Once wearied, they feel the inherent constraint and thence the obligation of a pretended docility that begets hatred. The primary stimulus of labor under such a system is enervating, unproductive fear. Rather too sanguinely, Weil suggests that "a moment comes at last when most of the population, youth excepted, does not wish for victory, nor even peace, but war and defeat so as to free itself of its masters."[56] Yet she realizes that, as Alain would say, a wish without action is not will but a nullity, and meanwhile tyranny will prove what few men wish to acknowledge, that "force can destroy spiritual values altogether, so that not even a trace of them remains."[57]

Weil also looks to the uneasy momentum of the oppressive state's machinery, suggesting that "what renders these regimes terrifying is also what enfeebles them with the years, that is, their prodigious dynamism. . . . Everything that assures the permanence of force is sacrificed to that which procures its progress. So, when progress has attained a certain limit, paralysis sets in."[58] The built-in contradiction of such a permanent atmosphere of revolution indicates an inevitable entropy of the totalitarian state. It is as though it is forced to pay for its excesses, its attempts to confound natural law.

She points to the lesson of these excesses: they show how cogently Anaximander's physics can be applied to history. It is certain that brutal systems of oppression have enforced upon modern consciousness the primacy of material force over mind. Good, reason, the life of the mind, culture, and all such appendages of the civilized person are ensured of nothing in this world, least of all a final triumph. And yet cruelty's excess must pay out.

Weil finds an Anaximandrian countervailing force to state tyranny in the tradition of the French Revolution. She calls it the indispensable offensive of liberty. Only the natural love of freedom can retard and perhaps arrest the march toward domination which has motivated nations for generations. France under Richelieu and Louis XIV had initiated that march so it would only be fitting that the France of 1789 be invoked to check it. She wants to propagate an image of her country that would advertise France abroad as "an interior source of energy," a phrase that betrays her preoccupation with mental orientations.[59] She wants France to become an ideal for contemplation, dynamic in its effects yet rather statically exerting "the principle of an irresistible attraction."[60] Not wishing France to be a modern nation-state, she prefers to conceive of it as an impersonal force of some higher physics. In that limited, purific compass where justice and humanity salve the conscience (Weil's conscience, at least) there may be found a defense from despots and the cult of grandeur which is their final cause.

If the France Weil wishes to conjure up has any social dimension it is that of the ideally free society she had set against the modern state, a society in which true individuality of mind is able freely to confront the world's fabric of necessity and to accept it with Stoic sangfroid and Christian humility. Still, it is difficult to understand how such an ideal could exert its presumed attraction unless clothed in the advertisements of nationalism, the very garb of collectivity Weil abhorred. She does not wish to tether her ideal to any social or political system—it is the business of ideals to serve as unattainable goals, she feels—and so the loftiness of her appeal seems to end in vacuity.

It had to be so because her true axis of freedom remains individual, if not individualistic; it depends on the single human mind's coming to terms with necessity. Social organization, no matter how minimal its collective harms, will always implicitly threaten that precious autonomy in which Weil sought to rehearse the old Greek drama of noble acquiescence to the mysterious dispensations of an ordered universe.

That is why even in *L'enracinement*, her final and most extensive effort to redeem history through a vision of Greek harmonies, Weil has scant success in locating society, in heeding the broad and complex dimensions of its real life, as though to do so would obscure the claims of necessity, which only the mind's untrammeled consciousness can meet.

Malheur

Weil's Greek cosmos might seem an academic preserve. Her recourse to Plato and the Stoics, her reach toward a universe of imperishable virtues, her fascinated longing for a transcendental order—all of this carries a *normalien* air of privileged access. It is the educated person's paradise. Since she sees modern social organization as only refined variations of collective tyranny and acknowledges in them no real advances of human awareness, she seems to leave us with no other option than to accept or reject her view of the world. Dismissing Enlightenment beliefs in a progressive eudaimonistic course of history, she sees humanity entering into a collectivized bondage more subtle and far more sinister than nature's dominion over earlier times. The only relief she knows comes in the contemplative wisdom of antiquity.

Fortunately for her readers, Weil does not intend a retreat into some cloud of higher learning. She is not interested in consoling the erudite or providing some Epicurean idyll of ataraxy. Necessity, as she sees it, weighs like the law of gravity, as heavily upon clever people as upon others. It is harbored in the incontrovertible fact of natural limit, of evil attending all of this world's good, and of death. She insists we cannot move an inch toward Plato's "other side of the sky"; we can only labor to find a more humane position on this side of it.

The illusion that necessity can be thwarted is not the exclusive property of collectivities; it is born first in the individual mind. In Plato's parable of the Great Beast, to which Weil refers repeatedly, a key role is given to the Beast's tamers, the sophists skilled in guiding its whims and duping its interests. Updating this spectacle, Weil finds the sophists' part in modern dictators and their bureaucracy and in all political propagandists. At a basic level, however, even these manipulators are the victims of illusion. In Weil's attention to necessity, the most melancholy fact seems to be that every human being insists on escaping from it into the protection, sometimes private but generally collective, of artificial constructs, fantasies that give the assurance of power.[61] Her remedy for this refuge in illusion is to look at a fact that does not offer the comfort of lies, and this is the presence of *malheur*.

She was not disposed to adversity by some perverse need to suffer. Her very insistence upon accepting fate implies in her an unwillingness to do so. Worse than any external harm, she felt, is the harm one does oneself from within by giving imagination leave to create havens from reality, and nothing does one seek to avoid so urgently as suffering, both in oneself and in others.

In a too brief sketch simply titled "Caractère," she sets out the problem of illusions:

> Our personality seems to us a sort of limit, and we love to figure that some day in an undetermined future we can get around it in one direction or another, or in many. But it also appears to us as a support, and we wish to believe there are things we would never be capable of doing or saying or thinking because it is not in our character. That often proves false. Witness St. Peter.
>
> Personality is continually modified in two ways, from within and without by the effects of freedom and of necessity. This second modification is very painful to consider because we don't know if something limits that which circumstances can make of us. We don't know how we can some day be transformed. What guarantee do we have that we won't one day become in spite of ourselves something that we hate, or at least something that is wholly alien to us?[62]

That interrogative marks a substantial move beyond Epictetus and the Stoic gospel of autarchy. While upholding Stoic submission to fate, Weil declines to stand on its bedrock of complacency and stiff confidence about virtue as life's guide. Necessity's lesson is that life lives us.

Still, acceptance of the world at every cost Weil made her own and never abandoned. This *amor fati*, the true province of freedom to her mind, she affirmed repeatedly in the last five years of her life. It was not solely a love of fate or things as they are but a consent to how they are. For example, a love of nature's rhythms means the harmonization of one's own life to a felt association with the seasons and the stars. Somewhere between affirmation and reverie, Weil seems to believe that one can cultivate an intuitive familiarity with the natural world. From that bond comes a perception of the world's order such as both art and science express.

The world's order, the material universe, presents no past or future; neither can its apparent design serve as an argument for God's existence.[63] Rather, it serves humanity as a model for the soul's contemplation. It purifies the ego: "Not to accept some event taking place in the world is to desire that the world should not exist."[64] Loving the world, then, purges the self of all egotistical refusals to accept necessity or to assert the will's desires.

This congeries of themes (release from illusion through renunciation of desire, a purifying liberation) seems to point clearly toward Eastern spirituality, toward Buddhism and Hindu monism. Indeed, Weil equates necessity with Indic *dharma* and *amor fati* with *nirvana*.[65] At times she seems to belong in succession to the nineteenth-century romantic cult which saw in the East an alternative to the European spirituality desiccated by the Enlightenment. She is not, however, Schopenhauer *redivivus* because she allows a good deal that is positive to the self. To love the world, she says, is to be its co-creator.[66] The self must, by its apprenticeship in Stoic *amor*, reconcile all contraries, see life and death as equivalents, endure evil—and love it. Only by undergoing such fire-and-water tasks can the soul apprehend the divine justice at work, through necessity, upon inert matter.

Though she finds analogies between Stoicism and Eastern traditions, Weil faults Christianity for its inattention to the material world: "Never has the Christian inspiration known how to give itself a relationship with the things of here below. Everything proceeds as if the Incarnation were a crowning, a fulfillment rather than a commencement."[67] Although God, the Christian's or another's, must not be confused with necessity, God may be read in necessity, in the sun shining upon the sinful and the rain falling upon the righteous. Weil calls this kind of action "necessity exercised," and she sees the crucifixion of Jesus as an example of "necessity endured."[68] In both aspects, God has a visible presence in the world's order, but it does not comfort or console, and never does it mitigate necessity's bitterness. One's love of the world may well be the basis for one's love of God, and yet nowhere, Weil insists, does God interfere (as in miracles) and co-opt that love.[69]

Weil wants no hint of theodicy. *Amor fati* involves no cosmic "payoff," no reward of personal immortality for the devout soul. Yet from the Stoic gospel of a virtuous life conformed to nature she extracts a peculiar dynamic of obedience to both necessity and God. She calls it "passive activity," a contemplative and accepting love of the world that cannot admit the will and still remain pure.[70] This static conformity cuts away the two mainsprings of egotistic illusion, desire and fear, the presumption of power and powerlessness alike. Weil calls it a necessary nurture for the soul.[71]

With a curious ambiguity Weil labors to distinguish obedience to necessity from slavery. As obedience implies consent, it is slavery's opposite, but her model of obedience is brute matter, the patent of a mindless congruence to necessity's limits.[72] Matter has no will or desire to suppress, so is it not casuistic to speak of its obedience to anything? As though anticipating such an objection, Weil holds that necessity obliges obedience whether we like it or not. Subjects by our very being, our only real choice is whether or not to desire that obedience.[73]

Lacking divine imperatives, Weil could only imagine them. The supreme example of obedience to fate she culled from the Christian gospels: Jesus' acceptance of God's will over his own and at the cost of his life. Not even the morbid Epictetus could match it. But without Jesus, and even without God, obedience to necessity can be taught—by *malheur*, the harsh school of suffering.

Difficult to define, *malheur* can signify harm or misfortune, unhappiness or woe. Weil's *malheur* has a metaphysical life of its own that resonates beyond any general meanings. More than merely pain (*douleur*) or suffering (*souffrance*), it denotes for her an overwhelming calamity, an affliction of both spirit and body, a paralysis that might have no discernible source and promises no discernible end. Inevitably, *malheur* has evil at its center, even as it has its root in *mal*. Weil's remarks are not consistent: at one point she writes that she does not see suffering in itself as evil; it is evil only for those who think it is. But she also claims that we should look upon suffering as "an evil endured completely against our will."[74]

Neither does she scruple to distinguish ontic evil (natural afflictions) from moral evil (human actions). The *malheur* of an incurable disease such as the enervating headaches from which she suffered (apparently an acute form of sinusitis) obviously differs from the *malheur* of an immoral condition such as slavery. The line between ontic and moral evil may sometimes be blurred: which evil is poverty? Is it subject to human remedy or finally in the nature of things? Weil seems not far from the Stoics' view that moral evils are the privatives of virtues: folly, injustice, intemperance, cowardice, and she reflects the view of Chrysippus that life affords no shortage of moral evil and misfortune.[75] More important to her than the occasions of *malheur* are their common proclamation of the human condition; they are necessity's primary text. The putrescence of Philoctetes and the dispossession of Lear say the same thing; they have the same soul-threatening power to reduce a human being to the state of thing. Weil fastens upon this condition and this threat for their educative value. The assumption that *malheur* does have this value she takes from the Greeks.

It is most economically expressed in Aeschylus's *Agamemnon*: "learning in suffering."[76] Weil's remarks on these words are inestimably important in showing how much her notion of *malheur* rests on her understanding of ancient Greece:

> The Greeks never attached value to suffering in itself, as do certain sick people in our time. The word chosen to designate suffering is *pathos*, which evokes above all the idea of submitting, more still than the idea of pain. Man must undergo that which he does not want, he must find himself submitted to necessity. Malheurs leave wounds that bleed drop by drop even in sleep, and thus gradually they train one by violence and dispose him in spite of himself to wisdom, which is defined by moderation. Man must learn to think of himself as a limited and dependent being; only suffering teaches him that.[77]

She iterates the point that submission, not merely suffering, holds the key to this enlightenment, for there may be those "who torment themselves with pleasure out of sheer perversity or romanticism."[78] These words suffice to remove from Weil the imputation of masochism or dolorism or any cultivation of woe for its own sake. *Malheur* must never be sought out.[79] Suffering holds no intrinsic merit for her, no benefit whatever; everything depends upon the afflicted person's use of it, and even then *malheur* must be loved for that use. In *malheur*, ulteriorly, lies what John Donne—a mind more akin to Weil's than George Herbert—calls the treasure of which no one can have enough.[80]

Malheur may, though, bite so deep that it arouses a disposition to itself.[81] Suffering in excess can prompt either rejection of it or a desperate clinging to its source. Weil says that the temperance which *malheur* rightly instills must be exercised toward *malheur* itself. There lies, for her, the peculiar genius of Job's story, that, repentant in dust and ashes, he is not overcome by *malheur*; at no time does he explain it away.

Malheur's victim must attain, as Job finally did, an equilibrium, a purifying void where affliction wins one's consent that it be. At times Weil suggests such consent is impossible; *malheur* is too profound for contemplation. One can only hold back one's energy, seeking not a freedom from suffering itself but from its effects. The pure void is, as it were, co-created by *malheur* and the self-arrested will. At the same time, it is right for the mind to seek understanding of its condition. Offering no consolation other than itself, knowledge of our wretchedness is the only thing in us, says Weil, which is not wretched.[82]

She also insists that divine grace be present to *malheur* as a requisite to understanding. In the *Agamemnon* she finds that grace itself provides understanding of suffering. It is possible, then, to suffer without illusion; the all-too-human penchant to rationalize suffering, either by denying it or perverting it with convenient meanings (including the belief that it is God's will) can be displaced, but only the foreign aid of the supernatural makes displacement possible.

With this assumption of grace, a substantial contradiction imposes itself: God is the source of good only, but of *malheur*, too.[83] Weil prefers to meditate upon this contradiction as an insuperable mystery; she relishes the tension that certifies our helplessness and enforces our wonder. Thus the acceptance of affliction, the Stoic *amor fati*, and the love of God amount to the same thing in her mind. That *malheur* should force the soul to face and accept contradictions such as God's goodness and the abiding power of evil gives *malheur* its peculiar value.[84] The Greeks had reckoned that affliction ennobles humanity because in the endurance of suffering one shows oneself superior to the gods, but Weil finds rather that suffering keeps us from becoming false gods because only suffering can convince us of our essential nothingness.

Weil urges that the reality of *malheur* not be cheapened by excuses or explanations as though it were a punishment or an occasion for expiation. In a time when the world's affairs had become a universal affliction, she wrote these striking words: "We must do our best to avoid affliction, only in order that the affliction we do meet with may be absolutely pure and absolutely bitter. We must do our best to avoid the affliction that befalls others, so that it may be for us a pure and bitter sort of affliction."[85] Acceptance of other people's suffering, however, means that one submits to it oneself, but Weil is not clear about how this sympathy, literally a shared suffering, can come about.

Her desire for absolutes in purity and bitterness expresses her unavowed wish that the lofty anguish she found in Greek tragedy, in Job and Lear, redeem the compromising sordidness of life. Although she writes against all consolation or compensation in suffering, it seems that the absolutes she seeks and would have us seek amount themselves to a consolation, however recondite. It is not surprising that she entertains an aesthetic of *malheur*, saying that even though suffering's invasion of the soul is hideous, a proper submission to the purity and bitterness of *malheur* brings the experience of *malheur*'s "savage beauty."[86] This is no quirk on her part, because necessity and the good are united in the world's order, and necessity therefore partakes of the beauty of that order, even in its direst form, as *malheur*. But in *malheur*'s assault, time and space—the universe itself, Weil says—enter the body, threatening to destroy the soul's divinity; it would appear impossible for anyone either to sense that terrible beauty in oneself or to behold it being borne in others. Weil admits as much and goes further: socially considered, *malheur* is degradation in extremis; it is a veritable branding that makes the afflicted person a kind of criminal, seemingly beyond all compassion. Like La Rochefoucauld or Vauvenargues, Weil chooses to dwell on ugly fact: to a person stricken by disease or overwhelmed by oppression we bring more contempt than pity.[87]

Precisely here, the Stoic's *amor fati* is put to the test. According to Weil, what is required is the perception that *malheur* is a gift of divine love. In exposing the soul to necessity as brute force, through physical pain and social debasement, *malheur* proves, in her phrase, a marvel of divine technique; it makes of one's compassion toward the afflicted (a miraculous response, to be sure) a kind of harmony extended over an almost infinite span, the distance between necessity and the good overcome as affliction and compassion are harmonized in the concreteness of experience.[88]

Weil's steady attention to the world as experience can be credited for giving her some insight into the implications of *amor fati* which the Stoics themselves perhaps did not fully apprehend. That is, she saw the positive value of suffering under necessity; she saw that when balanced by a love of necessity within the same person, it created a tension of harmonies analogous to those in the cosmos. One's own life realized as a microcosm of necessity and the good became for her a form of saintliness, a mimetic witness to the world's order. *Amor fati*, *imitatio mundi*, *imitatio Christi*—these terms attain synonymity in Weil's mind.[89]

Perhaps, as one of Weil's admirers claims, one of her foremost contributions is to bring "an idol-making civilization" to an authentic piety and wisdom by recovering Plato's distinction between necessity and the good.[90] Perhaps, too, as this admirer adds, her Stoic *amor fati* will help us "on the road to holiness," if that is the road we choose to take. But the twentieth century has offered rather too many tableaux of suffering to justify the limitation of *malheur* to an epistemological occasion for loving the world and seeing in it hidden harmonies, Stoic or Christian. One may wonder about the didactic value of purity and bitterness in suffering if it amounts to saying, finally, that all is well with the world. As to the ontic evil of, say, terminal diseases, surely the honorable response, the decent impulse, is to mitigate the suffering and to work in the hope of ending it. Weil's scorn of the illusions that inevitably attend progress make her reject progress itself. There is, it seems, something to be said after all for Alain's complaint that Stoicism invites resignation, and Weil's additive of Christian love does not convincingly deliver this resignation from a certain recumbence.

That an urgent seeker of justice, so demanding of herself and unsparing of others in its pursuit, could have found satisfaction, as though it were a respite, in the static and hierophantic visions of Greek sages seems an odd and disconcerting consideration and a melancholy one. From their vantage she could accept the mechanisms of necessity in both its divine and dire aspects. In the horror of *malheur* she could find an eerie redemptive beauty. She admired the onetime slave Epictetus for finding a higher guidance through a world in which slavery was commonplace. Believing herself a slave, perhaps she was trying to emulate him. It is not her fault, surely, that in the century of death camps and despoiled nature, this vision is one we must strain to appreciate, let alone comprehend.

SIX

Beauty, Bread of the Soul

Weil's Aesthetics, Her Poetry and Drama

La joie qui est une adhésion totale et pure de l'âme
à la beauté du monde est un sacrament.
SIMONE WEIL, *La connaissance surnaturelle*

First Essays on Beauty and the Good

From her earliest writing Weil regarded beauty as a puzzle. She gave herself the simple, not easy task of trying to understand what it is, how we apprehend it, and how it can be distinguished from and identified with the good. She never quite relinquished Plato's prejudice that the love of beauty is the one immediate avenue to the good vouchsafed to this life—a reflection of the Greeks' inclination to blur differences between the aesthetic and the moral. Through Kant she was able to place aesthetics beyond and above the empirically conceptual, and yet, thanks to Alain's influence, she gave no credence to Kant's notion of aesthetic experience as a free play of both the understanding and the imagination. Her intellectuality limited her to a beauty found chiefly in lines and proportions, a geometer's aesthetic; her moralism, wary of imagination, limited her to a beauty of actions. Her painter was Giotto, her music was Gregorian chant. Strangely, despite Kant's influence and her longing for transcendence, Weil neglected sublimity.

One of her first topoi for Alain, "Le beau et le bien," takes up both the beautiful and the good without seeking their identification and concludes by affirming it. Weil presumes that because a human being has ideas of the good, the beautiful, and the true, they have a kind of unity in the human, but she recognizes that a work of art might not be conformed to the good. Further, good conceived merely as morality is rigid and severe, yet the Jansenists' disapproval of art suggests to her that there might be a chasm between beauty and the good.

The example of arbitrariness in a temple's stones as "the game of mechanical forces" interests her.[1] Were they otherwise arranged, they would no longer form a temple. Hinting at Plato's notion of forms, Weil claims that the temple is eternal, outside of time and above existence. She skirts altogether his pejorative view of art as a third order (*Republic* 597 b–e), an imitation of the material world, which is itself an imperfect copy of the transcendent. She is close to the Neoplatonic view that art expresses an apprehension of the transcendent. Knowledge of Platonic forms alone, she realizes, does not help toward an understanding of this world's art as both material and absolute. We must accept art's impenetrability.

Perhaps better than architecture, music expresses this irreducible. To seize it we must move with it, yet we feel that it expresses us when in fact we are only imitating it. As with the templar stones, every note and rest is reciprocally means and end, perfect. What is beauty, then, but matter which art carries from mere sensation into object, a symbol, Weil adds gratuitously, of the universe's perfection. "Remove!" Alain urged in the margin for this last point, but Weil wishes to affirm, without developing the argument, that in art and in nature, beauty is always the same: form and matter are inscrutably one.

Here Weil is close to Kant's tenet that the beautiful symbolizes the morally good and is thus apprehensible to everyone and, beyond the mere pleasures of sensation, confers what he called "a certain ennoblement and uplifting."[2] But when she passes from beauty to the good in her essay, the discussion becomes more complex as she cultivates Alain's dialectical art of contradiction. She no sooner establishes a position than she undercuts it.

Taking for an example of moral action one's returning to a passerby some money accidentally dropped, she defines morality as an act's relation to its consequence, contingent by nature because all acts occur in existence. But (here is the first undercutting) what if morality requires certain knowledge not immediately perceived in the act, the motives of the one returning the money, for instance? If I am the agent, this difficulty vanishes because my movements are my intentions realized. As Plato would have it, morality is only for oneself. The good, it follows, lies in the subject or agent, whereas beauty inheres in the object.

If morality can be defined as conformity of one's actions to a rule, then each act is to morality like a particular circle to the idea of a circle. Obligation, though, not definition, is the issue. An act can be judged only in its particular reality, yet how can one judge except by moral law? That law can be found in oneself. Kant's influence could not be plainer, but Weil wants something more substantial than his "als ob" of universalized conduct. She plumps for the Stoic notion of true good, the act of a free will setting itself in obligatory adherence to moral law. Virtue lies in the force with which the worthy thinker's hand extends his thought. As though that were not rigorous enough, she throws in a caveat: the good is not a state of non-sin but a perpetual action. Once the extended moment is relaxed, morality no longer has meaning, and our actions can only be bad. Thus she invests Alain's athletic voluntarism with a hairshirt.

Beauty seems to have been forgotten, but Weil now prepares to examine it once more, in conjunction with good in a single act. She cites a story about Alexander the Great. Crossing a desert with his thirsting army, he was offered the only waterbag—and poured it onto the burning sand. His action was good, Weil says, because he delivered himself from the thirsty animal within him, he gave up the water on behalf of his men as they did for him. His action was beautiful because he and his men, like templar stones, serve in this story as means and end. Had any of them coveted the water, the action of pouring it out would no longer be possible. Weil's point seems obscure—"badly put, perhaps," noted Alain—but what she intends has nothing to do with whether anyone in that historic moment craved the water. Surely, they all did. What matters is that we behold the scene as ceremonial beauty, fixed and forever the same. History becomes art, action becomes sphinx. Like the temple, Alexander's body is matter informed by human spirit.[3] The moral action, the refusal of animal movement, presents itself in a sculptural immobility.

Weil considers Alexander's act a sacrificial, redemptive symbol. The acceptance of suffering is inextricable from the refusal to obey the animal self. In a school exercise we find in embryo her notion of decreation, and nowhere subsequently is its predication so bold:

> The good, then, is the movement by which one holds oneself back as individual, as animal, to affirm oneself as human, that is, a participant of God. But the good is possible only if we think God, who is humanity, the human spirit, present in each of our victories and making effort in us. . . . By the continual presence of the Spirit in us, each of our movements is ceremony; it's that which makes beautiful the just. So far as we act, that is, are free and equal to God, the beautiful and the good are one.[4]

This peculiar titanism, tinged with Platonic visions, seems even more emulous with God when Weil claims that, like God in Genesis, we create the world daily, separating object and spirit even as Jahweh parted lands and waters. Creation is the good, however, in that we move away from the object, thus allowing ourselves to look upon it as beautiful. The good lies in saying of all things, I am not that. The temple stands perfect in itself without me. One's own life becomes beautiful in the rejection of the object in the self, of that to which one's passions, feelings, thoughts would cling. Distance, as she affirmed later, is "the soul of beauty."[5]

In one of her last topoi for Alain, Weil resumed the theme that would continue to occupy her to the end, the magnum mysterium of beauty. The essay, "Commentaire d'une remarque de Kant," is brilliantly derivative, a synthesis of insights drawn from Descartes and Spinoza as well as Kant—these having passed through Alain's catalysis—and given Weil's usual energetic probing and intuitive flashes. She told Alain she intended to use the essay as part of a dissertation "on Poetry and Truth."

Weil again looks upon beauty as an intellectual puzzle but more now as an initiation. That is, she accepts Kant's argument that beauty does not hold the universal validity which logic brings to understanding but rests rather in the free play of intuition, both contemplative and creative. Kant mystified this nonconceptual realm by stating that the beautiful object is apprehensible without being known. As Weil's "Commentaire" illustrates, a triangle's properties can be defined and demonstrated but not derived. "Indeed, if Kant is to be believed, in these encounters resides the beauty of geometry, beauty being defined as a miraculous accord between necessity and finality."[6] Weil seems to be alluding to Kant's well-known characterization of beauty as "purposefulness without purpose."[7] The enchantment comes in one's own participation in this conjunction, which Weil would later call the meeting of chance and the good.[8] The mind creates a circle by forming an idea of it: "The circle is not an object which, like the moon or the stars, exists without the mind's participation; and yet, like the stars, it is for me, according to the poetic expression, an all-mighty stranger. It is unknown to me; it will always be impenetrable to me, even if I should live forever."[9]

Before this mystery, Weil acknowledges that "a theological penchant" inclines her to derive geometrical properties from "the divine understanding."[10] The inspiration for this derivation, as she admits, is Spinoza's notion of a third order of understanding, an intuition beyond reason, which takes God as its object. But then she gives way to what Kant might have called aesthetic play. In ideas such as primary number, circle, triangle, all "with eyes closed," "I see gods, as Homer's heroes saw gods in those they met who were unknown to them."[11] Geometry's hieratic language, its via media to divinity, showed her its affinity to aesthetics, both being immediate conduits to a supralogical reality. Using both she could hope to storm the "transcendent realm of truth" where her brother resided.

She resumes Kant's lead in distinguishing between the ordering of geometrical propositions, which being demonstrable do not dwell within beauty's province, and the totality of theorems themselves "turned to the world and, like it, blind, without reasons that might explain what they are." Here is beauty, "according to Kant's luminous view, the contrary of mind when it is found to satisfy the mind." She wishes to establish for mathematics the same element of chance which plays in a work of art and without which nothing can be beautiful. The mystique of mathematics "consists like every mystique in wanting to think by an intellectual intuition the constructions essential to demonstrations." Propositions and terms may serve the geometrician as brushes serve the painter, but the final, mystical, and aesthetic property of mathematics is that "existence is not involved," precisely the terms by which Kant said that every beautiful thing is mother to theology. Aesthetic enthusiasm belongs to this mysticism because its transport lacks "the counterweight which the idea of existence constitutes." "Yet, without this enthusiasm, without the unbearable astonishment caused by these mirrors of the mind which are its contraries, the idea of existence would undoubtedly never have been formed."[12]

If the notion of existence is derived from what is nonexistent, then it may be that what can be ordered by reason into knowledge is derived from what cannot be known but only represented. The intuitive or representational realm elevates the mind even as it enforces upon it a sense of weakness, a susceptibility that makes experience of the beautiful so overwhelming. Geometrical propositions are necessary only to the extent that the blind world puts up with them. They are as toys for the mind's sport, Weil asserts, of infinite application, yet they have an imposing beauty that belongs to the world of art and must be met there: "The mind's task is no longer to discover, a task to which undoubtedly the spinozist mind is condemned, but to invent. It is in surmounting the imperious feeling of the beautiful that the mind is thus delivered."[13]

A Mature Aesthetic

In Weil's later discussions of aesthetics there is nothing to rival the topoi for concentrated exposition, but if, as her efforts for Alain contend, beauty must be contemplated as a mystery, access to it will come by intuition's quick lighting, and in that the notebooks of her maturity abound.

Like Wittgenstein, Weil recognizes the limits of any talk about beauty. It escapes definition, she grants, just as contemplation excludes introspection. To recollect its existence is to have not the experience but only the recollection, and there is no demonstrable causality to link the one with the other. "One cannot then define aesthetic order as the condition of existence for producing an aesthetic feeling." The world's order, synonymous with its beauty, likewise does not prove God's existence, yet "the fact one may pass into a state of aesthetic contemplation before one of nature's spectacles as before a Greek statue is a proof of God."[14] In nature and in art alike beauty is the effect of reason persuading necessity, of purpose having its limited way in the house of matter where contingency and chance are permanent residents. In deferring in this way to Plato's *Timaeus* (48a), Weil commits herself to the classical view that art is mimetic, but she puts this imitation upon a far loftier plane than Plato allowed.[15]

Although beauty belongs only to this world, its meaning must be taken from the transcendent order it imitates. Thus, although Weil remains within the Stoic ambit in equating apprehensible beauty with perfect order, as though no reality obtained or needed to beyond this world, she wants to give it a hierarchic nexus to the divine. Indeed, it *is* that nexus by its mediation of so many contradictions.

Unless one dwells as securely as Weil did within Plato's semiotic world, it is not likely that a notion of beauty as either the imitation of a nonrepresentable or a knowledge of the nonexistent will say much. What, this side of Galileo's telescope, could it mean to claim celestial harmony as beauty's final reference? What does it mean to enlist beauty as the only sensible form of the intelligible world? Weil laments that since Ptolemy the poetry of the universe has been lost,[16] but what that really means is that since Copernicus human egotism can no longer claim to occupy the center of the universe. So, to assert that beauty is the manifest presence of being, "a souvenir of the beyond," as Weil notes from the *Phaedrus*, is to beg questions.[17] Fortunately, Weil never wholly loses sight of beauty as a human experience, that people are its necessary participants and its celebrants. We recall Alexander's ceremony in the desert.

Even more rigorously than Kant, Weil looks upon the apprehension of beauty as ethical in its effects: "Beauty is a sensual attraction keeping one at a certain distance and implying a renunciation, including the most intimate kind of renunciation, that of the imagination. One wants to devour every other desirable object. Beauty is something one desires without wishing to devour it. We merely desire that it be."[18] It would seem, then, that, as Plato supposes in *Hippias Maior* (295a–297d), beauty produces good. It arrests us in our predatory course through life. Desire is chastened; not destroyed, but elevated. In the aesthetic moment alone, desire is desirable. (It is no wonder that Weil esteemed Proust so highly.) For Goethe's Faust, a kind of salvation came in this desire that beauty not go beyond the phenomenal world, and Weil seems to evoke the Faustian moment when she says that beauty is what we do not want to change.[19]

Beauty itself, meanwhile, the being of beauty which is beyond particulars, as Plato would say, continues to elude. Weil continued to use contradiction as the method of pursuit because in finding equivalence in things radically different and opposed to one another, in contemplating them with no attempt at logical resolution, in accepting their interplay as contraries and thus achieving in herself a feeling of purificatory unity, she kept free from what she dreaded, the personal point of view.

What are the contradictions of beauty, its coherent tensions? Weil says they are the harmony of chance and the good, of the unlimited and the limited, the momentary and the eternal.[20] To this Pythagorean series Weil adds Kant's oppositions: beauty as finality without end, order without conceptualization, pleasure without attraction.[21] The Kantian finality, however, proves insufficient because beauty, in Weil's mind, is tethered to the divine: "Everything which has God for an end is finality without end," and that means that all sacred rites, prayer, and mystical awareness are inevitably beautiful.[22] But beyond or apart from these religious experiences, any occasion of beauty involves God's presence. Aesthetics for Weil is like faith in that it makes the object unique and exclusive. Whether in nature or in art, perfect beauty, itself a mystery, sensuously reflects the mystery of faith, for beauty, like faith, is the sustaining bread of the soul:

> When one pays perfect attention to a perfectly beautiful music (the same holds for architecture, painting, etc.) the intelligence finds there nothing to affirm or deny. But all the soul's faculties, including intellect, are silently suspended upon hearing. The hearing is applied to an object which, though incomprehensible, encloses reality and the good. And the intelligence, which does not get hold of any truth there, finds there nonetheless a nourishment.[23]

These remarks raise two problems. First, the conclusion that beauty nourishes the soul seems to differ from the earlier view that it is something we do not seek to devour but willingly let be. The mystery is that the source gives nourishment yet is never diminished. Like the infinitesimal point of light in Dante's vision of paradise, beauty suffers no reduction in its effects. That is, for Kant, its final disinterestedness. However often we hear a quartet of Schubert or look upon the blue glasses of Chartres, such works will remain as they are, constant amid the world's transience. Beauty, then, is not only "fruit one does not grab," but which one cannot grab.[24] Yet beauty is needed nurture. That means it must be contemplated, an object not of pleasure, Weil insists, but of attention. For her, beauty is conversion, not diversion.

The second problem lies in her use of *perfect*, a word rivaling *pure* for her favor and virtually its synonym. She provides no objective criterion for the perfect beauty of nature or art—how could she, after all, and continue to maintain that beauty is a mystery? Her reader is left with subjective categories and preferences. Her high estimation of Gregorian chant, for example: perfect beauty, perhaps, but how or why is it perfect and, say, Ambrosian chant not perfect? or opera, which has arguably surpassed church ritual as a ceremony that feeds the soul's hunger for beauty? "Basically, as to opera, apart from Wagner, I can put up with only sentimental comic things (Rossini and Mozart included)."[25]

Nevertheless, to music, the one transcendent art, she ascribes duly lofty properties. It is made up of relationships that cause us to weep, she says, in giving us an image of faculties harmonized to total order, an imitation of God's own composition.[26] Almost certainly, these assumptions Weil drew from hearing the architectures of Bach, which might also have inspired the following variations on Faust's "Verweile doch!" "Music unfolding itself in time, as it does, seizes our attention and delivers it from time's hands by bringing it to bear at each moment on that which is. The waiting is sustained in emptiness, a waiting upon the immediate. We do not want a single note, a single interval of silence to cease, while at the same time we cannot bear that either should continue."[27] Of all arts, music affords the ideal aesthetic for attention. It gives "our tense and undirected desire . . . the direction which is continually established and broken off."[28] All genuine art, according to Weil, instructs us in the indifference of time and space; it tells us where and what we are. Because its mission might be called sacred, Weil calls her favorite artists saints.

In imitating necessity's conformity to the good, art enforces upon us an awareness of our own subjection to necessity. The temple stones in "Le beau et le bien" are a supernaturally ordered heap of rubble, an abnormal good. Art of the first rank holds all the exception of miracle, but our experience of it includes "this core of bitterness," that beauty, like the love of God, can only be felt through the afflictions of necessity. There hides art's supreme contradiction, it is a pure joy that hurts. To borrow an example from Sartre: in listening to Beethoven's Seventh Symphony we are sustained by an unreal coherence, an order not of our ordinary world. When the concert ends, we have to reenter the disgusting tedium of the ordinary. One might wonder, faced with that wearisome return, whether the unreality of art should be entered in the first place. Even Schopenhauer admitted that art was a false exit from life's horror. But Weil values art exactly for the frustrations Sartre is pointing to, that necessity and the good grate upon one another in ourselves.[29]

The beauty of art springs from what Weil calls "an artificial world in which we try to teach ourselves to be truthful."[30] Art is the human device for directing one to the good, even as an understanding of necessity in the phenomenal world also directs one to the good. Weil holds that the truth which art instructs lies in its goal, which she characterizes as the *atman*, that immobile, universal self of Hindu monism in which all is indistinguishably a divine unity. To the endeavors of "perfect" art, Weil's genuine artist brings both a personality and a divine anonymity, the "me" and the *atman*'s "me outside of me." "An artwork has its author, but when perfect it has something essentially anonymous about it. It imitates divine art's anonymity. The world's beauty thus proves there is a God at once personal and impersonal, and not merely the one or the other."[31] A perfectly composed poem, Weil contends, one of the parts of which cannot be disjoined by analysis without a mangling distortion, amounts to an imitation of God. She even likens artistic inspiration to Christian incarnation, though she qualifies the analogy by noting that such inspiration is rare.[32]

That last point leads to her discrimination of a pure, perfect art that forms a hieratic link between necessity and the good, and all other art, which to her mind thrashes about in a failure to comprehend and balance the two. The flaws of her position, its circular argument, its subjectivity, are apparent enough, but they do not seem to have troubled her. She listed her "saintly" preferences as though they were unexceptionable, and who would cavil over her first-ranking of Giotto, Velazquez, Bach, and Mallarmé?[33] Yet to all these and other initiates into necessity and the good, creativity is as it were bestowed, mystically received. Weil takes inspiration in its primary, ancient sense: it is a divine infusion. Conversely, it involves decreation. In his frescoes, Giotto subtracts the self standing between creation and Creator. To inferior artists Weil ascribes imagination only, "Satan's gift," which fills the void of life with idols; these stopgaps of illusion, private or collective, prevent the furtive entrance of grace into the soul.[34] For Weil, imagination is antithetical to contemplation, to art itself, whether one creates or simply experiences an aesthetic object. It might be called "the me inside me," mortal, errant, up to no good.

Weil is thus not only taking the notion of mimesis to its logical extreme. She is taking a moral (or moralistic) position against the imagination. It is evil, she contends, in persuading us that final good may be secured in this world and so it prompts us to betray that good by attachments. The beauty of the highest art, on the contrary, has a quality of nakedness; it is unshrouded by imagination and thus affords us God's presence. It is "reality without attachment."[35]

The arts in excelsis may perform a didactic function, but whether we are morally altered upward, changed decently even by an iota in the embrace of art, must be questioned.[36] Plato himself was stubbornly dubious about the ethical value of the arts: Homer unexpurgated debauches our sense of the divine and the heroic, he said. Staged tragedy draws tears we should reserve for real suffering, and music, left to decadent modes, portends social chaos. Weil was familiar with Plato's brief, and she independently states that bad art has something demonic in it—that succubus, imagination, again.[37]

In her own attempts to create she looked to eternity—most unimaginatively, of course.

Her Poetry

The sum of Weil's poetic works is small, more a corpusculum than a corpus, and there is no indication she ever regarded most of her efforts as more than exercises. That does no mean she regarded poetry or her writing it as trivial. Her notes include countless recasts of lines and entire stanzas, as well as many metrical schemes. She tried to find publishers. But these poems interest us chiefly because she wrote them and because they shape with lyrical economy some of the themes of her prose. She knew that prose, not verse, was her medium, but in trying to attain an elevated, she might have said "pure," language, she was perhaps seeking a claim to that exclusive realm of truth where her brother was resident.

She attempts to place her metaphysics, ethics, and theology on the procrustean bed of poetic form, as though the limpidity of her prose might there find some suitable compaction. Her lyric range is tethered to an argumentative diction. Her poem on the sea, "La mer," for example, celebrates the sea's submission to necessity and bids its waters cleanse humanity with the justice of this obedience—a kind of Stoic baptism. With a common thread of didacticism, Weil's verse and her prose might be interlaced as exposition or commentary one upon the other, in the mode of Dante's *Vita Nuova* or the *Consolatio* of Boethius.

Seeking critical approval of her poetry (a sign she took these efforts seriously) Weil turned to Paul Valéry. Who could serve as a likelier judge of her verse than one whose poems, thoughtful without being thought, reflected the self scrupulous in its own suspension between ideation's elusive realm, that of *moi pur*, and the world, fluid and irrational, where the *moi spontané* takes its easy dwelling? Who else but Valéry, given his "prejudice in favor of absolute lucidity,"[38] the poet who addressed the experiential through a hierophantic "language within a language,"[39] even while disingenuously regarding his poetry as "a solemn, regulated and significant game."[40]

To an extent, Weil walks in Valéry's semantic ambit: his pursuit, with a concession to final impossibility, of what may be pure and absolute within the flood of ordinary impressions and discourse, the sound heard apart from the noise and distilled in its own universe—all this has an aural analogy to Weil's recondite good which necessity obscures. As instrument for access to that purity, Valéry's "attente active," a vigilant patience of the poet's sensibility, complements Weil's notion of attention as strenuous passivity directed to a cherished absence. Conjoined with such orientations in both Valéry and Weil is a chagrin, a disappointment never fully accepted "that the universe is but a defect in the purity of nonbeing."[41]

Technically, Weil's poetry, like his, follows a classical form; it submits to the exactions of metrical balance and rhyme. This attention inspired her to approach him.

Sometime in 1937 she sent Valéry a copy of "Prométhée," a poem of six stanzas celebrating the crucified inventor of arts, of the language where "L'âme se pale et tâche à se comprendre / Ciel, terre et mer se taisant pour entendre / Deux amis, deux amants parlent tout bas."[42] These lines fall between passages depicting in images of fire the Promethean bequest to humanity. The *malheur* that would attend human life without the divine gift finds balance in the final view of Prometheus suffering. Life's glories, the arts, require, if not expiation (the ancient motif of Prometheus' theft does not figure here), a recompense, but to what or to whom the poem does not say.

Valéry responded with praise for "the tightness of the whole, its plenitude and its force of movement," and noted "a *volonté de composition* to which I attach the greatest importance . . . something other than the logical or chronological succession which unfolds from a subject."[43]

Encouraged by this considerate reply, Weil, overcoming her fear of importuning him further, some months later sent him a second letter, this time including a much longer poem, "A un jour," "because I imagine, perhaps wrongly, that it responds in some measure to a certain, very striking view of poetry you express in one of your books à propos of painting."[44] Weil's appreciation of Valéry's preference of technique over inspiration is evident. That she upheld with him the classical standard of controlled, reflected, ever-conscious style even in prose is hinted in her postscript:

> You've written somewhere that you possess a small technical brochure which is for you a model of stylistic precision and rigor, a standard for comparing all prose writings in order to assess their value. Technique has always seemed to me a domain of choice where all the virtues of language ought to be able to appear, although that's generally not the case. Thus, I would give a great deal to know what this brochure is, so that I can procure it if it is still accessible.[45]

She never heard from him again.

Weil expended exceptional care on "A un jour." Two years after sending it to Valéry she was still revising it. Her notes include a far larger number of variants of this poem than of any other, and she had come to know it well enough to recast its 160 lines from memory after she had left her drafts in occupied Paris. Late in the summer of 1940, she wrote to a fellow teacher, now a Vichy bureaucrat, in the hope that he would retrieve all the poem's drafts at her parents' home, even though she felt that what memory had given her constituted the definitive version of what she wanted to say. She pressed him to circulate it among well-known writers and get it published, either anonymously or pseudonymously. "That doesn't concern me at all. I wish for no literary notoriety, and I no longer have at all the sense that this poem belongs to me to any degree. I would only like that it be read because in my estimation it would be a pity were it purely and simply to disappear." Besides, "events have given to this poem a good deal of timeliness."[46]

Written and rewritten in the time between the Popular Front's decline and the German invasion, "A un jour" sustains a bitter timeliness. The poem's beginning seems to herald the Stoic's *beauté du monde* while the nocturnal world of illusions is dispersed. In the three initial stanzas, supernal light brings a succession of sexual images, a kind of comforting violence: the chilling brightness of day penetrates the soul while "un silence monte et se mêle sans terme aux déserts transparents!" The hurtful grace of "la subite et douce atteinte du matin" causes the heart to bleed, and the light's splendor "comme une caresse en tous lieux / nous reviendra tendre et limpide."[47] Then, a Dantesque horror introduces and pervades the central tableaux upon which the transcendent day has arisen. It is as though the light of Plato's sun, having mystically ravished the soul, has somehow entered the cave. Arrived, unlike Plato's cave dwellers, from some better time, the earth's inhabitants now have nothing but "alarmes / Vains travaux, détresse et prisons."

Weil's dawn imposes upon the vanquished souls "Le cours affreux sans chanceler / Le coeur, les genoux leur défaillent. / Il faut pourtant debout qu'ils aillent / Où l'âme ne veut pas aller."[48] However timely these lines may have been to the German occupation, they were not intended as occasional verse. They depict a suffocating hopelessness that has attended the industrial age. In counterpoint to the luminous day, with all its birthing vitality, stand the man-made devices of confinement and oppression: "des murs en plomb . . . des prisons immuables. . . . Tout est clos sur la foule obscure / Dont tremblent les membres liés."

In her unpublished drafts Weil paints the day as both a victim and an accomplice of this inhumanity, and the theme subsumes not merely industrialism but the Babel-like vanity of all human aspiration. A passage recalling the queer light of Dante's Limbo depicts the "simple mensonge" which arrests the course of night and day to make "un crépuscule infini." The human face of necessity, the face of all tyrants and oppressors, arrests time itself. Hence in the published version, "En vain l'axe des cieux est juste."[49]

There is an obvious symmetry between this poem and "Prométhée." The divine gifts bestowed upon humanity have been abused. Now, instead of a deliverance from nature through art, a kind of anti-nature has been imposed through art, that is, technology. Humankind is itself impaled on the rock by a deviant will to power:

> "Si le sort, le fer, l'or, les lois
> Logent les longues destinées
> Dans l'espace d'un peu de voix,

Quand les lèvres inattentives
Laissant sur les âmes captives
Tomber ces mots, si lourd de temps."[50]

These lines recast a theme of Weil's "Réflexions" on freedom and oppression, that powers in nature when organized through society inevitably pass into unappeasable mechanisms of institutional force. But as in "Prométhée," where the god alone suffers in balancing payment for the boon he has brought, in "A un jour" one soul wins a mystical journey from the cave to the sun: "Ce jour de céleste silence / Livre à jamais au monde immense / Un esprit transpercé d'amour." That Weil intended this transfixion to be understood as a crucifixion—she was inclined to conflate the images of Prometheus and Christ—becomes clear from a variant to this published version: "Un fixe et céleste silence / A jamais cloué au monde immense / Un esprit transpercé d'amour."

Plato's Cave figures in another of her poems, untitled and never published. Beginning "Dans de sombres ténèbres ils vont," it runs to six quatrains, but its lines afford no rhythmic or metrical patterns. In comparison with her other poems, these verses fail, chiefly because they tell more than they show. No imagery is developed or even suggested by which the reader can engage in imaginative response. A lesson rather than a lyric, this poem argues an Eastern monism in Western terms.[51] It owes something to Plato's divided line (*Republic* 511c–e) in distinguishing those who languish in the phenomenal darkness of opinion and those who are awake to knowledge, but Weil wants to extend the line into Spinoza's world of third-order understanding, that mystical realm beyond reason toward which Plato's dialectic moves and never quite arrives.

Who walks in darkness? Not only the opinion-bound minds but "Ceux que le savoir satisfait." Counterpoised to their joyless, unawakened world stands the universal self: "L'atman, si elle le connaissait / Si elle disait, 'Je suis lui,' la personne / Souhaitant quoi, par quel désir / Peirerait-elle avec le corps?" Weil again hearkens to Plato (*Phaedo* 66b) in setting the body, domicile of ignorance and desire, against the soul, but the *atman*, the universal soul, has its corporeal prison, too—"dans cette glaise impénétrable est enfoui"—even though it is the world's creator and the world itself. Knowledge of the *atman* will make us immortal. The alternative is "grande perdition," a Dantesque finale: "Mais les autres, souffrir est leur partage"—an epistemological hell. Weil's final quatrain promises that whoever truly comprehends the *atman*, "Celui-là ne l'abandonne plus."

Although the conceptual focus here is Indic, and the congeries of ignorance, darkness, and perdition versus knowledge and deliverance is Platonic, Weil's language suggests Christian gospel. *Atman* is that truth which will make the knowing free (John 8:32, 14:6, 16:13), will not desert them (Matt. 28:20) but leaves all others wailing (Matt. 13:42, 50). As befits a monism, however, there is no eschatological moment, no world to be overcome (John 16:33), because *atman* is the world and subsumes even *maya*, the illusory show. The soteriology is limited, but it is sufficient knowledge, a surety against abandonment to ignorance and creation's clay. The poem amounts to a credo in verse, and its concentrated commingling of Platonic, Christian, Hindu, and Gnostic assumptions manifests Weil's eclectic if not syncretic energy.

More successful as poetry is its metaphysical companion, "Nécessité," which despite its portentous title does not sermonize and observes a conventional strictness: four quatrains of rhymed hendecasyllables. If "Dans de sombres ténèbres" argues epistemological grace such as Arjuna learns in the *Gita*, "Nécessité" offers not the slightest hope of rescue, even though the poem assumes at midpoint a petitionary, prayerlike mood.

Free of homiletic weight, necessity's image is the Pythagorean cosmos, the stars moving slowly in their dancing courses, "éclat glacé d'en haut."[52] It is a skyscape identical to the one Weil portrays in "Les astres," the same chilly fires of distance and indifference, but in that poem, a stumbling, plangent humanity fixes its eyes upward in the bitter posture of attention, and the divine fire makes sudden entry into the human heart at the closing line. In "Nécessité," though, the human terrain is so grim and violent the verses might be called a war poem. The stellar dance, "Immobilité qui change sans défaut," forever drags along an angry, thirsting mortality, but for what could humankind thirst to justify these awesome lines on the stars? "Qu'ils comblent la soif, s'ils déchirent les coeurs," and "Nos maîtres brillants seront toujours vainqueurs."[53] In the final quatrain, an apostrophe to the stars asks that they rend the flesh. The last image, one of Promethean recumbence, culminates the violence.

In her notebooks Weil wrote, "Gravity is the constraint we are subjected to, the chain; to ascend is supernatural; the sky, that's where we do not go."[54] In "Nécessité" she depicts gravity's pull as a magnetic force to which humanity is nailed. The unpublished version, a drama more vivid and excruciated than the printed, unfolds what one critic has aptly called Weil's poetics of "a revelation serene and at the same time tormented."[55]

Comparison of the final three lines of each version is instructive. The published version: "Cloués sans un cri sur le point fixe au Nord / L'âme vue exposée à toute blessure, / Nous voulons vous obéir jusqu' à la mort." The variant reading includes three revisions of the final line: "Cloués palpitants au point fixe du Nord / Sans cris nous chérirons la douce torture / Nous obéirons dans la vie et la mort" ("Puissions-nous vous obéir jusqu' à la mort," "Nous soyons obéissant . . ." and "Nous serons obéissant . . .").

The difference seems minor but is crucial. The martial step from a willingness to obey toward a resolution, from "nous voulons" to "nous obéirons," restates Weil's point that "the good commences beyond the will, as truth commences beyond intelligence," and obedience to that good, the Stoic *amor fati*, must be unreflected, not voluntary.[56] That is, obedience to the good means imitation of necessity, of nature's brute force (here, in its stellar emblem) understood not as sovereignty but as perfect conformity to God. The stars, "our brilliant masters," convey refractively the divine luminance. *Imitatio naturae* entails a heartrending renunciation of the will, that harbinger of futility. But why, in desire, must we "cherish the sweet torture"? It is because the obedience of creation, entering the body through *douleur*, is divine love's gift.[57]

Weil sets up basically the same choreography in "La porte," a poem that, although suggesting the gospel's open door (Matt. 7:7), apparently draws more inspiration from the door forever closed (Luke 13:24–28). An errant, suffering humanity seeks to enter an imagined paradise of orchards and flowers. It pounds, presses, pushes at the door, to no avail. Weeping eyes fixed in attention do not avail either. Only when hope and imagination's gardens are abandoned does the door open in a moment of mystic rapture: "Seule l'espace immense où sont le vide et la lumière / Fut soudain présent de part en part, combla la coeur / Et lava les yeux presque aveugles sous la poussière."[58] Even as Weil recasts Christian creeds to meet her own spiritual exigencies, so here she reworks the promise of faith, the seeking sufficient to finding, into something nearly its opposite. Only when we give up seeking, no longer impose our own terms upon the struggle, does revelation bring its bathing light to wash away mortality's dust. The self's struggle is necessary, if only to be renounced; it is illusion, the fond hope of garden comforts, which brings us to the gate. But no one in Christian gospels sat down in lassitude under a bo-tree.

Weil controls the imagery more ably here than in her other poems. "La porte" is perhaps the best specimen of what has been called Weil's "wild Platonism," that unrelenting drive to find release from the Cave of the phenomenal and illusory.[59] All of Weil's mature verse marks repeated attempts at such a breakout.

Typically, none of these poems, excepting the celebration of *atman*, consoles. Their steady motif is human subjection to necessity, *malheur* redressed only fitfully by celestial light and then on condition of obedience, the acceptance of true good as rare and fleeting to this life. In visiting paradise Dante learned how bitterly he would have to taste another's bread and tread another's stair. So in "Éclair," after the fulgent heaven initiates a series of births (Weil writes "naîtront" six times, in Péguy-like anaphora) we are in the end cast down to the Cave's adamantine chains and penal fire of deception: "Mais tout s'éteint, le monde est effacé / Les lendemains ont tissu leurs mensonges, / L'âme s'égare aux erreurs du passé, / Et le ciel même est terni par les songes."[60]

Obedience, Weil once told Perrin, is alone invulnerable to time, but art in her estimate also enjoys a kind of imperishability.[61] As harmony, as the coordination of necessary conditions on several planes—art is akin to politics, she says!—it plays beauty's game of transfiguring one's sensibility by an illuminating, universal light.[62] By forcing *malheur* into tandem with necessity, by making the horrible lovely, as the *Iliad* and the Attic tragedies do, art when perfect imposes upon matter Kant's finality without end.

Weil rehearses that imposition over and over in her poetry, hence the very narrow range of theme and image, as though she were constantly undertaking, like Socrates in the *Gorgias* (490c), to say always the same things about the same things: the tensions of necessity and the good; good and evil in human responses to these tensions; light and darkness, the human scenery arranged variously between them. Whatever readers she had in mind for her verses, she wrote to them in the urgency of a propagandist.

A moralist, Weil believed that artists must be accountable to their public. Nowhere is her case for art as a mimetic record of the human lot more forceful than in her attack on modern literature, in a letter she wrote to *Cahiers du Sud* in 1941, "Sur les responsabilités de la littérature."[63] She argues that writers must perform the ancient function of art, depicting the opposition of values, of good and bad; they must be faithful to the facts of human existence. She cites Dada and surrealism for expressing "the intoxication of total license." These movements had programmatically elected a complete absence of value as the supreme value, but their ideologies, she notes, gave merely the extreme representations of an essential tendency at work well before Tristan Tzara and André Breton issued their manifestos against the bourgeois order.

She makes two vital points. First, accountability for the betrayal of value belonged neither merely to writers, nor to France, nor to Europe alone but everywhere that Western influence pervaded. Rejection of the notion of good and evil constitutes, she asserts, the great disease of Occidental culture. Second, literature must not as antidote be narrowed to moralism (here she parts company with Plato). When indifferent to good and evil, it betrays its function; it gives the soul no orientation. Weil hails A *la recherche du temps perdu* for its abundant analysis of psychological disorientations and for revealing how rarely the good appears in this life, as by memory or a moment's beauty when eternity steals into time. But among moderns Proust is an exception.

A writer need not be exemplary of contingent or conventional good. Weil does not care that François Villon, one of her favorites, was a thief. His stealing was perhaps a matter of necessity, like Jean Valjean's; a sin, yes, but not "un acte gratuit." Above all, "the sense of good and evil impregnates all his verse, as it does every work which is not foreign to human destiny."[64]

Weil best conveys the feeling of her own mission as a poet in an unpublished, lengthy verse fragment on Arthur Rimbaud, *l'enfant sauvage* of the symbolist movement. Untitled, it survives in a single tattered version among her papers.[65] It is rhymed in couplets, but the lines run to an irregular length and have the aspect of statements or propositions. It might be called a meditation because it begins with an allusion to the well-known photograph of Rimbaud sun-burnished at work for the French National Geographical Society in Africa.

She announces the theme of questing, "le combat spirituel," upon which Rimbaud's life had shipwrecked before he was twenty.[66] She likens him to two parabolic figures in the gospels, the woman searching for a lost coin (Luke 15:8–10) and the man "seeking goodly pearls" (Matt. 13:45–46). But for Rimbaud, "un mystique à l'état sauvage" in Paul Claudel's profile,[67] there was no rest, only a succession of renunciations—of his home, of France, of poetry, "A cause de cette clef du festin ancien qu'il a perdue, / A cause de ce bonheur perdu jadis qu'il avertissait au chant du coq."

From this child too soon and too precociously out of Eden, Weil moves toward the first person through a brief reflection on the artist's sacred anonymity, as she saw it in Giotto, which sets God before creation:

> Ce qu'on appelle réalité des choses, à force
> de nous faire anonymes nous finirons bien
> par la trouver en défaut, nous finirons
> bien par la trouver assoupie
> A force d'être étrangèrs, les choses finiront
> bien un jour par le Paradis!

Before this domain of thing where necessity and hidden good are housed, she gives way to a Stoic assurance, an *amor fati* that for once has been budged from static awe into celebratory confidence: "Le delice qui est associé à leur être et la communication qu' elles contiennent, / Je finirai directement par l'entendre, autrement qu'au travers de ces paroles paiennes." Directly, however, the promise of afflatus is threatened: "Tant que je n'aurai pas trouvé le Paradis, la vraie place [pour] moi est ce qui ressemble le plus à l'enfer. / Rimbaud, pourquoi t-en vas tu. . ." But then she resiliently points to the sacred mystery of Rimbaud's suffering, that this "Furieuse esprit contre le cage, plein de cris et de blasphemes," could have found grace in the sensuous life he so rapidly consumed, in the very bounds of language he tried to break. It is the epiphany of Blake's minute particulars:

> Cet objet entre les fleurs de papier sec,
> c'est cela qui est la Suprême Beauté,
> Ces paroles si usées qu'on ne les entends plus,
> c'est en elles qu'était la verité . . .
> Le voile des choses pour moi en un point
> est devenu transparent.
> J'étreins la substance enfin au travers
> de l'accident.

In the manifest world of becoming, being lies hidden. In poetry's language, too, "ces paroles si usées," there hangs a "voile à l'Étre," that screen or veil which, as Weil notes in discussing Sophocles, is suspended transparent over truth. Language made beautiful through art becomes mediation of the otherwise impossible relation between God and time. The denomination common to time and God is the Christian *logos* found in the bread and wine of mortality: "Ne finirons pas par désirer ce qui est vraiment le vin et ce qui est vraiment la chair, / Quand Dieu même sur la croix pour nous s'est rompu et nous est ouvert?"

In effect, poetry performs this sacrament. It harmonizes the separation of matter and God. The same may be said for the *logos* of music, for the temple scanned in "Le beau et le bien," for Giotto's frescoes, for every intermediary that leads to God:

> Toutes choses sont situées dans une comparaison
> ineffable et c'est avec le coeur

Que nous nous sentirons faite de ce mot même
qui leur est intérieur.
D'où vient le surgissement en nous comme
une eau claire qui nous lave?
D'où cette initiative étrange et cette touche
sur notre coeur soudain si present et si suave?
Tu le savais, Rimbaud . . .

Although the erotic *surgissement* surpasses in boldness the luminous close of "La porte," and a now tactile initiation suggests the recesses of Plotinian mysticism, nothing proclaims itself more strongly in this poem than its achieved serenity, a wondrous tone near joy. It contrasts admirably with the stridency that mars the other poems, the desperate, almost shrill forcing of opposites. It seems a pity that Weil did not chisel down its propositional lengths with a concentrated imagery, lyric yet suggestive to her argument. That she was capable of such artistry is best revealed in her drama *Venise sauvée.*

Venise sauvée

Although this play contains many sketchy passages, it provides thematic contact with Weil's poetry and her notion of grace descending. As drama, however, it can do some special pleading. Not accidentally, Weil chose the most public of arts to portray the passage of the Holy Spirit through a single soul and the consequent preservation of a community.

By the time she began to write her play, in the summer of 1940, she had become disposed toward a mysticism that informed her writing in various degrees until her death. The action of *Venise sauvée* might be called religious, yet the mise-en-scène shows no trace or acting out of anything mystical. Rather, the spiritual dimensions of this work are like the harmony of the spheres, not heard yet there. They are to be inferred from the outside, chiefly from Weil's extensive notes on the play. Any drama requiring an apparatus to explain itself falls short, maybe fatally, of worthy theater, but Weil's apparatus is not indispensable. It remains a moot yet engaging question whether her play, dressed in the limbs of Greek tragedy and redolent of a highly personal, would-be Christian metaphysics, could be understood by a modern audience.[68]

As a historical drama it belongs to a genre that, except in operatic adaptation, has long passed from fashion. It succeeds two mediocre dramatizations of an alleged conspiracy to betray the Venetian Republic in 1618, the Abbé de Saint-Réal's *Conjuration des Espagnols contre le republique de Venise* (1664) and Otway's *Venice Preserved* (1682). In 1618 Venice was the only Italian state independent of Spanish hegemony. The plot to subvert it was discovered and ruthlessly crushed. Whether or not there was any basis to the allegation of conspiracy, the Spanish ambassador was sent packing.

A city isolated before a mighty and despotic foe—it is a mirror image of Paris in the spring of 1940. The conspiracy's strategist, Renaud, rationalizes that betrayal of Venice will unite all of Europe against Turkey, the Eastern menace. Embodying a will to universal domination that characterizes what Weil calls evil's illimitability, Renaud seems a transparent caricature of the slavophobic Hitler seeking to unify Europe against Bolshevism.[69]

Renaud's foil and the play's central character is Jaffier, who has joined the plot solely in friendship for another of its instigators, Pierre. Indeed, though Pierre is enticed like Renaud by a *libido dominandi*, his only dramatic function is to attest his loyalty to Jaffier, to reject Renaud's doubts that Jaffier is fit for the greatness of action the conspiracy requires, and, after Jaffier reveals the plot and Pierre is led to torture and execution, to express his anguish in not sharing his death with Jaffier, his friend's loyalty unquestioned—and rightly so, as tragic irony would have it.

Pierre's unqualified esteem for Jaffier provides an essential clue to the drama's almost furtive progression. This friendship not only surpasses the love of women (Pierre's attraction to Violetta, daughter of the Venetian Secretary, is more capricious than convincing), it approximates Weil's definition of friendship as a transcendent harmony. Jaffier's comradeship with Pierre anticipates in character his mystical bond with Venice. That is, genuine spirituality in a private devotion will not be distinct from the greater devotion shown to a community.

Weil's notion of friendship can therefore be related to the play's theme of redemptive suffering. The aesthetic corollary is that beauty is the fruit we look upon without trying to seize it. Both experiences, of amity and of beauty, are contemplative; they imply an unapproachable wholeness in a beloved person or in a beautiful object, before which the self must unequivocally yield its destructive urges by compassionate renunciation of desire. Jaffier's denial of his own will, the normal human urge to destroy, becomes the play's one true act of virtue: beholding the beauty of Venice he cannot go on in the plot to subjugate its people. He keeps the drive for power within himself rather than releasing it in violent action or in rhetorical imaginings that fire the other conspirators.

The play's central tension, as Weil's unpublished marginalia inform us, lies in Jaffier's interior progress set against the outward development: "Always pulsation between contemplations and levels of action—without interference in a return upon the self." It is that very epistemology of the mystical which sets Jaffier apart from all others: "What J. thinks all alone, ignored, an individual in the crowd, that's the only reality—what these people see as solid and eternal is already a shadow."

Isolated, Jaffier must redeem a world that the play fills with monsters, the ingenuous Violetta excepted as innocence personified. No one else remains free from a self-degrading need to deny the humanity of others. This dismal fact is clear (in the printed version) in the character of the Venetian artisan and his apprentice, who ignobly mock Jaffier toward the play's end. They revile him as a Judas even though he has saved them from destruction.

In Weil's unpublished drafts, a Greek courtesan, a Venetian subject barely outlined in the published version, best embodies the self-marring bitterness of brutalized humanity. "This city is going to be debased and stained as I have been. How its splendor has insulted me (develop). A slave from now on, it will after this night bear the accent of a foreign tongue without trembling or lowering its eyes." In her notes, Weil characterizes the courtesan as a female counterpart to Renaud. Despite her love of Jaffier she is driven to ambition and vengeance: "[She] has always been happy [Weil writes *heureux*, not *heureuse*] to lose and dupe men, to humiliate women, to see Venice's daughters begging. Such infamy can only be cured by vengeance and covered over by the glory of power." When Jaffier asks her if she is not touched by compassion for Venice, she responds like a heroine in Racine ("fierce, bitter replies") that "nothing is less accessible to a woman than pity when—what? Define well." When Weil adds that this character is later to be "put in prison or assigned to espionage," it is clear that in the courtesan she had written a part for herself and her fantasies, but she thought better of it, and the character is minor in the final draft.[70]

Even Pierre, recognizing in his friend's nobility that Jaffier "is more myself than I am," is contaminated in his inferior self.[71] When, at the play's climax, Jaffier confesses himself troubled by pity at the thought of sacking Venice, Pierre tells him Scipio Aemelianus wept before Carthage but did not hesitate to destroy it. Pierre insists that pity is not a feeling that penetrates the soul's depths. But that is just what it does to Jaffier so that when Pierre concludes to

Renaud that no one is made like Jaffier for great things, an ironic truth awaits exposure.

Dehumanization warps all the other characters, and Weil shows no sentimental indulgence toward the conspiracy's would-be victims. Just as cruelty inspires even the conspiracy's hirelings so that an officer among them speaks of Venetians as ants and shadows—"they believe they exist but they deceive themselves"[72]—so it infects the Venetians when the plot is exposed. Jaffier having secured from the Venetian Secretary an amnesty for his friends in exchange for revealing the conspiracy, the Council declines to honor it and orders the plotters executed. Sardonically, the Council grants Jaffier an unsought reward of gold and expels him to the frontier. Anguished over his unwitting deliverance of the conspirators to death, he is subjected to taunts and threats of murder from those whose lives he has saved. At the play's close he is given a sword and thrown into a street brawl.

In a world where cunning and hatred pervade, Weil dramatizes her conviction that though the good is abnormal—art alone makes us aware of the good—evil is compellingly ordinary. The Secretary's icy rejection of Jaffier's plea for Pierre and the others and the vicious mockery Jaffier suffers from the Venetian proletariat share with Renaud's lust for domination the definitive property of evil: a cheerless, unrelenting monotony of illusion.

Its epitome is Renaud, who claims that to conspire well, one must love nothing. It is not a withdrawal into indifference but a violent appropriation of what is not one's own, creating a void in others while filling the void in oneself through imaginative egotism. Behind his Machiavellian guile lies one of Weil's metaphysical deadweights burdening the shabby claims of the human self. The *malheur* of the "I," she writes in her notes on the play, wrests reality from the world. That process is exactly Renaud's intent when he harangues Jaffier on the advantage enjoyed by men of action, that they are dreamers who force the world to dream their dreams. Violence makes the dream stronger for the subdued and debased than reality itself; or, rather, the vaunting conqueror's whims become the only reality.

If Renaud, armed with self-excusing sophistries, exemplifies a belief in the external world's reality while affirming the will to annihilate it, Jaffier's response to that same reality is prompted by supernatural love. He is its unwitting agent. His pity frees his soul from the mist of illusions in which human actions are invariably cloaked, yet he remains to the end unaware of what has passed within him. He is no martyr conscious of some ulterior reward. Weil emphasizes that the play shows there can be no detachment without grief and no grief can be free of hatred and delusion except by perfect detachment.[73] This formula puts the drama in high relief as a Greek tragedy, but if Weil is sneaking an *imitatio Christi* through the back stage door, it is because for her the Hellenic spirit was at its greatest an intimation of the Christian.

God does make an appearance of sorts in *Venise sauvée*. At the climax but before the conspiracy is revealed, when Violetta's father, the Secretary, scorns her belief that the city's beauty would suffice to save it from its enemies (as in fact it will), she incredulously replies that God would not permit such beauty to be destroyed. In gospel fashion her faith saves her and Venice. As Weil instructs, Jaffier's response to Violetta must carry a "resonance de douleur": "Such a thing as Venice no man can make, God only. The most a man can do which comes closest to God is, since he cannot create such miracles, preserve those that exist."[74] That is Weil's instruction to Hitler before Paris and to all who would try to turn necessity by force against the good.

Structurally no less than thematically, her play recalls a Greek tragedy. It follows the convention of alternating episodes of prosaic speech, which further the action, and lyric stasima, which delay the action while elevating its meaning to a transcendent scope. There is no chorus for commentary, but the few characters who have soliloquies—Jaffier, Violetta, Pierre—function like an Aeschylean chorus in depth of feeling and acuity of vision.

Most important is Jaffier's elevation to a tragic isolation reminiscent of Aeschylean or Sophoclean heroism. In his helpless confrontation with power's cold immobility, Jaffier recalls Antigone before Creon; his vacillation between abject entreaties for mercy and a fierce nobility rests, like hers, on an appeal to the unwritten laws of another world. He is not unlike Oedipus when forced to assume cosmic shame and the burden of self-renunciation. Above all, he is Prometheus: having wronged a world order predicated upon violence and cruelty, he becomes an object so abominated that the earth itself, so his enemies hope, will be loath to sustain him. Unlike the Aeschylean hero, Jaffier enjoys no choral laments, no oceanid's sympathy. Earth and humankind do not bewail his ruin. Like the Prométhée of Weil's poem, he is "alone and nameless, flesh delivered to woe," and his sole crime is his pity.[75]

Imposing a dualism of pure and impure, Weil felt that subjective impulses to evil could be involuntarily passed into that part of the soul which has affinity with God, and thus transformed into suffering. Like Socrates' spiritual monitor or the *frein vital* of humanism, it is a negative check on action, partly intuitive perhaps, but finally the ineffable work of grace. Whether dismissed as a legerdemain of Weil's metaphysics or taken as an appeal to behold rather than to trample the lilies of the field, Weil's dramatic conception argues what may be a true stewardship, self-restraint from action against the world.

In more intimate terms, Jaffier's surrender to beauty is a form of friendship extended to all who might participate in that beauty. As grace mediates between the self and the world, so it mediates between self and self in another beneficent distance, the sacrament of suffering.

S E V E N

The Sacrament of Suffering

Weil's Friendships

Car l'amitié est pour moi un bienfait incomparable, sans mesure, une source de vie, non métaphoriquement mais littéralement.
SIMONE WEIL, Letter to Joë Bousquet, May 12, 1942

C'est ce qu'il a de plus difficile dans l'amitié de se defendre d'aimer le delicieux accord; et pourtant, si l'on ne s'en defend, toute amitié périt. Avoir un ami, c'est la seule manière d'aimer la humanité.
SIMONE WEIL, "Sur l'idée de Garuchaud"

In her last letter to Père Perrin, from Casablanca on May 26, 1942, Weil, seeking to express her deep gratitude for his friendship, wrote of how all the other friendships she had known had ended in betrayal of her. All her friends in some degree or other, wittingly or not, had amused themselves in giving her pain, "not by wickedness but by the effect of a well-known phenomenon which prompts hens, when they see a hen wounded among them, to overwhelm it with blows from their beaks."[1] Thus a mechanical necessity seems to pervade even the best of human relations.

Hyperbole, however rationalized, invites caution, especially in view of a time when Weil, obliged to face her Jewish status, could well feel betrayed by every human association. But Vichy had only dramatized outwardly the isolation which by her own temperament she had experienced long before. Her correspondence certifies how abundantly she gave of herself to others in thought and feeling, and Pétrement's biography reads substantially as the record of many friendships (including her own) which Weil sustained with her characteristic energy and devotion. But she intuited, at a level far deeper than ordinary human contacts would seem to tolerate, the spiritual demands of genuine friendship. She was able to write of them only when the desultory years of exile cut her off from any assurance of continuous affections.

Her most extended discussion of friendship figures in her well-known

"Formes de l'amour implicite de Dieu," one of the essays she left with Perrin in 1942 and which he published in *Attente de Dieu* eight years later. Heavily inlaid with Christian, especially Trinitarian conceits, *amitié* does not finally depend on any dogma save Weil's cherished Pythagorean schemes of contraries to be harmonized. Specifically, friendship is an equipoise of encounter and separation: "Indeed, when two beings who are not friends are near one another there is no meeting; when they are at a distance, there is no separation."[2] Weil explicitly rejects the Aristotelian claim that friendship requires proximity and equality (an embroidering of the Greek saw that a friend is another self); fixed upon the Pythagoreans, she insists that friendship as harmony unites things not alike, neither of the same nature nor rank.[3] She does not contend that Aristotle's notion of friends is impossible or false—experience argues too strongly for attraction by similarity—but her fondness for the putatively supernatural union of opposites implies his lack of poetry.[4]

The supreme friendship would lie in union with God,[5] but Weil is content to let God serve as mediator to human friendships.[6] A true friendship, the one legitimate exception to Weil's rule that only the whole of creation deserves one's love, reflects the divine union of necessity and freedom, the constituents of the world and the human will. One can rightly seek a good for oneself in another person and at the same time wish good for that person, but friendship is debauched when the other becomes so necessary as to impose constraint or domination upon the relationship. Then amity becomes its opposite, a hatred and disgust in which dependence allows no distance and force obtrudes upon consent. Weil draws from these commonplaces her argument that friendship requires "supernatural respect for human autonomy," that is, "the miracle by which a human being agrees to regard at a distance and without approach the very person who is necessary to him as nourishment."[7]

In that contemplative distance, the wholeness of each friend is preserved so that although the bond holds two people, it has an impersonal or universal aspect, one Weil likens to the universal properties of a triangle deducible from a particular geometric shape.[8] Nowhere perhaps does she apply her *esprit de géométrie* so boldly as here, but her essential thrust is spiritual: to desire the preservation of another's integrity and one's own is, she says, to transport the center of the world's order beyond the world itself.

If that characterization appears to make friendship unreally "heady" or impossibly ethereal, Weil simply intends a bond free of the fetters which circumstance and routine in all their loveless mediocrity cast upon ordinary human relations. Friendship's consent to mutual autonomy holds no utility, no privative advantage, no convenience, no contractual right, and no force. It is indistinguishable from justice, that supernatural principle which can be realized only furtively in a world where evil predominates.[9]

Distance, dissimilarity, and impersonality are odd predicates; friendship seems to demand some intimacy if it is to claim any meaning. Weil's Pythagorean harmony and Trinitarian mediation present fair symmetries, but it is hard to see how they can move about in the common human drama. It is not difficult, though, to sense how her noble extortionism, her inexhaustible longing for human accord, was disappointed even, or especially, in the presence of her most perspicacious friends. One thinks of Perrin, for example, to whom she had attested that "nothing is so powerful in human affairs as friendship for the friends of God in maintaining one's attention even more fixed upon God."[10] Yet so often the tone of her letters to him seems restive, defensive, almost resentful of some inevitable hurt, that she would wound him by remaining outside of the church, that she might if entering it be driven chiefly by a personal and therefore faulty desire to please him—a hopeless impasse. Her conception of friendship in "Formes de l'amour" may be an attempt to escape from this dilemma or to put the best face on it.

One kind of friendship she had discovered without fear of disappointment or henpecks. She did not mention it to Perrin; it occupied the esoteric removes of her sensibility. Superficially, it might be called *livresque*, but far more is at work in it than bookish matters of taste. Like all proud and lonely spirits, she found what company she best could, not in what necessity conceded as daily fellowship nor in the circuits of political activism (from which her intelligence and her sense of irony kept her at a final distance), but in the enduring society of the noble dead, especially in minds with whom she could readily establish an elective affinity by her own indispensable initiative. Weil followed the humanists' urge to exalt—Ficino and Erasmus had their "Saint Socrates"—but her chosen immortals satisfied in her more than intellectual appropriation; they spoke to her deepest personal needs. With them she could relax all diffidence as well as her penchant for unyielding arguments which Thibon found so exasperating.

In the *Phaedrus* (275de) Socrates complains that books cannot be interrogated. No matter what question one may pose, their arguments will always be the same. But he concedes that some works seem to have been "written in the soul of the listener" (278a), and such was undoubtedly Weil's ground for friendship with the dead. Her closest allegiances, those to which she expressly gave the name of friendship, belonged to writers who were not part of the cultures of antiquity she studied so approvingly. Rather, her favorites appear exceptional to the history of their times, isolated magnificently, and, most important, consecrated by a suffering Weil could make her own. On these terms, it is fair to claim that Théophile de Viau and T. E. Lawrence were among her few true friendships.

Another kind of friendship in suffering, one with the living and the dying, she invented. Better than her phantom literary friendships, it was her attempt to achieve intimacy with autonomy, a relationship free of contract, convenience, force, and emotive possession. It was her attempt to realize an inconspicuous justice that would allow her to contribute to the harmonies of beauty, goodness, and truth their human proportions. The choreography for this friendship was her nurses plan for front-line war service.

"One of my very dearest friends"

Théophile de Viau was born in 1590, died in 1626, and lives on in that marginal immortality accorded to poets who are enthusiastically anthologized within a few representative pages. The complete edition of his works by which Weil came to know him dated from 1856. She took pains to give him a revival.

Of Huguenot descent, he had been converted to Catholicism by political expediency, but his soul belonged to the materialism of Epicurus. In his intellectual and poetic libertinage he links the freethinking traditions of the Italian Renaissance and its romantic recrudescence in nineteenth-century France, but the milieu in which he had to work and which swiftly destroyed him was determined by increasingly constrictive religious and political orthodoxies. The muses themselves had lain in apparent bondage to François de Malherbe, whose conventions Théophile bearded with fresh, youthful élan. Although his satiric verse, including some drinking songs on Christian dogmas, had given him passing notoriety, Théophile also "possessed the secret of the stripped purity which is the sure note of classicism," his talent "instinctively attuned to the Attic compound of directness and grace."[11] Théophile apprehended the natural world with an intuitive sureness imbued with a kind of Lucretian assent. It seems a freakish mischance that Boileau's ridicule of some isolated verses in Théophile's drama on Pyramus and Thisbe succeeded in casting him into prolonged disrepute.

More to Weil's point was Théophile's freethinking. He wrote in a current of philosophical skepticism which challenged by salvos from the Platonic canon the Aristotelian underpinnings of Catholic theology. This process had been set in motion two generations before him by Petrus Ramus's *Animadversiones*. Ironically, in defense against the charge of atheism, Théophile composed a verse paraphrase of the *Phaedo*, entitled *Traité de l'immortalité de l'âme*, claiming through it proof that the pagan Plato believed in God and the soul's immortality.[12]

In the event, neither it nor his conversion to Catholicism saved him from an identification with libertinage. Having fled Paris, he was condemned to the stake on the charge of *lèse-majesté divine* (August 1623), arrested within a month, and placed within the Conciergerie, where he languished for two years. The parliament of Paris commuted his sentence to banishment from the city (September 1625), but there was no enforcement. He died in a fever the following year.

Modern judgment of his literary stature varies from commendation of his stylistic merits, his aesthetic of the idea "toute seule et dépouillée"[13] making him accessible to all readers, and censure of his youthful license: "Unfortunately, Théophile always confused independence with indiscipline."[14] Weil's defense of him presents a most idiosyncratic verdict: "He lacked baseness of soul to a singular degree; that's why he could not live on to an age when he might have been able to write poems sufficiently continually perfect to be kept by posterity."[15]

Théophile's time, the drama of his trial and imprisonment, and the pathos of his early death guided her judgment substantially. She blamed Richelieu, whose exercise of power fascinated her, for permitting Théophile's incarceration: "He thus deprived France of a poet of the very first order."[16] (In *L'enracinement* the anachronism of this charge becomes evident.) With Richelieu's deracination of France by a systematic accretion of state power, literature declined to the servility mirrored in Corneille's dedications to the Cardinal: "It has been imagined that that was simply the age's language of politesse. But that's a lie. To be convinced of this fact, one has only to read the writings of Théophile de Viau. Only, he died prematurely in consequence of arbitrary imprisonment whereas Corneille lived to a ripe old age."[17]

Weil also places Théophile in what she calls the prerevolutionary "subterranean history of France," including "everything which was related to the emancipation of serfs, freedom in the towns, and social struggles," and conjoins him with Agrippa d'Aubigné (another Huguenot) and Cardinal de Retz, that most able choreographer of his own egotism, on this front.[18] Théophile's voice was indeed the last before the onset of Richelieu's absolutism to express a compassion for his country that held in it "something exaltant, moving, poetic, and sacred."[19]

Of Théophile's verse she cited several passages at length in one of her letters. Apparently she had enjoyed them so much that she memorized them, for in one quotation she breaks off with the admission that she has forgotten the rest of it. Although these passages include poems celebrating natural beauty, and with a vivid lyricism that perhaps inspired Weil when she wrote Violetta's songs in *Venise sauvée*, the lengthiest derive as patents of his two years of suffering in prison. They vary from a disembodied Stoic equanimity—"What contentment sweet to human reason as to exhale so sweetly the pain which hate makes for us!"—to bitter grief over "the enormous course of woes."[20] It must have enchanted Weil that from his *malheur* Théophile retained unsullied his love of the sensuous world and an Epicurean's resignation to death's finality.

Théophile fulfilled an injunction that Weil set down for enduring *malheur*: he did not escape suffering, but neither was he spiritually contaminated by it. Perhaps his soul, torn by time's violence, had been opened to that transformation by eternity for which she herself longed. Her chosen texts allowed her to find in him, as in Villon, "the purity of soul manifested through the excruciating expression of *malheur*."[21]

It is not generally known that she attempted to promote Théophile's works for a modern edition. Her choice of an editor, André Gide, was apt. Like Théophile both in his Huguenot ancestry and in his firm refusal of orthodox Christianity (abetted by Claudel's endless importunate attempts to bring him to the "true faith"), Gide had also in his youth been a friend to a man whose life and ruin remarkably paralleled Théophile's, Oscar Wilde.[22] Gide himself stood in a kind of natural descent from seventeenth-century libertinage. Toward the end of her life, Weil would fault Gide's pride in his novels' corrupting influence on young people (the pride of Wilde's Lord Henry Wotton),[23] but she apparently did not allow herself scruples about his subversive powers when she wrote to him about Théophile. Besides, he rivaled Proust and Anatole France in literary stature, and he had shown in *Souvenirs de la cour d'assises* (1914) and *Voyage au Congo* (1928) that he had a social conscience which his fictions seemed to belie. Weil addressed this Gide: "It would be worthy of your generosity, and of the ardent interest which you bring to everything worth the effort, to make a new edition of Théophile . . . and to entrust him to the public with a preface that would get him read. . . . We have great need of free men about us, and of whom there are not many. . . .

Théophile was one of them, and one who knew no kind of baseness, he was made pure of it by the ruination of his life and his glory."[24]

No evidence survives that Gide ever responded to Weil's letter or even that she sent it. There remains, however, a list she composed of what she copied[25] from the 1856 edition of Théophile's verse. Under "Extraits de Théophile copiés pour Gide," she included strophes from odes, sonnets, lyrics, an entire scene from *Pyrame et Thisbe*, two poems on political themes ("Paix de 1620" and "Requête au parlement"), and much else. All this peculiar effort substantiates her touching commendation of the poet in a letter to a friend: "I hope that you love Théophile. He has become one of my very dearest friends."[26]

One Man She Loved

Weil believed that virtuous action imitates the harmony of necessity and the good. Outwardly, this view may be taken as a Stoic reformulation of Alain's voluntarism: the will, he taught, stands for nothing unless it translates itself into action. Kept within the strict bounds implied in Weil's formula, however, action belongs to necessity; it is not what the will realizes of itself but what the will must work with from the contingent world. Weil maintains that without the supernatural energy of virtue, that is, when we are nourished solely on "terrestrial energies," everything we can think or do is merely evil. All human action to some degree bears this *souillure*, and one's private history, unless renounced, continues to carry its sins and "their wretched fruit of evil and error. So long as we hold to the past, God himself cannot check this horrible fructification within us. We cannot attach ourselves to the past without attaching ourselves to our crimes."[27]

Weil sensed her Protestant need of atonement for the guilt of existence long before she wrote those words in her celebrated commentary on the Lord's Prayer. They might serve as an avenue for understanding why she responded with such fervent sympathy to the most heralded figure of her age.

Ned Lawrence of Oxford, Prince of Mecca, "of Arabia" thanks to his incontestable achievements in helping its tribes deliver themselves from the Ottoman yoke—this man Weil confessed to be "the one most famous in history, I won't say in our time, but in all times known to me, whom I can wholeheartedly love and admire; and I am scarcely able to bear the knowledge that he is dead."[28]

These remarks (in English) to David Garnett, Lawrence's friend and the editor of his correspondence, attest well enough the fascination Lawrence held for her when she read first *Seven Pillars of Wisdom* and subsequently *The Letters of T. E. Lawrence*. But hers was not the adulation paid to a heroic adventurer, least of all to the mythic figure promoted by Lowell Thomas in the insistent vulgarity of commercial exhibition.

She did not bewail Lawrence's strategic opposition to France's jockeying with Britain in the postwar Levant, his plan to "biff the French out of all hope of Syria," as he put it.[29] Lawrence had attempted to serve both British and Arabic interests, conceiving a policy in which Britain would retain influence and initiative in the Near East by an enlightened promotion of the Arabs' inchoate and unsteady moves toward autonomy. It was exactly the orientation Weil hoped France would assume toward its Indochinese and African colonies before World War II.

When in 1938 she wrote to Jean Posternak of having read *Seven Pillars of Wisdom*, Lawrence had been dead three years but a world celebrity for nearly twenty. His book, a generic mélange of journal, history, topography, and confession, and written in conscious emulation of *Moby Dick* and *The Brothers Karamazov*, records the Bedouin revolt against the Turkish Empire during the Great War. A British intelligence officer, Lawrence served in the event mostly as the Western confidant of Feisal, the revolt's leader. In Feisal Lawrence realized a bond of personal loyalty to a feudal ideal he had cherished from boyhood. (He carried Sir Thomas Malory's *Morte d'Arthur* into the campaign.) His record of the venture, however contrived, slippery in facts, and distorted in mystifying self-dramatization, conveyed that elementary fealty unsullied by the British War Office machinations in which he participated so that he attained an international esteem that outlasted the dismal story of British intrigue and final betrayal of the Arabs. Lawrence's book crystallized an anachronistic realization of individual conduct in war that now seems, as it perhaps did even in 1926, as remote as the chivalric medievalism that inspired it.

It is well known that Lawrence, for all his catty ambiguities and evasions, regarded his book as a failure. That Weil, whose reading knowledge of English was excellent, could hail *Seven Pillars of Wisdom* for "such complete absence of rhetoric, either heroic or hair-raising" suggests that she somehow missed the hallmarks of Lawrence's archly wrought style: syntactical inversions, overloaded epithets, precious diction.[30] Her praise of Lawrence seems hyperbolic: "I do not know any historical figure in any epoch who realizes to such a degree what I love to admire. Military heroism is something rather rare;

lucidity of mind is rarer; the combination of the two is almost without example, it is an almost superhuman degree of heroism."[31]

In a word, it was Homeric. And Lawrence's Bedouins assumed in his eyes a pristine simplicity recalling the warriors on Ilium's plain whom Weil loved and pitied. Indeed, confederates of Troy might well have been ancestors to such a fierce and grand swordsman as Lawrence's friend Auda abu Tayi, that Ajax of the desert. Not its rough chivalry, however, but the brooding in *Seven Pillars of Wisdom* won Weil its intellectual heroism. One of her references to Lawrence sounds the note that predominates in her study of the *Iliad*: of those many who worship force and those many who fear it, "who knows the full extent of its empire and at the same time scorns it? T. E. Lawrence, the liberator of Arabia, was that way, but he is dead."[32]

It is instructive to read *Seven Pillars of Wisdom* with Weil's eyes, as it were, to sense as far as intuition may allow what particulars informed her image of Lawrence as, in her words, "an authentic hero, a perfectly lucid thinker, an artist, a scholar, and above all that a sort of saint," the several selves she might have wished she could become and which many have seen in her.[33]

She provides a clue to "one great shock of recognition." "By nature and by will he had the most rare power of making himself at home among any men," she told David Garnett, and she remarks her own urge that carried her into the factories, "though of course no comparison is possible." But the character of that "at home," from Lawrence's years with the Arabs to the Royal Air Force barracks and its Rabelaisian fellows, had one steady motif: "abnegation, renunciation. . . . nakedness of the mind." The Saudis' wasteland became for Lawrence "a spiritual icehouse, in which was preserved intact but unimproved for all ages a vision of the unity of God."[34]

Although Lawrence retrospectively dismissed as affectation his romantic hope of assimilating himself with the Bedouins (the sartorial vanity of his most famous photo portraits speaks for itself), he became their intimate, "lived level with them, and yet appeared better in himself." Perceiving the Arab warriors individually, as their Homeric *arete* warranted, he wanted to minimize losses in battle by "arranging" the enemy's mind. Gratuitous killing was "not only waste but sin," and the Arabs were "not materials, like soldiers, but friends" among whom one death "like a pebble dropped in water, might make a brief hole, yet rings of sorrow widened out therefrom." Lawrence's lyric celebration of the Turkish dead after a raid might be cited as well and his longing to be one of them over against "the restless, noisy, aching mob" of his plundering Bedouin comrades.[35]

Here in Mohammed's deserts a solicitude throve, an elementary engagement of what is human such as governments, seeing only masses of people, could never comprehend. Here, too, was what Weil could not find in the Spanish war, an attempted Homeric equanimity, vested with the timocratic code of Arab warriors.[36] Lawrence set it down as his ideal "to make our battle a series of single combats, our ranks a happy alliance of agile commanders-in-chief"—a Homeric tableau, also an Arthurian, infused with a cultivated sense of doom, where failure becomes a desideratum.[37]

Beyond these chivalric accents and Lawrence's antiheroic, even comic self-effacements, whose bite Weil seems to have missed, many passages argue a close psychological affinity between Weil and her hero, particularly in negatives: their shame of the body's debilities, "the disgust of being touched," their mystical orientation to suffering and death as payment owed by self-convicted nobodies.[38]

Nothing impressed her more than Lawrence's assumption of an antiheroic position, that he could say, "I became a standing court-martial on myself," and on the Corneillian cult of heroism that had infected that other intellectual poet-saint, Charles Péguy.[39] For her, Lawrence's penetrating clarity in self-consciousness was "more heroic than his most heroic deeds":

> To be a hero, a conqueror, a great chief is, I think, relatively easy if one forgets the claims of that common humanity which in oneself and in others serves as material for glorious action; to remember these claims constantly, and yet perforce to trample upon them is almost impossible. Such is, to my mind, the unique greatness of that man; he paid for that greatness by ghastly sufferings and was of course misunderstood.[40]

His real heroism lay, to her mind, in his rejection of himself as a hero; his glory, in his contempt for glory. Further, his failure (Weil takes him at his word) made of him a metaphysical object lesson, an example of finite, exhausted energy.[41] It is because human society is forever limited, try though it might to pretend otherwise, and the good mysteriously absent from it, that "a man of purity achieves nothing, or whatever he does achieve turns to naught." She ranks Lawrence with Francis of Assisi.[42]

All the more commendable, then, was the sentence to self-degradation which Lawrence passed in his "court-martial," that mortification begun in the most notorious incident in *Seven Pillars of Wisdom*, his violation at Der'a. Bemused like any reader by that obscurely horrific story, Weil drew from it, through no strict process of logic, the conviction that Lawrence, thereafter given to voluntary suffering and self-debasement, longed for equality, he having come to realize "that among men in general not equality, but power and crushing subordination has been, is and will be the rule; so life was impossible for him; yet to seek a refuge out of life, either by dreams or theories or self-delusion, or forgetfulness, or voluntary death he thought cowardly."[43]

The course he undertook, "my urge downwards" as he called it, he set down in *The Mint*, a vivid glimpse of his term in the Royal Air Force (RAF), first under the name of Ross, subsequently as Shaw.[44] By the time of his death in May 1935, Lawrence had prepared a limited edition of this journal from a hand press but stipulated that *The Mint* not be given general circulation until 1950. Weil admitted to Garnett, "I would wish most eagerly to be allowed some time before 1950 to read *The Mint*," but she felt her admiration of its author did not suffice as a claim to that privilege.[45]

A reading of *The Mint* suggests Weil's and Lawrence's kinship. She was right, I believe, to feel that her factory work had initiated her into the mysteries of his kind of experience in the RAF. Resolved "to plunge crudely amongst crude men," he had arrived at insights that anticipate her amazingly: that "except under compulsion there is no equality in this world," that in playing "the game of mechanical toy" he could counter the effects of authority's aimless terror—not unlike the clock's tyranny at Alsthom—with the buoyant sense of "the feet on solid earth."[46] She shared with him a dedication to the steadying, sanctifying anonymity of manual labor (her one positive discovery beneath the factories' grinding inhumanity), even though she was as maladroit in many tasks as he was ungainly in drill and gymnastics. Both risked physical collapse: "This breaking point is always within reach," Lawrence wrote.[47]

Both, too, felt the allure of contact with simple, unassuming people—for Lawrence, enlistees seemed to carry into the service a permanent defeat in life—but in that very fascination which the unobstreperous and humble exert on their educated "betters," the ambiguity of a condition that could make one similar to them but never of them had to stay unresolved. Weil always knew that unlike her co-workers she could leave the factory behind her, and Lawrence had entered the RAF on condition of voluntary retirement. In both of them a pronounced indifference to their own well-being is evident in their attitude toward money. As one of his fair-minded biographers has observed, "Lawrence's generosity with money could only be described as saintlike, and he gave away any savings he might accumulate from his wages, royalties or other sources of income so readily that he was in fact constantly quite poor."[48]

That statement recalls Pétrement's description of Weil at Le Puy, where she gave her meager earnings as a teacher to unemployed workers. Further, their best biographies document a psychological effect that both Lawrence and Weil had upon many around them who shared in common tasks, that people felt elevated in their company, even though in both there lay a fundamental core of diffidence and final distance.[49]

Although it may be facile and unfair to see in their solicitude toward others the complement to their self-abhorrence, that darker side is there. For Weil, self-abhorrence found ultimate expression in theological formulas, but for Lawrence the burden proved differently complex. He had to live down the deceptions of his own lionized image, the conundrum of his identity with the Bedouins, the horror at Der'a, his illegitimacy. He told Charlotte Shaw he longed for people to look down on and despise him.[50] The theatrics, heroics, and politics of his years in Arabia mattered far less to Weil than the subsequent obscurity he so assiduously tended. She is explicit on this point in her letter to David Garnett: "What is to my mind most clear and natural is what seems strange to his friends and admirers, his years of voluntary suffering and degradation. Indeed, he seems still more human and at the same time greater in his slavery than in his glory; though his letters from the Royal Tank Corps hurt in an unbearable way."[51]

She refers, it seems, to letters Lawrence wrote to an Oxford friend, Lionel Curtis, in the spring of 1923. There, he admits to a seven-year plan of self-humiliation, to be realized in a military camp's milieu, where delusions could easily be mocked away: "Here every man has joined because he was down and out. . . . We are social bed-rock, those unfit for life by competition; and each of us values the rest as cheap as he knows himself to be."[52]

Lawrence set down in tandem with his private resolve some general observations on the human lot, the paltry limits of human knowledge, the miserable accountability of all mortal flesh that it can produce only what is mortal. In short, the mountainous *fastidium sui* of his own guilt-laden sensibility could pass over into a disparagement of humankind. He could even speak of "the fault of birth" lying in part on the begotten.[53] Weil herself was not altogether free of this tendency toward a cosmic bitterness. Unless one presumes that her gospel of decreation was intended solely for herself, it hints at misanthropy, a streak of which Alain suspected as early as her "Réflexions" on oppression and freedom. In their restive itinerant intellects, Lawrence and Weil found some relief from their disappointment in the human condition through mechanical forms of purity (or purification): he in hydrodynamics, she in geometrical problems and differential equations. For both, physical toil provided an expiatory self-forgetting.

Although she lived into darker times than Lawrence's, Weil did not embrace his pessimism. His life's example, its emblematic defeat—purity lost in the world of becoming—sustained her so intensely that "my admiration for him seems to me in such an unaccountable way to be akin to some personal link."[54] In the balance of things, it is not regrettable that these two votaries of the will to self-cancellation never met. Across an impossible distance Weil could find by her own projection a purity in human life (Stendhal's crystallized stick?) to emulate with her singular avidity. Whom else could she have extolled as much as this brilliant failure, the hero who mocked himself into slavery?

Lawrence had written:

> Free will I've tried and rejected (not obedience, for that is my present effort, to find equality only in subordination. It is dominion whose taste I have been cloyed with): action I've rejected: and the intellectual life: and the receptive senses: and the battle of wits. They are all failures, and my reason tells me therefore that obedience, nescience, will also fail, since the roots of common failure must lie in myself—and yet in spite of reason I am trying it.[55]

Weil could only have loved someone in whom "everything seems clear and transparent to such a degree that I cannot realize that he is a man made remote by greatness, glory and death, and not my most intimate friend."[56]

Her Amfortas

"The body's suffering is time's constraint upon humanity. The soul feels it."[57] This meditation on crucifixion might well have been prompted by Weil's meeting with a man who had given her its lesson in all its irreducible bitterness.

During combat in May 1918, a twenty-one-year-old French officer named Joë Bousquet was hit by a bullet that passed into his spine. From that day to the end of his life he was bedridden, half-paralyzed, forced to endure constant pain. In 1924 he took lodging in a room he was never to leave, in Carcassonne. Delivered to this private disaster, a victim of social violence at its acme, Bousquet in that same year signed André Breton's *Manifeste du sur-*

réalisme, not in anger or despair but in hope, and his example became infectious. He joined the editorial board of *Cahiers du Sud*, where some of Weil's most important essays first appeared. He is remembered for a novel, *La tisane de sarments* (1936), and a journal, *Traduit du silence* (1941), but it was not his writings or his surrealist affiliations that interested Weil. The opportunity to meet a man "born from his own death"[58] came when, late in March, 1942, she joined Jean Ballard, editor-in-chief of *Cahiers du Sud*, on a train from Marseilles to Carcassonne.

They arrived at Bousquet's lodging around midnight, and she talked with him until dawn in "impassioned exchanges."[59] She left later that morning, and they never saw each other again. Pétrement claims, "The one conversation she had with him sufficed to create a friendship. Each of them had recognized in the other a courage akin to each."[60]

Was Bousquet, then, in Weil's vivid apprehension, a Philoctetes lying in recumbent helplessness, abandoned to an impossible wound? Was he also the "other self" of Greek friendship, nailed to the cross she wanted to bear? Did she hope to assume his *malheur*? "One could make oneself pure enough," he noted in his journal, "to be all the happiness of someone who is among the very wretched."[61] Perhaps she passed on to him from her reading of San Juan de la Cruz the notion that purest suffering leads to purest knowledge and thus to purest joy. Could she purify his suffering?[62]

What enthralled her was this invalid's search for a revelation of things as they are; he desired a good beyond all appearances and illusions. Physical agony was his only instructor, but a good one. For Weil, the readiness of this spiritual desire, not the ripeness of any attainment, was everything, and that Bousquet's inexorable submission to the rack did not disturb his lucidity must have seemed to her a miracle. In fact, she saw him as Christ-like and told him so. His cruciform *malheur*, whatever the weight of its curse, had not become evil; that is, it had not poisoned his will with escapist fantasies, rationalizations, and vengeances. His was the "authentic grandeur" of one who, "even at the moment when he feels himself wholly abandoned by God and by men, is nevertheless preserved from all evil."[63]

With this, her encomium, she sent to him two weeks after their meeting drafts from *Venise sauvée*, some of her poems, verses from Aeschylus and Sophocles (Greek drama, she had long felt, was immediately accessible to those who suffer), and a *koine* edition of the New Testament. He responded to her poetry: "You are more clairvoyant in verse than in prose. One could say that for you poetic rhythm is the rhythm of consciousness," but gave himself mostly to personal reflections: "I am extremely happy to know you. And I believe in our friendship. More than anyone you will know how to help me annihilate everything that remains incomplete or inherited in me. . . . I have envied you your intuition of good and sense of evil. Never have I been able to raise myself so high as that."[64]

To her praise of him he demurred. No Philoctetes, no Christ, perhaps he was seeking only the happiness and forgetfulness of death—a third-act Tristan. As though emboldened to match her frankness, Bousquet makes a case for the illusions from which she presumed him free: to dream away one's life, to make a haven in one's heart. We are happy only in the way we have of playing host to ourselves, he insisted, but he also said she was the better judge, "more advanced than I." His only criticism of her was that she lacked self-confidence, a shortcoming he shrewdly assessed to be "the ransom paid for your moral qualities."[65]

Those qualities did not necessarily subsume an inclination to mysticism, but Bousquet had no trouble perceiving it in her; he even approved of the violence with which, as she had apparently told him, she had been visited by Christ in 1938: "I know full well how important it is to protect oneself against religious impressionism. But I don't fear for you this feminine complacency which all your aspirations belie." He had high expectations of her writings on divine love, characterizing her as one unwittingly pledged to reveal grandeur in "the most threadbare and disparaged subjects."[66] She was stripping the dogma of Christian trinity for her own Pythagorean reveting.

He closed his first letter to her with gratitude for her extraordinary offer to supply him with a drug he could use to end his life. No man had ever dared to avail himself that way, he said.[67]

Weil wrote two more letters to him within the following weeks; Bousquet's second and last is dated May 2, 1942. Her final letter in this intense exchange holds special importance (and has been duly anthologized) for its autobiographical statements, specifically in response to his criticism of her failure in self-confidence. She tries to deflect his remarks by a chronicle of her headaches. Regarding her suffering as a poisoning of body and soul, she found in her physical debilities an acute self-loathing because they distracted her toward idleness, which she considered a contemptible consolation. She tells him of her being overtaken in the midst of her pain by "a presence more personal, more certain and more real than that of a human being," an allusion to Christ's descent and seizure in 1938. She does not name Christ as this presence, but Bousquet knew whom she meant. Most important, she depicts this mystical moment as a kind of friendship, as the visitation suggested "the love which shows through the most tender smile of one beloved."[68] This final letter to Bousquet is a testimony of friendship, surcharged by her feeling that she serves as a medium through which God's love for Bousquet can be manifested to him. It is as though here she had effected on her own initiative that supernatural harmony she describes in a letter to Perrin: bound together by God's love, in encounter and separation, she and Bousquet undertake friendship's two motives, the search for good and the search for necessity.[69]

Weil felt Bousquet was privileged in his suffering; his agony had prepared him to bear the seed of divine love, to know, that is, and to contemplate through his affliction the kindred affliction of the world. She analogized that contemplation to a bride's consent. "For every human being there is a date, unknown by all and by oneself above all but wholly determined, beyond which the soul can no longer protect this virginity."[70] Striking and not entirely coherent images of generation succeed one another in this letter. Not only is Bousquet the seed-bearer and the virgin who must yield to the cross (she proselytizes expressly), he is also an embryo ready to break out from the shell of unreality, the world itself being an egg in which God has implanted divine love as an infinitesimal seed. Weil herself, like a mother hen brooding, bids him attend to his "instant limite." Her peremptory tone turns dramatic as she urges him not to miss his appointed time, that he understand the role of intelligence is to hate evil in oneself, that he recognize the danger that evil assumes in reverie. Only Weil with her athletic demands on mental vigilance could look at daydreaming as the root of evil. (Not even Dante, who knew well his own *superbia*, was so harsh toward *acedia*.) Her point is that consolation in affliction must be evil because it seeks, however covertly, to subtract from divine love. In effect, the gratuitous violence of her insistence was fueled by what she acknowledged to be her own susceptibility to inertia. As Bousquet's friend, seeing in him a plea for release from suffering, she inveighed against seeking any false exit.

Friendship lies at the heart of this message, but Weil's lockstep assertiveness, her categorical dicta, are not softened by her confessions about her own suffering. To hate oneself in one's weakness and pain is one thing; to exalt self-revulsion into an operating principle for enlightenment amounts to something quite other. How could she impose such seemingly cruel notions upon a friend, and one whom she had known only a few weeks?

In her self-contempt she figured that anyone's friendship for her was an impossibility, yet she was convinced of Bousquet's because she was inspired by the nobility she read in his fathomless pain. He was a living document of necessity's conjunction with the good, a miraculous occasion to be read. Although she could imagine herself a cipher by which Bousquet might apprehend God's love for him in affliction, he was in symbiotic turn a revelation; his friendship "literally gives to my thought all that part of its life which does not come to it from God or from the world's beauty."[71]

Bousquet later described her effect on him: "With her one could take leave from modern existence, rest one's eyes upon brilliant perspectives where all that we think and live, in spite of ourselves, is prolonged. She had the gift of uttering words in an illimitably human meaning. Her thoughts were mine but she settled in the ones which deprived me of repose."[72]

A Tableau of Friendship: Her Nursing Plan

Perhaps Bousquet never realized how immeasurably he had helped Weil in the project which since the spring of 1940 had become for her an *idée fixe*: her plan for the formation of a small corps of women to serve as front-line nurses. They were to give elementary first aid to the wounded and spiritual comfort to the dying.

The nurses plan might well be called Weil's essay on friendship, and one of her neglected masterworks. It contains virtually all that one needs to know about her personality: her *esprit de géométrie*, her longing for reckless courage, her indomitable, grandiose sense of personal responsibility, her need to create artfully a bridge to the world of others, especially where, with her Jewish sense of obligation to strangers, she would find them suffering.

For three years, in France, New York, and London, she worked to promote it, circulating copies, pressing friends and acquaintances with political influence so she could get a hearing. In America, she appealed to Jacques Maritain, whom she barely knew, to secure her an interview with Roosevelt. De Gaulle's "Mais elle est folle!" has often been quoted, but although a graduate of St. Cyr might be pardoned for forgetting that France's foremost saint was a woman in front-line combat, his view seems to have reflected a consensus among those upon whom she visited her importunate plea.

In part, her plan was unabashed propaganda. The presence of unarmed women risking or sacrificing their lives to help wounded and dying troops would provide a symbol of "authentic and pure inspiration" with which to confound the pseudo-religious inspiration of Nazism: "This corps on one side and the S.S. on the other would make by their opposition a tableau preferable to any slogan. It would be the most striking representation possible of the two directions between which humanity today must choose."[73] It is as though she were attempting to choreograph that "instant limite" for humanity when, like Bousquet, it would have to choose between good and evil.

Weil gives herself away in describing her plan as part of a tableau. Having rehearsed it so often in letters, she had made it a picture in her mind, and it might reasonably be called her work of art, a fresco like Giotto's *Lamentation*, a noble geometry. Her place in it would be, like the stations of Giotto's women, central but anonymous—all great art is anonymous, she believed. It would have been for her the culmination of Alain's voluntarism, an experimental action upon the world. In the nurse's anonymous calling, she could have found a *revanche* for the cruel fate that made her as a woman an outsider, and she would have remembered that in the Great War France had accepted and acknowledged the sacrificial services of its Jews. Above all, she could have offered in the battlefield's laboratory of *malheur* a friendship no soldier would refuse. No one would have scorned her for being a *normalienne*, a reader of Plato, an enthusiast of chant.

Bousquet not only listened to her without condescension; he told her anecdotes from his wartime experience that must have fired her with confidence. He recalled to her an officer's remark that nothing required a fighting soldier to attend the plaints of a dying fellow. The wounded had to be ignored to keep combat forces intact. Bousquet also recalled seeing automobiles driven by young American and British women who gathered up the wounded: "I won't tell you of the speed and calm of these lasses [fillettes], I would only stress the élan which their feminine presence communicated to us in the fighting."[74] He added that the character of men under fire posed no threat to women. Here was the vouchsafe for Weil's notion that friendship requires distance and impersonality.

Although Bousquet hailed the plan and believed nothing precluded its implementation, he criticized Weil's assumption that the corps of nurses' would be a sacrificial offering: "You seem to expect that women pledged to the moral solace of the wounded would stay continuously on the battlefield, without ever being relieved. That's a romantic and impracticable idea."[75] What he did not see was that the plan as a whole was impracticable. Weil's guiding vision was a Great War landscape with endlessly protracted trench lines. The German offensive of 1940 had ended within a few weeks, no front had been opened, and the character of modern war, mechanized and aerial, promised to be incalculably different from what Bousquet and his comrades had known in 1914–18. His paraplegia was an emblem of his fixity on an ever-dimming past.[76]

The Great War's significance to Weil's plan rests on two facts. First, the example of Alain's service in that war imposed itself upon her. Keenly resentful of generals and politicians who waged war at a distance, Alain profoundly respected the youths burdened with its immediate cruelties. Like many survivors, he felt obligated to speak on behalf of the fallen; his bitter *propos* of 1919, *Mars ou la guerre jugée,* forms a prose memorial. His influence on postwar youth at Henri IV can be measured by the scandal many of his students caused as *normaliens* when in 1929 they pledged that although they would accept their military obligations, they would refuse to become officers, even as Alain had refused.[77]

A second, far more intimate fact derives from Weil's childhood, when she experienced a good part of the war through her father's work as an army doctor. Contrary to regulations, the peculiarly willful Mme Weil and her children followed him from post to post. Simone and her brother took food and newspapers to soldiers in hospitals. They even adopted as "godsons" soldiers without families and sent them clothing and food. Once, when Dr. Weil was stationed at Chartres, Simone's "godson" came to visit during his leave. Pétrement describes "a friendship of great happiness, a shared pitying. The little girl (then seven years old) and her big godson took walks all the day, holding hands. The soldier did not stay long. She never saw him again; he was killed shortly afterward."[78]

The impact of his death on Weil's childhood can only be guessed at, not to mention the tacit heroism of her father, a healer. With his example, Bousquet's, and Alain's, her nurses plan in all its impracticality reads as a tribute to childhood memories, a "recherche du temps perdu," a longing to recover a brief, tender, dreamlike friendship.

Perhaps that *filleul,* her "godson," had given her the key to what friendship meant to her: the dissimilarity between her child-self and the soldier, the impersonality enforced by war's circumstance yet delicately countered by fleeting intimacy—the handholding is exceptional in a story of someone who did not like to be touched—and the distance ensured by death. Weil had no trouble befriending the doomed.

The strongest fact of World War II was that it seemed to promise her a career in friendship on her terms. The war had galvanized whole nations with moral imperatives nobler than the state propaganda that channeled them into action. As Freud noted in 1915, war's chaos brings coherence and purpose to those who live at random in peacetime. Weil, though in temperament at the farthest possible remove from a dissolute or haphazard existence, had nonetheless failed to find any way to make peace with society. (Her savvy dread of collectivity in part rationalizes that private failure.) Her unyielding need for autonomy had made her work in leftist activism and schoolteaching very mixed experiences, frustrating and physically exhausting. Her ungainliness had aborted her initiations into the violence of Renault and Catalonia. By the war's commencement, she had turned thirty, bound for spinsterhood—a dismal fate for a Jewish woman.[79] The war brought her a new sense of vocation.

One of the salient features of Weil's plan is her characterization of the sort of woman she believed necessary to make it work. As she made clear that she intended to serve, the plan is a kind of self-portrait, one more refreshing and positive than the lengthier and self-deprecatory "spiritual autobiographies" she offered in letters to Bousquet and Perrin. In one draft, written in English for an American army captain, she says it would not be necessary to enlist only trained nurses "since the work would essentially be first aid . . . spirit, devotion and courage are even more necessary than training."[80] (She in fact took first aid training in New York.[81]) Then she added a proviso:

> Of course the women must be carefully chosen. If they are, there is no danger either of their flinching under fire or of soldiers treating them lightly. They must have at the same time a stern, cold resolution, and a mother-likèd [sic] tenderness toward the wounded and dying. Both things at once are not easy to find in the same person, yet there are such women, and there is surely no fitter way to use them in this great struggle.

It seemed to her obvious that "there should be among them no mother, no wife and no young girl. Why should not women who are not tied by any family duty die as well as men?"

Here is another sort of friendship, what one might call a sisterhood but without broad feminist constructions. Weil was looking to a corps of women who, as in ecclesiastical orders, had rejected marital convention and could thus serve disinterested and lofty ends. At the same time they would have to show "mother-likèd tenderness" to young men—a telltale phrase from Weil's memory of her "godson." Her revolutionary originality came in the assumption that, weaponless, these women would share the odds of death with men.[82] As single older women without romantic expectations, they could be genuine friends to the troops.

Helpless as an exile, despised as a Jew, as a woman limited in opportunity, Weil had long had only words as weapons. Her nurses plan was her "letter to the world," an attempt to burst all bonds, not with a view to social acceptance but to realize in the most intimate way of friendship the yoking of necessity and the good, the conjunction of war's blind force and love's divine impersonality. The common denominator of her friendship with Théophile, Lawrence, and Bousquet was their out-of-the-way *malheur*, their afflictions sequestered by prison, self-exile, and a torturous bed: "All beautiful things, courage, fellowship, dignity, generosity have much more value among the unfortunate than the fortunate in this world."[83] Her nurses plan would have afforded her all of these in a host of anonymous friendships.

In the event, her plan came to nothing and she served at a desk, where, as though consigned to futility, she wrote virtually impromptu some of her most insightful essays. With *L'enracinement* the ripest fruit of that time, no one can regret that she was prevented from realizing her scheme. Likely, however, she would have given all her writing to befriend one battle-wracked soldier lying somewhere in her tableau of necessity and the good.

E I G H T

The Decline and Fall of Science

Ns. ne connaissons rien, du fait que ns. ne connaissons pas tout, pourtant tout se passe comme si ns. connaissons q. ch.—comme s'il y a des choses négligeables. C'est une condition de la vie—de l'action—que le monde se trouve ainsi—ms. c'est un hasard heureux pr. la vie, non pr. la pensée.

SIMONE WEIL, Cahiers divers, troisième series

Weil's writings on science are perhaps the most neglected of her works. As she had no training in any science, this neglect would seem justified. One might easily dismiss her thoughts as no more than those of a better than averagely informed layperson. The scientific community has paid her virtually no heed. Readers who are not scientists but are interested in the history and philosophy of science (as many scientists are not) may be titillated or outraged by her views.[1]

Although her theological notions carry an inebriant, at times liberating heterodoxy, her views on science give, at least initially, the impression of reaction; they seem hopelessly *à rebours*. Yet her arguments on science are of a piece with her religious views; for her, science and religion are not conveniently discrete from each other; both have necessity as a metaphysical linchpin. Thus a cosmopolitan, libertarian thinker set herself against some of the great intellectual revolutions of the twentieth century. It could be said that Weil wanted to establish a Christian science.

The nebulous word *science* holds a range of meanings. It can refer to exact sciences like physics, natural sciences like biology, or social sciences like sociology. All of these involve a systematic pursuit of knowledge through scrupulous and orderly observation of a problem, experimentation and tentative conclusions about it, or simply redefinitions of it.[2] One can, of course, think through a problem scientifically without being a scientist. The renowned example is Descartes, who in his autobiography, *Discours de la méthode*, tells how he spent his young manhood in continuous epistemological experiment, armed only with his resolve, a simple set of inductive guidelines, and a mind he thought average. Weil attempted to follow his example.

Beyond its disciplines and procedures, science has secured the imposing force of ideology, its most pertinent meaning to the present discussion. Science has in effect created a complex of values to which Western society adheres, however vaguely, without much protest. Its historical opponent, ecclesiastical authority, has been vanquished by generations of contempt and indifference. The ascendant prestige of science since the European renaissances, a prestige derived from discoveries in astronomy, physics, and biology in particular, from the compelling vigor of scientific reasoning and technological applications, has ensured science's displacement of religious belief as a way of understanding the world and, contrary to the religious disposition to fearful acceptance, of shaping it to human ends. The revolutionary advances in human consciousness over the past five centuries have come almost wholly from scientific inquiry or theory. Even Marxism has claimed legitimacy as a science. No one can contest the forceful appeal of science and its godchild, technology, to the primal urges of humankind as Pascal, objecting, defined them: to know, to experience, to master.

Because, when Weil was coming of age, the theories of quanta, probability, and relativity were confounding generations-old nostrums of scientific progress, there was a resumed open-endedness in scientific thinking almost everywhere but in France. After the Great War, France had lagged behind England, Germany, and the United States in industrialization and technological advances; it was also singularly parochial as a laboratory for research. War needs had tardily given birth (in 1922) to the Office national de recherches scientifiques, industriels et des inventions, but the age-old educational system resisted change.[3] Tradition was like a clenched fist: "In the traditional scientific institutions, old-fashioned ideas and a conformist outlook tended to neutralise research. In the name of common sense, and even the national genius and its peculiarities, the scientific establishment rejected all unorthodox discoveries, and even the most advanced teaching bodies spurned anything novel."[4]

A chauvinistic complacency about France as world educator, its self-assumed title since the Revolution, extended even to the sciences, as is clear from Lucien Poincaré's 1915 preface to a two-volume compendium of specialists' essays, *La science française*. French science, he asserted, "has often shown an extraordinary facility of adaptation and a perfect *souplesse*. . . . On the scientific terrain, as on others, France has been the most revolutionary of nations; it has broken down ancient cadres, set up new régimes, and without prejudice or partisanship, installed itself securely in conquered positions."[5] Even allowing for the puffery of wartime rhethoric, these remarks do not hold up to the facts, and it is significant that when a new edition appeared in 1933, the new editor observed that the professional scientists contributing essays "do not conceal the imperfections and the lacunas" in their fields.[6]

Eminence, of course, there was and had been, thanks to such pioneers as Jean Reclus and Paul Vidal de la Blache in geography, Alfred Binet in child psychology, Emile Durkheim in sociology and, in Weil's time, Louis de Broglie in physics and Claude Lévi-Strauss in anthropology. Within the academy, Léon Brunschvicq, Weil's thesis director at the Normale, had helped to overturn France's ancient allegiance to deduction and a priori reasoning in favor of what then was passing as modern scientific analysis. One of his foremost pupils, Gaston Bachelard, was emerging in the 1930s as a historian and philosopher of science with a sophisticated appreciation of contemporary physics.

Still, these were exceptional minds, and near consensual resistance continued against the current of new ideas, particularly those coming in profusion from the enemy across the Rhine. Daniel Berthelet, for example, assessed Einstein's theory of relativity as a species of alchemy and jibed at Einstein's membership in "a disturbed and disturbing race."[7] The French response to Freud in the 1920s was almost uniformly negative. Weil herself categorically dismissed his psychology as "suffused with the very prejudice he purports to combat, namely, that sex is dirty."[8] Alain, not above pettiness, grumbled whenever he read something from Einstein that seemed to entrench upon his philosophical preserve. What business did a mathematician have with metaphysics?

Circle versus Line

Before electing philosophy for her studies, Weil had considered pursuing mathematics. Years after she left the Normale, she continued to read in scientific literature, particularly classical texts. She has left extensive notes on Christian Huygens, a seventeenth-century physicist, and Daniel Bernoulli, an eighteenth-century Swiss who formulated a theory on the conservation of energy. She read Simon Stevin de Bruges, author of the first French book on mathematics, and dismissed him as a popularizer: "A strange thing: He deals with unknowns yet has no notion of them."[9]

When she met people trained in the sciences, she pursued them with her usual interrogative curiosity. Bernard, head of the foundry at Bourges and a chemical engineer, was one of her victims: "How did he study chemistry initially? subsequently? the manuals? what was it that amazed him, shocked him? what truly enlightened him? His intellectual adventures."[10] All this she wanted to know. She reminded herself to ask her brother about his psychological reaction after a discovery in mathematics.

Her wartime notebooks include several references to modern physics. They indicate a level of speculation well beyond what one might expect even from a well-informed nonprofessional. For example, of the famous Michelson-Morley experiment of 1887 she says that one might conclude the earth is motionless: "It is Galileo's system breaking down. But the crystallization of three centuries around Galileo has prevented it from being allowed to break down. . . . What ought one to think of the rotation of a sphere upon itself?" She notes that a gravitational field is created when "a system of reference" characterized by uniform acceleration has relation to a system in which everything is in repose or in steady movement. She found the idea so attractive that she would like to isolate it.[11]

This brief entry shows that Weil approached science as history, as politics, and as aesthetics. It is precisely because she brings a fresh, intrusive view to scientific theories and "advances" and because she is so alive to their implications, as perhaps few scientific specialists can be, that her thoughts warrant attention. She overcame French parochialism.

Her teaching also informed her thinking. Her philosophy syllabus at Le Puy included lectures on scientific method. She supplemented these with talks on historical developments in science. She quickly found that her students labored under the provincialism of textbook notions and lacked any awareness of the interrelations of scientific disciplines. Primarily, she spoke of Greek mathematics and Greek science: "I explained to them—what no one had bothered to tell them—how infinitesimal calculus had been the condition for applying mathematics to physics, and how consequently for today's developments in physics. All this everyone followed, even the most ignorant, with an impassioned interest."[12]

Her teaching required her to make complex matters comprehensible. She had had to do as much for herself. She realized fully her own limits in understanding the developments of mechanics and physics. More important, she learned from her students (*dum doceo, disco*) the value of a historical presentation: "They said that only such instruction could make science something human for pupils, instead of a sort of dogma one had to believe without knowing why."[13] Her students' very ignorance was an advantage to them: not only did it necessitate Weil's historical review, it kept them free of clever presuppositions.[14]

Weil's remarks on scientific dogma were more than a monitory note on the backwardness of French educational practices. She needed no reminding on that subject. For an antidote she prescribed, in a 1932 sketch on mathematical instruction, the following: a historical review of each science, including original texts when possible; experimental reproduction of discoveries in physics; a study of science's relation to technology; the student's apprenticeship and performance in a productive skill, to include a detailed education in its professional history relative to science and general technology.[15] In effect, she was trying to update Descartes's scheme for a workers' university.

Descartes had insisted that scientific understanding be made accessible to ordinary people. For him, experiment was the open sesame. What was one to do, then, when scientific learning had become specialized to such a degree that science itself assumed a mystique and knowledge became privileged and hieratic?

However typically French a reflexive individualism in the combat of ideas may be, Weil had a particular ax to grind when she tried to answer that question. As a lay outsider, her addressing the culture of science seems almost absurdly pretentious. How, not being a scientist, could she presume to understand the guiding assumptions at work within the sciences and only vaguely marketed without? She read widely, of course, if perhaps too impressionistically. And she intuited.

In her "Réflexions" concerning oppression and freedom she argues that technology's advent, having made capitalism an enlightened despot in Western industries, has given scientists a caste privilege that helps to keep science remote from public understanding. The public knows only the results of science, not its methods, and so it is subject to the delusions of continuous progress, that nineteenth-century shibboleth. Trying to probe the effects of specialization, Weil suggests that scientists themselves have become a laity, cut off from a comprehensive grasp of science as a whole. They are often made the cogs of industry, with no sense of the history and development of their fields. An abusive "new scholasticism" has arisen, from which only the impetus of individual genius can afford a rescue.[16] She is patently making the romantic's hopeful case for an intellectual revolution, a view one might expect from a lay mind made enthusiastic by the examples of Eudoxus and Copernicus. It is odd, then, that she goes on to condemn the work of Max Planck and Einstein, the revolutionaries who leveled the Bastille of classical (Newtonian) science.

In her analysis, science belongs to a discussion of oppression because it has warped its own practitioners by narrowing their range of vision and commitment and has become the henchman of capitalist technology. It has also become "the theology of a bureaucratic society."[17] More sinister than the hostility between science and religion—"the scandal of modern thought," Weil called it—is the likelihood (she sees no evidence to the contrary) that science will not be enlisted "on the side of the workers."[18] It is her concern for lycée pupils that scientific knowledge, recast on behalf of syndicalism, be popularized. Such a diffusion, a revolution in itself, though not ending the economic and political controls which corporate interests and the technocratic state exert, would at least enlighten their victims. That seems a piteous goal, but at the time of the "Réflexions" Weil could not justify any optimism about the liberating potential of scientific knowledge or the methods for its attainment. Also, she was reacting against the sanguine beliefs of Marxists on this subject. It is not surprising that some of her peers rejected the "Réflexions" for their apparent defeatism.

Subsequently Weil was concerned to preserve from total dissolution the tenets of what she called "the single Greek doctrine," that the universe is intelligible. The instruments of this intelligibility are word concepts she found in *logos*: relation, proportion, measure, analogue, law—all functioning under the canopy of necessity's eternal harmony. The Greek genius lay in geometrical invention, the ability to read number in the universe, number as key to the way things are, whether determinate or indeterminate.

At the center of this Greek endeavor was Pythagoras and his so-called school. All that remains of their work lies in derivative, fragmentary notes and, most important for Weil, in Plato. In him she saw a lone votary of a vanished world, a prophet after the fact, and one whose genius synthesized not only Pythagorean doctrines but also the Greek mystery cults and "very probably Egyptian and other Eastern traditions."[19] She seems to have strayed from science into spirituality, but for her—the point bears iteration—there is no legitimate division between them. The Greeks did not strictly divide them, and so Weil clings to preclassical or Greek thought as the standard by which to judge the subsequent history of science.

Her attitude to the "Greek doctrine" is tantamount to a profession of faith in it. Not incidentally, when discussing Catharism, she wrote that "nothing in my eyes surpasses Plato. Simple intellectual curiosity cannot put one in contact with the thought of Pythagoras and Plato; indeed, in respect to such thought, knowledge and adherence are but a single act of mind."[20] This remark reveals a romantic prejudice like that of Rilke, who dismissed aesthetic criticism on the ground that only love can grasp and fairly judge a work of art. Only one who adheres to Plato truly understands him. Like Alain, Weil is almost completely uncritical of Plato.[21]

Pythagoras and his followers were not the only practitioners of Greek science—in an empirical sense they were not even that—and the recruitment of Plato to science seems a bit forced. Weil was fully aware of the Ionians, the "pre-Socratics," and others who investigated the natural world and spun hypotheses in attempts to determine its constituents. In her "Esquisse d'une histoire de la science grecque" she duly credits Thales' work on proportional means and the measurement of pyramids, Menaechmus's discovery of the parabola, Eudoxus's development of an astronomical system, Archimedes' hydrostatics, and Hippocrates' advances in pathology. But her point in the sketch is to underscore how beholden they all were to "the Pythagorean inspiration" and its dogma of proportion.[22] Elsewhere she notes that Archimedes founded not only statics but "all of mechanics by his purely mathematical theory of the balance, the lever and the center of gravity" and likewise "all of physics" in his theory of the equilibrium of floating bodies.[23] The point of her sweeping remarks is to emphasize the brilliant anticipations of classical science, science from Copernicus until Planck, to be found among the Greeks. Oddly, however, what Weil does not say about Greek science, and especially about Plato's role in its course, most merits attention.

In effect, Greek science was not a uniform enterprise. Countering the naturalistic, that is nontheistic, Ionians and their successors, Plato undertook to bolster a theistic order accessible to the mind alone and thus independent of the empirical world. Nature he disdained as unruly and inferior to the constant and intelligible realm of forms. His idealism stood opposite the inquiring, experimental view of science, then in its inchoate stages, which has long been a commonplace of scientific method. Greek scientists had already employed it in technological inventions, in what Benjamin Farrington has called "a vigorous attack upon nature."[24]

Farrington contends that however halting, hypothetical, and finally short on factual contributions, Greek science might have reached a sophisticated level of technical advance had social crisis not furthered the institution of slavery: "One evil consequence of this was that control of techniques, knowledge of the processes of which is essential for many branches of science, passed into the hands of slaves, and an ideal of science was formed which was largely verbal and unrelated to practice."[25] Plato, according to this analysis, served as the philosophical apologist for a society built on servitude, and his "verbal" science diverted the impetus for an implemental science.

In his defense it should be noted that Plato's presumption of a universal order for the mind to apprehend and laws to which natural phenomena more or less comply reflects a humanistic attitude toward science, one not necessarily opposed to the naturalistic.[26] The Ionians had sought primarily to understand phenomena according to a universal *logos*. Common to both Plato and these naturalists ("physicists" in the Greek denomination, as first used by Aristotle) is an allegiance to the essential, not to the particular. Greek science remained hypothetical. There were, certainly, some extraordinary innovations in mechanics: Archimedes' war machines, the steam engine, and a host of other automata devised by Heron of Alexandria. Both men allegedly regarded their constructions as something like toys. Industrial application, or what Farrington calls "practice," did not occur to them nor to anyone else in their times, and so the effects of their genius remained negligible for centuries.

Although Plato can be credited with a high respect for mathematics and even with the invention of negative numbers, his view that the cosmos is a living organism with soul, body, and reason (the guiding myth of his *Timaeus*) was fantastically retrograde, but it was one with his theism. Within this vision, however, was that contemplative awe of the universe which Weil recognized as the hallmark of Greek scientific inspiration, the reading of *logos* in the world: "This is the discovery that intoxicated the Greeks: that the reality of the sensible universe is constituted by a necessity whose laws are the symbolic expression of the mysteries of faith."[27] One might say, rather, that it was the faithful intoxication of Pythagoras and Plato and of Weil, too.[28]

Superficially considered, this cosmic necessity, whether implied in, say, Anaximander's fragment on the succession of the seasons, or even Anaxagoras's *nous*, which is mind enthroned as the governing power over matter—whatever the nominal guise, this necessity seems nothing more than a metaphysical determinism for which a shackled rationalism implies "the mysteries of faith," and hypothesis becomes credence. What saved the Greeks from a too tidy rationalism was what threatened to destroy reason altogether, the mathematical fact of incommensurables, a discovery that, like the Pythagorean theorem, made Greek science, in Weil's words, the art of conjuring up the world in all its daunting mystery.[29] Greek reason met and overcame the challenge by establishing that a proportion can be determined between incommensurable quantities. The Pythagorean theorem signified a rational geometrical expression of an irrational magnitude: that is, the diagonal of a square with sides of one unit reveals the square root of two. The Greeks' fascination with reading reality mathematically was so thorough that it cannot be wondered that they made little effort to transform revelation into application, that for all their insight they neglected to think of "progress" in the modern sense of subjugating nature for a putative material good. Here is the trump card to be played from Weil's position against Farrington's, that the Greeks created a culture that seems anomalous to the modern mind: it looked to its gods and it did without comforts.

It may be difficult for modern readers to comprehend the nonprogressive Greek temperament as other than an arrest on human initiative, all the more difficult in view of the central role of mathematics, that most supple of mental arts, in Greek science. Like Plato, Weil had no gift for numbers, but for that very reason she could share his enthralled deference to mathematics. Whether mathematics itself involves mystery is secondary here to Weil's response, her perception of it as mystique.

In the *Republic* (509d–511e) mathematics lies on the positive side of a dividing line that separates what might be called animal faith (how we "know" the sun will rise tomorrow) and reflection from the divine heights of dialectical reasoning. That reasoning is an escape hatch from the sordid realm of time. Plato's God himself is forever geometrizing.[30] Weil picks up this accent in observing that mathematics is "thought not subject to imagination and to time." Its inventions are transcendent because they are derived from "absolutely nonrepresentable analogies." The mystical properties of number and harmony lie in the, for her, alluring absence of human predication. They harbor neither fear nor hope, neither desire nor aversion. They purify the mind of all its affective dross.[31]

The peculiar beauty of mathematics resides in what Weil calls the scandal of contradiction, a fundamental element in the world's order: it plays the harmony of contraries.[32] Humanity cannot create contradiction, it can only participate in it, and best of all through geometry. Weil's diction indicates her attempt to recover the Greeks' seismic enthusiasm about the beauty of number. It comes, she says, as reality's shock; the human response is one of *joie*, with a residue of wonder. Number has the koanlike power of inviting one's intuition while putting up "a stony resistance," as in the unity of a circle's various properties.[33] Mathematics is an intellectual's aesthetic, a formidable beauty that keeps the mind struggling toward an impossible attainment. Could anything be more terrible or more enchanting?

From here it is barely a step to Weil's spiritualization of mathematics. The koan of geometry, like mystical rapture, comes down and takes possession of the mind. Mathematics for her has the religious aspect of initiation; it is a purification from error, the conduit to God's impersonality, the image of faith's mystery and of supernatural hierarchy.[34] These highfalutin ascriptions are her signposts upward along Plato's divided line, from the conditionals of demonstration, which belong to necessity, to the elusive conformity that belongs to the good and forms with demonstration the contraries of mathematical harmony.[35]

As mathematics is reality's symbolic script, or, in Weil's description, a topology of supernatural truths, it follows that the proportions of number amount to a divine revelation. Here Weil gets her inspiration from the *Epinomis*, a work dubiously attributed to Plato, in which geometry is depicted as the likening of naturally dissimilar numbers according to the *moira* or destined nature of plane objects. The text concludes that "whoever is able to understand it sees clearly that this marvel is not of human but of divine origin." From there Weil makes her great leap of faith, or rather her yoking of faith, and asks, "Doesn't this show that the Greeks saw in the geometrical mean an image of the Incarnation?"[36]

In Christianity's human geometry, mortal and immortal find congruence on the plane of Christ the god-man, but this conceit is no proof that the Greeks saw and recognized this mean. Weil's peculiar wish is so intense it mothers the thought and the conviction. The Greeks, blessed (or cursed) with a restive intelligence—that unrest is the real gift of Prometheus's theft—must, she says, have been Christians without the name. They, as no one since, could read the divine code: "A variable proportion that includes an absolutely fixed relation, an indefinite increase, and between them a cyclical variation. A point, a circle, a straight line—the circle being the mediator. Circular motion contains all this. It is the image of God's relationship to himself (as seen in the Trinity) and at the same time of God's relationship to creation."[37]

Unfortunately, although geometrical mathematics occupied the center of Greek scientific thought, virtually everything about it prior to Archimedes and Euclid remains in the speculative limbo of hypothesis. There dwells the real mystery, and it was one too down to earth to satisfy Weil's exigent intuition.

But that cold fact did not dismay her; it encouraged her to hallow the Greeks' mathematical penchant. Because "mathematical invention is transcendent" and only "authentic genius" can approach the transcendent, "which is also sainthood's object," it became clear to her that the Greeks were intellectual saints.[38] They could not only read the universe as God's image, they had intimated "the universe as God sees it," in the contradiction known as *logoi alogoi*, ratios or terms that cannot be formulated. Weil is convinced Plato "used to try to discover inexpressible units."[39] One senses that, in Taoist fashion, the struggle to discover is or becomes tantamount to the discovery, that the way to truth is that truth itself. Plato's dialectic is both the way and the goal. Weil finds the *logoi alogoi* the purificatory agent in Greek thought.

The serpent in the garden of this strenuous contemplation of harmonies was algebra. Weil claims that Greek geometry, the employment of nonverbal axioms and postulates, was a refusal to use algebra.[40] But that statement concedes the Greeks' knowledge of it. As her brother has observed, Archimedes at many points supposes an advanced understanding of algebra, and Eudemus, a member of Aristotle's lyceum, wrote its history.[41] For her part, Weil supplies *refus* because she does not want to entertain the possibility that the Greek mathematical genius would forfeit its own contemplative vision as it was refracted through geometry. She considers algebra a debasement of mathematics because through it the *logoi alogoi* are given a name. It amounts to a profanation of mystery, analogous, one might say, to the Hebraic demotion, in her view, of God to a terrestrial power. Only such terms reveal Weil's animus in describing algebra as a leveler, a destroyer of the "inner hierarchy." She even compares algebra to money as triumphant signs of modern times: neither can represent "vertical distances."[42]

Algebra's reduction of intuition to reasoning marks the advent of classical science in the West. In chronology, it dates from the Greeks themselves, specifically from Eudoxus, a contemporary of Plato, but the Renaissance marks its coming of age. Classical science, by which Weil primarily means Newtonian physics, involved the study of natural phenomena as analogues of manual labor, but in fact it was conceiving work without a worker. As Weil neatly puts it, "One finds an impenetrable obscurity, even by running through a school textbook, in the simple, fundamental notions of mechanics and physics."[43] Mass, acceleration, and force have no one in charge of them.

Weil admits that scientific achievements since Galileo have been stunningly impressive. Joseph Lagrange's differential calculus, for instance, helped to create mechanical models for all imaginable conditions in which bodies, static or mobile, are subject to force, that is, to the velocity of other bodies. Nineteenth-century discovery of laws governing energy and entropy reimposed the notion of limit which Eudoxus came upon in working out an integral calculus. In short, classical science by the beginning of the twentieth century had fashioned a compelling view of necessity's dynamics. Was it, then, an advance from the mystical science promoted by Pythagoras and Plato?

At its Platonic best, ancient science had been a numerical road to God, a propaedeutic to a vision of the good. Classical science demystified the ancient tradition by concentrating on necessity rather than the good.

The effects were good and bad. Since necessity is opposite to the good, one term in the supreme contraries implying the other, it can have a purifying use, even as atheism purifies a mind seeking God. Classical science properly used, Weil says, "seeks to read through all appearances the inexorable necessity which makes the world a place where we do not count, where one works, a world indifferent to desire, to aspirations and to good. It studies the sun which shines indifferently on the wicked and the good."[44] For Weil, if science cannot serve as apprentice to the good, it can serve as a laboratory of human misery. Both services are manifestly religious.

Science since the Greeks, however, has not schooled humanity in humility. Evil ensued when classical science lost the spiritual perspective on necessity. How this falling off occurred Weil does not explain, but it is implied in her remark that whereas Greek science was, by its comprehension of contraries, related to Greek art, classical science was related to technology. That is, Greek science took as its subject the relation between order and its conditions, whereas classical science took its subject from the analogue of labor: desire and the conditions for its fulfillment. Both kinds of science confronted the same obstacles of necessity, but the Greeks contented themselves with contemplative affirmation of revealed laws: "Blind necessity which holds us by constraint and appears to us in geometry, is for us something to conquer; for the Greeks it was something to love, indeed it is God himself who is the eternal geometer. From Thales' flash of genius to the moment when the Roman armies crushed them, in the regular return of the stars, in sounds, balances, in floating bodies, everywhere they undertook to read proportions in order to love God."[45]

This romanticizing summary puts Weil in the company of an idealistic enthusiast like Johann Winckelmann, and it is not to be wondered that when she faults classical science for its want of beauty, its failure to touch the heart and confer wisdom, she cites Goethe and Keats for their scorn of Newton.[46] But her opposition to classical science derives not so much from the lovelessness she imputes to it or even from its lack of beauty, but rather to the attitude by which, she believes, it was practiced. Here we pass from the "pure science" of discovery and theory to an ideology and the presumption that everything can be explained: "Classical science wanted to take account only of blind necessity and abolish the notion of order."[47] To indicate its success in popularizing this mission, Weil cites a clergyman's approval of Renan's pronouncement that "the great reign of the spirit will begin only when the material world will be perfectly subject to man."[48]

Nowhere is Weil so contemptuous as when she confronts what she considers spiritual bankruptcy: "In fact nineteenth-century physicists believed there were no more things in heaven and earth than in their laboratory; be it added, their laboratory at the moment an experiment succeeded. Professional obsession was their excuse; those who, without this excuse, shared their credulity were fools."[49] In sum, nineteenth-century science assumed the guise of scientism, became an accomplice to bourgeois nostrums of progress which said that technology would increase wealth and leisure. Education would meanwhile make everyone rational, happy, and moral. Weil recognizes a limited worth in such values; she is careful not to take an altogether dismissive tone toward the recent past. Its central mistake, she feels, was to take these spiritually secondary goods as primary and unlimited: "It was less miserable than our century, but stifling; affliction is worth more."[50]

Weil is not, then, unsympathetic to the breakthroughs of Planck, Einstein, and others who soon confounded classical science and its reliance on the unity of calculable necessity. Modern physics demolished that reliance by reintroducing in discontinuity the Greeks' notion of the unlimited. It removed the illusion that in correlating contraries one term could be suppressed. A sufficient warning should have been discernible in the fact that the mechanical model of energy in classical science cannot account for the irreversibility (revealed in the second law of thermodynamics) that besets the world as we experience it: "We grow old, we die, ashes do not become wood, rust does not become iron."[51]

Chance could not be ignored. Modern science began by introducing probability as an experimental control on chance. It was furthered by refined measuring instruments and by discoveries like Brownian movement. Einstein's relativity theory applied to all possible movement what classical science had applied only to uniform linear movement: time itself became the fourth dimension of space—a paradox whose popularity in her day Weil, like Alain, derided, even as she lamented the implication that science was becoming meaningless or at least closed to common sense. Foremost in importance was Planck's use of probability to reveal discontinuity in energy (black-body radiation). The discontinuous varieties of energy and time (quanta) showed that energy could no longer be confidently related to the established denominations of weight, distance, mass, and velocity.

Weil wrongly assumed that Planck's quanta formulas "are valid for all the exchanges of energy taking place among atoms and radiations."[52] In a letter to her brother, circa 1941–42, she suggested that had Planck used a continuous calculus of probabilities (instead of a discrete number of microscopic states as postulates for the macroscopic "black-body" system he employed in his initial experiments), "One could have done without quanta. What was to prevent it? Planck says nothing about it."[53] This conclusion came from her understanding that Planck believed probability *required* discontinuity. In fact, he (and Ludwig Boltzmann) knew of continuous probability.[54]

Had she known Planck's theory fully and seen that a probability subsuming the continuous and discontinuous would have satisfied her view of necessity, Weil would not likely have attacked him and the scientific establishment of her day, caricaturing modern scientific endeavor as a closed world-village of egoistic specialists contriving hypotheses in a void.[55] (We recall Jonathan Swift's Lagado.) Erroneous as classical science was, Weil notes, it did try to represent scientific truth, but "today's scientists have nothing in their minds, however vague, distant, arbitrary or impossible which they can turn toward and call truth. Still less, therefore, have they any image of a path which could lead them toward it and by reference to which they could control each step of their thought."[56] The loss of scientific truth in an age enthralled by science seems the loss of truth itself, and so, unable to live without some notion of the good, society has substituted utility, not as the servant of intelligence but as its master. Weil compares her time to the age of the Greek sophists, violent in its propaganda and vulgar in its media.

In Weil's writing on science a kind of golden age myth is perceptible. Preclassical (Greek) science was directed toward the good. The two successive developments were degradations: classical science abandoned the good for necessity, and modern science has forfeited even necessity, thus losing its metaphysical way. Weil's polemical simplification of the history of science—she neglects the French and English academies of the seventeenth century—required her to omit facts that would have made a more complicated picture, but one not necessarily detrimental to her argument. For example, the Pythagorean dogma of intelligible harmonies lived on into the European renaissances in the work of Copernicus, Galileo, and Bode. The aesthetic and theistic mainsprings of this dogma were firmly in the mind of Kepler, a devout Christian. Yet Weil supports the church's opposition to Galileo (though not its persecution of him) because his notion of rectilinear movement destroyed the Greek balance or equilibrium of rest and motion which is expressed in uniform circular movement: "If we conceive a pure circle, homogeneous in all parts, nothing is changed when it turns. What thing more beautiful is conceivable? That is what is offered us each day."[57] Abandonment of circular for rectilinear motion became for Weil an emblem of science turning away from God, and she does not hesitate to accuse Newton of impiety for undermining the idea of rotary motion.[58] One need hardly wonder how she would have voted at the trial of Anaxagoras.

If Weil entertains a golden-age-and-decline view of science, she does not presume, as the myth has it, that the lost paradise (of Pythagoras and Plato) is irretrievable. To say, as she does, that "humanity is nostalgic for the circle" does not deny the circle's existence; it simply states that humanity no longer has a grasp of that circle but vaguely longs to.[59] It has lost the ability to read the universe because scientists themselves, society's mediators, cannot or will not read it, but the universe is still apparent.

That last clause should be good news for the Cartesian imperative that science be put within the grasp of the nonscientific or lay mind. Unfortunately, the prestige of science early in the twentieth century allowed what Weil calls an impish delight in the clash between science and reason, "that a single change of scale effects a radical transformation of nature's laws, whereas reason requires that a change of scale alter magnitudes but not the ratios between them . . . that necessities long considered evident become simply approximate when better instruments permit, thanks to the atom, further penetration into the structure of phenomena."[60] Weil argues a questionable dichotomy between reason and modern science. Why should reason not admit nonlinearity? She gives no answer to this question (she does not even pose it) because the intelligibility of the universe seems imperiled, at least for the nonspecialist. That is why she prescribes a return to basics, "a forced arrest . . . not to fabricate an artificial coherence but to make honestly a balance sheet of axioms, postulates, definitions, principles, without omitting those implied by experimental technique itself. . . . Such an effort would perhaps make science knowledgeable, allowing those difficulties, contradictions, and impossibilities to appear clearly which today are hastily cloaked in solutions beyond which the intelligence can no longer perceive anything."[61]

At stake, it seems, are two competing mysteries: on one hand, Weil's mystery, or the relation between the closed mathematical system of perfectly defined conditions and its application in physics to a world that admits no perfection; on the other, the mystery that recasts all thought to an equational level. The latter amounts to algebra's triumph over language, an ascendancy Weil considered catastrophic.

In classical science algebra had served physics as a convenient means of summarizing experimental relationships, but in modern science, Weil objects, it has displaced language itself. Rather, *it* has become a language that flouts common sense. Time as the fourth dimension of space is one such violence, the notion of curved space is another.

Weil seems to abandon her own cherished notion of contradiction. Why, relishing the lively contraries of the koan, does she apparently refuse to consider the possibility that absurdity obtains in science no less than in religion and may form their true common ground? Each has its own hieratic obscurity.

She contends that a profound thought cannot be expressed adequately in ordinary language because language cannot accommodate different levels of meaning. The logical difficulty is that a truth is destroyed when expressed on a particular level of meaning; it is true only when implied in a contrary assertion. Like Weil's God, it prefers to stay hidden and "can then be apprehended solely by minds able to grasp at the same time several superimposed rows of ideas."[62] In algebra, however, equations of letters allow no discrimination between a proof and a hypothesis, between a verification and a conjecture. "If the algebra of physicists produces the same effects as profundity, it is only because it is completely flat; thought's third dimension is absent."[63] By "same effects" Weil means the awe and reverence formerly associated with religious meditation. Modern scientific language has become the object of a mystified lay regard. Weil believes, however, that science has fashioned the emperor's clothes, and the otherwise thinking public, intellectuals in particular, have been duped by their own fear of becoming unfashionable if they do not applaud.

Carried along by her polemical scorn, Weil is unfair to Planck. She accuses him of eliminating humanity from science by promoting fictions and the algebraic disguising of "the human element."[64] It is interesting that she had already leveled the first charge at the classical science which Planck helped to overthrow, that is, the mechanical work models that suppressed the worker's role. Algebra, then, carried on the dehumanization of mechanical physics. But Weil ignores the early history of Planck's theory. When he first argued quanta, his international colleagues regarded his equation as "a lucky mathematical artifice" that classical physics would be able to explain.[65] After all, he had not proved his theory on the microscopic scale, where continuous emission was still assumed. Confirmation came only through experiments that could directly analyze elementary activity. Oddly, an aging scientific dogma had imposed an unwonted skepticism and thus gave birth to a new dogma, destroying itself. Although welcoming this liberation from a superstitiously held determinism, Weil wants "the third dimension of thought," an invocation of Spinoza's "third order of understanding," in which intuition, exalted above reason and imagination, finds special access to spiritual truths. It is clear that the lay reception of quantum theory and of relativity theory recapitulated in her mind the popular response to the discovery of incommensurables in ancient Greece: in each instance, a sophisticated discrediting of the idea of truth ensued.[66] But it remains unclear whether she is expecting scientists to attain the Spinozan higher reaches or merely castigating them for the popularization of their arcane formulas and their elevation to the status of seers. When she says the vulgarization of Einstein's paradoxes is the source of his "rather evil renown," it is difficult to discern whether Einstein or the gullible public stands more to blame in her eyes.[67]

She further charges that modern science has substantially damaged the practice of philosophy and done so with the deferential connivance of philosophers themselves. So that philosophy remain invulnerable, she stresses, like Alain, its territorial integrity, particularly its immunity to the bacillus of progress. She wants to reassert philosophy's primary role of setting limits to what can be thought and not thought, said and not said.[68] Ancillary to philosophy, science builds analogical bridges between the reality of particular objects and universals, or between objects as natural phenomena. Unless we return to this Greek way of science, Weil warns, we shall break our heads against necessity's walls.[69]

Armed with that imperative, she redefines science in Stoic terms. Its aim is "the study and theoretical reconstruction of the world's order . . . relative to the mental, psychological and corporeal structure of man. Contrary to the naive illusions of some scientists, neither the use of telescopes, microscopes, nor the most extraordinary algebraic formulas, nor even the contempt of the principle of noncontradiction allow an exit from the limits of this structure."[70]

Basically, this Stoic enterprise is aesthetic, an apprehension of the universe's beauty. Weil holds to it so tightly that at times she denies that the most ennobling accomplishments in art and science are themselves beautiful.[71] Just as she rejects consolation in religion, so she seems to reject a participatory joy in creative response to the universe. Her intent is corrective: modern science is based on pride, not, like the Greek, on piety: "An original sin adheres to modern science."[72]

Of the three ways in which Weil finds that science can have practical interest, two are implicitly negative. One she calls the chess game of competing theories, in which winners are awarded Nobel prizes.[73] Another is technical application. She saw as clearly as anyone in the prenuclear age that technology could have evil effects as well as good.[74] The likelihood lay with evil because technology "puts force and civilization on the same side. . . . It is accursed."[75] This statement remarkably anticipates the course of "atomic diplomacy" less than five years later, but it is also a corollary to her *aperçu* that every advance away from human bondage to nature brings a more subtle enslavement within social organization. The only remedy is the third application, that science become, indistinguishably from religion, a road to God.

Weil believes that science itself shows the way in the noncommutativity principle of physics: energy in various forms leads to entropy, not to material conversion. Science must exhaust the second order of understanding, the discursive reasoning that apprehends the world's order as mechanical necessity, so as to reveal what part of that order is indemonstrable. It is as though science must go on a quest that will leave it weary, like Siddhartha under the bo-tree. Weil means that it must cultivate mystery and the impossible, "pursue a higher source of inspiration than itself or die."[76] Not incidentally, this peremptory call for a new philosophy of science parallels Weil's call for a new religion: Christianity must either supersede itself and become truly catholic or die. It is because the Greek (Platonic) model of science remains so vividly before her that Weil can affirm that true science is a contemplative, obedient love of the divine.[77]

Science must reestablish the Pythagorean notion of a vertical hierarchy and the humbling sense of limit. It should not seek to be satisfying and coherent—the error of classical science's claim to unity. Weil even suggests that primary schools should inform pupils by a list of "things about which science is in no position to provide any information whatever." Yet science can help to make more precise our relation to the supernatural. Weil epitomizes her position: "A science that does not bring us closer to God is worthless."[78]

In her essay on quanta she notes that the ascent of a nontheistic science is due primarily to negligence by "the official guardians of spiritual values."[79] In *L'enracinement* she takes up the consequences of this debauch in the sociology of science.

Her analysis threatens to demolish all hope for the theistic science she wants to restore. If science has emptied the churches, if its research demonstrates no love of truth, how is science to bring humanity nearer to God? Clerics and theologians, she notes, defer abjectly to their debating opponents in the sciences: "In all the polemics where religion and science appear to be in conflict, there is on the church's side an almost comic intellectual inferiority which is due not to arguments from the other side, generally very mediocre ones, but solely to an inferiority complex."[80] Weil overcredits the decline of faith within the working classes to their awareness of scientific views. (Péguy knew better when he reproached the church for its alliance with propertied interests.) It is not that science has entirely dispossessed churchgoers of their faith: "Whoever has no faith cannot lose it. With few exceptions religious practices have been a convenience for the bourgeoisie. The scientific worldview does not hinder the observation of convenience . . . by those who exploit the people."[81] Tepid middle-class faith would not explain why even among serious believers science has brought a bad conscience. Too few of them, says Weil, dare to be certain their Christianity would survive as the truth in their eyes if, in a genuinely scientific spirit, they started from zero and considered every issue impartially. It is the very fault she found in Pascal, who, although or because he was informed by scientific discipline, did not dare to hope that his intelligence, let free, could arrive at certitude about his religious faith.

It was intellectual certitude that brought Weil her own spiritual affirmations. It does not seem peculiar, then, that when she considers, quite superficially, the modern scientific practice of studying what she calls "only facts as such," she objects: "Facts, matter, force, isolated in themselves, without relation to anything else—there's nothing there that a human thought can love."[82] The dynamic openness of scientific inquiry, the self-correcting skepticism of its methods—none of this satisfies her demand for a fixed, transcendent orientation. A kind of neo-Christian Platonism would make for a rather woolly ideology among modern scientists, and it is strange that Weil, so wary of collectivized (and therefore perverse) expressions of truth, should want to promote what could easily degenerate into another scientism, one perhaps more dangerous in its pretensions than was classical science.

In *L'enracinement* she recalls the chessboard on which the prestige of a false grandeur (false because independent of all thought of the good) exerts its sway like a magnetic field. Some scientists bedazzle the public with the technological applications of their discoveries. Like politicians in an earlier age, they now enjoy the intoxicating power of shaping human destiny. Worse in Weil's estimate are those who feel or affect indifference to the implementation of their theories or findings. She likens them to a race of gods that has reduced humanity to an ant heap. Others, stimulated by technology's potential, do not hesitate to pursue it, regardless of social consequences.

Weil's blurry charges take on forceful relevance; she set them down at the time of the Manhattan Project: "A scientist who feels himself on the point of making a discovery capable of devastating human life exerts every effort to arrive at it. It scarcely or never happens that he stops to weigh the probable effects of this devastation, good and evil, and gives up his research if evil seems the more likely."[83] In this context, religious attention to the good hardly seems anachronistic; it would exert a vital check on whatever egotism propels scientists. Weil is shrewdly aware of the allure of public status. In a passage inspired by Plato's comparison of the truly just man put to torture and the apparently just but wicked man who thrives in popular esteem (*Republic* 360b–362c), she hypothesizes a choice for scientists: either to dwell once and for all in idiocy's darkness but with enough presence of mind to feel its bitterness, or to enjoy in oneself an efflorescence of intellectual abilities bringing worldwide acclaim and lasting glory but with the qualification that one's thoughts are always a little outside of the truth: "Can we feel that many would sense the slightest hesitation before making such a choice?"[84] Only a hairshirt like Weil (or Plato) could conceive such scenarios, but she makes a point worthy of La Rochefoucauld, that people are inclined to love the error which is their own rather than the truth which belongs to no one.

She resumes the attack on specialization and the isolated village of each discipline where collective opinion rules. "That is especially the case in physics, where the very means of research and control are a monopoly in the hands of a very closed milieu."[85] It is as though she had found in the scientific professions a vulgarized version of that "transcendent realm" that admits only geniuses like her brother. Instead of a supernal light, however, a Darwinian contest was at work: "Theories push on as though by chance and the fittest survive. Such a science can be a form of *élan vital* but not a form of the search for truth."[86] Here she betrays her impatience with the fundamental task of scientific methods, to submit theory to experimentation in order to verify, modify, or reject it. That must be the work of a limited number of people, and it is hard to conceive how such a group could be effectively extended. Quantum theory "survived" because laboratory instruments became refined enough to address it, but Weil regards the quantum revolution as a change of fashion: "If people hadn't been so infatuated with quantum theory when Planck first proposed it, even though it was absurd—or because it was absurd, indeed people were tired of reason—it would never have been known how fecund this theory was."[87] But these remarks avoid two facts: Planck's theory was not initially given a welcoming band's reception, and Planck himself, conservative in temper, was no fashion designer.

Weil's charge that scientific consensus is fashion obviously exaggerates. A fashion is aimless, capricious, short-lived, but thinking in science proceeds generally by slow accretions of evidence. Of course, a revolutionary theory or discovery by definition confounds nearly all that has preceded it. Perhaps it is science's revolutionary thrust, overriding the past, that most distresses Weil. Contemporary scientific theories constitute, like a martial triumph, that victor's camp from which justice seems to have fled. As Thomas Kuhn has observed, "Scientific education makes use of no equivalent for the art museum or the library of classics, and the result is a sometimes drastic distortion in the scientist's perception of his discipline's past."[88] Weil denies the future toward which science's linear advance is directed the name of progress because she is convinced that the disinterested love of truth does not figure in the scientist's motivations, and so it will not be found in science itself.[89] The objection seems odd because Weil had not long before criticized Augustine for inverting the Christian message, "by their fruits ye shall know them." Augustine had contended that an evil tree cannot bear good fruit, and that seems to be Weil's assumption about modern science.[90] But one can be mistaken in premises and still arrive at a sound conclusion, and much substantial work in science has likely been achieved without its agents reflecting upon their love of truth or even presuming to know what it is. Yet it is to the loss of that love in science, in religion, in contemporary thought that Weil, looking to Vichy and the war, attributed "the atrocious evils in which we are now struggling."[91]

Weil's criticism of modern science peculiarly fails to appreciate its similarity to Greek science in seeking a fundamental law governing material movement. Even as early Hellenic thinkers attempted to identify a primary constituent in all substances (Thales was first, nominating water) and then looked to a governing law at work in all substances (characterized in Anaximander's fragment on the seasons), so early twentieth-century physicists attempted to determine whether motion could be explained in terms of known waves (protons and mesons) or of a universal substance in which elementary particles would have no priority relative to one another. As Werner Heisenberg has noted, the notion of harmony as the maintenance of opposites in a tension of constant exchange (the dogma of Heraclitus) anticipated the modern idea that strife between opposites is at work in two different forms of energy. More intriguing, when Heisenberg predicted that quantum theory would identify elementary particles as mathematical forms rather than substances, he alluded to Plato's mathematics of particles in the *Timaeus*: "If we follow the Pythagorean line of thought we may hope that the fundamental law of motion will turn out as a mathematically simple law. . . . It has hitherto always been possible to write the fundamental equations in physics in simple mathematical form. This fits in with the Pythagorean religion, and many physicists share their [the Pythagoreans'] belief in this respect, but no convincing argument has yet been given to show that it must be so."[92] What more could Weil have asked?

These words help assess strengths and weaknesses in Weil's thinking about science not because they reveal an ongoing or neo-Pythagorean orientation that might have appeased her (it enjoyed a greater life in Germany than in France) but because they succinctly provide a professional's view of how science really works. Whatever the accumulated facts, the conceptions of science, like those of religion, require some inspiration and must overcome a good deal of superstition. Anyone familiar with the history of science in the West knows that much has been owed to false starts, luck, and intuition (guess). As Goethe, himself no mean student of science, once remarked, there are positive uses for error. They may even be indispensable correctives. Heisenberg shows that there are indispensable elements of scientific thinking one generally associates with religion: hope and humility. The *libido sciendi*, which must fuel all theory and research, is tempered by awareness that a chosen line of thought may prove unfruitful. Dogma, in science no less than in religion, tends to ossification. Weil saw that classical science had nowhere to go, yet she was impatient with the apparent aimlessness of modern science. What perhaps most annoyed her was the open-ended skepticism in scientific thinking which theories like Planck's and Einstein's renewed and energized. She could not wait for a "convincing argument" to validate her Pythagoreanism because it was her article of faith.

Heisenberg's tentative, qualified tone suggests the necessary route of adventure; the scientist does not know in advance where facts and theories may lead. Methodical willingness to follow them shows a humility toward truth rivaling, if not exceeding, any religious credo of love, Weil's included. She expressly required a vertical goal, the Stoic love of universal order and of God—a difficult, dubious business. Although scientists would not likely agree to tailor theory and research to an exclusive metaphysical donnée, that does not mean they have been blind to mystery or the inexplicable within the phenomena of their inquiries. Weil gratuitously ascribes to science a blindness that is simply procedural caution or, in the case of indigestible notions like curved space, hypothesis which is as worthy of doubt (in Alain's positive sense) as any other.

As to mystery, the history of science contains many examples of illustrious minds confessing awe before natural wonders. Jean Henri Fabre, for instance, physicist turned entomologist, marveled at the god he believed responsible for insects' cross-pollination. Thales had led the way in saying that all things are full of gods. Still, scientists' fascinations lie within phenomena; they belong to the world of necessity, not to God or an a priori truth.

Heisenberg's experiment of an imaginary microscope capable of observing and measuring electrons ushered in a new metaphysics that complements Weil's notion of necessity. In Karl Popper's words, "We try to catch the thing in itself, but we never succeed. We only find appearances in our traps."[93] Weil might say that any number of empirical truths do not add up to the truth she means. The hazard is to presume that empirical truths lead to metaphysical ones. Truth, in her estimate, lies beyond intelligence; its value can be apprehended only indirectly, by its effects, but as we are condemned to illusions ("our traps"), truth may seem false. Only a loving intuition or desire of it makes it accessible.[94] This mystical, as opposed to scientific or demonstrable, truth awaits, Weil insists, anyone who attends to it. It helped her overcome the crushing failure of her intellectual inability to follow her brother into the "transcendent realm" reserved for genius. Suspicious of consolation in religious feelings, she seems to have been consoled by her own notion of mystical access. A good deal of her resentment toward science seems to lie as a kind of residue in this uplift. Although she untiringly pursued what Aristotle called the natural human desire to know, she distrusted and so deprecated those who seemed gifted in satisfying that desire.

In an essay on wave mechanics, she says:

> One is undoubtedly deceived in believing he finds in these strange games of modern science secrets known only to initiates. Notions of space, time, causation are the same for the most eminent physicist as for an illiterate peasant; all the physicist possesses more of is the precise knowl-

edge of instances where these common notions are incapable of organizing into a coherent system the ensemble of experimental données and their simplest interpretation.[95]

But such a difference puts considerable distance between physicist and peasant, not to mention the rest of us who might not have thoughts on causation, space, or time worthy to be called ideas. Weil makes the very point she wishes to contest.

Her scorn of chess game laureates prompted this gloss: "Passion for the chase. We mustn't wish to find. As with an excess of devotion, we become dependent on the object of our efforts, looking for some extrinsic reward which chance occasionally provides and which we are ready to take at the cost of distorting the truth."[96] It is as though the brilliance of a scientific theory, especially when recognized, demotes the supernatural. The wonders of the inquisitive human mind do not figure as part of the universal beauty Weil would have us contemplate. This position is wholly consistent with her conviction that human existence is an ontological offense and can manufacture only illusions. It is also consistent with her notion that a genuine love of truth is a consent to death: Christ's cross is the sole avenue to knowledge.[97] This statement concludes Weil's arraignment of Descartes for promoting the idea of progress and celebrates the past as "real and better than we are, [and] able to draw us upward, something the future never does." What, then, of science, which implicitly shortchanges its past by correcting and reformulating problems and discovering new ones? Its "ewig Weibliches" resides in today and tomorrow, not in yesterday.

There is yet another reason for Weil's uneasiness about science. Whatever the limits which theory or experiment impose on consciousness, whatever the constraining wonder a scientist might feel before mystery, there is an élan or creativity in scientific effort that runs against Weil's program of decreation and truth through the cross but which is also integral to that sense of beauty which her devotion to Plato could never deny. Why should the world's beauty not be present in scientific theory? When Einstein proposed his theory of relativity some physicists said it was too beautiful to be false—the very criterion Weil used for accepting gospel stories: they were so beautiful there had to be truth in them.[98] Paul Dirac, first theorist of anti-matter (particles have complementary, that is, positive and negative values), once claimed it is more important that a theory be beautiful than that it be true.[99] Harmony and symmetry being desiderata in scientific theory, a scientist's work is akin to art.[100] Weil argues as much in saying the business of science is to seize hold of the universe, not merely to study but to reconstruct the world's order, to find out what mathematics gives us of transcendent truth. The practice of modern science is no less devoted and is surely immeasurably better equipped than was Greek science in the reading of the world, but Weil, precipitous and anxious, does not appreciate that fact.

Just as her new religion would constitute primarily a restoration of the mediated mystery she found everywhere in antiquity save Rome and Israel, her new science would serve chiefly as reaffirmation of the ancient Greek notions of limit, proportion, and equilibrium. It would correct the human imposition of absolutes upon the finite, a practice Weil says is the source of the world's sin and suffering. Science rightly understood is antidote to despotism by pointing to the *délivrance* of "reading limit and relation in all sensible appearances without exception, as clearly and immediately as a meaning in a printed text."[101] To an age threatened by political or religious fanaticism, science could perform as a cautionary break. This chastening is not a function one might associate with science, but it is as vital as any liberating dynamic.

Considering the social uses of science, Weil is caught between a Platonic elitism of static, theoretical contemplation and a Cartesian dynamic toward democratic implementation of scientific understanding. The antinomy is not obvious or even inevitable. Why should anyone not be able to go the length of Plato's divided line, master dialectic, and gaze upon the divine harmonies? But Plato was no democrat; he presumed the anagogic way so steep that few would last its course, and even in his republic of the mind it is not clear whether leadership belongs to a corps of matriculated guardians or to dialectic's sole surviving pupil, the philosopher-king. Yet none of this argues decisively against a widely disseminated instruction and popularization (in the positive sense) of science. Even in an age of specialization, the educable mind could be expected to know something about everything and one thing well.

In her "Réflexions" on oppression and freedom Weil commends Descartes for seeking the common sense of science so that it might help every artisan understand his craft. Descartes, she submits, showed himself more a socialist than did all of Marx's disciples. Mind and world are conjoined in work; through physics and mathematics, science interprets that conjunction. In tandem with Weil's endorsement of Descartes runs her Goethean view of life as one's continual self-creation, a dynamic that attains a quasi-socialist dimension in Faust's cooperative labor.

Weil did not give up her early Cartesian enthusiasm for a socialized science. Indeed, toward her life's end that enthusiasm found a major key that the gloomy dissonance of prewar industrial capitalism had made impossible. But she could not see how modern science could inform the syndicalist ideal. Einstein and quanta, she claims, cannot be integrated into the workers' culture. So the mechanical model of classical science, which she knew was now discredited, served her as the analogy tying human toil to nature: "Classical science belongs to the workers, if one knows how to present it to them, far more naturally than to students of the lycée."[102] That means the workers' university she envisions would be condemned to an intellectual anachronism. Here her love of the past is recidivist, as though she wanted to situate the workers' culture in a world that Planck, Einstein, and modern physics could not penetrate, where classical assumptions about space and time, and therefore about labor's essential bondage to necessity, could still operate. Inversely, she wanted human work to remain the indispensable model for science: "The idea of work resides at the root of physics and governs it completely. . . . 'Classical mechanics' represents a particular relationship between work supplied and work restored. There lies, apparently, the essence of our compact with the world."[103] Modern science violated this compact, it seems, and therefore must have abandoned the love of truth.

She finds Descartes culpable. Though she hails his populism and his pleas for common sense, she traces to this workers' champion the idea of progress, which she calls "the poison of our time." She also finds him guilty of making algebra a dogma: "Descartes's mistake, in mathematics as in mechanics and physics, was the belief that all quantitative ratios are composed with a straight linear movement as number is with unity, and that therefore algebra affords the key to everything."[104] Worst of all, he was an example of the view that science is the method for mastering nature. Weil subscribed to Bacon's dictum that nature is overcome only by submission to it (*natura non nisi parendo vincitur*), yet she gave final emphasis to submission, not mastery. *Parendo*, the submissive means, became an end in itself through her sacrament of labor. She would not have sacrificed *parendo* for a scientist's *intelligendo* any more than she would have entrusted postwar laborers to a lesson in quantum mechanics.[105]

A Cartesian popularization of science would help workers understand the techniques of their labor, but it would not give them revolutionary power. The social business of science, according to Weil, is to advance a conscious, rational method that will ensure work as a human value and its organization as a cooperative use of human intelligence. In her conjunction of science and work, each establishes an equipoise between mind and body. In some notes on work as the paradigm of classical mechanics, Weil claims that "nonqualified work, the most elementary, the grossest form of work," is the model for technology. She exemplifies the relationships of mind and body: "I want to move a matchstick. I do so. I think of a melody, and without even knowing it, my fingers strike the notes. The second instance requires apprenticeship, the first does not. Science is constituted entirely upon the first model, magic upon the second: magic, the efficacy of disciplined thought. Greek aesthetics is related to both. Every action, a mélange of the two (even mechanics)."[106] Scientific practice, necessarily voluntarist, will always be modeled on work. It is an exertion on the world that, as exertion, implies submission, even in the playful, inductive experimentation (what would happen if?) which Bacon performed. But surely technology has the efficacy of magic. The "Greek aesthetic" Weil refers to has its first exemplum in the shop of Hephaestus (*Iliad* 18.417–21) where maidenlike automatons carry out his metallurgic bidding. The Greeks dreamed of release from toil, but Weil does not explore or even countenance the implications of a modern technology that might provide the leisure her beloved Greece could maintain only through slavery.

She might even have challenged Alfred North Whitehead's statement that "Civilization advances by extending the number of operations which we can perform without thinking about them."[107] Such an extension (call it progress) is linear and indeterminable, and it threatens the balance she would uphold in her Greek aesthetic mélange. Contra Whitehead, she would have humanity learn, in the words of a Nobel chess player, "to think about, adjust, subdue and re-direct activities which are thoughtless to begin with because they are instinctive. Civilization also advances by bringing instinctive activities within the domain of rational thought, by making them reasonable, proper and cooperative."[108] This cooperation is exactly what Weil intended as the social task of science, especially in its humane rationalization of work processes. Yet she did not ascribe to science the meliorism implied in this social service. It is as though all she would ask of an applied science—and all she would grant it can legitimately do—is the discovery of some recondite balance to harmonize the worker and his labor's object. To give the mind full consciousness of its operation upon the world must not signify the world's subjugation. Weil would amend Bacon's dictum to *Natura non vinci potest*, nature cannot be overcome. At no point does she entertain, as popular fictions in her time provided, that technology could supersede nature.

The shortcomings of the splendid architectonic beauty of Greek science, which Whitehead appreciated no less than Weil, have been exposed by Erwin Schrödinger, the Austrian mathematical engineer who theorized on wave mechanics. He is another Nobel villager, but no cramped specialist. Like Weil, he notes that the Greeks knew about irrational numbers, the infinite, and even relativity (he cites the Sophists as first to state problems not by "yes" or "no" but "that depends"). The Greeks' very fear of limitless process, says Schrödinger, caused them to deny their physics a dynamism. Zeno's paradox of Achilles and the tortoise terrified them because they refused to analyze movement in single successive phases. The aesthetic criterion is inextricably involved in this refusal in that the Greeks "thought of the path along which a body moved as a whole, not as something that develops but as something that is already there in its entirety. In looking for the simplest type of motion the rectilinear one was excluded because the straight line is not perceptible in its entire range—rectilinear motion is never completed, can never be grasped as a whole."[109]

These are exactly the terms of Weil's prejudice: modern science's rectilinearity was, she feared, literally going nowhere, or rather to a not apprehensible "there." As Schrödinger adds, the Greeks saved themselves by presuming that the circular path of heavenly bodies is both natural and perfect and is propelled by a yet greater central mechanism. There resides Weil's God, like Dante's "Amor che muove il sole e l'altre stelle." Her theistic science of contemplated symmetries and vertical direction is medieval.

What, then, of work as a model for science? In her *cahiers* Weil continues to regard the idea of work as basic to popularized science, but as she moves toward a theistic philosophy of labor that makes work a consent to death, a habitual elimination of "I," and a descent into matter—in all this the limitation she would set upon science is clear. Science must not shape a technology to free workers from their labor because leisure, being negative (not work), is not an object of desire. Science's proper object is the world's providential order; it must experience the reality of the Word; its destiny is to be a bridge leading to God. But this mystery is static, even as its mechanical expression in natural phenomena and in work is circular and reciprocal, not linear.[110]

"If priests were to show young mechanics learning their trade images of the highest religious truths. . . ?" Thus begins one of Weil's reflections on science as a falling off of attention to mystery. Astronomy, she notes, came from astrology, chemistry from alchemy, but both are debasements because they lack the contemplative symbol-reading of "truth" once known to astrologers and alchemists.[111] It seems that the *Urwissenschaft* of the zodiac is more scientific than astronomy. Weil could "read" zodiacal signs and interpret them as God's symbolic movement through history. She even contrives to find a liturgical symbolism in them.[112] She implies that science, once it becomes theistic, is the preserve of hierophants. She does not see that nothing could more likely alienate workers from science than this privileged access to its supposed arcana in higher astrology and alchemy.

That point recalls the elitism of Platonic science, which had no room for Descartes's university for workers. To some degree Descartes's own conception of science worked for this elitism and against the popular enlightenment he hoped to promote. He had come to it, as Weil knew, through an almost mystical revelation early in his adulthood when he realized that mathematics holds the key to the order of the universe. Such was the Pythagoreans' credo two thousand years before him. It made Plato require mathematical acumen of his academicians. Descartes believed mathematics could explain everything, from the solar system to barnyard chickens, as a mechanism, but he was so entranced with the overarching scheme of mathematical principles that he slighted the particulars of observation and experiment. He criticized Galileo for seeking particular effects at the expense of nature's "first causes."[113] Yet it is Galileo's orientation, his efforts at exact quantitative measure of rolling bodies on an inclined plane, for instance, or his improvement of Hans Lippershey's telescope, that would make immediate, demonstrable sense to lycée students and factory workers—far more sense than the contemplation of universal harmonies and "first causes." As a teacher Weil had at least nominally recognized the value of experimentation, but lacking laboratory training, she felt the hieratic pull or "mystery" of a presumed aesthetic in nature. Like Descartes she wanted to reach immovable a priori truths. She went further, however, by entertaining the fantasy of an intuitive geometry, wordless and free of demonstration, the mathematical exercise, it would seem, of Spinoza's third order of understanding. What could be more elitist than a silent science for initiates?

That initiation, however, would be, like labor, a consented obedience. Weil would sequester scientific genius to limbo, secure at least from the hubristic pull of Nobel prizes and popular esteem. It is not in whimsy that she commends the nineteenth-century German mathematician Karl Gauss for having pocketed a discovery that years later someone else made and publicized. Not only was his gesture a show of disinterested love of truth, she says, it was a vote for eternity.

She decried the vulgar treatment of science in her day as "a sort of supernatural oracle," yet she herself was disposed to recast modern scientific notions into the oracular terms of ancient Greek thought.[114] For example, Niels Bohr's discovery of complementarity between matter as wave and as corpuscle was "nothing but the ancient correlation of contraries which was basic to the thinking of Heraclitus and Plato."[115] Brownian movement simply restated the ancient discovery that the atom is always accompanied by chance, and chance, as she knew from Plato, governs all our lives.[116] Modern physics, then, tends willy-nilly to reassert the old Greek philosophical verities about necessity. All that is missing for Weil, fatally, is a transcendence that will allow analogies between natural phenomena.

Her Platonic science would be an a priori contemplation of the universe, an orientation to a dialectic that dispenses with hypothesis, an aesthetic of love, a mathematical mysticism. It is a Christian science as well, in that Weil reads in Archimedean mechanics a divine symbolism: Christ's cross is the fulcrum, a descending movement being the condition for an ascending one.[117] Weil's imagined priest entering a factory to explain to workers the spiritual import of their machinery's rhythms might be called a practitioner of this Christian or Platonic science. One may wonder whether Weil's Cartesian university for workers would have amounted to anything more than this kind of instruction.

To some people in the late twentieth century, however spiritually astray they may be, this hierophantic science probably bears no more relation to science than star-gazing or symbol-reading astrology does to astrophysics. Perhaps even Teilhard's enthusiasts would be hard put to endorse it. This "bridge toward God" would not materially improve humanity's lot on earth, including that of working people. Weil writes of the Greeks having turned all activity save manual labor toward God. Ancient Greece had no spirituality of work, "which is why its cause was betrayed by its workers and manufacturers."[118] Oddly, unable to bear the fact of Greek slavery, the economic basis of the Greeks' contemplative life, she blames its victims. It would have been far more reasonable of her to reproach Plato for having exempted his guardian-theoreticians from technical work and thus from a collaboration between thought and manual labor.[119]

Weil's theistic science of symbols and analogies may best be understood as a defense against the *libido sciendi*, the irrepressible urge to know that gives scientific inquiry its momentum, whether an individual's theory or a laboratory's teamwork. Why did she oppose this urge?

In the *via negativa* of mysticism she had followed the traditional response to God's unknowability: because God cannot be humanly comprehended he must be desired. But in science, theory itself becomes the desired reality, a working construct ever subject to imaginative transformations. Knowledge comes by equation, not description. As Bachelard wrote, the scientist believes in the realism of measurement more than in the reality of the object.[120] As though in retort to Bachelard (whom in fact she never mentions), Weil attacks what she perceives to be the psychological mainspring in the elastic, skeptical, questing efforts of science: the pleonexia at the root of human life itself: "No one is long satisfied with living pure and simple. One always wants something more. One wants to live for something. It's enough not to lie to oneself to know there's nothing here on earth to live for. Imagine all one's desires satisfied. After a while, one will be dissatisfied. Wanting something else, one will be wretched in not knowing what to want."[121] It is hard to place scientific endeavor within this context of sin and suffering. Weil, herself so restless, was impatient with the elementary restlessness of human imagination and human curiosity, and nowhere is this more apparent than in her attitude toward modern science.

She would allow it to go anywhere provided religious inspiration guided it toward God. Curiously, this predetermination of the course of scientific thought recalls her own criticism of Pascal, that in searching for God he had betrayed his intellectual probity: "Having had an intelligence shaped by scientific practice, he didn't dare to hope that in leaving this intelligence to its own free play it would recognize a certitude in Christian dogma. And he didn't dare moreover to run the risk of having to do without Christianity. He undertook an intellectual search deciding in advance where it had to lead him."[122] Weil provides in her theism an egregious example of what Bachelard called an epistemological obstacle, an irrational preconception imposed on the open course of scientific reasoning. Bachelard saw that the scientific community often creates its own impediments, makes sacred cows of its own predominant theories, and he would perhaps have seconded Weil's criticism of the closed village of specialists. But the renewal ensured by questioning gives scientific thinking its vitality.

Weil was not alone in her reaction. If she is dismissed as a crank, she shares distinguished company. "It isn't absurd . . . to believe that the scientific and technical age is the beginning of the end for humanity; that the idea of great progress is a delusion, just as it is a delusion that man will ultimately know truth; that there is nothing good or desirable about scientific knowledge and that mankind, by striving for it, is running into a trap."[123] This gloomy caveat against the Faustian impulse comes from Weil's fellow Jew and fellow exile

Ludwig Wittgenstein. It seems particularly relevant because it came late in his life (1947), when he had passed from positivism's athletic logic to mystical preoccupations that banished metaphysics and ontology altogether. Thus he might stand accused of retreat into the irrational even as Weil, superficially considered, can be arraigned for giving up Cartesian rationalism and Alain for Christian mysticism and Perrin.

Given her unqualified allegiance to a Platonic view, her call for a new science is suspect. Her devotion to antiquity exposes a neglect or unawareness of science as teamwork. Even Descartes's genial presumption that society's good might be advanced through letters exchanged among savants belongs to a vanished world, where confident individual minds could go their own heroic way. In Weil's time, science harnessed to capitalism and the bureaucratic state bore a sinister aspect. Supposedly scientific rationales for social, political, and economic organization masked totalitarian intents. Whether her theistic science harbored another form of totalitarianism is a delicate point.

Its libertarianism should not be shortchanged. Her science is fully legitimate in its procedural rigors, but it is not an open sesame. It elucidates problems; it does not resolve them. In her "Réflexions" on oppression she calls for a methodical study of what technical progress amounts to and what can minimize social and economic bondage. She feels the scientific study of history aids these endeavors. Let science give to the mind what truly belongs to mind alone, she enjoins, and let it be secure from collective and automatic procedures. If science can serve despotic interests, why should it not serve humane ones as well?[124]

Her many subsequent references to method offer a good indication of how she continued to maintain an experimental orientation together with the Platonic or contemplative. "Is it necessary to act methodically? That's it, to act. The world exists only as object of a methodical action."[125] That is the Cartesian way, but it is also the way of a scientific inquiry that might be divorced from all moral concerns. Weil's antidote to a potentially amoral *libido operandi* and a science used for world subjugation is an attention to the good, which is beyond all human capacity for manipulation. She characterizes this attention as a humbling submission to time, immobile yet creative. As intuition, it supplies apprehended truths to the discursive intellect and so can be called ancillary to scientific reasoning.[126] It is theory in the old sense of the word: it beholds.

It would not be fair to say that Weil gave up Descartes for Plato, retreating from a dynamic humanistic science to a static, theistic one. Rather, she was fusing them into a sort of experimental theism. She made a science of religious sensibility.

To take a dramatic example: she asks herself, How is one to know God's will? She answers that by producing in oneself a silence free of all desires and by giving full attention to "Thy will be done," one can be confident that whatever one feels impelled to do thereafter is God's will.[127] This procedure belongs to faith, not to science. It is hardly disinterested and remains open to autosuggestion. It presupposes a divine will, and it even co-opts the grace most believers would regard as a sheer gift. Weil admits that one may be mistaken about one's agenda after such an exercise, but this example also shows her faith in what she termed experimental certitudes.[128] In another instance, she ascribed to an attentive recitation of the Lord's Prayer the experimental value of effecting "an infinitesimal but real operation within the soul."[129] One of the most fascinating claims of her fideistic empiricism is that an undiminished attention to the mistakes one makes in school exercises would induce a feeling of humility far superior to physical mortifications such as fasting. This belief prompted her to an essay on how schoolwork, properly used, prompts a love of God and puts one on the way to truth: "When one is constrained by violence to fix the eyes, including that of the soul, on a classroom exercise stupidly botched, one feels with irresistible evidence that one is something mediocre. No knowledge is more desirable. If one comes to know this truth with all one's soul, one is well established on the true way."[130] It is a Calvinistic application of Descartes's truism that one cannot grasp anything from someone else so well as when one finds it out for oneself. The humiliations an instructor might visit on a blundering student are nugatory in comparison with this inner "purification."

Many instances of such private experimentation can be drawn from Weil's notes and essays. One's aesthetic sense, for example, can be used to secure "experimental verification" of purity in "religious things." With love and faith (that is, attention) one arrives at a kind of proof for Christianity through Romanesque architecture, Gregorian chant, and the Lord's Prayer.[131] In her meditation on that thoroughly Jewish prayer she remarks that the petition "lead us not into testing" is grounded on the fear of one's abandonment to oneself upon contact with evil, a condition in which "the nothingness of man is then experimentally verified."[132] The point is that the individual sensibility is engaged in all such conditions of learning. One does not merely perform experiments; one lives them. The Cartesian imperative is preserved against the collective dogmas of science.

In a sense, the whole of Weil's writing life can be read as an attempt to maintain the experimental initiative. As early as her *normalien* thesis on Descartes she posed the question: "Must we submit ourselves blindly to these scientists who see for us, as we once submitted ourselves blindly to priests who were themselves blind, if the lack of talent and leisure keeps us from entering their ranks?" Or has the scientific revolution given the egalitarian lesson that the domain of pure thought is the sensible world itself? Can we presume that this supposedly hieratic and privileged knowledge is in fact "la pensée commune"? "Nothing is more difficult, and at the same time more important for every person to know. Indeed, it is a matter of nothing less than knowing if I must submit the conduct of my life to the authority of scientists, or to the exclusive lights of my own reason; or rather as it is up to me to decide that, if science will bring me liberty or legitimate chains."[133]

Weil found in and beyond science both the liberty and the chains, both the imperative to discover and the grounds for acceptance. Necessity and *malheur* gave her the laboratory structures for determining the limits of human existence. Within these prisons, reason must pursue not only its discursive path to "laws" but also "the irreducible logic of absurdity" in human life.[134] Beyond science and reason Weil followed intuition in the belief that it alone when "pure" approaches the transcendent. She wanted to make of Spinoza's third order a new science for discovering "the mysteries of daily life" and determining where a good becomes evil.[135] As a contemplative, not corrective enterprise, it does not pose problems for resolution but dwells on insolubles. But the insoluble is a nonproblem for scientists; it belongs to philosophy.

It seems that science as a problem-setting task, using analogical models and theoretical constructs, is for Weil exclusively an aesthetic, not an epistemological business. Indeed, she remarks, as though in accord with Dirac, that the goal of science is beauty, not truth. It must create a system of necessity's images. Truth is the goal of philosophy, but it is attainable only by intuition, when one not only knows but apprehends: "To contemplate the difference between knowing and knowing with all of one's soul. When one is surprised by something foreseen (it happens to me frequently in these tempestuous times), it's that one had not foreseen it with all of one's soul."[136] The paradox is that what one grasps so totally has no determinable significance, no formulaic meaning. It is beyond science. Suffering offers the capital example: it is unavoidable, irreducible, foreign, but real. Its supreme value for Weil is not, as often alleged, masochistic but epistemological.

Weil's "new science" extends the mind beyond reason's limits even while it denies the mind categorical affirmations and all the apparatus of hypothesis, demonstration, and proof. If scientists are compelled by questions they cannot yet answer, Weil holds out for contemplation the void where nothing can be answered. Like Proust, she knows that nothing is so satisfying as the desire that is not satisfied. For her ontology of mediocre human existence, she finds a complement in the radical inadequacy of human inquiry. Here she owes something to intentionality and its author, Franz Brentano, or at least to his successor, Edmund Husserl, whom we know she read. According to this dogma, all mental acts are fallible; the objects of one's thought do not necessarily exist, nor are they necessarily true. The implication for science is that its practitioners are not so much world discoverers as they are storytellers and imagemakers—these being positive, not pejorative, denominations. Dirac's remarks on beauty and Bachelard's on measure over the thing measured support this point. Weil says intentionality must be applied to all things, and she shows the way by resuming Plato's lesson that nothing but the good is the object of human endeavor. What one believes to be good might be wicked, but it is nonetheless pursued as a good.[137] Weil argues that since the world is imperfect, all we seek within it is imperfect, and so every presumed good is inadequate. Imagination, especially when it addresses a collectivity's needs, disguises this inadequacy by making relative, conditional goods into apparent absolutes. Science works to similar ends as its technology serves up a limited good to society with the promise of something better to come. It is the feeding of the Great Beast in Plato's parable.

No contingent good is ever adequate. To cite Weil's example, one eats bread but is soon hungry again. Only the will to good goes on, and without one's knowing what the good is. Even God is not the good as far as we think of God. The good is not an object but something unobtainable within the need of it. Necessity continues to supply the will a means through energy and gives it short-term ends in particular objects, but the will cannot escape the iteration of pleonexia, of needing ever more. Science is an epistemological pleonexia. Weil did not appreciate that the aims of science amount to something more than the accretion of loveless data and that it has to move in a linear progression. She realized that to arrest this *libido sciendi* would be to deny the distinctly human, but she thought it far better to give up the unsatisfactory vicissitudes of human striving than to go on with its piecemeal benefits: "We must renounce existence. Return from rectilinear movement to circular movement. Want solely to direct our steps above—where it is impossible to go. Want the impossible. Embrace absurdity with one's mind. Love evil."[138] One of her definitions of decreation is pertinent here: it is the certitude that comes when all temporal desires have been rejected and one is living in "truth."[139] Obviously, no scientific truth is meant.

Conclusion

Weil's metaphysics either cancels science altogether or absorbs it into a contemplative exercise. That exercise is not necessarily a pretext for mysticism. Indeed, Weil upholds reason because it is exacting, and the attraction of Greek geometry for her lay not only in its symbolic imagery of the supernatural but in the demonstrative rigors by which such imagery is fashioned. Still, her entrancement with the circle as mediator between the finite and the infinite, her desire to resume the Greek craving for "an identity of structure between the human mind and the universe," argues a very confining axiology of science.[140] The cosmic breadth of her conception of science ironically shortchanges science in its rag-and-boneshop daily life as work. The same may be said of her slighting of technological applications of science for ameliorating the conditions of daily living. A theistic science, serving as "a symbolic mirror of supernatural truths," does not concern itself with such an effort.[141] In that negligence it remains loftily free of the idolatry Weil associated with science in her time.

A final example of what she saw as idolatry concerns the public adulation of Louis Pasteur. He had done much to relieve physical ailments, but "if the intention to succeed in doing so wasn't the principal motive of his efforts, we must regard the fact of his success as a simple coincidence. If it was the principal motive, the admiration owed him has nothing to do with the greatness of science, it's a matter of practical virtue, and so Pasteur would belong to the category of a heroically devoted nurse, and would differ from her only by the extent of his results."[142] With syllogistic force it is clear that science in Weil's mind does not belong to the world of *vertu pratique*. Her science is anomalously pretechnological, yet that anomaly is wholly in keeping with her conviction that science must not be progressive. Without technology it cannot be. It is perhaps impossible to imagine such a rarefied science, but it is not so difficult to glimpse some sinister implications in its indifference to the material world and concrete human problems.

To resume the example of Pasteur and disease: if suffering is of incomparable value as a gateway to understanding, it may be wondered what value Weil would attribute to medical or psychiatric sciences in combating that suffering. Is not a denial of a progressive or meliorative science as dangerous a perversion as, say, the pseudo-science promoted in authoritarian cultures such as Hitler's Germany or Stalin's Russia?

Weil's attempt to restore a Greek science was meant as a stay against the drift of her time and a generation beset with political menace and economic chaos. Scientists had won theoretical and experimental grounds for a skepticism far more sophisticated than the methods required only decades before. To Weil's lay mind, the "nouveau esprit scientifique" reflected disarray, not adventure. She was not alone in discounting the Enlightenment's dogma of progress, both technical and moral, but she was not given over to pessimism or to a cult of the irrational made fashionable by Pareto, Spengler, Sorel, and Bergson. It seemed to her that science had betrayed reason and common sense.

She wanted to tether reason to intuition so that discursive reasoning would find its own limits and thus defer to an apprehension of the divine mystery encoded in nature. If her view seems constrictive, if she could not endorse science in its technological dimensions, she did perceive the need for awe, reverence, and humility in scientific practice. Her intent was positive: as humanity must seek sources of inspiration higher than itself, so must scientists. The Greeks were her exemplars. One could hardly do better, but her Platonic bias that God, not man, is the measure of all things forbids its own retrieval.

No one can cavil about her call for the democratization of science. It is surely in the interest of science that it be intelligible to the layperson, that by its own procedural doubts it debunk its sacred cows and imbue an expectant public with a skeptic's appreciation of what its technological apparatus can and cannot, should and should not do. It is a happy fact that everything in science, methods included, calls for revision.[143] Concomitant with this renewal is the braking action of caution; the tone of any theory should be tentative. It tempers *élan vital* with *frein vital*. Besides, the foremost theories of modern physics have reinforced the sense that knowledge is subject to limit. Even Heisenberg's principle of uncertainty has been qualified with the view that a particle does in fact have an exact position and velocity, and both are inscrutable.[144] What more could Weil require for her desiderated mystery?

It bears repeating that she was responding to certain popular assumptions about science in her time, some fostered by scientists themselves. Had she enjoyed the freedom and leisure to read more widely than she did, she might have relaxed some of her adversarial strictures. She would have profited greatly from more discussions with her brother; wartime exigencies limited their correspondence. How she would have addressed post-Hiroshima science and the moral implications in technological "advances" can be guessed no more accurately than how she would have responded to the Second Vatican Council.

The central problem of her thoughts on science remains how science is to be accommodated to her uplifting theism. Not by the state's decree, certainly. By some profession of faith? Is the work of the nonbelieving scientist *eo ipso* invalid? Is a farrago of Pythagorean balances and Christian symbols the only source of inspiration? To assume that scientists must be aware of or accountable to extradisciplinary "truth" is to shackle them with an ideology that is at best impertinent and at worst dangerous. It savors of fanaticism and the very mentality which Weil herself opposed with all her temperament and intellect.

She stands with the exponents of philosophical idealism—Plato and Hegel, F. H. Bradley and Josiah Royce—who insist that science necessarily lacks perfectibility. That is surely true, but it does not justify an attack on the autonomy of science itself. Scientists in their right minds are not looking for perfection or completion; they make do with what is conceptually workable. Scientific reasoning cannot solve all problems, but any constriction of its vitality may forfeit even the ability to pose them.

Whatever its mystical content, Weil's third order of understanding seems too nebulous to serve as a safeguard against its own dark twin, the irrationalism which, lacking mystical exaltation, threatens both reason and her Pythagorean inspiration and a good deal more.

Weil's writings on science, like those on religion, deserve respectful attention but also a cautionary distance. Judged fairly, they might well afford a good tonic, but it seems doubtful they would make a good diet.

PART THREE

Spiritual Crises

N I N E

A Stranger unto Her People

Weil on Judaism

Les Hébreux ont nommé leur propre âme collective Dieu, feignant et se persuadant qu'elle avait créé et gouvernait le ciel et la terre.
SIMONE WEIL, *La Connaissance surnaturelle*

Weil's hostility to Judaism became evident to her first international generation of readers when Gustave Thibon published *La pesanteur et la grâce* (1948), a posthumous selection from the notebooks she had given him when she left France in 1942. In a miscellany entitled "Israël" her astonishing castigations are gathered up like a court brief, and since 1948 publication of her other works has done nothing to alter the image she created of Judaism and of herself. This uncongenial subject has been addressed only occasionally since then, but it must continue to figure in any attempt at an honest, inclusive assessment of Weil's thought.

The central issue, the character of her statements concerning Judaism and the Bible, requires caution. It would be easy to presume she was anti-Semitic or to take up a psychology of Jewish self-hatred and portray her as a victim. Aware of her family's Jewish roots, she may have felt a need to get free of them by condemnation. Her insistent claim that she was fully assimilated into French culture perhaps failed to convince her.[1] In a matter too complex to warrant one-sided answers, several approaches may be helpful.

This chapter briefly reviews the historical background of anti-Judaism in France from the Revolution to Weil's time. Her family's relations with Judaism must be considered within the crisis of assimilation. Weil's feelings about Judaism were undoubtedly affected by the xenophobic atmosphere in Paris when she was growing up.

Next, the range of her arguments on Judaism and Scripture is examined to establish Weil's position in relation to the Christian church's historic abuses of Jews and Judaism. The appropriation of Weil as a saint in some Christians' views and her manifestly widening influence suggest that her voice may have some impact in the tenuous "dialogue" of Jews and Christians willing to confront together some unhappy facts. Unless her writing can be examined fully and openly, her influence might well prove as baneful to Christians as it has been hurtful to Jews.

This chapter concludes with a review of some Jewish writers on Weil, from the time of *La pesanteur et la grace* to the recent past. In their varied and compelling remarks these critics set the agenda. They indicate that for any reader of Weil her relationship to Christianity and its church should be considered secondary to her relationship with her own people.

Hating the Jew in France since 1789

The modern history of anti-Jewish attitudes in France might arbitrarily be dated in the first year of the Revolution credited with the emancipation of Jews. A statement of Comte Stanislaus de Clermont-Tonnerre summed up the assimilationist dogma which told Jews to cease their life as a community, to cease being Jews: "The Jews must be refused everything as a nation and granted everything as individuals. . . . They must form in the State neither a political group nor an order, they must be individual citizens."[2] For the greater part, French Jews adhered to that injunction in the generations subsequent to the Assembly's conferral of rights in September 1791.

Anti-Semitism did not abate, however. It planted substantial roots in both the French Left and Right during the nineteenth century. Among utopian socialists "la question juive" defined much of the antagonism between Saint-Simon, who looked upon Judaism and Christianity as precedents for his own vague messianism, and Fourier, who despised Jews as exemplars of bourgeois individualism. In 1845, one of Fourier's epigones, Alphonse Toussenel, set down in *Les Juifs rois de l'époque* a leftist caricature of Jews, drawing on their medieval image as nonproductive middlemen in the trading world. As merchants and speculators they had to be opposed no less than factory owners and financiers. Socialist opposition to Jews seemed a logical function of anti-capitalism.[3]

However rationalized, Toussenel's anti-Semitism had only limited resonance among socialists, but its virulence was there awaiting occasion. It is helpful to remember that Proudhon, a furious hater of Jews, in his *carnets* anticipated Hitler by setting down as alternatives the expulsion of Jews from Europe or their extermination.[4]

For many on the Left, Catholicism no less than the Jew barred the way to a harmonious new order, and the anticlericalism running as a strong current in the Revolution prefigured many socialists' efforts to make of themselves a new priesthood. The church did not condemn the view that Jews had organized an international conspiracy to destroy soi-disant Christian nations and dominate the world. Père E. A. Chabauty's *Les Juifs nos maîtres* (1882) typifies this xenophobic certitude about secret societies.

Far more important than the effusions of one camp or another was the effort to unite them in a common front. Edouard Drumont's *La France juive* (1886) was aimed to please revolutionists and conservatives alike by calling for the nationalization of Jewish property. Taking up Marx's notion of a Jewish fetishism of money, Drumont concentrated on Jews the laborers' resentment of capital. The confiscation of "Jewish" factories, presumably in a peaceful revolution, would permit workers "to experiment with their social doctrines in conditions better than any violent revolution that's taken place." The wealth of Jews, after all, was parasitic and usurious, not created but "sponged."[5]

Drumont's two volumes of twelve hundred pages initially attracted little notice when Flammarion published them, but timely criticism won for Drumont the support of the Catholic press. Within weeks he became at forty-two the most popular writer in France, and in the following generation upward of 2 million copies of his works were sold.

In 1889, Drumont helped to found the Ligue nationale antisémitique française but with the Dreyfus Affair in the succeeding decade, anti-Semitism was absorbed into a more broadly conceived nationalism that would find its most influential voices in l'Action Française, the royalist vehicle of Charles Maurras.[6]

The Dreyfus Affair, lasting over a decade, embedded itself deeply in the national consciousness, split the socialists, and galvanized the Right. "La question juive" thereafter served continuously to prompt in many a need for national identity that could be called wholly and purely French. Jews, Maurras wrote, were like metics, foreigners who had employed "their insolent grandeur to impose and propagate a brutal contempt or ironic indulgence toward our national heritage."[7]

Like Drumont, Maurras shrewdly couched his appeals to all classes, furthering the notion Sartre was to dissect in *Réflexions sur la question juive*

(1944), the anti-Semite's claim that he possesses the real France, that he alone serves as guardian of its storehouse of irrational values. One of Sartre's most important insights reveals the anti-Semite's need of the Jew so that he himself can affirm identity with others of similar rage who form "a tradition and a community, those of the mediocre."[8] In that sense, the exoneration of Dreyfus gave incalculable impetus to anti-Semitism, for it stood as a conspicuous symbol of legal processes supposedly debauched by Jewish influence. The anti-Semites took up permanent residence in the rightist camp, fusing their own animus with patriotic harangues for the disgraced army and a strong, xenophobic France.[9]

Characterization of the post-Dreyfus years as "a golden age of symbiosis" for French Jews must be weighed carefully.[10] True, most were middle class and nonobservant; their "religious and cultural indifference" to their Judaic heritage seemed to further their assimilation.[11] But while Jews native to France were substantially achieving assimilation, it remained remote to the larger number of Jews who immigrated there from Eastern Europe, predominantly from Russia, in the 1880s and after 1918.[12]

Immigrant Jews, although valued as laborers in France's war-depleted industries, fueled the Maurrasian fire by their persistent otherness, their retention of their *shtetl* identity, and their Yiddish. Persecution in their homelands and the vociferations of l'Action Française (as well as those of kindred crypto-fascist groups[13]) reinforced the defensive, insular posture of these immigrants and maintained a gap between them and native French Jews. Exploiting these differences, anti-Semitism condemned Jews on both counts: the assimilated had taken over France, the unassimilated were an abiding foreign menace.

Jews for their part labored helplessly in their differences. Those "inauthentic" Jews (Sartre's denomination) for whom assimilation signified an escape from their Jewishness were faced with the perpetual reminder of it in their immigrant kinsfolk.[14] It was the "authentic" unassimilated Jews whom the Vichy régime would later so willingly hunt down for the Nazis.[15]

Weil's background was mostly "inauthentic." Although her maternal grandmother observed Jewish dietary laws and made sure they were kept for her grandchildren, both of Weil's parents, like most Jews of bourgeois professional rank and education, were nonpracticing. Her father, of Alsatian ancestry, enjoyed telling anti-Semitic jokes (not an uncommon practice among Jews) and was "an agnostic, indeed a convinced atheist."[16] Mme Weil, born in Russia, had grown up in Belgium. Simone thus had within her own home representative members of the two Jewish communities of France, one native, the other alien. Her parents spoke German (not Yiddish) at home whenever they wished to communicate something exclusive of their children. In that way André and Simone learned German quickly.[17]

In such a home, Weil naturally grew up with a keen ambivalence common to Jewish experience: the liberating diversity of cultural backgrounds allowed her in maturity to distinguish between nationalism and true love of country, between *l'état* and *patrie*. Yet that very freedom imposed upon her a sense of not belonging—precisely what anti-Semitic chauvinists of her father's generation and her own intended. The equation of *métèque* and *youpin* ("yid") was as automatic to xenophobes like Drieu la Rochelle as it had been to Maurice Barrès.

The dark side of cosmopolitanism, the consciousness of being nowhere truly at home Weil spoke of later as her destiny, "that it had been prescribed to me to find myself alone, a stranger and in exile in relation to any human milieu whatsoever and without exception."[18] Her error lay in not recognizing that she had made herself an exile among exiles.

In that singular apartness, her claim to Perrin that she had been Christian in sensibility from childhood is not cogent. Her identification of Christian love toward others as justice, as a rigorous look at "problems of this world and this life"[19] without resort to dogmas, suggests that she had assumed what Sartre calls the Jewish role as "a missionary of the universal."[20] She spoke of her pursuit of "pure truth" as a vocation she sought according to "common morality."[21]

Because Weil subscribed to the universalistic perspective with which Rousseau endowed the Revolution, she could disdain political partisanship, but she could not attain comparable distance in what the government decreed about race. In response to the *Statut des Juifs* (October 3, 1940), wherein a Jew was defined as anyone with three Jewish grandparents, she spoke to its arbitrary and absurd character. Two of her grandparents were freethinking so she could not be an "official" Jew. She denied any racial link with "the people who inhabited Palestine two thousand years ago." To the minister of public education, the renowned Latin scholar Jérôme Carcopino, she stated the bizarre view that since Titus had exterminated the Jews so thoroughly in the wars of 66–73 C.E., "it seems unlikely that they left many descendants." Besides, heredity had no inevitable connection with religion: "I myself, who profess no religion and never have, have certainly inherited nothing from the Jewish religion."[22] Asserting that she had virtually learned the French language by reading Pascal and Racine, she concluded that the only religious tradition she could consider her own was the Catholic.[23]

Transparent and pathetic as this protest was, it accorded fully with Weil's striving for intellectual honesty. She was not rejecting Judaism; she had been raised without any allegiance to it. Her self-imputed identity as French and implicitly Catholic came from the affirmations of experience. In a freethinkers' household, education was as much what one chose as what one was given. For her, a freethinking Jew must have cut an oxymoronic figure: no one could be both freethinking and Jewish at the same time.

Her ultimate decision to remain outside of Christendom rested on a rationalized defense of the freethinking she inherited from her parents. There lay her true patrimony, and she remained loyal to it to the end. She could affiliate herself to French traditions only to the extent that they sustained the individualism necessary to her intellectual conscience. That individualism has long been at the heart of French culture, and Alain epitomized it. Similarly, Weil's interest in Oriental religions was predicated on her convenient distance from them. Her abstract loyalty to, for instance, Vedic or Egyptian religions was matched by her insistence upon intellectual autonomy, which kept her from any immediate obligations to community.[24]

Weil glimpsed Judaism as an outsider but also forced on it an unreal historical distance, as though it had no more present life than, say, Druidism. But she could not possibly have kept herself deaf and blind either to the existence of Jewish communities in Paris during the 1930s or to the anti-Semitism that was then increasingly resurgent against them. She surely knew of the Mouvement populaire Juif, which paralleled the Popular Front; concurrently, of xenophobic resistance in the trade unions toward Jewish immigrant workers who, concentrated mostly in shops rather than factories, were accused of weakening labor's unity against capital.[25] At union meetings and conferences she would have observed the spectacle of Jewish aliens cut off from the proceedings by their ignorance of French. And she could not have been ignorant of so prominent an organization as the Ligue internationale contre l'antisémitisme (founded in 1928), which sent members into public meetings and onto streets to confront rightist gangs. A hawker of anti-Semitic papers caused her to blush.[26]

Still, Weil might not have perceived immigrant Jews as living adherents of Judaism. Eastern European Jews had kept in Judaism a defense not only against anti-Semites. Judaism was their community set at odds with French

Jews who had traded it for the conveniences of assimilation. Of that fact Weil seems to have had not the least appreciation.

There is a curious anecdote about her attitude toward Jews. In March 1936 she managed to invite herself to work on a farm in the Loire-Cher district. Although a hard worker, she soon wore out her hosts with her interrogatory importunities, "and especially she spoke as far as the eye can see about the coming martyrdom of the Jews, about suffering, deportations and a terrible war that she situated in the near future."[27] During a vacation in Spain in 1933 she offhandedly remarked to her friend Aimé Patri that "one day we will perhaps be tortured, so we ought to prepare ourselves for it. Do you want to drive some pins under my fingernails?" Patri, on the spot, threatened to slap her.[28] Perhaps only in her fascination with suffering ("obsession" is a clinical term) could she overcome the distance between herself and other people.

After Vichy legislation stripped Jews of their professional lives, Weil was obliged to give up teaching. It is instructive to note how little her perspective on Judaism changed in the year subsequent to her letter to Carcopino.

She had begun harvesting grapes for Thibon, the Pétain régime's unofficial sage. In October 1941 she wrote an unsolicited letter to Xavier Vallat, Vichy's anti-Semitic minister of Jewish affairs:

> I suppose that in some way or other I have to consider you my boss. . . . The government has made it known that it wants Jews to enter into production, preferably on the land. Although I do not consider myself a Jew, indeed never entered a synagogue, was raised without any religious practices of any kind by freethinking parents, feel no attraction to the Jewish religion nor any attachment to the Jewish tradition, and was nourished since infancy only in the Hellenic, Christian and French tradition, nevertheless I have obeyed. . . . I regard the Statute on Jews as generally absurd and unjust, for how can one believe that a mathematics teacher can harm children learning geometry simply by having had three grandparents who went to synagogue?[29]

The protests to Vallat are virtually identical to those of the year before to Carcopino.

Yet there is evidence to argue that Weil's attitude toward Judaism was mixed. If, as she claimed, she abhorred the nationalism of ancient Israel, why, in her "Essai sur la notion de lecture" did she cite as her sole literary example of a psychological reading Esther's approach to Ahasuerus (Esther 5:2)? Weil observes that Esther, alone and defenseless, "advances not toward a man who, as she knows, can put her to death, but toward majesty itself, terror itself, which by the sight of him penetrates her soul."[30] And this, from perhaps the most triumphalist text in Scripture, with the Jewish people victorious over their would-be oppressor! Is not Esther's courage the very sort Weil herself longed to realize in military service, with Spain's anarchists in 1936 and with the Free French in 1943? Or was it merely Jahweh's absence from Esther's story (in the original version) that made it so attractive to her?

Another instance occurs when, in a letter from early 1940 to her brother, she objects to the idea that the Greeks had an intense feeling of the disproportion between humanity and God. In one draft of this letter (there are three) she adds parenthetically, "They were not Hebrews!" But in another draft after the same remark on the Greeks she says nothing about Jews but generalizes to include them: "All men have the feeling both of an infinite distance and an absolute unity between man and God."[31]

As to the love and knowledge of God, she contends in her letter to the Dominican Père Couturier that there were men of an indeterminate number in Israel perhaps as spiritually advanced as Christendom's saints.[32] That, given the general tendency of her remarks on Israel, weightily qualifies her charge that Israel indulged in self-idolatry. She could perceive, or at least suppose, a saving remnant of individuals within the Jewish collectivity as within any other.

These few examples may not mitigate the essential harshness of Weil's anti-Judaism, and they cannot be offered in its extenuation, but they do indicate that her position, however violent, was not unequivocal.

One of the most striking documents from her time in New York is a letter in which she advised her brother, who had married a nonpracticing Roman Catholic, on whether his infant daughter should be baptized. André, an agnostic like his father, was amenable to baptism but did not want his children exposed to a fanatical inculcation of religious dogmas. Weil suggests that his daughter

> would not have the shadow of a reason for regretting baptism by a priest unless she were to be converted to fanatical Judaism. If she is converted to Buddhism, Catharism, Hinduism, or Taoism, what good could it do her to have been baptized? If she is converted to Christianity, Catholic or Protestant, which is her right, she would be quite happy. . . . If more or less anti-Semitic legislation accorded advantages to baptized half-Jews, it

> would probably help her to have the advantages without having committed a cowardly act.[33]

The absurdity of conversion to Taoism or Catharism must have been apparent even to Weil's lively imagination, but why did she write of Judaism alone as fanaticism?[34] As it was at this time that she was making her most vigorous protests against the church's history of *anathema sit* (in her letter to Couturier), was she perhaps feeling in some atavistic way the pull of the heritage she so insistently had denied to Vichy? Was she at last aware that the church's chief victims of exclusion were not heretics but Jews?

She had undoubtedly learned of Drancy and the trains destined for the East (Auschwitz) while she was still in France, in the spring of 1942. (The first deportations occurred on March 28.) Her papers include hearsay reports of brutality visited upon Jews in a detention camp in the Ruhr the previous year:

> The Jews of Rhenanie [the Rhineland] arrived in a state of extraordinary spirit. Many till then had lived quietly at home. On arriving they demanded their shoes, they gave orders to interns to carry their bags, etc. (not obeyed, of course). They took a long time in learning, then fell quickly into filthiness, an indescribable degradation. Women who had only a little time previously been ladies relieved themselves anywhere, in front of the barracks, within them.[35]

What startles in this passage is the almost sardonic tone in her description of a scene far more piteous than any she could have found in the tableaux of the *Iliad*.

In America she would have learned even more from the many exiles whose addresses she recorded in her notebooks. It is impossible to determine how much she would have known about the "Final Solution" when she was working for the Free French in London.

Paul Giniewski, in his bitter polemic on Weil, relates testimony about her he received in 1976 from a Dr. Kac, a physician who worked for the Free French. Kac had examined her on two occasions, they worked in the same building, and he shared with her some of his philosophical and political writings. He came to know her attitude toward Judaism and held up for her the example of Henri Bergson, another freethinker who had almost embraced Christianity but finally affirmed his Jewish inheritance when Jews began to suffer from the Nazis. Kac discussed the atrocities with her. "She took refuge in a complete dumbness. When I pressed her, she showed herself profoundly irritated." He concluded that the death of Jews did not interest her. "After thirty years, I still see her frozen stare. I felt I was facing two machine guns."[36]

A horrific scene, but it may be that Kac (and Giniewski) misread Weil's agitated silence. As Thibon and others have testified, Weil was not accustomed to yield an argument and was never inclined to be silent in the midst of one. In a wholly uncharacteristic reaction, dumbfounded and furious, she had been forced to recognize the cruel irrationality of her feelings. Perhaps she had already come to that awareness privately but could not bare it even in her notebooks. Was she groping with it at all at last?

There is some evidence of that possibility. In one of her essays in the spring of 1943, "Légitimité du Gouvernement Provisoire," reviewing the inadequacies of the Third Republic's penal system, she observes that no provisions were made for injustice. A law, she says, could have been passed condemning Jews to death without regard to sex or age. "Will it be said that this hasn't taken place? Is it certain that measures haven't been taken, though less visibly, approximate to the level of atrocity? For instance, in the treatment of the colonies and of foreigners?"[37] To whom does "foreigners" refer but to the immigrant Jews Vichy was helping the Nazis deport?

Another document must be examined, one from which all who admire Weil can only cringe. During her work for the Free French, she was given a proposal from a group known as l'Organisation civile et militaire (OCM). One of several Resistance factions created in northern France from the beginning of the Occupation, the OCM bore a distinctly rightist character. Its proposal centered on "non-Christian minorities in France" with the intention of ensuring that in postwar France they would not be able to retain their prewar status.[38] Weil's résumé puts the matter bluntly. As to non-Christian minorities, "In fact it concerns French Jews. The central idea is that the cohesion between Jews is not racial but religious, and this in spite of the great number of atheistic Jews. Indeed, when a religion disappears, replaced by atheism, the mentality corresponding to that religion abides.[39] There's a change of mentality only when there's a change of religion. Thus only those Jews (sincerely) converted to Christianity, or on the point of being, are assimilated." She notes that the proposal rejects charges made against Jews but claims that a majority can legally take measures toward a minority "in order to avoid certain eventual inconveniences" such as a disproportionate number of Jews in elected bodies and the presence of Jews in educational services. The proposed statute would forbid Jews from entering either government or educational office.

Regarding the professions, Weil, daughter of a reputable physician, notes that the proposal "shows that while admittedly the Jews behave badly as doctors, lawyers, bankers, teachers, etc., the remedy ought not to be sought in a struggle against the Jews but in the prevention and repression of harmful conduct among the doctors, lawyers, bankers, teachers, etc."

The proposal would totally ban Jewish immigration and allow only Christian foreigners "chosen among the populations most akin to the French temperament" to enter France. Foreign Jews would be expelled.

This not so astounding proposal, patently rooted in the old xenophobic and anti-Semitic tensions of the Third Republic, won a sympathetic but cautious response from Weil. In her "Commentary," she defined the issue by questioning the very existence of a Jewish minority or of any group whose identification would be "a certain mentality responding to the absence of a Christian heritage." In her view, no modus vivendi could remain stable because "the existence of such a minority does not constitute a good; so the object must be to provoke its disappearance, and every modus vivendi must be a transition toward this objective," lest recognition of the Jewish minority allow it to "crystallize." (She recommends parenthetically the creation of a new judiciary to help in this matter.) Mixed marriages and "a Christian education" for future generations of Jews would ensure assimilation or at least that "neither the so-called Jewish religion nor the atheism characteristic of Jews emancipated from their religion would have enough strength to prevent contagion."[40]

The medical term closing this statement is illuminating, however naturally it might have come to a doctor's daughter. It hints that Weil, viewing cultural allegiances as a kind of pathological warfare, saw Judaism as a condition or disease from which one might be relieved. Oddly, however, Christianity here plays the part of the germ that cures, a desired contagion that a Jew, so Weil dreamed, cannot resist: "Jewish racism wouldn't have enough strength for that. At the end of two or three generations, the only ones to remain conscious of being Jews would be fanatical racists. At this time the problem would be to find a criterion to pick them out so as to deprive them of French nationality." Weil urged that Jewish parents of sufficient intelligence be encouraged not to tell their children that they were Jews—a kind of autobiographical obtrusion, for she and her brother did not realize they were Jews until they attended school. Such was Weil's tribute to her upbringing, that she wished every Jewish child in France could have a similar one.

Finding that the OCM had not provided a psychological profile of Judaism, Weil supplied one in terms that mirror her notebook entries. Its distinguishing features are deracination and "irreligion," the latter meaning that "the so-called Jewish religion is a national idolatry that has lost all reality since the destruction of the nation. That is why a Jewish atheist is more atheistic than any other. He is so less aggressively, but more profoundly." With these hallmarks, Jews, according to Weil, had naturally and therefore legitimately attained a disproportionate eminence in French culture, but reactions against them were no less natural and legitimate. Again, the image is of contestant germs, and the antidote would be "an inspiration of authentic spirituality," but because Weil believed most Jews incapable of associating with Christian bacilli, she felt it proper to push them aside (*écarter*) from positions of public instruction, precisely the fate she had suffered in 1940. She rationalized this measure, saying that in "purifying" the national life "almost all the inconveniences tied to a minority's existence will be suppressed." Conversely, accusations against Jews by "the most clairvoyant anti-semites" would constitute "a precious repertory of the nation's ills."

Weil concluded her commentary with a defense of non-Jewish minorities, Spanish refugees from the Civil War and Russians exiled by the Revolution. It would be cruel, she maintained, to deprive them of the native cultural life they had imported into France. Spain and Russia were real countries to which Judaism had no claim. "A band of fugitives" had no comparable good to lose. "In dissolving the Jewish milieux without brutality, they will not be deprived of a country but prepared to have one for the first time."

That a project such as the OCM's could be authored by a Jew, Maxime Blocq-Mascart, and endorsed in substance by another Jew tells how deeply the virulence of racism had worked in France from Drumont's time. Assimilation had gone so far that some Jews either had no sense of their heritage or ardently wished to destroy it. Contagion, indeed.

This document, Weil's only officially proffered view of Judaism, shows how she determined her response to Judaism on two related lines, the chauvinistic prompting for assimilation which Clermont-Tonnerre first articulated and the call for the total displacement of Judaism by Christianity's "authentic" spirituality. In effect, Weil wanted to rescue Jews from Judaism; she also believed she was rescuing them from those who would persecute them as Jews.

That becomes clear in another OCM proposal, on postwar constitutional reform. It seemed so patently fascist in conferring six years of total power upon the executive that Weil looked back to the first proposal and perceived "these people's real thinking about Jews."[41] "Realizing that anti-Semitism of the German kind is impolitic at this time in France they pretend to make a serious, objective study of the problem. But their aim is only to set up a crystallized Jewish minority as a ready preserve with a view to future atrocities." Her rejection of the first plan's scheme of crystallizing a Jewish minority thus takes on an almost positive aspect. Undoubtedly, she regarded her own scenario of assimilation and conversion for all of France's Jews as utmost charity.

That does not, however, address the animus she felt toward "the so-called Jewish religion." Why did she set herself so implacably against Judaism?

Jahweh, the Great Beast

Because she regarded the Torah as alien in spirit and in substance to the New Testament, Weil has sometimes been identified with Marcion and the Gnostics of the early centuries C.E.[42] On the basis of that apparent affinity, she has been charged with anti-Semitism.[43]

Her censures of Judaism complement a trend in modern Christian theology. It is well known that the foremost historian of church dogma, Adolf von Harnack, a generally sympathetic scholar of Marcion, followed him in the belief that Jewish Scripture should be demoted from canonical to apocryphal status. The modern church, he reasoned, has sufficient distance from the historically necessary rooting of Christendom in Judaism to break the tie. After Harnack, Rudolf Bultmann carried on the Lutheran antithesis of law versus gospel which relegates the Judaic heritage to a merely pedagogical function.

The effect of stressing differences between Judaism and Christianity has inevitably been "to tear Christianity from its rootage in history and thereby to run the risk of turning it into a system of philosophy or a sect of eternally valid principles."[44] Such deracination also makes evident Christianity's affinities with other revelatory faiths, mystery religions, and salvific cults. Weil pursued those affinities with singular fascination, hoping to establish through them a non-Hebraic provenance for Christianity.

In a letter she wrote from New York to the eminent professor of philosophy Jean Wahl, she reviewed her belief that a common thread of truth binds the ancient thought of Egypt, Greece, China, and India and is carried on in Christian tradition to its mystical flowering in San Juan de la Cruz but also in the heresies of Mani and the Cathars. She presumes that modern science may work to articulate this "truth." Then, "As to the Jews I think Moses knew this wisdom and refused it because, like Maurras, he conceived religion as a mere instrument of national grandeur; but when the Jewish nation had been destroyed by Nebuchadnezzar, the Jews, totally disorganized and mixed up with all sorts of nations, received this wisdom in the form of foreign influences and, as far as was possible, brought it into their religion." On that basis she singles out what she presumes to be non-Jewish texts: Job, the Song of Songs, the sapiential books, Daniel and Tobit. "Almost all the rest of the Old Testament is a tissue of horrors."[45]

Those last words recall a more extensive gloss on the Bible, Voltaire's "Catechisme d'un honnête homme," in which the histories of Israel's kings are dismissed as "a tissue of cruelties."[46] The mock-pious deist's inventory of all that seems absurd and horrible in the ancient stories anticipates Weil's own review in her notebooks,[47] but the thesis in her effort differs fundamentally from Voltaire's non-Christian appeals to "sagesse."

Weil's "tissue of horrors" amounts to a peculiar propaedeutic. Following John 12:40, she contends that the passion of Jesus required Israel's ignorance of its significance so that Israel would have no supernatural part in God and be kept in the darkness of its exclusive, collective spirituality. "For this reason everything in Israel is contaminated with sin, for there is nothing pure without participation in the incarnate divinity, so the lack of any such participation may be manifest."[48] Weil thus sets out a predestinarian scenario for Jews in antiquity. Israel was Zionist from the first, and its Jahweh was the sum of its own nationalistic impulses. She seems to follow Paul's characterization in Romans 10:3–4 that an alleged Jewish self-righteousness is set in opposition to the incarnation. Hence, bizarrely, Israel was indeed a chosen people.[49]

Yet Weil is also inclined to hold Israel accountable for not conducting itself by supposedly Christian standards: "If the Hebrews, as a people, had carried God within them, they would have preferred to suffer the slavery inflicted by the Egyptians—and provoked by their own previous exactions—rather than to win freedom by massacring all the inhabitants of the territory they had to occupy."[50] On that basis she compares Israel to Rome, where power rather than good held sway. When she writes of the Israelites' God as "heavy," she means that preexilic Jews could not distinguish between God and the devil, between transcendent good and shows of might.[51]

Regarding Jahweh as a demon born of this confusion, she makes a pithy, trenchant comparison: "Jahweh made the same promises to Israel that the devil made to Christ," the offers of miracle, mystery, and authority taken up by Dostoevsky's Grand Inquisitor against Jesus.[52] The covenant means that God is under contractual obligation to make virtue, as adherence to the covenant, prosperous, whereas Christianity at its true, Greek center affirmed "an essential truth, the possibility of a suffering innocence."[53] The Jewish conjunction of prosperity and obedience implied the equation of misfortune with sin, and such a notion would make charity impossible.[54]

Israel's covenantal God offends Weil by his presence in the patriarchal stories. She prefers the Father hidden and secret (Matt. 6:6). Jahweh seems the cause of Israel's "contamination" with sin. She directs an accusing finger at Abraham's abuse of his wives, at Lot's offer of his daughters, at Jacob's deceit and extortion, at Simeon's slaughter of the Hivites, concluding that "everything is of a polluted and atrocious nature, as if intentionally so . . . as though to indicate absolutely clearly: Beware! There lies evil."[55]

Seeing these stories as cautionary tales, she does not realize the Hebrews might have seen them that way, too. She allows no extenuations for all-too-human figures: Abraham's fear before Pharaoh, Lot's observation of hospitality rituals, Jacob's trickery as just recompense to Laban. Her indignation, deeper than Voltaire's, also precludes appreciation of the pathetic beauty in some of these narratives: the anguish of Esau in loss of Isaac's blessing or the reconciliation with Jacob speak from and to the heart no less eloquently than many passages in Weil's faultless Homer.

Of course, the issue comes to more than literary appreciations. At the heart of her "catalog of crimes" view lies her failure to understand that, as Scripture attests, the miserable sinfulness of Israel makes it representative of all humanity; it is still loved by God and summoned to service. Weil did not recognize—as even her most eager friends concede—the full length, breadth, and depth of Judaism. The daily life of halakhah rooted in the Talmud, of mitzvoth, the practical exigencies of a high moral sensibility—all this was wholly unknown to her. She gave no heed to the abundance of midrashic literature; no heed (surprisingly, given her interest in folk wisdom) to the wealth of Hasidic lore; and the Kabbalistic tradition finds virtually no mention in her papers. She simply did not accommodate anything Jewish in the otherwise cosmopolitan reach of her intellectual fervor because she did not see in what little she knew of Judaism anything compatible with her conception of a genuine, that is, mystically centered, religion.

She would not, then, have known that her notion of *kenosis*, of creation as God's withdrawal, can be found in the Kabbalah, so interpreted by the sixteenth-century mystic Isaac Luria: the world came to be through God's self-limiting, a consent to exile such that creation signifies the place where God is not. Weil's theology holds this kind of cosmic atheism at its center.[56] But she could not have accepted Luria's corollary to God's withdrawal, that the world, devastated by God's absence, must be restored by human agency; humankind by strenuous moral effort seeks to gather together the divine order. Such progressive voluntarism, especially in a social context, was anathema to Weil.

In her vigorous partisanship for the oppressed, how could she have ignored the *tsedeka* of the Deuteronomic laws, their compassionate justice extended to foreigners and slaves, proofs of a far loftier moral sense than is found in her florilegium of favorite texts, including the *Gita* and Egypt's Book of the Dead? In her concern for the integrity of thought free of all collectivist persecutions, how could she have refused attention to the woeful history of Jews at the mercy of Christian Europe for nearly two thousand years and to minds such as Maimonides, whose works were banned and burned near to the very time and place where her friends, the Cathars, fell?

Had Weil known the ethical core of Judaism, she would have seen beside its concern for social justice a respect for manual labor much like her own. Unlike Greece and Rome, Israel extolled the dignity of labor and honored those who performed it. In working out a theory of labor as obedience to God, Weil was more Jewish than she knew.[57]

And yet, however awesome her ignorance of Judaism, appeals to an "if only she had known" argument do not help much. It is more useful to look at the exceptions she makes to her censure and see why she makes them. For example, using John 3:14 she finds a symbolism in Moses' bronze serpent and analogizes it to the healing power of the cross.[58] She sees in the elusive Melchisedek an earlier incarnation of the Johannine *logos* and fantastically entertains the possibility of a connection with the Hellenic mysteries.[59] She presumes that Noah's drunkenness and nudity are mystical, and she inflates that notion into a wild exercise of supposition.[60] Accepting a non-Hebraic origin for Job (a standard practice among commentators), Weil can see in Job Plato's just man who seems unjust on one hand and on the other a version of the Oriental theme of a dead and resuscitated god.[61] The common denominator in such instances, a non-Judaic tradition, only reinforces her antipathy to Judaism. One might paraphrase Origen's response to Celsus's attacks on Christianity: Weil seems to believe the Hebrew Scriptures whenever she wants to do so in order to assail Judaism and to disbelieve they are Jewish when she finds in them something lofty and inspiring.

Apart from the incidental horrors in biblical history, Judaism as a collectivity provoked some of her harshest remarks. In that her assaults on collectivity, denominated as "a powerful beast" in Plato's *Republic* (493b), extend throughout her works, Judaism as one of its imputed manifestations shares its general character: a superstititous regard for convention, a deprivation of the supernatural, and legitimation of all crimes according to the needs of prestige.[62]

As nothing here seems pertinent to any fair-minded understanding of Judaism, it is important to see what Weil means when she tars Judaism with the brush usually applied to modern authoritarianism.

The pharisaic punctilio of observing the Law seems to conform to Weil's allegation of superstitious convention. She finds the craving for prestige at the expense of the spiritual in Judaism's "thirst for carnal good," the shalom of earthly abundance secured in the land Jahweh promised the patriarchs.[63] The connection between shalom and crime lies in the *herem* recorded in Joshua: that God should ordain acts of cruelty and injustice contradicts, says Weil, the essential truth about God.[64] Just as Plato censured Homer's depiction of the Olympians' wanton behavior, so Weil rejects a God who sanctioned the deaths of Canaanites in order to give land to Jews.[65] She says the Jewish *herem* is far more reproachable than the *luxus* of pagan cultures—as though such indulgence were their worst fault.

Construing the "chosen people" motif in the way of dramatic irony, Weil believes she sees what Jews presumed in this title. The idol Israel worshiped was itself: "The Hebrews named their own collective soul as God, pretending and persuading themselves that that soul created and governed the heaven and the earth."[66] This conception of God as an exclusive national fetish not only strengthened Jews in their times of trouble but implicitly sanctioned an unlimited imperialism.[67] Ancient Rome, Israel's twin in idolatry but atheistic (its worship, Weil says, was directed solely to the state) could not appropriate the Jewish fetish until it took over Christianity under Constantine. Weil contends that the church's historic persecution of Jews lay in its contest for what Judaism had kept to itself, a totalitarian deity.[68] Imperial Christendom thus reflected mirror images of Rome and Israel.[69]

In the belief that Judaism corrupted the Christian mystery religion, Weil would welcome a purgation of the Jewish heritage, ignoring the central fact that the church, Jewish in its origins, grafted Greek culture onto its Jewish trunk. She does not suggest how the church would accomplish such a drastic and absurd volte-face or how most Christians could be expected to welcome the departure of so-called "Old Testament" readings from their lectionaries.

In substitution she would perhaps have supplied the Book of the Dead for the "evangelical charity" she saw it evincing in the soul's ritual confession to

Osiris.[70] Convinced that in animal sacrifice the Egyptians had learned how humanity might see God as a redemptive mediator, Weil assumed what might be called a collaborationist posture toward the first of Israel's oppressors. Indeed, as the Vichy experience informed all of her late writings, it is not surprising that she saw the first generation of Christians in a borrowed perspective: "There was once a nation that believed itself holy and it succeeded very badly, and on this subject it is very curious to think that the pharisees in this nation were the resistance and the publicans were the collaborators, and then to recall Christ's relations with each of these groups."[71]

Where Judaism exerted influence beyond Israel Weil sees only an "inderacinable nationalism" that, she claims, perverted the gospels' transmission by the inclusion of Jewish references.[72] It is as though Judaism had somehow forced Christians in the first century C.E. to appropriate Jewish texts as their own in composing the New Testament. Jesus' own many references to the Torah and his identity as a Jew she avoids altogether. "Ye do err not knowing the scriptures" (Matt. 22:29) aptly suggests Weil's strange and tragic blind spot. As Perrin wondered, "Why does she forget that our Lord willed to be a Jew even to the fringe of his cloak and to the manner of his discussions, parables and arguments?"[73]

Perhaps she did not forget but at heart knew too well so that it would be almost captious to conclude that Jesus himself as we know of him in the gospels confounds her notions of Judaism and of Christianity as well. Perrin's conception of her "inclination to deprecate everything that touched her" might be invoked as a key to the reason for her decision not to enter the church.[74] She told him she felt appointed to remain "at the junction of Christianity and all that is not Christian."[75] She was caught cruciform between her cherished mystery cult and an ancestry she knew was her own but could not name. Even as the OCM report showed her desperate eagerness to remake Jews into her own assimilationist image, so, behind all the bitterness of her views on ancient Israel, this "saint of outsiders" (Gide's words on her) was perhaps at last educating herself, with angry resistance, to accept history's foremost outsiders in their darkest hour.

Jewish Writers on Weil

Speaking for Europe's surviving Jews, the late Wladimir Rabi has recalled that when *La pesanteur et la grâce* appeared in 1948, "We had emerged from the greatest catastrophe of our history. And the dozen pages its author devoted to the Jewish people constituted an insupportable outrage. I believe it is fair to say that almost no one, excepting a few rare individuals, ever got over the vexation and grief they felt then. Don't say that we were deceived and that in reading the texts better we would have come to other conclusions. If only that could be."[76]

Yet the partial and inadequate character of Weil's understanding of Judaism became immediately apparent, and prominent Jews began to address it. As Armand Lunel observed in 1950, her condemnation of Israel is confined to its early, preexilic history, before Judaism had become fully educated by its prophets and its suffering to an encompassing missionary love of humanity. (The influence of Renan's *Histoire du peuple d'Israël* informs Lunel here.) But that does not explain why Weil refused to credit Judaism for those books in Scripture which she commended, such as the Psalms, Isaiah, and Daniel. Had she been blinded by Alain's rationalist prejudices against the Bible? Lunel, it seems, wishes to believe so, and yet Alain inspired her to the unrelenting urge for truth, which, in Lunel's view, keeps her from the stigma of "a doctrinal and metaphysical antisemitism."[77]

Although that latter point might be contested, Lunel scores brilliantly on a historical point, remarking the peace and friendship which Weil's beloved heretics, the Cathars of twelfth-century Languedoc, enjoyed with their Jewish neighbors. More, he suggests the possibility of "a common climate of mysticism" linking Albigensians and followers of the Kabbalah.[78] Had Weil looked more closely at what she praised and what she execrated, she would have perceived a common ground to unsettle her biases.

The nature of Weil's ignorance of Judaism has received special scrutiny from Martin Buber. He maintains that like Bergson, another almost Christianized Jew, Weil did not reject Judaism in any real form but rather the Christian church's caricature of it. There is much to support Buber's point, save that Weil did not subscribe to the church's supersessional dogma; she vigorously denied the identity of Jahweh with God the Christian Father. Her notion of a carnal Jahweh, a god of thunderbolting cruelty, bears no relation to the God superior to nature and spirit alike. In Buber's eyes, Weil's protests reflect an abhorrence not only of the natural world but of reality itself, and he feels that God became for her a release from both. He regards her negation of individual and collective egoism as so sweeping that she could not admit any legitimate relations of, in his well-known coinage, I and Thou.

Had Buber known it, Weil's *L'enracinement* would have gone far to qualify, if not confound, this criticism. Indeed, Buber's celebrated Hasidic models of "little communities bound together by brotherly love" seem not far removed from the syndicalist anachronisms in Weil's prescriptive vision of postwar France.[79]

To her charge that preexilic Judaism embodied a totalitarian nationalism, Buber rejoins that Jews labored under the covenantal obligation to materialize love and justice, to make them active in daily life. The Ten Commandments, he adds, speak not to a people but to every individual. Thus, "precisely in the religion of Israel it is impossible to make an idol of the people as a whole, for the religious attitude to the community is inherently critical and postulative."[80]

Emmanuel Lévinas makes even more of this point. Not pride but an answering to strict justice separated the ancient Jews from other peoples. He further argues that as the Bible, far from praising God's people, directs invectives against their waywardness, it indicates Israel's uniqueness, "to have chosen this book of wrath and condemnation for its message."[81] How could Weil have missed that elementary and iterated fact, in Deuteronomy, Isaiah, and Amos? It is even in the Bible that her preferences of other Mediterranean cultures finds some justification: through Malachi, most nationalistic of prophets, God says he is known of all the earth's peoples and is better served by them than by Israel. Weil did not, therefore, need what Lévinas mordantly terms "morceaux choisis" from texts like the Book of the Dead to find transcendent justice in antiquity.

Lévinas's most daring argument takes up Weil's accusation that Judaism means uprooting, from early Christianity through the modern gospel of progress and the world's colonization: "The Jews," she had hyperbolized, "this deracinated pack, have caused the deracination of the whole globe."[82] So be it, answers Lévinas, if deracination amounts to liberation from cultural parochialism. He even makes the case that such freedom is vital to Christianity: a true society is one in which everything comes from within oneself. Paganism in its very etymology implies rootedness. Scripture signifies not the subordination of spirit to letter but "substitution of letter for soil. The spirit is free in the letter and chained in the root. It is upon the desert's arid ground where nothing is fixed that the true spirit descends in a text for its universal realization."[83] Lévinas's argument, recalling Gide's famous exchange with Barrès on the virtues of vagabondage, runs totally against Weil's urge to define a vital parochialism barely distinguishable from *la belle France* of Bernanos, Thibon, and Pétain, a France where, as we have seen, she would have Jews wholly assimilated.

Ironically, on this very point Rabi claims Weil for the Jewish community of France. Even as before the war, Jews proudly referred to the first Jewish premier of France as "notre Léon Blum," so, as early as 1951, Rabi boldly spoke of "notre Simone Weil": "If I have recourse to this term, it is that I have always considered Simone Weil as a formative part of our destiny and that our French Judaism was guilty of her. The enfeeblement of French Judaism for 150 years, its weakness and spiritual vacuity, were such that she ought to be considered the end product of a community aspiring to extinction."[84] Hence even her approbation of the OCM plan takes on the bizarre aspect of a cultural suicide, with Weil an almost imprecatory voice that cries, Yes, let Jewry in France be no more.

In his function as "long-time critic of the French Jewish establishment," Rabi drew upon Weil to chastise the community for its assimilationist apostasy.[85] How bitterly this issue has continued to rage was shown as recently as 1978 in a *Le Monde* exchange with Weil at the storm's center. The assimilation controversy need not concern us here, but the precipitant article, by Arnold Mandel, offered some penetrating remarks on Weil and one of the severest judgments of her.

Mandel resorts to a bogey of Jewish folklore, the dibbuk, which possesses a soul and uses it to blaspheme. In prosaic terms, the blasphemy amounts to an impassioned contempt for Jews and Judaism. Mandel concurs with Theodor Lessing's view in *Der jüdische Selbsthass* that "this phobia runs consecutive to the ultra-assimilation which produces an excessive, sometimes frantic estimation of values in the gentiles' culture."[86] Weil wanted to identify herself with French Catholic culture, a ready accomplice to and victim of its Judeophobia.

While conceding that Weil does not conform herself to the conventional racist mold or stand *à plein temps* like Drumont or Maurras or Céline, Mandel cautions that the paucity of her anti-Judaic writings might give the false impression of mere "occasional manifestations of temper." For him the dibbuk came to an all too willing, predisposed victim. He is incontestably correct in any case when he asserts that no one who admires Weil may approve of her Judeophobia: "In this instance, to absolve is not yet to render innocent."[87]

With Weil still in the docket, Mandel presses his case further. He distinguishes anti-Semitism and anti-Judaism: the anti-Semite sees "the content through the container," the anti-Judaic sees the other way about.[88] Did Weil have any substantial notion of the "container" at all? She gave Judaism many glosses as an idolatrous or "natural" religion, but never did she attack Jews as people. Even when she upheld the scenario of the early church in which the chosen people serve as blind agents who bring Jesus to crucifixion, as though stooges of providence, they were faceless.

Mandel notes that within Jewish tradition one can contest its values without ceasing to be Jewish. He cites as an example the translator of Homer, Saül Tchernichovski, who wanted to be a Greek but lived in Israel; for all his rebelliousness, "un bon juif." One might add Heinrich Heine, Benjamin Disraeli, Moses Hess, and Theodor Herzl. And the excommunicated Spinoza? Surely, but not Weil: "Those who abandon the pavilions of Israel or never entered them pointing a finger from afar and saying 'There is evil,' they are enemies of Jewish humanity. That is what Simone Weil did."[89]

But she did more. She recognized well enough the Greek tradition at work in Christianity's metaphysics, as well as Gnostic soteriology. She wholly denied the plainest of facts, that Christianity's ethical source, its very center, is Judaism. What irony that her own ethics, in much of her life and the best of her writings, should be so very Jewish. In tearing Christianity from its true roots, she was herself deracinated. It is as though in this bemusingly willful endeavor she was practicing a form of self-mutilation for entry into some mystery cult of her own fashioning.

That a mind of abundant energy, a mind that has cast brilliant lights on some of the abiding problems of this century, could do itself harm and give hurt to the Jewish people must be reckoned one of the intellectual and moral catastrophes of a dark age. It should also serve as one of the saddest of cautionary tales, not least, perhaps, for those who go looking for saints.

Nowhere is the acute bitterness Weil aroused among Jews better revealed than in Paul Giniewski's polemic on her life as, to quote his subscript, *haine de soi*. Unfortunately, it cannot be called a study or a clinically dispassionate examination of Weil as a subject of Jewish self-hatred, comparable to, say, Kurt Tucholsky or Otto Weininger. Burdened with journalistic excesses and, by the author's admission, fueled with an anger that courses flamelike through 350 pages, the book lacks any critical disposition to balanced judgment. Giniewski shows neither an interest in the dazzling variety of Weil's intellectual pursuits nor, consequently, in the ideas they spawned, not even in those so clearly informed by her Jewish heritage: her passion for justice, for example, and her fealty to the purity of universals and absolutes.

For all that, he makes some telling points against Weil, that she "deprived God of all power over man and man of his role beside God. . . . She condemned man to despair, to wander, literally as a soul in pain, in the expectation of God and the certainty that God will not answer." Her intellectual errors, he concludes, "have added not only to the Jews' *malheur* but to the world's as well."[90] Giniewski's distortions are obvious, but they remain unsettling.

The most lucid of Weil's recent Jewish critics is the late Jean Améry, an Austrian (née Hans Maier) who survived Auschwitz, Buchenwald, and Belsen. Impatient with hagiographic legends, he endorses Giniewski despite the excesses, and he seeks to expose Weil as a forerunner of what he calls neoirrationalism, a movement he elsewhere credits with a forgetfully immoral rehabilitation of postwar Germany. To evade the moral lessons of the not so distant past (the Holocaust) is to contribute to "historical entropy," the process by which time makes us indifferent to what the past teaches. Weil herself would surely have taken up this argument for sustaining moral judgment in historical awareness; it is implicit in her wistful plea for lost cultures such as the Albigensian. Who cares now about the Cathars? Who, Améry worries, will care about Auschwitz a few generations hence?

He objects chiefly to Weil's mysticism as a retreat from existence, and a blind alley, too, because she does not seem to countenance salvation in or for this world. Her *attente* closes the door not only to logic and responsibility but to the immediacy of things she could accept only in perfection: "She lost from her sight all that's really beautiful, good, just, only because it can never be perfect."[91] This is a shrewd if not entirely accurate estimate. Améry can imagine loving Weil as a person and pitying her, but he concludes that her thought has no value for anyone interested in humanity's good—an extreme judgment, perhaps written in despair (Améry died by his own hand before it was published). Most important, it comes from a freethinking and violently deracinated Jew. An outsider like Weil, and even more so because he had to endure postwar disillusionment (he came to doubt that the non-Jewish world had grasped the war's moral lessons or even cared to), Améry rejects Weil from her own vantage.

Strangely, the most lamentable position of all comes from Weil's friend Gilbert Kahn. He is, of course, a sympathetic critic, but he is also one of her most astute readers, consistently attentive to the many nuances of her writing. No one has expounded and defended her more ably. To expound, however, is to expose, and even Kahn's rationales do not help Weil in the matter of

Judaism. Against Giniewski's attack, for example, he says that Weil's point is not to make a critique of Judaism but "to question Israel's heritage in Christian-inspired Western civilization."[92] One labors to appreciate this distinction, not to mention the spurious questioning. Her efforts were not purely theoretical, he goes on, but a response to "la crise de la civilisation." Worse and worse: Kahn's points do not excuse Weil, they inadvertently accuse her. Was Judaism responsible for the European crisis of the 1930s?

Weil, Kahn says (and rightly), was concerned about Israel's "capitalist and totalitarian heritage, and not about contemporary Jews." Ergo, she was no anti-Semite. She was simply imputing the worst of civilization to Judaism, as Marx had before her. That she felt no vulgar animus to "des Juifs actuels" does not extenuate the fact that she was furthering an intellectualized argument that could be used by others to cloak their racist hatreds. In pointing to Hitler's historical antecedents, Rome and Richelieu, she deflects the Nazis' personal accountability, all the while ignoring the predominant role of the Christian church in tolerating, sometimes promoting, an anti-Semitism of the heart.

Kahn acknowledges that Weil was sometimes irrational in her feelings, but he says Giniewski's constructions of her words are "almost always forced and sometimes extravagant." That is true, but far more harmful to Weil than Giniewski's writhened words are Kahn's uncritical iterations of her position. Jews did not, he repeats, constitute a true *patrie* in her eyes because their dream of temporal domination precluded rooting and "authentic spiritual inspiration." This is to say that Jews, uprooted and uprooting, bear the burden of ancestry to Nazism. From there it is not a large step to one of the truly monstrous sophistries of this century, that Europe's Jews brought the Holocaust on themselves.

Kahn asserts that Weil's sundry remarks on Judaism cohere, even if "very often impassioned and rather facilely unjust," and that they are not mere expressions of some psychosocial personality problem. But that is an implicitly antihistorical view. We need not subscribe to Giniewski's blackwash to glimpse the tragedy of time and place at which it tears, the tragedy that made Judaism the cross Weil refused to carry. Incredibly, Kahn concludes the opposite, that "the question of Judaism and even the question of Israel in general" do not hold "a central position either in Simone Weil's thought, of which they indicate only a backside, nor in her all too brief life."[93] Such a sweeping under the rug is inadmissible.

In a profound and lasting sense Weil's story is part of the family tragedy of European Jewry. The issue goes far deeper than her outlandish and rebarbative words on the Torah. Her ignorance of Judaism, partly circumstantial, partly willful, reflects the horror many Jews have had to face and internalize when assimilation into a "Christian" culture becomes limited and complete integration is made impossible. The Nuremburg Laws of 1935 indicated how quickly Jews could be forced into the psychic imprisonment of inferiority and self-destruction where Weil languished. Weininger, Kafka, and countless others had been obliged to tread this sinister path well before the Nazis came to power. Hitlerism compelled many who might otherwise have gone their own way of denial to discover they were Jews. These were, in Améry's telling words, "catastrophe Jews." Bergson is an example, and his tardy but noble course, as Buber suggests, does not elevate Weil. That is because she spent so much of her indomitable energy on behalf of a Christianity faced with nearly complete moral bankruptcy.

Concurrent with Jewish censure has come approbation from many Christians who either sidestep Weil's hostility to Judaism or covertly sanction it with rationalizations. It has been written that she united in herself "the glow of the Old Covenant's prophets in an implacability toward its own people, and a dominican pathos of Truth."[94] Gustave Thibon has remarked: "I'm astonished that many people who take seriously a lot of what Simone Weil has said don't take seriously what she has said about the Old Testament. I believe one must practice toward what she has written about it the attention she recommends for practice regarding geometrical paradoxes, antinomies and every sort of contradiction."[95] That point is well taken, but Thibon neglects to recognize that our attention is necessarily informed by awareness of Weil's time and her pathetic status as a "catastrophe Jew." Her words must be taken seriously and not hermetically sealed off as though there has been no Chelmno, no Treblinka, no Auschwitz.

TEN

Waiting, with Vichy, for God

Je trahirais la vérité, c'est-à-dire l'aspect de la vérité que j'aperçois, si je quittais le point où je me trouve depuis la naissance, à l'intersection du christianisme et de tout ce qui n'est pas lui.
SIMONE WEIL, *Attente de Dieu*

L'ennemi du catholicisme est catholique essentiellement, citoyen du monde, frère et ami de tous les opprimés, contre tous les oppresseurs.
ALAIN, "La vraie foi" (1913)

Just as her god, like Krishna before the prince in her beloved *Gita* or Proteus before Menelaus in the *Odyssey*, is a polymorph, so Weil the believer constantly eludes any certain grasp. That fact owes nothing to her neglect or *refus* of what is called systematic theology, it simply owes a great deal to the way in which she thought about divinity: chiefly, by the occasions of reading many texts, only some of which are conventionally regarded as religious or spiritual, and particularly by intuitive flashes sparked in that reading or in the broader reaches of daily experience. She reworked her thoughts, recast them as though like geometric shapes they might afford many symmetries. She was fascinated with Lagneau's cube: hold it whatever way one wishes, one can never see it fully as a cube yet it is experienced as a cube. Weil and her god are rather like that cube, and nothing could be more wrongheaded than to assume that any angle taken affords comprehension of the whole. There is a tendency to regard Weil as some sort of Christian, manqué or otherwise, because she was often inclined to express her thoughts in the language of the Christian faith. This tendency must be resisted.

Perhaps no one understood her better than her brother, André, not only because of the identity of their upbringing but because he, too, pursued a spiritual itinerary with as cosmopolitan a reach as her own. When she once told him, during the war, that she would have been baptized into Christianity except for the problems the church posed to her, he replied: "I see only one difficulty in that; it's that you would have the same reasons for adhering to Hinduism, or Buddhism, or Taoism."[1] But the "problem" remains only for those who do not admit that she continued to be as open to those isms as to Christianity. Their common denomination lies in their mystical awareness of what Evelyn Underhill has called "that human incompleteness which is the origin of our divine unrest."[2] The Christian mode predominates in her writing because she was the stepdaughter of a mostly Catholic culture. It is vital to understand that fact in its historical context.

Nothing in Weil's thought has so steadily sustained general interest and critical attention as her reflections on the Trinitarian God, on Christ, and the church. If Weil is known for any work, it is either the collection of essays and letters, *Attente de Dieu*, or Thibon's selections from her *cahiers*, chiefly on moral and religious topics, *La pesanteur et la grâce*. Both works were published within a few years after her death and went far to crystallize Weil's reputation as a "religious writer." Yet the historically obvious has not been remarked: these writings belong to the Vichy years.

Weil was not working out a theology for Vichy or against it, but her thoughts on religious matters must be situated in the *années noires* during which they developed. Studies of Weil as a "religious writer," a genius of love, have been antiseptic to historic facts. Usually, she has been confined to the vacuum of an enthusiast's creedal presuppositions or prejudices—an ironic limbo, indeed, for a mind of such breadth.

She spent nearly two years, from June 1940 to May 1942, under the dismal Pétain regime, one member of a vast audience for its *fuite en arrière* propaganda. Unemployed because she was a Jew, she remained a tacit victim of the New Order in which Vichy played the abject partner. That such degradation affected her sensibility seems indubitable. Actually she saw it in a peculiar light: "Present events are an affliction, and that is an unbearable fact. We must contemplate this affliction in all its bitterness and without consolation, while loving God as the author of all things—including this same affliction—and as the author solely of good."[3] It is hazardous to conjecture how official oppression, the Nazi menace, and the tensions of collaboration and resistance may have shaped her thinking about God and belief, but it hardly seems incidental that a centerpiece in her thought, the ontological penance called decreation, removal of the self as a blemish upon being, as obstacle between God and the world, reads like a metaphysical improvisation upon a theme that Vichy thrust on defeated France, the need for repentance for all the Third Republic's crimes, chief among them that the Troisième had existed at all.

Her fascination with toil, the more grueling the better, antedated the war by many years, but only in the Vichy years did she come to understand work as a spiritual exercise, a working off, one might say: the emblem of decreation. That she labored in Ardèche vineyards for some of that time provides a curious conjunction: she had experiential access to the agrarian world that suffuses New Testament metaphors and she carried out at the most immediate level possible the Vichy injunction (which expressly included Jews), back to the land. Weil was at work simultaneously in the fields of the Lord and of the Maréchal. It is no small irony that one of Vichy's victims transcended its shibboleths on labor and articulated a philosophy of work aimed toward a genuine spiritual rebirth of France.

To love the good and at the same time accept necessity at its most harsh, in the degradation of soul, mind, and body: such was Weil's vocation as a Jew in a sordid and dangerous time. To say that she stayed out of the church is not enough: not *hors de l'église* but *hors de l'église vichyssoise*. She struggled to love the God who sent the sun to shine on the Nazis and the rain to fall on the French. Like Pascal she kept Christ on the cross. And she did not flinch when Krishna in his theophany proclaimed himself Death, destroyer of worlds.

Confronting the Church

If, as is sometimes argued, the Great War signaled the passing of a golden age in French letters—who, coming of age in the 1920s, would rival Proust and Gide in prose or Valéry in verse?—Weil's generation was eloquent in what might be called the genre of spiritual thirst. It would be convenient but misleading to call the young writers of that time *déracinés*, to use Barrès's surcharged word. They were not barren of options; they faced all too forceful ones: old-guard Catholicism, Marxist materialism, wave-of-the-future fascism. These ideologies claimed to satisfy the necessity of social cohesion and individual purpose even while dissolving that purpose into the requirements of church, party, or state. Weil is one of the few who made the suasions of these collectivities submit to the rigorous scruples of a singular intellectual sensibility.

She and her contemporaries inherited a top-heavy literature of social prophecy, from Rousseau (Weil called him a Christian genius), Fourier, and

Saint-Simon to Sorel. Major editions of Proudhon and Marx appeared throughout the 1920s. Jaurès had asserted that socialism was the realization of Christianity, and Weil's early understanding of Christianity as the pursuit of justice on earth could be called a voluntarist adaptation of socialism: "It will suffice then to be just and pure in order to save the world; that is expressed in the myth of the Man-God, who redeems human sin by justice alone and without any political action. It is necessary therefore to save oneself, to preserve in the self the Spirit of which outward humanity is the myth. The sacrifice is the acceptance of pain, the refusal to obey the animal in oneself, and the will to redeem suffering people by voluntary suffering."[4]

These words from a topos for Alain hint at Weil's subsequent commitment to activism and her resistance to its organizational, authoritarian forms. The will to justice had to be kept individual so as to vouchsafe its spiritual source, a personal revolution to redeem suffering. How her remarks here pertain to her final distance from Catholicism can best be seen in what she denied in the church's doctrinal tradition, what she expressly rejected or merely ignored.

Perhaps most surprising, in view of her interest in Greek mysteries, is her indifference to the idea of the soul's immortality. But, in fact, adopting Plato, she does believe in an immortal part of the soul, uncreated and impersonal. It is the divine constituent of our being, *le sacre*, not be to confused with the subjective makeup of personality, *la personne*. In the *Republic* Plato speaks of human misdeeds as so many barnacles on the soul, but for Weil everything that can be identified with the perishable ego is a barnacle. That is why she does not admit an afterlife in any personal terms.[5] A fortiori, the resurrection of the body is meaningless to her. From one of her favorite Christian texts, Philippians 2:5–9, she drew much joy because Christ's incarnation is depicted as that of a self-humbling slave, but she did not go on to address the passage's conclusion in Christ's glorious resurrection.[6] What Christians account the greatest of miracles did not interest her.

She dismissed the gospel miracles altogether. Better, she felt, to regard miracles as Hindus do, events too banal to be interesting. Besides, the Western notion of miracle is tied to a scientific worldview with which miracle is incompatible because there are no grounds sufficient for its affirmation or denial.[7] She contended that the popular notion of miracles "either hinders an unconditional acceptance of God's will or obliges one to be blind to the quantity and nature of evil existing in the world."[8] Devoted to the Platonic separation of good and necessity, she denied that there could be any overt divine interference in the contingent world of relative good and evil. This is the basis of her attacks on Judaism's intrusive God and his manifestations of power. Good can be present in necessity only covertly, infinitesimally: God is incarnated as a slave and killed as a criminal.[9]

Although Weil gave profound attention to the eucharist and to baptism, she paid no heed at all to sacramental confession and absolution. Not that she was without a conviction of sin; her *cahiers* abound in references to it: as one's identification of self with what is not God, as the transference of one's own misery into another person, as the use of false goods to hide from God (putting the illimitability of imagination into something finite), as failure to recognize human hurt, even as a favor from God in showing human imperfection.[10] She had an anguished sense of her own sinfulness. She once told Perrin that she felt all her sins were mortal and that she was committing them incessantly. She even acknowledged a certain pride in her awareness of sinning.[11] Because she considered sin to be, like virtue, not an act but a state of being or orientation, confession was bootless. The foremost sin for which she held herself accountable was her existence.

Weil did not, could not participate in the orgiastic penance that became fashionable in the first years of Vichy, but this atmosphere informed her. As a prominent historian has written of that time: "The churches had not been so full for years; sin, retribution and penance were the themes of many sermons. Prayer was in fashion—for families to be re-united, for the million and a half prisoners of war to be swiftly released. . . . Processions, pilgrimages and retreats became the vogue."[12] It is helpful to recall these popular manifestations of piety. Weil's Great Beast of collectivity, apart from its authoritarian guises, wore a human face she could not help but notice.

Religiosity under Vichy may account for Weil's hostility to religion as consolation, where belief in miracles plays a major part. The folk cults centered on Lourdes, Thérèse of Lisieux, and Jeanne d'Arc perhaps never flourished so well as in this time of national prostration and impotence. They provide a context for Weil's criticisms without which her dismissal of miracles, seemingly unprompted, has a gratuitous, almost truculent aspect. Escapism, whether in cult worship or I-centered rituals of penance, repelled her.

Folk religion has a life of its own, and Weil could not have faulted the official church for vulgar shows of enthusiasm. These displays of *croyance* were the faithful equivalent of Pétain's innumerable parades, where uniforms and banners gave ordinary people some importance to cling to. Weil, though critical of the common believer's need of solace, directed most of her attention to the formal church and its handling of mystery and authority.

What might fairly be called the "protestant principle" (Paul Tillich's words) Weil exercised against the church in its self-arrogated role as mediator between God and humanity.[13] While recognizing the church as repository for sacraments, she believed it had no privileged authority by which to deny these to anyone. She has sometimes been criticized for this belief on the presumption that, rather than humbly acceding to the church, she was trying to make it come to her on her terms. But it is more fair to suppose she wanted the eucharist, the sacrament that mattered most to her, to be a truly catholic gift, one of transcendent purity, to the countless people of France who, though not communicants, were as beleaguered and debauched as any Catholic under the Occupation. Yet when she read the gospel story of the centurion (an Occupation agent par excellence) who witnesses Christ as Son of God, she noted privately that it "suffices to show that we exaggerate the role of the sacraments."[14] Her denunciation of the ecclesiastical practice of anathema suggests her fear that if she received baptism, she might later be excluded from the sacraments. Once in, she could be cast out. So long as she remained outside, nothing she believed, thought, or wrote could be condemned as heresy.[15] She did not wish to give the church the institutional power over her which Vichy held.

She was possibly no less fearful of how confession might bind her to the church. It is not certain that all the objections she enumerated against organized Christianity were the only ones she had, or even the most important. Her brief against the church's totalitarianism, for example, rests mainly on historical rather than contemporary practices: the supposed contamination of Christendom by Rome and Israel; the church's culturally subversive missionary tradition; its Thomism, which she found as intellectually stifling as Hitlerism; and the "poison" of its eschatological idea of progress, including universal conversion and the world's end.[16]

Since, according to Weil, the church has too many bad fruits by which it is known, it is no wonder she rejected its claim to be the mystical body of its savior. Our true dignity, she told Perrin, lies not in any such collectivity but in the Christ-in-us. One can be loyal to Christ unto death without being a part of the Body, she insisted. As far as the church is a social institution (Plato's Great Beast) rather than a spiritual authority only, it would be best not to offer oneself to it as a martyr.[17] These remarks are the prolegomenon to her comparing medieval Christendom to modern totalitarianism: she likened the apocalyptic heroism of early Christian martyrs to that of communists in her own day who acted on behalf of a presumably imminent revolution. But that comparison is disingenuous: she well knew that the Communist party in France, hounded by the government since 1938, had become the first effective cadre of the Resistance, its members imprisoned and frequently shot by the Nazis in reprisal for sabotage. Putting their lives on the line, they did not have the Christian martyrs' expectation of a glorious reward in the hereafter and precious little hope (in 1942) of a revolutionary overthrow of fascism.

In Stoic fashion Weil believed that virtue should have no extrinsic reward, no comforting or alluring compensation. Expectation of reward vitiates the good in one's acts. She stated confidently that most of the church's saints will not enter heaven. Her categorical exclusion implies, of course, that there is a heaven some few do enter. Just as she acknowledged the church's legitimacy in administering sacraments and serving as a source for "inspiration," so she recognized a true membership or saving remnant in the church, consisting solely of those who have risen above the level of what she called social participation; in effect, those who would be Christians even (or especially?) if there were no congregated body.

When she insisted to Perrin that she was remaining outside of the church because of her imperfections, she referred not to the collective body that confused the impure and the pure and belonged, she said, to Satan; she referred to the church of an exalted few, those she knew individually and regarded as authentic Christians.[18] It was another august group occupying a transcendental realm, like that of the intellectual saints of her adolescent fantasy whose genius made her feel cut off and excluded. At the same time, she felt that she, too, belonged to the church's "sacramental life" because of her "implicit faith," which informed her youth's "Christian inspiration," her perception of the world's problems in an explicitly Christian way, and her three "contacts" with Christianity in adulthood.[19] Though she felt unworthy of baptism (as though one had to be pure to receive its cleansing), she took the church to task for its parochialism, particularly its contempt for other mystical religions. If she resisted the church because she sensed her impulsion toward it was also carrying her toward acceptance of Israel, she did not say so, but she did say that Christianity, "catholic by right but not in fact," did not embrace "so many things I love and don't wish to abandon; so many things God loves, else they would not exist": despised cultures and races, heretical traditions such as those of Mani and Albi, the antiquity of Greece, Egypt, India, and China, the world's beauty and its reflections in art and science. With so extensive an inventory of loves for which she saw no place made in the church, it seems strange she ever gave herself so much trouble about whether to accept Christianity formally. She concluded to Perrin that it was legitimate, even obligatory, that she remain a member of the church "by right but not in fact."[20]

Perhaps, she speculated, in a materialistic age, God wants some people to love Christ and yet stay outside of the church. Because she never felt God wanted her within the church, she believed she was a chosen outsider. She called it her vocation. Most odd is her desire not to be cut off from "the immense and wretched mass of nonbelievers," as though membership in the church would somehow isolate her from them.[21] It is instructive that she stated this concern to Perrin in a letter of January 19, 1942, the month she was distributing the *Cahiers du Témoignage chrétienne*'s denunciation of anti-Semitism. In a nation ostensibly Catholic, who more than Jews could be called "a wretched mass of nonbelievers"? If the Judaic roots of Christendom kept Weil from entering the church, could it be that the suffering of Jews worked on her as well?

If, in all her objections to the church, Weil seems to have protested too much, it would also seem that the church offered her abundant occasions for creative intellectual response and interrogative curiosity. Despite her own contention that the mysteries of faith belong to supernatural love rather than to intellect, her attempts to yoke Christianity to pre-Christian Greece amount to an intellectual task. They also indicate that she approximates within her own thought much within the Christian theological tradition. That point is easily obscured, however, because her affinities lie far more in the non-European or Eastern church than in the Western.

Her reading in patristic literature perhaps made her aware of this difference. Attempts at a *syncrétisme* of Hellenic and Christian beliefs "like that of which Nicholas of Cusa dreamed" were mostly the work of Eastern theologians.[22] Weil herself was not inclined to syncretism—her fondness for analogy precluded identity, and she always delighted in difference—but she was completely receptive to the Greek patristic practice of making symbolic constructions from commonplace terms like *logos* and *pneuma*. Justin Martyr's deference to the Greeks, his belief that the Christian *logos* had, in the guise of eternal reason, inspired Heraclitus and Plato anticipates Weil's persuasion.

She hails Porphyry's statement that Origen had interpreted Scriptures symbolically according to secret Pythagorean and Stoic texts and Melito's that Christian "philosophy," though sprung from Judaism, flourished under the gentiles. But nothing she read could satisfy her desire to conjoin Christianity and other mystery religions of the ancient Near East. Because this conjunction had only apparently been suppressed or denied by the early church in Rome, she was left with "a tissue of suppositions" and the suspicion that the church had camouflaged or destroyed much of its own spiritual vitality.[23]

Her efforts to recover that vitality strikingly recapitulate many of the fundamental issues and tensions of patristic literature East and West. It might be said, for instance, that like Irenaeus she tried to unite the mysticism of sacramental union and the Jewish (also Stoic) laws of righteous conduct to an obedience owed to a higher, universal law. Her desire for newness—a new *sainteté,* a new religion to supersede Christianity—has that synthetic freshness. Like Arius she looked upon the abyss between God and humanity which requires the soul's total submission to God, but like Athanasius she upheld divine immanence and the implicit ontological identity of Christ with God and of the human soul (in its uncreated substance) with both. Like the renegade Tertullian, she rejected the church as too worldly.

It is a strange fact that on many points she is like Augustine, the church's hatchet man as it struggled to define itself against heresies. Her printed remarks on him are almost entirely censorious,[24] but she knew that his thought never lost the Neoplatonic orientation it had early assumed. Weil's identification of the divine *logos* as the one legitimate goal of the mind; her Platonic bias about mathematics as key to transcendent truth; her view that the object of science and religion are one; that knowledge is divine illumination, with the prevenience of grace enabling intellect; that perfect freedom lies in total submission to the good; her theodicy of the world's beauty participating in the divine—all of these cardinal notions have antecedence in Augustine. Had she been able to read him less politically than she did, she might have found in him the model of an ongoing intellectual quest within the Christian faith such as she feared she could not pursue if she entered the church.

The point is crucial because her *hors de l'église* reticence has helped too many readers, Christian and otherwise, to assume that her basic affinity is with heresies such as gnosticism. But the Gnostics were an amorphous gaggle of outsiders, and her points of agreement with them are few and mostly negative: she appreciated Valentinus's condemnation of the Hebrew God and of Joshua's *herem,* but she did not reject the whole of the Torah. She did not fully subscribe to the Gnostics' ethical dualism; she said we cannot see the world in black and white because we are ourselves subject to illusion. She also rejected the Gnostics' metaphysical dualism, which condemns the material world as evil, even while acknowledging a satanic power in the world. She saw it as a political and psychological, but not a material, evil.

It is true, however, that she placed gnosticism within the magic circle of Oriental mystery cults from which she was convinced Christianity was derived.[25] In that circle, too, she located the Cathars of twelfth-century Provence, but her inspiration in doing so came secondhand, from reading a booklet on Catharism by Déodat Roché, editor of *Cahiers d'études cathares*. He had described this movement as a form of Christian Platonism,[26] precisely the sort of phenomenon Weil could seize upon in her efforts to supplant the Judaic foundations of Christianity with Hellenic. But her enthusiasm for the Cathars rested substantially on extraneous grounds: they had imputed to Judaism an adoration of force, and they were persecuted to extinction by the Inquisition. Besides, her intellectual honesty forced her to concede that her central assumption of a sacred band threading its way across diverse cultures into medieval times stood on very exiguous evidence: "Of course, given the scarcity of documents, such an opinion can hardly be proved."[27] She also realized the impossibility of modern adherence to cults such as Catharism because "one cannot, indeed, support what doesn't exist."[28] To call Weil a neo-Gnostic or Cathar, as friends, foes, and others sometimes do, makes no more sense than to call her a Church Father. Neither can her hypothetical attempts to conjoin Christianity with history's victims obscure her romantic sentimentalism, which found in their losing and their otherness a quixotic butt against the entrenched triumphalist church. If the church, militant and expectant, smelled of mortality more rankly under Vichy than before, Weil knew she could neither sanitize it nor find a substitute for it.

She was not lost in pedantic fantasy, but she tended to overstep the bounds which the paucity of historical evidence set on her conjectures. Why she overstepped them is a question that has not received much attention. An answer may be found in her two essays on Languedoc published by *Cahiers du Sud* under her anagrammatic pseudonym, Emile Novis, in the late summer of 1942.

The first, "L'agonie d'une civilisation vue à travers un poème épique," draws on a fragmentary *chanson* as a kind of medieval *Iliad* in which the chivalric culture of Toulouse succumbs to the treachery and force of papal Rome. It was a subject of transparent significance to any reader in 1942. Despite her own caveats—"we can merely attempt to guess what this civilization was like"—she infers from the fragment that following the church's destruction of the Languedoc culture, "Europe never again recovered to the same degree the spiritual freedom lost through this war."[29]

In her other essay, "En quoi consiste l'inspiration occitanienne?" she states confidently that Languedoc realized the rebirth of Greek ideas of proportion and mediation between divinity and humanity. This Romanesque civilization was "the true Renaissance" of Pythagorean and Platonic idealism, succeeded after "the murder of this country" by the "false" Renaissance of non-Christian humanism and the church's Gothic "attempt at totalitarian spirituality."[30] The constituents of the Cathars' "inspiration" were an understanding of force, the "supernatural courage" that rejects force even while acknowledging that force reigns virtually uncontested in the world, and finally, compassionate love for all victims of force. Weil arbitrarily equates the cult of chivalric love with the *eros* in Plato's *Symposium*—each was a spiritual counter to force. As Toulouse was situated in the world of necessity, its society was not free of "pollution," but the inspiration, Weil says, was "pure." It was a communal alternative to Great Beast collectivity. Such is Weil's recreation (or projection) of a genuinely spiritual culture, one such as the authoritarian church, in all its centuries, has failed to produce.

It becomes clear why Weil passed beyond thin historical records to philosophical incantation. In her discussion of the poetic fragment, she concluded that though a dead culture cannot be revived, "piety preserved through the ages allows its equivalent to arise one day, when favorable circumstances are presented."[31] Weil revered the past, saw most of it as bleak—conquerors write history—but gave a special value to its moments of exceptional nobility, as she saw them, so as to draw some inspired sense of direction in the days of Vichy.

In her second essay, she recognizes that the Cathars' desire for purity went too far in discarding dogmas altogether, but laments the church's choice of force in dealing with them: "It is infinitely painful to think that the arms of this murder were guided by the Church. But that which is painful is sometimes true. . . . The Church chose badly. It chose evil. This evil bore fruit and we are in evil's midst. Repentance means returning to the moment which preceded that bad choice."[32]

These essays on Languedoc are a species of Resistance document, written both against the contemporary church and on its behalf: against, while Catholicism was officially lined up behind Vichy (how could it not be, since Pétain was pledged to restore a church battered by republican anticlericalism?); and for, because Weil had come to know in the Unoccupied Zone groups within the church that were fighting to preserve its spiritual integrity even at the cost of its episcopal authority. These groups—the *jocistes*, the members of Témoignage chrétien—were, if any, capable of that penance for an evil choice. This context shows Catholicism as Weil experienced it, as an institution rent like France itself by collaboration and *résistance.*

Performing under constraint as an accomplice to an evil too great to name, the church incurred continuous suspicion from German overseers: "It was a force to be reckoned with, sustained by a creed far more venerable than Nazism, run by a Hierarchy commanding an absolute obedience and with world-wide contacts."[33] But Vichy had its outspoken supporters in high church offices: Lyons's Cardinal Gerlier, for example, who embraced Pétain's *Travail, Famille, Patrie* slogan with "These words are ours";[34] Monsignor Dutoit, archbishop of Arras, who, as late as December 1941, issued a pastoral letter calling for collaboration through a "free and fair desire for understanding";[35] and Cardinal Baudrillat, rector of the Institut Catholique in Paris, who contributed articles to the pro-Nazi journals *La gerbe* and *Le nouvelliste.* Official deference to Pétain was hardly involuntary, especially after June 1941, when Nazism took on the guise of a universal crusade against Bolshevism, the church's deadly rival in confessional totalitarianism.

Individual profiles amount to only a very small part of an extraordinarily complex picture.[36] Many clerics were courageous renegades, the most famous among them Cardinal Salièges, archbishop of Toulouse, the Cathars' homeland, and Monsignor Théas of Montaubon, but it was the *jocistes,* ever suspect to the Nazis because of their close contacts with labor movements, and the participants of Témoignage chrétien who gave Weil concrete examples of the love and higher obedience she saw, or chose to see, in Catharism. Beside them was the liberal, heterogeneous culture around Marseilles: Weil's affiliates at *Cahiers du Sud,* the members of the Société des études philosophiques, friends such as Bousquet, Lanza del Vasto, and the Sanskrit enthusiast René Daumal, all of whom contributed to Weil's intellectual vitality in an adverse time and gave her some intimation that the "spirit" of Languedoc was being sustained for a time of "favorable circumstances." They also imparted some fear that this fragile world, like that of twelfth-century Languedoc, might quickly be destroyed.

Covertly, Weil addressed her words on the Occitanian inspiration to an intellectual community in the Unoccupied Zone that was fit to uphold that inspiration and overcome what in her conclusion she called "the ignobilities which make up the air we are breathing."[37] She offered scant hope that this inspiration would last because, like Catharism, it confronted force and the sword. Nothing is more terrible, she feels, than the church's ambivalence in the modern confrontation. In the Languedoc essays, Weil offers her most devastating criticism of Roman Catholicism, a refracted glance at its spiritual default, its near decrepitude. It seems fitting, too, that she was writing from Marseilles, which, having taken in thousands of Jews, was derided by the Nazis as the New Jerusalem of the Mediterranean.

If the Vichy years exposed to her the susceptibilities of the church as an institution, they did not teach her that a Great Beast collectivity can be rendered piteous, fragmentary, and, however beset by evil, open to regenerating good. That she could continue to esteem the church as a treasury of dogmas and sacraments shows how strongly the church was drawing her to itself. Yet the positive examples of believers like Perrin, the Honnorats, the *jocistes*, "the six or seven Catholics of an authentic spirituality," did not suffice to convert her.[38] She refused to be converted to please someone, and as such pleasure would have been the inevitable effect of her conversion, she seems to have nursed an instinctive horror of her Catholic friendships.

Her observation of the church's sacramental legitimacy was never more than observation. Respectful, even reverent attention always implied a safeguarding distance, as though the church was not so much a house as a museum gallery. Her position was that of a transient visitor, and seldom, despite her frequent attendance at masses, does she suggest awareness of a present, daily community of the sinning faithful. Her struggle was wholly her own, and she did not and perhaps could not conceive of a communal struggle. That seems the oddest fact of all because her own crisis or time of judgment coincided with the church's.

In the end, her standing outside the church owed much to Alain. His name is usually ignored in the innumerable discussions of her relations with Catholicism, but it can be assumed that she was familiar with his *Propos sur la religion*, gathered in 1938. During the Vichy years she read his *Les Dieux* and told Gilbert Kahn that some of Alain's views were still her own; others she no longer admitted. It is in *Les Dieux* that Alain observed: "Reproached by one's own piety, one surely grasps it is a great crime to be ignorant of the true god, but one grasps much more, that it is an even greater crime to belong to the people of God. One cannot."[39] No communicant, Alain was well disposed to the church on his own outsider's terms. His model was the non-Catholic Auguste Comte, whose humanist balance and impartiality he admired. Alain commended the early church for struggling against what he called *croyance*, credulity which is the opposite of faith. Expressly influenced by Hegel's dogma of intellectual progress, he saw the church's proper role in the successive development of the mind, but he also saw the hazards of collectivity and "the God-thing."[40] He asserted that many formal believers, "the inhumane and obstinate crowd of Catholics," were not aware of genuine spirituality.[41] His religion was a belief in *volonté* and the heretical power of *refus*. Mind is by nature a sacrilege, he said; it is atheistic. Christianity's development lies in free thought. The true gods, he claimed, are "the genuinely mystical ideas of faith, freedom, equality and justice," and for official saints he would substitute a cult of the illustrious dead.[42]

An apologia he wrote in 1923 anticipates Weil's own cosmopolitan heterodoxy as she revealed it in her *Lettre à un religieux*: "If you propose a religion to me, I examine it, not with the idea that it is false, but rather that it is true. So how is it that I pass for an unbeliever? It's that I think the same of all religions. Each of them is only a more or less deformed perspective in which it is necessary that I rediscover the unique object."[43] Weil's contention that religions of various cultures hold explicit and implicit truths vis-à-vis one another, that the essence specific to each religious tradition is finally the same in all, follows Alain's assumption of a unique object. But she also knew what Alain's insouciant humanism did not allow him to admit, that every religion can be known only from within—a concession that makes Weil's own sense of herself as a Christian dubious.[44] Alain's uncommitted intellectual politeness toward institutional Christian faith must be set in contrast to Weil's confrontation of it with the whole of her sensibility, with its Pascalian need to examine and freely believe and its Cartesian autonomy reinforced by doubt.[45] Her fundamental protestantism had its domicile in her own nature, and she knew intuitively that had she entered the Christian church she would have betrayed not only her Jewish family, not only the beauties of the non-Christian world, not only the countless, wretched outsiders. She would have betrayed herself.

Christ and Evil

Near the center of Weil's religious thinking is Christ, but this Christ is always refracted through the complex prism of her temperament. She does not write of Jesus, the Jew of Nazareth. She read the gospels, but she seems not to have comprehended them as personal histories. (Had she read Renan?) Like many who approach Christianity from outside its traditions, she looked on Christ as a model, a source of metaphors, an embodiment of philosophical truths. Because, as she told Perrin, he was the truth before he was Christ, she did not ask if Christ was the incarnate God. She was even willing to suppose there were incarnations before Christ's time; that cultures such as those of ancient India and China had revealed scriptures; that the Spirit of Christ came to those who called on Krishna or Buddha. She read this universal Christ in (or into) the lore of ancient myths, where he was Dionysos, the suffering god, where he embodied Tao as the Way, where as Osiris and *maat*, he was truth.[46] All of these analogies deny the uniqueness of the Christian incarnation, with Jesus rooted in Jewish culture and its history.

Nowhere are her efforts more bold, one might say flamboyant, than in the "intuitions pré-chrétiennes," which she imputed to classical Hellenism. An instance she lengthily presents almost as a defense of Greek "intuitions" of Christ is the recognition scene from Sophocles' *Elektra*. Loving the absence of her brother Orestes more than anything else, Elektra awaits in him a deliverance from slavery, debasing toils, and humiliations. So intense is her desire that Orestes, having returned in disguise from exile, is compelled to reveal himself to her. Having seen, heard, and touched him, "she will no longer ask if her savior lives." This epiphany signified to Weil the divine reward to the soul's indefatigable yearning for God. She read this drama as her own story, a scenario of the soul's loving expectation of the divine *parousia*. In her own testimony, "each word had at the center of my being a resonance so profound and so secret that the interpretation likening Elektra to the human soul and Orestes to Christ is almost as certain for me as if I myself had written these lines."[47] The broader context of the play, whose dénouement is matricide and a party, mattered not at all to her. A French critic has charitably characterized Weil's interpretation of Elektra and Orestes as "a singular adventure," but in fact it recalls the fantastic allegorical feats of patristic exegesis.[48] Like the tortuous efforts of Cyprian, Justin, Irenaeus, or Origen to impose a Christian anagogy upon innocuous and resistant Jewish scriptures, Weil's reading of Sophocles conveys little more than her imaginative ingenuity in establishing a meaning ulterior, not to say anachronistic, to the drama. It is better to draw a curtain over such fancies.

Although Weil's Christ is universal or catholic in meaning, he is not impersonal. How could he be, having come down and possessed her in 1938? How, then, did she see him subsequent to this rapture? The answer requires a brief review of the biblical Christ, how Weil selectively recognized him and then recast him in her reflections on theology and ethics.

She was especially fond of the Johannine gospel. With its dogma of the divine *logos* it is the most Greek of the gospels and the most hostile toward

Jews. But her *cahiers* and other writings show that each of the four gospel accounts contributed substantially to her understanding of Christianity.

She read in Matthew 5:45 a witness to the mechanism of necessity: the sun and rain fall on good and bad alike. In the lilies of the field (6:26) she read a witness to the world's beauty that she believed the church, excepting Francis of Assisi, had lost. In this gospel hides Christ's unseen Father (6:6), the *deus absconditus* she took as the true god absent from Judaism; and in Christ's promise that everyone who asks for bread shall not be given a stone (7:8–9) she found release from her adolescent destitution. Christ's exemplary slave waiting for the master's return (24:46)—a text one could read with a difference in the Vichy years—she saw as herself prescribed. Matthew 25:35, "I was hungry and you fed me," carrying the *deus absconditus* into the daily ethics of Jewish *tzedakah*, she might have heard in her service to the dispossessed, from Le Puy in 1931 to the Annamite camps ten years later. It was one of her favorite passages, and the extent to which her life answered its message, long before Vichy, seems to ratify her claim to Perrin that she had long lived in "the Christian inspiration."

Yet she feared she was the fig tree Christ condemns in Mark: "I never read the story without trembling. . . . I think it is my portrait. In it, too, nature was powerless, and yet it was not excused. Christ cursed it. . . . The feeling of being for Christ like a sterile fig tree rends my heart."[49] The old conviction of inadequacy and exclusion now assumed a terrible force. In Mark's brooding, elliptical version she also found attributed to Christ the logical absurdities known as koans, and they fascinated her no less than comparable utterances she found in reading about Zen Buddhism: "To him with nothing it shall be taken away" (4:25) may well have terrified her. She noted of the paralytic who could not walk that he was "merely too lazy to move. But that is my case." Then, in the Greek, she records his response to Christ: "If you are willing, you can heal me."[50] But she fastened upon Christ's fate in the Markan story far more than upon his words.

The Markan Christ is isolated; helplessly subjected to necessity, with Jews and Romans its agents; falsely appropriated and misusunderstood by his disciples; ingloriously traduced and crucified, mocked even by those dying with him. Most significant, there is no triumphant resurrection. Her faith, she wrote to Père Couturier, would be "easier" without the resurrection. The "perfect beauty" of the Passion and the cross alone sufficed for her.[51] Mark's gospel, nonecclesiological, bitter, and without consolation, most closely prefigures Weil's Christ and his eerie perfection in agony.

St. Luke's gospel afforded her a cutting edge against the church's exclusive triumphalism. It prophesies (3:6) that all humanity would be witness to God's salvation. Further, the contrast the Lukan Christ makes between new wine and old (5:38–39) underscored the Christian departure from Judaic traditionalism. Some enigmatic texts in this version prompted her to ask questions: what was the key to the house of knowledge (11:52) which Christ said the Pharisees held? What did Christ mean in saying (12:49) that his mission was to set the earth afire? Her questions came not from intellectual curiosity but from an intellectual hunger. That so much in the New Testament remains obscure to Christians seemed to her a reproach to the church as guardian of the Scriptures. She did not expressly accuse the church of blurring possible non-Judaic sources, but she did find it guilty of slovenliness scarcely less objectionable than dishonesty. It was scandalous that the church no longer understood much of what its savior imparted.

To most Christians the question of whether Melchisedec was a prototype of Christ probably matters little, but for Weil the absence of clarity and the suggestiveness of some texts, as she posed them either to herself or to bemused clerics, prompted her to fill in the gaps with her own speculations. Asking, for example, about Christ's unknown years in Egypt led her not to answers but to intriguing implications. (Did she know Freud's essay on Moses?) Such musings left her frustrated, but they also left open a door to the would-be heterodoxy she developed in her theology.

Before a discussion of that theology, it is useful to address a brief work unlike anything else Weil ever wrote and to which she gave particular importance by insisting to her mother that it be placed at the beginning of her seven volumes of American notebooks. Although it defies generic classification—it is neither memoir nor fiction nor allegory nor reverie—it might be called Weil's version of a gospel episode, with herself cast at the center, with Christ as "He."

"He came into my room and said: 'You poor wretch, who understand nothing and know nothing, come with me and I will teach you things you have no idea of.' I followed him."

They go to a church altar and he orders her to genuflect. "I told him: 'I have not been baptized.' He said: 'Fall on your knees before this place, with love, as before the place where truth exists.' I obeyed."

They ascend to a garret overlooking a town. They talk. He gives her bread. "That bread truly had the taste of bread. I have never found that taste again. He poured wine for me and for himself, which tasted of the sun and the soil on which the city was built. Sometimes we lay down on the wooden floor, and the sweetness of sleep descended on me."

Despite his pledge to teach her, there was only desultory talk in the way of "old friends." "One day he said to me: 'Now go away.' I threw myself down, clung to his knees, begged him not to send me away. But he flung me out toward the stairs. I descended them as if unconscious, as if my heart was torn in shreds."

She then feels it was a mistake that he had come. Her place was anywhere but that garret. Yet she troubles herself trying to remember what he had told her: "I well know that he doesn't love me. How could he love me? And yet there is something deep in me, some point of myself, which cannot prevent itself from thinking, with fear and trembling, that perhaps, in spite of everything, he does love me."[52]

If "He" is Christ (who else could give her the bread and wine?), he is also a cad and a bully. Not even the eucharistic sharing, the old friends' talk, the stretching out on the floor (a tableau of adolescent sexuality) can overcome his peremptory tone and violence. Why should she want this creature to love her? This curious story is ammunition for those who presume Weil was masochistic.[53]

It seems obvious that this composition interprets her experience of Christ after the visitation in 1938. The entry into her room is the mystical rapture; the altar and the garret are settings for an initiation to which she feels inadequate. They might respectively symbolize the church she finally could not enter and the intimacy within it which she feared might leave her complacent and compromised. Her expulsion, a casting out into the wilderness, is an involuntary *imitatio Christi*, an indication of how emulously she looked upon Christ, the suffering servant. The loves-me, loves-me-not conclusion marks a furtive confidence in her own position beyond the church, that she had been divinely appointed to an itinerary away from the deceptively comforting garret. She has a mission "in spite of everything"—a phrase that says much about her sense of inadequacy and failure and her being a Jew. Unlike the transcendent realm of genius to which she had not won admission in childhood, the garret was accessible but turned out to be a mere way station, and she leaves it, although precipitously, as an initiate. The very exclusion adumbrates acceptance: it is the Christian paradox of being chosen an outcast. Weil had discovered that Christianity does not evade suffering but uses it. The prologue, apologia for all ensuing notes, suggests that Weil felt she had been put to use. She no longer needed to know whether her place was within the formal church. Instead, Christ had sent her out into the world in the terms of a supreme contradiction: she was a slave on her own.

Why, then, Christ the bully? Alain had written that "what is received and submitted to isn't faith. In short, there's only one value, the free man, and such is the object of faith."[54] Surpassing Alain, Weil found in her Christ the peculiar reconciliation of submission and freedom. In that sense, "He" does teach her after all, and she continues to follow him. As to his apparent cruelty, another remark from Alain may cast some light. Speaking of the Jansenist, Alain describes him as "a coarse, pitiless friend who looks not to your weakness but who strikes always at your strength and so honors you. Fearsome, because he demands exactly what you can't refuse, which is that you be a free person. . . . You will love him at once without knowing why, and perhaps after twenty years you will discover that he alone loved you. An ironsmith."[55]

Weil's Jansenist Christ is this taskmaster: the bread that feeds and the stone that wounds, she wrote, both come from Christ's hand as a love the soul must receive to its depths.[56] Not even her trouble, at the story's end, in remembering what Christ had told her really mattered: true faith, she was convinced, is a secret between God and us in which we have no part.[57] This is a Christ of no compromise, at a world's remove from the humanitarian phantom of all smiles and no agony and even from the Great Teacher of colorless humanism. Weil has the courage to conceive of Christ as many professional Christians would be loath to admit him, one conjured up in bewilderment and anger over the loneliness of humankind on earth.

Given Weil's dramatic account of her initiation into Christian mystery and this story, it is strange that some critics have either denied altogether that she was a mystic or have denied that she belongs to the contemplative tradition.[58] Underhill's remarks on mystical sensibility show how well Weil conforms to it: "Mystic conversion is a single and abrupt experience, sharply marked off from the long, dim struggles which precede and succeed it." The mystic's personality is generally of "a nature capable of extraordinary concentration, an exalted moral emotion, a nervous organization of the artistic type." However quaint these terms (they belong to the age of Matthew Arnold), they do not obscure Underhill's point that for all mystics, a higher reality overtakes the self and compels it beyond its will to "intense poverty and pain, as the only way of replacing false experience by true," to "the deliberate embrace of active suffering . . . seized as a splendid opportunity, a love token timidly offered by the awakened spirit to that all-demanding Lover."[59] These words profile Weil incisively.

Questioning her status as a mystic belongs of course to the issue of whether she was a Christian or something else. It is a hollow issue, but persistent. A substantial book could be written on Weil, much like René Etiemble's on Rimbaud, addressed solely to what others have presumed or manufactured about her, whether benevolently or otherwise—reputation made myth—and most of such a review would concern attitudes about her Christ and her god. Her Christ belongs to the Vichy years, a period fertile in analogies to the first-century Roman occupation of the Near East. Much of what Weil writes of Christ takes a vivid, compelling sense in this context.

Weil identifies two forms of wretchedness, that of distance from Christ and that of sharing with him the sinful human condition. They are identical, and to apprehend that identity amounts, she claims, to saintliness. Christian *malheur* she defines as an overwhelming, ineradicable sense of deprivation, that God has abandoned us. Christ felt his *malheur* so dreadfully he begged God to be spared it. "Christ's story is the experimental proof that human wretchedness is irreducible, that it is as great in the totally sinless person as in the sinner."[60]

Because Christ is man-without-God, it is impossible to conceive of him as God and man at once, yet much if not the whole meaning of the incarnation for Weil is that Christ gives humanity the divine response to God's distance and abandonment: he overcomes evil by submitting to it. His consent to unjust punishment is more than Stoic *amor fati* put to its greatest test; it is the ultimate manifestation of love as willingness to become "a thing in space."[61]

For Weil, the incarnation as divine submission to necessity is tantamount to crucifixion. Christ is God become slave. As he is mortal, his earthly presence is not perfect and pure, so Weil concludes from his reproach (Matt. 19:17) of someone who called him good. The Satanic temptations in the gospels prove that God gives free play to necessity. Christ, subject to it, was other than the good: he was the divine surrender of the good. In a reprise of Alain's humanism, Weil even goes so far as to disjoin Christ from the *logos*. The Word is "the light arising within everyone; and that is true always for everyone, without exception. . . . Regarding the common identity joining the Word and [Christ], nothing shows that affirmation of such a junction is a condition for salvation, and that would be absurd."[62] In a Vichy world, Christ does not save, he suffers, but human suffering is so unbearable to the human mind that it recoils from Christ's passion. How could it be otherwise, since fidelity to Christ occurs in a void?[63]

Weil's notions of sin are closely bound to Christ in this void. Because the void shows the world's need of God, sin attempts to fill it. Sin is passively a failure to recognize the human woe Christ epitomizes and actively the transference of one's own woe into another person. (How well that sums up anti-Jewish legislation in Occupied France.) It is not so much an act as an orientation or allegiance to what is not God, to, for example, all collectivities that use the prestige of force. Hence society is the mirror of sin, and all its false gods serve one's attempt to hide from God.

It is noteworthy that Weil writes nothing to indict Vichy's collaborators. To the contrary, she points to Christ's attitude toward the Resistance of his day, the pharisees, and to the Romans' henchmen, the publicans. The former he reproaches harshly; the latter, objects of common contempt, he does not. As the pharisees had their "reward," "Christ could as well have said of the publicans and prostitutes: Truly I say to you, they have their punishment—that is, social reprobation. So far as they do have it, the Father in secret keeps from punishing them. . . . Thus, social reprobation is destiny's favor."[64] In God's absence there is no black and white, only shades of gray—a moral chiaroscuro. This fact was no commonplace in a time when opposition to the *boche* was righteous, but the unhappy implication of God's absence from the world is that true justice is not to be realized, and God changes nothing. Neither does Christ. To be a slave is not to be a miracle worker or a Resistance zealot. As Weil puts it in a *boutade*, "Christ was killed in fury that he was only God."[65]

Those words go to the center of Weil's Christology, the cross. In one of her most quoted passages, she confesses that she envies Christ crucified.[66] This remark must be rescued from its apparent perversity. As her criticism of early Christian martyrs makes clear, the cross must not be desired; there can be no pharisaic or ulterior reward in seeking it. In a voluntarist vein, she says one must cut down the tree of self, make a cross of it, and carry it to life's end, but she is wary of atonement or expiation precisely because the "I" at sin's center continues to lurk in such efforts. Her perception of a cryptic egoism in confession might have been prompted by the disingenuous religiosity of Vichy, but its focus is obviously not limited to that time.

Her way to the cross—God did not reserve it for Christ alone, she says—is complex. One must be aware of sin in oneself and make a mental affliction of it by meditating upon the ontological offense of the "I," its pretense to being something. More positively, this meditation involves steady gazing turned toward God yet free of imaginative constructions. Christ's cross symbolizes attainment of this effort because it is grounded in an affliction that does not lie. Weil insists that only crucifixion's nakedness is not subject to "imaginary imitation": "It is a lot easier to imagine oneself in the place of God the Creator than in that of Christ crucified."[67] Only in the cross is the misery of humanity's contradictory nature comprehensible. In a key passage Weil moves from what initially reads like an existential statement of ethical and epistemological despair to a peculiar imperative: "Our life is nothing but impossibility, absurdity. Every thing we desire is contradictory to the conditions or consequences attached to it; every statement we make implies its contradiction; all of our feelings are mixed up with their opposites, because we are made of contradiction, being creatures and at the same time God, and at the same time infinitely other than God."[68] To apprehend the reality of this wretchedness is to love it. Christ crucified instructs in that love.

The cross itself is a corollation of contraries, both a union of humanity and God and their separation, and the unity subsuming unity and separation, just as God, through necessity, subsumes good and evil. The cross's affliction as Archimedean fulcrum—one sinks to rise—is much to be desired. Weil wrote to Perrin of her desire to arrive at this "good port," of wanting to be by Christ's side at the crucifixion, a station she considered far preferable to the glorious resurrection.[69] Superficially considered, her *theologia crucis* seems masochistic, but it is not clinically so; there seems to be no relish here in suffering as the occasion of an exotic eroticism. Neither does Weil argue for dolorism. She urges that one approach Christ "not through degradation, staining [*souillure*] and distress but in an unbroken joy, purity and sweetness."[70] If the crucified soul is fixed in love of God, free of self-serving illusions, it is rent yet transformed.

In Greek terms, the soul delivered into being ceases to become. (St. Paul enjoined Christians to put off mortality and put on immortality.) Weil found warrant for this transformation in Orphism, a nebulous mystical tradition that included belief in the soul's immortality. An Orphic text she transcribed into her *cahiers* bids the initiate rejoice in suffering as the way to godhead. Specifically, the soul must restore, by its own love of God and by the impulsion of grace, the unity of opposites which sin has broken down: these are power and love, Zeus-Jehovah and Prometheus-Christ: "We've become separated from God by wanting to share in his divinity through power, not love, and through being, not nonbeing." Repairing the harmony of power and love, the soul learns to imitate God: "Then God refashions in and with the soul what previously he had fashioned without its assistance."[71] Crucifixion reveals the arcana of divine wisdom.

Potentially, every human being is a Christ. That introduces the most dynamic of Weil's contraries, the Christ's passion as historic event and the passion that, with original sin and resurrection, goes on through time: "Creation itself is already a passion. God is an eternal act always and continuously unmaking and remaking itself. In God there are perfect and infinite suffering eternally and simultaneously, and perfect and infinite joy."[72] Pascal's Christ on the cross to the end of time becomes, in Weil's conception, only part of a cosmic, Heraclitean rhythm of the *spiritus sanctus*. That is why she diminishes Christ's incarnation as a historic event and rejects the Augustinian division of history into profane and revealed epochs: Osiris and Melchisedec were incarnations, too. Likewise, she sees the Christ's passion in Herodotus's account of Egyptian animal sacrifices; the Trinity in Cleanthes' Stoic hymn to Zeus; the cult of the Virgin in Plato's *Timaeus*.[73] By such readings she convinced herself that the sum of Christian faith can be found in Greek thought.

Her Christ seems both less and more than the gospels' savior; less, when she places him in succession to mythic avatars to whom ancient lore assigned historical origins; more, when she elaborates the Johannine *logos* of Christ as mediator between the Father, humanity, and the Holy Spirit. Her Christology is composed, on one hand, of lively paradoxes, on the other, of rather stiff propositions *in more geometrico*. Christ on the cross is the sacrificial animal that consents to its suffering; his cry of abandonment is the perfect praise of God. Like God, Christ has both personal and impersonal divinity; he is both the slave and the mediator assimilated to the constellation at the equinox. If the gospels' passion narratives are beautiful, so, too, is the cross as cosmic balancing point, the equipoised junction of contraries: being and nonbeing, necessity and the good, time and eternity.

Whatever these notions mean, they have a jolting freshness that enlivens the threadbare *croyance* it would have threatened in any of the great ages of faith. It likely offends no one that Weil pours her new wine into very old skins: she does not hesitate to conjecture that Pythagoreanism is at work in the New Testament: the Pauline "breadth and length and height and depth" of Christ's love (Eph. 3:18) suggests to her a Pythagorean symmetry in early Christian thought which soon became incomprehensible. She construes the Johannine *logos* itself to be analogous to the Pythagorean trinity of relation, proportion, and harmony. But who can credit her claim that the whole of Christian faith lies in Greece? Her equation of faith with thought says enough.

Her Greek Christ is the indispensable mediator between God and time;

without him, all religious feeling would be directed to a tribal collective god such as Jahweh. The world itself is a mediator between the soul and God, and so loved: *amor fati* and *amor mundi* are one, even though from the cross the created world seems an obstacle because the soul must traverse an infinite distance of time and space to the divine source of its love.

Weil's Johannine formulas on mediation and the aesthetic she reads from Stoicism would alone make a static tableau, a universal architecture in which everything would hang like a pattern from the cross. Fortunately, her reflections on evil and *malheur* rescue her from such cosmetics.

The evil in oppressors is obvious. Far more engaging to Weil is the psychological mechanism of illusion shared by evil's agents and victims. She speaks of evil in Dantesque terms: it is monotonous, empty, trivial, vulgar, but it is also a false infinitude, a response of illimitable imagination to the void God's apparent absence from the world imposes on the mind. Imagination creates idols to fill the holes where grace might enter.[74] It cannot be otherwise in an existence determined by necessity and the illusory wielding of power. This evil contaminates even the relatively just, and it is inescapable: "It is for that reason that Christ did not come down from the cross, and did not even remember, in the moment of his greatest agony, that he would return to life."[75]

Weil makes worldly good and evil equivalents as contraries. A degraded good, "good of the penal code sort," actually conceals the higher good, which is inviolable, mysterious, and not to be sought or realized by human action. Christ's rejection of the title "good master" bears this lesson.[76] One's consciousness of doing any good in the world amounts to violence done to the true, supernatural good. It is the pharisee's reward. The efficacy of contingent, worldly good requires a total, it would seem impossible, absence of one's awareness in carrying it out.

If evil is tedious and ugly, how can imagination impose it on the individual or collective sensibility? Weil says that imagination recasts evil as a good; it imitates good by projecting the "I" upon the world without constraint. Evil is a bad imitation of God, a substitute creation that can only be destructive. All vices and crimes, she claims, are attempts to devour beauty, rather than to contemplate it.[77] They deny the burden of necessity. Hitler, with his mistaken assumption of good in thing (that is, race, analogous to Marxist assumptions about material progress), succeeded in forcing the world to live out his dream, but each of us, on a far smaller scale of performance, works to similar ends.

That home truth leads to Weil's distinction between evil inflicted (sin) and evil endured (suffering). The victim of another's sins, while suffering, may respond to affliction by the most subtle of sins, an attachment to self: "The life instinct survives the attachments torn from it and clings blindly to everything that can give it support, like a plant fastening its tendrils."[78] Weil calls this a needless suffering because the victim is clinging to the illusions of self-preservation. It is the last desperate playing out of "earthly energies submitted to necessity," which, when they alone sustain human action, lead only to evil in thought and deed.[79]

Weil believes that the evil we initiate escapes our awareness but also that we cannot even contemplate evil suffered by another. The human response to another's woe is revulsion or pity's distance. Sympathy, shared suffering, is impossible unless grace brings the soul to expiatory suffering and the awareness of "I" in the self. We become experimentally aware of evil by rejection, when we transfer evil to other things: "But things becoming thus ugly and contaminated in our eyes send back to us the evil we have put into them. They send it back increased. In this exchange, the evil in us grows. It seems then that the very places where we are, the very milieu we live in imprisons us in evil, more and more each day. That is a terrible anguish. When the soul worn down by this anguish, no longer feels the evil, there's scant hope of its salvation."[80] Whatever its bearing on *la condition humaine*, the vividness of this passage owes much to Vichy's daily inner prison.

Weil gives special value to the Vichy world of delusion and compounded evil: evil becomes a proof of God's reality by showing his absence. Evil paradoxically works as a purificatory route to the good: "I am absolutely certain there is no God, in the sense that I am absolutely certain there is nothing real that resembles what I can conceive when I pronounce that name, since I am unable to conceive God."[81] Weil says that this impossibility is more immediate to her than the feeling of her own existence; it marks not an end, however, but a beginning: it obliges the self to attend to God. Weil leaves the Cartesian *cogito* on the cross.

She sets up a conundrum from which there seems to be no escape. We need Christ's mediation as an *imitatio dei*, but we must not desire to imitate Christ or seek his cross lest we fall into the delusion that the pursuit of good does not entail acceptance of the most bitter suffering. Crucifixion is "salutary bitterness," "something immeasurably greater than martyrdom," because it annuls the will and prepares the soul for acceptance of the distance between necessity and the good, between creation and God.[82] In a passage evocative of Plotinus, Weil observes: "There are many degrees of distance separating the creature from God. A distance where it is impossible to love God. Matter, plants, animals. Here evil is so complete it cancels itself; there is no longer any evil: [it is a] mirror of divine innocence. It is a great privilege, for the love which bridges is proportionate to the distance."[83] Christ, becoming the slave crucified, traversed the extremities of innocence, from God to matter, and took evil as sin and as suffering into himself. Weil weighs upon the paltry human soul the burden of making a return journey to God, and this she calls decreation.

God and Decreation

God is the only worthy object of human love, but God does not exist except as imagination's fantasy. Faith must therefore be negative, and prayer must have no "I" to delude the mind. Weil thus overcomes by mystery the scruples she felt in adolescence that "the problem of God" not be posed lest it be falsified.[84] Humanity's relation to God remains wholly unfathomable. Better, says Weil, going one better than Hebrew piety, not to speak of God even within the soul. The only knowledge humanity has is that God is what it is not.

This granted, Weil cannot help flouting her own precepts. She writes of God with exfoliating abandon, working out the implications of divine polarities: God hidden and God manifest, impersonal and personal, nonexistent and exclusively existent. These opposites the soul must ponder; they are incompatibles to be reconciled in God alone. The effort in the pondering is a kind of love, for loving and knowing God are finally inseparable acts.

The road to faith is atheism, the recognition that one cannot identify God by any human faculties. Its contrary is an intuitive affirmation: one's love of God is so real it must have an object. God is impersonal like the sun and rain, and yet the sun is an emblem of God because it gives and does not receive. Nature thereby affords the divine analogue: God is personal, God seeks us and not we him. This dynamic works at the very center of Weil's credo because it is the effect of Christ's taking possession of her, an encounter for which she claims, despite her living so long in "the Christian inspiration," she had been entirely unprepared. It had convinced her of divine mercy.[85]

She was pleased to find the searching God motif in myth and lore, in the story of wandering Demeter, for example, and in the requiem mass: *Quaerens me, sedisti lassus.*[86] But her Hound of Heaven does not run; it does not even bark. God shows no providential intent whatever in the world, no violation of necessity's causality in the manner of Jahweh or Christ the miracle worker. God wishes to remain hidden, and God's "will" does not cause any one thing.[87]

God's hiddenness, whatever its scriptural warrant (Matt. 6:6) abounds in paradox. Our only contact with God seems to be through a sense of his absence, compared with which "presence becomes more absent than absence."[88] This absence constitutes proof of God's love, the true miracle that allows us to be and so to consent by the cross not to be. It follows that the greatest possible love from God requires his greatest possible distance from us, and everything making God remote is thus beneficent. There lies the real value of necessity—Weil criticizes Alain for ignoring it—that its noises, being meaningless, allow us to hear God's silence. Christ's abandonment, his unanswered cry, brought him to divine silence: "The Word is God's silence in the soul. That is what Christ is within us."[89]

God's absence has a corollary, if not an identity, in his hiddenness as a secret presence. The "superabundance" of God's mercy is here on earth, not only in the left-handed gift of suffering but in the human capacity to love God with a certitude that has for its substance "real, eternal, perfect, and infinite joy." Weil also finds divine mercy in the world's beauty and the inspirations of art and language, "favors God grants to beings capable of contemplation."[90]

So far, little or nothing in this exposition would likely offend a Christian sensibility. Many of Weil's notes simply embroider gospel texts with ontological threads, and the motif of God's absence owes much to the Torah's psalms, not to mention the *noche oscura* of San Juan de la Cruz, the mystic with whom she felt a deep affinity. Far different, however, is Weil's god when she resorts to a rather Hegelian portrait of sublime egocentrism. Creation is the act of God knowing, loving, and creating himself in the frigid hypostases of good, truth, and being. The Trinity's perfection amounts to its circularity: "Saying God thinks of himself means 1) he is nothing other than thought, and 2) he doesn't think of anything other than himself. All affirmations concerning God are, in their true sense, negations."[91]

The implication lingers that the created world is superfluous. Weil does not explain why God created the world other than to extort love from it. Creation seems a crime; it is the undoing of divine harmony. It might be called God's original sin because God bears responsibility for what is not God. God and creation are less than God because creation means limitation of God, an ontological privation. It seems God does think of something other than himself and commits a felony in doing so. One of Weil's witticisms (even her humor had to be intellectual) suggests that we forgive God our sins. But because human existence is itself an offense and diminishes God's glory, it seems divinity and humanity are partners in crime. That again begs for a theodicy Weil seems reluctant to provide. What she does provide is theater, a theological Grand Guignol in which excruciation supplies the tension. "My existence crucifies God," she writes, and so she has prayed: "O God, grant that I become nothing." In becoming nothing, she will become the agent for God's self-love.[92] This drama goes full circle back to the divine Hegelian Narcissus. Even Christian incarnation must be understood as a gaze into his pool: it was meant not to save humanity, says Weil, but to attest the love between Father and Son.[93]

The epitome of Weil's wish for annihilation comes in what Pétrement calls her "terrible prayer," a long, dithyrambic plea that God reduce her to unintelligible matter, stripping her of all intelligence and sensory awareness "since you are the Good and I am mediocrity."[94] At first wince, one might wish to escape these excesses, but for all their shrillness, they make the point that an *imitatio Christi* means that like Christ one must consent to become a nothing. To pray is not to wish. Prayer is a counterwish, made to destroy all the assertive resilience of the ego. The forcefulness of Weil's personality is particularly evident in her prayer to have that personality rendered eucharistic stuff for divine and human sustenance. She is in covert rivalry with God here because God himself can be present to humanity only in a piece of matter, the host. As the last shall be first, "the love of the most wretched is most precious of all." Coveting that position, Weil informed Perrin she was exceptional only in her inferiority to others.[95] Such was the pride of her ferocious humility.

Mercifully, Weil's god is not merely self-regarding, and she does not leave humanity out in the cosmic cold. God loves creation through its creatures and pities human misery. Incarnation is God's voluntary entrapment by the evil of suffering as he looked upon creation: "The Creation is an act of love, and something that is going on perpetually. At every moment our existence is God's love for us." Yet, no sooner does she affirm that than she recalls that anything said about God is a negation: "God can love only himself. His love for us is love for himself through us. So, he who gives us being loves in us our consent not to be. . . . Our being is nothing other than the will that we should consent not to be. He is forever begging from us the being which he gives. And he gives it so as to beg it from us."[96]

Weil's god is not only a Narcissus but a neurotic and a tease. That impression is reinforced in a passage that borders on theodicy:

> Anyone who believes that God has created in order to be loved, that God cannot create anything that is God, that God cannot be loved by anything that is not God, is faced with a contradiction. That contradiction contains necessity within it. Yet, every contradiction is resolved through the process of becoming. God has created a finite being that says "I" and cannot love God. Through the action of grace the "I" gradually disappears, and God loves himself through the creature which empties itself and becomes nothing. [Then] God goes on creating other creatures and helps them to decreate themselves.[97]

With these words Weil can fairly be ranked with Pascal as a sublime misanthrope. They say her deity is far more jealous than the Jahweh of *Exodus* she denounced. Her god will have no humanity before him.

Even though she believed that one's love of God would be supreme perfection if only it could be attained, she could not accept an imperfect, impure, all-too-human love of God—better to assume a total incapacity. Better than to love like God, or humanly with heart, soul, and mind, is to be like mud, obedient to God. It is oddly touching that Weil can liken God in relation to the human soul as a mother to her child and yet not understand that a parent's genuine love gives freely and without extortion, without expectation of some reward or payback. She seems not to have understood love in this essential unselfishness. Never married and (probably) a virgin, she had no active experience in the caring of parental love, in which her own parents seem to have been unstinting. Neither, it is certain, did she know the intimacy of sexual love. These facts tell against her.[98]

Perhaps such limits help to explain why she conceives one's response to God to be chiefly a matter of complicity, of obedience to divine will or consent to divine beggary. In his wish is our command, in his will (human decreation) a peace of *Schrecklichkeit* as profound as anything Goethe could object to in Dante.

Weil makes a great deal of obedience to God, especially in her letters to Perrin. As though to confound in him any sense of her obduracy toward the church, she sets out fantastic hypotheses of submissiveness to God. Here are three discrete instances:

> If it were conceivable that one damn oneself by obeying God and save oneself by disobeying him, I would even so choose obedience.

> If I had my eternal salvation put before me on a table, and I had only to put out my hand to obtain it, I wouldn't stretch out my hand as long as I did not think I had received the order to do so.

> I would joyfully obey the order to go to Hell's center and dwell there forever. I don't mean of course that I prefer orders of this kind. I'm not so perverse.[99]

Although she surely meant such declarations to convince Perrin of her willingness to obey God and of her inner need to obey so that she might finally find acceptance, she did not realize that the extremities of her if's depict God as a kind of *Oberkommandant* who plays the cat-and-mouse game of Nazi sadism: torment coyly mixed with toleration. Vichy France obeyed this god for four years without choice.

Because we are bound by necessity, Weil says we have no escape from obedience to the god beyond its mechanism. The only choice is to desire or not desire obedience. Weil almost embraces Spinoza's world, where there is no free will. Indeed, the desire for obedience has no voluntary element; it is an imitation of nature, either through the body's submission to *douleur* or, more rarely, through the soul's *joie* before the world's beauty, each of these serving what Weil calls a transforming apprenticeship. But not to desire obedience is a willful act. Weil states explicitly that to imitate nature requires a renunciation of the will. When she describes consented obedience as a sword cutting away all illegitimate desires, she subsumes everything which intellect or imagination provides as finite ends for the will's action.[100] In sum, the will itself must be destroyed. The paradox is that the will itself must be recruited to that end, set to the impossible task of agreeing to its own nonbeing.

As the Christian cross offers the imitative model of obedience, a totality of silence, attention, and immobility, the purely disinterested act (hence Weil's envy of Christ crucified), one can infer that the destructive will is equivalent to existence itself.[101] Weil's brief against the will focuses on its moral inefficacy: the will cannot overcome its sinfulness, cannot produce good in the soul, cannot diminish suffering. She derides the muscularity of lay morality for its voluntarist underpinnings. Willing good constitutes the secret lie of the soul's inferior part, the personal self that fears destruction. At times, Weil sounds like Schopenhauer: will cannot escape the bondage of the self, it is in fact a principle of violence in the self. It should be turned upon the sensibility's desires and aversions and forced to obey reason.

If the will can be put to such use, it would seem Weil qualifies her own dogma that the will's destruction is an exclusive desideratum, "our only right."[102] In fact, she concedes that it is more than a device for constraining the irrational; it has positive functions, duties such as consent to the autonomy of other people. Concerning God, the will must be impressed to love the void which is his absence, as manifested in the extreme *malheur* of personal pain, distress of soul, and social degradation—life as Weil lived it under the Vichy regime.

The will, arrested by *malheur*'s irreducible nature, can be transmuted into love. Less dramatically, it can simply be worn down by the futility implicit in contingent goods. Again, Weil seems to traverse Schopenhauer's bleak landscape of human endeavor, where misery is not so much created by contingency as revealed by it. The difference is that Weil not only describes, she prescribes. She believes that the will, however obliquely, operates for good without being or achieving good. That is why she makes it imperative that the will be directed above itself, "that it be stretched and stretched and not attain. It must feel its limits and be knocked against them continually."[103] Such exertion becomes finally a precondition to the soul's reception of divine grace in its "dark night": "It's after a lengthy, fruitless straining that ends in despair, when one no longer expects anything, that the gift comes from without, gratuitously, as a marvelous surprise."[104]

While seeming to invoke the weary Siddhartha under the bo-tree, soon enlightened because he has given up all attempts to become so, Weil's words have a peculiar authority that goes beyond mere allusion. Her urgent expression and confident tone argue that in decreation she had found what she told Perrin "the present moment requires," a new saintliness of miraculous novelty, something analogous to the Copernican or Galilean revelations about the universe: "The world needs saints of genius just as a village where there is a plague needs doctors."[105]

It is no surprise, given the "present moment" of Vichy and the war, that the saintliness of decreation is a gospel of death. The cross as symbolic self-abdication implies as much, but Weil comes back repeatedly to the equation. She is careful to note that death must not be wished—we must beg in all natural willfulness not to undergo decreation—it must be accepted. Perpetual consent through conviction of one's nothingness is a remedy for sin.[106] The supernatural awareness that we are dead allows us to see things in their essential nakedness. Whatever the antecedent forms of this awareness (Plato's, in the *Phaedo*, that philosophy is a practice for death), Weil does not leave it suspended in meditative abstraction: "Death is the most precious thing given to humankind. That's why the greatest impiety is to make improper use of it. Dying mistakenly. Killing mistakenly." She rejects suicide, however admissible to the Stoicism she cherished, as a false decreation.[107]

Genuine decreation requires violence to the soul, a killing of its mediocrity. Because one cannot will this process, only consent to it, Weil makes God the agent. Reflecting on the gospel koan of the dying seed that is reborn, she bids us "ask God to kill us and plant us spiritually here below . . . in total renunciation and silence."[108] Decreation must not admit illusory consolations. That is why Job is, after Christ, the biblical model she most treasured—and one most appropriate to despoiled and afflicted France. That is why she rejected personal immortality; it cheated death of its pure bitterness.

However somber these accents, decreation would seem to be, finally, the most positive of acts. It is a reverse imitation of God's *kenosis*, that divine self-emptying that lets creation be. She likens it to the withdrawal of a screen so that God can see the world. Hence, for all the words on death, decreation should not be understood as destruction but its opposite, the abolition of the evil "I." Unfortunately, her most eloquent reflections on decreation reveal a morbid self-disparagement inextricable from the process:

> I can't conceive the possibility of God loving me, when I sense so clearly that even the affection people show for me can only be a mistake on their part. But I can imagine quite well that God loves that particular perspective on creation which comes only from where I am. But I act as a screen. I must withdraw so that God may be able to see it. Those whose inner gaze isn't directed to the fount of grace so as to receive the light can still experience a genuine contact with God if, by a wondrous meeting, they become the object of an act by someone who through perfect obedience has become a mere intermediary. I must withdraw so God can enter into contact with human beings whom chance places in my path and whom he loves. My presence is tactless, as though I were to find myself between two lovers or two friends.[109]

It seems a peculiar despair in Weil that, devaluing her friends' affection for her and concluding from that that God, too, does not love her but does love everyone she meets, she proceeds to elevate herself to a Christ-like intermediation, the "perfect obedience" of a "someone." The confessional tone of the first and third statements cited above, counterpointed by the detachment of the second, raises the issue of whether Weil intended decreation as a prescription primarily for her own wounded self, the Jewish exile who could never be certain that the solicitude of her Christian friends was more than a benign condescension, or whether she was seeking to formulate a new spiritual witness that could be realized as Vichy's "present moment requires."

Could only those who, like Weil, felt themselves rejected by God and not loved by humanity serve in this new sainthood? If so, then Weil's position regarding her fellow Jews carries an even richer ambiguity than the evidence suggests.

Although she tends to be most harsh and exacting when focused on herself—witness the "terrible prayer"—there is nothing to indicate she precluded others from drawing on her words. One might wish that like Kierkegaard or Nietzsche she would have anticipated cultists and would-be disciples with horror and aversion, warning them away from an *ipsa dixit* acquiescence.

A discriminate study of Weil's use of "I" and "we" in her religious writing might afford many helpful insights, but it is not needed to establish that, as she reckons, the final aim of imitating God is that the human soul, mine or ours, become God. Sinking to nothing, the soul attains (or recovers) its pristine divinity. This notion is hardly original with Weil, but she may be credited with giving it renewed life centuries after it had slipped away from theological discourse.

One of her best of many characterizations of decreation (best, because it betrays her hidden voluntarism and an ambiguity that leads to monism) is that it is the refusal of the permission God gives us to exist as other than he. To abolish the mortal self is to desire to live while ceasing to exist.[110] Christ's promise of abundant life is, in this reading, covalent with the crucifixion. Another divine absurdity such as Weil loved to ponder, this koan points to Zen Buddhism and to other Eastern cultures of wisdom in which she was interested even as she was working out a mysticism of the Christian cross.

Turning East

"I believe the mysteries of the Catholic religion are an inexhaustible source of truths about the human condition. Besides that, they are to me an object of love. But nothing keeps me from believing the same thing in regard to other mysteries, or from believing that some of these truths have been revealed elsewhere."[111]

Nothing reveals the cosmopolitanism of Weil's freethinking Jewish temperament so well as her devoted interest in Eastern religious thought. It would be easy to misconstrue this interest, to argue that subconsciously she pursued the Vedas and the *Gita* as safeguards against a surrender to Christianity and church authority. True to herself, she remained independent, but one might unfairly infer that, like Alain, she subscribed to a flaccid, uncommitted, all-religions-are-one version of humanism. Her words above indicate the opposite, that for her, religious traditions reinforce one another at their source in mystery. One of her fundamental objections to Christians is their inability to respect mystery beyond their faith: "In saying Catholicism is true and other religions false, one does injustice not only to the other religious traditions but to the Catholic faith itself by putting it on the level of things that can be affirmed or denied."[112]

She did not regard all religions as valid. Tailored to her dogma of mystery, the "true" ones show God's voluntary distance from necessity, his apparent absence and secret presence; the "false" show divinity exercising its power in human events. Thus she demoted Judaism—but not altogether.

In a key passage she accords Judaism a place within the religions of antiquity, noting how from each great Oriental culture came a vocational idea: "Israel: God's unity. India: the soul's assimilation to God in mystic union. China: God's way of action . . . which seems inaction . . . the presence which seems absence, the void and silence. Egypt: immortality, salvation of the just soul after death, by assimilation to a suffering, dead and resuscitated God. Greece (which was greatly influenced by Egypt): human misery, distance, God's transcendence."[113] While admitting that a religion's sustaining life can be known only from within, she characteristically practiced for herself the legerdemain of special access: the study of religions requires that one transport oneself into their "center" through "faith," the latter a synonym for the attention intellectual love concentrates on its object.[114] As attention, that study is artificially exclusive: "Each religion is alone true, meaning that as we are thinking of it we have to bring as much attention to it as if there were nothing else. . . . A 'synthesis' of religions implies an inferior kind of attention."[115]

Weil's toil over Sanskrit shows how willingly she took up the challenge of a complex otherness in non-Western spirituality. Commenting on the apparent identity of the idea of good in Plato and the Upanishads, she rejected syncretism: "We ought to conceive the identity of various traditions, not by reconciling them through what they share, but by comprehending the essence in what is specific to each. For this essence is one and the same."[116]

These remarks show why she insisted upon giving to Eastern mysteries a "religious attention" and tried to come to them on their own exigent terms, learning an unusually difficult and subtle language and incorporating many of its word concepts into her daily reflections. Having no spiritual dogmas instilled in her from childhood, she could undertake her studies free of prurience and condescension. That she was aware of these traps in Western attitudes is clear in this tableau of Catholic provincialism: "Suppose I find myself in a room through whose window I can see the sun, and there's a door open between this room and another one, where there is someone else, with its window facing the same way. Through the door I can see a rectangle of light projected on the wall. I might say: That wretch! Here I am, able to see the sunlight, while all he sees of light is a dimly lit surface on a wall. That is precisely the Catholics' attitude in regard to other religions."[117] Aware of it or not, Weil has brilliantly conflated two gospel lessons, "In my father's house there are many rooms" (John 14:2) and Luke's story (18:9–14) of the publican and the pharisee. Not even Perrin had been exempt from her charge; she expressly accused him of being a church patriot.[118]

At the same time, she did not believe in ready conversion. She said it was as dangerous an undertaking as for a writer to give up his native language for some other. The point needs emphasis: Weil was not of that Western bourgeois intellectual's disposition which, burdened by security without responsibility, grows bored and resentful, then embraces something that entices by its sheer or modish otherness, as many French youths took up the new religion of fascism in the 1920s or as many of a later American generation took up Eastern guru sects. Of course, having grown up without any catechism, Weil had nothing to reject, but she did not counsel escapism of any kind. The most fascinating aspect of her delving into Eastern texts is how she used them to support what she believed to be Christianity.

From an old Sorbonne acquaintance, René Daumal, she borrowed a number of Sanskrit texts early in her stay in Marseilles. She later wrote of her "thirst for this language and this thought" and of the "treasures of an inestimable price, of which I've absorbed very little. May Krishna grant that someday I get back to it."[119] Her notebooks and countless fragments contain the record of her industry: Sanskrit lines transcribed with meticulous clarity, usually with parallel transliterations and sometimes translations. The major source of her understanding of Hindu religious and philosophical terms was René Guenon's *L'homme et son devenir selon la Vedanta* (1925). From Guenon she gleaned the meanings of words that were to have recurrent and profound reference in her *cahiers*. What immediately strikes the reader of Guenon's book is the rather artificial correspondence he assumes between Vedic words and Western religious and philosophical terms and which facilitated Weil's predisposition to see common "revelations" and to argue that religions hold explicit and implicit truths vis-à-vis one another. She seems to have been a too ready victim of his semantic conveniences.[120] But Guenon cannot be held accountable for Weil's extravagant belief that Christ sends his spirit to all those who call on Krishna or the Buddha, as in times past they called on Dionysos or Osiris: "And the Spirit acted upon the soul, not in bringing it to abandon its religious tradition but in giving it the light—the plenitude of light in the best cases—within this tradition."[121]

It is instructive that Weil's attitude on pre-Christian incarnations reflects Hindu views on avatars. The Hindus believe that godlike figures such as Rama and Krishna have historical origins. They took worldly birth, led moral and compassionate lives, taught righteousness against the evils of their age, and died. Their role was to restore *dharma*, harmony between the universe and human society. They exemplify the human potential for disinterested action and *bhakti*, devotion to God.[122]

Weil's idea of decreation draws more from Eastern traditions than has generally been recognized. She qualified her claim that the Christian cross is the only way to knowledge in her notes on the koans of Zen Buddhism. Her principal source was Daisetz Teitaro Suzuki's now classic *Essays on Zen Buddhism*.

In her Marseilles journals she observes that contemplation of logical absurdities like the noise of one hand clapping involves a search "of such intensity it displaces all attachments." It is an intellectual mysticism that leads the mind to exhaustion and a "dark night" succeeded by illumination, "when searching and the thing sought merge in a single perfect identification."[123] The effect, says Suzuki, is what Japanese Buddhists call *satori* or peace—a quantity most elusive to Weil's temper.

She was deeply impressed by Zen Buddhists' efforts to attain the highest degree of mental attention and a purity of perception free of imagination and reason. She found no comparable technique in Christian tradition. During her months in New York, her remarks on koans reached conclusive focus: the contemplation of impassable contradictions destroys not only the intelligence but the soul as well. For contradiction "experienced right to the depths of one's being means spiritual laceration, it means the cross." One might call it decreation by contemplation, even as *malheur* furthers decreation by one's acceptance of its pain. The koan, then, ranks with accepted suffering and rapt joy as a path to reality.[124]

Contradiction, the koan's heart, became one of Weil's major theological themes. Even before she began reading Suzuki she wrote: "Contradiction is our road to God because we are creatures, and because creation itself is a contradiction. It is contradictory that God, being infinite and all and lacking nothing, should do something outside himself, not himself, yet proceeding from himself."[125] Ontology becomes, in Weil's mind, a science of impossibilities. As a creature of necessity, the human mind is not disposed to dwell on contradiction; it seeks convenient causalities, but the mighty otherness of contradiction imposes itself upon reality, and so Weil would have us seize it. Even the jungle of absurdities in ordinary living, the cross-purposes, misunderstandings, and conflicts between intent and act (as though life had been scripted by Flaubert) all come from human existence as itself a contradiction.

Absurdity, then, offers an instant conduit to the supernatural if only the mind fixes full attention on it. Weil sees that the real difficulty in summoning this attention is not so much intellectual as it is moral: how do we deal with the inextricability of good and evil? "Evil is the shadow of good. All genuine good . . . projects evil. Only imaginary good does not project any. . . . A good without the merest shadow of evil in it must be something impossible to desire."[126] Every desire for good must accordingly entail acceptance of its concomitant evil, internalized as suffering: "We have to love evil as evil. But our attitude can only be pure when evil is a physical pain one endures and has not sought, a pain one would do anything in the world to elude."[127]

To bear the sins of the Vichy world, to transform them into one's own accepted *malheur*, was part of the new saintliness Weil prescribed. This toleration, seemingly passive and defeatist, amounts psychologically to a lived-out koan: it is an active passivity, an endurance of evil that conceals a strenuous, unremitting desire for good, the real good that lies in the supreme harmony of opposites. *Dharma* was not for her some listless metaphysical principle but "a truth of the utmost importance for conducting one's life."[128]

As though by serendipity Weil turned to the text that puts the question of individual conduct into a war's setting, the *Bhagavad Gita*. She had a close personal reason for attaching herself to this book. Her brother André had studied it at the Sorbonne. Though like most French intellectuals in the late 1930s he was antifascist yet pacifist, his sister took upon herself an acute sense of guilt for his pacifism when the realities of war overtook France. The *Gita* exposes the illusion that one can sit apart from the world and its evil actions.

In the *Gita*'s story, a fragment of the vast *Mahabharata*, Prince Arjuna faces imminent war with his cousins. He foresees that the battle will bring only disaster because no matter the victor, the *ksatriya* or warrior caste will be destroyed and social ruin will ensue. How can he take on responsibility for such devastation? His servant, Krishna, then reveals himself as the avatar of Vishnu, come into the world to right wrongs, which in this instance seem to be nothing other than Arjuna's prevarications. Through the rest of the poem, Krishna instructs Arjuna on the way things are. In a climactic theophany, Vishnu reconciles all contraries, for he is the source of all things, including pain and death. Implicitly, whatever is, is right. There remains, however, the suffering of those in bondage to desires (such as Arjuna's desire to prevent the battle) and illusions (such as Arjuna's that he can prevent the battle). For their remedy, the prince learns that the highest human achievement is action without attachment to its fruits. Weil interpreted this to mean the pure obedience of self-renunciation.[129] Disinterested action, says Krishna, is an overcoming of one's birth by indifference; it is a discipline in self-purification, the goal of which is fixing oneself upon brahman, the ground of reality where sin is destroyed by the inner joy of nirvana.[130]

This exposition, though brief, suffices to hint at the *Gita*'s appeal to Weil and its challenge. Renunciation, both of evil and of earthly good, of knowledge no less than of ignorance, a constant ataraxia or imperturbability of mind to all things—there lies the way to God and the perfection of beginningless brahman. Weil says that the *Gita* poses the problem of how finite means can possibly be ordered with a view to transcendent ends. Her answers seem inconclusive: "To let Necessity act within the self. (Renunciation of personal will.) Everything is good for one who knows that everything is good. (And still: 'Why hast thou forsaken me?')"[131] She believes the *Gita* complements the gospels because it, too, shows that contact with force deprives one momentarily of God. The *Gita*'s lesson comes from the sword's handle (Arjuna must fight) rather than from its point (Christ must die).

In fact, however, there is no such deprivation in the *Gita*. Weil's contrast between Arjuna and Jeanne d'Arc—"he goes to war although inspired by God, she because inspired by God"—is also mistaken.[132] Weil is on surer ground in stating that the *Gita* teaches that we must not seek good in our own acts, but she seems to sense that Arjuna's pity, however objectionable to the divine scheme, has no alternative: "It is evident that Krishna reproaches Arjuna for wanting to perform a false kind of decreation. (And yet, for the most part, it is precisely killing that constitutes this error.)"[133]

In the *Gita*'s last book, Arjuna is told that the slayer without self (ego) does not slay, but Weil refuses to infer from this the Nietzschean dictum that everything is permitted. Her own conclusion is interrogative and pertinent to Vichy: "Are there certain things we can do without wanting success, and others we cannot do that way? Does this criterion permit us to distinguish between our actions? It is not certain. . . . We can attribute some things to limited injustice, required by the social order. But how much? That's the whole question."[134] Her inability to answer these questions to her own satisfaction may have fed her sense of guilt in accepting Vichy and in resisting it through Combat and Témoignage chrétien.

Although the *Gita* ends with an evangelism of knowledge as worship, exactly the exalted faith in epistemology Weil was pursuing, it was the message of obedience to God that continued to preoccupy her even to her final months in exile. One should obey an order one believes to be divine, she writes, without attachment to belief or to action, ever desiring more light but holding fast to what light one has, even if in fact the inspiration comes from a devil. Arjuna initially fails to act according to the light of his soldierly resolve. His pity deprives him of energy, but Weil knew that was not the central issue: "If one does something with the certainty of obeying God and without any other motive or intention than obedience, it is certain that one is obeying God. But does that mean one may do anything at all with this intent? That is the big problem, the problem of the *Gita*. I still don't really understand it."[135] She might more accurately have said she did not accept the problem's implication, for then she would have had to accept as well the actions of Hebrew patriarchs whom she condemned for presuming to act by divine orders.[136]

If the *Gita*'s gospel of obedience to God means carrying out prescribed acts, how does one recognize such acts? "One must carry out human obligations, in the cadre of social relations where one is situated, unless God specially commands that one leave it. Arjuna's fault was to have said he wouldn't fight, instead of begging Krishna—not then, but long before—to prescribe to him what he had to do."[137] It is difficult, not to say impossible, to see how such intervention differs in kind and in effect from the interventions of Jahweh which Weil found so offensive in the Torah. It is important, then, to observe how Weil distinguished between the Hebraic and Hindu forms of divine intrusion. It rests upon mysticism, here to be understood as a safeguard against reading divine mercy into nature. Weil faults Jews, Muslims, and even Christians for falling into the erroneous belief that God's mercy can be read beyond a private or privileged mystical contemplation and into the world. That belief is the source of human pitilessness, she claims. Although Arjuna achieved contemplative perfection, he had to go on committing evil acts and yet by his detachment he remained undefiled by them. Here was the kind of purity within time and space—Weil calls it vertical progress—which she longed to attain for herself in all its absurdity.

In this positive dynamic of decreation, the soul's perfectibility, the Hindu accent is no less pronounced, perhaps is more so, than the Western or Christian. Although Weil often writes within the Christian convention, that perfection, for example, comes through the Holy Spirit and the power of prayer, that God can be imitated only through a Christ-like powerlessness, that the abdication of self means its reduction to the mystical matter of communion—still, a mystical detachment points her to the arcane "transcendental intellectualism" of the East.[138] When, for instance, she urges that to perfect the soul one's motives for action be put outside the self, she suggests one imitate God's impartial sun and rain. The allusion is obviously Christian (Matt. 5:45), but it is the disinterested Arjuna or Rama who comes to mind, not Christ. Similarly, though she has the Judaeo-Christian deity in mind when she says that we become images of God in renouncing the will and consenting to be nothing, her prescription for doing away with the will closely follows the psychology of the Hindu *gunas*.[139]

Once beyond the *gunas* one would not even have the satisfaction of having performed a duty. This supreme austerity of disinterestedness exerted a tremendous appeal upon Weil, not only in its giving primacy to the noetic life as opposed to the affective or emotional, but in its finally dissolving all the contraries and opposites of the phenomenal, illusory world of *maya* into a monism.[140] The impersonal, immortal soul of Greek tradition is here only a portion of transcendent being. Further, there is the promise that short of transcendence, the soul abiding in *sattva* ascends upon earthly death to *atman*. In short, the *Gita* and its kindred texts, the Upanishads, offered Weil the lofty equanimity she had found in the monism of Spinoza.[141]

Hindu preoccupation with escape into a nescient participation with the infinite served Weil's intellectual sensibility by providing a counter to, if not a release from, the affective turbulence of Western mysticism with its propulsive desire for union with God. Vishnu, for all his incarnations, is peculiarly inactive, wholly unlike the god who in Weil's lively imagery plays the role of a woman whispering to her lover, or a child hiding from its mother, or the mendicant seeking bread, or the soul's rapist.[142] In the Upanishads, Weil observes, the gods do not wish to unmake creation by drawing near to humanity. If, then, in Hinduism there are ways to purification, such as the mantras and the exercise of believing that nothing exists, if self-annihilation is immortality, and the disciplined obedience of attention has a place, there is still no mediator, no suffering, redemptive go-between, only the *atman* as a kind of world soul. There can be no *attente de Dieu*, no expectant longing that prompts God's coming and prepares the soul to receive supernatural good. Such facts pose a problem Weil does not address: since she insists that mediation or a suffering mediator between God and humanity is necessary to preclude worship of a collective, tribal god, it would seem that Hinduism, lacking mediation, is collective and tribal. Krishna and Rama, Vishnu's incarnations, are not true mediators by Weil's definition: absolutely god and absolutely man.

Like Hinduism, Buddhism offered Weil a particular intellectual satisfaction: enlightened beyond reason, purpose, and voluntarist effort, the intellect is aimed only to the good for its own sake. God is forever absent. Suzuki had written: "In Christianity we seem to be too conscious of God, though we say that in Him we live and move and have our being. Zen wants even this last trace of God-consciousness, if possible, obliterated."[143] As though in echo of that, Weil wrote that "Christianity (both Catholics and Protestants) talks too much about holy things."[144]

In the Eastern texts Weil had only herself to confront. There was no Hindu or Buddhist Perrin to remonstrate with her, no mundane society of believers around her constituting a nation to which she could not belong. Because the Indic world was not too much with her, she was free to respond to it on her own scholastic terms. It is interesting that she remained completely uncritical of Hinduism. She did not see that the psychological strata of the *gunas* corresponded to and thus rationalized an adamantine caste system, with the goodness of *sattva* implicitly resident only in the righteous brahmans and the downward torpor or *tamas* in the slavish class of shudras.[145]

Sociology apart, it must be admitted that despite (or because of) her belief in an essential identity in spiritual traditions, Weil did not recognize a fundamental antithesis between Eastern and Western religious philosophies. Occidental religions tend to seek humanity's deliverance from the fear of death; Oriental religions aim to deliver humanity from the pain of life. The realization of the soul's nescient fusion with brahman could hardly be more remote from the belief in a personal immortality and a last judgment. How could Weil, with her unrelenting *fastidium sui*, so repelled by her own self that she was convinced she had a natural disposition to crime, burdened with a permanent tristesse over her sins, and unable to conceive the possibility of her salvation, bear the Christian belief in an afterlife?[146]

Was it perhaps some dread of that cardinal belief in Christians which moved her to hail in Eastern spirituality the dismissal of miracles, among which resurrection from death is primary; to proclaim the Upanishads' affinity with San Juan de la Cruz; to imply that there is as much love and knowledge of God in Hinduism as in Christianity; to assert that Hindu texts tell better than Christian ones why virginity has a spiritual value and show better than the Pauline letters the connection between law and sin?[147] These utterances are final maneuvers of protest in exile, points Weil was scoring against a church she had already decided she would not enter. More imposing than these random theses nailed on Catholicism's door are her notes to herself while she was still in Vichy France, when she sought help from Hinduism in determining an agendum within the Occupation's net of complicity.

There was, for example, the need "to attach ourselves to the All" of *atman*: "What at present we hate, we shall manage to be capable of loving. We have to feel our hate to the hilt; know what it is we are hating. Through every feeling, going downward to join with the atman."[148] As to the *dharma* of righteous acts, every possible action commingles good and evil: "Dharma is a law for choosing the appropriate mixture," but how can one do so in the midst of social upheaval: "What happens to *dharma* in a conquered country? and what are one's duties to the conquerors? (Have to find out.)"[149] It is as though Weil sought some doctrinal relief from her qualms over her Resistance activities, but these *cahier* notes predate her involvement with Témoignage chrétien. Surely in *sattva* "the sacrifice where no fruit of any sort is sought," she found a vital resource against the gravity of Vichy collectivity, for as a constituent of every soul, *sattva* prompts everyone to weigh "the scales of dharma," to love necessity and to give "free play to one's capacities for action and for suffering."[150] In Vichy, Arjuna and Christ complement one another.

Given this complement, Weil recasts the Hindu trinity into terms analogous to the Christian: Brahma is the sacred Word, the world's order; Vishnu as creator is God the Father; Shiva, who figures as a violent and epicene deity in Hindu lore, becomes the god of decreation, the Holy Spirit.[151]

It seems remiss of Weil that she does not mention Krishna in this trinity, he being the god incarnate. In the *Gita* he is the prince's charioteer, but he assumed a different role for Weil as she tried to realize her own *dharma* in the midst of a cataclysm far more terrible than the one Arjuna faces. From the first days of World War II until the last weeks of her life she appears to have kept a peculiar, almost affectionate regard for Krishna. Pétrement recalls that in discussing religion, Weil often used Krishna's name rather than Christ's. In a

1941 letter to Pétrement, Weil cites a Sanskrit text in which Krishna, known as a sovereign to the gods and a child to old women, is called the beloved by young women who tend cattle. Undertaking farm labor in the Ardèche, Weil hoped that her new found lowly status would bring her closer to Krishna. Yet, as she complained, half-jokingly it seems, she did not have Krishna at hand, as Arjuna did, to reveal whether her true station, her *dharma,* was indeed this servitude in the fields. Not that Krishna's guidance was indispensable because "my feeling is in accord with the social order at present. If to the French people at this moment it seems good that I be among the *çûdras,* it's perhaps good that I conform myself to this."[152]

Is there a private code at work here? If Weil spoke of Krishna rather than Christ out of what Pétrement calls shyness, was she similarly prompted to speak of *shudras,* the lowest Hindu caste, in place of Jews? She had wanted to believe that Christianity is inevitably the religion of slaves, but events had told her that her own people were now debased to their ancient bondage, *super flumen Babylonis.* Why, then, in her letters to friends and to family did she enjoin them to think of Krishna and to take comfort in him? Is it simply the beloved of milkmaids she intends? The *Gita*'s Krishna, in his epiphany as Vishnu, exposes all earthly striving as illusion or *maya.* But as brahman subsumes *maya,* it may be said that illusion and all its attendant evils have a place. The Hindu teaching apparently agrees with the Stoic: everything that happens can be called part of the divine will.[153]

The point here may lie as much with the messenger as with the message. Krishna, the incarnate god appearing from age to age, speaks directly to errant, suffering humanity. And when was a theophany more urgently needed than in Hitler's time? Weil's Christ could not come down—she never credits a second coming—because his station was one of torment (along with millions of fellow Jews), at that greatest distance from God which, for her, argued God's love. Perhaps in Krishna, dispenser of *dharma,* she found a foil to the horror in her own Christian scenario, where, while God's infinite remoteness from the cross vouchsafes his innocence of evil, here below cruelty and death abide, according to Weil, as proofs of his love. Krishna does not do away with suffering, but he does come and proclaim its necessity and the human role to be played in it. There is a great difference between apparently meaningless suffering (suffering in the void) and suffering in theodical knowledge; it is the difference between utter abandonment and revealing light. Weil is not careless of words when she tells her family to take comfort in Krishna.

Since God's will can be known only by looking to the past, how can humanity place its present spiritual wretchedness in contact with God? There is some evidence that Weil, in struggling to answer this question, grew impatient with her Hegelian-Christian deity. She says she cannot understand God's love of himself through human woe—a remark suggesting that perhaps she cannot accept him either. Within a few pages of this concession she admits to the severe limit of her love for all but a few people. When on such occasions as these she attains some distance from her own view of Christianity, she becomes more human. She is not always the Love Bolshevik portrayed by her Christian appropriators. One might say that just as she delights in Krishna, the accessible god and the milkmaid's *bien aimé*, so in every show of recalcitrance or confusion she comes closer to Arjuna. Her well-known belief that it was her fate (her *dharma*) to stand at the intersection of Christianity and all that is other than Christianity should be taken in full view of her Judaic need of God and her comforting affirmation of the *Gita*.

Conclusions

Many of Weil's critics have characterized her life as a series of blunders; she seemed to fall short in everything she tried to do and to be. She even failed to become a Christian. Her own god rejected her, so she thought. But for a person of such indomitable will and intellectual vigor, this assessment does not seem valid. That she did suffer from a native cultural shock is demonstrable. It was her fate to find herself a Jew at a time when T. S. Eliot's "Christian Europe" was entering a dark night different from the kind she read of in San Juan de la Cruz. What compels amazement (in some critics, revulsion) is her willingness (or willfulness) in going so far to recreate Christianity, to revitalize it according to the exigencies of her own very Jewish sensibility. She thus appears an apologist of the culture that, by its final indifference and no small hostility, victimized her people.

Were that the whole of her spiritual history, it would be pathetic indeed. It is not. If it is one irony that she tried to embrace Christianity and, having set down her own terms, could not do so, it is another that what kept her independent was the deep-rooted Judaism she resented and rejected. Though exiled in her own country she exemplified par excellence the cosmopolitan reach of freethinking Jewish culture. As she once wrote, "The clearest idea of existence is that nothing of it can be neglected."[154] It is as though existence itself were one great Talmudic lesson for her to learn, and she brought all the avidity requisite to the learning. Her months in the lively milieux of Marseilles (probably, after the lycée Henri IV, the most stimulating time of her life) gave her at an intellectual level a complement to her Jewish passion for universal justice and charity. There, she found in Tao, Zen, and Hindu texts "sources of wisdom and serenity toward which, happily, the present distress is now pushing many minds."[155]

They took her, as they had taken her brother, to the East, and toward that contradictory ethic which denies all claim to personhood while demanding one's compassion for the personhood of others. Arguably, this ethic is Christian as well, save that the wayward, sinful self in Western tradition is to be redeemed, not annihilated. From Hinduism Weil took what she wanted, the texts but not the tribal taboos, the *Gita* and the Vedic hymns but not the proprieties of an iron caste system. In Zen she found a perky hostility to all dogmas and conventions, an intellectual holiday from metaphysics and reasoning to satisfy her antinomian temperament.

Though Suzuki's essays informed her study of Buddhism, as Guenon's her study of Hinduism, neither text gives more than an oblique indication of how very closely Weil's *metaphysique religieuse* shows as great an affinity to the East as to Christianity. Buddhism, centered on the contemplative discipline of individual consciousness, provides the best evidence for this affinity. In the words of a classic study, it "mixes metaphysics and psychology" in a way unknown to the West: the empirical self is not the real self, and yet a mode of living is prescribed.[156] Is not Buddhist detachment the pragmatic equivalent of Weil's decreation?

Although, like Christianity, Buddhism appeals to the disillusioned, to those with a keen sense of *malheur* and a capacity for renunciation, it does not exalt a personal savior. The historic Buddha is of no account save as *tathagata*, an archetypal divinity. Buddhism prescribes intellectual precision and leaves pious devotional practices to the masses. The precariousness of the body, the horror felt at one's constant subjection to the sensuous world, require a mental violence to protect one in seeking the true self within—*le sacré*, as Weil called it. Her cultural isolation and her stringent intellect predisposed her to this austere pathmaking toward an absolute. Cut off, self-exiled, she fashioned from lost times and distant cultures an intellectual's spirituality that was exclusive and forbidding.

Like Guenon, one may risk some semantic analogies. The Buddhist notion of *samadhi*, a narrowed attention of the will to an alert receptivity, is Weil's *attente*. One may object that Weil is waiting for the master, for God, whereas

Buddhism recognizes no master, but like the Buddhist, Weil required of herself an apophatic contemplation that would strip away all delusions and comforts, including any idea one entertains of the absolute. Further, *apramana*, an unconditional goodwill to all that lives, an unbounded compassion for all, is Weil's ethic as well. Morally, it is indistinguishable from a Christian love that extends itself even to one's enemies. The difference is that Christianity recognizes that one has enemies to forgive; in Buddhism, everyone is to be pitied as a kind of ontological victim. Weil is especially Eastern in this respect. For all her contentiousness, she does not give an impression of personal hatreds and enmities, even in her irrational flings at Judaism.

Far more acutely than Christianity, Buddhism perceives the reality of universal suffering, and accordingly it prescribes a rejection of all worldly pleasures and an extinction of all desires. One might say that in response to the proclaimed calamity of existence it personalizes monasticism. Weil's life, a series of withdrawals, of *refus*, her cultivated apartness from the very milieux, political and religious, in which she worked and lived, her apparent denial of any sexual life for herself, her intellectual pathfinding—all this might be read as a movement toward Eastern asceticism. Perhaps she failed as a syndical militant, as a teacher, and as a factory worker, but she succeeded brilliantly as an itinerant. It was, of course, the fate of her people to become expert wanderers.

History caught up with her as it had with them. She did not find in the "intense inane" of Eastern transcendence any final answer to the vicious realities of her time. The *Gita*, in its implicit anything-is-permitted message remained as problematic for her as her self-regarding god, who battened upon human suffering. Oriental otherworldliness, like the Christian, might have given "wisdom and serenity" to Marseilles intellectuals, but its *dharma* of detachment could only at best pacify the victims of oppression and official cruelty. It may seem captious to submit Weil's spiritual beliefs and her *lecture orientée* to political and historical contingencies for validation, but her own insistence, following Alain's, upon experimental truth rather than abstraction, warrants this direction. She looked hard to find Christ and Arjuna in Vichy, but she also indicted Christianity for failing to relate itself to "the things of this world."[157] How disastrous this failure was she did not live to realize, but Christianity (Christendom, rather) was not singular in this deficiency. Weil's own gospel of acceptance must be weighed in the balance of historical fact. Whether Stoic or Hindu in formulation, a determinism that includes evil in its rationale (whatever is, is right) has been forever invalidated in the events of 1939–45. Weil believed, or wanted to believe, that, as she put it, "everything that happens is God's caress."[158] If that is so, then, after Auschwitz, one must ask, What God is this?

It is exactly at this point, where Weil's attempt at a theodicy may seem outrageous, if not obscene, that one must try to be fair to her. If reality becomes brutish and murderous, then voluntary obedience to it amounts to little more than the suicide which Mohandas Gandhi prescribed to Buber as the proper response of Jews to their Nazi tormentors. But Weil, as has been noted, considered suicide a false exit. What, then, of love? She did not fondly presume that loving an enemy can disarm him; she did not even believe that love can transfigure the misery of others. On the contrary, she said it cannot. She believed humanity is the only proper object of love, even though it be not ourselves but God within us who does the loving. One's love for God, in turn, though ontologically impossible (only God can love God), must include acceptance of all irremediable suffering, sorrow for human pain, and active charity. That is, love must suffer and can do so only when it is mediatory. True religion, and Weil would include true justice, requires mediation, where God renders himself a victim.

Did Weil, one must wonder, in her *emulatio Christi*, will herself by obedience and love to be such a victim? Is that the recondite sense of her decision to stand at the cruciform intersection of Christianity and everything else? Was she attempting at some atavistic level of consciousness to sanctify God's name by the Jewish martyrdom known as *kiddush ha shem*? It is not certain. It is certain, however, that although refusing Judaism she could not refuse the imputation of being a Jew. Her self-denomination as a Christian *extra ecclesiam* by God's will, and a Hindu *shudra* by the French people's will amount to rhetorical evasions of a cold fact, but, as evasions, a tacit acknowledgment as well. She was a Jew. The cruelest irony of all may be that: she did not see that being a Jew could have placed her in the role of suffering mediator she so much desired. *Shema, Israel,* the apostrophe many Jews uttered on their way to the gas, was a *Schiksalslied* she did not hear. Neither did she perceive that the swastika superseded in her time the cross as the emblem upon which innocence was nailed.

These are strident words, but they reflect historical facts. They also refer to an experimental truth such as Weil wanted to find. The proof lies in a story more terrible and poignant than any she could have found in the *Iliad* or Sophocles.

At the beginning of the Jewish New Year, September 25, 1941, near the

Lithuanian town of Ejszyszki, German officers massacred several hundred local Jews. Having fallen into the prepared pit unscathed, a youth named Zvi Michalowski crawled out at nightfall, naked and covered with others' blood. He went to several homes of Christian peasants. He was repeatedly turned away and at one door told, "Jew, go back to the grave where you belong!" At another, an old widow chased him away with burning wood. Desperate, he returned to her door and said, "I am your Lord, Jesus Christ. I came down from the cross. Look at me—the blood, the pain, the suffering of the innocent. Let me in." The old woman fell at his feet, crossing herself and exclaiming, "My God! My God!" She took him in. He promised to bless her and her children if she kept him hidden for three days. Upon leaving, he told her his visit must remain a secret because he had a special mission on earth. He escaped to the forest, joined some partisans, and survived the war.[159]

Here, with the force of a scriptural parable (it recalls the story of the resourceful steward, Luke 16:1–7, commended by Christ for his shrewdness), a number of injunctions come to mind: to knock that one might enter, to be as gentle as a dove and as subtle as a serpent. Following them is a parodic *deus absconditus*. One even finds a *dharma* for the tormented: resistance and survival. Above all, there is the suffering mediator—as before, a Jew.

Whatever Weil might have read in this story, it seems a pity that she missed it.

PART FOUR

Resolutions

ELEVEN

Prefaces to *L'enracinement*

La partie que nous jouons, révolutionnaires et Français, est une partie infinie, parce qu'elle est une partie d'un enjeu infini.
CHARLES PÉGUY, *Par ce demi-clair matin*

Weil wrote her only book-length work, *L'enracinement*, in the limbo between the Third and Fourth Republics, but she was recasting a problem that had beset France more than three generations before, beginning with the defeat it had suffered from Prussia in 1870. In less than a century, France, having inspired the world by its Revolution and set upon a new course of empire while maturing toward a parliamentary republic, had to seek its identity anew after that crushing reverse. The ensuing eradication of the Paris Commune, that ill-starred experiment which Engels called the intellectual child of the First International, prompted the question Ernest Renan took up in a tract, "What is a Nation?"

Reflecting a militant chauvinism that throve as France struggled to recover its pride, Renan prescribed a collective glorification of the past and a national will pledged to great deeds. Curiously, with an eye to Vercingetorix, Roland, and Sainte Jeanne, he saw that French glory lay mostly in defeats, but he drew a spirited conclusion: "As to national memories, times of mourning are worth more than times of triumph, for they impose duties and command common efforts."[1] This cult of glory in defeat has had a long pedigree in France—it consoled Bernanos in exile during the Vichy years[2]—but it has also rationalized defeat itself. Schoolchildren in la Belle Epoque, the generation of Barrès, Maurras, and Péguy, read in their history manual, *Le petit Lavisse,* that they should love their ancestors who had built France more in suffering than in joy. Such a lesson gained a renewed if pathetic vitality from Maréchal Pétain's exhortations to Nazi-occupied France.

Weil remained free of the allure of this Gallic defeatism. With the *Iliad* her text for a definitive pathology of war, she looked on the claims of wounded chauvinism and addressed more lucidly than could Renan his query. On behalf of a France that would have to overcome not only the Nazi darkness and its own complicity within that darkness but also decades of social and political turmoil, Weil posed the question, How can there be justice in this world? Her late essays, written in the last eight months of her life, try to conceive of justice in personal, social, and international terms. These works can be read as ancillary efforts toward what she would attempt in *L'enracinement*. Indeed, one of them, "Etude pour une déclaration des obligations envers l'être humain," succinctly formulates the justice of what Weil meant by being rooted: "The human soul needs above all to be rooted in many milieux," as for example those given by "language, culture, a common historic past, a profession, a locale. . . . All that in effect uproots people or prevents them from taking root is criminal."[3]

Barrès could have written those words; he would certainly have given them his assent, but Weil does not follow his lead toward a committed nationalism. Her sense of ultimate reality rests not on nationhood but on a conjunction of Platonic and Christian visions. Following Kant's dualism of the phenomenal and the noumenal, she recognizes in the reality of this world "the sole basis of facts," including the wretchedness of all earthly needs. To the Platonic, transcendent reality belongs all beauty, truth, and justice, as well as the imperative to subordinate human conduct to obligations. Patently, these are the realities of Plato's Cave and his sun, apprehensible to anyone who consents to love the good. All human beings, whatever their differences, share "a central need of the good" that constitutes their bond to "the reality foreign to this world," but only those genuinely attentive to that other world can recognize the perpetual obligation to remedy as far as possible "all privations of body and soul susceptible of destroying or of mutilating the earthly life of any human being."[4] In short, Weil weighs religious injunctions upon the guardians of Plato's republic.

A society can be good, she maintains, only in proportion to that part of it which has a consenting access to the "other reality." Any society, state, or legal system lacking such orientation must be illegitimate and criminal. The aim of public life must be to place all forms of authority in the hands of those who know their Kant and their Plato.

Looking to remedy "privations of body and soul," Weil sees that it is perhaps more important to assuage suffering than to explain its merits, but she drastically limits the effectiveness of any attempt toward that assuagement because she sets up as a precondition a mystical clear-sightedness that is likely granted to very few in any age and seldom to a nation's leadership. She remembered that Plato himself, the author of this *sagesse oblige*, had failed dangerously in his one attempt to implement a government by philosophy. Perhaps only a theocracy, of which Islam has afforded some models, would suffice for Weil's ideal of lofty leadership.

As a sketch for *L'enracinement*, the "Etude" is more than a metaphysical cloud passing by. It concludes with an "application pratique" referring vaguely to a broad range of economic and technical powers and "spiritual" agencies, but all of these are significantly without rank relative to government authority. A Rousseauist assumption about popular sovereignty emerges in Weil's belief that for a declaration of obligations to have any practical bearing, "the first condition is that it be adopted in this intention by the people."[5] It is a condition that Plato, no democrat, would never have dreamed of.

To ensure that obligations have force, she calls for institutions and customs (requiring, she grants, generations to develop) to punish infractions. In 1943 any talk of punishment would have smacked of *revanchisme*, of some need, private or partisan, to get even with enemies after the war, but Weil is, in her unique way, free of such meanness and yet relentlessly insistent upon *le châtiment* as a measure of society's commitment to justice.

In *L'enracinement* she attacks journalistic distortions of truth, noting that calculated lies find acceptance with the public when they go unpunished. She prescribes "special tribunals, highly honored and composed of specially chosen and trained magistrates," and would call Jacques Maritain before them as a model offender for having said in print that the greatest thinkers of antiquity did not condemn slavery.[6] She takes his remark as an unconscionable slur against her beloved Greece. For this "atrocious calumny against an entire civilization" her tribunal would censure him.[7] What form such censure would take remains unclear, but Weil does present a rationale for punishment derived wholesale from Plato.

Punishment has only one legitimate social function, to restore and reintegrate the deviant soul into the social matrix. As a corrective instrument, it is as indispensable to the criminal as to society. Wholly free of sentimental indulgence, Weil requires that the criminal consent to suffering. Society for its part must not be vengeful or terroristic in punishment lest the criminal be cut off from any hope of rejoining it. Through the notion of consenting acceptance, the centerpiece of Weil's *theologia crucis* and *amor fati*, punishment becomes a sacred process of reinitiation. She boldly characterizes it as an honor because it effaces the crime, purges and reeducates the soul to the public good. Properly administered, it restores justice to the soul.

Weil shows a high estimate of the criminal's mind; she presumes him predisposed to the rite she envisions. Her criminal recalls those souls in Dante's *Purgatorio* who sing Scripture in the midst of their agony, but it is hard to imagine Maritain in some prison joyfully penitent for having slandered truth and the Greeks. In fact, he did not slander them—a particular that suggests that Weil's special tribunal would quickly become a literary and philosophical debating society and a world apart from the rough justice of French courts in 1944 and 1945.

Because she does not elaborate a scheme for corrective justice, it is uncertain how Maritain, left hapless in the docket, would have been punished for what Weil regarded as sacrilege (a capital offense in Plato's book). But it can hardly be doubted that the issue weighed heavily upon her because it was a conspicuous part of the postwar agenda. How was liberated France to be judged? What corrective justice could be applied to men like Pétain and Laval or to Maurras, who for over two generations had propounded an ideology serviceable to the Occupation? How to judge the far less visible and innumerable accomplices? If a government is evil, Plato contended (*Timaeus* 87), the community it governs must be reckoned in its guilt for tolerating it. Some French people considered the Occupation itself a punishment, and Pétain rationalized the Nazi presence as a deserved chastisement for the Third Republic. But now it would not suffice merely to call up the accusations of betrayal and arraign everyone who seemed to have contributed to the debacle of 1940.

Mindful of the *Iliad*'s imperishable words, that justice always flees the victor's camp, Weil, foreseeing the end of Nazi domination in Europe, dared to ask if the Allies were fighting for justice. In view of a barbarism that had threatened to destroy Western civilization and nearly succeeded, it seems a captious if not foolish question, but Weil, not one to admit rhetorical questions, was not interrogating the political intents of those who would reconstruct postwar Europe; she was addressing instead the moral character of their presuppositions. She argues that the issue of justice is indissolubly bound to and identical with the demands of love.

That may sound ridiculous. Weil insists that it is ridiculous but commends it for that very reason. If the universe has a wise order to it, as she stoically suggests, there must be moments when from reason's mundane perspective the folly of love is alone reasonable. This folly of love requires compassion for the enemy—a tall order, indeed, in view of the Nazis—but what it chiefly solicits is love's free consent as the indispensable mechanism of justice within any society or between any individuals. Weil holds that a nation must at its heart and in the depths of its past contain something for the love of which its people will consent to obedience, else there can be no true liberty. This means that she conceives of freedom not as a throwing off of restraints but as a voluntary assumption of them—a freedom at the greatest possible remove from its flattering caricatures in partisan lies and propaganda. On that score she faults the old quarrels of Left and Right as contentions between the urge for social constraint and the urge for individual caprice, both alike void of justice and charity. She attacks as well the predominance of money in most aspects of social activity, especially in its debasement of labor. As oppression or forced consent is like rape, money's influence as a motive for work is like prostitution.

Hearkening to the Revolution's trinity, Weil claims that *liberté* means simply the genuine possibility of giving one's consent to obedience; *égalité* makes sense only in relation to that possibility; *fraternité* means one wishes that possibility for everyone else. Clearly, *liberté* thus conceived was not the *clef de voûte* in the Revolution, and Weil argues that a central blunder of 1789 lay in making right, rather than obligation, an absolute principle, but that only signifies the betrayal of the Revolution from the start, well before Robespierre appeared. The task of the post-Vichy generation, Weil asserts at her most pithy and audacious, is to reinvent liberty.

How that invention may proceed she indicates only sketchily. In looking to the nation's fidelity to its past, to those wellsprings where, as she so charmingly puts it, love is imbibed as naturally as milk, she regards a rebirth of the syndicalist movement and of universal suffrage as vital. And without making specific injunctions, she anticipates that the future of the French empire must be considered with a rigor free of lies.

Obligation and obedience are requisites of justice but in Weil's lexicon they have discrete meanings. Obligation involves a hierarchic leadership down to familial paternalism. Obedience does not work upward in a social stratum; it signifies deference on everyone's part to the universal law of necessity, the very condition which exposes everyone in this world to suffering and possible injustice.

How can obedience to necessity constitute justice and be made the nexus for *liberté*, *égalité*, and *fraternité*? It would seem rather to constitute abject submission or a sensational quietism. The answer lies in Weil's idea of love, a folly that by its voluntary power can transform evil into good, injustice into justice, suffering into beauty and even happiness. True to Plato, Weil regards this process as wholly the soul's operation. She does not contend that this ethic enjoys efficacy in any practical context, and she frankly admits that the French people have been too exhausted by the Occupation to achieve what her strenuous kind of liberty entails. She expressly states that one cannot run the risks inherent in this justice and this love if one gives allegiance to any cause or nationalism, or even to a religion, all of which offer pharisaical rewards for one's fealty. Consent to necessity, mighty in its absurdity, cannot be bought or sold.

One might assume that by 1943 Weil had lost touch with sordid reality. If now she wrote in the outdated academic currency of metaphysical abstractions, Platonic, Kantian, Stoic, was she really aware of the world at war and of the France she had left behind less than a year before? Fortunately, the eloquent proof that she was lies in a very hard and down-to-earth look at Vichy.

"Impressions" of Vichy

During her exile in America and Britain, Weil wrote a small but important number of essays in English for a readership, of one or many, English and American, who, immersed in their own propaganda and prejudices, did not have sufficient or impartial witness to what was happening in France. She knew that official French propaganda, from Vichy and from de Gaulle's Free French, was tainted with expediency. With a fairness and balanced judgment such as few in positions of authority could presume or pretend to show, she was in effect writing against French propaganda.[8] What she modestly calls her "impressions of a Parisian" have the vivid freshness of historical witness.

In one of her essays she observed that only a decade before the war France "seemed the ruler of Europe; the French people were so unconscious of any danger to national independence that they did not know they needed it, as one does not know he loves to breathe till he is being strangled."[9] Hence, *patrie* and a rootedness in French national life would have to be, like freedom, reinvented. Weil saw that restoration of the sense of belonging to a cohesive culture would be perhaps the major desideratum of postwar leadership. Although she underrates the French people's ingenuity in devising strategies for accommodation and survival under the Germans, she is implicitly pointing to the divisive consequences of lost nationhood: the exacerbation of tensions between classes, between regions (people in the Occupied Zone presumed those in the Unoccupied were well off), and between town and country.

She acknowledges that in some ways the war only intensified the malaise of the 1930s, the "moral and mental drowsiness" brought on primarily, in her view, by "boredom, lack of interest in things in general, anxiety about the near future, lack of intensive spiritual life." This syndrome amounts to no more than a petty selfishness but Weil, with her moralistic concern to look to the incriminating past more than to a vague, possibly redemptive future, is making no partisan indictment. There is no embittered, accusatory tone, and she tags no one group or class or party as culprit or traitor. She sees that far more to the point than class antagonisms or factional differences are the common denominators of suffering: "There is incredible national humiliation. And there is hunger, which came slowly, first merely imaginary, then more and more real every day, till it has become the chief fact of nearly everybody's everyday life." She comes back to this "chief fact" again and again. Pervasive hunger, it seems, was the abiding impression she carried with her into exile. It became fatefully bound up with her own life. As is well known, in her last months she restricted her daily diet to what she believed was the common level of rations allowed to her compatriots. But, as may be less well known except in France, a substantial underground quickly developed in both zones. One historian reckons that "due to the organizational failures or incapacities of the French Ministry of Provisions, less than half of the available food in the country was distributed through officially approved channels. The black market was a vast uncoordinated area of business in which the remainder was bought and sold."[10]

Weil was surely aware of the black market and that its benefits were not evenly distributed and enjoyed. The very private enterprise Jean Dutourd satirized in *Au bon beurre* did not extend to the working people of Marseilles, for example, and it is the real suffering, as opposed to the contrived, which fixed Weil's sympathy. It transcended all class differences in her estimation because before the defeat no one had ever imagined he or she would suffer genuine privation: "Hunger, except from extreme poverty, was a tale of far-off countries or ancient times, for schoolchildren, a thing to be found only in books. Unemployment was nearly the only possible cause for real and lasting hunger: even the poorest could at least get plenty of bread. There has scarcely been any lack of bread in France for two centuries. Who would have dreamed that some day well-to-do people would long for dry bread and in vain?" Hunger, according to Weil, was the ever-imposing factor that contributed to one's sense of the nightmarish reality of the German presence in France.

The emblem of that unreality was the daily queueing necessitated by the Nazis' extortionist demands upon the French economy. In the Marseilles region, where food cultivation was limited to citrus fruits and wines, shortages were more acutely felt than in other urban areas: "Some years ago Marseilles was one of the noisiest cities in Europe; everyone shouted in anger or in merriness out of sheer animal spirits. Now people speak low. In the 'queues' every day, the people are standing still and silent, during hours and hours. Such silence is sinister because it means that, even though there are no striking marks of distress or famine, life is ebbing away." She adds that only when she had seen the faces and comportment of ordinary people in Manhattan did she realize how miserably low the French people had been brought.

It would be gratuitous to object that she had oversimplified these circumstances, as though since the summer of 1940 *malheur* had descended upon France with the uniform outrage of tragic drama. She was registering at the immediate level of daily life one of the emergent causes of general disillusionment and bitterness toward Vichy and even toward Pétain in early 1942. Her concern about hunger dwells not on dietary deficiencies but on the connection between physical and psychological suffering. As in her remarks on well-to-do Jews suddenly debased in German camps, there is here a moralist's fascination with the calamitous reversal of fortune.

She contends that no one, not even its factotums, were taking Vichy seriously: "It is mere administration. There must be some administration as a matter of course. . . . That one is bad, but no one thinks there could be a better one in the present circumstances. On the other hand, most people think, rightly or wrongly, it could not be much worse. It is borne with as a necessary feature of the nightmare." Weil makes scant mention of Resistance movements, perhaps because although they were winning tacit support from the general population before she left France, there were no widely based movements. Also, she did not wish to give them a premature celebration, and it is certain she resented those at home and in exile who "resisted" Vichy by the cheap comfort of carping about it. Her perceptions are brilliantly unsparing: "Many of those who use the most violent terms of abuse against the cowardliness of the Vichy government are very glad in the bottom of their hearts that there is such a cowardly government to stand between them and even greater misery; they speak only because they know that their words cannot possibly have any effect. If it was in their power to destroy the government they would not do it." This is a shrewd judgment and one that shows how nuanced the term *collaboration* must be in reckoning the meaning of Vichy.

All genuine enthusiasm for Pétain had vanished by 1942. Holding back from an adversary's contumely, Weil gives an "impression" so extraordinarily temperate that it might well figure in history's verdict on France's most contested national figure: "The people have nearly ceased to love and respect him, yet neither do they hate or despise him. They merely do not care about him any more. They do not look upon him as a traitor, but as a very old man who probably does his best, and whose best is not good. They are all so weary that they can understand an old man's weariness." Weil is not interested in exculpating the Vichy regime but rather in marking the true dividing line in the French national crisis. It does not, she insists, concern collaboration. As there were once "quarante millions de Pétainistes," so in varying degrees of necessity there have been 40 million *collaborateurs*. The only real difference lay between those who wished for Germany's defeat and those who presumed its triumph. By this demarcation it is evident that she refers to those who, like Pierre Laval, had openly and publicly cast their lot with Hitler.

Weil is characteristically free of rancor toward such people as she analyzes the motives of their allegiance. First of these was the pecuniary gain which Germans had brought, not only to industrialists but to small shopkeepers as well. Second was the old dread of communism, "but that is becoming lesser every day, as present ills put possible ones out of mind." However deep-seated and reflexive one's fear of Bolshevism—it had long been a bogey of Catholicism, of professional rightists and the bourgeoisie—it lost some of its vividness before the ongoing terrorism of the Gestapo and the Milice. Third and most important, those who had committed themselves totally and enthusiastically to collaboration knew that Hitler's defeat meant death. Weil shows how by honest intentions they had followed Pétain's disastrous lead: "Many hoped that France would find fairness and regard and even respect among the Germans and agreed wholeheartedly with collaboration. Most of those would now strongly deny that they ever had such feelings, and quite sincerely, too, for man is a very forgetful animal. But the well-known political men . . . cannot take refuge in forgetfulness. They went upon that side with a numerous following. . . . They are unlucky traitors indeed." If this is not an apologia for Laval and thousands of others behind him (and it is not), it is a witness to their pathetic misjudgment. History does not forgive such errors.

Yet Weil's instinctive sympathy for history's losers is not wanting here, and neither was it lacking in de Gaulle. Most of those "unlucky traitors" who escaped street vengeance after the Liberation and came to trial received short sentences or acquittal.[11]

Looking to a post-Vichy France, Weil shows little optimism. She believed the French people put little stock in de Gaulle as a political leader, and she may have shared their doubts. Much as she could appreciate in him the conjuror of symbols, she could not become enthusiastic about him as a political leader or policy maker. She is also expressly dubious about the emergent leadership from Resistance cadres, claiming that their popularity rests mostly on their being anti-German. Few are involved in the Resistance, she notes, simply because the risks are not commensurate with the results. It would "most probably be a dangerous mistake" for the Allies to presume the Resistance could provide "a machinery for selecting adequate leaders" because its most notable organizers "are not at all looked upon as future political leaders." It is within that perceived void that Weil would seek a nonpolitical coherence in *L'enracinement*, but she knew that the strongest faction within the Resistance was the Communist party. That she would discount its postwar leadership (Maurice Thorez spent the war in Moscow) seems disingenuous, and the fact is that she would not have wanted to see the Communists ascendant and dominant. She had not forgotten their usurpation of the CGT during the Popular Front.

At the same time she regarded the inauthenticity of all political parties as self-evident: "The old political functions are now nearly corpses, except in small towns where 'left' and 'right' go on hating each other and even, I have been told, storing arms in secret against each other." The likeliest prospect was that the nightmare years would culminate in "much blind and random cruelty." If the French people had any preoccupation other than food, it was the longing for "freedom to kill scoundrels, the list of scoundrels being of course arbitrary."

In such an atmosphere no political leader would prevail. Weil realizes this melancholy fact, and she does not share leftist hopes that Germany's defeat will usher in a revolution like that of June 1936. As to a communist revolution, whatever the hold of 1917 on the imagination, inspiring hope in some and terror in others, the general lassitude made it improbable: "The dreadful thing is that any leadership in France after the war will probably establish itself not through the trust, but through the weariness and indifference of the people."

To Weil's mind, the capital irony was that, for all its barbarism, Nazi Germany had seemed to monopolize the spiritual energy necessary to wage war. Against it the Allies were able to muster only what she called "a gross materialism":

> Hitler always promised victory to his people as a result of their faith and their unbounded devotion to a great ideal, while [French Premier] Paul Reynaud made up the most unhappy slogans. "We shall have victory because we are stronger." And the commentaries showed that stronger chiefly meant richer. Money had to win the war. Even now after nearly three years, how often do we read, "Food will win this war." Yet the French were much better fed than the Germans in 1940.

Here is the axial point upon which *L'enracinement* will turn, the restoration of a vital spirituality to France, without which all political and economic adjustments would go for nought. The French long for freedom, Weil says, but she warns that freedom could entail great dangers: "To be used rightly its nature must be known." Hence a return to basics, to abstractions long manipulated in propaganda, was Weil's self-assumed task, a *débrouillement*.

Weary of suffering and evil, France could not have been receptive, even in the war's aftermath, to Weil's exhortations to voluntary, consented obediences and obligations. Although her compatriots' acquiescence to Vichy was a kind of basic training in consent, the diametric difference between complicity and voluntary accord became too clearly drawn. Weil could, however, appeal to the nation's conscience in examining the issues of liberty and consent in another context, that of French colonialism. It was a matter of utmost importance to her throughout and even before the war, yet it has been largely neglected even by her most enthusiastic critics and commentators.

Colonial Disasters

From the time of Jules Ferry's expansionist program in the 1880s, France had gained in Africa and Asia some recompense for pride lost in the war with Prussia. Colonies had partly assuaged the spirit of *revanche*. With these acquisitions France irreversibly entered nationalism's colonial game, in rivalry with England and Germany. But with neither a surplus population to release nor evident pressures for new markets, France could not make its colonial efforts part of the lives of the French themselves. Colonial policy was the artifice of a few, and "colonists were dreamers and adventurers inspired by hope which seldom had a sound basis in reality."[12] However fascinating to schoolchildren Pierre Brazza's exploration of West Africa, however charming Louis Lyautey's gallicization of Morocco, France took a long while in facing the dirty realities of its distant possessions. In 1939, less than a decade after the Colonial Exposition was mounted in Paris, a poll indicated that only two of every five questioned felt that France should go to war for its colonies.[13]

Weil's concern about the colonies dates from the exposition. In a 1936 letter to a journal in Indochina, she recounts how for more than five years she had been burdened with grief and shame. She had gone to the exposition and observed crowds admiring reproductions of the temples at Angkor Wat, the French "stupidly indifferent to the suffering caused by the regime thus symbolized."[14] This was only one occasion for her revulsion.

A bloody uprising in Vietnam, documented in an article by Louis Roubaud and published by *Le petit parisien*, occupied her one day at breakfast: "In haste I devoured Louis Roubaud's article. I saw how coolies were recruited, how they were beaten and how the white overseers maimed or murdered the Vietnamese workers with kicks before comrades too frightened to intervene. Tears of shame stifled me, I could no longer eat."[15] In this oblique contact with colonial life at the Homeric level of brute force, she addresses Indochina's hopes of liberation. Although the Blum administration, having won many concessions for French workers, might help to end the disgrace of France's foreign labor, the prospects were not sanguine. She warns the Indochinese that though the French government is socialist, its colonial offices are not, and yet she urges them to use colonial journals to express themselves openly. With typical naïveté and candor, she concludes that one must flatter tyrants, but one may speak freely to friends. In her mind the faceless Indochinese had become her friends and their remote suffering immediate.

In her lycée classes at Roanne in 1933–34, she had drawn upon her reading of Roubaud to create a balanced view of what colonization meant. The manifest benefits of education, highways, health, and the abolition of superstitions did not compensate for violence French officials visited upon subject peoples.[16] The substantial drawback to colonization was this sustained terrorism, made worse to Weil because it remained so remote to the indifferent French at home. She concluded to her students that the colonial problem had to be made part of France's self-transformation—hence her subsequent hope that Blum would alleviate the colonial crisis.

One of the bitterest lessons she learned during the Popular Front she recorded in a series of short essays in 1937–38, three of which were published at that time. Alsthom and Renault had taught her that awareness of suffering requires proximity to it. But she had not realized that indifference to suffering in Tunisia or Indochina—where, she notes acidly, the dying do not count for the French as dead—pervaded the Left no less than the bourgeoisie. Worse, as the bourgeois could pretend that the workers' physical and moral anguish did not exist so long as they remained silent, so the Left in loading upon colonial laborers "the same pitiless constraint" could rationalize or minimize colonial servitude. To Weil, the leftist complacency showed itself more culpable than the bourgeois: the concessions Blum had won for unions had required years of organization and a wave of strikes that eventually confounded the shareholding classes, but the impetus for organization had also required an elementary sense of outraged justice. Where was it now that millions abroad "from an abyss of woe and misery turn their eyes to us?"[17] In sum, the Left decried the domestic oppression of labor without seeing that oppression abroad was identical: "It is always and everywhere the same problem which is posed. Always and everywhere where there are oppressed."[18]

After 1937, Weil was less disposed to consider French colonial rule beneficent. She had hoped that France, faced with the growing menace of Nazism, might reclaim the Revolution's heritage of freedom and brotherhood. Her criticism of colonial policy recalls some inspired pages of Condorcet 150 years earlier.[19] The Popular Front seemed to be the one substantial basis for reclamation of revolutionary idealism. When, after June 1937, its momentum was dissipated by Edouard Daladier's regime and when another general strike in 1938 failed drastically, exposing weariness and cynicism among the unions themselves, an enlightened policy toward the colonies seemed no longer likely.

In remarks on "anti-French intrigues" in the colonies Weil cites instances of violent protests against France. She iterates her feeling of shame at French colonial exploitation and the Left's indifference to colonial facts. She expressly includes the Popular Front in her claim that the French government has provoked colonial hatreds.[20] Now, relishing the prospect, she fancies that colonial peoples may go on a general strike comparable to what French workers achieved in June 1936: a shutdown of the colonial economy takes on axiomatic inevitability in her assertion that all men (and all women, too?) are by nature proud enough to revolt in the face of oppression. In fact, as she notes in another essay, Algerian workers had played an important role in the occupation of Parisian metal factories in June 1936, even though they had long been victims of racist contempt from their French co-workers.[21]

How great a debt, she mused, did France owe to its foreign peoples for instructing it in its own fair history of liberation. Besides, as she remarks of Vietnam, some colonial peoples could claim an ancient culture as noble as any in Europe. Through Chinese, Hindu, and Buddhist influences, Vietnam had learned the doctrine of *karma*, that universal law of measure which, like the Greeks' nemesis, punished excess. The course of empire demonstrated how well Europe had forgotten that law.

Munich was the proof. In the wake of France's abject concession to Hitler, Weil's writing on the colonies assumed an urgent perspicacity. France, she believed, still had a chance, barely, to direct reforms that would help the colonies to autonomy. The alternative might be a totalitarian revolution within a colony that would exploit its people under a new form of statism: if France went to war with Germany, the drain on her armed forces might precipitate a violent effort in the colonies toward emancipation. Alternatively, colonies kept impotent and passive would be ready victims for the predations of aggressors more powerful than France. Far better, therefore, first to afford colonial peoples an active part in their own political and economic life. Ironically, in thus divesting itself of empire, France would enable its colonies to acquire a freedom worth defending against all forms of oppression.

Although the prestige of France as educator of nations keeps a low profile in all of Weil's considerations, it is clear that a colonial overthrow of all foreign domination stayed foremost in her mind. It seems she did not care that France might lose its imperial status, but she earnestly hoped, even in noting the lateness of the hour, that her country might at least be an accomplice to colonial freedom: "From the French point of view, such a policy is necessary; from the humane point of view—which, let it be said in passing, is naturally my own—whatever the consequences for France, it will be a happy one."[22]

Weil wanted France to pursue a decreation policy, but nowhere did she assume that an appeal to a national conscience, if such a beast existed, could suffice. In the face of German and Japanese expansionist ambitions, France awaited colonial dismemberment, yet the alternative, in Weil's analysis, came to political realism at its best, the coincidence of expediency and morality: "Humanity in politics consists not in incessantly invoking moral principles, which are usually fruitless, but in undertaking to consider first all the motives of a low order which, in a given situation, can act in the sense of moral principles."[23] In Weil's reckoning, statesmanship meant realizing that the freedom and well-being of alien peoples in Asia and Africa would indirectly benefit France's own national security.

Weil did not pretend to know how a policy of enlightened rapprochement might be effected, or even when, or how (this was most important) the French public could be educated in that policy, but she was quick to condemn obstructions, namely, official lying about colonial realities.

A notable instance of lying occurred in November 1939. Jean Giraudoux, a dramatist Weil admired and a fellow veteran of the Normale, just appointed first commissioner general of information in Reynaud's new Ministry of Propaganda, broadcast an address on the duties of French women in which he asserted that the colonies were bound to France by "ties other than those of subordination and exploitation." To any informed person, Weil wrote to him, the truth was otherwise. Regarding the Indochinese, for instance, "We have murdered their culture, forbidden them access to writings in their own language, imposed upon a tiny number of them our own culture, which has no roots in them and which cannot do them any good."[24] She likens France to imperial Rome in the thoroughness of its oppression. No graver charge could she have imagined; it anticipates a no less severe indictment three years later, when she equates French colonial policy with Hitlerism. Her patience and the *drôle de guerre* were ending; now she denies to wartime France any real potential for beneficent action in the colonies. Not even the importation of French culture any longer provided a rationale. "Can we say we have carried culture to the Arabs, who preserved the Greek tradition for us in medieval times?"[25] The colonies were, in fact, the bearers not only of their own venerable cultures; they carried an important lesson for France, and she refers to Giraudoux's attention the message of Vietnamese *karma*.

Whether Weil would have welcomed some grand chastisement of France's colonial crimes can only be conjectured, but she did feel implicated in them. Her reaction to Roubaud's articles years before suggests how viscerally the issue affected her. As to Giraudoux's rosy view of France's relations with "la France d'outre-mer," she told him, "I would give my life and more if it were possible to be able to think it so. It is indeed painful to feel oneself guilty by involuntary complicity."[26]

More than painful, this complicity linked her to the historical statism she denounced in the example of Rome. Her hatred of Rome might be considered a deflected hatred of the French colonial system. On despotism's family tree Richelieu and Louis XIV occupy for Weil a median position between the

Caesars and the Führer. To feel herself an accomplice to the colonial machine must have been more than *douleureux* for her because she virtually invites Giraudoux to arraign her for treason: "I'm aware that this letter puts me on the spot by the decree of May 24, 1938, providing penalties of one to five years' imprisonment. I'm not troubled in this regard, but if I were, what do I care? Unending imprisonment wouldn't hurt me more than the impossibility, because of the colonies, of thinking that the cause of France is just."[27]

In the event, not until three years later, when she joined the Free French, could she feel she was fighting for a just France, one, that is, newly recreated in her own vision. Within that time she as a Jew was reduced to quasi-colonial status by Vichy statutes that severely restricted or expressly excluded Jews from nearly all of France's professional life. Having been officially dispossessed, her life as a French citizen irremediably degraded, Weil going into exile in 1942 had won at great personal cost a peculiar insight into the colonial problem. It is fitting that her most eloquent writing about the colonies was done in a foreign language, English, itself the *lingua franca* of subject peoples around the world.

Like her nurses plan, "The Colonial Problem" addresses the need for a candid view of what the war against fascism is really about: the struggle for freedom. The French empire seemed to have been built without anyone's awareness that it set France against that struggle. Consequently, Weil writes, most French people "feel that after being a French citizen the next best thing is to be a French subject. They believe that the people which France have [sic] conquered are grateful for that privilege."[28] The rest of her essay attempts to undermine what she calls the French people's "naive complacency."

Drawing on her talks with natives of French colonies, Weil avoids sentimentality about them and their culture. (She is also attentive to some of the good achieved by French policy, such as the abolition of slavery and tribal war in West Africa.) In 1939 she talked with two Senegalese students whose principal grievance against France was its demolition of their ancestral status as warriors and slaveowners. "Those two boys were quite willing to recognize the fundamental superiority of the French people, provided their own superiority upon [sic] the less well-born Negroes was firmly established." Colonial students in France enjoyed complete equality with the French, a privilege that reminded them of how poorly their compatriots at home were faring.

Weil is unsparing in her review of official cruelties. She notes, for example, how in Africa France imposed forced labor in building roads and railways.

Worse, the colonial authorities, in deference to business interests, cleared land around the Niger "in true Hitlerian style. They rooted up by sheer force whole villages, transported them and put them to work in that place. . . . The letters of Lyautey written from Madagascar and describing Gallieni's methods of conquest could have provided good schooling for Hitler." In addition to these sources, Weil cites the reports of Albert Londres and André Gide on Africa; the navigator Alain Gerbault on French islands in the Pacific, where "illiterate policemen remained absolute lords and masters over one of the most refined, subtle, poetical populations in the world" (Weil speaks for Gauguin here); and Eugène Fromentin on the sorrows of Algeria late in the nineteenth century.

Little of her *tour du monde coloniale* would have been news to an informed French reader, but she insists that "at least ninety-nine out of a hundred well-informed Frenchmen know nothing whatever about Indochina." Exaggeration apart, it was probable that not many in France either knew or cared about forced labor on Vietnamese plantations or the starvation imposed on northern Vietnamese peasants during a drought—that measure in retaliation for the aborted 1931 revolt. Few would have cared to learn how fortunate Indochina was and how splendid its culture before the French arrived, but Weil seized upon this tragic incongruity of past and present and later identified it as a principal effect of deracination. In this essay she puts the matter most vividly when she recalls Indochinese students telling her

> wonderful tales about the management of their country before the French came. They have those tales from their fathers. It may all be exaggerated, of course. At any rate it expresses the feeling of the educated youth. Although they have studied in France, they can never willingly bear an alien rule. They submit only because they feel helpless . . . And what would French fathers feel if their children had to say in school, "Our forefathers the Germans . . ."? Yet it is the subject of a common joke that all over the French Empire little black, brown or yellow boys are forced to learn and repeat the meaningless words, "Our forefathers the Celts had a fair skin, blue eyes and blond hair."

Weil learned that one effect of this subjugation was an indifference to competing masters. Students even told her they preferred Japanese overlords because the Japanese were at least of a kindred race: "Of course their real wish is to have done with all and any alien rule. . . . For they are not being educated under French rule; they are being corrupted. The educated youth is spiritually routed [sic] up and without any moral support. The next generation would be worse."[29]

Closer to home, the three North African colonies (Tunisia, Morocco, and Algeria) had problems that could lead France to fatal mistakes. Weil details pungent ironies. She had seen postcards caricaturing Arabs during the 1925 Moroccan war (in which France used tanks and bombers against the tribesmen): "The Arabs were drawn exactly like the Jews in Nazi magazines, with the same grotesque and loathsome figures and faces." And yet Moroccan horsemen took heavy casualties trying to stop German tanks invading France in 1940. Weil notes their bitterness in being looked upon by the French as "equals only for death."

She cannot resist comparing the French presence in North Africa to the German occupation of France, which she does to undercut the apparent sincerity of Arabs who accept French rule: "We know that most French collaborationists hate Germany in their heart [sic], and are led to such behavior only by fear of danger and thirst for gain. We may suppose that the same thing is true of most of the Arab collaborationists, I mean Arabs who accept collaboration with France." The analogy could not have been more blunt: only now under the heel of Nazi extortions could the French realize what it is like to hate and to be hated, and even as there was a Resistance emerging within France, Weil picked up signs portending rebellion in North Africa during her brief stay in Morocco en route to America: "There are no open acts of hostility as yet, but a very uneasy atmosphere which the French people established in this country begin to feel acutely." As some Vietnamese looked to Japan, she figured that Germany, with its active propaganda in Arab countries, exerted considerable sway in North Africa. Besides, Germany's superior military strength sufficed: "Men may choose the weaker side for the sake of freedom and of their country, but they cannot be expected to do so where those incentives are lacking. No one displays heroic vertues [sic] when under restraint and without any hope of getting out of it."

She ends her essay by implying that the struggle for freedom she had identified as the Allied war aim belonged to the colonies more than to their French and English masters. That is why she looks to the United States for a promise of freedom to sustain the Arabs.

"The Colonial Problem" deserves the lengthy attention given it here because it shows in concrete terms what *l'enracinement* meant to Weil, if only by its negation in French colonialism. As in her writing on Vichy, the tone is intimate but not partisan, and the content is vividly detailed, bidding comparison on both counts with her *journal d'usine*. She felt and avowed a moral imperative: "I am French, but I believe in seeking for justice and truth before power and prosperity for one's self, one's family and one's country." These are admirable words and wholly in character. Here is Weil at her libertarian best and in sharpest contrast to the authoritarian Weil who attacked political parties.

Homage to Rousseau, or Suppressing the Parties

Weil's "Note sur la suppression générale des partis politiques" requires a substantial review of its historical context. In part, it recalls the anarchist view of men such as Bakunin and Proudhon that political parties offer nothing but various disguises of absolutism. In part, it evokes the latent antiparliamentarianism that has run as a strong undercurrent in French society since the time of the Girondins and Montagnards. Fundamentally, it reveals Weil's debt to Rousseau in shaping her political philosophy.

The very title of this essay might bemuse Anglo-American readers, who, well situated in an almost exclusively bipartisan tradition, have little appreciation of the byzantine vagaries of Continental politics.

The suppression of political parties, the end of parliamentary democracy itself, had for over two generations served the intent of political theorists (Georges Sorel chief among them) seeking to destroy the bourgeois materialism predominant in France since the Revolution. Against the individualistic cult of money they propagated cults of work aimed to enlist the proletariat and cults of blood and sacrifice (rhetorical therapy for the humiliations of 1870–71) intended to coalesce all classes under a mystique of *étatisme*. In such ideologies France begot Europe's first generation of fascists. They opposed political parties in the conviction that *politique d'abord* always served the interests of a degenerate, self-seeking middle class. A Marxist expectation that the working class would initiate the new revolutionary order gave way to the more encompassing and conveniently nebulous vision of nation. The state was not to be violently overthrown; it was to be regenerated, and all class antagonisms, all partisan differences would be overcome in that renewal. Implicitly, it was an antidemocratic, antiliberal crusade.[30]

Weil has much in common with those who "ni droite ni gauche" wanted to elevate France above the chaos and chicanery of political parties. Like many of them, she had moved from a Marxist view of class struggle toward corporatism. Like them, her orientation was *au fond* psychological: her ideas for a postwar France in *L'enracinement* speak to spiritual needs and do not amount to a political platform. But her differences with these national socialists are far more profound than any similarities. She rejected *étatisme* in any form, most emphatically one, like fascism, with pretensions to a collectivist spirituality. Also, she abhorred the cult of progress which fascists vivified in the expectation that new technologies would ensure social cohesion. She saw through the viciousness of this myth of efficiency in her attacks on the Taylorization of industry. Finally, she was no dupe to the fascist cult of unity through warfare.

Why, then, did she play the totalitarians' trump card and call for the suppression of political parties? A brief glance at the 1920s may begin to answer this question.

The crises convulsing France after the Great War—the strikes of 1920, the political incohesion of trade unionism after a disastrous national conference at Tours, the heavy indebtedness of the government and the franc's corresponding instability, the sometimes chaotic succession of administrations (five in less than a year, 1925–26), an inchoate resistance in the colonies, then the attempted or seemingly attempted coup by the Right in February 1934, the Popular Front's failure to reconcile socialists and communists within its troubled camp, the ascendant threat of Nazism—all reflected ill upon the partisanship of a weary Third Republic in its third generation.

The so-called Radical party in the 1920s and 1930s offers a sorry and telling lesson. Straddled between Right and Left, this most temperate of factions, one seeking to centralize the state while securing an illusory provincial republicanism of small shops, claimed its denomination by hearkening back to the Jacobins' bourgeois utopism. Alain, the most discriminate of rationalists, was one of the Radical party's tutelary spirits, but he could not help it arrive at any political or economic theory to buttress its venerable libertarian resistance to the church, the business culture, and the Two Hundred families. The Radicals' critical sense, self-consciously Cartesian, worked well against the dogmas of the obscurantist Right of Maurras and the dialectical Left, but it provided no fuel of its own. The Radicals influenced the ministries, especially those of the interior and public instruction, but never once secured the presidency between 1900 and 1939. Shifting and seldom resolute, they occupied an increasingly weak and anachronistic center.[31]

Coming of age in this fretful time, Weil in her political writings before 1940 shared many of its disappointments and refractory hopes, but she drew her inspiration first and above all from Rousseau. More than anyone else, Rousseau cultivated the French habit, so alien to Anglo-American practitioners of compromise and muddle, of casting politics into an absolutist's mold, of fighting ideas rather than things, and ferociously. This habit took a dark turn in the Terror, in Louis Saint-Just's chilly logic, in Robespierre's abstract visions, even in de Sade's plea that the Revolution put an end to Christianity. Rousseau, godfather of these aberrations, "confessed" he could find no mediation between everything and nothing, and his method in his *Contrat social*, where, as Alain put it, "all streams of revolt have their source," documents that incapacity.[32] It also reveals the ground of Weil's affinity for him reflected in her "Note."

In Rousseau's vision of a voluntary collectivity, the sovereign authority of the *volonté générale* ensures everyone's participation as a citizen and submission as a subject of the law. But the hypostasis of a general or popular will posed difficulties Rousseau could not overcome, namely, that this will could be only approximated in actual political practice: "The more that agreement prevails in the assemblies, that is, the more that opinions approach unanimity, the more, too, is the general will predominant; but lengthy debates, dissensions and tumult anounce the ascendance of particular interests and the decline of the State."[33] Hours before he went to the guillotine, Saint-Just drew the conclusions Rousseau implied: "The factions are the most terrible poison of the social order . . . they make a question out of lie and truth, vice and virtue, what is just and what is unjust. It's force that makes the law."[34]

The general will, then, was indispensable to social order, the precondition to justice. According to Weil, Rousseau fathered "the true spirit of 1789" in proclaiming "not that anything is just because the people will it but that under certain conditions the popular will has a greater chance than any other of conforming to justice."[35] She also credits him with the Hobbesian view that a popular will works by mutual neutralization of partisan passions, but she realized that such an equilibrium is destroyed when passions are collectivized by a single party. This totalitarianism, "the original sin of political parties," had found a voice in Saint-Just's own appropriation of the masses during the Terror: "Since the French people has manifested its will, all that is outside its sovereignty is the enemy."[36] Once a party or faction equates its own aims with the general will, it is a short step to proclaiming that whatever "the people" wills is just. "One People" ends with one Führer.

Rousseau knew all this. A keen student of ancient politics, he heeded the lesson of Rome's chaos during the late Republic. Factionalism's effect was, paradoxically, a new unanimity: "It is when the citizens, fallen into servitude, no longer have either freedom or will."[37] Weil might have foreseen this lesson in her firsthand observations of Weimar's death throes in 1932–33. The possibility that acute factionalism in France during the 1930s would prompt a fascist revolution had been real enough to give substance to the charge (not Weil's) that Hitler's triumph in June 1940 signaled also the triumph of the French Right over socialism and the *syndicats.*[38]

As Weil was writing in wartime, the position of the Free French, for whom she was ostensibly working, must also be considered. Specifically, the issue was de Gaulle's relations with the Resistance movements. To counter charges from Vichy and its foes alike that he aimed to impose his own dictatorship via the Allies, de Gaulle had to encourage through his mainland agents the continuation of the very factions that had vitiated the Third Republic. He could then call on diverse parties in the name of a new postwar republicanism and legitimately claim to be speaking for all of France, a habit he had been confining to first-person utterances. In finally choosing accommodation he went against the advice of his confidant, Philippe Leclerc, who in 1941 had urged him to suppress all political parties. De Gaulle's parliamentarian advisers and his own savvy won out, but that did not keep Weil from taking up Leclerc's advice. Without ascribing a crystal ball's prescience to her, it may be supposed that behind de Gaulle's chosen strategy she foresaw the Fourth Republic's ruinous debilities. Perhaps, hoping there was still time, she intended her "Note" for a single addressee.

Although derived from historical contexts and immediate circumstances, Weil's "Note" does not argue for an empirical solution to a crisis. That does not mean it was intended for the limbo of abstract theory. It carries out what Weil called "the formula of the lesser evil," which distinguishes opposing alternatives "as a function of a clearly and concretely conceived ideal."[39] As every political party, says Weil, works toward an idolatrous image of itself that will promote it to greater power and allow it, when predominant, to tyrannize over all other parties and the public, it is a greater evil than the people as a collectivity that follows its own moods. A political party cannot be enlightened, but a popular will might be. The "concretely conceived ideal" for Weil is Rousseau's vision of humanity harnessed to the Stoic dogma of a natural law that argues all people are sociable and beneficent. History regularly confounds this view but not conclusively. To turn a phrase of Abraham Lincoln, all of the people can be foolish but not all of the time. In *L'enracinement,* Weil looks to Rousseau and his Stoic antecedents for an image of postwar France hallowed in virtue, even though she remains fully aware of what collectivity has come to historically.

She is candid in her awareness. If the efficacy of Rousseau's popular will depends upon a unity of expression, France has never known anything resembling democracy. Weil claims that *le peuple* has never enjoyed either the means or the occasion to express itself on any public issue. (She allows one brief exception from the Revolution, noted presently.) Whatever has escaped partisan interests has been fashioned into collective passions, officially guided and encouraged. Weil logically should have concluded that the masses themselves are finally responsible for modern despotism. If *le peuple* were sufficiently conscientious about the *volonté générale*, the parties and the State would perhaps be incapable of whipping it up. But Weil does not follow Plato and identify the Great Beast with the people. If she is not wholly one with what Barrès, during the Revolution's centennial, called "the holy rabble of 1789, 1830, and 1848," she is not antidemocratic.[40]

It would be unfair to say, however, that her thinking here is *antipolitique*; it is wholly at odds with the cultivated indifference toward parties that pervaded *l'Ordre nouveau* and the *spiritualisme* of Dandieu, Aron, and Daniel-Rops. Suppression of the parties, Weil hoped, would prevent the ultimate cynical scenario of totalitarianism as Hitler staged it: one faction in power and the others in jail. A democracy determined by parties cannot prevent the formation of one pledged to destroy it: "If it makes laws of exception, it strangles itself. If it does not, it has the security of a bird before a serpent."[41]

The dilemma she presents gives democracy little hope, and it implicitly justifies Plato's belief that democracy in all its variety and disorder inevitably leads to anarchy and thence to tyranny. Weil does not concern herself with the sociological and economic factors Plato identified in this degeneration, but she subscribes to his reductionist view of political strife. If, as America's constitution makers wanted to believe, freedom thrives when government is limited and weak, then the way lies open to "the game of parties."[42]

Whether they call themselves Jacobins, democrats, or Bolsheviks, the game's participants share, according to Weil's analysis, three fatal designs: fabrication of collective passions, organized pressure of conformism upon all members (it drove Péguy from the socialists' camp), and unlimited growth. A party must be in essence a cryptic form of tyranny if only to compete with its opponents. Weil never suggests that partisan politics can pursue anything other than a pitiless law of the jungle. Compromises of policy or even the sharing of limited objectives (the 1875 Constitution was such a masterwork) she does not consider at all. One is left to infer that give-and-take can only be a sham, a maneuver to conceal dark ulterior intents.

It follows that Weil is no friend of the so-called open society of democratic liberalism. Dismissing the English party system as a bizarre anomaly, she does not entertain the possibility that the social conflict in partisan differences might be no less creative than destructive, that conflict is inevitable and must simply be afforded channels adequate to its expression. Would the suppression of parties be feasible, or would it not likely entail consequences as grievous or worse than any partisanship? Most basic of all, who is to suppress the parties? The Vichy regime had succeeded in outlawing them but only by having the rather convincing proximity of German force to back it up.

It was a common assumption in wartime France that the parties bore much if not most of the blame for the debacle of 1940. As Léon Blum lamented from prison, Vichy and Gaullist propaganda alike fueled this view.[43] Some in the Resistance itself supported at least a wartime suppression of the parties, and one underground journal even commended Vichy for its success against them.[44] Assumptions changed when de Gaulle received the Communist party's representatives and got their full support. Resistance leaders realized they could not erect barricades among factions patriotically working together. By the end of 1942, the leaders of Combat, the foremost movement in southern France, conceded that although "fundamentally hostile to the political parties, it must nonetheless resign itself to their resurrection and accommodation."[45] What distinguishes Weil's rationale for suppressing the parties is that she was arguing for a prejudice that had ceased to be a realistic goal. Her absolutist view that parties are potentially totalitarian and need only the opportunity to become so smacks of what Thibon has called her "passionate apriorism," as though she had some textbook dogma she wished to impose or graft upon elementary political realities.

Because she sees parties as ideological contestants, not as groups organized around concrete economic issues and interests, she remains within the traditional French republican context in which parties have long stood for well-entrenched biases resisting education of the people's everyday lives and needs. Hence she does not examine why the French parliamentary system failed to be genuinely representative of its constituencies. Her Rousseauist popular will is the only alternative she can find both to the hidden despotism of parties and to the bureaucratic megalith of *étatisme* which she denounces in *L'enracinement*. Just as for Rousseau, the *volonté générale* was the only way to escape the parties, for Weil it is the only means for suppressing them.

That leaves her with the task of distinguishing a legitimate general will from collective passions. She says the two indispensable conditions for determining the general will are that public awareness and public expression be entirely free of any impulse to crime or lies and that it engage problems of public life and not merely choose leaders. Both the parties and the state fail on both counts: they perpetuate themselves by manipulating emotions, and they make use of a *Führerprinzip*.

One alternative Weil seems unwilling to countenance is the savior. Why, enthusiastic reader of Plato that she was, did she not consider a philosopher-king, the enlightened leader Plato set at a diametric distance from the tyrant? The answer lies in modern French history: the Third Republic, for all its parliamentary woes, had survived crisis through individuals such as Poincaré (Alain's bête noire) and Georges Clemenceau, but no one of their ability emerged in the 1930s. Pétain, the vaunted savior in 1940, needs no comment, and it would be ingenuous to suppose de Gaulle did not see himself in the deliverer's caste. In one fleeting moment Weil suggests that De Gaulle might be capable of contemplating the Platonic forms, but her instinctive horror of any final political authority vested in one man wins out over any possible nomination.[46] She resists the temptation to pass à la Péguy from *politique* to *mystique* on de Gaulle's behalf. Besides, in the twentieth century a great man alternative to partisanship has been permanently discredited by the predators who managed to institute it. Weil suggests a look back to the featureless men of 1789 who worked through the *cahiers de revendication*, an improvised nonrepresentative system of popular agents who were, as she hallows them, "conscious that the country was attentive to their words and jealously watchful to make those words translate exactly the country's aspirations." Too briefly, the *cahiers* provided "simple organs of expression for the public thought."[47] Such, if any, are the true voices of a popular will. For Weil, politics at its best, like art, is anonymous. That the Revolution made occasion for such politics seems to have redeemed it in her eyes from all its subsequent errors and excesses.

In an ancilla to the "Note," entited "Le devoir des représentants du peuple," Weil pursues her idea of 1789's heroes. This short work indicates how the example of Roman republican tribunes influenced her.

Her sketch calls for an indeterminate number of men to safeguard the people: "But it is necessary to ensure that these watchmen remain citizens, without ever forming a corps. For that, they must be elected, not so much because the people will always choose well as that they will always feel themselves at the disposition of the people. Necessarily having the leisure [for this task], they must nonetheless work in such a way as to remain citizens among citizens." These representatives, in judging whether legislators and executors are carrying out the popular will, "must never decide in advance according to a set doctrine but must offer a new judgment for each occasion." If, for instance, a representative approves government actions for war when the people wish to avoid it, he is a traitor. The representative must be able to denounce the government if it fails to abolish remediable injustices. Weil excludes factory owners, generals, and bankers from this office, assuming they can never represent the people. Only those with neither power nor the desire for it could serve, their selection to be made "according to firmness of character and judgment, and the absence of political passion." Unlike the Roman tribunate, Weil's corps of representatives would be legion: "There would have to be a deputy for each social group, for villages, neighborhoods [*quartiers*], even in some instances occupations, in such a way that everywhere the man who has influence due to his firmness of judgment receives the obligation to surveillance."[48] This is only one example of her notion of an extragovernmental group of overseers, an idea that fascinated her as she sought alternatives to the parties.

It is useful to see how this toy-republic sketch complements the "Note." There, Weil's only antidote to partisan evils seems to be the individual's very private "exclusive fidelity to the inner light," a devotion that evokes Rousseau's religion of the natural man "bound to the purely inner cult of the supreme God and to the eternal obligations of morality."[49] In "Le devoir" the highest duty in serving the popular will amounts to what Weil elsewhere calls her own vocation, "to remain in some fashion anonymous, fit to commingle at any moment with the paste of common humanity."[50] She remains so wholly immersed in and loyal to Rousseau's pious vision of virtue and fraternity that both essays have an almost unreal purity about them. They contain a deontological rigor that makes them seem fantastic, if not obscure, to any modern context.

These facts point to another mainspring in Weil's political thinking, the Stoicism that assigns the duties of government exclusively to the sage. Her lengthy notes on Stoicism form an indispensable complement to the late essays.

Weil records the fundamental principle of Stoic reason as *to akolouthon en tei zoei*, an ordering of life in accordance with nature: "In effect, officium (duty) concerns all the functions of life." The sage, wholly conformed to nature, free of passions and appetites, stands above convention and does what he wishes. But his lofty wisdom obliges him "to descend into the swamp of public responsibilities and determine them for others."[51] With that descent a difficulty arises.

The Greek tradition distinguished virtue's upright actions, *katorthoma*, from actions performed in conformity to law, *ta kathekonta*. The latter lack the spirit of justice, the "intention droite" of the former. Indeed, the Stoics wrote of *katorthoma* as the completion or perfection of *ta kathekonta*. It may fairly be assumed that Weil thought she was opposing the parties from the higher vantage of final, or to use her cherished term, pure justice, and saw in the parties the degenerative tendency of mere legalism.

For the Stoics, the final dependence of law as practice upon law as justice was mirrored in a community's dependence on its sages. The "esprit de justice" could not be easily distinguished from noble, rational minds. As Weil noted, "By *katorthoma* one acts in respect for a law of which one is oneself the author." But how could Stoic wisdom, with its *sagesse oblige*, be reconciled with the law of daily practice and not force it to become virtuous?

At the heart of this problem lies Stoic logic:

> With Aristotle, logic demonstrates properties apart from essence, [but] the Stoics, being teachers, transform all logic into dialectic, which does not invent but transforms a common opinion into a firm conviction. This is, however, not an art of persuading but of demonstrating, a science of true and false—that, thanks to the *koinai ennoiai* [general ideas] whose ensemble constitute reason itself. The aim of the Stoic is to bring round his view to reason itself.

Mediator between reason and the world, the Stoic sage is much like Plato's guardians in the *Republic*.[52] Armed with "right reason," Zeno's sole criterion of truth, the sage's authority assumes a formidable position in the face of circumstance, or so it seems.

The sage's privileged access to *koinai ennoiai* recurs in the Rousseauist dogma of *volonté générale*. That is, the general or popular will is not simply the sum of the community's wishes as determined by votes. It occupies a hypostatic life in the mind of the people's sagely friend, and that is how Robespierre saw it in himself: the wise man who knew the people's will even in spite of them. In this realm of stiff virtue, reason works not at all in a people or its history and surely never in political parties; it must be, as it were, translated for the people.

Weil's representatives, with their "fermeté du jugement" as sole qualification, are the translators. Like tribunes between a people and its government, they wait to impose virtue upon the law's daily life. They never become part of the government's machinery. Far from being civil servants (bureaucrats), they perform their monitory obligations only to withdraw to occupations apparently more worthy than political posts.

Although she presents her Stoic worthies in earnest, Weil does not presume that any practical means exists for creating such a body until she draws up her plan for a postwar French constitution. If pressed, she might have answered, like Socrates, that however difficult and remote an ideal may seem, it is not impossible; what matters is that it serve as a constant corrective. As she noted in her "Réflexions" on oppression: "One can only direct oneself toward an ideal. An ideal is wholly as unrealizable as a dream, but it differs from dreaming in that it concerns reality." In that essay a heroic voluntarism is conjured up to parry the thrusts of modern collectivism—"we live in a world where one must expect miracles only from oneself"[53]—and it reappears in the late essays as Weil profiles a kind of people's sage akin to those enlightened minds whom Plato intended as society's saviors.

Meanwhile, the central evil of political life, the parties, abides, and government's legalities remain vulnerable and available to cunning. (Hitler came to power by constitutional means.) If Weil could not realistically hope that the parties would be suppressed, she could at least identify them as the bacilli thriving at every center of power, as though that sufficed to establish once and for all that from them no good can ever come. Her "clearly conceived ideal" was the Stoic's world of reason, where justice alone could be sovereign. Imagining a corps of dedicated, selfless servants in a reprise of the *cahiers de revendication* she might have believed she had followed her "formula of the lesser evil," replacing the parties, but in fact she saw no evil in her vision. The real "lesser evil" lay in government itself, and so, thinking of a new constitution, she sets out to punish it.

Weil's republicanism is Jacobin: in a chosen number of virtuous men, her watchdog representatives, a conformity to justice may be possible. But these men, more akin to Robespierre's lawgivers than to François-Noel Babeuf's leaders of pliable masses, belong to 1789 and no later. It does not slight her to say she might have felt at home with disciples of Rousseau such as Robespierre and Saint-Just, people, in J. L. Talmon's words, "too cosmopolitan and rationalist in their outlook to admit a historic, racial or any other irrational basis for national unity."[54] Like them in ignoring the force of social and economic realities on political processes, Weil subjects everything to the will's energy and its enlightened power to inform, if not transform, institutions and the social order. Like the Jacobins and Rousseau, she fails to harmonize the notion of freedom as an inner law of obedience and the inclusive moral authority of a general will. The almost irresistible temptation to construe one's own rational vision as the general will, somehow privately revealed and then set against the divisive interests of society's *volonté de tous*, unmasks the totalitarianism implicit in Rousseau's apparent democracy. *La volonté, c'est moi*, says the craftsman of this new statism. Weil's "Note" does not escape a sinister ambiguity. Perhaps it was with an eye to that ambiguity and to Robespierre, who died in consequence of it, that she defined her own role as an activist of theories: "Those preparing for the arrival of a new political regime are not the ones suitable for directing it once it is there, and yet they are the ones summoned to do so by the automatic play of circumstance."[55]

In her still youthful ardor and her righteous sincerity, she recalls the young Proudhon, who claimed that with a hundred followers he could within a decade banish prostitution, exploitation, and despotism: "J'expurge la France pour l'éternité."[56] So, too, in her categorical moments, Weil seems to want to sweep the boards of history clean, the stakes being, as Péguy said, infinite. The peculiar importance of works like the "Note" and "Le devoir" lies not only in their historical importance and in the inexorable logic she uses to press her case. Rather, it is that these works reveal her authoritarian liberalism—not that of a power-driven despot bent upon forcefully maintaining prestige but of a personality pledged to institute a transcendent ideal at whatever cost. Such a mind is fixed on an unshakable notion of justice and is compelled by its own assumptions to deem its program or cause exclusively legitimate over and against all opposition.

It is not incidental that Weil admired Robespierre. He, like Oliver Cromwell, exemplifies this liberalism. Significantly, neither he nor Cromwell sought the supreme office or the formal title of power (Cromwell was offered kingship); each considered himself a guardian or caretaker of a new order, a post rather like that of the forerunner Weil describes in the remarks just cited. Characteristic of an antipartisan or suprapartisan stance is the conviction one can hold of its purity. Weil's intolerance of parties was entirely free of dissembling or hypocrisy; she had not the slightest ambition for herself, but there remains an unsettling ruthlessness in her devotion to the general good. Although she supported losing causes like syndical anarchism and pacifism, causes eschewing power, she had some of the bullying righteousness that those purist ideologies occasionally reveal through their proponents. It is strange that Weil, who skirted formal association with any party, condemned the parties without qualification at the very time that Léon Blum, a victim many times over of the party system, wrote an eloquent defense of it from a prison cell.

If her devoted waiting for God, truth, and other verities and her attendant rhetoric of purity have enlisted many admirers, those people should be no less compelled by her waiting for justice—unswervingly, implacably, and a bit ferociously. In that waiting she set down her thoughts for a new constitution for France. Her essays on this subject are lively, savage, and generally ignored.

On the Reconstitution of France

At Grenoble on March 19, 1941, Pétain announced, "I have the duty of preparing a new constitution for the day when France shall again be free."[57] He was not alone in assuming that obligation. Making a preemptive claim on the shape of France's postwar government became a Resistance activity as vital as sabotage. Constitution drafting became a major part of the Resistance cadres' propaganda, not only against Pétain and Vichy but against each other. Weil's writing for a new French constitution came in response to proposals given her by the Free French in London and through them from the Organisation civile et militaire, the French Resistance group, decidedly rightist, whose anti-Semitic program for the postwar she denounced.

A historical background is necessary to an understanding of the problems Weil, the Free French, the OCM, and others were trying to address. After November 8, 1942, when the Germans occupied all of France in response to the Allied invasion of North Africa, all of Vichy's pretenses to legitimacy could be swept away, and with the consequences of Hitler's two-front war becoming evident, plans for a new France and a new Europe gained fresh impetus.

In a larger sense the reconstitution of France was not only an attempt to cancel the Vichy record but to overcome as well the profound weaknesses endemic to the Third Republic.[58] The Troisième was kicked about a good deal in Weil's time, and it is easy to forget by hindsight that for all its faultiness, compromises, and neglect of elevating abstractions, the Constitution of 1875 had served France workably for three generations.[59] It was the product of precisely the kind of partisan dealing Weil despised and distrusted, an unseemly (or pragmatic, depending on one's viewpoint) arrangement between Left and Right to avert a return to the Bonapartism they feared more than they abhorred each other.

Between the Revolution and the Troisième, France had known upward of ten constitutions, mostly the products of singular men of vision: Victor Mirabeau, Jean Antoine Condorcet, Emmanuel Siéyès, Benjamin Constant, Alphonse de Lamartine, Napoleon Bonaparte himself. The Third Republic produced no one comparable, but it did prove the brilliant success of mediocrity. The makeshift plan has a strange way of outlasting ideas built on eternal truths. Horse traders, not idealists, tend to get things done, and many men in the Third Republic made careers in horse-trading. Last of these was Laval.

Like Rousseau, an outsider to the politicians' world of deals, Weil was prone to set aside the facts of power and turn to fundamentals of theory. She was no dreamer; she was simply trying to get around the elementary fact of government, which is power. In her "Note" on suppressing parties she saw in all partisanship per se an implicit urge to domination; in any government she was ready to scent swindle and deceit. She is the model of Jefferson's citizen-democrat, ever vigilant against government's tyranny. Her writing on a new French government is a kind of citizen's constitution. As though in conscious disregard of the Troisième, she hearkens back to the individual constitution makers who preceded the Second Empire.

As early as 1929, in defending La ligue des droits de l'homme, she had argued that all power (government) seeks to perpetuate itself.[60] Accordingly, it declares popular claims, however just, to be impossible of realization. Backed by its police and soldiers, the government retains the exclusive power to act. More sinister is the fact that it alone knows the conditions for acting. The public knows neither all the facts nor the workings of political machinery. Kept guessing, the public must gratuitously assume either that the government is infallible or that it is at least acting in good faith. Weil regards acceptance of either assumption as a tacit alliance with power. (How fortunate for rulers, Hitler once said, that people do not think.) Weil found in the Ligue a commendable example of vigilantism as an antidote to popular passivity and government complacence: during the Dreyfus Affair it had forced the government to review Dreyfus's case, thus showing that a demand for justice can be efficacious.

In the 1943 essays she looks within government for some agency to perform the Ligue's role. Given her assumption that government means power, not justice, the effort seems pointless. What prompted her to relax her old suspicion of authority? She realized that by reverting to the separation of powers principle embodied in the 1789 Declaration of the Rights of Man she might find in the judiciary an office sufficiently elevated to serve as monitor of an overweening legislature or executive.

De Gaulle had set up a commission to propose a new constitution. In reviewing its draft, Weil mercilessly exposed in it some of the weaknesses carried over from the Third Republic's parliaments. She is particularly concerned about partisanship, including a loyal opposition, as a straitjacket on individual conscience. The real partisan betrayal in the proposal's draft was the preponderance of power it gave the Assembly, at the judiciary's expense. It invited a return to the disastrous 1930s: she recalls how Daladier, successor to the Popular Front in 1938, had turned judges into rubber stamps for repressive legislation, including provision of six months in jail for aliens who did not comply with expulsion decrees.

Weil is suspicious of the de Gaulle commission's identification of the supreme judiciary as a court of "political justice." Why the adjective, and why was the court to be composed of "representatives of the majority and the opposition"? "It is to introduce political passion under the most arbitrary, least legitimate, purportedly official form, in what ought to be the very seat of impartiality."[61] As to the legislature, she holds that "majority" and "opposition" work only in a bipartisan system such as Britain's, where the parties are opposed free of passion (relative to the French, that is) and fanaticism. By giving constitutional sanction to the parties under these titles, the commission was preparing the way for totalitarianism: a minority officially crystallized would be wide open to persecution. She did not need to adduce the fate of the German Communist party under Hitler.

She concludes that no mechanism of government can of itself ensure conformity to the public good. At best, a constitutional arrangement can only serve to bring to authority people who are solely concerned for that good. It is Plato's ideal once more: people must be found who do not want office but are able and willing to serve in it for the community's sake. Weil does not presume that once in power such people will be corrupted—she is too earnest to be cynical—but she believes they will carry a Sisyphean load: "Human intelligence—even among the most intelligent—is wretchedly below the great problems of public life."[62] De Gaulle's commission, she remarks, had fallen below even the motley standards of 1875, as though to prove just how great those problems had become.

Worse, however, was the OCM proposal. The Organisation civile et militaire, it will be recalled, was composed mostly of middle-class professionals and civil servants, people like herself who did not know intimately the workings of power and who therefore, in their constitution making, recast it to suit their own needs. Weil found the OCM plan so objectionable that she thought its opponents must have submitted it to the Free French in an attempt to discredit it.

The Gaullist scheme proclaimed that sovereignty resides in the nation, but this, Weil insists, is a fiction: "These empty formulas have done too much harm to merit indulgence."[63] Justice should be the only sovereign but in brute fact, force is sovereign, and exercised by the few. In the OCM scheme, this fact is covertly recognized, but now "popular sovereignty" is invoked. This, too, is a fiction: "The state is always an entity distinct from the people; relative to it, the people and each citizen need protection."[64]

Weil endorses the OCM's criticisms of 1875, that the legislative chambers were beyond constraint so that nothing kept them from enacting the most criminal laws from which victims had no recourse. The president of the council, as the legislature's executive agent, could pressure the judiciary into docile conformity to the law. This is the very point Weil made to the de Gaulle commission about Daladier. But in seeking to correct the past, the OCM proposed to reduce the chambers to regional authority only, while raising the executive to supreme power by plebiscite. Since all court appointments, in the OCM plan, would come from the chief of state, there would be no judicial curb whenever the executive chose to dissolve the legislatures. Stipulation of a six-year term for the executive was, to Weil's wary eye, a mere fictive limit upon what she called a constitution "du bluff."

Her capital objection concerns the role the OCM would give to a party (composed of OCM members, of course) denominated "Groupe révolutionnaire des Républicains de France." It would admit as members only Resistance militants but would not refuse governmental association with members of other Resistance groups accepting its constitution. In Weil's résumé this means "it recognizes the rights of the opposition on condition that the opposition not make itself harmful." Such a semantic blur was, to Weil's attention, a giveaway of the menacing intent she inferred from the Gaullist draft on "majority" and "opposition." For the rightist OCM the opposition could only mean the Communists, its foremost rivals, and its frank admission that it would need "revolutionary methods in order to set up the new legality" did not indicate (Weil misses this point) what role the opposition-to-be would perform in this violence.

Worse still, as head of this party, the chief of state would have absolute control over the nation's economic life. Unions, organized by métier, would be controlled by contracts the executive imposed on them. The bourgeois reactionary, Weil must have seen, was still taking revenge on the Popular Front. Whatever, then, its positive elements (Weil approves of its ministerial structure), the OCM's proposal was transparently totalitarian: "These people are completely, exclusively, and consciously fascists. When they say that they intend their party not to be the only one, it's clear they are lying. And that's the one point where they make an effort to keep away from the appearance of fascism. All the rest is fascist unadulterated, unattenuated, and avowed. . . . They admit their intention to take power by violence."

The most abused branch of government in the OCM plan was the judiciary. Whereas the Gaullist proposal reduced the high court to partisan factions, OCM judges, *la Pairie*, would be executive appointees. In both submissions, the judges would be selected for their professional reputations in science, letters, and any area other than government. Weil ridiculed this bias: "It is one of the stupidest prejudices of our age to accord a spiritual value to reputations made from jobs so narrowly specialized that they are denuded of all relation with the spiritual life." The OCM's Collège des Pairs, a body of 150 people over forty-five years of age, would be dressed up in uniforms and insignias and hold ceremonial meetings; all of its members would be known as "excellency." In this innocuous hokum it is easy to see the OCM's bourgeois professionals feathering their beds, but Weil is looking to the telltale fact that the OCM's judges do not have any substance. All power resides finally with the executive. A despot in that office could appoint 150 criminals, who could then, in Weil's worst-case scenario, "whenever they wish, dishonor with infamous calumnies every honest deputy and senator who displeases the President. . . . Friends like these could really give some lessons to Hitler."[65]

Weil learned alarming lessons from these would-be constitutions. The Gaullist commission report showed her that the old parliamentary chaos of the parties had a good chance of resuming course after the war (it did so as the Fourth Republic). The OCM plan, as though to provide a remedy, gave all real authority to the executive, the "fascist" alternative to government by partisan intrigue. Both plans co-opted and corrupted the judiciary, making it either the extension of partisan rivalries in the legislature or a dictator's tool.

When Weil set down her own "Idées essentielles pour une nouvelle constitution," she was responding to both proposals. This point needs emphasis because the draconian measures she includes among her "essential ideas" clearly took inspiration in her reaction to the OCM's unbridled executive.

Paramount among her "essentials" is that every government office be limited in its power, controlled by separation of functions, subject to penalties. She takes Alain's recumbent hostility to government and sets it on its feet. She recommends that a court of "particular justice" ensure conformity of laws to the 1789 Declaration. In a conflict between this court and the Assembly, the issue would go to a popular referendum.

Oddly, this provision seems to run against Weil's second point, that the legislature's job is "to think the essential thoughts of a country's life." She says that people have aspirations but not the possibility of making clear ideas out of them. The people must name men, not to 'represent' them (what can this word mean?) but to think for them. For that, it is necessary to designate men, not parties. Parties don't think. They think less than the people."[66] Tilting against the parties, Weil is only too happy to imagine Plato's sort of willing good men capable of thinking "the essential ideas." Her view of government is more republican (and elitist) than democratic. This point gains weight in her outline of the legislators' tasks: "to know the people's needs, aspirations, and unspoken thoughts"; "to translate them into clear ideas in the form of laws"; and to see that the government "instructs" the people regularly about legislation.

All this seems to answer her question, What does "represent" mean? except that she is not clear about how much the people think, if at all. If the people do not have the "possibility" of thought (does she really mean "capability"?), how can they be expected to name the thoughtful to legislative office? If the people fall short of clear ideas, does it help that legislators "instruct" them? Weil wants to substitute this vague uplifting process for what she calls the "prostitution" of political campaigns, but the result is, if not *mystique d'abord*, a programmatic assumption or hope that "le peuple" is something other than a blind collectivity.

Weil's qualifications for judges are instructive. They must have "a spiritual, intellectual, historical and social education, more than a juridical one." Where these lofty creatures are to be found she does not say, but not even their credentials suffice for her. She would have another court specially appointed "for the judgment of judges, with very severe punishments."[67] The OCM's vicious toadies on the bench gave her an image so frightening that she could not rid herself of it. Her "special court" amounts to a paragovernmental body, significantly without a popular basis. It is as though Weil, ever ready to be disappointed with life, is inclined to throw over her own exalted vision of government-by-inspiration, or at least not be seduced by it. Her view of the judiciary is acutely moralistic. She not only provides judges for judges but makes clear the judicial obligation "to punish everyone who does evil to the country."[68] She cites as examples of malefactors a journalist who lies and a factory boss who harasses his workers. Mercifully, if unhelpfully, she does not indicate penalties ("pour encourager des autres") to fit these crimes. Instead, she recommends that "little groups of men specially charged with the work" should set down norms of conduct "oriented to the public good."[69] Independent of the three government branches, these groups would form yet another corps of watchdogs. In conceiving of such agencies Weil hopes to minimize government authority and activity; she does not see that they would likely encourage the gigantism of a self-perpetuating bureaucracy, one of the phenomena of the modern state she most loathed. Similarly, in view of how far-reaching her notion of evil-done-to-the-country extends, it takes little effort to imagine a substantial body of parapolice and informers springing up, as though Vichy's bands of such agents, Joseph Darnand's Milice and Georges Groussard's "Groupes de protection," were not adequately threatening examples.

Still another overseer is Weil's president of the republic. A lifetime appointee, he has the particular job of "surveillance" of the judiciary. Drawing from Anglo-American models, she provides checks and balances in case of "grave conflicts" between branches, forgetting for the while that such arrangements work best in predominantly bipartisan systems.

The most striking feature of Weil's constitution is this: "Every twenty years, the people are invited to say by referendum if they think—relative to the imperfection of human affairs—that public life is satisfactory. The referendum is preceded by a lengthy period of reflection and discussion, when all propaganda is forbidden under penalty of the gravest punishments."[70] A negative vote in the referendum would entail the president's expulsion, a tribunal to hear charges against him, and provision for his "social degradation" and condemnation to death. A death penalty for one man, stipulated in popular dissatisfactions about *la vie publique*, seems rather excessive, much like Plato's provision (*Laws* 907a–909a) of the death penalty for recalcitrant atheists. It looks like scapegoating.

In Weil's defense (and she seems to need it) it might be assumed that such a measure is cautionary. Anyone in the Damocletian seat of this presidency would have to be a paragon of morality. But the same holds true for her legislators and judges, not to mention her judges of judges and her "little groups of men." Is it too cynical to suppose that all this piety, virtue, and spiritual training would go awry, ending in a nightmare of Robespierres and Saint-Justs?

Her final words stun: "All this seems fantastic but isn't. The most difficult thing would be to imagine a transitional régime before such customs could be set up."[71] But what is really difficult to imagine is an enactment of the "customs" in Weil's constitutional scenario. She would populate the government with the high-minded, broadly educated, and well-intentioned, but French history, from Babeuf to Blum, has tended to make short shrift of such people. Her checks and balances, given the preclusion of partisan bartering, are redolent of her suspicion of government itself; there are more checks than balances. Fearful of power, she tries to hedge it in by creating corps upon corps of *normalien* overseers, thus ensuring exponential increases of "spiritual" authority. If 1789, 1917, and 1933 show that revolutions end by devouring their own believers, a constitution that becomes a contest for purity of vision may do the same thing.

As well as any of her writings, these "idées essentielles" show Weil's fastidious nobility and her longing to give justice a corner in the world. Wanting to make justice sovereign, she seems to have taken it by the throat. It is a pity that with admiration for her efforts comes a shudder.

On Being Human: "La personne et le sacré"

Weil's subscript for *L'enracinement* promises words on obligations to the human being. Her psychology of the individual is distilled in an essay whose title, "La personne et le sacré," is better rendered by commentary than by translation. She keeps Plato's familiar company, but it is Thomas Aquinas who more accurately anticipates the sense of her dualism of personality.

Aquinas distinguishes personality (*persona*) as a spiritual entity independent of matter and individuality as a principle of matter. In the one, humankind exists in God's image; in the other lies the precarious and puny ego. This Thomist division of the self is ontological and moral: personality belongs to heaven as "that which is most perfect in all nature."[72] Individuality, where sin and evil win out, goes to hell.

For many people today, it is probably difficult to entertain such a dualism, even if the tags are changed to, say, "immortal self" and "mortal self." Even those who believe in the soul's immortality would be hard put to imagine it without their own earthbound taxpaying selves somehow given a part in the perpetual holiday. However irrational, the tendency to assign very human faces to whatever lies beyond death is profound and persistent. What makes Weil's psychology intriguing is that she sets up a dualism much like the Thomist, its predicates so ancient that they take on the aspect of novelty to modern readers. By "la personne" she designates the cramped egotism of individuality. By "le sacré" she means something impersonal and transcendent of mortality. Her "sacré" has the definitive aspect of the Thomist *persona*, perfection, but it is not the perfection of the "I."

Weil's ontology is rigidly moralistic. In a note on Comte, whose notion of a *humanité* served by the individual's obligation undoubtedly appealed to her, she wrote:

> Altruism, when it is energetic, always shows itself fitter than egoism in directing and stimulating the intellect. It furnishes the intellect a greater field, a more difficult goal, and even a more indispensable participation. . . . Egoism hasn't any need of intellect to appreciate the object of its affection, it needs only to discover the means of satisfaction. On the contrary, altruism requires, besides, a mental assistance so as to know even the external being toward whom it always tends.[73]

In these terms she seems to intend a Kantian distinction between the phenomenal, percipient self, the ego "für sich," and the noumenal or substantial self. Only in the latter does morality impose itself. It is unclear, however, whether altruism is an expression of reason or of the will or of some higher imagination. Some *tertium quid* to mediate between Weil's two moral and ontological categories would be helpful, but she is not interested in giving a tidy, fully accounted scheme of human psychology. What most matters for her is that "le sacré," or one's true self, is in effect God. The immortal soul is divine, not really human at all, and yet all human endeavor must be aimed toward it by overcoming the *moi*. Implicitly, Weil is entertaining a monism: in one's true self lies the ultimate source and nature of being. Contrary to Christian tradition, this monism means that God does not create the immortal soul. In the old Greek way, immortal for Weil means uncreated—something pure, par excellence—and that suggests why she ignored the dogma of resurrection. The errant, all-too-human person is not to be forgiven and redeemed but renounced.

Weil sees in "la personne" a life of false pretenses. She considers sin nothing more than "identifying oneself with what isn't God," that is, sin means not being one's true self: "One is never oneself. One is always something else. There is no egoism. But this something must be God. Only thus can one truly be oneself." Decreation is a kind of ontological homecoming. If by self-renunciation she understands a casting off of the old Adam, she expects to find no new Adam. The casting off is not penitential but mystical: by isolation, silence, and rapt attention, one achieves what Weil calls moral solitude.[74] Lest it seem that she has wandered to a final distance from Christian tradition, it should be noted that in this mystical hollow she arrives at her ethic of charity to others: the mystical disappearance of the petty, mortal self allows one to love what is indestructible in others, the true self of "le sacré." Also, it gives God access to others, because the vain self-assertiveness of "la personne" is removed like a screen: "Each of those who have penetrated into the domain of the impersonal encounters there a responsibility toward all human beings, that of protecting in them, not the person, but all of the fragile possibilities of passage into the impersonal covered over by the personal."[75] The imperative of this mystical ethic recalls the obligation of Buddhism's *boddhisattva*, once enlightened, to descend back into the world of mortality's pains, the same journey Plato's initiate into the supernatural light must take (back into the Cave) to impart to others the mystical good he has received.

The *Republic*'s text is especially apt because Plato goes on to speak of the dangers an enlightened person must face from the unenlightened. Weil identifies them in her bogey word, *collectivity*. Although this word denotes any social organization, with the individual tacitly subordinate to the group, its existence, says Weil, is abstract, "a fictive operation," because it is the creation of "la personne," the expression of the miserable ego in search of something larger than itself. Weil sees that collectivity's menace lies not so much in its designs on the individual as in the individual's own disposition to rush into the collective. One's very identity depends on collectivity, and Weil shrewdly notes that even the self-estimation of one who defies convention (a dandy like Wilde or Gide) requires a collectivity to supply that convention.

To Weil, every modern ideology, being collectivist, must be suspected, not least those that propose to reclaim human dignity from the centrifuge of standardization. What makes them particularly suspect is that they cater to "la personne" by invoking rights.

Weil equates the notion of rights to sharing and exchange. It has, she observes aspersively, something commercial about it. As Spinoza recognized, a right can be sustained only by a claim on force, but as its possession implies possible use for either good or evil (for example, the right to bear arms may proceed to defense of one's country or to murder), it cannot be identified exclusively with the good.[76] That was the mistake of 1789. Much though she approves of the Revolution's emancipation of those oppressed by political and ecclesiastical tyranny, she identifies its fatal illusion as the conception of rights as absolutes, an idea all the more monstrous because in it a collectivity, calling itself the Revolution, masqueraded as something sacred. Perhaps every totalitarian collectivity has made a similarly false claim, but the historic advance of rights can be traced well before the materialism of Diderot and *les encyclopédistes*. Weil locates the notion of rights at its lexical source, in ancient Rome.

Her indictment of Rome runs to many counts throughout her *cahiers*, her essays, and, as a setting for French imperial history, in *L'enracinement*. Rome imperialized Christian faith into triumphal forms of power. Freighted with that crime, Rome stood in her mind beyond appeal. That the modern idea of rights dates from the Romans' *ius* sufficed to make it suspect, and Weil makes an adroit if unconvincing connection between Rome and Nazi Germany: "The Romans who, like Hitler, understood that force has its full efficiency only when dressed up in certain ideas, used the notion of right this way. It lends itself quite well. Modern Germany is accused of contempt for rights, but it has helped itself abundantly to them in its demands for a proletarian nation. For those it subjugates, indeed, it recognizes no other right than that of obedience. So did ancient Rome."[77]

By diametric contrast, the Greeks, in whom Weil had as much trouble seeing evil as in the Romans she had seeing good, possessed no word for rights. They contented themselves, she says, with justice at its proper transcendent remove. The proof text for this argument comes from her beloved Sophocles, in Antigone's confrontation with Creon. He pleads for conventional justice, she for the "unwritten laws" of the gods to which only one's obligation to love others can respond. Justice is inextricable from love because it involves fulfillment of obligation toward "le sacré" both in oneself and in others, and this is everywhere and always a good. This is the absolute which the Revolution missed.

The Greeks claimed no rights because they knew none, and neither, Weil suggests, does anyone who loves according to genuine spiritual dictates such as the imperatives of Christ. As love is bound with justice, it thrives at the greatest possible remove from any sentimental condescensions with which it sometimes suffers popular confusion. Witness Antigone's love for the dog-torn corpse of her brother; it costs her everything. With characteristic severity Weil comprehends the relentless exactions of love, its near impossibility and its violence, its poetry and terror.

The object of love and justice is *malheur*, the woe that penetrates the soul's innocent depths, making it cry out, "Why am I being harmed?" For Weil this is the most important question in human history; it is history itself. She distinguishes this cry from the plea of rights that seeks a tribunal's redress, asking, "Why does he have more than I?" She grants that we should hear such claims (or clamors) and try to minimize conditions provoking their contest, but that effort would take us to Creon's sort of court, and she offers little hope of rectification. She remarks with mordant ambiguity that for this vulgar sort of justice law schools suffice.

As to that deeper cry, in "le sacré," she offers the following: "In every human soul there arises continually the plea that it not be harmed. The text of the Lord's Prayer addresses this plea to God. But God does not have the power to preserve from evil anything save that eternal part of the soul which has entered into real and direct contact with him. The rest of the soul, and the whole soul of anyone who has not received the grace of real and direct contact with God, is abandoned to the wills of men and to the hazards of circumstance."[78] This passage suggests that Weil is not quite sure about her own ontology of an uncreated, eternal, impersonal part of the soul. If it is eternal and impersonal, how can it cry out that it is being harmed? She contradicts herself in saying that "the rest of the soul" is "abandoned." And just what is "the rest of the soul"? Not the egotistic, illusion-driven *personne*, surely, but where else is the hurt self? Again, a human *tertium quid* is needed to make full sense of Weil's drama of the self, but had she considered the self *ni ange ni bête* she would have had to relinquish her compulsive sense of the divine and pure.

As it is, between the recondite ways of grace and the legalisms of *l'école de droit* there is a great gulf fixed; or rather, a broad plane where most evil occurs. Weil includes as evil acts all the uses of status, comfort and pleasure, anything that promotes the egotism of "la personne," but her larger concern is the evil that people do to each other. Her remedy for this hurting is abstruse. First, it goes beyond the etymological fog of *mal* and confronts the measureless pit of *malheur*. Thought, she states, avoids *malheur* because it means death; the soul is compelled to recall its own nothingness, "the state of extreme and total humiliation which is also the condition of passage into truth."[79] More than *douleur* (grief) or *souffrance* (suffering), *malheur* is a cosmic disaster concentrated on the soul. Weil speaks of it as a leprosy so dire that even its victims recoil in abhorrence of themselves. The afflicted tend to be dumbstricken or at least unheard by the fortunate. Weil cites lofty literary examples of what *malheur's* children would say if only they could cry out: the *Iliad, Job, King Lear,* Aeschylean tragedy, *Phèdre,* but no quotation rivals the image she recalls from a visit to a courtroom, where she saw an ignorant vagrant standing helpless before a judge who spun out patronizing witticisms. The defendant's stammerings went unheard at the bench and throughout the courtroom because the spectators, including those as wretched as the vagrant, were deafened by a pervasive indifference.

In this tableau "la personne" is stripped of every illusion or pretension, including the collectivity's shelter of rights. To put oneself in the place of anyone thus afflicted requires more than the idle pity of words. It requires sympathy in the root sense, a suffering with and annihilation of one's own "personne." Genuine self-annihilation, Weil admits, is as unlikely as the suicide of a happy child; it is impossible. Only grace can make one's soul become the beheld. *Malheur,* being hideous, needs besides grace the supernatural expedient of beauty. True to Plato, Weil unquestioningly believes in the coherence of beauty with justice and truth and also, by its eliciting one's attention, with love. In her favorite literature of *malheur* "the éclat of beauty is extended over woe by the light of the spirit of justice and of love, which alone permits human thought to look upon and reproduce woe such as it is."[80] These words are contrary to Plato's aesthetic,[81] and if beauty does work as an operational principle within the pathos of drama, it resembles Aristotelian *katharsis,* except that the justice and love Weil wants to derive from this beauty pursues a nobler calling than the pleasure Aristotle finds in pity and fear.

She does not say just how the experience of beauty through her literary canon, having quickened one's desire for truth and therefore for justice, will transform one's conduct. Does she assume that rapt attention to the sorrows of Philoctetes or Lear will make us hear more acutely a kindred though not so eloquent sorrow from the vagrant detained in court? Because she wants to endorse an art for action's sake, the action of attentive sympathy, she is far from what Pétain called a "pseudo-culture livresque," but it remains unclear whether once *malheur's* cry is heard, a moral act responsive to that experience follows necessarily. Beauty might arouse a thirst in the sacred part of the soul, and if one can sustain "the delicious torment it inflicts," as Plato depicts it in the *Phaedrus*, that thirst might indeed turn to love, "the faculty of pure and gratuitous attention." But what of the beauty in *malheur*? The nexus Weil wants to hold so tightly between beauty and justice lacks motivational cohesion. She says: "Justice, truth, beauty are sisters and allies. With three words so beautiful there is no need to seek others."[82] In an age contaminated with official deceit and programmatic lies to subtract all sense from words like *right* and *democracy*, these hieratic words, emanating from Platonic forms, offered Weil a mantric power in their incorruptibility, as though of themselves they might induce action. She thought that as some words have the power to delude or pervert the mind, others (her Platonic triad) possess an uplifting virtue for good because they point to an absolute and incomprehensible perfection. Hence the person not afflicted with *malheur* can be brought to look on it only when guided by surrogate "Great Book" texts that reveal its hidden beauty. An aesthetic response (attention) implies a moral response, as though someone who truly reads Homer or Shakespeare becomes a better person—a dubious matter. That the aesthetic response is not enough (how can it help the vagrant?) means only that in "La personne et le sacré" Weil has not developed a psychology of moral action. She attempts to do so in *L'enracinement*. For now she prescribes: "To preserve justice, to protect people from all harm, that means above all keeping them from being hurt. For those who have been hurt, it means effacing the material consequences, putting the victims in a situation where the injury, if it has not pierced too deeply, may be healed by natural well-being. But for those whose whole soul has been lacerated by the injury, it means more and above all satisfying their thirst by giving them drink from a perfectly pure good."[83]

In moving from the mundane to the mystical, from "material consequences" to the sacramental draught of absolute good, and in making that sequence an issue of social justice rather than private miracle, Weil almost breaks free of her assumptions about the inefficacy of human endeavor toward the good, but her hortatory notes here (too vague to be called a program) depend not on acts of will but on the effort of attention she wants to place mystically above and beyond all voluntarism. She would relieve those in *malheur*'s depths by another aesthetic: the very naming of justice, beauty, and truth will assuage the soul's hurts, much like Moses' bronze serpent in the wilderness (an image that fascinated her) curing the stricken Hebrews who saw it uplifted. She is inclined to a kind of public mysticism (a true oxymoron, but how else to speak of the eucharist?) as she seeks agents of this "perfectly pure good." She wants to ensure their authenticity by limiting their number to a miraculous few. She suggests that public leaders become a corps of guardians charged "to show the public things for it to praise, to admire, to seek, to request."[84] This suggestion returns in *L'enracinement* when she says that de Gaulle's name holds such authority as the symbol of France's lost fidelity to itself that anyone using it may take inspiration from "the region situated above the heavens."[85]

Such was the language of her exile and the zeal in her anguish.

T W E L V E

L'enracinement

Les phénomènes sociaux échappent à l'intelligence humaine. L'esprit humain est par nature hors d'état de penser ce tout dont il est une partie.
SIMONE WEIL, *Cahiers*, 1

L'*enracinement*, known in translation as *The Need for Roots*, is Weil's Summa. Her longest essay, it is a synthesis of her religious, social, and political views as they had matured in the years since she left the Ecole Normale. Whether, burdened with refractory energies, she was consciously writing a valedictory summing up is questionable. From first to last Weil's intellectual self-assurance is evident, but this work is buoyed with a peculiarly affirmative tone absent from the 1934 "Réflexions" on oppression and freedom, which might be called its dark companion.

Even as she had seen the need for a new religion and a new science, so now she took up the task which the war, the Occupation, and Vichy's sorry example required of everyone, "to invent a new France."[1] The impulsion to sweep all boards clean—a gesture common to the young anywhere but especially, it seems, to French intellectual youth in the 1930s—was carried over, indeed galvanized by the disaster and humiliation of *les années noires*. For Weil the national crisis warranted every effort "to think of fundamental notions as if they were new things."[2] She was a veteran of such efforts, and she knew she could sustain it. It is as though catastrophe summoned her gift. Exile gave her a perspective and critical detachment that might not have come readily had she tried to think things out during her time in Marseilles and the Ardèche.

L'enracinement can be closely identified with Weil's activist assumptions in the prewar decade. Because she never pledged herself to the constraints of any party membership and yet seemed fully at home in an age of manifestos (when she was their author), she could now envision a postwar France ready for reclamation in a spirit akin to Saint-Simon or Fourier, of Proudhon and the syndicalists above all—reclamation not through political parties but through social transformation.

A fair number of books written in French during the war spun recriminating variations on the theme of treason. Someone had to be blamed for the fall of France and Hitler's triumph over democratic Europe. Concurrently, other books addressed the postwar and attempted a prognosis of impending political and economic difficulties in a more or less sanguine way as it became evident that Germany would not prevail. As there had been prewar betrayals to allege, there was a possibility of postwar betrayals. Reconstruction toward a United States of Europe, under American hegemony, appealed to Europeans who had admired the industrial efficiency of *fordisme* in the 1920s and the reform capitalism of Roosevelt's New Deal in the 1930s. Weil was not one of them. The prospect of a Taylorized or New Deal capitalism imposed on Europe's economies was as distasteful and frightening to her as their possible reduction to Soviet bureaucratic controls in the wake of postwar revolutions. *L'enracinement* reveals a fearful *antiaméricanisme* (an extension of the *antiétatisme* Weil felt with many on the Left) as the United States, "the cancer of the modern world," as Aron and Dandieu put it, threatened the coming peace.[3]

Weil's unpublished reading notes show a substantial debt to E. H. Carr's *Conditions of Peace*, published in Britain in 1942.[4] Carr, subsequently professor of history at Cambridge and author of a multivolume study of Soviet Russia in its first generation, argued that the economic and political crises of the century were essentially moral crises. This was exactly the sort of message Weil, ignorant of economics and hostile to political mechanics, was ready to receive. Carr reviewed eighteenth-century laissez-faire capitalism and its elevation of maximal production of wealth into a moral imperative. He noted that nineteenth-century liberal democracy, in its heyday of expansive prosperity and rapid industrial development, had complemented the gospel of rights and benefits with a responsible sense of public service and personal sacrifice: largesse oblige. Laissez-faire ethics, in tandem with nostrums of scientific and industrial progress, had operated within a self-regulating machinery that made the moral direction of society itself unnecessary. In the twentieth century all these assumptions were rapidly unraveled. Modern mass democracy, matured in war and depression, witnessed the dissolution of belief in progress through profits and a freely realized harmony of interests.

Another ideal, the rights of nations, once dispossessed of its capitalist foundations, collapsed into a nationalism of supremacy, making international cooperation impossible. Weil quotes from Carr: "The twentieth century has brought an ever growing recognition that 'patriotism is not enough'—that it does not provide an intelligible moral purpose and cannot create a cohesive international society."[5] The war showed how even supposedly decrepit parliamentary democracies could organize their economies for war production, but there was no concomitant organization of individual and collective morality beyond vague slogans about defending democracy. Carr sought William James's "moral equivalent of war" to supply a postwar dynamic, even while noting that "the popular demand, not for more unrestricted liberty, but for more authoritative leadership" explained the appeal of Stalin, Roosevelt, and Hitler.[6] There was thus a general but blurry yearning for direction and a new order. Carr presumed it would depend on some great leader, but he also saw the need for a common consent to "gradual and almost imperceptible transformation of the climate of thought and action. . . . Anyone who can by deed or word promote and hasten that transformation, even though he may himself have no claim to the role of prophet and no clear vision of the social philosophy and moral purpose of the age, is rendering service."[7]

Weil seems to have taken these words to heart; indeed, she went further and required of herself the prophet's "clear vision." Although relegation to a desk frustrated her activist schemes for the Free French, the intellectual momentum she gave to writing *L'enracinement* was not simply displaced energy. In July 1943, answering a letter in which her mother expressed confidence in her having something to give, Weil acknowledged "a kind of growing inner certitude" that she had within her "a deposit of pure gold to be handed on." She was doubtful about how or even whether it would be received and even predicted a postwar time when "the publications and manuscripts of our age will undoubtedly have disappeared."[8] The implication is that Weil knew her "deposit of gold" lay in her writing. It lies substantially in *L'enracinement*.

There she takes up Carr's call for a "moral purpose powerful enough to generate self-sacrifice on the scale requisite to enable civilisation to survive."[9] Of the world's competing ideologies he perceived that only Christianity and communism had any likelihood of offering a vision to ensure peace, but there would be needed "a transformation of Christianity or a revival of its primitive spirit, which would in itself amount to a revolution."[10] Weil saw the same need, and she might have characterized herself as a revolutionary on behalf of a "primitive spirit." Like Carr, she understood moral purpose in terms of obligations, not rights. That emphasis is clear in *L'enracinement*'s programmatic subtitle declaring duties to "l'être humain."

This subscript signals how closely (and just as important, how distantly) she keeps company with eighteenth-century utopists. An assumed universality of principles offers the possibility (or threat) of their uniform application. Yet the conceptual hingeword in Weil's book is *devoir*, and it is obligation that sets her at odds with past visionaries such as Condorcet, who looked to an inclusive scheme of rights as the basis of a new social system.

Carr's influence is again notable in his outline for "a new faith," the necessary fuel to get Weil's "new France" going. Carr admitted that setting down criteria for a viable future seemed presumptuous, might be ineffectual, and would perhaps meet only with indifference among those too helpless or too busy amid the war's immediate tasks. Weil is similarly caught between a sense of futility and a sense of mission. The war taught her the Jansenist lesson that humanity is powerless yet responsible.[11]

She summarized Carr's agenda: the goals of the "new faith" must be positive, to achieve good rather than avoid evil; the new faith must speak to the "little man" rather than the organized powers of capitalism, unions, and political parties (this point wholly conformed to Weil's rejection of collectivist power in any guise); it will remedy unemployment and inequality; and as social obligations must take precedence over rights, so the egoism of nations must yield to international needs. Ultimately, liberty and authority must attain a new synthesis. Weil works toward it in her discussion of obedience, responsibility, and hierarchy as "vital needs of the human spirit."

These "needs" form the rubric of *L'enracinement*'s first part. From it the rest of the book depends in two lengthy sections, on *deracinement* or the historical and contemporary deprivation of the soul's needs, and *enracinement*, their rooting in a new soil of the spirit. By writing a kind of ontological constitution of needs, Weil was addressing every nation devastated by war (hence her large readership in postwar Germany and Italy), and her discussion of the soul's needs is almost entirely free of French references. Yet her analyses of order, freedom, honor, and equality are inextricably bound to the very concrete issues of public and private property. One might suppose that Plato's aporetic dialogues reminded her that virtues such as courage or temperance require cohesive relation with justice and wisdom in order to be understood; each term implicates all the others in its definition. Weil presents the soul's needs as a series of harmonized Pythagorean contraries: freedom with obedience, equality with hierarchy, security with risk.

Needs, she says, are wholly distinct from desires or fantasies in that they are as limited as their source of sustenance. One's need of bread is not the same as the miser's need of money. Also, needs are complementary; they require the equilibrium of *le juste milieu*. That is why, in sounding the Pythagorean chimes of balance and proportion, she qualifies a libertarian concern for freedom of opinion with attention to social order.

At points this construction almost betrays her to artifice, as when she discusses the inevitable aspiration of some to rise in the social scale: "A social malady results from it unless a descending movement creates equilibrium with the ascending. To the extent it's really possible for a farmhand's son to be a state minister someday, to that extent it ought really to be possible that a minister's son someday be a farmhand. The degree of this second possibility cannot be considerable short of a very dangerous degree of social constraint."[12] Accordingly, proportion must be a combination of equality and inequality; everyone is answerable, but differently. A factory boss guilty of an error should be required to suffer more in body and soul than a worker guilty of some blunder: "The degree of impunity for crimes and misdemeanors ought to increase, not as one rises but as one descends the social order."[13] Weil knows that is not the way the world works, but the consequence of this maladjustment is that punishment amounts to an abuse of power rather than an exercise of justice. Weil implies that when the socially powerless commit crimes they do so in the face of injustice and their own hopelessness, even as the powerful can commit crimes with a cynical trust that status will protect them.

Most surprising in Weil's list of needs is punishment. Following Plato's argument that punishment must correct the errant soul, she even calls it an honor in that it educates the soul to a high devotion toward the public good. No less significant is her utilitarian justification for a social scale of impunity. It complements the deontological position she takes in stating that everyone must be respected as a person without degrees. Her ethic is a balance between arguments of utility and of a priori, what ethicists call a mixed deontology. Such a combination does not mark a departure from her previous writing, in which the deontological or the utilitarian perspective predominates according to the topic. Here she tries to temper her strait-gated moralism with an attention to circumstances and real needs.

An outstanding instance of this attention is her revised view of collectivity. In her earlier work, collectivity is the social mechanism that blinds people to the elementary difference between necessity and the good. It hinders the soul's true salvation by erecting ersatz forms of deliverance, be it through party, church, or state. It is the modern face of totalitarianism derived from imperial Rome. All these assertions Weil iterates in *L'enracinement*, but she now adds positive remarks on collectivity. One owes it respect, she says, no matter what form it takes, "country, family or all other forms—not for itself but as nourishment for a certain number of human souls." Attitudes and actions in response to that obligation may vary, but it is in itself "absolutely identical for everyone."[14]

War and exile had imposed this new perspective, but it was also required by the essay's programmatic intent, the restoration of France. Only in the cultural collectivity of *patrie* can the past's treasures be retained and given over to succeeding generations. June 1940 taught Weil a lesson that all the chaos of the preceding decade had obscured, that a collectivity can be threatened with destruction. Disposed to self-sacrifice, she had not conceived so great an object for her efforts. She did not relax her objections to the sinister kind of collectivity she had always attacked. What better example of a soul-devouring entity than Vichy, propped up by the church, a sham "national revolution," and the Nazis? Yet when she writes of a collectivity needing surgical treatment, the reference is clear.

On a smaller scale she remembers Carr's "little man" and writes that everyone should feel a part of collective ownership in public gardens and monuments so that "the luxury which nearly everyone desires is thus accorded even to the lowliest." Not just the state but every collectivity must afford this satisfaction. It seems a trivial, almost ludicrous matter, but it is integral to Weil's larger point that everyone must have multiple roots in "a moral, intellectual and spiritual life by the mediation of milieux one is naturally a part of." This is no snobbish plea for "culture," which she defines as "an instrument manipulated by professors who make more professors."[15]

No milieu was dearer to her than that of the French working classes, but by 1943 she had won some critical distance from the workers' movement, chiefly because the Communists had taken over the CGT. In *L'enracinement* she notes that before 1914 syndicalism had in it "a lot of purity" (political separatism) it subsequently lost because of "the poisons of the social environment." Specifically, trade unions failed to show as much concern for "the truly wretched members of the factory population, young people, women, immigrant and colonial workers" as for wage increases for those already better paid. This failure instructed her on how difficult it is for a collectivity to be oriented to justice.[16] She reaches a seasoned judgment. Collectivity is no longer a bogey; it has a very human face, one that she had seen among her friends at the workers' bistro.

Could there be a truly healthy collectivity? Weil's enlistment of such "vital needs" as order, responsibility, and hierarchy suggests that she wanted to believe in the possibility, but she also insisted that an ideal must be upheld for the direction it gives; to force it on the procrustean bed of reality is to court disaster.

Her notion of *obéissance* is instructive. Obedience is not an obvious need of the soul, surely. She distinguishes it as "consent and not the fear of punishment or the bait of recompense, so submission may never be suspected of servility."[17] For a corollary she adds that those who command obey in their turn, a notion borrowed from Plato's *Republic*. The novelty is her conclusion that people are now starving for obedience. There have been dictatorships aplenty, but they have run on slavery's forced or indoctrinated (fake) consent. True obedience for Weil is the political expression of *amor fati*, an informed acquiescence.

That point leads to the *clef de voûte* of her argument for replacing rights with obligations. Carr had emphasized the need to reverse "the nineteenth century trend" that exalted benefits gained from society over services rendered to it. According to him rights lost their claim when they began to endanger social cohesion; economic expansion and profit-fueling were curtailed in cycles of depression and war.[18] But though he implies that a new stress on social obligations would be only a seasonal adjustment to contain a crisis, Weil pushes on to lasting affirmations.

Right, being conditional, is tied to particular facts and situations. Obligation is unconditional, universal, eternal: "A man, considered in himself, has only obligations, among which are some he holds toward himself. Other people, from his viewpoint, have only rights. He has rights in his turn from their viewpoint as they recognize obligations to him. A man who would be alone in the world would have no rights but he would have obligations."[19] She does not explain why one's viewpoint does not include a recognition of others' obligations, but this shortcoming simply shows she is rejecting a contractual view of social order. She wants to keep the intimate focus of the self facing another person: obligation's object is always the human being as such, without regard to convention or custom, and is derived from each person's "vital needs." All of this complements her argument in "La personne et le sacré."

Weil believes people feel born for sacrifice. However dubious that assumption, it is a reminder that *L'enracinement* is in part wartime rhetoric, addressing a time when sacrifice had become so commonplace as to be a way of life. Perhaps she was confusing willingness with wish. She notes, though, that the only sacrifice people can conceive is one of military necessity, a form of service to the state. Patriotism has become indistinguishable from statism and has caused the neglect of moral limits to one's ambitions and appetites. In short, one can lead a patriot's life and simultaneously play the scoundrel to one's neighbor. Concurrently, the decline of religion has its certain hallmark in the privatization of conscience; it is no longer regarded as "something too sacred for the intervention of any external authority, rather it's listed with things the State leaves to everyone's whim [*fantaisie*] as being of little importance relative to public affairs."[20] Weil thus provides some light to the question frequently posed after the war of how a supposedly Christian Germany could accommodate an official and murderous racism.

Weil admits that though obligation, being universal, is infinite, none of its earthly objects can be. That opens the way to two deadly evasions. The first is to pretend that the only obligations are transcendent ones; this leads to a false mystique or to the self-deception that any good works one does count as a show of one's love of God. People in need become occasions for attesting one's goodwill. Weil says one must feel an obligation to serve one's neighbor, not Christ.[21] In that action, love for God takes care of itself.

The other evasion amounts to the idolatry of false absolutes, putting perfection within some human vessel. The histories of party, church, and state amply document this waywardness and the human craving for illusion that keeps it going. Weil's prescription for a new *patrie* is accordingly hedged with caveats.

Déracinement

The second and longest portion of *L'enracinement* concerns the uprooting of the urban and rural proletariat and French history since Louis XIV.

Deracination is an ancient story, of course. It is the history of military conquerors subjugating whole nations. Weil distinguishes conquering peoples who settle among and commingle with subjugated natives (the Hellenes in Greece, the Celts in Gaul) from those who remain aliens in the conquered land and thus bring "an almost fatal malady for the conquered." Without specific reference to Jews, she recognizes that Nazi Germany's mass deportations constitute "the most acute degree" of deracination.[22]

A more subtle but no less devastating aspect of uprooting is economic, through money and the domination it imposes on whole classes and, colonially, whole peoples. Weil was no economist. However wide-ranging her intellectual pursuits, they did not include economic theory, but she was keenly interested in the psychological constituents of economic practice and the force money exerts on those who have it and those who need it. One might say that money is necessity transmuted into human relations at the most immediate and intimate level.

As a preface to her discussion of the deracinated workers of factory and farm, an unpublished fragment she entitled "La monnaie" deserves mention.[23] It begins with the dramatis personae of what initially looks like a parable: the relationship between someone who has money to employ another and that other who, having once lived by hunting, now has a broken bow and must seek hired work. But then Weil shifts exclusively to the employer in a first-person "interior monologue." Because of the hunter's need, I can have him do any work I wish: useful but not indispensable work too painful or hazardous for my own undertaking; or useless work. "I can even, if it amuses me, have him perform a useless action but one I can take pleasure in seeing because of the pain it gives him, as in moving a heavy rock. I can have him begin a job and then leave it, half done, for another."

In a few lines Weil catches the essentially capricious and even sadistic power exercised within Carlyle's "cash nexus." What outwardly looks like a contractual relationship, in which the employer can even boast he has saved a life by employment, is in fact a slavery that can be renewed indefinitely. Having to work all day to survive, the hunter-now-hireling never gains the leisure to fashion a new bow and regain independence.

Weil embroiders the theme of this despotism. Hiring out one's slave to a third person brings more money and the power to procure others for labor. "So I am soon at the head of an army of slaves, for whom the greatest misfortune [*malheur*] would be that I not accept their service." This is Marx's Lumpenproletariat under Sade's scrutiny. Human beings have become capital. The difference here from ancient slavery is in the contract. Most sinister of all is the warped voluntarism implied, not only on the employer's part but on that of his victims. It is the peculiar moral ugliness of the oppressed: "Not one of my slaves will cease for one day celebrating the enslavement of praising and flattering me, else he'll make himself unworthy of the favor I'm doing in having him as a slave." The worker participates in his own transformation into a thing, an accomplice to his own deracination.

In *Conditions of Peace* Carr followed his review of the moral crisis with a discussion of industry, agriculture, and a history of British rule, domestic and colonial. Weil sets out the same sequence but unlike Carr does not concern herself with the mechanics of policy and the new dynamics of state controls.

Instead, she looks at the "little man's" crisis: her focus is not industry but the factory worker, not agriculture but the farmer.

Carr had written that a "new faith" must appeal to the "little man," as though it were a product to be sold. The consumer's passivity is patent. Weil writes not only for and to the "little man" but from his cramped world. By subordinating politics to psychology she gives her arguments a much wider application than the national. The deracination of labor is not only a French problem. The forcefulness of Weil's presentation comes not only from her usual mental acuity but also from her years-long experience of the working world and its *déracinés*.

The melancholy fact, she notes, is that the world is diseased. The uprooted might be called germ carriers. They are subject either to spiritual torpor, "an inertia of soul almost equivalent to death," or to the deracinating violence of revolution.[24] She takes the French proletariat as an example of the first syndrome, the German proletariat since 1918 as an example of the second. Hitler's rise resulted, she says, primarily because of the Versailles humiliation, inflation, and massive unemployment. There could be few better lessons of how economic and political disasters beget a moral crisis. Historians might quibble that Weil's causality is inadequate or simplistic; many other factors would have to be adduced to explain why revolution overtakes some countries but not others. Weil indeed simplifies when she claims that England, buffeted by unemployment, strikes, and depression between the world wars, held out against revolution because in Britain "tradition is the most alive and best preserved."[25] She does not consider that tradition itself may deracinate, and this amounts to a substantial weakness in her thesis: tacitly she appears to excuse all centuries-hallowed caste or class systems. It is not incidental that her favorite religious cultures of antiquity—Greece, Egypt, and India—all rested on the shoulders of slaves. She fails to come to terms with that fact. The Platonic each-in-his-place notion of justice to which she adheres is a suitable lining for the oppression within a well-rooted tradition.

Simply put, her placement of tradition in a dynamic opposition to revolution is an attempt to uphold the past, not against the future but against the revolutionary's assumptions about the future. Her often-cited remark that revolution is the twentieth century's opium of the people refers to the foolish belief that the future will clear away the past: "The opposition between the past and the future is absurd. The future brings us nothing, gives us nothing; it is we who in order to build it must give it everything, our very lives. But to give it is necessary to possess, and we possess no other life, no other sap than the inherited treasures of the past, ingested, assimilated and recreated by us."[26] Here she posits a conservative revolution against statism, big industry, and the unions. She hearkens to the corporate syndicalism of medieval times as a past in which working people can reclaim their roots. She insists that revolutionary or reformist measures like nationalization of industry or abolition of private property or collective bargaining are all juridical and do not address proletarian *malheur* at its daily sources.

Her disdain of revolutionary catchwords is commendable, but she does not see beyond them to the very concrete matter of political action. Having called for the abolition of parties, she must have hoped that conventional instruments of institutional power would somehow go away, that the Third Republic and Vichy were so totally discredited that they would also discredit *étatisme*. She finds no authoritative substitute for the state or the parties directing it because her focus is intentionally on local or regional associations. She believes that centralized government, despite the historical momentum of its ascendance, should reverse course and yield to these smaller constituents. How big industries would be reconstituted to a smaller scale she does not say, and her neglect in this matter is curious indeed, given her inside familiarity with monstrosities like Renault. In her scorn of revolutionary deracinators and the expropriators of capital, she forgets to consider the very material object of their rhetorical heat. In place of what she calls the "apocalyptic reveries" induced by propaganda, she tries to recast the medieval trade corporation into the daily life of modern labor and technology.

For all her rejection of the intellectuals' Marxism and her denial of its coherence as a doctrine, she holds fast to Marx's insight that class relations cannot be changed without a transformation in the instruments of production. Considering machinery from the workers' point of view, she sets down three criteria for determining the benefits of technology: first, that the machine cause no physical or psychological hurt; second, that it be adjustable to many purposes—this to remedy monotony; third, that it require professional training. Her neosyndicalism would necessitate an end to unskilled labor. Once laborers are educated to a sophisticated grasp of their work in all its dimensions, they will no longer be a proletariat.

These are utopist accents, but Weil's intimate awareness of factory life keeps her clear of abstract dreamlands. What she wants in and through the machinery is a humane psychology of work. Her position is basically identical to the one she argued nearly a decade before. Wartime production demands had not qualitatively altered the situation of labor; they had simply carried its absurdities to a higher degree, forcing skilled workers down and unskilled workers up to the uniformity of quotas set by the military. (Weil carefully avoids reference to Vichy's German overseers.) The generations-old syndrome besetting the industrial worker continued: the *vertige intérieur* which took away all love of work; the loss of all initiative and reflection; the impossibility of understanding the productive process as a whole, including its ultimate social value; and the total disjuncture of labor from the worker's family life.

Regarding this last disaster Weil makes her most radical proposals. Only decentralization of industry, its transfer from capitalist interests to the level at which workers can enjoy steady contacts between technical schools and their own working places, will ensure their well-being. Only then, to resume the parable of "La monnaie," will they be able to refashion the bow. The scale Weil envisions involves the preindustrial *atelier*. Workers are to carry out their skilled tasks not in miniature factories but in "industrial organisms of a new kind, where a new spirit can breathe." "Some workers could work at home, others, in small shops that might often be organized on a cooperative model."[27] In these conditions the baleful demands of speed at all costs would be void.

Inspired by the June 1936 sit-in strikes at the Parisian metal industries, where workers brought their families to see their machinery, Weil almost rhapsodically entertains such a tableau as a commonplace. She claims it would ensure that children become familiar with their parents' work and thus be set early on apprenticeship: "Work would be illuminated with poetry for all their lives by this marveling, instead of forever taking a nightmarish color through the shock of first experiences," that is, when youths enter factories to assume the role of regimented piecemeal hirelings.[28] It is clear that only someone born and raised outside the working classes could presume that work can be regarded as marvelous and poetic.

Weil paints a pretty picture of an anachronistic idyll, but in ironic fact, the notion of working at home was realized when the war's exigencies forced such innovations and proved their efficacy. While Weil was in Britain, for example, housewives assembled airplane parts on their kitchen tables while their children played beside them. She might have seen propaganda films showing "Mum" working on a fuselage—an indication of how Vichy's trinity of *patrie, famille, travail* could be given some integrity, at least in England. Whether she knew about these domestic arrangements, she did believe that technology could work in and contribute to decentralization, as in the electrification of the countryside.

It is important to note that her proposals are as much "against" as they are "for." Work will belong to the home or the *atelier* because factories must be abolished. Trade unions must resume the medieval neighborly corporatism whence they came so that the moral death in their collective bargains, their wage demands, and the innate corruption in their organizational hierarchy can be ended. The *syndicat* should have a say in the creation of new machinery so that capitalist interests are no longer primary. For Weil decentralization is imperative because it is her only remedy for dehumanization. Above all, a spirituality of work must be attained because it is the only alternative to totalitarian idolatries.

The *malheur* of laborers must not be appeased with wage increases and spurious "benefits"; it must be cured. Weil's orientation seems novel, not to say off-putting, because she is not interested in what has for generations served as the unions' primary agendum, ensuring workers' participation in consumer materialism. As far as capitalism and socialism alike aim at the *embourgeoisement* of labor, Weil rejects them both. She feels the dignity of labor must be rooted in something other than the standard and cost of living.

She creates a peculiar difficulty for herself. On one hand, she wants the unions to participate in public life and decisionmaking, else they will lose all legitimacy and cease to exist. They must not take refuge in old-style anarchist separatism. On the other, she does not want them to assume an official, national authority that would make them a mere rival collectivity against the state. Syndicalism, as mediator between government and workers, must restore the old denominators of tradition that had long ceased to count: the village, the town and province, and the family. It would also admit the vision of a united Europe, to which the unions' claim to internationalism had long pointed.

Although Weil does not presume to set up a workers' paradise free of the state and *patronat*, she assigns very little to government and the bosses. The state is to dispense lifelong gifts of machinery, housing, and land to each worker who marries and passes proficiency tests. The *patronat* is to help the union administer taxes on products and profits. Weil keeps government and capital on the periphery in at best auxiliary roles because she is not so much interested in political and economic organization as in the ends they pursue, and she defines these ends within the workers' community of shops and schools.

She knows that in eschewing capitalism and socialism she exposes her corporatist ideas to inconsequence; they have no likelihood of "passing from the domain of words unless a certain number of free men have in their hearts' depths a burning, unquenchable desire to make them pass."[29] Who these men are she cannot say, no more than could Plato in setting up his republic of guardians. Perhaps neither the trade unionist nor the Parisian intellectual would be fit for her summons because her inspiration, her attempt to use and transcend the blind mechanisms of necessity, is Stoic. The very image of rooting someone in a social order that can correspond to the cosmic order is no more modern than the ultramontanist views she got from Gustave Thibon and which he espoused in *Diagnostiques* (1942).

Appropriately, the static, one might say recidivist life of rural France provides the setting for Weil's appeal for a new spirituality. Composed of Christian symbols and rituals, this appeal is centered on work, which Weil makes into the redemptive source of *enracinement*.

Work

Weil infuses her conservatism with religious zeal, and it is no afterthought that she would have the *syndicats* cooperate with the church in labor's spiritual transformation. She is not promoting a revival of Catholicism; adverting to the lay "poisoning" of French rural culture, she does not call for restoration of the clerical influence in education which the Third Republic and Jules Ferry had stripped away generations before. Her middle way between an anticlerical secularism and the church is her own cosmopolitan regard for Christianity as "one treasure of human thought among others."[30] The compromise she would effect, however, amounts to more than special pleading for her idiosyncrasies. There was fear that France, once free of Nazism, would descend into a civil war in which bourgeois reactionaries would enlist a not unwilling church against the Communist party, the most powerful Resistance faction. Weil could not, of course, presume to forestall this conflict, but she invested her hope in educating France toward a *christianisme authentique*.

Doing so involves a very delicate balance. Priests should have no place in public education, but public school instructors should not be ordered to speak to their pupils about God, a Vichy practice Weil dismissed as a bad joke. She writes that "a priest who having the natural occasion to do so, would abstain from talking about Christ to the child of a non-Christian family would be a priest who hardly had any faith," yet she says that students of a strictly

Christian education would be abused if it kept them from appreciating the "pure gold treasures of non-Christian civilizations."[31]

What she means by authenticity is her own cosmopolitanism. Unfortunately, it would confound the particular, specifically local life of genuine roots. It is a contradiction she does not overcome. She sees the need for some antidote to the intoxicants of totalitarianism which carried off her fellow intellectuals either to Moscow or Berlin, but she can offer only a vague theism resting on the historic fact that religion has everywhere had a dominant role in the development of civilized cultures. "If we get children used to not thinking about God, they'll become fascists or communists out of the need to be given something."[32] Hence, competent and disposed educators should be allowed to speak to pupils "not only about Christianity but also, though much less insistently, about any other current of genuine religious thought." She explicitly excludes Judaism, the most deeply rooted spiritual life, because it is "tied to the notion of race."[33] Thus she tacitly endorses the 1935 Nuremberg Laws' definition of Jews.

Apart from her telltale disqualification of Judaism, Weil's program for thinking about God in the schools is so tepid it can only be wondered what good she expected of it. She ignores the fact that fascism and communism exert their appeals not merely because they are ersatz faiths but because they are so in an impassioned way. People do not turn to them for *pensées* but for marching orders, and their appeal, far more demonstrably than "authentic" religious traditions and "genuine religious thought," is universal. In her humanistic attention to pedagogy, she almost passes by the primitive and irrational fundament of religious and pseudo-religious faith.

Writing about a peasant lad who begins fieldwork at fourteen, when such labor is still, she claims, "une poésie," she urges that this first contact with the land be "consecrated by a solemn festival that will make it forever penetrate the soul's depths. In the most Christian villages, such a festival ought to have a religious character."[34] It is the kind of secular religiosity that Robespierre programmed in public festivals. In one of her Marseilles essays, however, Weil casts the peasant youth's initiation within an explicitly Christian context of rituals.

"Le christianisme et la vie des champs" is a prolegomenon to *L'enracinement*'s gospel of work. Weil wrote it as a prescription for the ennui that, in her estimate, dogged French country life: drudgery relieved only by drunkenness, narrow concerns about money. The church's authority had dwindled to Sunday masses. She submits two "reforms" to give Christianity a natural place in the peasant worker's daily life. First, village priests would relate all the New Testament parables about seeding and viticulture to their due seasons: the mustard seed story belongs to the time for tree planting, for example, and the story of the Cana wedding to winepressing. These commentaries would supposedly "transform daily life itself, to the greatest possible degree, into a metaphor of divine significance." The farmer's life would itself become a parable. Second, the eucharist would assume the central position in the cycle: "If Christ chose bread and wine for his incarnation after death . . . it was not without reason."[35] The eucharist symbolically complements the passage of the worker's flesh and blood into the objects of labor. Work passed into wheat sowing or grape harvesting signifies that the worker attains a sacramental bond with Christ, becomes Christ's blood and flesh given back. It is a kind of reverse communion, a decreation by sweat.

Weil believes that work, if regarded as a sacrifice, can be rescued from degradation; it can transform the worker's daily life. That this transformation presupposes a rather sophisticated, *normalien* consciousness and attention does not deter her. She feels that thinking about God should be like the leavening in bread, infinitely small. Besides, the priest would keep the faithful going with ceremonies and readings. But it is exactly these reflective exertions that betray the scheme: the farmer reckoning his labor a sacrifice, the priest delivering homilies on labor's religious symbolism—Weil forgets that symbols and rituals work best, if at all, on a nonreflected level, where considerations and reminders have no part. To rationalize a mystery is to destroy it. In her uncompromising way of uniting thought and action, Weil does not appreciate the irrational dynamic at the root of religious culture. Nowhere does her estimate of Christianity as a "treasure of human thought" go farther astray than in the field, where any curé would know that the proprieties are chthonic and silent, like the plaster, epicene deity that keeps a tutelary station over the barn doors of France, even today.

The urge to uplift the farmer's mental life, to make a program of rituals, is an intellectual's mistake. But, like the nurses plan, this Christian life in the fields became particularly vivid in Weil's mind:

> Every Sunday, the priest would announce: 'Today the bread to be consecrated comes from such and such a farm; by their labor this farm's men and women have given of their vital substance to God so Christ may be incarnated on the altar.' On that day, the men, women and children of this farm, overseers and servants, would be of the first rank. This honor

> would be unconditionally accorded at least once to each farm, but more often to those where piety and, above all, neighborly charity, were greatest.[36]

How piety and charity would be measured in this pharisaical show can only be imagined. Weil's usual disdain of reward is, like her judgment, strangely absent. In *L'enracinement* she separates the wheat from the chaff: the piety contest is not mentioned, but the sacrificial and sacramental idea of labor is elaborated.

As she acknowledges, Weil owed much of her inspiration to the *jocistes*, whose concern for the plight of young factory workers, in whose ranks they themselves stood, suggested to her that Christianity was not entirely dead in France. Their conception of Christ as a worker "intoxicates them and carries them to a degree of purity in our time that is incredible."[37] Their example prompted her to seek the model of an agrarian Christ, and she found him in the harvester of communion bread and wine. When she met some *jocistes* in Marseilles she saw them through Vichy's refractory lens: with them Christianity had assumed what she called "its true accent, that which gives supernatural liberty to slaves." As workers they knew, so she claims, it was matter that weighed upon them, and they responded in conscious submission. That constituted "an immense superiority," where "what remains pure is truly pure." Of their nonpartisan, nonproselytic example she wrote in 1941: "One would only with difficulty imagine something more moving or more comforting in the present hour."[38]

For Weil, the oppression peculiar to Vichy—abolition of trade unions, exorbitant production quotas set by the Germans, forced labor—was, finally, incidental. What remained was the need to maintain "the pure worker spirit" as the *jocistes* exemplified it, in an accepting submission to matter. Even while presuming to ensure a postwar *enracinement* for workers through decentralization, cooperatives, and ownership of tools, Weil does not believe these melioristic adjustments would change the nature of work. It goes on being hard and necessary. Abolition of exploitative production systems will not change that fact *au fond*. The servile humiliation in piecework and all divisions of labor might find amends in workers' initiative and responsibility, but such reforms cannot end work itself. It is a malady of modern civilization, according to Weil, that human toil has not been granted its rightful position as a chastisement for human disobedience to God. It is a kind of daily death because it requires that one put oneself into inert matter: "The worker makes of his own body and mind an appendage of the tool he wields. The body's movements and the mind's attention are functions of the tool's requirements, the tool itself being adapted to the work material."[39] Weil is at the greatest possible distance from Marx: the worker *wills* to become an extension of a tool, and this consented obedience to work as necessity is tantamount to obedience to God. That is why work must occupy the spiritual center of society. In no way does consent mitigate work's essential violence in binding human beings to matter. Work becomes in effect an ontological penance, and so, in *L'enracinement*'s closing pages, Weil judges physical toil spiritually superior to all the gifts of science, art and philosophy. Her hostility to technological progress comes from her assumption that to release people from labor's penitential bonds would endanger the sacramental obedience within work. Humanity's ancient dream of a release from toil is, for Weil, a will-o'-the-wisp, and an evil one at that.

Because in her intellectual fashion, she regards a mental disposition as itself ethically sufficient, it would seem that obedience, fully consented, does nothing but rationalize drudgery. Of course, Weil denies that is the case. With penance and the bondage to time goes, peculiar as it may seem, joy. Weil did not forget her own infrequent moments at Alsthom and Renault when she had the thrill of achievement in the midst of frustration and exhaustion. Her program for workers' ownership of machinery, for cooperatives and educational research would obviously facilitate that release. It gives to her discussion of *liberté* and *égalité* a very tangible, earth-bound sense quite different from the employment of such terms in partisan platitudes.

She makes her point with a striking comparison. Imagine two women sewing. One is a happy young expectant mother preparing a layette. Despite all the difficulties of sewing technique, she does not for a moment forget the baby. At the same time, another women, a convict in a prison, is also sewing. She is no less attentive to sewing's technical demands; in fact, she fears punishment for bungling her job. An abysmal difference lies between the two seamstresses. Weil says that work will have won its proper place in society when working people have been enabled to pass from the convict's condition to the expectant mother's: "What would be necessary is that this world and the other, in their double beauty, be present and associated in the act of work, as the expected infant is present in the making of the layette."[40] Weil's suggestions for interpreting agrarian labor through New Testament parables show how an awareness of the *beauté du monde* might be conjoined to concrete tasks. Indeed, the world's beauty penetrates a human being through the pain (not wretchedness) that inevitably attends work. This ache is integral to all true dignity, Weil contends; the pain and the dignity both have their root in supernatural order. Workers must be given (back) a full consciousness of their work so that through it they can make an affirmative response to reality itself, an *amor fati.*

In this conception Weil shows herself a unique revisionist of Marx. Complementing her final position on Marx and Marxism as stated in *L'enracinement* is an unfinished essay from the same period, asking whether there was such a thing as Marxist doctrine. There she identified Marxism as the bourgeoisie's highest spiritual expression, its negation and therefore its justification—a kind of redemptive self-cancellation. But as Marx was a bourgeois, he could not escape susceptibility to bourgeois nostrums, particularly those of material progress. He believed that progressive changes in social organization (class relations) depend on technical changes in productive forces. Weil submits that Marx placed an unwarranted confidence in those forces as guarantees of progress—unwarranted because even the most sophisticated machines could be used to oppress rather than emancipate labor. In fact, specialization of functions, like the modern parcelization of knowledge, tends to ensure the former rather than the latter.

Marx further erred in hypostasizing a collectivity, the proletariat, as the medium for individual action. Although Weil had early recognized the fact of class antagonisms, she came to feel that Marx's idea of a class struggle had no conceptual substance. Worse, it had been put to use by his bourgeois followers, who accepted the unexamined "struggle" to promote a false apocalyptic, their own belief in automatic mechanisms of force as the instruments of justice: "Marxism, in offering workers the pseudo-scientific certitude that they will soon be the sovereign masters of the earth, has stirred up a workers' imperialism very much like that of the nationalist imperialisms."[41] Ironically, by advancing the false grandeur of force, Marxism betrayed the true grandeur Marx had discovered in the spirituality of work. In company with Rousseau, Proudhon, and Tolstoy, but far more profoundly than they, Marx articulated the one value unknown to ancient Greece, only to surrender it, in Weil's reckoning, to a spurious materialism. The result, she says, is a confused mélange of ideas foreign to working people themselves and which, because it is so readily convertible to propaganda, actually becomes a factor in deracinating labor.

Her attempt to redirect Marx's insights leads to what might be called a Stoic revision of Marxism. Because it is not normatively revolutionary, this attempt might seem reactionary, at least not Marxist. In her 1934 essay on oppression she had cited approvingly Marx's Goethean notion that one creates oneself in producing the conditions of one's own existence. In *L'enracinement* that liberation is furthered in a program of decentralization, cooperatives, and workers' private and collective ownerships, but it is also qualified by the Stoic gospel of accepting the conditions of existence as determined by work. Work must be conducted in a spirit (*le mot juste*) of humility, obedience, and love, directed not to a *patron* or commissar but to God and the divine providence constituting the world's order. Weil puts it best in saying that we must receive our human joy and human grief with the same internal gratitude. Work is a fundamental educator in that receptivity. It is the key to *enracinement*.

Sustained with the hope that once the Vichy regime was swept away, all things might be made new, *L'enracinement* has a forward, confident tone that suggests Weil was working for a practicable utopia quite different from the ideal society she knew to be hopeless in her 1934 "Réflexions." To be sure, utopia may be defined either as an ideal society that no one, including its conjuror, expects ever to realize (Plato does not consider implementation of his republic a vital matter), or as a guide to what might be possible. As early as 1934, Weil stated that idealism functions as an orienting vision, not an attainable goal, but it must be worked with and not simply entertained as an armchair reverie. Marxism itself, she holds, should be regarded as a method of social analysis, not as a doctrine. Outwardly the work economy she sketches in *L'enracinement* is utopist. Statism has conveniently disappeared, and the Stoic overlay of universal order provides a spirituality of *amor fati* for the soul's perfectibility. And yet what other utopia has ever been constructed in the conviction that pain, grief, and suffering are a natural, ineradicable part of human life?

The State Monster

Another element contributing to Weil's confidence was the Free French Movement under de Gaulle, or rather her perception of it as a symbol of France's fidelity to itself. As her English writing on Vichy shows, she felt de Gaulle had little support in France, and she was sure very few looked to him for postwar leadership. These assertions do not contradict her lofty estimate of the Free French in *L'enracinement*. There, the very absence of political power in any parliamentary sense becomes an asset, if not a virtue, as though de

Gaulle and his fellows in exile were placed above the compromises of political life which Weil found so hard to accept. She in fact attributes to the Free French a kind of spiritual authority, claiming they are ideally placed "to make the world hear the language of France." Their mission, she says, is to inspire France in the midst of its *malheur*, appeal to its genius, speak the people's mute thoughts, and even issue orders without fear of tarnishing "the kind of pure and lucid intoxication which attends one's free consent to sacrifice."[42]

From someone else these words might sound like propaganda, but from Weil they carry the ring of a deep, personal investment. She admitted that the Free French got their spiritual mission by default; de Gaulle had little leverage before Churchill and Roosevelt, and American policy was, to de Gaulle's humiliation, particularly indulgent toward Vichy. At the same time, the force of these circumstances enabled her to see politics itself in a new and positive way.

Her essays on the parties and a new constitution point to a suprapartisan leadership, a governing board of sages. Such government would rest on the Stoic worldview she promotes in her gospel of work. Whether she imagined or hoped that the Free French might carry on in their "spiritual" way after the war and function as a Stoic agency of justice and truth may be doubted. She was a veteran of disillusionment. But the Free French likely prompted her idea that politics has an affinity with art and science; it requires an elevated attention and the ability to achieve "logical coordination of different planes." The sense of the last phrase is vague, and Weil gives no details to support her comparison, but the direction she is taking is clear: "Whoever finds he has political responsibilities, if he has in him the hunger and thirst for justice, must desire to receive this art of composing on many levels, and must thereby infallibly receive that art in time."[43] Politics is not only, as the cliché has it, the art of the possible. It is a calling visited upon the just (not the ambitious), and the only proper response is a forceful desire for justice that might be analogized to prayer. There is even, in the last words just quoted, prayer's certitude of an answer. For Weil, politics allows no partisan maneuvers, only a statesmanship of utmost probity—and passivity: the lover of justice "finds" himself responsible, he desires and receives. Weil's politician scarcely acts at all; rather, he inspires in others the motivations for right action.

Weil is again erecting a guiding utopism "beyond the possibilities of human intelligence," but it is a vision for one's orientation and contemplation so that decisionmaking, however imperfect, may be good: "Only the desire for perfection has the virtue of destroying in the soul the evil part which contaminates it."[44] She cites Christ's impossible injunction to perfection, but the inspiration here is really Platonic in that it suggests that one's political responsibility is privileged by one's access to immutable truths.

Because she makes statesmanship a requisite to all political action, it appears strange that she gives the state itself a very low working profile. Like Plato she disdains detailed means, but her essay on a new French constitution shows she could understand government as a nuts-and-bolts operation. Her intention in *L'enracinement* is primarily to indict the state as chief culprit in the soul's deracination. Only after she has piled up a number of charges against it will she consider the state positively.

In her mind, "état" is virtually a synonym for totalitarian power. Rather than define it abstractly, she looks to its work in history, beginning with its French inventor, Richelieu. He subordinated everything to the state's interests, power, and prestige. Displacing the interests of a presumably once sovereign people, the seventeenth-century state became the sole object of allegiance, devoured the country's moral and physical resources by creating an oppressive police, and furthered its own authority by provoking war. Weil observes that, unlike individual egotism, national egotism has no legal and social sanctions to check it and no will to admit its errors or limit its desires—it does not need to do so if it can sustain itself by conquests. Richelieu and Louis XIV were Hitler's precursors; Napoleon's wars, masked as campaigns of liberation, were a prototype of the blitzkrieg.

Even as Hitler's ascent to dictatorship by clever and duplicitous use of constitutional procedures permanently discredited partisanship in Weil's eyes—as though his example would inevitably inspire others—so his conquest of Europe retroactively discredited the past to which that conquest afforded imposing analogies. But since she had already identified Hitlerism as the creation of the imperial Roman republic, why does she now locate it on French soil? The answer is bound to her notion of *patrie* and her concern to invent a new patriotism. This patriotism would be a sine qua non for every nation that had participated in what she calls the ersatz grandeur of conquest.

France had exemplified that false grandeur from Richelieu to Napoleon. Even in its subsequent decrepitude it had continued to sustain a colonial empire in Asia and Africa. Accordingly, it carried as great an obligation to penance as the more recent totalitarian contestants, Soviet Russia and Nazi Germany. Like the ancient Hebrew prophets, Weil sees the iniquity of her nation at a wide, encompassing angle: "Many things can be said about our suffering, but not that it is undeserved."[45] That is not a verdict on Vichy only, or on the years *entre deux guerres*, or on the Third Republic. It refers to three centuries of bad fruit that happened to fall in 1940.

In sketching Richelieu's *étatisme* Weil traces totalitarianism much farther back than J. H. Talmon and Hannah Arendt have taken it in their now classic studies. It has become a commonplace that the totalitarian state depends on mass support, a conspiracy of mob and elite. In modern contexts this assumption holds weight, but Weil does not entertain it. She situates totalitarianism within a French monarchic tradition that was hated for centuries before the Revolution (in the south, for example, from the thirteenth century). No less important is her point that the loveless bondage of the people to the state, once inflicted, persists through all vicissitudes, chiefly because the state has made itself inextricable from *patrie*: "Thus we have seen this strange thing, a state, object of hate, repulsion, contempt and fear, which, in the name of country, demanded absolute loyalty, the total gift, the supreme sacrifice, and got them, from 1914 to 1918, to a point surpassing all expectation. It posed as an earthly absolute, that is, an object of idolatry, was accepted and served as such, and honored by a frightful amount of human sacrifice. An idolatry without love, what is sadder and more monstrous?"[46]

What, then, of revolution, the most dramatic break with the state? Weil had already answered that question in her "Réflexions" on oppression: the state's established engines of despotism (the army, police, and bureaucracy) are merely taken over, virtually intact, by new masters. The Girondists, in promoting foreign wars, were resuming Richeliu's policies.

If Weil's analysis is correct, a totalitarian regime's support rests as much on a people's sullen complicity as on its fervid devotion. Alain's grudging deference to the state will not suffice to check it. Weil sees that popular moods fluctuate according to the state's apparent success or failure with the imperial agenda, but the support continues because there is no perceived alternative, certainly none admissible to the state. Vichy is a textbook on this melancholy fact. As has been noted, Weil contended that by 1943 the Pétain-Laval government was almost completely discredited, yet it went on, its artifices buoyed by German force, of course, but also by popular lassitude. It is Weil's insight that that lassitude preceded Vichy. She holds the French people responsible for "opening its hand and letting its country fall to the ground. . . .The French had nothing else but France to be loyal to, and when they abandoned it, in June 1940, one saw how ugly and piteous is the spectacle of a people tied to nothing by any loyalty."[47] In these vivid words *L'enracinement* displays a psychological breadth and depth far greater than Weil achieved in the 1934

"Réflexions." Historical events had informed her perception and judgment, of course, but the drift toward war and war itself did not, curiously enough, reinforce the dark view she held in 1934, that the state had become a permanent mechanism of oppression, with totalitarianism owning the future. This fact is the more remarkable since she now adds to the apparatus of statism (army, police, bureaucracy) the ingredients of *déracinement*: the degradation of work, the absence of religious inspiration, the cult of false grandeur. It would seem that an age beset with all of these viruses is incurable, yet Weil writes with the certainty that it is not. She is trying to demonstrate in *L'enracinement* that if we look honestly at a problem, here a syndrome of historical ills and evils, we can find some light emerging, however faintly, from the darkness. History can provide a way out of its own impasses. *L'enracinement* is an argument against historical fatalism.

She courts the regionalism that has been long and deeply rooted in French consciousness, a mighty prejudice with which to erode or at least contain the centripetal power of the state. What validates the regional is clear enough: it is (literally) the ground of *l'enracinement*, it provides the social and economic measure within which workers' cooperatives can function. Implicitly, Weil is tugging at the old Left's nostalgia for the Paris Commune three generations before. The Commune's violent destruction by the armed state, a spiritual disaster that blighted the workers' movement for decades, had been redeemed but only briefly in 1936 and the Popular Front. Weil's idyll of a provincialized authority of skilled labor is in some ways an attempt to repeat the experiments of 1871 and 1936. Although she believed that history was not in itself an adequate guide in preparing France for the postwar, her decentralization scheme is an attempt to roll back history, to undo the unification imposed by the state's internal conquests. Her regionalism is premodern, almost medieval; it seems not very distant from the antiurban fetishism of the old Right.

Vying with Weil's awareness of an inevitable *souillure* in all human actions is her passion for history making. She takes encouragement from the Revolution's initial or "pure" development in 1789, when France assumed the role of thinking for the world and defining justice. To her, 1789 signified inspiration, not institution (this is her dichotomy), and could thus, she hoped, further France's recovery from Third Republic chaos and Vichy squalor. Even though, as she admits, the Revolution's course through Europe involved a prolonged and violent *déracinement*, 1789 gave France for generations afterward a reputation for justice and liberty, one she earnestly wanted it to regain.

The Occupation had created an artificial intensity of emotions that could not be sustained after the war. The need to find some legitimate orientation of motives for the *patrie* and the individual became, in Weil's estimate, paramount. She sees that motivation finds its reality only through action. In Sorelian fashion she states that action "does not merely confer reality upon motives which previously existed in a semi-phantom state. It also causes to arise in the soul motives and feelings which did not previously exist at all."[48] In this notion she complements the mystique of a symbolic leadership that merely has to issue orders with a mystique of obedience. Indeed, the symbolic leader is obedient to a transcendent authority: "There are those who obey an order that has come directly from God."[49] What these orders are, how they are conveyed by leadership, what "motives and feelings" they might prompt in the obedient all remain undefined; hence the mystique. Whether domiciled in Christ, Arjuna, some Platonic guardian, or a conflated image of all these in her mind, Weil's politics of an all-sufficient *logos* is far more than a utopic design to end mass slavery and the baleful constraints of totalitarianism. It is an attempt to conform politics to an ancient world of vanished harmonies, to make motivation and action reflect the Stoic virtue of compliance with an intuited order. All of Weil's "vital needs" of the soul imply theocracy. That is why she invokes the anomaly of a society rid of parties. They have nothing to do with her Stoic cosmos and a *patrie* mediated by learnèd, disinterested, powerless leaders, where the only real entities are a *res divina* of symbols and a *res plebeia* of cooperatives.

Little is left of the state in her vision. She says it is entitled to one's obedience not for its own sake but for the conservation and peace of the *patrie*. In a telling phrase she likens the state's claim on the people to that of a mediocre governess on children. She allows that the state is sacred but not as an idol, only as a repository of symbols. This radical surgery is analogous to her stripping down the Catholic church to a sacramental storehouse barren of all institutional dynamics. The state is, finally, without power and authority. Unlike the constitutional essays, *L'enracinement* does not even offer the prospect of effectual government by seers in place of bureaucrats.

Patrie is no surrogate for statism. In seeking to empty it of all false pride and the glory of conventional patriotism, Weil wants the country to serve chiefly as a cadre for the formation of attachments to "every kind of milieu other than itself."[50] This amounts to one more plea for regionalism and for that sense of provincial identity which the war's partition of France had reinforced. Weil looks upon local loyalties as sick plants to be nourished. She bids the French people affirm themselves as Bretons, Alsatians, Provençals, according to wherever they live, so as to transplant patriotism from the desolate soil of *l'état*. She disclaims xenophobia, but it is hard to see how she would mitigate age-old provincial resentments toward the capital, as though Paris were another country—as it still is to many in France.

Since the state, whatever its modern guise, is a persistent bogey in her eyes, it is no surprise that in the amplest scope of her vision she makes no reference to a United States of Europe. The postwar economic Americanization of the Continent already figured in her prophetic dread, and as she wanted regionalism to triumph as a check on a central national authority, so she would surely have wanted the diversity of European cultures kept free even of the artifice of political consolidation. She had identified the mission of the Free French as the prevention of postwar fascism and communism in France, and she hoped for comparable safeguards in every other *patrie*. If she is not explicit about the European renaissance for which, as it seemed to Camus, *L'enracinement* provided essential criteria, it is because her vision extends to a universal compass. If work, secured against oppression, and community, secured against the state, provide the soil in which the soul's needs can take sustenance, the air for the soul's breath, once cleared of partisan lies, will be filled with the cerulean *amor fati* of Stoicism. The last word belongs to Weil's friendship with antiquity.

Conclusion

A lasting assumption of Stoicism through each of its successive periods, Greek and Roman, was that human life and the universe are coherent and correspondent, held together in a transcendent order, the rational principle of *logos*. Cosmology (or physics) and ethics are complementary; both are structured in conformity to divine law. Wisdom, the conscious assent that this is the inevitable way things are, is tantamount to virtue.

Nowhere else in Weil's writing is this Stoicism so pervasive as in *L'enracinement*, even though its explicit references to Stoic dogma are few. *Amor fati* or Stoic obedience to the cosmos of reason she construed as the Christian response of humility and love. There are gaping defects in this construction but also some ground of correspondence wide enough for the Stoic and the Christian to share: cosmic determinism in the one, for example, prefigures predestination in the other; the Stoic doctrine of assent anticipates the Christian dogma of free will. In both views, evil is primarily an indisposition, a dissent from the divine, even though Stoic logic dictates that in a divinely ordered world evil plays a necessary or complementary role to the good and is not, therefore, what a Christian would understand as sin. It might rather be analogized to the Hindu notion of *maya*, the illusion subsumed in brahman.

It is curious, however, that in *L'enracinement* Weil seems to have demoted Christianity. Why does she not include in her list of the soul's vital needs the Christian trinity of faith, hope, and charity? Her words on the church (she is writing for a public now, not for Perrin or herself) are harsh and dismissive: though its Romanism has persisted intact, it is more subordinate to the state than ever before. Her dismay at and scorn of churchmen feeling inferior before scientists, the bourgeois Christian's complacent exploitation of the workers, the comic inadequacy of "dialogues" between the faithful and the unbelievers—all this she sets down in *L'enracinement*. One's religious affiliation nowadays, she says, has no more profundity than one's choice of a necktie.

To this melancholy prospect her own strictures would appear to bring no relief. Identifying Christ's resurrection in glory as the real attraction for conventional devotion (an imposed false grandeur?), she states that there is no need of resurrection (Christ's or one's own, presumably) for genuine faith. She delivers a lengthy attack on the belief in miracles. She scores both points on behalf of what Christianity seems to have lost or abandoned: *kenosis*, or the Christ-like consent to be nothing. In Stoic terms, this means *amor fati*, accepting the beauty of the world through the *douleur* of work, finding one's true dignity at its supernatural root in the cosmic order.

Typically, her attitude toward Christianity is fraught with ambivalence. She remarks, for example, a phrase from Pius XII, "Not only from the Christian viewpoint but more generally from the human viewpoint" as implying that the former has a smaller range than the latter, and she concludes, "One cannot conceive a more terrible admission of bankruptcy." Yet she had already admitted that in the face of modern lay philosophy the only "authentic" attitude toward Christianity is to present it as "one treasure of human thought among others." *Treasure* may carry greater connotative weight than *viewpoint*, but there is the same relativizing dilution in her statement that she objects to in the pope's.[51]

She claims that Christian faith is without defense against lay ideologies. She does not mean that it is irrational or insupportable but rather that point-by-point ripostes diminish it at the core, just as arguments for God's existence impoverish all around. Its only true function for her is basically Stoic, to illuminate all profane life, public and private, without ever dominating it. (Stoicism has never sponsored an auto-da-fé or an *anathema sit.*) This is to say that Weil's Christianity is aesthetic rather than didactic, it is the perception, Stoic through and through, that the brute force of nature is not sovereign but rather in perfect obedience to the divine *logos,* the sovereignty of limit. Whether construed passively as the consent to eternity which Weil read in St. John, or actively as the study of supernatural mechanisms which she found in Plato's *Timaeus* and in San Juan de la Cruz, it is the same static and timeless contemplation of necessity as the only reality of this world but one in which divine thought is made materially present.

Here at last is the ultimate rooting, as much for workers in their medieval cooperatives as for their symbolic guardian leaders who know no party or bureaucracy. This rooting holds together all the strands of daily life that sustain the soul's vital needs. Its true need, Weil indicates, is intellective:

> So far as one puts up with having the soul filled with one's personal thoughts, one is wholly submitted, even in the most intimate of them, to the constraint of needs and the mechanical play of force. To believe otherwise is a mistake. But everything changes when, by virtue of true attention, one empties the soul to let thoughts of the eternal wisdom penetrate. One then carries in oneself the very thoughts to which force is submitted.[52]

Kenosis becomes *l'enracinement*; *la personne,* decreated, becomes *le sacré.* If any one passage in Weil's writings could be taken as an epitome of her thinking, it might be this one.

But if *L'enracinement* can be taken as a final statement, it is not an exclusive one. Although the state has obligingly withered away or has at least diminished itself by some mysterious fiat to the contemptible role of governess, Weil's constitutional essays outline some form of central government and implicitly open the door to the very *étatisme* she hated. Likewise, if she is not concerned here about individual regeneration as a prerequisite to the renewal of society, "La personne et le sacré" serves eloquently to signpost that regeneration. If, finally, her sketch of French history, from Richelieu to Pétain, seems too sweeping an indictment, her "impressions" of Vichy France show that she could look hard at piteous present realities and the dismal future they promised. All of this needs saying lest *L'enracinement,* taken by itself, seem rooted only in an anachronistic Stoic vision.

Yet it is the Stoicism in Weil's orientation that sets her singularly apart from her contemporaries, giving *L'enracinement* the aspect of a lofty disinterestedness. She cannot be enlisted for the so-called Christian existentialism of Gabriel Marcel or for the *personalisme* of Emmanuel Mounier; neither does she belong to the revitalized Marxism of Paul Nizan. It cannot even be said that she is trying to straddle or reconcile the differences between these camps (in the ecumenical way of Roger Garaudy) because she would have disdained the tacit allegiance of these individuals to Rome or to Moscow. In her book she attempts a twentieth-century impossibility, conceiving of the world without a Great Beast so that divinity can still be read. If this is utopism, then the worse for the twentieth century.

It is an appropriate irony that the only time Weil was given a government task, looking to postwar France, she succeeded in arriving at a coherent vision that took her well beyond that scope. Politically considered, *L'enracinement* is a grand piece of impertinence. Putting aside the elementary facts of human power seeking, she exposes her vision to the charge that she rationalizes the brute world of oppression. Hegel had already exposed Stoicism's fault, that an acceptance of necessity, an identification of oneself with a universal reason, does not transform human relationships. A slave at Alsthom or Renault might gain access to eternal wisdom by the utmost attention but he (she) goes on being a slave. *Amor fati* aborts the will to change the world. To invoke cosmic justice and order is to cheat the earthly justice needed here and now. Weil would respond that to accept is to transform, it is to make *malheur* into the sacramental *douleur* of work. Her own writing, especially in the centripetal fury of her last months, was a kind of sacramental effort. It warned that to ignore suffering's redemptive value as necessity's gift to human mortality is an offense—what Plato would call the lie in the soul. Conversely, to cause suffering so that it bites so deep as to arouse a disposition to itself is to bring disaster upon the oppressor and the oppressed alike. Weil's notion of attention points to God's harmonies, silent and recondite in nature. She knew that this orientation made her a fool, but, as she hoped, Lear's kind of fool, one who sees what others do not or will not. She also knew that refusal of attention leads, at whatever tempo, to the world Hitler made.

T H I R T E E N

Inconclusions

> There is a relation between discipline and the theatrical sense. If we cannot imagine ourselves as different from what we are and assume the second self, we cannot impose a discipline upon ourselves, though we may accept one from others. Active virtue, as distinct from the passive acceptance of a current code, is therefore theatrical, consciously dramatic, the wearing of a mask. It is the condition of an arduous, full life.
>
> W. B. YEATS, *Autobiography*

Were a final estimate of Simone Weil possible, something of the following remarks might figure in its shaping. Although they may serve to recapitulate what I have argued in this book, I hope they will also stimulate the reader toward what is more important, his or her own estimate of Weil. Any critic presuming to serve as mediator between her and her reader knows that it is best to withdraw finally into the supreme discretion that is silence, rather as Vergil withdrew from Dante upon the approach of Beatrice. Let me add with some haste that I do not—and the reader who has come this far has likely guessed as much—regard Weil as a Beatrice. I am dubious that she has a beatific vision to offer us. She does not solve problems, but she can more than occasionally help us in trying to face them.

One lesson she gives us, and perhaps it is the most important, is that of doubt. She was Alain's faithful pupil and invites us to be. Everything she wrote, even though so often in the limpid style of French analytical tradition, deserves to be held at an intellectual arm's length. Throughout her brief maturity she wrote skeptically, that is, experimentally. She set down ideas as they came to her, in bold intuitive strokes that resist systematic development. Significantly, many of her writings are entitled "reflections," and the aphoristic brilliance that frequently flashes out in them (and even more in her *cahiers*) might be likened to the commanding lines of a sketch. There is consequently an attractive incompleteness in her work. The judicious reader senses that Weil is not attempting to impose an argument or a set of convictions she holds in peremptory readiness but rather that she is taking one along the uncharted course of her thoughts. The steadfastness with which she looks at a problem or an issue becomes the guide. Doubt is a kind of mainspring to this steadfastness, a vigilant reckoning (or intellectual fussiness) that kept Weil from being taken in by easy resolution of very real difficulties. She always preferred the harder way, that of keeping the difficulties in focus. This dubitative power of her intellect kept her finally free of the mighty fanaticisms that beguiled so many of her fellow intellectuals. By reading her skeptically, we are not only responding to her in kind; we assume the necessary distance of doubt from which to assess the value of her ideas.

Her style is in a sense a snare. The clarity of her presentation and its intellectual forcefulness may be too easily taken (impetuous readers as we are) as evidence of final conviction, as though she had assumed some definitive vantage, just as her longing for purity, intellectual, spiritual, and otherwise, may be too easily construed (and has been by some) as evidence that she was a pure being.

Take, for example, her many references to *amor fati*, the Stoic dogma of accepting a putatively rational universe. They are no proof whatever that Weil was a Stoic or that she even practiced Stoic deference to the cosmos. They indicate her awareness of this dogma and they imply an affirmative response to it such as she might have called *attention*. She drew upon elements of Stoic philosophy for inspiration, but she did not argue for Stoicism as an inclusive system. Indeed, she could not have done so and continued to believe in divine grace, a most un-Stoic entity.

Her writing at its best has a meditative quality, and meditation forbids the snatching which, in Blake's terrible words, "doth the wingèd life destroy." That is why, again following her example, we do well not to grasp her and her thinking in an appropriative way, putting her under a house arrest convenient to our own sensibility. This point must be underscored if only because she has so often been seized upon or pulled at, particularly by Christians with canonical urges. It should be caution enough that none other than André Gide, whom she primly dismissed as a corrupting and irresponsible writer, was first in this line, calling her "the saint of outsiders." I suggest that this remark would have bemused her and that, like Kierkegaard and Nietzsche, she would have fled the embrace of the devout and the enthusiastic, whether of the inside or the outside. In her advocacy of an out-of-date anarchism, a Hellenized and bogus Christianity, a *patrie* of pastoral industries, she was not writing programs; she was championing lost causes. It was her way of wearing the mask of what Yeats calls "the arduous full life." Like Blake, she remains a creature of private fervors and singular visions, an unlikely recruit for others' intents.

Weil is nothing so dull as a saint. The happy fact is that she went her own way, and reading her guarantees an adventure free of ideological signposts and the deadly finality of tags. That is why taking her writings as dispensed dogma does particular and violent injustice to them and to her. She did not achieve—or even try to achieve—the magisterial ease of Alain because her whole effort was that of a student, in the old root sense of that word: she had an insatiable, unyielding zeal for testing, for finding out. She once remarked that she did not read books that truly interested her, but rather devoured them, and the same holds of her responses to the political, social, and religious issues that compelled her decision, putting her intellectual and personal integrity to the test.

Given her *libido experiendi*, it seems amazing that she was able to sustain a poised and lucid style. It argues a great deal of restraint. And yet hers is a surcharged clarity, as though, like Rousseau, she had an arcane ability to set reason afire. Many of her readers may well feel a profound ambivalence toward her, at once applauding her, as Camus did, for her exalted vision, and deploring her, as Améry did, for the subtle menace of irrationalism within it. This ambivalence may be the more marked because of the very clarity of her thinking: her horror of *souillure* kept her free of the jargon, slogans, and shibboleths of an era in which many other thoughtful people were engulfed. Irresistibly they were pulled toward commitments. She felt the pull, too, but resisted. Much of the continuing freshness of her writing is surely owed to this resistance, to the fact I have already noted, that she wrote problematically rather than programmatically. Even the minor and topical *feuilletons* she contributed to leftist journals early in the 1930s hold up in this way, altogether justifying (if justification were needed) Gallimard's at-long-last critical edition of her complete works.

The Gallimard series not only gives us the length and breadth and depth of Weil as a writer, it also gives us through her refracting lens some clearer focus on the dark years in which she wrote. The point bears repeating that during her fifteen years of work, from the time she entered what Paul Nizan called "the allegedly Normal and supposedly Superior Ecole" to her last weeks with the Free French in London, Europe moved from crisis to crisis and then on to the disasters of war. France, torn by the libertarian and reactionary urges of its political ancestry, remains the most fascinating barometer of tensions both before and (through Vichy) during the war. For Weil, only once in all that dismal time, during the euphoric first months of the ill-fated Popular Front, did the sun break through. By the spring of 1943, when it was becoming apparent that the Axis powers would eventually be defeated and that France and Europe had some promise of rebirth, Weil believed she had only a few years to live—in the event, a too generous estimate. The point here is that throughout her maturity, Weil as one "in situation," to use Sartre's term, was a catastrophe writer, even as she was a catastrophe Jew.

Accordingly, I have tried to relate Weil's writing to the time in which she was living. More is involved here than a mere succession of backgrounds or a mise-en-scène of various contexts. Weil's insistence, passed on to her by Lagneau and Alain, that the mind submit its ideas to experience, that it confront the world, implicitly recognized that the world meets the mind and does so rather more than halfway. Her notion of necessity is no abstract or academic figment. It points to a reality weighing daily on human consciousness. The record of her time, as she saw it, was one of futile and cruel resistance to reality, a great age of lies and false turns. Her own progress through it, a course not free of its own false turns and illusions, makes a compelling story and one that goes much deeper than the sensational biographical surface data so often cited about her, in her roles as factory worker, Spanish war partisan, hunger artist, and so forth. Even (or especially) the most apparently abstract or "metaphysical" of her writings and also the most private and personal, such as her letters to Père Perrin on Christianity, sustain historical reference and therefore historical interpretation.

Such an approach may serve to give these writings some *enracinement* and should thereby help to discourage the anti-historical cultism that thrives on the mythification of isolated facts. Of course, a lurid glamour will continue to hang over the record of her life: by outward account she was a failure several times over, yet in her true vocation as a writer she succeeded brilliantly. As one of death's discoveries, she has the allure of the tragic artist or neglected genius, one upon whom it may be hard not to bestow a solicitous awe and hallowing sentimentality. It is far easier to admire her for those grueling months of work at Alsthom and Renault than to dwell on her courting of anarcho-syndicalist visions that put her in succession to Proudhon. It is far easier to imagine her reciting Herbert's "Love bade me welcome" than to weigh the many cold facts that kept her from sitting down and eating at the Christian banquet. One is reminded of Descartes's complaint that people were more interested in his face than in his ideas, as though he were an animal caged in a zoo. Weil, unfortunately, has had a good deal of face in this regard. In attending rather to the ideas she was trying to think through and live out, we can appreciate both her independence and her derivation, her lone-wolf integrity and her pathos as an errant Jew on one hand and on the other her privileged life as a bourgeoise and a *normalienne*.

Perhaps in no way is she so unique to her generation as in her entertainment of ancient Greek wisdom, of Platonic necessity and Stoic *amor fati*, with their attendant philosophical constructs so imposingly rationalizing the social, no less than the cosmic, way things are. It seems odd that Weil, who never quite abandoned anarcho-syndicalism—indeed, reaffirmed it in some of her last essays—should have esteemed most highly the elitist Plato and the slave Epictetus; odd, accordingly, that she did not appreciate the materialist philosophy of Epicurus and Lucretius, which went far to subvert the collectivist bugaboos of an oppressive religious and social "order" and did so on behalf of the soul's autarchy. (How, in this matter, could she have missed Nizan's lead?[1]) If, by invoking transcendent, "other side of the sky" Platonism Weil became in effect an apologist for existing hierarchies, like St. Paul advising Christian masters and Christian slaves on how to get along, one might wonder whether she was so much an outsider as her reputation purports her to have been. Her love of the past, her celebration of regionalism and the old *artisanat*, her distrust of partisan politics and modern collectivities all conspire to suggest that in her own way she perhaps heeded too well the Vichy radio's injunction to "penser Pétain." And yet no one more than she has been a persistent and exemplary champion of intellectual freedom (she includes it among "the soul's needs") so that if she is to be deemed a reactionary, she is, however anomalously, a libertarian reactionary.

That she thought hard and on her own is clear enough. She owed no subscription to any organized groups, and she spent a good deal of effort defining herself and her thinking against them. It would be possible to caricature her life as one *refus* after another. At the same time she was sensitive to a kind of chameleon susceptibility in her response to the collectivities she strove to despise. In one of her letters to Fr. Perrin she confessed to "a strong gregariousness," that "by natural disposition I'm extremely influenceable, to excess, especially regarding collective things. I know that if I had before me at this moment twenty young Germans singing Nazi songs, a part of my soul would immediately become Nazi. That's a very great weakness. But that's the way I am."[2] This is someone quite other than the person who made a career of *refus*, who had rejected her comfortable middle-class status and professional life within it, who had resisted the seductions of the Communist party and the Christian church.

How, then, can we explain why Weil, one of the century's most forceful voices against social and political conformism, ended her life with a Marxist vision of labor and a profession of Christian faith? These are the effects, of course, of her very personal, on-my-own-terms views: she heralded a proletariat redeemed without revolution and a Christianity shorn of Judaism. We might go further and say that this defender of history's lost causes and of the oppressed everywhere was also, again on her own terms, a consummate middle-class intellectual, for although she rejected the bourgeois fetish of progress and scorned its material blandishments, she clung to Alain's verbal universe in which salvation lies in a disposition of mind, and this refuge belongs only to the well-educated. In minds less vigilant and less restive than Weil's, less insistent on clarity of vision, this disposition could readily become a storehouse of clichés and rationalizations, a comforting and complacent bulwark against real problems and real suffering. We need only refer to Christians who tell Jews that forgiveness and love are owed to Nazis to wonder how many steps away from this patronizing sits Weil's *amor fati*. Her own explicit desire that all the Jews of France tear up their roots and graft themselves to the tree of French Catholic culture (an inverted Pauline *enracinement*) is about as thorough a program for *embourgeoisement* as one can imagine, and it is simulatenously an indication that for her, acceptance of the world did not include acceptance of oneself. Was decreation her prescription for the woes of all human egotism or did she intend it primarily for herself as the self-loathing *écran* between God and the world?

This point brings us around once more to her Jewishness. Judaism, it has sometimes been said, is a club one does not quit. Weil once conceived of herself as a Christian outside of Christendom, but to remember her as a Jew kicking against the pricks of Judaism may be more helpful to a sound estimate of her life and work. In ironic fact, much that is so positive and attractive in the balance has to do with Weil as *tzeddik*, the just person. Her biographers offer many instances of her alms-giving, her help, often material, given to oppressed people, to unemployed workers, and to exploited colonials exiled in France. She did not preach love and salvation to them; she gave them money, food, ration coupons, and her time. These actions are not isolated instances; they are what Blake calls "the minute particulars" that finally count. Arguably, it was as a *tzeddik* that she went to Alsthom, to Spain, and to London, seeking the all-important experiential ground of justice.

How Jewish, too, we find her passionate wrestling, often bitter and violent, with God. Her *attente de Dieu* itself barely conceals a plea that God issue her a command, make, as it were, a covenant with her. This is egotism of the highest order; in Donne's words, "a most desireable covetousness." Perhaps something in her dislike of the Hebrew patriarchs points not to their lives of crime, as she reviewed them in her *cahiers*, but to an emulous resentment of them, that they had a terrible, spoken intimacy with their God. In any case, much of the poetry and danger of her life, the real poetry and the real danger as opposed to the bunkum of myth, have simply to do with the fact that she was a Jew.

Let one final observation suffice. What is her *attente de Dieu* but an halakhic receptivity, an altogether Jewish waiting in the certainty that, because God descends, God is not to be sought? Weil, to be sure, had her own special way of waiting. Like Maine de Biran's *croyance*, her *attente* is an admission of ontological need, a concession of radical insufficiency in the human condition, and hence, as she remarks, it is more intense than any seeking. It is not the merely receptive, submissive waiting assigned to women in fairy tales but a tautly pitched expectation. We are reminded that *attente* shares an etymological home with Weil's *attention*, which stretches out and reaches as though to grasp.

If we could altogether separate her ideas from her fascinating life, what might we identify as truly valuable? This may be a foolish question because every reader will surely discover in Weil something that speaks best to her or his own sensibility, and so my plea that she not be shortchanged by an imposed aura of saintliness will likely fall idle before some readers. She is bound to enthrall or irritate even as her ideas are variously strange, penetrating, ridiculous, brilliant. In my estimation, one of her most important *aperçus* comes from her 1934 "Réflexions" on the causes of oppression and freedom: as we free ourselves from the bondage of nature, we deliver ourselves into a more subtle bondage of our own contrivances, in increasingly sophisticated forms of social and economic organization. In an age that has become idolatrous of technological "advances," this perception should serve as a caveat. But it is only one instance in an abundant number of her thoughts that are not out of season. It may be more useful in a summary to note that the salient character of all Weil's writing is what might be called its kinesis: the effect of her setting herself the difficult task of thinking is that she prompts us to do the same. That is so, I believe, even when she is outrageous or especially demanding of modern wits, as when she passes into the stratospheres of Plato and of

Pythagorean "inspiration" or speaks as the votary dwelling in some mystical recess. If she was a slave, finally, to her own freedom of mind, we continue to benefit from her drudgery. That we can do so in a way exciting and fruitful to our minds and to our daily contact is really all the tribute Weil needs.

Not that she would have asked for it.

Notes

Abbreviations

Manuscript Sources: The following abbreviations refer to labels on the *boîtes* containing the unpublished Simone Weil Papers I have consulted at the Bibliothèque Nationale in Paris. All of these labels are to be found in the microfilm copies of the Simone Weil Papers at the Institute for Advanced Study in Princeton.

AHS	Articles historiques pour *Syndicats*
CD 1,2,3	Cahiers divers, trois séries
CG	Correspondance générale
CO	Condition ouvrière
CSWAW	Correspondance Simone Weil–André Weil
DB	Documents biographiques
DH	Donation Honnorat
ELM	Ecrits de Londres et de Marseille
EHP	Ecrits historiques et politiques
HS	Histoire et syndicalisme
P	Poèmes
TPAG	Textes philosophiques antérieurs à la guerre
TS	Textes sanskrits
VS	*Venise sauvée*

Published Primary Sources: The following abbreviations refer to the texts of Simone Weil published in France and to the major biography.

AD	*Attente de Dieu*. 3d ed. Paris: Fayard, 1966.
C 1, 2, 3	*Cahiers* 1, Paris: Plon, 1951; 2, Paris: Plon, 1953; 3, Paris: Plon, 1956.
CO	*La condition ouvrière*. Paris: Gallimard, 1951.
CS	*La connaisssance surnaturelle*. Paris: Gallimard, 1950.
CSW	*Cahiers Simone Weil*, quarterly journal of L'Association pour l'étude de la pensée de Simone Weil
E	*L'enracinement*. Paris: Gallimard, 1949.
EHP	*Ecrits historiques et politiques*. Paris: Gallimard, 1960.
EL	*Ecrits de Londres et dernières lettres*. Paris: Gallimard, 1957.

IPC	*Intuitions pré-chrétiennes*. Paris: La Colombe, 1951.
LR	*Lettre à un religieux*. Paris: Gallimard, 1955.
OC, 1	*Oeuvres complètes: Premiers écrits philosophiques*. Paris: Gallimard, 1988.
OL	*Oppression et liberté*. Paris: Gallimard, 1955.
PSO	*Pensées sans ordre concernant l'amour de Dieu*. Paris: Gallimard, 1962.
PVS	*Poèmes suivis de Venise sauvée*. Paris: Gallimard, 1968.
S	*Sur la science*. Paris: Gallimard, 1969.
SG	*La source grecque*. Paris: Gallimard, 1969.
Pétrement 1, 2	Simone Pétrement. *La vie de Simone Weil*. 2 vols. Paris: Fayard, 1973.

English Translations: The original French texts are indicated in parentheses.

First and Last Notebooks. Translated by Richard Rees. London: Oxford University Press, 1970. (CS)

Intimations of Christianity among the Ancient Greeks. Translated by Elizabeth Geissbühler. London: Routledge & Kegan Paul, 1957. (*IPC*)

Letter to a Priest. Translated by Arthur Wills. New York: Putnam, 1954. (*LR*)

The Need for Roots. Translated by Arthur Wills. New York: Putnam, 1952. (*E*)

The Notebooks of Simone Weil. Translated by Arthur Wills. 2 vols. New York: Putnam, 1956. (C 1, 2, 3)

On Science, Necessity and the Love of God. Translated by Richard Rees. Oxford: Oxford University Press, 1968. (Portions of *S*, *SG*, *PSO*)

Oppression and Liberty. Translated by Arthur Wills and John Petrie. Amherst: University of Massachusetts Press, 1973. (*OL*)

Waiting for God. Translated by Emma Craufurd. New York: Putnam, 1951. (*AD*)

Chapter 1

1. I paraphrase a remark from Eugen Weber, "Reflections on the Jews in France," in *The Jews in Modern France*, ed. Frances Malino and Bernard Wasserstein (Hanover, N.H.: University Press of New England, 1985), p. 27.

2. *AD*, pp. 38–39.

3. C, 1:206.

4. Pétrement, 1:23.

5. Ibid., 21.

6. Ibid., 27.

7. EHP, pp. 220–24, 109.

8. Jacques Cabaud, *L'expérience vécue de Simone Weil* (Paris: Plon, 1957), p. 18.

9. On Le Senne's influence on Weil's teaching see Rolf Kühn, "Dimensions et logique interne de la pensée de Simone Weil," in *Simone Weil: philosophe, historienne, et mystique*, ed. Gilbert Kahn (Paris: Aubier Montaigne, 1978), p. 339, n. 19.

10. Cabaud, p. 21, n. 2.

11. Pétrement, 1:70.
12. Ibid., p. 65.
13. Quoted in ibid., p. 67, from a letter of June 21, 1914.
14. André Weil, "Lettre à Jean Guitton," February 9, 1979, in CSW 2 (June 1979): 54.
15. Pétrement, 1:69.
16. Ibid., p. 68.
17. Cabaud, p. 22.
18. Ibid., p. 34.
19. Ibid., p. 33.
20. Pétrement, 1:106.
21. Ibid., p. 115.
22. Ibid., pp. 122–23. Simone de Beauvoir's own account comes from her *Mémoires d'une jeune fille rangée* (Paris: Gallimard, 1958) pp. 236–37.
23. Cabaud, p. 38.
24. Ibid.
25. *OC*, 1:265. It is instructive that here Weil contrasts Greece, her emblem of adolescent freedom, not with Rome but with Egypt and servitude—an identification that would come naturally to a Jew.
26. *OC*, 1:267.
27. Her classical text is Bacon's formula "Natura enim non nisi parendo vincitur," from the *Novum Organum* I, aphorism 3. She uses it again in *OL*, p. 140. During her teaching at Roanne she assigned it as a dissertation topic.
28. *OC*, 1:273.
29. Ibid., p. 271.
30. Pétrement, 1:170–71, 178–79.
31. *OC*, 1:377.
32. "La marche vers l'unité syndicale," *L'effort*, November 21, 1931, p. 2.
33. "La vie syndicale: en marge du Comité d'Etudes," *L'effort*, December 19, 1931, p. 2.
34. "Les modes d'exploitation," *L'effort*, January 30, 1932, p. 1.
35. "Le capital et l'ouvrier," *L'effort*, March 12, 1932, p. 1.
36. "La Conference du Désarmement," *L'effort*, February 20, 1932, p. 1.
37. "L'U.R.S.S. et Amerique," *L'effort*, July 2, 1932, p. 1.
38. *Le Charivari*, January 23, 1932, quoted by Pétrement, 1:243.
39. Pétrement, 1:251.
40. The story comes from a fellow teacher and labor activist, Jean Dupperay, "Quand Simone Weil passa chez nous; témoignage d'un syndicaliste," *Les lettres nouvelles*, 12 (March–May 1964): 85–101 and (June–August 1964), 123–38.
41. Cabaud, p. 80. The dossier is now at the National Archives and cannot be examined.
42. *Lectures on Philosophy*, trans. Hugh Price (Cambridge: Cambridge University Press, 1978), pp. 98, 164.
43. Quoted by Cabaud, p. 99. These remarks should be compared with those of four Le Puy students, C. Claveyrolas, S. Faure, Y. Argaud, and M. Dérieu on "Simone Weil

professeur," *Foi et education*, May 1951, pp. 170–73: "The instruction and personality of Simone Weil had a most profound influence upon us. We owe to her a love and respect for moral and intellectual probity in all forms. Thanks to her, we foresaw that it is true thought which seeks passionately, if not always successfully, to recognize the true from the false, the pure from the impure."

44. Pétrement, 1:415.

45. Quoted from her dossier by Cabaud, p. 104.

46. Pétrement, 1:412–13.

47. Ibid., p. 188.

48. The journal's content appears to have dictated its form. Alongside lists of tools and parts Weil recorded the names of co-workers—two inventories, in effect, set down the more tellingly for their matter-of-fact simplicity.

49. *AD*, p. 42.

50. The *fado* is defined in the *Dicionario de Morais*, 5 (q.v.) as a popular song of sad, mournful music.

51. *AD*, pp. 41, 43.

52. Pétrement, 1:431.

53. Letters to Jean Posternak, *Nuovi arggomenti* (Rome) 2 (1953): 80–99. It is a pity that Weil does not elaborate on her admission of what appeals to her in Italian fascism. See Pétrement, 2:53.

54. Quoted by Pétrement, 2:151.

55. *AD*, p. 43.

56. For an excellent analysis of the Popular Front's economic and political difficulties see Jean-Marcel Jeanneney, "La politique économique de Léon Blum," in *Léon Blum: chef de gouvernement*, 1936–1937, ed. Pierre Renouvin and René Remond (Paris: Presses de la Fondation Nationale des Sciences Politiques, 1981), pp. 207–32.

57. In 1940, as Vichy's minister of labor, Belin oversaw the dissolution of the CGT.

58. See the anniversary issue, "Sur les Nouveaux cahiers," *Nouveaux cahiers*, no. 2 (March 1, 1938), p. 14.

59. Cabaud, p. 180, is surely correct in assuming that Weil's pacifism led her to tailor facts according to her desires. Pétrement's defense, 2:171, of Weil's "moderation" and objectivity is less imposing.

60. *AD*, pp. 43–45.

61. Pétrement, 2:217.

62. See her letter to Joë Bousquet, quoted by Pétrement, 2:207.

63. Pétrement, 2:252–53.

64. *AD*, p. 45.

65. Ibid., pp. 99–100.

66. In an unpublished note in DB, Weil comments on her "feeling of impossibility in physical pain. Thought is violently deprived of everything it clings to. Deprived of orientation. Passive thought—deprived of that which it needs for existence. Mélange of being and nonbeing. Waiting without hope. Thought close to thing."

67. Quoted by Pétrement, 2:234.

68. Pétrement, 2:235.

69. If Alain was right that war totally cancels justice, then individual acts of justice within war foredoom their agents. This fatalism informs Weil's drama *Venise sauvée.*

70. Letter to Jean Wahl, quoted by Cabaud, p. 204.

71. André Weil had read these works at the Sorbonne under the eminent Sylvain Lévi. While teaching mathematics in India (1930–32) he had pursued his interest in Eastern religious culture. He also preceded her in reading the Spanish mystics. Why, given her brother's interest in this literature, had she not read it before 1940?

72. This is the title of an excellent discussion of Weil's nonpolitical wartime writings, Miklos Vetö's *La métaphysique religieuse de Simone Weil* (Paris: Vrin, 1971).

73. Quoted by Pétrement, 2:333.

74. Quoted by Pétrement, 2:346.

75. Jean Rabaut, "Simone Weil, anarchiste et chrétienne," *L'âge nouveau* 61 (May 1951), 21. Rabaut believes that Weil suffered from feelings of inferiority because she was "ugly" and that her "masochist preponderance" determined in her "an extreme generosity."

76. Letter to Gilbert Kahn, quoted by Pétrement, 2:346.

77. Peter Novick, *The Resistance versus Vichy* (London: Chatto and Windus, 1968), p. 134.

78. Quoted by Pétrement, 2:119.

79. Quoted by Pétrement, 2:307–8 (original English version with French translation).

80. There is some evidence to support Weil on pro-British attitudes during the Occupation. See the memoirs of Frida Knight, *The French Resistance, 1940 to 1944* (London: Lawrence and Wishart, 1975), p. 81.

81. Pétrement, 2:326.

82. The journal was begun in November 1941 in Lyons, edited by R. P. Chaillet and Louis Curvillier. Chaillet claims the Témoignage was founded autonomous of Combat and other Resistance movements, but Combat did help in diffusing the Témoignage *Cahiers*. See Henri Noguères, *Histoire de la Résistance en France de 1940 à 1945*, (Paris: Robert Laffont, 1969), 2:209, 634.

83. For a comprehensive history of the movement see Renée Bedarida, *Les armes de l'esprit: Témoignage chrétien, 1941–1944* (Paris: Les Editions Ouvrières, 1977). On p. 103, n. 28, David says that when Weil left France, she passed her distribution tasks to an agnostic, Jean Tortel of *Cahiers du Sud*.

84. "Simone Weil, la Résistance et la question juive," Entretien entre Marie-Louise Blum et Wladimir Rabi, *CSW* 4 (June 1981): 80.

85. According to Dr. Louis Bercher, one of Weil's syndicalist friends, who saw her in Marseilles in July 1941, Weil's "preoccupations had assumed maximum intensity" despite his assurances given "since 1938, or perhaps even before" that just souls are saved even beyond the church. The church's ambivalent responses gave her no rest. See Pétrement, 2:338–39.

86. Cabaud, p. 305; Pétrement, 2:408. Her acquaintances in Combat could have afforded her many opportunities for service and danger at home.

87. *AD*, p. 30, no. 1. See Pétrement, 2:408: "In the situation of that time, she could still reckon that if her parents settled in a village, they would not run great danger." If Weil thought that, then her awareness of reality was fantastically limited. It is hard to believe

that either she or her parents were deaf and blind to what was happening. One of her letters from New York in English, quoted in Pétrement, 2:426, indicates at least her parents' awareness: "Although my parents, who wanted to escape anti-Semitism, put great pressure upon me to make me go with them, I would never have left France without the hope that through coming here I could take a greater part in the struggle, the danger and the suffering of this war."

88. See the unpublished letter to a friend, quoted by Cabaud, p. 305.

89. Letter to Perrin, May 26, 1942, *AD*, p. 69.

90. Letter to Maurice Schumann in *EL*, p. 199.

91. Pétrement, 2:487: "I remember she once told me that remorse was what she feared most in the world."

92. Ibid., p. 429.

93. Cabaud, p. 310.

94. Quoted by Pétrement, 2:432.

95. At the Information Department she had regular access to such underground organs as *Liberté, Pantagruel, Valmy, Socialisme et liberté,* and even, from the Sorbonne, *Défence de la France.*

96. *EL*, p. 212.

Chapter 2

1. Quoted by Jacques Cabaud, *L'expérience vecue de Simone Weil* (Paris: Plon, 1957), p. 383.

2. The definitive biographical study is André Sernin, *Alain, un sage dans la cité* (Paris: Robert Laffont, 1985). It draws upon many of Alain's unpublished works, including his journal. For a comprehensive bibliography see Suzanne Dewitt, *Alain, essai de bibliographie (1893–juin 1961)* (Brussels: Commission Belge de Bibliographie, 1961).

3. Alain, *Histoire de mes pensées* in his *Les arts et les dieux* (Paris: Gallimard, 1958), p. 69. Hereafter the Pléiade editions are designated as follows: *Les arts et les dieux* as LA; *Propos* (Paris: Gallimard, 1956) as *Pr*, and *Les passions et la sagesse* (Paris: Gallimard, 1960) as *PS*. Dating from 1906, Alain published over three thousand *propos*, running two to three pages each, in Rouen's *La dépêche*, only a fraction of them edited for the Pléiade edition.

4. *Les sources de la mythologie enfantine* in LA, p. 1147.

5. From notes labeled "Cours Sevigné," DB.

6. *LA*, p. 29.

7. André Weil has suggested to me a reason for her indifference, that Aristotle has no place in Greek mathematical tradition. Interview of July 23, 1985. Some of Weil's notes from Alain's lectures on Plato and Aristotle survive in CD.

8. *LA*, p. 69.

9. Ibid., p. 30.

10. *Définitions* in LA, pp. 1052, 1057–58.

11. *Souvenirs concernant Jules Lagneau* in *PS*, p. 774.

12. *LA*, p. 185. On p. 85 he suggests that mathematics might be styled "an eyes-closed practice. . . . The mathematician vaunts his ignorance; such is his constant method."

13. *Les idées et les âges* in *PS*, p. 66.

14. *LA*, p. 175.

15. Ibid., p. 59. Weil uses the same metaphor in describing the proper employment of irreconcilable terms in a contradiction.

16. Ibid., pp. 43, 42. The model of this detached but dedicated effort is Alain's essay on Spinoza.

17. Ibid., p. 23.

18. Ibid., p. 162.

19. *Définitions*, p. 1032.

20. In his study *Alain* (Paris: Domat, 1956), p. 21, André Maurois notes that the master scorned the presentation of ideas "en résumé" and graced his own "not by logical framework but by metaphors and parables, and by profound poetry."

21. All these remarks are in CD.

22. André Maurois in his preface to Alain, *Propos* (Paris: Gallimard, 1956), p. xiv.

23. *AD*, pp. 38–39.

24. Ibid., p. 39.

25. *Définitions*, p. 1098. That God, too, can be apprehended not as fact but as the object of a consciously free will is posited in Alain's note on "spiritualisme," p. 1092.

26. Alain, *Propos sur la religion* (Paris: Rieder, 1938), p. 173; *AD*, pp. 132, 144.

27. *LA*, p. 109.

28. Alain, *Les saisons de l'esprit* (Paris: Nouvelle Revue Française, 1937), pp. 284, 90; see also *LA*, p. 182.

29. Alain, *Entretiens au bord de la mer* (Paris: Nouvelle Revue Française, 1930), p. 271.

30. Simone Pétrement, "Sur la religion d'Alain," *Revue de metaphysique et de morale* 60 (1955): 321.

31. *Les dieux* in *LA*, pp. 1323, 1056.

32. This essay is discussed in "Beauty, Bread of the Soul," Chapter 6 in this volume.

33. The essay, running to five legal-sized pages, is in TPAG. It might date from the time Weil was studying Kant under Léon Brunschvicq at L'Ecole Normale.

34. Weil forgets that Berkeley's God is beyond nature, beyond ideas and ourselves. Her complaint belongs at Spinoza's door.

35. This twelve-page essay, with Alain's marginal remarks, is in TPAG.

36. Weil's terms might be transposed into Spinoza's: thing and idea have discrete existence. Thought and extension, although united in substance (God), are independent modes or attributes of being.

37. Gilbert Kahn, in a discussion of Jeanne Alexandre, "Rencontre de Simone Weil et d'Alain," in *Alain: philosophe de la culture et théoricien de la démocratie*, Colloque de Cerisy-la-Salle July 21–August 1, 1974 (Paris: Association "Les Amis d'Alain," 1976), pp. 201–2, characterizes their differences as philosophical, that in Alain a Cartesian optimism predominated. Weil was "perhaps spinozist, rather without wishing to be." Kahn's distinction between Alain's "certaine prudence" and Weil's "engagement total"

seems overdrawn, for it was Weil's prudence that kept her free of party memberships in the 1930s and church affiliation later.

38. See the preface to his *Spinoza* (Paris: Mellottée, 1949, and Gallimard [augmented ed.], 1986).

39. "Le vrai de l'homme," ibid., pp. 166–67.

40. "Spinoza," *propos* of July 12, 1921, in *Pr*, p. 250; see also "vanité" in *Définitions*, p. 1097.

41. Emile Chartier, "Valeur morale de la joie d'après Spinoza," *Revue de metaphysique et de morale* 7 (1899): 759–64.

42. Alain, *Spinoza*, pp. 80–81. These remarks paraphrase the discussion in Spinoza's *Ethics* IV, proofs 50, 54.

43. *Vingt leçons sur les beaux-arts* (sixteenth lesson) in *LA*, p. 581.

44. *Propos* of February 28, 1922, "Le grand crystal," included in *Spinoza*, p 160. In *PS*, p. 1272, Alain describes Spinoza's system as a kind of imprisonment; time itself dies, "everything is made and without remedy."

45. "Spinoza" in Alain, *Abrégés pour les aveugles*, in *PS*, p. 808.

46. *Souvenirs concernant Jules Lagneau* in *PS*, p. 777.

47. Pétrement, 1:128–29. "His method of instruction consisted chiefly of telling stories whose relevance to the question at hand it often seemed difficult to grasp."

48. Pétrement, 1:157–58, defends Brunschvicq from this charge by suggesting that he had an intellectual prejudice, that "it was the ideas and methods of Alain's disciples which displeased him, as his displeased them."

49. "Science et perception dans Descartes" in *S*, pp. 24, 29.

50. Ibid., p. 45.

51. Ibid., p. 56.

52. Ibid., p. 61.

53. See *CS*, pp. 47, 274, 297 (the soul is murdered by contact with God), and 305.

54. *S*, pp. 68, 71, 74.

55. Cf. Alain on imagination in *Définitions*, p. 1064. His remarks are wholly negative. This faculty tortures us with anxiety and "passions," he says. It can be killed only by action. Weil accepted this psychological estimate and gives to imagination scarcely any positive value as a creative or harmonizing force.

56. *S*, p. 74. In "Le beau et le bien" she characterizes aesthetic contemplation as the identification, by distancing, of all that is not me.

57. *S*, p. 83.

58. Ibid., p. 95.

Chapter 3

1. Even in midcentury, the grip of that spirituality exerted itself, as in Vichy's back-to-the-land injunctions. De Gaulle's quixotic referendum on decentralization is a more recent, if oblique, expression of this physiocratic bias.

2. See George Lichtheim, *The Origins of Socialism* (New York: Praeger, 1969), pp. 60–

62, and the discussion by Tony Judt, *Marxism and the French Left: Studies on Labour and Politics in France, 1830–1981* (Oxford: Oxford University Press, 1986), pp. 24–114, esp. pp. 60–68.

3. Judt, pp. 96–97.

4. On women, see ibid., pp. 44–46, 123. On peasant emigration, see Philippe Bernard and Henri Dubief, *The Decline of the Third Republic, 1914–1938* (Cambridge: Cambridge University Press, 1985), p. 142.

5. Georges Lefranc, *Le syndicalisme en France* (Paris: Presses Universitaires de France, 1953), p. 63.

6. This essay was published by the teachers' union periodical, *Bulletin de la Section de la Haute-Loire* (Le Puy) 13 (November 1931): 69–72. All translations in the text are from the six-page typescript in AHS.

7. Ibid.

8. Ibid.

9. Ibid.

10. In her last year at the Normale, she included Lenin on the list of authors "to relearn well." See Pétrement, 1:165. She might also have been familiar with Rudolf Hilferding's theories on finance capital.

11. See her 1934 essay on a "proletarian" uprising in 1378, in *EHP*, pp. 91–92, in which she compares the workers' insurrection in Machiavelli's Florence to those in Paris in June 1848 and in Moscow in February 1917. She credits Machiavelli's analysis of the uprising with "an astonishing precision in everything that corresponds to our present preoccupations."

12. Weil's view does not do full justice to Gisors, the elder who takes opium not to overcome a sense of his own nothingness but to suppress the intolerable tension between the mind's sense of its own eternity and the anguished awareness of life's mortality.

13. The essay is simply titled "La condition humaine" and is located in HS.

14. *L'effort*, no. 288 (January 2, 1932), pp. 1–2. The article is unsigned. In HS there is a "deuxième ébauche" of this essay, in Weil's handwriting. Translations here are from this second "sketch."

15. See Ernst Nolte, *Three Faces of Fascism* (New York: Holt, Rinehart and Winston, 1965).

16. *OL*, p. 32. See the prospectus of Dandieu and Aron, *La révolution nécessaire*, which extols *personalisme*, and Weil's assertion in *OL*, p. 84: "The enlightened goodwill of men acting as individuals is the only possible principle of social progress."

17. Quoted by Jean Touchard in "L'esprit des années 1930: une tentative de renouvellement de la pensée française," in *Tendances politiques sans la vie française depuis 1789*, ed. Guy Michaud (Paris: Hachette, 1960), p. 93.

18. From the staff of *L'ordre nouveau*, Henri Daniel-Rops, Denis de Rougement, Alexandre Marc, and Dandieu himself contributed essays to Mounier's *Esprit*. Other collaborators included Raymond Aron, Nicholas Berdyaev, Henri Guillemin, and Jacques Maritain.

19. Quoted by Touchard, p. 114, n. 31.

20. Quoted by Pétrement, 1:401.

21. This review may be found in HS. It runs to three legal pages in Weil's longhand.

22. The pathetic vagaries of Drieu la Rochelle and Robert Brasillach suggest the prophetic force of this statement.

23. *OL*, p. 117.

24. Although Weil has often been denied the title of humanist and never claimed it for herself, "Réflexions" remains one of humanism's triumphant expressions. See Marcelle Monseau, "L'humanisme de SW dans la condition ouvrière," *Revue de l'Université Laval* 12 (January 1958): 454–62: "There triumphs here a humanism profoundly respectful of human worth" (461); R. J. Mostyn's review of Richard Rees's *Simone Weil*, in the *Humanist* 82 (October 1966): 298, contending that Weil's "stoic" acceptance of "human impotence in the face of intractable contradictions" betrays an "anti-Humanist" attitude; Kathleen Nott, "Religious Humanist," *Observer*, June 19, 1966, p. 27, where Weil, for all her rejection of collectivistic progress, is tagged "a new and genuine kind of Humanist—a unique person trying to re-define the human universal"; Rosalind Murray, "The Onlooker," in *Tablet*, June 13, 1953, 516, identifies Weil's expressed obstacles to religious orthodoxy as "common ground among contemporary humanists."

25. A one-page unpublished essay in HS. Pétrement, 2:282, dates this work to the autumn of 1936.

26. See Lefranc, *Le syndicalisme*, p. 64.

27. Pétrement, 2:84–85.

28. This phrase comes from her "Réflexions brutales."

29. George Orwell, *The Road to Wigan Pier* (1937; rpt. Harmondsworth: Penguin, 1984), p. 103. This quotation might be challenged as unfair because Orwell is writing about the English working classes, not the French. But in the case of Weil and Orwell similarities far outweigh differences: he wrote at the same time as she and about the same problems. Both were leftist mavericks. Both were bourgeois educators who tried to escape what Orwell called the "class racket" by taking on *la vie ouvrière* at quixotic personal extremes. Some of Orwell's apprenticeship in the proletariat he learned in Paris as a *plongeur* or bottlewasher, a term of trial he partly fictionalized in *Down and Out in Paris and London*.

30. Founded in Belgium in 1925, the JOC quickly spread to France. Until the Fourth Republic it eschewed political partisanship (for Weil, a point in its favor) and served as one of the most influential Catholic Action groups. By the mid-1930s its membership exceeded sixty-five thousand. With parish clergy backing it, it formed an invaluable nexus between the generally conservative church hierarchy and the alienated proletariat. See William Bosworth, *Catholicism and Crisis in Modern France* (Princeton: Princeton University Press, 1962), pp. 35, 106–7.

31. A one-page typescript of "Sur une tentative" may be found in AHS.

32. It begins, "Ce qui est regrettable, s'il faut tout dire, dans les organisations ouvrières," in CG, with Weil's letter drafts to Emmanuel Mounier.

33. The typescript ends here. I have not been able to locate a handwritten copy. This fragment is probably a variant sketch of her undated letter to Emmanuel Mounier discussed below.

34. Quoted by Pétrement, 2:128–29.

35. Undated, unpublished letter to Emmanuel Mounier, CG.

36. Aquinas learned this from Aristotle, she says. She seems to refer to the *Politics* 1334a 11–18, that many necessities of life are prerequisite to leisure, which is the condition of virtue.

37. As she says they were chastised "in June," a clear reference to the sit-in strikes of June 1936.

38. From the draft she quotes, Pétrement deletes the following question, which comes directly after the remarks on love of others: "Why isn't there a Christian separatism, why no question of founding a Christian nation in respect to the gospels' morality?" Few of her remarks better indicate how remote Weil was from conventional Christian assumptions.

39. *AD*, p. 37.

40. "A propos du syndicalisme unique, apolitique, obligatoire," in HS. Subsequent quotations are from this essay. The archival note suggests that this five-page essay dates from 1937, the year of the Statut du travail to which Weil briefly alludes.

Auguste Detoeuf, director at Alsthom, was a manager of unusual sophistication and receptivity. Because Weil had no experience of the roles managers and technicians played in industrial organization, her understanding of them was marginal and abstract. When she came to know Detoeuf, she gave way to fanciful scenarios for creating optimal relations between the *patronat* and the workers, as indicated by her plans in an undated letter to Detoeuf in *CO*, p. 253. Her corporatist notion of a nonarbitrary subordination of labor, in which workers understood and accepted "orders corresponding to necessity," owed much to Detoeuf's openness and sharing of ideas.

41. See Plato's *Republic* 454e: the equality of men and women in the state's guardianship; 457c: the community of parenthood; 473d: the equation of philosopher and monarch.

42. *OL*, pp. 115–16.

43. Roy Pierce, *Contemporary French Political Thought* (London: Oxford University Press, 1966), p. 104. Pierce writes of Weil's "Utopia," but his own analysis shows she is no programmatic utopist, and his qualifying language (pp. 94, 106) seems to concede as much. The basic point is that she sees a utopic *model* as a necessary but unrealizable goal for social organization. Never does she presume all would be well once or if only her Cartesian paradise could be set up.

44. These and the subsequent unpublished notes come from "Feuilles détachés sur le travail en usine," the archival rubric for a series of notes in HS.

45. "La classe ouvrière et le Statut du Travail," dated February 1938, HS.

46. "Feuilles détachés." These remarks may be compared with Weil's first letter to Jacques Lafitte, dated to the spring of 1936 by P. Guillerme, "Deux lettres inédites de Simone Weil," *Dialogue* 12 (September 1973): 454–64. Lafitte, author of *Réflexions sur la science des machines* (1932), had hypothesized an organicism in the construction and use of machinery. It implied that division of labor could follow what he called "technomorphic organization." Weil's letter took up the need to seek "a superior form of mechanical work where the worker's creative power has a much greater field than in artisan's work" (p. 461). This remark suggests that Weil, no Luddite, was willing to entertain the positive potential of technology, perhaps in order to stay its menaces. Thus the utopic sketch she sends to Lafitte includes, like "My utopia," a definitive role for technology: "I imagine a de-

centralized economy where our industrial prisons would be replaced by shops scattered all over. In these shops you would find extremely supple automatic machines to satisfy in large measure the region's industrial needs. The workers, all very highly qualified, would pass most of their time in regulating. The distance between the worker and the engineer would be effaced in such a way that their two functions could perhaps be assumed by the same man" (p. 462).

47. Georges Sorel, *Matériaux d'une théorie du prolétariat* (1921; rpt. Paris: Slatkine, 1981), p. 138.

48. CO, p. 109.

49. "A propos du syndicalisme unique, apolitique, obligatoire," HS.

50. The journal entries are in Weil's neatest hand, but the writing is at times almost illegibly small. Peculiarly, this is true even when she has a good deal of space left on the page. The Gallimard texts give a very imperfect idea of the open spaces. The impression of brevity and incompletion recalls Weil's physical debilities through most of her factory days.

51. See, for example, CO, pp. 156–57, where she sets down a procedure for each kind of work: to make a clear account of possible difficulties, to note how the machinery can get out of order, what mistakes to avoid, and so on. There follows a list of no less than sixteen "stupidities committed."

52. CO, p. 45.

53. Ibid., pp. 88, 96, 142.

54. Ibid., pp. 52, 67.

55. Ibid., pp. 48, 117.

56. Ibid., p. 124.

57. Ibid., pp. 55, 56. These words underscore the need for autonomy in work, without subjection to another's orders. The factory could have been a decent place to work had there been no overseers.

58. Ibid., p. 66.

59. Ibid., pp. 108, 110.

60. See Anne Reynaud, "La joie chez Simone Weil," CSW 10 (June 1987): 139–52.

61. CO, pp. 52, 53, 60, 142.

62. Ibid., p. 72.

63. Ibid., p. 144.

64. Ibid., p. 154.

65. Ibid., p. 164.

66. In CO, p. 164, she faults Alain for his "superficial" view of mechanics. When he heard of her factory jobs, he grumbled that surely she had better things to do. See André Sernin, *Alain: un sage dans la cité* (Paris: Robert Laffont, 1985), p. 345.

67. CO, p. 167.

68. "Un appel aux ouvriers de R." in CO, p. 177.

69. Camus may have drawn upon these insights in *L'homme revolté* (Paris: Gallimard, 1951), p. 256: "Misery and degeneracy have not ceased to be what they were before Marx and what, contrary to the usual view, he did not want them to be: factors of servitude, not of revolution."

70. "Lettres à un ingénieur directeur d'usine" in CO, pp. 191, 193.

71. Ibid., p. 197.

72. Ibid., p. 206. For an extended attack on Weil's letters to Bernard and the essays of *Oppression et liberté* see the Stalinist critic Jeanette Colombel, "Simone Weil et la condition ouvrière," *La nouvelle critique* 8 (February 1956): 46–66.

73. He did, however, welcome her essay on Antigone to his factory periodical, *Entre nous*. Jacques Cabaud sees in Weil's characterization of the Sophoclean hero a kind of self-portrait, but her exchanges with Bernard suggest that her closing remarks on Creon were meant as a caveat to him: "This man who knew so well how to speak like a boss collapses, annihilated by grief." With the final choral admonition that proud men pay "through terrible suffering" the point could not have been lost on Bernard. Like Antigone before the unbending king, she had found him intransigent to her pleas for more humane concessions to his workers.

74. See Lefranc, *Le syndicalisme en France*, pp. 70–72.

75. CO, p. 231.

76. "La victoire des métallos" exists in an elegant longhand copy done by Mme Selma Weil in HS. The upper-right-hand corners are paginated, from "36" to "56."

77. Ibid., p. "39."

78. Ibid., p. "48."

79. Ibid., p. "56."

80. For a review of various rightist responses to the Popular Front and the strikes of 1936 see Charles Micaud, *The French Right Wing and Nazi Germany, 1933–1939: A Study of Public Opinion* (1943; rpt. New York: Octagon Books, 1972), pp. 108–11.

81. For a succinct and helpful review of political and economic issues, see Gordon Wright, *France in Modern Times*, 3d ed. (New York: Norton, 1981), pp. 386–405.

82. Pétrement, 1:277.

83. Her six published essays on the situation in Germany are gathered in *EHP*, pp. 117–96 and are translated in Dorothy T. McFarland's *Simone Weil: Formative Writings, 1929–1941* (Amherst: University of Massachusetts Press, 1987).

84. The unpublished review of Trotsky's *Histoire de la Révolution russe*, 1 (Paris: Rieder, 193?) is in AHS: "He applies better than any so-called impartial historian Spinoza's beautiful formula 'Concerning human actions, do not weep, do not laugh, do not become angry, but understand.'"

85. See, for example, her letter of April 1930 to R. Louzon, quoted by Pétrement, 1:263–65. Trotsky did not demonstrate that Russia was incapable of sealing itself off from the world and realizing a socialist state "en vase clos."

86. Weil seems to be adverting to chapter 7 of volume 1, "Five Days: February 23–27, 1917." See the Max Eastman translation, *The History of the Russian Revolution* (1932; rpt. New York: Pathfinder Press, 1980), esp. pp. 111, 117 ("Without a look back, the masses made their own history") and p. 118 ("We must lay it down as a general rule for those days that the higher the leaders, the further they lagged behind"). In chapter 8, however, Trotsky emphasizes that the substantial leadership of the revolutionary parties, including Lenin and Martov, was in exile. He opposes the contention that the revolt was spontaneous; rather, the workers and soldiers had been for years seasoned to "an accumulation of experience and creative consciousness which the revolutionary insurrection and its victory only completed" (p. 152).

87. "Premières impressions d'Allemagne," *EHP*, p. 124, a series of excerpts from a letter to her parents, quoted in its entirety by Pétrement, 1:280–83. Weil observes that the *Arbeitsdienst*, a virtual "military enslavement," might be the only way to sustain the most demoralized among the unemployed. *Chomeurs* still propagandizing (i.e., communists) would not be able to tolerate it. "But it is to be feared that they are fighting all alone and will be exterminated." Weil read the Nazis' intent with prophetic accuracy.

88. Weil's analysis is the more striking in view of the substantial growth of the Communists' representation in the Reichstag. Between 1928 and 1932, their numbers nearly doubled. The 6 million votes won by their presidential candidate, Ernst Thälmann, in the last republican election frightened the financial and industrial powers into dumping Weimar democracy and supporting Hitler.

89. "L' Allemagne en attente," *EHP*, 141–42.

90. "La situation en Allemagne," *EHP*, p. 155.

91. See *La critique sociale* 9 (September 1933), p. 137.

92. "La situation en Allemagne," *EHP*, p. 157.

93. Quoted by Pétrement, 1:281.

94. "Faisons le point," HS. This two-page unpublished essay probably dates from February 1933, after Hitler took power (January 30), but before the Comintern, reacting to his triumph, recommended in March that its European affiliates now make common cause with leftist reform parties against national socialism.

95. "La situation en Allemagne," *EHP*, p. 182n.

96. CG; the addressee, if in fact one was intended, is unknown. Subsequent quotations are from this source.

97. "La situation en Allemagne," *EHP*, p. 150.

98. This passage comes from an unpublished and fragmentary essay, "Front unique et unité syndicale," included in a folio entitled "Tentes pour l'unité syndicale—1933," HS.

99. V. I. Lenin, *The Proletarian Revolution and the Renegade Kautsky*, in *Collected Works*, 28 (Moscow: Foreign Languages Publishing House, 1965), p. 477.

100. "Faisons le point." See note 94.

101. This letter is dated "1932—début 1933?" in CG. Weil's most substantial attacks on bureaucracy come in her essays gathered in *OL*. She emphasizes bureaucracy's ubiquity, that it enjoys a soulless autonomy in any modern economy. In the United States and the Soviet Union, its three forms—unions, industry, government—have attained a unifying perfection. She also notes apparently contradictory tendencies of bureaucracy, that its unlimited parasitism entails anarchy as it takes over the initiatives proper to individual thought and transforms them into collectivity: "Thus in all the domains of thought, individual privilege is subordinated to vast mechanisms which crystallize the collective life, and this to the point where the sense of what true thinking is becomes almost lost" (*OL*, pp. 146–47).

102. Her penchant for categorical, sweeping statements might owe inspiration, for example, to his attack on centralization: see Pierre-Joseph Proudhon, *Capacité politique des classes ouvrières* (Paris: Riviere, 1924), p. 297, and the attack on the state's tyrannical parasitism in his *Idée générale de la révolution* (Paris: Riviere, 1923), p. 376. On Proudhon's influence in the 1930s see Touchard, p. 105, n. 19.

103. Pétrement, 1:357–58.

104. This essay, reprinted in *EHP*, originally appeared in *L'école émancipée*, July 23, 1932, a journal of the Fédération unitaire de l'enseignement. Although a CGTU member, it did not follow the "Moscow line." See Pétrement, 1:297.

105. *EHP*, p. 208.

106. *OL*, p. 28.

107. Ibid., pp. 33, 37–38. It is the language of someone awaiting a firing squad in the resolution not to accept a blindfold. As Pétrement, 1:153, notes, many of Weil's leftist comrades were daunted by her vigorous defense of positions that her own analysis showed to be virtually hopeless.

108. Quoted by Pétrement, 1:355. In another article the same month, Trotsky equivocated about Soviet bureaucracy. It was irresponsible, he granted, but at the same time legitimate because it was not derived from property relations set up by the revolution. Its extirpation could only be achieved by police action. It is possible that Weil had read this article and used it when she confronted him. Of Trotsky late in the 1920s, Robert Wistrich, *Trotsky: Fate of a Revolutionary* (New York: Stein and Day, 1979), p. 161, remarks: "He seriously underestimated the power of the bureaucracy and its autonomy, the degree to which it had created its own social support, independent of other class forces which it kept fragmented and powerless through terror and repression." This observation substantiates Weil's position uncannily.

109. Weil parenthesizes this remark in her notes, so it is not clear whether she was bold enough to make it in Trotsky's presence or simply interpolated it as a subsequent reflection. There is no evidence to support Isaac Deutscher's claim, in *The Prophet Outcast* (New York: Oxford University Press, 1963), p. 270, that Trotsky "spent many an hour in discussion with Simone Weil, a 'Trotskyist' at this time." She talked with him subsequently but only briefly, at a meeting where he tried to promote his pet scheme, a Fourth International, before some socialists.

110. Simone Weil to Emile Chartier, October 13, 1934, quoted by André Sernin, *Alain: un sage dans la cité* (Paris: Robert Laftont, 1985), p. 330. Alain passed Weil's recommendation to André Malraux, then a Stalinist, at the *Nouvelle revue française*, which rejected Souveraine's manuscript. Plon accepted it in 1935.

111. See George Orwell, *The Road to Wigan Pier* (1937; rpt. Harmondsworth: Penguin, 1984), p. 155: "As for the philosophical side of Marxism, the pea-and-thimble trick with those three mysterious entities, thesis, antithesis, and synthesis, I have never met a working man who had the faintest interest in it."

112. A four-page essay in Weil's tiniest longhand, in HS. Subsequent quotations are from this source.

Chapter 4

1. Pétrement, 2:94.

2. See his letter to Mme Morre-Lambelin, August 8, 1915, quoted by André Sernin, *Alain: un sage dans la cité* (Paris: Robert Laffont, 1985), p. 175.

3. Alain to Marie Salomon, November 13, 1915, quoted ibid., p. 179.

4. On Alain's comparison of factory work with war service, see his *propos* 13, "Mécanisme," in *Mars ou la guerre jugée* (Paris: Gallimard, 1936), p. 41.

5. "Réponse à une question d'Alain," *EHP*, p. 246.

6. See the *propos* "Des sacrifices humaines" in *Mars*, p. 45.

7. "Quelques réflexions concernant l'honneur et la dignité nationale," a variant of the "Réponse," *EHP*, p. 396.

8. "Réponse au questionnaire d'Alain," yet another variant of the "Réponse," *EHP*, p. 396.

9. "Réponse à une question d'Alain," *EHP*, p. 245.

10. Georges Bernanos, *Les grands cimetières sous la lune* (Paris: Plon, 1938), p. 154.

11. Ibid., pp. 99, 113.

12. Ibid., p. 155.

13. "Lettre à Georges Bernanos," *EHP*, p. 220. The letter is undated. There is no evidence that Bernanos replied, but see Jean-Loup Bernanos, *Georges Bernanos: À la merci des passants* (Paris: Plon, 1986), pp. 291–92.

14. *EHP*, p. 223.

15. They are amply documented in Hugh Thomas, *The Spanish Civil War*, rev. ed. (New York: Harper & Row, 1977), pp. 258–81.

16. *EHP*, p. 209.

17. Simone Pétrement, "La pesanteur et la grace," *Cahiers du Sud*, no. 289 (1948), p. 499.

18. *EHP*, p. 215.

19. Ibid., p. 214.

20. Ibid., p. 217. The communist rank and file in Madrid, instructed by Moscow's concern for its own foreign relations, sought to minimize the war's revolutionary potential.

21. *EHP*, p. 217.

22. Thomas, pp. 319, 430.

23. *EHP*, p. 219.

24. Five years later, Orwell, in "Looking Back at the Spanish War," *Homage to Catalonia* (1938; rpt. Harmondsworth: Penguin, 1962), p. 235, summed up the meaning of the deceit: "The very concept of objective truth is fading out of the world. After all, the chances are that those lies, or at any rate, similar lies, will pass into history." This grim conclusion coincides with Weil's own assumption about the historiography of the mighty. If justice runs fugitive from the victors' camp, it takes truth with it. Did Spain give her this insight or had it been implicit in her 1933 essay, "Réflexions sur la guerre"? There, she argues that if a revolutionary war necessarily entails the erection of oppressive machinery to serve its ends, those ends are debased into a counterrevolution.

25. Franz Borkenau, *The Spanish Cockpit* (1937; rpt. Ann Arbor: University of Michigan Press, 1963), pp. 288–89.

26. Ibid., pp. 291, 292.

27. Orwell, *Homage to Catalonia*, p. 173.

28. Michel Collinet, "Simone Weil: anarchiste et chrétienne," *L'âge nouveau* 61 (May 1951): 25.

29. *C*, 2:165.

30. See *E*, p. 49, and Alain's *Definitions* in *Les arts et les dieux* (Paris: Nouvelle Revue Française [Pleiade ed.], 1958), p. 1064.

31. *C*, 1:56.

32. Weil supported the CGT-CGPF collaboration in her "Principes d'un projet pour un régime nouveau," *CO*, p. 286, urging them to address the professional retraining of the unemployed.

33. David Thomson, *Democracy in France since 1870* (New York: Oxford University Press, 1964), p. 198.

34. *OL*, p. 155; see also pp. 17–21.

35. It was no solitary apprehension. The Committee of Vigilance of Anti-Fascist Intellectuals was formed shortly after the February riots, but Weil was one of perhaps few who had a vivid image from Germany of the true face of fascism.

36. Notes on "Fascisme—mouvement ultraréactionnaire" in AHS.

37. "Nouvel état du capitalisme" in AHS.

38. Notes on "National socialisme die 'Fat' mystique du travail" in AHS. In a letter to Perrin, *AD*, p. 24, she admitted to a natural and dangerous inclination to crime and gregariousness: "By natural disposition I am extremely influenceable, influenceable to excess, especially in collectivities. I know that if I had before me at this moment twenty young Germans singing Nazi songs, part of my soul would immediately become Nazi."

39. "Sur les contradictions du Marxisme," *OL*, p. 202.

40. "Nouvel état du capitalisme" AHS.

41. V. I. Lenin, "The War and Russian Social Democracy," in *Collected Works* (Moscow: Foreign Languages Publishing House, 1964), p. 21.

42. See "Réponse à une question d'Alain," *EHP*, pp. 246–47.

43. She ignores the Spartans' enslavement of Messenia. This is but one instance of her uncritial regard for the Greeks.

44. "Quelques réflexions sur le patriotisme" in HS.

45. She had already made this point in her essay "Après la mort du Comité des 22," discussed in the previous chapter.

46. All of these notes come from AHS.

47. "La déclaration de la CGT," *Le libertaire*, no. 519 (October 23, 1936), p. 8. It should be read in tandem with "Projet d'une section de consultation pour les conflits sociaux." Both are in HS. Weil understood the excesses of agitation and abdication as functions of the workers' helpless ignorance in assuming new tasks subsequent to their June victories. While scolding them for giving the country "this impression of agitation and of weakness which is the best encouragement for fascism," she does not identify the communists' responsibility in furthering that impression.

The value of "Projet" is its indication of what "worker control" meant. Weil points to the CGT as an aid to workers' cohesion, furnishing the unions "precise instructions" on how not to become intransigent at a false turn and how to resist the baiting *patronat* with arguments.

On labor's resistance to the *patronat*'s production plans and the CGT leadership, see Michael Seidman, "The Birth of the Weekend and the Revolts against Work: The Workers of the Paris Region during the Popular Front (1936–1938)," *French Historical Studies* 12 (Fall 1981): 249–76.

48. "Faut-il graisser les godillots," *Vigilance* 44–45 (October 27, 1936), reprinted in *EHP*, pp. 248–49.

49. "Quelques remarques sur la plan de C.G.T." in HS.

50. "Va-t-on reparler du plan?" in HS.

51. "Il faudrait aussi un plan de la C.G.T. pour la politique internationale" in HS.

52. "Non-intervention généralisée," *EHP*, p. 252.

53. Yet, in "A quoi correspond l'organisation des tendances dans notre fédération?" (dated "1933?" in HS), she remarks that in 1914 the CGT, despite its independence and revolutionary spirit, capitulated to the general war fervor, though less dishonorably, she adds, than the Second International.

54. "Les dangers de guerre et les conquêtes Ouvrière," published in *Syndicats* 28 (April 22, 1937); the manuscript is in HS. It has the novelty of ending mid-word.

55. "Prestige national et bonneur ouvrières," published in *Syndicats* 26 (April 8, 1937). The manuscript is in HS.

56. This unpublished essay in HS bids comparison with Robespierre's final address of July 28, 1794 (8 Thermidor, II), which Weil copied out. Her two-page draft is in AHS. Subsequent quotations are from the essay in HS.

57. "France-Allemagne et lutte de classes" in AHS.

58. "Ne recommençons pas la guerre de Troie" was published in *Les nouveaux cahiers*, April 1 and April 15, 1937. The first quote is from the reprint in *EHP*, p. 257. The post-Homeric *Schadenfreud* begins with the sixth-century poet, Stesichorus, is mentioned by Plato (*Republic* 586c) and figures in Euripides' farce about Helen in Egypt.

59. "Ne recommençons pas la guerre de Troie," *EHP*, p. 259.

60. On the modern, thoroughly communist CGT and its recent problems with the *patronat*, see John Ardagh, *France in the 1980s* (Harmondsworth: Penguin, 1982), pp. 93–115. Little seems to have changed in worker-boss antagonisms over the nearly sixty years since Weil wrote about them.

61. *EHP*, p. 271.

62. Ibid., p. 272. For a comparable pessimism, see George Orwell, "Arthur Koestler," in *Collected Essays, Journalism and Letters of George Orwell*, ed. Sonia Orwell and Ian Angus (New York: Harcourt Brace Jovanovich, 1968), p. 243: "Since about 1930 the world has given no reason for optimism whatever. Nothing is in sight except a welter of lies, hatred, cruelty and ignorance, and beyond our present troubles loom vaster ones which are only now entering into the European consciousness."

63. This fragment, in HS, bears the archival note "1937?" but internal evidence argues early 1938, possibly at the time of the Anschluss (March) and Blum's second administration.

64. "Pour une négotiation immédiate," *Feuilles libres de la quinzaine*, no. 54 (March 25, 1938), p. 90. Listed with other antifascist intellectuals, Weil expressed revulsion toward dealing with Hitler but felt negotiations were the only means of reaching "a first international détente," which could serve as the basis for "a progressive and controlled disarmament."

65. "Meditations sur un cadavre," *EHP*, p. 327. On the circumstances of Blum's departure, see Irwin Wall, "The Resignation of the First Popular Front Government of Léon Blum, June 1937," *French Historical Studies* 6 (Fall 1970): 538–44. Wall argues that Blum resigned in fear of his administration's defeat on the nonintervention issue regarding Spain, which was soon to be raised at the Marseilles Congress.

66. "L'Europe en guerre pour la Tchécoslovaquie?" *Feuilles libres de la quinzaine* 4 (May 25, 1938), reprinted in *EHP*, pp. 273–78. The quotation is from p. 274. D. W. Brogan, *The Development of Modern France*, rev. ed. (New York: Harper & Row, 1966), 2: 724, includes among the pre-Munich elements of French attitudes "the human hope that things could not be so bad as they seemed." Weil's projection of a Czech culture preserved under Nazi authority suggests she was not immune to such hope.

67. "Lettre à Gaston Bergery," *EHP*, p. 286. Bergery, editor of the weekly *La flèche* had argued that an increase in German territorial demands would lead to an attack on France.

68. "L'Europe en guerre pour la Tchécoslovaquie?" *EHP*, p. 276. Weil went so far as to suggest privately, in a letter to René Belin (Pétrement, 2:133), the experiment of giving Germany all Hitler demanded. She reasoned that the risk of reaching the point at which demands became unacceptable would be no greater than the risk of provoking war by resistance.

69. "Lettre à Gaston Bergery," *EHP*, p. 287. Her assumption about Nazism's instability has been corroborated by Joachim Fest, *Hitler*, trans. Richard Winston and Clara Winston (New York: Random House, 1975).

70. "L'Europe en guerre pour la Tchécoslovaquie?" *EHP*, p. 278. That concession marks an abrupt change from the argument of "Ne recommençons pas la guerre de Troie," where humiliations depend on chauvinist phantoms.

71. Undated letter to Jean Posternak, quoted by Pétrement, 2:186. On 2:187, Pétrement cites these words as evidence of Weil's "désintéressement," when, facing the alternatives of war and a French rightist regime, she preferred the one that would have made her personally a victim. And what of her family? Was she willing to have it victimized as well?

72. "Désarroi de notre temps," *EHP*, p. 290.

73. "Fragment," *EHP*, p. 293.

74. With another of Alain's students, Michel Alexandre, Bouché espoused an ultrapacifist position in *Vigilance*.

75. "Réflexions sur la conférence de Bouché," *EHP*, p. 280.

76. Pétrement, 2:189, says these views were "relatively new at the time," but Weil was well read in ancient historiographical accounts of guerrilla warfare.

77. "Réflexions en vue d'un bilan," *EHP*, p. 304.

78. Ibid., p. 296.

79. Undated letter to "Chère petite," CG.

80. Orwell, *Homage to Catalonia*, p. 246.

81. "Réflexions en vue d'un bilan," *EHP*, p. 300.

82. Ibid., p. 310.

83. In her London notebooks, *CS*, p. 317, she writes bitterly of being "thrown into the mistake of criminal negligence toward the nation." She blames "my criminal error before 1939 regarding the pacifist milieux and their activity" on her physical exhaustion, which

had kept her from an awareness of the pacifists' "inclination to treason." She probably refers to Alexandre's circle at *Vigilance* and her pacifist colleagues in the teachers' union. It is unusual for Weil to condemn other people for her own shortsightedness. Her violent self-censure suggests she had forgotten the grounds for her pacifism: the memory of World War I, the dread of a militarized state, her concern to preserve the unions' reforms of 1936.

84. "Réflexions en vue d'un bilan," *EHP*, pp. 311–12.

85. Undated letter to André Weil, spring 1940, CSWAW.

Chapter 5

1. Weil cites these passages with her commentary in "Dieu dans Platon," *SG*, p. 82.

2. For Zeno see Lactantius, *De vera sapientia*, 9 in *Stoicorum veterum fragmenta*, ed. Johann von Arnim (Leipzig: Teubner, 1921), 1.42, para. 160 (hereafter cited as *SVF*). For Chrysippus see Philodemus, *De pietate*, 11, in *SVF* 2, 315, para. 1076.

3. The following quotations come from notes found in TPAG.

4. See Plutarch's *De Stoicorum repugnanda* 47, in *SVF* 2.292, para. 998.

5. See Epictetus 1.12.15: *hekasta houтos thelein hos gignetai*. The issue is discussed in admirable detail by J. M. Rist, *Stoic Philosophy* (Cambridge: Cambridge University Press, 1977), pp. 112–32.

6. For her references to Cleanthes' Hymn see *AD*, p. 236; *CS*, p. 132; *LR*, p. 30; *SG*, pp. 151–53. J. H. Randall, *Hellenistic Ways of Deliverance and the Making of the Christian Synthesis* (New York: Columbia University Press, 1970), p. 41, says that Cleanthes' Hymn "displays all the moral strength and much of the intellectual weakness of popular Christianity."

7. *C*, 3:322.

8. André Jean Voelke, *L'idée de volonté dans le stoicisme* (Paris: Presses Universitaires de France, 1973), p. 97, characterizes this consent as the "acte volontaire par excellence."

9. Seneca, *De vita beata* 15.4–15.7: *Deo parere libertas est*.

10. This undated fragment, located in TPAG, carries several grammatical notes on the Greek text. That suggests Weil was perhaps preparing it for discussion with Gustave Thibon.

11. Seneca, *De providentia* 5.4: *Non trahuntur a fortuna, sequuntur illam et aequant gradu; si scissent, ante cessissent*.

12. Epictetus 3.24.104–6. In an epistolary fragment, *EHP*, p. 107, Weil says, "I have quite often bitterly regretted that we don't have precise information on the life of Epictetus; to my knowledge it's the sole example of a man reduced by fate to extreme woe—there cannot exist a more base and grievous condition than that of a Roman slave—and of whom one has serious reasons to suppose, according to the tone of his writings, that he always bore himself perfectly well." For Epictetus's remarks on his own death, see 2:10.5.

13. *CS*, pp. 204–6. The predominant motif in the prayer is a Stoic desire for conformity to God's will by anticipatory consent to the worst. Epictetus himself (4.89–100) said he wanted to be tortured and die if thus he could be attached to God. Even Weil's notion of becoming Christ's body upon which others might feed (a strange heresy, indeed) has a Stoic resonance in its straining toward a union of God and creation (or of Christ and the

wretched), the *syntonia* that makes the individual soul one with God and the universe. The agent of that union, according to the Stoics, is the divine breath or *pneuma*, the very spirit Weil identifies as her prayer's dictator. Stoicism is one obvious road that must be taken for access to Weil's extraordinarily heterodox views on Christianity. See *CS*, p. 201, where Weil claims the incarnation is not meant to save humanity but to witness the truth that the love between God and Christ is stronger than that between Creator and creature and that "the thought of separate thinkers is one"—a clear reference to the Stoics' *koinai ennoiai*, the assumption of a universality of reflection that truth ratifies.

14. *CS*, p. 299. For an attack on this Stoicism, see Robert Rouquette, "Mystère de Simone Weil," *Etudes* 268 (January 1951): 88–106.

15. *AD*, p. 107. Theism plays no part in the initial discussions of Weil's essay on liberty and oppression. There necessity as an idea seems to be applied only to matter. In the London fragments (1943) included in *OL*, the Platonic unity of necessity and the good beyond this world is stated as open to experimental verification.

16. *OL*, p. 98.

17. In "Réflexions sur la guerre," *EHP*, p. 239, Weil takes up Engels's notion that war can be an occasion for the proletariat to exact concessions from the state, but her conclusion is pessimistic: "Every attempt at reform seems puerile in the face of blind necessities implied by the game of this monstrous meshwork. Modern society resembles an enormous machine snatching up people incessantly, without anyone knowing its commands."

18. See A. W. Gomme, A. Andrewes, and K. J. Dover, *A Historical Commentary on Thucydides*, 4 (Oxford: Clarendon Press, 1970), 173–74. Weil's translation of 105.2, "always, by an absolute necessity of nature, everyone commands wherever he has power to do so," occurs in her essay "Réflexion en vue d'un bilan," *EHP*, p. 303.

19. The brave Melians chose to perish. This grim episode, like Thucydides' account of the civil war in Corcyra (3.81–83), Weil accepted as proof that the Greeks were not the sublime creatures of Winckelmann's fantasy.

20. In a series of notes entitled "Idées essentielles à faire apparaître," TPAG, she sketches out the Baconian thesis that one commands nature only when one obeys it: "Nature wills nothing. To the extent that one believes he acts in opposing will by will he is defeated in advance (Xerxes); whether he revolts or reigns himself, it comes to the same thing. When he believes he commands, he serves. When he knows how to obey, he commands. He triumphs over nature by ruse and not by force. . . . Attention. All our mental life depends upon it."

21. *OL*, p. 117.

22. Ibid., p. 129.

23. Ibid., p. 137.

24. Ibid., p. 155. One recalls the famous image of the future which O'Brien gives to Winston in *Nineteen Eighty-Four*, a boot forever pressing upon a human face. Weil might be accused of hysteria, as Orwell has been, but Orwell was reacting to the world of Stalin's purges and Hitler's camps; Weil was foretelling them.

25. Pétrement, 2:60, dates Weil's reading of Hamp to 1935, directly after she had ended her work in the factories. "A very beautiful novel," Weil called it (2:69).

26. Her notes on *Glück Auf!* are in TPAG. Her mystification of power here indicates a

significant departure from the Marxist view she had presented only two years before in "Réflexions sur la guerre," where she identifies machinery, including armaments, as the means by which capital subordinates labor. There is no hint in that essay that the state and bosses are victims of their own power in waging war upon their soldiers and factory workers. Socialists, Weil observes, *EHP*, p. 234, were mistaken to see war as a function of the state's foreign relations: "It constitutes above all a fact of internal relations, and the most atrocious of all." On war as an intensification of internal oppression see Weil's 1933 "Fragment sur la guerre révolutionnaire," *EHP*, p. 241.

27. Weil saw Chaplin's film several times and conscripted friends and students to see it with her. Pétrement, 2:91, reports that Weil, "doubtless joking, said Chaplin was next to Spinoza the only great Jew." In fact, Chaplin was not a Jew.

28. Ibid., p. 21.

29. "*L'Iliade* ou la poème de la force," in *SG*, p. 35.

30. Ibid., p. 32. In the notes on Hamp she refers to "la puissance," in the essay on Homer to "la force," but these terms are clearly equivalent as "power."

31. *SG*, p. 29.

32. Ibid., p. 18.

33. This fact warrants George Steiner, *Language and Silence* (New York: Atheneum, 1967), p. 8, to dismiss Weil's essay as a "perverse reading" of Homer. As he remarks, "disaster, and the routine of flight and exile," familiar scenes of the present century, have prompted us to look more attentively to Vergil, and Weil's reading of Homer does seem peculiarly Vergilian. Specific points in her interpretation do not hold up when we examine the passages to which they refer. As Michael K. Ferber has shown, "Simone Weil's *Iliad*," in *Simone Weil: Interpretations of a Life*, ed. George Abbott White (Amherst: University of Massachusetts Press, 1981), pp. 70–71, Priam is not, as Weil contends, reduced to a thing in Achilles' tent. This is a sufficient clue that Weil either ignored or did not perceive the operating norms of the Homeric warrior's code, honor and shame. Ferber objects that Weil's moralism is too desperate, that it leaves no option for working against force through the nonviolence of a Gandhi or King. But that she was aware of that strategy is clear from her notebooks, as is cited in another excellent essay, Joseph H. Summers, "Notes on Simone Weil's *Iliad*," ibid., p. 91.

34. See Hermann Diels, *Fragmente der Vorsokratiker* (1903; rpt. Berlin: Weidmann, 1956) 1:89. This is the text Weil used.

35. *SG*, pp. 98 (on Anaximander) and 19.

36. The manuscript, with variants, is located in the archival boîte for *SG*.

37. Fragment 53 in Diels, 1:162. Weil faithfully translated nearly all of the 137 fragments of Diels's edition, but it seems she was at least occasionally dependent on Diels's own translation of the frequently elliptical Greek into German. For his entries in numbers 64–65 and 68–69 she brackets her translation according to his italicizations. She omitted number 42 (43 is misnumbered as 42 in her list) in which Heraclitus says that Homer deserves to be cast out of the contest of singers.

38. In Weil's drama *Venise sauvée*, Renaud rationalizes the terror to be imposed on the conquered Venetians: "The ground must be lacking to their feet suddenly and forever, that they might find an equilibrium only in obedience."

39. Quoted by Weil in *E*, p. 302. See Adolf Hitler, *Mein Kempf*, trans. Ralph Manheim (Boston: Houghton Mifflin, 1971), p. 245.

40. These lines occur in the manuscript after the reference to "l'amour du maître," which is printed on p. 17 of the Gallimard text of *SG*.

41. Succeeding these lines is the quotation from the *Iliad* 2:160–162 (Hera's fateful goading of Athena), found on pp. 29–30 of the Gallimard text.

42. "Méditation sur l'obéissance et la liberté," *OL*, p. 191. This splendid little essay offers a kind of résumé of themes she expounds in larger works.

43. In "Poème de la force," Weil emphasizes how exceptional all relations of love and personal loyalty are to the war's course: the bond of hospitality rescuing Diomedes and Glaucon, the love of Thetis for Achilles, of Achilles for Patroclus. These affections at times threaten to arrest the bloody action.

44. *OL*, p. 193.

45. *E*, pp. 304–5. She attributes Hitler's failing to the allure of modern scientific conceptions of nature and their vulgarization into a belief that history can be "baptized" as an automatic mechanism of justice. She chastises Hitler on this point by citing Anaximander's fragment, p. 361.

46. See Weil's discussion of Rome's influence upon the Church, *CS*, p. 67; on unconditional love of the Church as a form of idolatry, pp. 79, 220; on its historical tyranny as a function of its temporal expectations, p. 173.

47. "Fragments de Londres," *OL*, p. 206.

48. "Réflexions sur les origines de l'hitlérisme," *EHP*, p. 24. Weil's ascription of racism is unfounded. As to propaganda, Caesar's commentaries on Gaul provide an excellent example of the "fides populi Romani" (4.21).

49. *EHP*, p. 28.

50. Ibid., p. 32. In *E*, p. 135, Weil likens the Roman reduction of Greece to Germany's occupation of Vichy France.

51. *E*, p. 285. Weil's is a moralistic gratitude toward a brilliant exemplary evil.

52. *EHP*, p. 16.

53. In *LR*, pp. 49–50, Weil says that Rome's assumption of Christianity as an official religion is something that Hitler would have dreamed of.

54. "Réflexions en vue d'un bilan," *EHP*, p. 303.

55. "Fragment," *EHP*, p. 293.

56. *EHP*, p. 308.

57. Ibid., p. 309. That, for her, is the lesson to be drawn from the papal suppression of the Albigensians.

58. Ibid., p. 306.

59. "Fragment," *EHP*, p. 313.

60. Ibid., p. 314.

61. She anticipates the thesis of Ernest Becker's *Denial of Death*, that the individual seeks to overcome the imminence of mortality by taking refuge in religious or political cults that confer the faith in one's immortality by adherence within them.

62. This essay, odd to say, comes from TS.

63. *C*, 2:85, 153–55. In assuming neither past nor future, Weil seems to be moving

toward an Eleatic oneness of being, yet her final allegiance is not with Parmenides but Heraclitus, perhaps because of his influence on Greek Stoicism. In rejecting the ontological argument from design she seems at one with Hume (or Philo) in the *Dialogues Concerning Natural Religion*.

64. *C*, 2:240. See also *AD*, pp. 115–16, and *E*, p. 331.

65. *C*, 3:210. See also *C*, 1:153.

66. *C*, 2:240. She traces this idea to the *Upanishads*, but it is also to be found in the Jewish Kabbalistic idea of restoring the world together with God.

67. *CS*, p. 226; *AD*, p. 150.

68. *C*, 2:75.

69. Ibid., p. 77; *C* 3:39.

70. *CS*, pp. 38, 166.

71. *C*, 1:160.

72. *E*, pp. 24, 358–59; *AD*, pp. 112, 114. In *CS*, p. 166, she writes: "There is no good in the universe but this universe is good." The paradox follows from the nature of blind matter's relationship to the transcendental order which informs it. Necessity is good only in telling us it is not the good.

73. *AD*, p. 113. In scriptural terms, one may kick against the pricks (Acts 20:14) or conform oneself to the divine will (Rom. 12:2). Weil does not cite these texts, but they make her point.

74. *C*, 2:106, 278; *C*, 3:33.

75. See Stobaeus, ecl. 2.57, para. 19, in *SVF* 3.17, para. 16–21. For the passage from Chrysippus, see Plutarch, *De Stoicorum repugnanda* 31, in *SVF* 3.167, para. 21–24.

76. *Agamemnon* 176, in the chorus on Zeus, 161–257. For Weil's notes on specific passages in this play see *C*, 2:375–77.

77. "Zeus et Prométhée," *SG*, p. 44.

78. Ibid., p. 45.

79. *C*, 1:211. For her explicit rejection of masochism see *CS*, pp. 222–23; also "L'amour de Dieu et le malheur," in *PSO*, p. 108.

80. See his Meditation 17, *The Complete Poetry and Selected Prose of John Donne*, ed. Charles M. Coffin (New York: Modern Library, 1952), p. 441.

81. *E*, p. 126. Such a disposition, Weil believed, figured in the rise of national socialism in Germany.

82. *C*, 1:168; *C*, 2:135; *C*, 3:18.

83. *C*, 2:317–18.

84. *C*, 2:128, 159, 201–2.

85. Ibid., 236.

86. *CS*, p. 89.

87. *C*, 1:40; *C*, 2:369; *PSO*, pp. 88–90; *AD*, pp. 69, 98, 100.

88. *AD*, pp. 82, 135.

89. *C*, 2:375. Her *imitatio Christi* is a concentrated image of her *imitatio mundi*. It can be interpreted in four dimensions: 1) suffering under necessity means that the soul is threatened with reduction to matter; 2) love of necessity is like Christ's love for his

persecutors; 3) suffering from the good comes to distance from and abandonment by God; 4) love of the good means acceptance of the divine will, the negation of one's own.

90. P. Savinel, "Simone Weil et l'héllenisme," *Bulletin de l'Association Guillaume Budé*, 4th ser., no. 1 (March 1960): pp. 143, 132.

Chapter 6

1. *OC*, 1:61.
2. Immanuel Kant, *Kritik der Urteilskraft* (Berlin: Lagarde, 1793), p. 258.
3. In *C*, 2:256, she describes beauty as a part of matter that makes spiritual perfection sensible. She is working toward that idea in this early essay.
4. *OC*, 1:71.
5. *C*, 3:305.
6. *OC*, 1:94.
7. Kant, p. 61. The conclusive formulation reads: "Schönheit ist Form der Zweckmässigkeit eines Gegenstandes, sofern sie, ohne Vorstellung eines Zwecks, an ihm wahrgenommen wird" (Beauty is the form of an object's purposefulness insofar as it is perceived without the introduction of a purpose).
8. *C*, 2:192.
9. *OC*, 1:94–95.
10. Ibid., p. 95.
11. Ibid.
12. Ibid., pp. 96, 97.
13. Ibid., p. 98.
14. *C*, 2:153.
15. Her characterization of beauty in *C*, 2:343, as a divine seduction of the flesh is obviously indebted to the *Timaeus*.
16. *C*, 3:195.
17. *CS*, p. 149; *C*, 2:293.
18. *C*, 2:293.
19. *C*, 1:65, 3:339.
20. *C*, 2:192, 301; 3:216.
21. *C*, 3:172.
22. *C*, 3:301–2.
23. *LR*, p. 67.
24. *C*, 2:218.
25. Quoted by Pétrement, 2:144.
26. *C*, 3:112, 180.
27. *C*, 3:215–16. Her subsequent remarks in this passage, that "perfect music" is maximally bearable monotony minimally changed, seems to refer to the linear simplicity of chant.
28. *C*, 3:272.

29. Jean-Paul Sartre, *L'imaginaire: psychologie phénoménologie de l'imagination* (Paris: Gallimard, 1940), pp. 244–45.

30. C, 2:87.

31. C, 2:153–54; on the *atman* see 1:193.

32. *E*, pp. 357–58; CS, p. 102. On her belief that the artistic sensibility receives "aesthetic analogies" to spiritual truths, see *CS*, p. 334.

33. For her ranking of French prose and verse writers, see *E*, p. 297.

34. C, 1:226–27, 2:122–23.

35. C, 2:272, 3:34–35.

36. For two penetrating discussions, see George Steiner, *Language and Silence* (New York: Atheneum, 1970), pp. 3–11, 55–67.

37. C, 3:48–49. On a strictly mimetic view, the existence of bad art argues an inferior beauty, a point Weil concedes in *IPC*, p. 158.

38. Marcel Raymond, *From Baudelaire to Surrealism* (London: Methuen, 1970), p. 140.

39. Paul Valéry, "Poetry and Abstract Thought," in Valéry, *The Art of Poetry*, trans. Denise Folliot (New York: Random House, 1961), p. 64.

40. Quoted by Raymond, p. 139.

41. These lines are from Valéry's "L'ébauche d'un serpent." For a discussion see D. J. Mossop, *Pure Poetry: Studies in French Poetic Theory and Practice, 1746 to 1945* (Oxford: Clarendon Press, 1971), pp. 204–9.

42. *PVS*, p. 23.

43. Paul Valéry to Simone Weil, September 1937, in *PVS*, pp. 9–10. Pétrement, 2:165, says that Weil showed Valéry's letter to her, asking "if I did not find it astonishing that someone who wrote such a letter showed no desire to meet the person to whom he sent it. She would surely have been happy to make his acquaintance."

44. Simone Weil to Paul Valéry, CG. Valéry never answered this letter. According to Jean Hytier, *La poétique de Valéry* (Paris: Armand Colin, 1953), p. 20, he preferred to keep his readers in the dark about his poetic method.

45. Simone Weil to Paul Valéry, CG.

46. Simone Weil to G. Guindey, CG.

47. All published quotations are from *PVS*, pp. 25–30. The unpublished variants are from P.

48. The last lines are clearly reminiscent of John 21:18. In C, 1:206, she says we must love time as it takes us where we do not wish to go, but in this poem time itself is violated.

49. Two possible references here are the cosmic spindle of necessity in Plato's *Republic* 616b–617c and the wheel of fortune in Dante's *Inferno* 7:73–96.

50. This unpublished variant forms most of the third stanza in one of Weil's drafts.

51. The poem is located in VS. Its theme, deliverance through *atman*, seems to belong to the first Vichy years, when Weil was absorbed in Vedic hymns and learning Sanskrit.

52. This unpublished variant and all others come from P; the published version is in *PVS*, p. 33.

53. The less forceful, published version has "furent" for "seront."

54. C, 1:116.

55. Adriano Marchetti, "Simone Weil, poeta e critico," *Revista di letterature moderne e comparato* 30 (September 1977): 191.

56. *CS*, pp. 166, 191, 228; *E*, p. 363.

57. *AD*, p. 116.

58. *PVS*, p. 36.

59. Marchetti, 201.

60. This final quatrain is an unpublished variant of the much less dramatic one in *PVS*, p. 21.

61. *AD*, p. 28.

62. *C*, 1:124; 2:49, 215. On art and politics, *E*, pp. 273–74.

63. It was reprinted in that journal in its number 310 (1951), pp. 426–30, and appears in *CSW* 10 (December 1987): 354–57.

64. "Sur la responsabilité," *CSW* 10 4 (December 1987): 357.

65. In P, under the heading, "Copies de textes poétiques."

66. In his "Adieu" concluding *Une saison en enfer* he had written, "Le combat spirituel est aussi brutal que la bataille d'hommes; mais la vision de la justice est le plaisir de Dieu seul." In her essay "Morale et Littérature," *CSW* 10 (December 1987), 349–53, Weil judges Rimbaud a specimen of demonic genius.

67. In a 1927 essay introducing Pascal Pia's edition of Rimbaud's *Poésies complêtes* (Paris: Gallimard, 1963), p. 5.

68. The play was rescued from closet drama status and given a translation adapted for the BBC by Sir Richard Rees in 1957. In 1965, a performance based on a completed version was given at Marseilles by the Théâtre Universitaire. To date there has been no published translation.

69. In her notes on Renaud, Weil has Trotsky in mind. Her unpublished notes and lines omitted from the published version are in VS. Published notes are in *PVS*, pp. 43–53.

70. It is easy to assume that Weil would have identified herself with the Promethean redeemer Jaffier, but at a deeper, subrational level, she perhaps held a greater bond with the courtesan, whose bitter words on the women of Venice, her longing to see them debased, recall Weil's adolescent poem "A une jeune fille riche." There, in vindictive tones, Weil's speaker desires to see a young woman of ease reduced to hunger and humiliation. But as rancor toward others is far less characteristic of Weil than rancor toward herself, "A une jeune fille riche" may be a self-reproach that she, well-educated and comfortably bourgeois, was at a definitive distance from the factory women and prostitutes the "jeune fille" has not noticed.

71. *PVS*, p. 66. The phrase recalls the "me outside of me," the *atman* of self.

72. Ibid., p. 93.

73. Ibid., p. 46. Detachment, or setting of distance by self from its object, is for Weil central to aesthetic experience, but in this play she seems almost too concerned to emphasize the social consequence of detachment, that it amounts to a kind of lèse majésté against collectivity.

74. Ibid., p. 89. Weil's published notes say (p. 47) this is "the moment when reality enters him, because he pays attention. . . . His recoil is supernatural." But the unpublished notes show he is motivated by the elementary decency of conscience: "End of 2nd act: I

renounce power and glory; history will not remember me, though such an occasion a man's life does not find twice. I'll go on leading my mediocre and arduous life in obscurity, but at least I'll have peace of soul."

75. Ibid., p. 122.

Chapter 7

1. *AD*, p. 73.

2. Ibid., p. 108.

3. *CS*, pp. 327–28.

4. The gods are so vastly superior to humanity that no one can be their friend, Aristotle says, but John 15:14–15 makes Weil's case for mediation. Since Weil used a Thomist commentary for her attacks on Aristotle, it may be doubted whether she read the *Ethica Nicomachea*, Books 8 and 9. Their wide-ranging and sensible discussions of friendship could not have inspired her rash conclusion (*CS*, p. 328) that Aristotle was "the bad tree which carries only rotten fruit."

5. *CS*, pp. 31, 173.

6. Just so, Plato in his dialogue on friendships, *Lysis* 219ab, considers a mediation by love of the good, which is superior to two friends. There is unfortunately no evidence that Weil read this work.

7. *AD*, p. 204; *CS*, p. 292.

8. *AD*, p. 205.

9. *C*, 3:69. Weil does not share Plato's moralism that makes friendship the model for a well-regulated society. Determined to anchor friendship in the heavens, she neglects (or refuses) to anchor it in the world at large. It is too precious to bear translation into any collectivity.

10. *AD*, p. 51.

11. L. Cazamian, *History of French Literature* (Oxford: Clarendon Press, 1955), p. 127. For a negative view of Théophile's highly subjective style see O. de Mourges, *Metaphysical, Baroque and Précieux Poetry* (Oxford: Clarendon Press, 1953), p. 74.

12. It has been conjectured that he was upholding the Greek mysteries against scholasticism. See Antoine Adam, *Théophile de Viau et la libre pensée française en 1620* (Paris: E. Droz, 1935), p. 175. I have not been able to determine whether Weil read this study. It does not support her suggestion (*E*, p. 150) that Richelieu was responsible for Théophile's death. See p. 410, esp. n. 2.

13. Adam, p. 321.

14. L. Petit de Julleville, *Histoire de la langue et de la littérature française des origines à 1900* (Paris: Armand Colin, 1897), 4:65.

15. "Ebauches de Lettres," in *EHP*, p. 111.

16. Ibid. She might more justly have accused the Jesuit Garasse, whose printed attacks led to Théophile's trial, or those henpecking friends who either withdrew from him in the face of danger or, like Guez de Balzac, openly sided with his prosecutors. Richeleu arrived late on the scene, and there is no clear evidence of his direct responsibility for Théophile's fate.

17. *E*, p. 150.

18. Ibid., p. 143. It may be questioned whether Théophile, who received some of his patronage from the Huguenot Duc de Montmorency, was a partisan for social and economic justice at the expense of the nobility's privileges.

19. Ibid., p. 228. See *EHP*, p. 112, for citations of the verses from Théophile's "Sur la paix de l'année 1620" to which Weil refers.

20. *EHP*, pp. 111, 113.

21. *E*, p. 297.

22. Weil linked Gide with Wilde, *EL*, pp. 18–19, as writers whose cult of personality made them not independent of public taste, as they fancied, but slaves to it. For a brief comparison of Gide's spirituality and Weil's see Jean Guitton, "André Gide et l'éternel présent," *La table ronde* 83 (November 1954): 175–77.

23. *E*, p. 38. She is attacking the shallowness of *l'art pour l'art* arguments that would defend writers from moral responsibility to their readers.

24. Undated letter to André Gide, CG. An archival note suggests that this letter was written around 1938–39, but, according to Gilbert Kahn, there are in fact two letters to Gide, both written from Marseilles, that is, from the Vichy period.

25. I have not found any of these copies in her papers. In reading through the poems of Théophile she listed as "copied for Gide," I have calculated that she must have written out over six hundred lines of verse.

26. *EHP*, p. 113.

27. *AD*, pp. 222, 224.

28. Undated letter to David Garnett, CG. Portions of Weil's letter are reprinted in Louis Allen, "French Intellectuals and T. E. Lawrence," *Durham University Journal* 19 (December 1976): 61.

29. Quoted by David Garnett in his edition of *The Letters of T. E. Lawrence* (London: Jonathan Cape, 1938), p. 182.

30. For a discussion of Lawrence's style see Desmond Stewart, *T. E. Lawrence* (London: Granada, 1977), p. 246. A trenchant examination of the psychology at work in this style is by R. P. Blackmur, "The Everlasting Effort," in his collection *The Expense of Greatness* (Gloucester, Mass.: Peter Smith, 1958), pp. 1–36. Lawrence himself, quoted by William Rothenstein in *T. E. Lawrence by His Friends*, ed. A. W. Lawrence, abridged ed. (London: Jonathan Cape, 1954), p. 244, wrote: "My style is a made-up thing, very thickly encrusted with what seemed to me tit-bits and wheezes of established authors."

31. Letter of late March or early April 1938 to Jean Posternak, reprinted in CSW 10 (June 1987): 130.

32. "Descente de Dieu," *IPC*, p. 52. She goes on: "Perhaps some Christians are very near to God and sainthood. But probably few. Yet this double knowledge is perhaps the purest source of the love of God." Reared free of organized religion, Weil naturally found a mirror of her own religious sensibility in unorthodox figures, of whom Lawrence, no formal believer at all (he detested his mother's cloying piety), was one.

33. Letter to Posternak, 130.

34. T. E. Lawrence, *Seven Pillars of Wisdom* (1926; rpt. Harmondsworth: Penguin, 1962), p. 40.

35. Ibid., pp. 161, 168, 199, 201, 315. Weil has Lawrence's notion of "arranging" the enemy's mind when she writes of war as only one means of persuasion, *C*, 1:57.

36. Lawrence's characterization of the revolt (*Seven Pillars*, p. 149) as not a war but "a national strike, perhaps" must have intrigued her.

37. Ibid., pp. 348, 421–22; see p. 529, on the death of Farraj: "triumphal weakness coming home."

38. Ibid., p. 547. On p. 193 Lawrence's sickness "made my animal self crawl away and hide." Cf. Weil at Solesmes, *AD*, p. 43, "able to go out of this wretched flesh and let it suffer alone, heaped in its corner." *C*, 1:24: "Not incidentally doctrines with a mystical content are more or less oriented toward death. Cathari. T. E. Lawrence." Weil's "I truly count for nothing" where God is concerned, *AD*, p. 49, should be compared with Lawrence's most pithy autobiography, quoted by Irving Howe, "T. E. Lawrence: The Problem of Heroism," in his *A World More Attractive* (New York: Horizon Press, 1963), p. 38: "I was an Irish nobody. I did something. It was a failure, and I became an Irish nobody."

39. Lawrence, *Seven Pillars*, p. 583.

40. Quoted by Allen, p. 60. Weil's own greatness comes in her next words: "I won't say I understand him. How can I know if I do?"

41. *C*, 2:54, 70–71.

42. *C*, 3:110.

43. Quoted by Allen, p. 60.

44. T. E. Lawrence, *The Mint* (Harmondsworth: Penguin, 1978), p. 136.

45. Quoted by Allen, p. 61.

46. Lawrence, *The Mint*, pp. 40, 44, 93, 155.

47. Ibid., pp. 160, 180.

48. John E. Mack, *A Prince of Our Disorder: A Life of T. E. Lawrence* (Boston: Little, Brown, 1976), p. 323.

49. See the letter from Selma Weil to André Weil, quoted in Pétrement, 1:221. On the affect of Lawrence and Weil on others, see Mack, pp. 401, 457, 458, and Pétrement, 1:263.

50. Mack, p. 357.

51. Quoted by Allen, p. 60.

52. *Letters of T. E. Lawrence*, ed. Garnett, p. 413.

53. Ibid., p. 414.

54. Quoted by Allen, p. 61.

55. *Letters of T. E. Lawrence*, ed. Garnett, p. 419.

56. Quoted by Allen, p. 60.

57. *C*, 2:354.

58. Gaston Massat, "Reconnaissance à Joë Bousquet," *Cahiers du Sud* 303 (1950), 204.

59. Jean Ballard, introductory note to "Correspondance entre Simone Weil et Joë Bousquet," *Cahiers du Sud* 304 (1950), 420.

60. Pétrement, 2:398.

61. Joë Bousquet, "Fragments du journal," *Cahiers du Sud* 303 (1950): 207.

62. *C*, 2:113–14. In her first letter to him after this meeting she mentions the Parzifal

legend and its wanderer, who, feeling accursed, must pass through a dark night, but finally comes to cure another's suffering.

63. Simone Weil and Joë Bousquet, *Correspondance* (Lausanne: Editions l'Age d'Homme, 1982), p. 20. Toward the end of 1942, he wrote ("Fragments," 209), "To my taste for death, which was a defect of my will, I substituted a longing to die that it might be the will's apotheosis." This was Weil's sort of glory—recondite, untrumpeted, giving the lie to Corneille, to Péguy, and to all banner carriers.

64. *Correspondance*, pp. 23–24.

65. Ibid., p. 25.

66. Ibid., p. 27.

67. Weil's thoughts on suicide are equivocal. Suicide must not "thicken the ignorance" of those who do not know necessity and *karma* (C, 1:160). But suicide is also "the most precious gift to humanity" and so its abuse constitutes "the supreme impiety" (C, 1:163). We may presume Weil knew of Plato's view in the *Laws* (837cd) that suicide is sanctioned for one who is compelled by incurable pains—Bousquet's own case, but in C, 2:187 she says suicide is a false decreation. Her notes on the Stoic perspective, in CD 1, deserve mention: "Suicide—virtue in oneself without relation to life—the affliction in oneself hasn't any relation to the obligation to leave life. It's not in ceasing or continuing to live that one does an act of philosophy. One doesn't put an end to life's *bonheur* or *malheur* by dying."

68. *Correspondance*, p. 45.

69. See *AD*, pp. 80–81, 108–9, 199–201.

70. *Correspondance*, p. 41.

71. Ibid., pp. 46–47.

72. Letter of January 26, 1943, to Pierre and Hélène Honnorat, DH.

73. "Projet d'une formation d'infirmières de première ligne," *EL*, pp. 192, 193. She enclosed with this draft and her letter to Maurice Schumann Bousquet's letter of recommendation, which apparently has not survived.

74. *Correspondance*, p. 34.

75. Ibid., p. 35.

76. On Alain's similar limitation, see André Sernin, *Alain: un sage dans la cité* (Paris: Robert Laffont, 1985), p. 311.

77. Ibid., p. 283. Out of 165 students, 83 signed this manifesto, including Robert Brasillach.

78. Pétrement, 1:38.

79. The first of the laws by which Judaism is lived enjoins its people to be fruitful and multiply. For all the indifference of its nonpractice, Weil's family, including her brother, offered positive models of married life.

80. "A plan for a group of volunteer fire-line [sic] nurses," ELM. The following quotations are from this source. Several drafts of the plan can be found in her papers.

81. Among her papers in DB is a list of twenty-eight first-aid questions for review, including "how long does it take for blood to clout [sic]?"

82. Richard Rees, *Simone Weil: A Sketch for a Portrait* (Carbondale: Southern Illinois University Press, 1966), p. 56, contends that in her last years Weil showed "an unbalanced

tendency towards self-immolation, an intensity of sacrifice which cannot be regarded simply as a high degree of any common virtue such as unselfishness or courage." This "death wish" view seems to me unfair, certainly as regards the nurses plan. One might be indifferent to personal danger without seeking self-destruction. Repeatedly in her plan Weil points to "vital" alternatives to German ruthlessness, for a new courage that would sustain rather than destroy. How could she have expected any success for her plan if death was a certainty? The very desiderata, to help the wounded and comfort the dying, presupposed, however unrealistically, a high survival rate among the nurses. But Weil did not consider the helplessness of wounded and dying nurses and the demoralizing effects of such casualities in the scheme of a vital propaganda.

83. Unpublished fragment in CO. She goes on: "Lindbergh, Costes, Bellonte [the latter two were France's first successful transatlantic flyers] were powerfully stimulated by the prospect of winning wealth and glory; they knew in advance that if they succeeded, the whole world would celebrate them, the crown would acclaim them, money would come flooding in to them. . . . Fishermen or miners who save their comrades, often on terms of almost improbable prowess, are treated by life and men exactly the same way afterward as before."

Chapter 8

1. For enthusiastic approval see Malcolm Muggeridge, "Agonies and Ecstasies," *Observer*, September 22, 1968, p. 31: "One reads on, I find, with a kind of avid delight, leaping almost hilariously from sentence to sentence—like a man leaping from ice-floe to ice-floe on a swiftly flowing icy river." For an undelighted view see John Wren-Lewis, "Breakthrough Wanted," *Guardian*, November 1, 1968, p. 6. He says Weil deplores modern science because it has taken away "the classical picture of a world of iron necessity before which the human spirit must prostrate itself."

2. In *Pluto's Republic* (Oxford: Oxford University Press, 1984), p. 80, Sir Peter Medawar, biologist and Nobel laureate (1960), questions whether the scientific method exists: "Only a minority of scientists have received instruction in scientific methodology, and those that have done so seem no better off."

3. Theodore Zeldin has related this depressing story in abundant detail in his *France, 1848–1945* (Oxford: Oxford University Press, 1980), 3:139–204.

4. Philippe Bernard and Henri Dubief, *The Decline of the Third Republic*, 1914–1938 (Cambridge: Cambridge University Press, 1985), p. 165.

5. *La science française*, ed. Lucien Poincaré (1915; rpt. Paris: Larousse, 1933), p. x.

6. Ibid., p. iii.

7. Bernard and Dubief, p. 165.

8. C, 3:91–92.

9. The notes on Huygens, Bernoulli, and Stevin are in CD 3.

10. "Questions à Bernard," CD 3.

11. C, 1:107.

12. "Lettre à un camarade," S, p. 104.

13. Ibid.

14. Thomas S. Kuhn, *The Structure of Scientific Revolutions*, enlarged ed. (Chicago: University of Chicago Press, 1970) p. 167, n. 3: "Because science students 'know the right answers,' it is particularly difficult to make them analyze an older science in its own terms."

15. "L'enseignement des mathématique," S, p. 109.

16. "Réflexions sur les causes de la liberté et de l'oppression," *OL*, pp. 62, 70, 159.

17. "Sur le livre de Lénine, 'Materialisme et empiriocriticisme,'" *OL*, pp. 51–52.

18. "Sur les contradictions du Marxisme," *OL*, pp. 202–4; and "Fragments, Londres 1943," *OL*, p. 220.

19. "Dieu dans Platon," *SG*, p. 70. Weil does not note that in the *Republic* 531bc Plato criticizes the Pythagoreans for not passing from numbers in harmonies they hear to problems "considering which numbers are harmonies and which not, and why."

20. "Lettre à Déodat Roché," *PSO*, p. 66.

21. One exception: in C, 1:12, she notes the "insufficiency" of the *Republic*, that Plato analyzes sin but not *malheur*.

22. "Esquisse d'une histoire de la science grecque," *IPC*, pp. 173–80.

23. "Science et nous," S, p. 136.

24. Benjamin Farrington, *Greek Science* (Harmondsworth: Penguin, 1949), 2:7.

25. Ibid., p. 8.

26. John Losee, *A Historical Introduction to the Philosophy of Science* (London: Oxford University Press, 1972), p. 18, contends that though Plato was "dissatisfied with a 'merely empirical' knowledge" of phenomena, it does not follow that he would have dissuaded others from inquiring into sense experience; he might even have granted that a rational pattern lies hidden within nature. Richard P. Gregory, *Mind in Science* (London: Weidenfeld and Nicolson, 1981), pp. 558–559, suggests that the defects of Greek mechanical inventions might have hinted to Plato's mind a dualism of reality and appearance present in technology itself, earthly contrivances being only imperfect representations of a universal design.

27. "La Science et nous," S, p. 144.

28. Weil's case for the laws of necessity could rest as substantially upon Greek literary texts as upon philosophical ones. It is peculiar that she did not adduce them in her discussions of science. The case is put in A. N. Whitehead's *Science and the Modern World* (Cambridge: Cambridge University Press, 1926), pp. 12, 13, where Attic tragedians are "the pilgrim fathers of the scientific imagination," using theater to reveal the natural order. Whitehead even likens a meeting of the Royal Society's fellows to a Greek chorus, when they discussed photographs verifying Einstein's theory on the curvature of light rays in proximity to the sun.

29. C, 1:21. The ancient scandal of incommensurables might be compared to the scandal of Heisenberg's principle of indeterminacy, which collapsed classical notions of causality at the level of atomic activity. One of Weil's shortcomings in discussing modern science is her neglect of Heisenberg's revolutionary discovery.

30. Plutarch, *Symposium* 8.2. For an engaging review see E. R. Dodds, *The Ancient Concept of Progress and Other Essays on Greek Literature and Belief* (Oxford: Oxford University Press, 1985) chap. 1, esp. pp. 14–15.

31. *C* 1:110; 2:171; 3:310.

32. *C*, 2:331, 370; 3:173.

33. *C*, 3:147; cf. 2:371, 373, 402, and 3:64–65.

34. *CS*, pp. 35, 36.

35. *C*, 3:153.

36. *CS*, p. 259; *C*, 3:42.

37. *C*, 3:311.

38. *C*, 2:183.

39. *C*, 1:110.

40. *C*, 1:64.

41. "If nothing remained of it all, it is undoubtedly the success of Euclid's *Elements* which is responsible," according to André Weil, quoted by Françoise Armengaud, "Simone Weil et la science grecque: richesse et ambiguité d'une interpretation," *CSW* 6 (March 1983): 15–16.

42. *C*, 2:7; 1:225.

43. "La science et nous," *S*, p. 126.

44. Ibid., p. 131.

45. Ibid., p. 146.

46. Ibid., p. 139. She ignores the fact that Goethe's dislike came from his self-appointed rivalry with Newton over theories of light. Cf. *S*, p. 266: "Keats hated Newton (perhaps she meant Blake), what Greek poet would have hated Eudoxus?"

47. "Réflexions à propos de la théorie des quanta," *S*, p. 202.

48. In a review of *L'avenir de la science* by Louis de Broglie et al. (Paris: Plon, 1941), in *S*, p. 148.

49. Ibid., p. 181.

50. "La science et nous," *S*, p. 175. *Malheur* is a gratuity in this discussion. The opposite of scientism's overweening confidence would be a renewed skepticism, not misery.

51. "Réflexions," *S*, p. 202.

52. Ibid., pp. 193–94.

53. "Extraits de lettres à A.W.," *S*, p. 254.

54. André Weil, as quoted by Armengaud, p. 16, has stated that their paucity of letters during 1941–42 did not help him to disabuse his sister on this point. In another letter, *S*, p. 256, she tells him of reading Planck's four-volume textbook on physics in which "he says explicitly that probability requires the discontinous; he makes no allusions to the slightest attempt to employ probability in conserving continuity. If he had made such an attempt and it had failed, it seems to me he would have said so."

55. As J. Bronowski observes in *The Common Sense of Science* (1951; rpt. London: Heinemann, 1982), pp. 100–101, the presumption that specialization means no one can master the sciences may be an illusion. He submits that we simply lack a unifying method and optimistically notes how in the seventeenth century the sciences seemed no less specialized than now until Descartes and Hobbes "introduced the unifying concept of cause and effect."

56. "Réflexions," *S*, p. 206.

57. C, 2:399.

58. C, 3:75.

59. Ibid.

60. "La science et nous," S, pp. 158–59.

61. "Réflexions," S, pp. 206–7.

62. C, 1:129; see 2:34. One might compare the remarks on the "slippery texture" of logical problems as linguistic phenomena in Ludwig Wittgenstein, *Culture and Value*, trans. Peter Winch (Oxford: Basil Blackwell, 1980), p. 30e.

63. "Réflexions," S, p. 195.

64. C, 2:85.

65. See the discussion in Albert Messiah, *Quantum Mechanics*, trans. G. M. Temmer (Amsterdam: North Holland, 1961), 1:10–11.

66. See her letter to André Weil, S, p. 216. She concludes her essay on quanta, S, p. 208, by remarking that the ninth book of Plato's *Republic*, a profile of social degeneration, "seems to describe current facts."

67. "Réflexions," S, p. 188.

68. See Ludwig Wittgenstein, *Tractatus Logico-Philosophicus*, trans. D. F. Pears and B. F. McGuinness (London: Routledge & Kegan Paul, 1961), p. 49, nos. 4.114 and 4.115.

69. AD, pp. 178–79.

70. Ibid., p. 160.

71. Ibid., pp. 167–68.

72. C, 3:206. She forgets the egocentrism of Heraclitus, Parmenides, Zeno, Empedocles, and other "pious" Greeks, who, recording their own views (or revelations), made sure to set down everyone else as a fool. See G. S. Kirk and J. R. Raven, *The Presocratic Philosophers* (Cambridge: Cambridge University Press, 1962), pp. 266–67, 323 (fr. 11, esp.).

73. The physicist Lewis Ryder, reviewing S in *New Blackfriars* 50 (February 1969): 272, says Weil "shows in this book an understanding of science we expect from Nobel prize laureates—and we don't always find it there."

74. She wants to credit the Greeks' indisposition to technology to this insight but cites no evidence to support it, in C, 3:204.

75. Ibid., p. 213.

76. Ibid., p. 275.

77. CS, pp. 23, 24, 319.

78. C, 2:39–40, 78.

79. "Réflexions," S, p. 208.

80. E, p. 301.

81. Ibid., p. 312. These should be sufficient words for those who believe Weil gave up her interest in social justice and retreated into the private comforts of mysticism.

82. E, p. 320.

83. Ibid., p. 322.

84. Ibid., p. 328.

85. Ibid., p. 325. Her complaint recalls a similar one in her essays on the prewar international crisis, that secret diplomacy was depriving the public of understanding and control of the issues.

86. *E*, p. 326.
87. Ibid., p. 325.
88. Kuhn, p. 167.
89. *E*, pp. 326–27.
90. *CS*, pp. 64, 310.
91. *E*, p. 328.
92. Werner Heisenberg, *Physics and Philosophy* (London: Allen & Unwin, 1963), p. 69.
93. Karl Popper, *The Logic of Scientific Discovery* (London: Hutchinson, 1972), p. 453.
94. *LR*, pp. 55; *CS*, pp. 132, 270.
95. "A propos de la mécanique ondulatoire," *S*, p. 270.
96. *C*, 2:43.
97. *C*, 3:50. On scientific activity divorced from spiritual life see Georges Cattaui's defense of Weil, *La table ronde*, no. 255 (October 1966), p. 158. Wren-Lewis (see note 1) counters that the resurrection, not the passion, serves as guide to science so far as true science is "the dominion of creative personality over Nature in ordinary human life."
98. Richard Morris, *Dismantling the Universe: The Nature of Scientific Discovery* (New York: Simon and Schuster, 1983), p. 182.
99. According to Charles Hartshorne, who heard Dirac lecture, in "Science as the Search for a Hidden Beauty of the World," in *The Aesthetic Dimensions of Science*, ed. Deane Curtin (New York: Philosophical Library, 1980), p. 88.
100. For a physicist's discussion see William N. Lipscomb, "Aesthetic Aspects of Science," ibid., pp. 1–24.
101. "Du fondement d'une science nouvelle," *S*, p. 275.
102. *E*, p. 94.
103. *C*, 1:16, 17.
104. *E*, p. 290; *C*, 3:147–48.
105. Ironically, it is in quantum mechanics that she finds her idea of limit best realized. Quantum physicists realized that there is a limit to the degree of accuracy with which phenomena can be measured. Besides, she notes in *S*, p. 183, observation will always disturb the phenomena observed. This remark suggests that she knew Heisenberg's principle of uncertainty, yet nowhere does she credit its achievement.
106. *CD*, 3.
107. A. N. Whitehead, *An Introduction to Mathematics* (New York: Henry Holt, 1911), p. 61.
108. Peter Medawar, *Pluto's Republic* (Oxford: Oxford University Press, 1984), p. 196.
109. Erwin Schrödinger, *Science, Theory and Man*, trans. James Murphy (London: Allen & Unwin, 1957), p. 102.
110. *C*, 2:40, 41, 45, 190; *C*, 3:44, 46, 79.
111. *C*, 3:152.
112. *CS*, pp. 329, 330; see also pp. 183–88.
113. See his letter to Père Marsenne, October 11, 1638, in *Oeuvres de Descartes: correspondance*, ed. Charles Adam and Paul Tannery (Paris: Vrin, 1969), 2:380.
114. "Réflexions," *S*, p. 200.
115. "L'avenir de la science," *S*, p. 183.

116. "La science et nous," *S*, p. 150.

117. *C*, 3:220–21.

118. *C*, 2:248.

119. On Plato's neglect of the necessary connection between theory and laboratory work, Gregory Vlastos, "The Role of Observation in Plato's Conception of Astronomy," in *Science and the Sciences in Plato*, ed. John Anton (New York: Eidos, 1980), p. 16, observes that "a man of Tycho Brahe's intellectual powers would have qualified as a theorist and hence, on Plato's principles, would never have done the work of a Tycho Brahe."

120. Gaston Bachelard, *La formation de l'esprit scientifique: contribution à une psychoanalyse de la connaissance objective* (Paris: Vrin, 1938), p. 213.

121. "Pensées sans ordre concernant l'amour de Dieu," *PSO*, p. 14.

122. *E*, p. 314.

123. Wittgenstein, *Culture and Value*, p. 56e. See p. 63e: "Perhaps science and industry, having caused infinite misery in the process, will unite the world—I mean condense it into a single unit, though one in which peace is the last thing that will find a home."

124. *OL*, pp. 47, 61, 71, 123–24.

125. Untitled fragment, CD, 3.

126. *CS*, pp. 35, 47, 57, 274; *C* 3:45–46, 248.

127. *C*, 2:141. Determining God's will was very important to her. Only by knowing that will could obedience make sense, and only in obedience could she hope for God's acceptance of her.

128. *AD*, p. 87.

129. Ibid., p. 228.

130. Ibid., p. 90. See *C*, 3:13 for the germ of this essay.

131. *AD*, p. 182. Exemplary beauty, she notes, is not absolute purity. It is precisely the conditional aspect of the examples she cites which gives them experimental value.

132. Ibid., p. 226.

133. *S*, pp. 12, 13.

134. *CS*, p. 236. One might compare Wittgenstein, *Culture and Value*, p. 76, his interest in *Unsinn* and "the greening valleys of stupidity."

135. *C*, 2:22, 333; 3:211. See "Fragment d'une lettre à un étudiant," *S*, p. 117, where she credits de Broglie for intuitive genius in seeing that "the appearance of whole numbers in atomic phenomena, since Planck's sensational discovery of the stable movement of electrons, implies something analogous to wave interference. This intuition has been notably confirmed by the prodigious experience of electrons diffracted by means of crystals or optic nets. All that is physics, and most beautiful."

136. *C*, 3:108. On beauty in necessity see *C*, 1:131; 3:155, 205.

137. *CS*, p. 319. This notion is highly dangerous because it negates moral responsibility. One could exculpate the Nazis from the Final Solution's evil by saying they felt it was for the good of Europe.

138. *C*, 3:123.

139. *CS*, p. 284.

140. *S*, p. 219.

141. *E*, p. 369.

142. Ibid., p. 327.

143. See the conclusion of W. V. Quine's "The Scope and Language of Science," in his *The Ways of Paradox and Other Essays* (Cambridge, Mass.: Harvard University Press, 1975), pp. 242–45.

144. See W. V. Quine, "The Limits of Knowledge," ibid., pp. 66–67.

Chapter 9

1. For the view that her hostility to Judaism was part of a tendency to self-accusation see J. M. Perrin, *Simone Weil telle que nous l'avons connue* (Paris: La Colombe, 1952), p. 59: "She was harsher toward some person or institution the nearer they touched her."

2. Quoted in Patrick Girard, *Les Juifs de France de 1789 à 1860* (Paris: Calmann-Lévy, 1976), p. 51.

3. Marx himself argued in 1843 that the true self-emancipation of the age would be a deliverance "from haggling and money, from practical, real Judaism." See "On the Jewish Question," in *Karl Marx: Selected Writings*, ed. David McLellan (Oxford: Oxford University Press, 1977), p. 58; also McLellan's *Karl Marx, His Life and Thought* (London: Macmillan, 1973), pp. 80–86. For the most exhaustive discussion, see Julius Carlebach, *Karl Marx and the Radical Critique of Judaism* (London: Routledge & Kegan Paul, 1978). This book, graced by an important annotated bibliography, surveys anti-Semitism and Jewish self-hatred from Marx's time into the twentieth century.

4. See George Lichtheim, "Socialism and the Jews," *Dissent* 15 (July– August 1968): 314–42, esp. 322.

5. Quoted in *Le Nationalisme Français: Anthologie 1871–1914*, ed. Raoul Girardet (Paris: Seuil, 1983), p. 149. On Drumont's career and influence see Robert F. Byrnes, *Antisemitism in Modern France* (New York: Howard Fertig, 1969), pp. 137–55.

6. Beyond the political mainstream but important in contributing to racist nationalism, Arthur de Gobineau's *Essai sur l'inégalité des races humaines* (1851–1855) deserves mention, for there is evidence that Weil knew this work. In CD, 1, she records (without endorsement) the "conception ethnique de la patrie," adding: "*Gobineau*. The white race, superior to all others, has let itself be corrupted by blacks, semites, yellows. The Germans have let themselves be penetrated by the Slavs and Celts, the Latins by the Jews. Only the Anglo-Saxons are virtually pure."

7. Quoted by Girardet, p. 211.

8. Jean-Paul Sartre, *Réflexions sur la question juive* (Paris: Morihien, 1946), p. 27. In the Weil archives I have been able to find only one reference to Sartre, in CD, 1: "Sartre: imitation: possession, imitator: possessed."

9. For two excellent discussions see Eugen Weber, "Nationalism, Socialism and National Socialism in France," *French Historical Studies* 2 (Spring 1962): 273–307; and Stephen Wilson, "The 'Action Française' in French Intellectual Life," *Historical Journal* 12 (1969): 328–50.

10. See Paula Hyman, *From Dreyfus to Vichy: The Remaking of French Jewry, 1906–1939* (New York: Columbia University Press, 1979), chap. 2.

11. Ibid., pp. 40–42.

12. For comparative figures see David H. Weinberg, *A Community on Trial: The Jews of Paris in the 1930s* (Chicago: University of Chicago Press, 1977), p. 4.

13. See the discussion of anti-Semitism in Robert Soucy, *French Fascism: The First Wave, 1924–1933* (New Haven: Yale University Press, 1986). Stephen A. Schuker, "Origins of the 'Jewish Problem' in the Later Third Republic," in *The Jews of Modern France*, ed. Frances Malino and Bernard Wasserstein (Hanover, N.H.: University Press of New England, 1985), pp. 135–80, contains an excellent discussion of immigration as an issue of conflicting rights, a matter Weil took up in her work for the Free French in 1943.

14. Sartre's prescription, p. 178, of the "authentic" Jew, who is "apart, untouchable, disdained, proscribed," describes the Eastern European Jew, not the native French Jew, but Sartre makes no national distinctions. Weinberg shows how important they are.

15. See the concluding discussion in Michael Marrus and Robert Paxton, *Vichy France and the Jews* (New York: Basic Books, 1981), pp. 363– 72, and Lucy Davidowicz, *The War against the Jews, 1933–1945* (New York: Holt, Rinehart and Winston, 1975), pp. 483–91.

16. Pétrement, 1:16.

17. Interview with André Weil, July 23, 1985.

18. *AD*, p. 26.

19. Ibid., p. 37.

20. Sartre, p. 146. He affirms this freethinking or humanistic role of Jews at the expense of the Jewish community. The Jew is to him an invented object, someone made "other" by anti-Semites.

21. *AD*, pp. 37–38.

22. Simone Weil, "What Is a Jew?" in *The Simone Weil Reader*, ed. George Panichas. (New York: David McKay, 1977), p. 80.

23. The *Statut des Juifs* was authored by Vichy's minister of justice, Raphael Alibert, a Jewish convert to Christianity. For Xavier Vallat's defense of Vichy's anti-Jewish legislation as "approximately within the dispositions already taken by the Church throughout the ages," see *France during the German Occupation 1940–1944*, trans. Philip W. Whitcomb. (Stanford: Stanford University Press, 1957), 2:629.

24. In *AD*, p. 56, she says that the proper function of intellect "requires a total liberty, implying the right to deny everything, and without domination." She was apparently unaware that Judaism, free of dogmas, has encouraged intellectual independence in its rabbis. By consistently going her own way, Weil was very Jewish.

25. See Weinberg, pp. 110, 130.

26. Pétrement, 1:105. On the rightist bias of the French press in the 1930s see Henri Noguères, *La Vie Quotidienne au temps du Front Populaire* (Paris: Hachette, 1977), pp. 260–64.

27. Cabaud, p. 131; cf. Pétrement, 1:75. The latter cautions that the hosts' reminiscence may be a mixed memory of Weil and what they later learned of her and of Jews during the war. Weil's visit to Germany in 1932 had apprised her of the Nazis' anti-Semitism, yet in

her fondness for the German people, she believed, or wanted to believe, that "anti-semitic and nationalist sentiments don't appear at all in personal relations" (Pétrement, 1:281).

28. Pétrement, 1:351. Pétrement offers this story as an example of Weil's desire to share others' suffering.

29. Letter to Xavier Vallat, October 18, 1941, in CG. Fr. Perrin in *Mon dialogue avec Simone Weil* (Paris: Nouvelle Cité, 1984), p. 97, says that Vallat, seeing the letter in print years later, remarked, "If I had received it, I would certainly have answered it."

30. *Études philosophiques* 1 (January–March 1946), 15.

31. S, pp. 232, 248. Only the first draft was published in an English translation, in Richard Rees's collection *Simone Weil: Seventy Letters* (London: Oxford University Press, 1965), pp. 119–27, thus giving a damagingly incomplete view of Weil's thinking in these drafts.

32. *LR*, pp. 70–71.

33. Undated letter, CSWAW. Her reference to "half-Jews" shows that at least here she recognizes that Jews are not merely believers but a consanguine people.

34. In *C*, 3:236–37, having reviewed Jewish patriarchs as criminals, she notes that there was no fanaticism in Solomon, implying that his predecessors were fanatics, yet his taxation policies make him seem to her "a sort of Louis XIV." She does not censure the one biblical figure who brings to her mind the model of authoritarian dictatorship she attacks in *E*.

35. CD, 2. This entry includes a reference to an *Histoire du peuple Hebreu* published by Desnoyers. Gilbert Kahn, "L'idée d'une beauté diabolique chez Simone Weil," *Entretiens sur l'homme et le diable* (Paris: Mouton, 1965), p. 124, says Weil knew about the horror of the camps enough to consider sending tracts to them urging revolt, but that simply shows how little she knew of the real situation. Jacques Adler, *The Jews of Paris and the Final Solution* (New York: Oxford University Press, 1987), pp. 46–47, maintains that "no news had reached the Jewish population of Paris before the end of 1942 about labor and extermination camps," but Weil, living in the Unoccupied Zone, might have learned a good deal before her departure.

36. Quoted by Paul Giniewski, *Simone Weil ou la haine de soi* (Paris: Berg International, 1978), pp. 48–49.

37. *EL*, p. 68.

38. No. 658, "Bases d'un statut des minorités françaises non chrétiennes et d'origine étrangere," in ELM. Subsequent quotations are from this source. Pétrement's abridgment of Weil's résumé (2:477) unduly moderates it.

39. At this point, Weil notes marginally, "This study unhappily does not undertake to define precisely the mentality corresponding to the Jewish religion."

40. The French word is *contagion*. Vallat, arguing that Jews were unassimilable, also used a pathological image, when he stated his resolve "to defend the French organism from the microbe which is leading it to fatal anemia." Quoted by Robert Aron, *Histoire de Vichy, 1940–1944* (Paris: Fayard, 1954), p. 208.

41. No. 657, "Les bases de la réforme constitutionelle," ELM. Weil's commentary on this document is discussed in "Prefaces to *L'enracinement*," Chapter 11 in this volume.

42. Pétrement, 2:218; on Weil's alleged Catharism see *PSO*, pp. 63–64, and her interest

in Marcion, p. 71. Pétrement, 2:434, quotes a letter from Weil to her parents in which she supposes that Perrin's neglect of his correspondence with her is owing to his conclusion about "my spiritual affiliation (the devil via Marcion)."

43. For example, Hans Meyerhoff, "Contra Simone Weil," *Commentary* 24 (September 1957): 240–49. For similar charges see the annotated bibliography of secondary essays.

44. John Bright, *The Authority of the Old Testament* (Grand Rapids: Baker Book House, 1975), p. 78.

45. Letter to Jean Wahl, *CSW* 10 (March 1987): 4. Weil's perspective here is not one of historiography but of historicism. She exercises a keen but selective knowledge of historical processes and then becomes an advocate. An impressionistic view in itself does not invalidate the argument it would further. Weil's presumption that Christianity's true home is with Greek mysteries may well rest on shaky, even false assumptions about history and yet retain insight and validity. Christians who reject Weil's view that Judaism is alien to their faith face a similar contention from Jews who understandably resent the claim that Hebrew Scriptures find their genuine meaning and fulfillment beyond their Jewish tradition in the New Testament.

46. Voltaire, *Oeuvres complètes* (Paris: Garnier, 1879), 24:527.

47. *C*, 1:165–67.

48. *C*, 3:231–32. Weil's attempt to isolate Judaism from other ancient religious cultures is identical to the intent of Jewish tradition. See Abba Hillel Silver, *Where Judaism Differed* (New York: Macmillan, 1956), pp. 183–234, for the argument of Judaism's thorough distinctiveness from Christianity and from other Oriental escapist cults of mystery and transcendence.

49. In Matthew 8:12 Jews are cast into outer darkness in consequence of the crucifixion. In Romans 11:8 Paul cites Deuteronomy 29:4 and Isaiah 29:10 as evidence that God had blinded the Jews. Such passages suggest how Weil's conceptualized hostility to Judaism is rooted in the New Testament.

50. "Israël et les Gentils," *PSO*, p. 54. The reference to "previous exactions" indicates that Weil subscribed to the view that the Hyksos were Jews. The notion of "God within" (Gal. 2:20) argues a kind of mystical participation impossible for large numbers of people in any culture, but Weil implies that Jews should have been collectively capable of it. She seems close to the position of Ignatius of Antioch that "to live Jewishly" meant not to live in grace. See William Schoedel, *A Commentary on the Letters of Ignatius of Antioch* (Philadelphia: Fortress Press, 1985), p. 119.

51. *C*, 2:27.

52. *PSO*, p. 50.

53. *LR*, p. 72.

54. Ibid. In *CS*, p. 147, Weil notes two contradictory views of God: in one, God is submitted to laws, as by recitation of magical formulas; in the other, God bestows favors capriciously like a king. As church sacraments may be considered a formulaic compulsion of God's presence, Christianity follows the first view. Jahweh's covenant with Israel puts Judaism under the second. Although urging a mediating unity between these contradictions, Weil did not perceive a cohesion of Judaism and Christianity on exactly these lines. It is a strange failure because she adds that magical (sacramental) knowledge is not a

technique of co-option but a form of love, and the seemingly capricious favor (the covenant) is not arbitrary but just.

55. *C*, 3:237. Thus Weil does not employ the patristic legerdemain that separates the pre-Mosaic patriarchs from Jewish history to claim them as ancestors of the "true Israel," the gentiles' church. On that tradition see David Efroymsen, "The Patristic Connection," in *Anti-Semitism and the Foundations of Christianity*, ed. Alan J. Davies (New York: Paulist Press, 1979), pp. 98–117.

56. On God as not existing, as nothingness, see *C*, 1:213, 222; 2:121– 22, 148. Instances could be multiplied, all in the direction of Weil's pivotal idea, that the true *imitatio Dei* must be a self-renunciation, an affirmation of one's own nothingness.

57. See *E*, pp. 372–80, and *CO*, pp. 327–53.

58. Weil's belief that Moses knew of an Egyptian religious tradition but yielded to the Hebrews' nationalistic needs strongly suggests the influence of Freud's 1939 essays depicting Moses as an Egyptian of royal descent who passed on Ikhnaton's exalted monotheism to the Jews. But in *CS*, p. 212, Weil aligns Moses with "the sacred wisdom of the Egyptian priests," the "establishment" Ikhnaton opposed. In *LR*, p. 17, she asserts that all peoples in history have been monotheistic.

59. *LR*, pp. 21–22.

60. Ibid., p. 47, and "Les trois fils de Noé et l'histoire de la civilisation méditerranéenne," *AD*, pp. 229–46. Perrin, *Mon dialogue*, p. 98, includes her interpretation of the Noah legend as one of her "inventions which border on bad faith."

61. *CS*, pp. 218, 289–90. See the Talmud, *Baba Bathra* 15b on Job as a heathen prophet.

62. *C*, 2:311; 3:106, 211, 229. Her equation of collectivity with idolatry may owe something to Alain's definition of idolatry, in *Les arts et les dieux* (Paris: Gallimard, 1958), p. 1064: "It is a gluttony for valuing what pleases you, and this appetite for thinking agreeably is the basis of idolatry." A collectivistic example would be the belief that one's nation or people is favored by God or by some privileging "manifest destiny."

63. *LR*, p. 19. Weil's Platonic disdain of the corporeal and material seems to inform her prejudice here.

64. Ibid., p. 15.

65. Did Weil know Spinoza's argument in his *Theologico-Political Treatise* (New York: Dover, 1951), p. 47, that "the Hebrews' choice and vocation consisted only in the temporal happiness and advantages of independent rule"? To him, Jews were a chosen people only for a limited time but on exactly the terms Weil abhors, the apparent chauvinism of national well-being. She would have rejected Spinoza's belief that in intellect and virtue they were no different from their neighbors.

66. *CS*, pp. 171–72. Her view that Jews contributed nothing to the Canaanite civilizations they took over echoes the charge of Apollonius Molon in Josephus's *Contra Apionem* 2:148. For a "Christian" deprecation of Judaism for self-idolatry see Arnold J. Toynbee, A *Study of History* (London: Oxford University Press, 1939) 4:262–63.

67. She may have known Philostratus's *Life of Apollonius* 5:33, which says Jews are "in revolt not only against the Romans but against humanity . . . a race that has made its own a

life apart and irreconcilable." The Christian source for the view that Jews are "contrary to all men" is 1 Thessalonians 2:14–15.

68. *CS*, p. 173. In the same passage she says that Hitler, in persecuting Jews, "would like to plagiarize them and baptize the collective German soul Wotan, and say that Wotan created the heavens and the earth." Carl Jung, in "Wotan," *Neue Schweizer Rundschau* (March 1936), 668, compares Wotan to Jahweh as a god into whose hands it is terrible to fall.

69. Weil was not original in claiming, *E*, p. 206, that Hitler's racism was inspired by the idea of a chosen people. Jacques Maritain, *Antisemitism*, (London: Centenary Press, 1939), p. 11: "The Germany of Hitler, in seeking to reject Israel, has embraced the very worst of Israel. I mean that sentiment of racial pride which is in some carnal Jews the naturalistic corruption of the supernatural idea of divine election." George Steiner, in "One Definition of a Jew," *Cambridge Opinion* 39 (1964): 16–22, says the "poison" of the "chosen people" notion may be remedied in what he sees as "most profoundly" Jewish, a universal humanism.

70. *LR*, pp. 16–17. Raised in ignorance of ritual recitations, Weil did not realize that for the Egyptian confessor of the rite-of-passage formulas, there may have been no more force of truth felt in the words than for a Christian reciting the Nicene Creed. On the personal strength of the Hebraic psalms in contrast to Egyptian formulas see André Barucq, *L'expression de la louange divine et de la prière dans la Bible et en Egypte* (Cairo: Institute Français d'Archéologie Orientale, 1982), p. 505.

71. *E*, p. 188.

72. *LR*, p. 35.

73. J.-M. Perrin, *Simone Weil telle que nous l'avons connue* (Paris: La Colombe, 1952), p. 70.

74. Ibid., p. 69.

75. *AD*, p. 54.

76. Wladimir Rabi, "La conception Weilienne de la Creation: Rencontre avec la Kabbale Juive," in *Simone Weil: philosophe, historienne et mystique*, ed. Gilbert Kahn (Paris: Aubier Montaigne, 1978), p. 141.

77. Armand Lunel, "Simone Weil et l'Israël," *Revue de la pensée juive* 4 (July 1950): 50.

78. Ibid., p. 52. Cathars were called "Judaizers" by their foes.

79. Martin Buber, "The Silent Question: On Henri Bergson and Simone Weil," *The Writings of Martin Buber*, ed. Will Herberg (New York: Meridian, 1958), p. 313. The original essay appeared in German in 1952.

80. Ibid., p. 310.

81. Emmanuel Lévinas, "Simone Weil contre le Bible," *Evidences*, February–March 1952, p. 163.

82. *C*, 3:246.

83. Lévinas, p. 165.

84. Rabi, p. 154.

85. Michael R. Marrus, "Are the French Antisemitic? Evidence in the 1980s," in Malino and Wasserstein, p. 232.

86. Arnold Mandel, "Le dibbouk en Simone Weil," *Le monde*, April 19, 1978, p. 1. The year was notable for a number of violent anti-Semitic incidents in Paris, Avignon, and Marseilles.

87. Ibid., p. 22.

88. Arnold Mandel, "Repliques à . . . Oscar Wolfman," *Le monde*, July 19, 1978, p. 2.

89. Ibid.

90. Giniewski, *Simone Weil ou la haine de soi*, pp. 338–39.

91. Jean Améry, "Jenseits der legende," *Merkur* 33 (1979), 84.

92. See his review of Giniewski's book in CSW 1 (September 1978): 35, 38.

93. Gilbert Kahn, "Limites et raisons du refus de l'ancien testament par Simone Weil," *CSW* 3 (June 1980): 110.

94. Ernst Küller, "Das Zeugnis der Simone Weil," *Evangelische Theologie* 10 (1959): 482, quoting E. Przywara's *Humanitas gestern und morgen*, p. 567.

95. See his discussion of "Le problème du judaïsme," in Kahn, p. 159.

Chapter 10

1. Pétrement, 2:440.

2. Evelyn Underhill, *Mysticism* (1911; rpt. New York: E. P. Dutton, 1961), p. 93.

3. *C*, 2:317–18.

4. "Le beau et le bien," *OC*, 1:71.

5. When her friends the Honnorats said good-bye to her in Marseilles, "Au revoir, Simone, in this world or the other," she replied, "No, in the other world one is not seen again" (Pétrement, 2:414). Her position has been defended as agnostic. Bernadine Bishop, "Exchanges: Bernadine Bishop and Hilda Graef, *New Blackfriars* 48 (October 1966): 55–56, fairly observes that Weil did not deny an afterlife—how could she?—but "found it more helpful to discount the possibility, as any finite interpretation of the infinite would be more misleading than nothing."

6. In CS, p. 175, she says that Christ's example teaches us our nonbeing, but she makes of his humbling not merely an ethical lesson (service to others) but an ontological one, the fundamental nothingness of self. In *LR*, p. 62, she claims that "Hitler could die and be resurrected fifty times and I would not regard him as the Son of God."

7. Discussing Osiris, CS, p. 213, she raises the same points about redemption: is it a historical memory or a presentment of the future? "Perhaps we don't have the données necessary to make even a supposition on this subject."

8. *LR*, pp. 55, 58, 63. Her discussion of miracles is the lengthiest of her thirty-five points in *LR*; one might infer that they were more of a sticking point than is evident in her other writing. In C, 2:158, she indicates her real difficulty with miracle. She suggests that the idea of miracles argues an unmaking of creation and violates God's established order. Miracle means supernatural action in nature, an absurd contradiction in terms. Here she is with Hume, but she realizes it is impossible to deny miracles altogether by reducing them to natural explanations. She submits that the scientific mind's hostility to miracles recapitulates the church's hostility to Galileo's astronomy. Finally, she settles for miracle as a

natural phenomenon manifested in hysteria, ascetic exercises, and (begging the question) sainthood.

9. Necessity is not lovable, she says in *CS*, pp. 95, 293, but we love it by accepting Christ as a condemned criminal.

10. *C*, 2:145, 245; 3:108, 313–14, 316–17; *AD*, p. 15.

11. *AD*, pp. 49, 91.

12. W. D. Halls, "Catholicism under Vichy: A Study in Diversity and Ambiguity," in *Vichy France and the Resistance*, ed. Roderick Kedward and Roger Austin (London: Croom Helm, 1985), pp. 133–34.

13. She rejects historical Protestantism as a species of nationalism, *CS*, p. 261. Because the Catholic church monopolized the sacraments, those who broke with it were left with "la morale au premier plan," a morality doomed, in the absence of "the sacramental life," to degeneration.

14. *C*, 2:172. In counterpoint to this remark, her "Théorie des sacrements," *PSO*, pp. 135–45, argues why their importance cannot be exaggerated. In fact, Weil concerns herself only with holy communion. The eucharist becomes agent of the soul's perfection if one believes in the "supernatural possibility" of contact with God, but to the degree that one truly desires contact with God, "the soul's mediocre part" fights this process with hate, fear, and repulsion. Weil regards this contest as benign (provided the soul not heed its own mediocrity) because the eucharist destroys much of the soul's evil. How this happens, how she knows it happens, she does not say.

15. Gabriel Marcel, "Simone Weil," *Month* n.s, 2 (July 1949): 16, concludes, "Without going so far as to say that she was formally heretical, I should be inclined to say that she was constantly on the fringe of heresy." Weil's own view of heresy, *CS*, p. 81, should be added: the only true heresy is a speculation that "diminishes the reality of divine things by covering them over with an apparent reconciliation of the contradictions constituting their mystery."

16. *CS*, pp. 67, 173; *LR*, pp. 44–45, 49–50; *C*, 2:315; 3:305–6. The eminent Frederick Copleston, S.J., "The Existentialists Once More," *Month* 9, (June 1953): 370–71, says Weil "did not really understand the Church and its place in the divine plan." It would be more accurate to say she refused to accept the church's claim to a part in the so-called plan. She rejects an eschatology or teleology for the human condition in any historical sense.

Regarding missionary imperialism she excepts the Jesuits in China, *LR*, p. 37. Their respect for Chinese culture brought them severe criticism from the Vatican. The Jesuits, she says "fulfilled Christ's word" because they saw that the injunction to instruct and baptize did not require baptizands to renounce what was regarded as holy in their native traditions.

17. *LR*, pp. 35–36; *AD*, pp. 59–60; *CS*, p. 265. In *AD*, p. 253, she says she is more ready to die for the church than to enter it. Her church was made up of the two or three who would gather in Christ's name. In *C*, 2:153, 230, she read this Scripture (Matt. 18:20) as an implicit denial of Christ's presence in "the social element" and a point for comparison with "Socratic tradition."

18. *AD*, pp. 17, 23–24, 26. As for her sense of inferiority, she once noted to herself, *C*, 2:300, that she would have to enter the church if being outside it made her feel superior.

19. *AD*, pp. 37, 75. On p. 248 she maintains that Christian dogma is an object for

contemplation, not belief. On that basis, an outsider might be as privileged, if not more so, than the church's indoor believers.

20. *AD*, pp. 52–53.

21. Ibid., pp. 19, 65.

22. *LR*, p. 84.

23. Ibid., pp. 85–86, 94. The distinguished historian of ancient philosophy Emile Bréhier, reviewing *LR* in *Revue philosophique de France et de l'etranger* 147 (1957), 79, compares Weil to non-Christians of the early centuries C.E., such as the emperor Julian, who wanted to find in paganism "some of the fundamental beliefs and practices of Judaism."

24. *CS*, pp. 64, 67, 68, 79 (his "totalitarian use of mystery"), 172. On p. 311 she upholds Augustine's "just war" doctrine.

25. *PSO*, p. 65. Even that does not suffice to warrant Rosalind Murray's implying in "The Onlooker," *Tablet*, June 13, 1953, p. 516, that Weil "has certainly expressed the mind of a contemporary Gnostic in an arresting and compelling way." Weil shared little with ancient Gnostics so it seems unlikely she would have much in common with modern ones.

26. Roché's booklet was *Le Catharisme* (Carcassonne: Gabelle, 1937). She may also have read his *L'église romaine et les Cathares albigeois* published the same year. In her letter to Roché she expressed interest in meeting him, but nothing came of it.

27. Lettre à Déodat Roché, January 23, 1941, in *PSO*, p. 64.

28. *C*, 2:315.

29. *EHP*, pp. 67, 68.

30. Ibid., pp. 78, 79.

31. Ibid., p. 74.

32. Ibid., p. 79. Such remarks are grist for the mill where Marcel Carrières grinds in "Simone Weil et nous," *Cahiers d'etudes Cathares* 7 (Autumn 1950), 157–62. He says Weil was "not only a great Christian. Dare we say: a Perfect One [*une Parfaite*] in the purest Cathar tradition? And isn't it permissible to ask what would have been the definitive orientation of her thought if, instead of R. P. Perrin [sic] she had followed up her relations with M. Roché, for example, or more simply if she had lived?" But Weil, once resolved not to enter the church, did not go on to call herself a Cathar, and the presumption of "l'orientation definitive de sa pensée" remains only that.

33. Halls, p. 133.

34. Jacques Duquesne, *Les Catholiques français sous l'Occupation* (Paris: Grasset, 1966), p. 44.

35. Quoted by Halls, p. 137. See also John Sweets, *Choices in Vichy France* (New York: Oxford Universty Press, 1986), pp. 56–57.

36. For a brief but telling summary, see the results of a December 1944 questionnaire on the clergy's views of Vichy, the Occupation, and the Resistance, in André Latreille, *De Gaulle, la libération et l'église Catholique* (Paris: Editions du Cerf, 1978), pp. 56–59.

37. *EHP*, p. 84.

38. *AD*, p. 21. By contrast with this "authentic few" position, she could tell Maurice Schumann that as businessmen are by definition honest and soldiers brave, so Christians

are by definition saints. This Platonic absolutism-by-definition, unless tinged with irony, shows how Weil's inability to admit qualification finally allowed her to remain *hors de l'église*. If one can be a Christian outside the church as well as within, what need is there of a church? On her remarks to Schumann, a converted Jew, see F. W. J. Hemmings, "Sainte Simone," *New Statesman* 72 (July 15, 1966): 99.

39. Alain, *Les Dieux* (Paris: Gallimard, 1947), p. 203.

40. Alain, *Propos sur la religion* (1938; rpt. Paris: Presses Universitaires de France, 1969), p. 23. See pp. 235–37 on *l'orgeuil de pouvoir*.

41. Ibid., p. 277. See p. 208: "Many who call themselves Catholics are not so at all."

42. Ibid., p. 273. For Alain, ideas are the object of faith; for Weil, they are the modes of faith.

43. Ibid., p. 153. In *E*, p. 120, Weil says that in the face of lay philosophy the only authentic attitude to Christianity is to present it as "one treasure of human thought among others." Those could be Alain's words.

44. *LR*, pp. 38, 39. In *AD*, p. 178, however, she suggests that in studying religions, one must transport oneself to their center by faith. That implies that an intellectual attention to a religious belief is, for her, tantamount to its affirmation.

45. Pierre Marin, "D'Alain à Simone Weil," *CSW* 3 (March 1980): 59–64, unfairly says Alain regarded religion as nothing more than an element of culture like the fine arts. Alain believed religion had been superseded, not invalidated, by philosophy; intellectual progress—the only kind he recognized—meant that the divine increasingly takes a human form. He believed in saintliness, which he defined as living for the good alone and giving oneself up to God. He defended the cult of the Virgin, and he delighted in the rich, psychological truths of religious legends. He scorned those who sought to demythologize faith or mocked it as fanaticism. See *Propos sur la religion*, pp. 91–93, 130, 223, 257.

46. *LR*, pp. 21, 22, 25, 32–34.

47. *AD*, p. 64.

48. Georges Hourdin, "Simone Weil et l'église catholique," *Le monde*, May 9, 1950, p. 5.

49. *AD*, pp. 83–84.

50. *C*, 3:8.

51. *LR*, p. 62. Let a Christian imagine Good Friday forever without Easter. An anonymous reviewer of "The Paradox of Simone Weil," *Times Literary Supplement*, May 6, 1955, p. v, contends that "it is the absence of hope that makes her charity almost inhuman and her work 'contemporary,'" but he (or she) goes too far in concluding that Weil had no apparent need for hope or its promise, that the New Testament was no more essential to her than the Torah.

52. *CS*, "Prologue," pp. 9–10. For a reading of this work as a mystical journey, see Hélène Honnorat, "Un poème en prose de Simone Weil," *Cahiers universitaires catholiques* 2 (November 1968): 101–9. Honnorat loosely alternates biographical reminiscences with the reading of symbols. The absence of a consistent level of interpretation or even a coordination of levels is disconcerting. In the midst of her discussion of Weil's humility and rejection, Honnorat remarks, p. 108: "On the eve of departing from France, she greatly feared escaping from the Nazis' rage, should it spread throughout France." Honnorat's

intent is hagiographic, but what the statement means is that Weil did not wish to miss the supreme choreography of humiliation and rejection.

53. Martin Jarrett-Kerr, "Martyr to Masochism," *Guardian*, December 18, 1964, p. 7. Reviewing Cabaud's biography, he caricatures Weil's life as "a calculated course in outrageous masochism, but what a magnificent masochism. . . . Her mystical experiences, self-authenticating, give a beauty to her harsh, cruel love." The latter phrase suggests the harshness and cruelty of love in "He" may have been projected from Weil's own uncompromising temperament.

54. Alain, *Propos sur la religion*, p. 231.

55. Ibid., pp. 156–57.

56. *AD*, p. 146.

57. Ibid., pp. 196–97.

58. Elizabeth Jennings, "A World of Contradictions: A Study of Simone Weil," *Month* 22 (December 1959): 349–58, says Weil's unremitting stress on intelligence argues "little of that total abandonment to God which is so shiningly evident in every Christian mystic who preceded her." She ascribes to Weil "the wish for an autonomous world created by the mind for the mind"—Alain's influence is clear, even when Weil's reader evinces no awareness of him. Finally, Jennings charges that Weil, "a mystic manqué," "longed to surrender herself completely but lacked the ultimate confidence to do so."

Albert Béguin, "La raideur et la grâce," *Témoignage chrétien* December 2, 1949, p. 5, objecting to the fast-flourishing Weil cult of that time, denies Weil status as "un maître de spiritualité." Like Jennings, he finds in Weil an impenitent intellectuality but adds that her desire for "the complete suppression of personal consciousness so that only divine impersonality subsists" reveals a mysticism "du type asiatique."

59. Underhill, pp. 90, 178, 200, 221.

60. *C*, 2:145.

61. Ibid., p. 390.

62. Ibid., p. 161.

63. Ibid., p. 11. Weil remarks astutely that Peter's denial that he would betray Christ was itself the betrayal because he supposed that the source of faith was in himself and not in grace.

64. Ibid., p. 254. This remark might suggest how Weil would have reacted to the orgy of vengeance that ensued after the Liberation in August 1944.

65. Ibid., p. 123. See also *C*, 3:146: Christ's existence as a pure being was itself an incitement to crime among the wicked.

66. *AD*, p. 62.

67. *C*, 2:407.

68. Ibid.

69. *AD*, pp. 31–32.

70. Ibid., pp. 61–62. See also her censure of *tristesse*, in S, pp. 232–33, 241: sorrow is sterile and impious, a sign of pride, a refusal of obedience to necessity, and a denial of God. Neurosis implies atheism. Weil's severity recalls Dante's—he put full-time melancholics in *Inferno*, 9—but her philosophical source seems to be Spinoza's *Ethics* 4, prop. 42. To Spinoza, melancholy is always bad.

71. *C*, 3:192–93.

72. Ibid., 3:225.

73. *AD*, pp. 235–37. She seems unaware of the central role of sacrifice in orthodox Judaism, but on Abel's murder as a prefiguration of Christ's, see *CS*, p. 212.

74. She is expressly indebted to Plato's idea of the soul's irrational power and its striving into the unlimited, as expounded in the *Philebus*.

75. *C*, 1:46–47.

76. *AD*, p. 93. On degrading the supernatural by searching for it, see *C*, 2:50.

77. *C*, 2:65; *AD*, p. 156. In *C*, 2:20, Weil uses this idea to explain why evil is so attractively represented in fiction and why good is so boring. (The reader might recall Milton's Satan and Milton's Christ.) If there were no such thing as gravity, good would be commonplace, and evil would have the allure of surprise and thus please us. But in this life, the good is exceptional. That is why all great literature—Weil mentions Sophocles and *King Lear*—represents the force of gravity. It is truly mimetic, "supernatural," and not imaginative.

78. *C*, 2:125.

79. *AD*, p. 222. Perhaps only with her firsthand awareness of Vichy's internment camps could she have come to this stark intuition of Nazism's greatest horror, making the soul at bay both thing and accomplice. Her own degradation in the factories should also be reckoned. Fatigue and headaches gave her "a keen desire to make some other person suffer by striking him in exactly the same part of the forehead . . . to say words that cause pain" (*C*, 2:18).

80. *AD*, p. 185.

81. *C*, 1:200.

82. *C*, 2:413. At best, it would seem Weil's only remedy for evil is to put up with the discord between imagination and the facts, but at times Weil gives her not so cryptic voluntarism a tether in order to "cut away energy's bonds" and choose God over Mammon. Likewise, to love God's indifference to the play of contingent good and evil means that one must refuse "complicity" in human destiny. See *C*, 2:123.

83. *C*, 3:307.

84. *AD*, p. 36.

85. *AD*, pp. 45, 69; *C*, 2:201–2; cf. *LR*, p. 79.

86. *AD*, p. 192. See *A Book of Showings to the Anchoress Julian of Norwich*, ed. E. Colledge and J. Walsh (Toronto: Pontifical Institute of Mediaeval Studies, 1978), 2:420: "For as truly as ther is a propyrte in god of ruth and pyte, so verely ther is a properte in god of thurst and longyng."

87. *LR*, pp. 62–63; see also *C*, 2:195, 264.

88. *C*, 2:152. Cf. Alexander Kojève's maxim that desire is the presence of an absence. Weil's God must be absent, otherwise he could not be desired. One senses that for Weil the desire for God is more precious than God himself.

89. *C*, 3:323.

90. *AD*, pp. 70–71; *C*, 3:58.

91. *C*, 2:326. Paul West, "Simone Weil," in his *Wine of Absurdity* (University Park, Pa.: Pennsylvania State University Press, 1966), p. 153, contends: "All told, she was more

concerned with perfecting God's geometry than with confronting the human lot." Consequently, "I find something monstrous in Simone Weil, something that doesn't respect an ordinary human joy." Thibon had anticipated this criticism. It might be added that for all his self-regard, her god does not seem to show any joy, either; no joy in creation, no looking upon and seeing it as good.

92. *C*, 3:230; 2:232.

93. *CS*, pp. 200–201.

94. Ibid., p. 205.

95. *C*, 2:290; *AD*, p. 27.

96. *C*, 3:303. Cf. *C*, 2:334: "It is not my part to love God. Let God love himself through me as a medium."

97. *C*, 2:289–90.

98. Gustave Thibon, *Simone Weil telle que nous l'avons connue* (Paris: La Colombe, 1952), p. 134, notes that though Weil was profoundly self-concerned and regarded other people as preferable to herself, she did not have the sense of another person as another. Thibon's statement bears witness to Weil's God as well, for it seems he has no sense of humanity as another. That holds despite Weil's many words on divine love. It is strange that this God loving only himself is so human, and all the more so that he is a bungler; he cannot make a creation capable of loving him. Besides, Weil at times is close to the ancient Greek prejudice that humanity is superior to divinity in having to suffer and struggle. Such, she felt, is the scandal that necessitated the incarnation and crucifixion. Yet at other times she writes as though the scandal continues: "Love is a sign of our wretchedness. God can love only himself. We can love only something other than ourselves" (*C*, 2:205). She also strikes the note of pathos, comparing God and humanity to two lovers missing a rendezvous (*CS*, p. 92). God and humanity are like two prisoners communicating between prison walls (*C*, 3:129).

99. *AD*, pp. 18, 29, 52. See also her statement, p. 38, that the most beautiful life would be one of total constraint, where one would be moved either by circumstances or by impulsion and not by choice. Terence de Vere White, "Saint Simone Stylites," *Irish Times*, September 21, 1968, p. 8: "One must weep for Simone Weil; so blundering, so earnest and so good; but there is sufficient evidence in what she wrote to suggest that she rather liked the idea of going to hell." Apart from the fact that she believed suffering is to be used, not enjoyed, and accepted, not cultivated, it seems unlikely she relished damnation. After Baudelaire, there was some fashion in posing oneself as a damned soul, but surely one has to have been born into the Christian faith in order to pervert its spirituality by such attitudes. Weil was not, and her sense of heaven and hell as any Christian would understand them (whether believing in them or not) is simply not evident.

100. *AD*, pp. 14, 171; *CS*, p. 111.

101. *AD*, pp. 29, 190. Cf. p. 31, where Weil, about to leave France, writes to Perrin that "my greatest desire is to lose not only all will but all being proper."

102. *CS*, p. 169.

103. *CS*, p. 179; *AD*, p. 190. Cf. *C*, 3:284: "It is certain that I must work at transforming the feeling of effort into a passive feeling of suffering."

104. *C*, 3:180.

105. *AD*, pp. 81–82.

106. *C*, 1:92; 2:180. T. S. Gregory, "Both Sides of the Threshold," *Tablet* 198 (October 27, 1951): 289, suggests that the only baptism Weil could conceive was Christ's baptism into death: "She would not grab at God. . . . For such inexorable piety, death is the only possible reception."

107. *C*, 1:162. Joseph Blenkinsopp, "The Frustrated Pilgrim," *Wiseman Review*, no. 489 (Autumn 1961); pp. 277–85, perhaps overstates "the will-to-death deep in her temperament." Like John Donne, Weil in her debility and bouts of sickness may have developed a fascination with death and a perception of spiritual treasures in an acceptance of it, but she did not try to embrace it. She did not take up self-mortificatory practices like fasting. The imputation of anorexia remains hollow.

108. *CS*, p. 227.

109. *C*, 2:335.

110. *CS*, p. 176: hell she defines as our refusal to accept our nonbeing.

111. *C*, 2:75–76. Cf. *LR*, p. 21, on the possibility of revealed scriptures among the Chinese and Indians. This receptivity likely offends some Christians. Bede Griffiths, O.S.B., "The Enigma of Simone Weil," *Blackfriars* 34 (May 1953): 232–36, says Weil is wrong to see the level of contemplation among Eastern mystics as equal to that of Christian, but he does not say how or why she is wrong. It is strange to read his charge (p. 236) that her intelligence was "in many ways defective and blinded by ignorance and prejudice." Weil would have confessed to a learner's ignorance about the East. As to prejudice, hers was a prejudice for, in this instance, not against. One wonders how Griffiths would have characterized his own attitude to Eastern religions.

112. *C*, 2:156.

113. "Dieu dans Platon," *SG*, p. 67.

114. *AD*, pp. 177–78; *LR*, p. 39.

115. *C*, 2:134. By synthesis Weil does not of course mean analogical parallels such as she draws freely between religious, mythological, and philosophical traditions.

116. *C*, 3:137.

117. *C*, 2:307.

118. *AD*, p. 78. That verdict should be kept in mind in view of Donald Nicholl's claim, "Simone Weil, God's Servant," *Blackfriars* 31 (August 1950): 364–72, that her relationship with Perrin allowed her to pass from "a somewhat Kantian sense of duty" to "love as a person loving persons . . . the metallic tones of the female intellectual, unconscious echoes of a heart empty with longing, are unmistakably softened into the fuller notes of the woman deep in understanding of others." Apart from the assumption here that women who think are somehow unnatural or undeep, the sentimental, almost mawkish language reflects the attitude that gave Weil a cultish aura in the Catholic revival movement of the late 1940s.

119. Letter of August 3, 1941, to René Daumal, quoted by Pétrement, 2:345.

120. In CD there is a list of some of the most important terms: *samâna*—harmony; *sandhya*—intermediary; *prasada*—spiritual grace; *sattva*—conformity to pure essence; *rajas*—expansive impulsion; *tamas*—tendency to descent. The last three are known as the *gunas* of *prakṛiti*, states in which all beings participate variously. On *prakṛiti*, see C, 1:148–49.

121. *LR*, pp. 33–34.

122. The Hindus drew no line between myth and historic fact, and neither, it seems, did Weil. See David Roper, "L'interprétation des traditions hindoues et bouddhiques chez Simone Weil," in *Simone Weil: philosophe, historienne et mystique*, ed. Gilbert Kahn (Paris: Aubier Montaigne, 1978), p. 98.

123. *C*, 2:382, 383.

124. *CS*, pp. 233, 258, 295. The koan's lesson complemented Lagneau's: just as it is what we think we know that we cannot be certain of, so we can be certain of what we do not comprehend. See p. 30. This might be taken as an example of the Cartesianism that Weil has been accused of relapsing into after she was no longer in Perrin's company.

125. *C*, 2:368.

126. Ibid., p. 411.

127. *C*, 3:30.

128. *C*, 2:370–71.

129. *CS*, p. 230. As a tacit apology for the Indian caste system, the *Gita* urges a positive delight in carrying out one's allotted actions: the *ksatriya* must fight with an elevated self-abandon. In *C*, 2:112, Weil says Arjuna's feelings of pity show he "wasn't worthy of not making war."

130. The latter is not, as commonly supposed, a mere nothingness but, in Guenon's definition, "extinction of agitation."

131. *C*, 2:180.

132. *C*, 1:46.

133. *C*, 2:231.

134. *C*, 1:89.

135. *CS*, p. 258. This remark indicates that Weil's distinction between Arjuna and Jeanne d'Arc had been false. Both acted under divine compulsion.

136. See *C*, 3:65, on Dante's consignment of righteous pagans to Hell, and Joshua's destruction of Jericho as "a wholly illegitimate use of the idea of mystery." Yet she grants that she has no criterion for differentiating "absurdities that project light . . . and those that project darkness."

137. *CS*, p. 306.

138. This term comes from D. T. Suzuki, *Essays in Zen Buddhism: First Series* (London: Luzac, 1926), p. 217.

139. *CS*, p. 296. Weil frequently reproached herself for the spiritual torpor of *tamas*. Exertions such as her paramilitary schemes might be interpreted as attempts to stretch her will to a point of maximal tension (*sattva*) in the hope of its annihilation.

140. The Upanishads do not present a uniform, coherent reality, but it may be said they tend toward the monism of brahman-*atman*, a union of the eternal soul with the eternal ground of the universe, at an absolute remove from nature (*prakṛiti*). It is difficult to determine the extent to which Weil embraced the theistic or personalized monism of the *Gita* over against the non-theistic harmony of *om* in the Upanishads, where the soul becomes a co-creator affirming the world as it is. Perhaps no line need be drawn. Weil herself equates *atman* with God (*C*, 1:200). What matters to her is the purifying acceptance or love of reality.

141. It is no accident that she ends her notes on the *Gita*, *C*, 1:151, with a citation from Spinoza's *Ethics* 5:23, *sentimus experimurque nos aesternos esse*, we feel and sense we are eternal.

142. *CS*, pp. 77, 91, 205, 222. See p. 46 on God as mother to the infant soul, and p. 253 on God the parasite planting the Son's sperm in humankind.

143. Suzuki, p. 236.

144. *C*, 1:236.

145. For a discussion of these correspondences, see R. C. Zaehner, *Hinduism* (Oxford: Oxford University Press, 1962), pp. 110–11. Weil's inattention to these elementary facts complements her ironic assumption that a Christian is a slave—this in the face of contemporary evidence to the contrary, that Jews were being forced to that degrading station and worse.

146. *AD*, pp. 20, 27, 54, 71. She could countenance salvation for an atheist, but she told Père Couturier, *LR*, pp. 12, 41, that her own was of no importance.

147. *LR*, pp. 53, 55, 57, 71, 75, 76.

148. *C*, 1:41.

149. Ibid., pp. 81, 82.

150. Ibid., p. 151–53.

151. *C*, 2:190.

152. Pétrement, 2:345.

153. *AD*, pp. 13–14; *CS*, p. 223.

154. Fragment in CD, 3.

155. See Weil's report on the Société d'études philosophiques, *Cahiers du Sud* 19 (May 1941): 288. Her interests at this time were not confined to philosophy and religion. In her unpublished papers one finds dozens of pages of transcriptions and reading notes: twenty-five on Bernal Diaz's account of Cortez's conquest of Mexico; nearly as many on Persian grammar, including conjugations in original and transliterated script, with English translations and French commentary; an extensive transcription of the *Nâtya Çâstro*, the most ancient Hindu treatise on theater, which her friend René Daumal had translated. It is unlikely that these vast exercises will find a place in Gallimard's edition of Weil's *Oeuvres complètes*. That is a pity, for they record convincingly her boundless inquisitiveness.

156. Edward Conze, *Buddhism: Its Essence and Development* (Oxford: Bruno Cassirer, 1951), p. 17.

157. *CS*, p. 226.

158. *C*, 2:277.

159. This story is recounted in Yaffa Eliach, *Hasidic Tales of the Holocaust* (New York: Oxford University Press, 1982), pp. 53–55.

Chapter 11

1. Quoted by Raoul Girardet, *Le nationalisme français* (Paris: Seuil, 1983), p. 66.

2. Knowing the difference between the humiliation France suffered in 1940 (the sources of which he savagely attacked) and its history of defeats, Bernanos claimed in defense of his

compatriots that their suffering not only made them more human, it helped them survive. Weil admired Bernanos and read with appreciation his *Lettre aux Anglais* during her own exile.

3. *EL*, p. 83.

4. Ibid., pp. 76, 78.

5. Ibid., p. 84.

6. *E*, p. 54.

7. Ibid., p. 55. And what of her calumnies against Israel?

8. It was almost fashionable in that time to blame one's political or ideological opponents for the disaster of June 1940. On the respectable Left, Léon Blum, in *A l'échelle humaine* (1942) scored the bourgeoisie for giving itself over to reaction and the ruin of the Popular Front. In his *Lettre aux Anglais* (1942) Bernanos saw the defeat as a result of the elites' betrayal of Ancien France and its chivalric code of honor. Maurras, in *La seule France* (1942), rehashed the old Jewish–international conspiracy argument. Grudges quite ulterior to the immediate issue were thus dredged up and kept going by adding the national woe to one's list of the opposition's crimes. A rare, fair-minded contemporary assessment is Louis Levy's *The Truth about France*, trans. W. Pickles (Harmondsworth: Penguin, 1941). A socialist and ardent admirer of Blum, Levy is nonetheless able to judge Left and Right equanimously.

9. The untitled manuscript is in ELM. Subsequent quotations are from this source. The first sentence reads: "These are the impressions of a Parisian who left Marseilles last May, having lived in unoccupied France, chiefly in Marseilles, since the armistice."

10. H. R. Kedward, *Occupied France: Collaboration and Resistance, 1940–1944* (Oxford: Basil Blackwell, 1985), p. 15.

11. As Robert O. Paxton notes in his indispensable *Vichy France: Old Guard and New Order, 1940–1944* (New York: Columbia University Press, 1972), p. 333, France after liberation "punished a smaller proportion of its total population with prison terms than any other occupied Western European country and executed a smaller proportion than Belgium."

12. Theodore Zeldin, *France, 1848–1945: Anxiety and Hypocrisy* (Oxford: Oxford University Press, 1981), p. 174.

13. Ibid., p. 176.

14. "Lettre aux Indochinoise" in EHP. A sumptuous work published for the Exposition Coloniale International de Paris is Sylvain Levi's *Indochine* (Paris: Société d'Editions, 1931). This volume's review of Vietnamese history, literature, art, and religion was probably one of Weil's major sources for her high esteem of Annamite culture.

15. Petrément, 2:118.

16. For a thorough account of the spurious benefits in France's "development" of Vietnam, see Robert Sansom, *The Economy of Insurgency in the Mekong Delta of Vietnam* (Cambridge, Mass.: Harvard University Press, 1970), pp. 18–52.

17. "Le sang coule en Tunisie," *EHP*, p. 337.

18. Ibid., p. 340.

19. In his *Esquisse d'un tableau historique des progrès de l'esprit humain*, completed in October 1793 (Paris: Flammarion, 1988), p. 268, he wrote: "Go through the history of our

undertakings, our establishments in Africa and Asia, and see our commercial monopolies, our treacheries, our bloody contempt for people of a different color or a different creed, the insolence of our takeovers, the extravagant proselytism and intrigues of our priests destroying the feeling of respect and benevolence which the superiority of our knowledge [*lumières*] and the advantages of our commerce had at first obtained."

20. "I'm ashamed of French democrats, French socialists and the French working class" (*EHP*, p. 341).

21. "Ces membres palpitants de la patrie," *EHP*, pp. 344–50, is chiefly a celebration of the radical Algerian newspaper *Etoile Nord-Africaine*, whose staff, Weil observes with delight, consisted wholly of workers, not one of whom was a white or an intellectual.

22. "Les nouvelles données du problème colonial dans l'empire français," *EHP*, pp. 355–56.

23. "Fragment," *EHP*, p. 360.

24. "Lettre à Jean Giraudoux," *EHP*, pp. 361, 362. This letter bears Weil's disarming candor and wit. She tells Giraudoux: "Although my admiration for you obliges me to write to you, it is not my admiration that I am going to express. . . . I have always been proud of you as one whose name can be pronounced when one seeks a reason for loving present-day France. That's why I would like you always to speak the truth, even on the radio."

25. Ibid., p. 362.

26. Ibid.

27. Ibid., p. 363.

28. I have arbitrarily entitled this essay, from ELM, "The Colonial Problem" on the basis of its first sentence: "Among the many difficult and dangerous problems of this war, few are so difficult and dangerous as the colonial problem." Subsequent quotations are from this source.

29. For an analogy to Vietnamese preference of Japan see *The Collected Essays, Journalism and Letters of George Orwell*, ed., Sonia Orwell and Ian Angus (Harmondsworth: Penguin, 1970), 2:253: "Many, perhaps most, Indian intellectuals are emotionally pro-Japanese . . . it is merely that the nationalism of defeated peoples is necessarily revengeful and short-sighted."

30. For a thoroughly documented review see Zeev Sternhell, *Ni droite ni gauche: L'idéologie fasciste en France* (1983; rev. and enlarged ed. Paris: Editions Complexe, 1987).

31. Alain's shortsightedness as a Radical substantially limited Weil's political perceptions. A year after his death, Alain was bitterly attacked by Raymond Aron, "Alain et la politique," in the Nouvelle revue française's collection, *Hommage à Alain* (Paris: Gallimard, 1952), pp. 155–67. In Alain's dogma of resistance to the state as a citizen's moral duty Aron saw the ruin of all moderate government and an open invitation to a ruthless, reactionary one. He contends that Alain never outgrew the position he took in the Dreyfus years, when Radicals mobilized against the authority of the army, the church, and the government. That resistance was legitimate before the Great War, says Aron, and disastrous after it. He concedes that Alain's preaching against powerseeking in the parties held a great deal of truth. "It is weak when it disregards the particularity of institutions or of ideas and gives them a universal meaning. It is strong when it sifts out certain abiding characteristics not so much from society as from the condition of the people within it."

32. Alain, *Les arts et les dieux* (Paris: Gallimord, 1958), p. 39.

33. Jean-Jacques Rousseau, *Du contrat social* (Paris: Garnier Frères, 1962), p. 309.

34. Antoine Louis Saint-Just, *Saint-Just: discours et rapports*, ed. Albert Soboul (Paris: Editions Sociales, 1977), p. 209.

35. "Note sur la suppression générale des partis politiques," *EL*, p. 129.

36. Saint-Just, p. 118.

37. Rousseau, p. 309.

38. Léon Blum, *A l'échelle humaine* (Paris: Gallimard, 1945), p. 83 says the bourgeois "nourished the secret hope that Hitler's fist would make the rebellious working class tow the line for a long time." On p. 101 he exonerates the parties from blame for the Republic's terminal illness: "They presented themselves in compact blocs, they practiced strict unity in their tactics and voting, and in their actions they conformed themselves to programs publicly debated and defended."

39. "Réflexions sur les causes de la liberté et de l'oppression sociale," *OL*, pp. 85–86.

40. Quoted by Sternhell, p. 143.

41. *EL*, p. 126.

42. Ibid., p. 142.

43. Léon Blum, letter to de Gaulle of March 15, 1943, quoted in *Les idées politiques et sociales de la Résistance*, ed., H. Michel and B. Mirkine-Guetzévich (Paris: Presses Universitaires de la France, 1954), p. 110.

44. See *Verités*, August 25, 1941, quoted in *Combat: Histoire d'un Mouvement de Résistance de Juillet 1940 à Juillet 1943*, ed. M. Garnet and H. Michel (Paris: Presses Universitaires de la France, 1957), p. 94.

45. Quoted by Garnet and Michel, p. 105.

46. *E*, pp. 244–45.

47. *EL*, p. 131.

48. This fragment is in EHP. In the same *boîte* are Weil's brief sketches on Roman history, including "Une république en proie aux soudards: Marius et Sylla," and "Un mouvement revendicatif dans l'armée romaine de Germanie."

49. *EL*, p. 137; Rousseau, p. 331. There is a reminiscence in both texts of Plato's saving remnant of the philosophical life, *Republic* 496e, 500c–d.

50. *AD*, p. 20.

51. Notes in CD, 1. Subsequent quotations are from this source. The relevant Stoic texts may be found in *Stoicorum veterum fragmenta*, ed. Johann von Arnim (Leipzig: Teubner, 1921), 1:55, para. 230 (Zeno on conforming life to nature), 3:4, para. 4 (Chrysippus on the same), 3:40, para. 169 (Stobaeus on life free from passions).

52. See Chrysippus in von Arnim, 2:154. A crucial difference between Plato and the Stoics is that for him, the good, the beautiful, and the true are apprehensible within the human soul, through whose training one becomes a participant in them. The true reality is "intelligible and bodiless forms" (*Sophist* 246b). The Stoics, however, looked to the material world and to experience as sources by which a higher reason is comprehended. They are the authors of common sense, and upon the sharing of reason they erected a truly cosmopolitan justice. Plato's guardians would entertain no such materialism or its comforting faith in nature informed by divine will. Weil does not quite settle in either the Platonic

or Stoic camp. However attractive the Platonic dogmas, she was powerfully drawn to the Stoic ethic of accommodation and submission to the world as it is.

53. *OL*, pp. 113, 119. On an ideal's remoteness see *Republic* 450c, 472c, 502d.

54. J. L. Talmon, *The Origins of Totalitarian Democracy* (London: Sphere Books, 1970), p. 110. Like these men, Weil entered the very center of a revolutionary disjuncture in French history, when the immediate past was totally discredited and the door stood open for profound political transformations. Also, the impetuosity of youthful brilliance was coupled with inexperience: Saint-Just died at twenty-six, Danton at thirty-four, Robespierre at thirty-six. Weil's most important political writing occupied her last two years, when she was in her early thirties.

55. *C*, 3:81. Cf. *EL*, p. 126.

56. *De la justice*, 6, quoted by Georges Sorel, *Matériaux d'une théorie du proletariat* (1921; rpt. Paris: Slatkine, 1981), p. 428.

57. *Messages d'outre-tombe du Maréchal Pétain: textes officiels, ignoré ou méconnus, consignes secrètes* (Paris: Nouvelles Editions Latines, 1983), p. 244. The new constitution was not signed until January 30, 1944. The text is on pp. 251–59.

58. As Paxton has ably shown in his *Vichy France*, a good deal of Vichy's legislation was carried over to the Fourth Republic and remains on the books to this day.

59. See the assessment of Jacques Castenet, foremost historian of the period, in his *Histoire de la troisième république* (Paris: Hachette, 1952), 1:190.

60. "Pour la ligue" in AHS. For its background see Pétrement, 1:134.

61. "Remarques sur le nouveau projet de constitution," *EL*, p. 88.

62. Ibid., p. 90.

63. "Remarques," *EL*, p. 86.

64. "Commentaire" on the OCM constitution in ELM. Subsequent quotations are from this source.

65. These remarks are in typescript, on the reverse side of Weil's typed outline of the OCM proposal, headed "Schéme de la constitution hitlérienne française."

66. "Idées essentielles pour une nouvelle constitution," *EL*, p. 93.

67. Ibid., p. 95.

68. Ibid. Her words "fait du mal" could be rendered "does harm" or "does injury" but it seems clear from her examples that she means "does evil."

69. Ibid., p. 96.

70. Ibid., p. 97.

71. Ibid.

72. *Summa Theologica* 1: q. 29, a. 3.

73. "Comte," in TPAG. For Alain's discussion of egotism and altruism, see his essay on Comte in *Idées* (Paris: Hartmann, 1939), p. 353.

74. "La personne et le sacré," *EL*, p. 17.

75. Ibid., pp. 19–20.

76. Weil's position on rights in "La personne et le sacré" rests on the early essay "D'une antinomie du droit," *OC* 1:255–59. There as here she starts with Spinoza's view that right is a function of power. The dignity of a thinking person lies in freedom: no one has a right to impose on another's thoughts. Justice belongs to the domain of thought, but right applies to

people's interactions. Hence the element of irreducible force and the equivalence of right to cold fact. Weil does not recognize any "natural" right. Right springs not from mind or from nature, yet the mind conceives nature only by means of right. The notion of right must, she concludes, be set at the level of action. By implication, nothing absolute can be appropriated as a right.

77. *EL*, pp. 24–25. She ignores the fact that Rome extended citizenship to many non-Italic peoples subjugated throughout the empire in the first century, C.E.—a process that ended in universal enfranchisement in 212. Inclined to be neither humane nor sentimental, the Romans thus simplified their administration and filled imperial coffers with much needed revenues, but the status of citizen did entail substantial benefits. The forced Romanization Weil decries is, however, easily documented. Julius Caesar's advice to the peoples of Britain before his invasion, "ut populi Romani fidem sequantur" (*Commentaries* 3:10), exemplifies the euphemism of force clothed in an idea which Weil denounces as Hitlerism.

78. Ibid., pp. 38–39.

79. Ibid., p. 35.

80. Ibid., p. 37.

81. Weil does not mention Plato's thorough censorship of *malheur* in the *Iliad* (*Republic* 388a–391e), nor does she heed his argument against tragedy, that the imitative poet is "a manufacturer of images and very far removed from the truth" (605b). Weil's notion argues the opposite (*EL*, p. 37), that such "images" although "without power to contain the truth inspiring them have with it a correspondence so perfect by their arrangement that they furnish support to every mind seeking to discover the truth."

82. *EL*, pp. 37, 38.

83. Ibid., p. 39.

84. Ibid., p. 42. Her diction is instructive: *montrer* (showing the public) has an ecclesiastical ring to it, as in revealing the sacramental host (*faire voir*), and a pedagogical one, as *montrer* may denote *enseigner*. Her public leaders are like priestly educators.

85. *E*, p. 245.

Chapter 12

1. *EL*, p. 63.

2. Ibid., p. 66.

3. See Robert Aron and Armand Dandieu, *Le cancre americain* (Paris: Rieder, 1931).

4. Her notes, in ELM, identify only "Carr," but her paginated quotes allow easy identification of their source.

5. E. H. Carr, *Conditions of Peace* (London: Macmillan, 1942), p. 107.

6. Ibid., p. 110. This is another passage Weil copied verbatim.

7. Ibid., pp. 112–13.

8. *EL*, pp. 250, 251.

9. Carr, p. 116.

10. Ibid., pp. 116–17. These words are quoted in Weil's notes.

11. *C*, 1:154.
12. *E*, p. 27.
13. Ibid., p. 34.
14. Ibid., p. 15. For other positive views of collectivity see pp. 167, 176, 243, 310.
15. Ibid., pp. 51, 61, 92.
16. Ibid., pp. 74, 86.
17. Ibid., p. 23.
18. Carr, pp. 121–23.
19. *E*, pp. 9–10.
20. Ibid., pp. 164, 178.
21. *C*, 2:327.
22. *E*, p. 62.
23. The manuscript of "La monnaie" is in EHP. Subsequent quotations are from this source.
24. *E*, p. 66.
25. Ibid., p. 68.
26. Ibid., p. 71.
27. Ibid., p. 82.
28. Ibid., p. 83. She goes on: sown among small country shops would be workers' universities, with a corps of intellectuals to help promote a new workers' culture. She looks to the educated young (the *jocistes*, apparently) to resume in peacetime the contacts they have made with workers during the war. Work would be limited to half days so that workers could pursue their education and develop "un patriotisme d'enterprise" with their comrades.
29. Ibid., p. 103.
30. Ibid., p. 120.
31. Ibid., pp. 118, 120.
32. Ibid., p. 119. She is still haunted by the sense that oppressive systems have a peculiar élan, a compelling albeit false spirituality against which a true spirituality must be invoked and lived out.
33. Ibid., p. 121.
34. Ibid., p. 110.
35. *PSO*, p. 24.
36. Ibid., p. 27.
37. Ibid., p. 31.
38. "A propos des jocistes," *Cahiers du Sud* 19 (April 1941): 246.
39. *E*, p. 378.
40. Ibid., p. 124. It might seem that the convict's work, far more than the mother's, has the penitential quality Weil saw in the nature of all work. But penance requires consent, and the continuing threat of punishment in the convict's case reveals a degraded relationship of worker to work.
41. Ibid., p. 194.
42. Ibid., pp. 250, 259.
43. Ibid., pp. 273–74.

44. Ibid., pp. 274, 275; cf. *C*, 3:125, on the desire for good as an agency for destroying the evil of the self.

45. *E*, p. 113.

46. Ibid., p. 165.

47. Ibid., pp. 131, 147.

48. Ibid., pp. 264–65.

49. Ibid., p. 258.

50. Ibid., p. 210.

51. Ibid., pp. 120, 163. Similarly, she cuts the ground from herself in a kind of credo published as her "Dernier texte," *PSO*, pp. 149–53. She mentions her conflicts with the church and her study of "the truth enclosed" in non-Christian religions, but she also concedes that as her cowardice has left some evil in her, "I doubt in a sense the very things which seem to me most manifestly certain." But then she validates the doubt (true student of Alain) as an indispensable part of her "vocation" to "an absolute intellectual probity," a position that cannot be demonic, she feels, because it has cost her only "pain, moral discomfort and isolation."

52. *E*, p. 366.

Chapter 13

1. See Paul Nizan's introduction to *Les matérialistes de l'antiquité* (Paris: Editions sociales internationales, 1935).

2. *AD*, p. 24.

Bibliographical Essay

Unpublished Primary Materials

All of Weil's papers—her notes, essays, and letters—are reposited in the Manuscripts Division of the Bibliothèque Nationale, Paris. It is timely that these papers are now finding their way into publication (see Published Primary Materials), for many of them, after fifty years, are yellowed and so brittle that they crumble in the reader's hand. Some are either so ink-blotched or their script so faded as to be illegible.

Fortunately, microfilm copies of the Weil archives are available for consultation at the Historical Studies and Social Science Library of the Institute for Advanced Study, Princeton. The library's microfilm reader does not improve the legibility of faded papers, but the efficient staff and a file indicating the subject matter of each of the thirty-three microfilm reels will help the consultant who does not have the advantage of visiting the Nationale, undergoing its byzantine clearance procedures, and enjoying prolonged waits for requested materials.

Most of the papers are in Weil's tidy longhand but the script varies in size from conveniently large blocklike characters, as in her essays for Alain, to the minuscule. Lecture notes, however, come in a jerky, irregular script, the obvious sign of haste. The greater number of the 1930s writings, denominated Textes philosophiques antèrieurs à la guerre, has a fully legible and almost elegant neatness. There are typewritten copies of many of the essays she intended for publication, and Mme Selma Weil transcribed many more in her careful hand.

What in the archives is designated "Cahiers divers," in three series, deserves special mention. A miscellany, these pages contain a large number of reading notes on philosophers seldom mentioned in Weil studies: Aristotle, Berkeley, and Hume, Maine de Biran, and many secondary authors, of whom Octave Hamelin and René Guenon are particularly important for their studies of Aristotle and the Vedanta, respectively.

The consultant of these papers will be surprised to find a substantial number of doodles among them. Many of these are stylized letters, geometrical patterns, or, most arresting, floating humanoid shapes about which only an intrepid psychologist would speculate.

Published Primary Materials

In 1988, forty-five years after her death, an edition of Weil's *Oeuvres complètes* at last began to appear from Gallimard. The first of the projected thirteen volumes, *Premiers écrits philosophiques* is abundant in promise for the series to come. The volumes are scheduled to appear at eight-month intervals. The editors are André-A. Devaux, who has contributed a preface, and Florence de Lussy, Weil's archivist at the Bibliothèque Nationale, who has composed an invaluable eighteen-page chronology of Weil's life. The large amount of previously unpublished material in this first volume alone suggests that the completed edition will likely alter, if not transform, present and long-held assumptions about Weil. At the least, in supplying a trove of unexamined works, Gallimard has ensured a scholarly industry for generations. Furthering that industry are the notes, supplied for the first volume by Gilbert Kahn and Rolf Kühn, a precious aid to readers weary of searching for the sources of Weil's countless allusions.

In the meanwhile, we have a large number of "standard" texts.

La pesanteur et la grâce occupies a definitive position in the canon of Weil's works. Published by Gustave Thibon in 1947, it is a topical arrangement of extracts from the *cahiers* she left with him when she went to the United States in 1942. More than any other volı me bearing her name, with the possible exception of *Attente de Dieu*, published three years later, *La pesanteur et la grâce* shaped Weil's image and reputation for her first generation of readers. Yet, however favorably one may respond to Thibon's selection (François Mauriac regarded it as a masterwork), the fact remains that not even the convenient rubrics overcome one's impression of *disiecta membra*. To presume otherwise in effect relegates the writing to the belletristic genre of aphorisms. Regarding Thibon's work as an anthology, we may take some caution from Alain, who groaned at the "title vulgaire" and admitted he found little in the volume (see his "Simone Weil," *La table ronde* 28 [April 1950]: 48). But Claude Mauriac spoke prematurely in claiming of *La pesanteur et la grâce*, "Ici s'arrête le domaine d'Alain." I shall note why presently.

The *cahiers* themselves in their full integrity quickly confound the impression that Weil was a *maximiste*. The topics listed by Thibon reflect problems upon which Weil expended much thoughtful energy. This is to say that nothing Weil wrote can safely be extracted as though it had attained resolution. Not that her entries seem tentative; they prove unfailingly direct, and their expression bears all the force of her probity, but they remain in a sense experimental. Not the dicta of Thibon's production, these exercises, no one of which finds final articulation, compel the reader to participate in Weil's restive iterations.

That process may well frustrate, but it does not cheat, and the impatient need only recall that in these notes Weil does not invite one's prurience. Indeed, when leaving France in 1942 she wrote to her friend Gilbert Kahn about the writing left with Thibon: "On reflection I regret having authorized you to read my *cahiers*. Please regard this authorization as null and void. They are too intimate and would not help you. I'm writing to Thibon about not showing them. Don't be angry with me. I sincerely think that you will miss nothing in them."

In fact, the *cahiers* are a treasure one would not wish to miss, and surely no one can honestly regret their serial publication by Plon in three volumes: *Les cahiers de Simone*

Weil, 1951, 1953, and 1956. It stands as a measure of Weil's status in the English-speaking world during the 1950s that a translation by Arthur Wills of all three volumes appeared in 1956 as *The Notebooks of Simone Weil* (London: Routledge & Kegan Paul). This translation was reprinted in 1976 but unfortunately not updated to include a notebook that Plon had for some reason initially omitted but later included in its revised edition of *Cahiers I* (1970). A translation of that notebook begins Richard Rees's *Simone Weil: First and Last Notebooks*, the latter referring to Weil's writings in New York and London, published by Gallimard as *La connaissance surnaturelle*.

Plon's setting of the notebooks in order must be commended, for each of them on many a page presents a dazzling chaos. Weil seems to have abhorred a vacuum. She fills some pages with vertical entries, many in an infinitesimal script. She passes from French to Greek to Sanskrit, boxing in here and underlining there. Many of these pages include differential equations and geometrical exercises which Plon saw fit to ignore. In the Wills translation, omission of these mathematical passages is indicated by a row of dots across the page. More to be regretted are the many passages in Sanskrit which Weil meticulously set down and which deserve translation. Even though they are not *ipsissima verba*, it helps us to know what she took care to record from the Vedic texts and from the *Gita*.

Everyone interested in Weil owes an enormous debt to the late Sir Richard Rees, who translated some of her most important writing. *Selected Essays* (London: Oxford University Press, 1962) derives from Gallimard's collection *Ecrits historiques et politiques*, including her two essays on Languedoc, "La personne et le sacré," "Ne recommencons pas la guerre de Troie," the brilliant "Réflexions sur les origines de l'hitlerisme," and many shorter pieces. *On Science, Necessity and the Love of God* (London: Oxford University Press, 1968) contains "L'amour de Dieu et le malheur," the essay on quanta, "Science et nous," and a host of sketches taken from Gallimard's *Sur la science*. It is a scandal that these translations have been out of print for years. Alas, the same is true of Rees's translation of *Seventy Letters* (London: Oxford University Press, 1965). They include her letters to the *patrons*, Detoeuf and Bernard, the charming last letters to her parents (a window on her capacity for tenderness and common affections), letters to her brother, and the indispensable letters to Bernanos, Bergery, Roché, and Bousquet.

There are three recent anthologies in English. George Panichas's *The Simone Weil Reader* (New York: McKay, 1977) draws from previously published translations, some of which had not been accessible for years. The introduction indicates Panichas's preoccupation with Weil's "spiritual progress," but his selections are of a range sufficient to suggest that she also took up political, social, and psychological *topica*.

Siân Miles's *Simone Weil: An Anthology* (New York: Weidenfeld and Nicolson, 1986) is disappointing. Not only does it merely resume Panichas's scissors-and-paste effort, it makes many of the same selections. The abundance of published material as yet untranslated could have served for a selection of wholly other yet no less representative work.

The special merit of *Simone Weil: Formative Writings, 1929–1941*, edited by Dorothy Tuck McFarland and Wilhelmina Van Ness (London: Routledge & Kegan Paul, 1987) is that it addresses that large store of literature long available in French yet incredibly neglected. These editors give us Weil's thesis on Descartes, her reports on Germany's convulsions just before Hitler became chancellor, the *journal d'usine* (a challenge for any translator), and essays on the political crises of the 1930s. This ingathering is hardly for the reader seeking spiritual guidance, but it is an invaluable source for anyone genuinely interested in Weil.

Books on Simone Weil: A Selection

Four of these have become indispensable companions for the serious student, and all but one appear in an English translation.

First in chronology and foremost in insight is the memoir composed by Fr. J.-M. Perrin and Gustave Thibon, *Simone Weil telle que nous l'avons connue* (Paris: La Colombe, 1952). Perrin's is the definitive respondent to Weil's struggle with the Catholic church. Thibon's recollections provide an abundance of insights into Weil's character and thinking. Both men have written further about her (Perrin at book length in *Mon dialogue avec Simone Weil* [Paris: Nouvelle Cité, 1984]), but neither, in my estimation, has matched his own *coûp d'essai*.

Jacques Cabaud's *L'experience véçue de Simone Weil* (Paris: Plon, 1957) and Simone Pétrement's *La vie de Simone Weil* (Paris: Fayard, 1973) are complementary in excellence. Cabaud drew upon a wealth of interviews and documents, Pétrement upon a long friendship with Weil and many unpublished papers in the Weil archives. Both studies present a matrix of biography and discussion of Weil's writings that sometimes obscures alternately the narrative thread and the coherence of Weil's thought, but both are rich in information, and one might excuse in each of them a virtually uncritical admiration of their subject. Cabaud recast his book into English as *Simone Weil: A Fellowship in Love* (New York: Channel Press, 1965). Readers should be aware that Raymond Rosenthal's translation of Pétrement, *Simone Weil: A Life* (New York: Pantheon Books, 1977), omits substantial portions of her French text.

The best exposition of Weil's philosophy remains Miklos Vetö's *La metaphysique religieuse de Simone Weil* (Paris: Vrin, 1971). Although his topical presentation may give a deceptive semblance of a system to Weil's thinking, it is easy to follow. As the title indicates, Vetö does not address Weil's activist writing, and the discussion is concentrated almost entirely on the wartime essays, but the imbalance is not to be regretted. Unfortunately, this valuable ancilla has not been translated.

In addition to these four indispensable books, there are several others worth reading.

Despite its years and the small number of Weil texts to which it refers, E. W. F. Tomlin's essay *Simone Weil* (Cambridge: Bowes and Bowes, 1954), in the excellent series Studies in Modern European Literature and Thought, is still useful and full of insights. Concentrating on her "spiritual itinerary," which at the time he was writing was still a source of controversy, Tomlin is commendably evenhanded, but he also knows how to speak eloquently for Weil's many unique merits. "No one was less of a 'realist,' yet no one had a greater sense of reality." This may be hyperbole, but it invites reflection, and in his too few sixty pages there is scarcely a thoughtless or superfluous remark.

Richard Rees's *Simone Weil: A Sketch for a Portrait* (Carbondale: Southern Illinois University Press, 1966) sensitively and intelligently poses Weil's arguments but in the uncritical tone of an advocate. Perhaps in a full portrait Rees would have admitted some chiaroscuro, recognizing like Tomlin where Weil tends to extravagance and perversity. He passes by, for example, her telltale remarks on Judaism without demur and swallows whole her plea for a science of the "supernatural." In his ready agreement with Weil Rees represents enthusiasts who see in her ideas the corrective to the twentieth century's many ills.

For a splendid review of Weil's thought relative to ancient philosophical and religious traditions Marie-Magdalene Davy's *Simone Weil: sa vie, son oeuvre avec une exposé de sa philosophie* (Paris: Presses Universitaires de France, 1966) cannot be surpassed. Davy, a medievalist, shows how Greek patristic literature established the connections between pre-Christian and Christian thought for which Weil has often been reviled. Davy draws several interesting parallels between Weil and Plotinus, Meister Eckhart, and Malebranche. Her defense of Weil's thought, its "caractère métahistorique," is vigorous, knowledgeable, and concise. Fortunately, this excellent little book, in the Collection "Philosophes," is still readily available.

One of the best short accounts of her life and thought is David Anderson's *Simone Weil* (London: SCM Press, 1971). This clergyman does not look upon her activism in the 1930s with much sympathy. He feels that her efforts contained an element of the perverse and grotesque and that she was unconsciously courting martyrdom, yet he commends her for seeing, subsequent to her mystical experience, religious implications in every subject. He also defends her from the allegation of gnosticism which recurs often in the early criticism (see Selected Essays) and asserts that her theological use of mathematical analogies will likely hold up because the members analogized do not have to be true in the same way in order to be valid. He feels that the particular value in Weil's thinking lies in the revelation of correlations in ideas we would not usually make.

Eric O. Springsted's *Christus Mediator: Platonic Mediation in the Thought of Simone Weil* (Chico, Calif.: Scholars Press, 1983) provides, as its title promises, discussion of Weil's inreading of Plato and her Platonized Christology of *metaxu*. He duly attends to the influence of Pythagoreanism, too, though not, for some reason, to Heraclitus. He argues that Weil early saw mediation as a technique for harmonizing the individual to the world. Her initial optimism about finding a proper method of work through social reorganization collapsed with her discovery of *malheur*. Her mystical experience of Christ led her to recast the terms of mediation, from the conjunction of mind and matter to the descent of transcendental good in Christ, the *metaxu* of humanity and God. This thoughtful study presents perhaps the best case for regarding Weil as a Christian thinker, but it does so by passing over too much else that was integral to her spirituality, particularly the influence of Stoicism and of Eastern religions. Springsted reiterates Weil's urgings for a greater Christian appreciation of other religious traditions, but he does not point to where such an effort must begin—with Judaism, where Weil never conceived that it could.

Although it belongs to the Radcliffe Biography Series, Robert Coles's *Simone Weil: A Modern Pilgrimage* (Reading, Mass.: Addison Wesley, 1987) is not biographical in approach. Rather, it is a series of topical essays, presented in a relaxed, ruminative tone. Coles attempts some psychoanalytic insights based on his own practice and conversation with the late Anna Freud, who was suitably cautious in her responses to the data about Weil which Coles provides. Coles is shrewd enough to avoid diagnostic tags, and he goes a good way to make Weil accessible to intelligent, nonacademic readers.

Peter Winch's *Simone Weil: "The Just Balance"* (Cambridge: Cambridge University Press, 1989) is of particular merit. It eschews biographical data and concentrates on Weil's thinking as the occasion of philosophical problems. Nevertheless, the reader fearful of abstractions should not be deterred. Winch writes in a straightforward and engaging way, and his attention to Weil's semantics is never pedantic. He is admirably sensitive to some of the difficulties and irresolutions in Weil's arguments. Wittgenstein makes a few guest appearances.

Gabriella Fiori's *Simone Weil: An Intellectual Biography* (Athens: University of Georgia Press, 1989), is substantial in narrative but short on analysis. Far more satisfying is David McLellan's *Utopian Pessimist: The Life and Thought of Simone Weil* (New York: Simon and Schuster, 1990). The noted scholar of Marxism brings the judicious sympathy indispensable to a study of Weil and balances the life chronicle with an astute discussion of Weil's writing. This work will be the standard reference for many years to come.

Of particular topical interest is *A Truer Liberty: Simone Weil and Marxism* by Lawrence A. Blum and Victor J. Seidler (New York: Routledge Press, 1990). They update the influence Weil exerted on Catholics, especially worker priests, in the postwar generation: they note her apparent influence in Latin American and European radicalism upsurgent against totalitarianism on both Right and Left. It may be doubted, however, that the spirituality of any new collectivity would have satisfied her stringent need of absolute integrity. The Great Beast takes many forms, and humanity can never entirely free itself of illusions.

Three collections of essays deserve notice. The most substantial is Gilbert Kahn's edition of papers delivered at three conferences (held in 1974, 1975, and 1977), *Simone Weil: philosophe, historienne et mystique* (Paris: Aubier Montaigne, 1978). Most of the participants are veteran scholars of Weil, and the value of their contribution is matched by some stimulating and well-nuanced discussions. Half of the book addresses Weil's thoughts on Christianity, Judaism, and *l'universalisme religieux*, and so it might be considered an antidote to an earlier collection, *Réponses aux questions de Simone Weil* (Paris: Aubier Montaigne, 1964). The *réponses* come from Catholics, most of them clerics, apparently eager to address (correct) Weil's heterodox views of Christianity, the church, and Judaism. A battery of ecclesiastical documents, including statements from three popes on church doctrine, makes plain how powerfully Weil's objections to the church had registered. That fact (and the book's appearance in the wake of the Second Vatican Council) points to the real significance of this collection, but the essays themselves deserve attention, especially those of the Jesuit J. Daniélou, "Hellenisme, judaïsme, christianisme," and of the Dominican B. Hussar, "Israël et l'église."

George Abbott White's *Simone Weil: Interpretations of a Life* (Amherst: University of Massachusetts Press, 1981) serves as a counterpoint to the *Réponses* and a complement to Kahn's collection in that most of the essays address the non-mystical Weil. There are three essays on her politics and two on "The *Iliad*, Poem of Force" alone. Of particular interest are two contributions from Michele Murray, who died while composing a book on Weil. The general orientation is away from Weil as a "case" or problem and instead to Weil as a poser of problems, as the outsider who challenges those within. The thinking and the writing in this volume are consistently high, and the reader is mercifully spared hagiographical jaunts.

Published Secondary Writing: A Selection of Criticism

The essays and reviews listed below fall mainly within the first generation of Weil's readers. As indicated in the Preface, I have attempted to lay some groundwork for a *Rezeptionsgeschichte* of Simone Weil, and this task centers on those who in their writing served to crystallize Weil's present reputation. Many of them wrote in substantial ignorance of the Weil now known to us in biography. They were responding to a legend in its birthing, and they were helping to form it. It is one measure of Weil's first decades of fame that she drew so many vigorous and varied reactions. Even as her works were appearing piecemeal through the 1950s, her critics, favorable and otherwise, seemed eager to set down final judgments about her, as though what one of them called the "cocksureness" so often apparent in her writing had assumed an infectious dynamic. All the essays I note here have nonetheless, I believe, something valuable to contribute, even when judgment yields to caricature, simplification, hagiographic rhetoric, or other misdemeanors. The annotations are not, of course, intended as summaries of arguments. I have cited what I find of particular interest, and where the author seems to me in error, I say so.

Essays and reviews mentioned in the chapters of this book or in the footnotes are not included in this listing.

The indispensable aids toward a *Rezeptionsgeschichte* are J. P. Little's two volumes, *Simone Weil: A Bibliography* and *Simone Weil: A Supplement*, published in London by Grant and Cutler in 1973 and 1979 respectively. The first lists, in addition to translations, books, and dissertations, over a thousand essays and reviews in several languages. The second updates and recovers many more, includes an index nominum and an index to reviews of all of Weil's works then published.

The bibliography is, of course, not without some errors. Some of the secondary entries are erroneously paginated or misdated. But this is to cavil. Little's valiant effort indicates to the consultant how quickly interest in Weil extended beyond France. The multitude of entries in German and Italian alone invite the writing of a history.

Useful though these books are, the proliferation of writing on Weil since 1979 would seem to make further supplements a gargantuan undertaking. Fortunately, at least for readers of French, l'Association pour l'étude de la pensée de Simone Weil, founded in 1974, has been regularly issuing notices and reviews of everything published on Weil, both in France and abroad. The association's quarterly, *Cahiers Simone Weil*, begun in 1976 (from 1974 to 1978 there was a *Bulletin de liaison*), includes thematic and comparative studies on Weil, book reviews, and references ("Echos et nouvelles") to all events, such as seminars, public lectures, and television programs, in which Weil's name is involved. This is a thorough and fascinating index to her current international profile.

Abosch, Heinz. "Wandlungen einer Anarchisten." *Die Zeit*, August 18, 1972, p. 18.
Contends that Weil's notion of *déracinement* would not have been possible without

Marx's theory of alienation. But there is no evidence that Weil drew specifically from Marx on this point (which he derived from Hegel and Feuerbach). Besides, the social contexts of deracination which Weil addresses had French precedents, for example in Rousseau's distinction between *l'homme naturel* and *l'homme policé*; and the Barrès-Gide exchange can be read without Marx. Abosch believes that Weil's "vorherrschende mystische Tendenz" closes her off from sociological thinking. See Hunter, below.

Ahemm, Hildegard. "Zur Analyse der Gegenwart." *Deutsche Rundschau* 82 (July 1956): 793–95. Sees in Weil's work a "rebirth of Christian mysticism" in that "in more than one regard it passes from a change of mind to a change of power [*Machtveränderung*]."

Arcangeli Marenzi, Maria Laura. "Simone Weil." In her *Linguaggio e poesia* (Florence: Libreria Universitaria, 1966), pp. 51–92. A challenging study that seeks to interpret Weil through her style. Weil's language, she writes, "builds and unbuilds itself at the same time." The author seems to be fond of semantic pranks, as when she writes of *attente* and a tension that "indurisce, disincarna e disumanizza." And she seems to exaggerate the difficulty of understanding Weil. This book includes studies of Eluard and Saint-Exupéry.

Bachmann, Ingeborg. "Das Unglück und die Gottesliebe—Der Weg Simone Weils." In her *Werke* (Munich: R. Piper, 1982), 4:128–55. A radio essay composed of a narrative on Weil's life, quoting from her writings and commentaries. Concludes it would be senseless to assume that Weil's path is one that can be followed by many; only a few can pursue it and in different ways. But Bachmann, whose own life was, like Weil's, immensely creative, cosmopolitan, and tragically short, maintains that we can receive from Weil the beauty that dwells in what is "purely thought and lived." From Weil there shines out "the indestructible countenance of man in a world that pledged itself to his destruction." And hers.

Bady, René. "Reticences en face de l'église de Péguy à Simone Weil." *Cahiers universitaires Catholiques*, January 1951, pp. 197–209. A judicious presentation of Weil's objections to the church as she put them in *Attente de Dieu*. It points to her essential agreement with Péguy that many people are to be found in grace outside of the church. Bady puts her in the tradition of Christian humanism that would baptize antiquity and revere Socrates and Erasmus as saints. He concludes that Péguy and Weil would concur that a true Christian cannot show either a systematic defiance or harmful suspicion toward the church (is it certain that Weil posed neither of these?) or a lazy, timid submission to it based on fears not respect.

Balla, Borisz de. "Simone Weil, Witness of the Absolute." *Catholic World* 179 (May 1954): 101–9. Presumes that Weil belongs to the "invisible community of saints" and agrees with Perrin that had she lived, she would probably have formally entered the Catholic church. Unusual here is the gratuitous assumption that Weil was "reared in a spiritually dead environment . . . a typical product of the post-Proustian age" and its denial of transcendence. The real meaning behind such words is transparent enough.

Bataille, Georges. "La victoire militaire et la banquerote de la morale qui maudit." *Critique* 5 (September 1949): 789–803. As one would expect, this is a penetrating essay, also a savage one. Most of his assessments (of *L'enracinement*) are negative. He identifies first the present (postwar) moral crisis: the impossibility of giving to moral law an unimpeachable foundation. Obligation, a matter of great moment to Weil, no longer imposes itself without discussion. Weil's "blind passion for lucidity" often conceals the obscure depth of her thought. In *L'enracinement* it has "an odious and immoral aspect," that is *l'outrance autoritaire*. Further, she is given to trite (*rebattu*), irrelevant, and paradoxical formulas, a touching quixotism, and "une merveilleuse volonté d'inanité." Bataille says that Weil's intangible faith cannot be of use to anyone who searches for the good without knowing it in advance. For her obligation he would substitute loyalty and generosity as the basis of communal interests. This is one of the indispensable essays on Weil.

Blanchard, Anne. Review of *Attente de Dieu*. *Cahiers du Sud* 299 (1950): 359–60. Weil, she says, will confound "those who glory in choosing, willing, creating and thinking by themselves." But, like Bataille, she finds Weil's preoccupations anachronistic. Twentieth-century thought is before a void, and each of us must make a solitary quest. Weil's voice seems "égarée en ce siècle." Did she come too soon or too late?

Blanchot, Maurice. "L'expérience de Simone Weil." *Nouvelle nouvelle revue française* 5 (August 1957): 297–310. Some excellent notes on *attente* and *malheur*. Points to the absurdity that Weil speaks openly and assuredly about a God she insists is hidden.

———. "Simone Weil et la certitude." *Nouvelle nouvelle revue française* 5 (July 1957): 103–14. The affirmative nature of Weil's remarks suggests that answers came before questions or even without them, but Blanchot recognizes that affirming is often for her the procedure for questioning and testing. What makes her exceptional among moderns, he adds, is that she could never doubt the good.

Bloch-Michel, Jean. "L'expérience ouvrière de Simone Weil." *Revue de la pensée française* 11 (March 1952): 8–14. Her moral and intellectual concerns for the reform of workers' lives constitute the truly liberating revolution. What counts in her work is not her proposed solutions but that she denounced evils and gave voice to workers whose condition was fundamentally a silence. Her factory journal is a detailed description of that silence.

Blumenthal, Gerda. "Simone Weil's Way of the Cross." *Thought* 27 (Summer 1952): 225–34. A good summary of Weil's use of analogy and contradiction in fashioning her heterodox theology. Suggests that Weil's mysticism is joyless; she construes the experience of grace and love in negative terms so that they may be acceptable to intellectual purity. Her preference for universal harmony (Stoicism) to a personal, sacrificial God (Christianity) "accounts for her anti-humanism."

Bodart, Roger. "Simone Weil ou la prière dans les orties." *Revue générale belge* 64 (February 1951): 581–91. Defends her from already surfacing charges of Catharism and masochism, compares her *violence d'esprit* to Péguy's; criticizes her intense need of purity as a "péché d'angelisme." She was not hostile to the church, Bodart claims, only mistrustful of it. Its way of access to God was too easy to please her. She was Jewish in her restless, intuitive urges and in her "stiff-necked" Talmudic requirement of countless proofs.

Brée, Germaine. "A Stranger in This World." *Saturday Review*, February 20, 1965, pp. 26–27. In this generally favorable review of Cabaud's biography, the eminent scholar of Gide and Camus gives some explanation of why Weil's influence waned after the first few years of enthusiasm. Brée points to the fragmentary character of her writing, the abstruseness of her philosophical interests, and the diverse and recondite sources of her inspiration such as the *Gita* and the pre-Socratics. To those factors could be added the hostility to Judaism which Weil's *cahiers* evinced far more imposingly than Thibon's selection, "Israel," in *Pesanteur et la grâce.*

Bréhier, Emile. Review of *Pesanteur et la grâce. Revue philosophique de France et de l'étranger* 140 (July–September 1950): 389. The noted French historian of ancient philosophy makes two seemingly contradictory points: that Weil's "gout de l'universe" scarcely belongs to the Christian sensibility (Weil herself knew this and faulted the church for its indifference to the world's beauty) and that her attention to methods for looking at images and symbols so that illusion gives way to reality shows that she understood "l'essence de la méthode symbolique si répandue dans le christianisme."

Cabaud, Jacques. "Albert Camus et Simone Weil." *Kentucky Romance Quarterly* 3 (1974): 383–94. According to Jean Grenier's memoir *Albert Camus, souvenirs* (Paris: Gallimard, 1968), p. 142, Camus said the two keys to his work were "the myth of Moby Dick and the thought of Simone Weil." Proceeding from there, Cabaud likens Camus and Weil in moral temperament and suggests possible influences of Weil in Camus's writing. But he also draws essential lines of difference, noting that Camus confounded the sacred with the human and rejected God out of love for people without God. He notes that Camus once thought of completing *Venise sauvée.* See Davy and Rustan, below.

Carrouges, Michel. "Religion et religions." *Le monde nouveau-paru,* nos. 53–54 (1951), pp. 223–28. Seeks to identify Weil's appeal and sees it in Protestant terms: Weil shows that faith is a very long road. Notes that in her *Lettre à un religieux* Weil looks for dogmatic answers at the same time that she deplores dogmatism in the church. Regarding the "intuitions pré-chrétienne," were the Greeks themselves "on the watch" for the mystical sense of their own stories? Weil does not and cannot say, but she has a habit of putting questions in a way that presupposes answers.

———. Review of *La condition ouvrière. Le monde nouveau-paru,* no. 57 (1952), pp. 123–26. Weil's program of voluntary collaboration between workers and bosses recapitulates the old syndicalist view of the CGT before the Communist party's takeover in 1938 that political struggles for power must not be confused with the social struggle to weaken the power structure in favor of local control and authentic cooperation. Weil's writings recover for the postwar labor generation "une loi vitale et primordiale pour le mouvement ouvrier." These remarks fail to mention that the CGT had not been (and still is not) free of the Communist party's mortmain since the time of the Popular Front.

Chaning-Pearce, Melville. "Christianity's Crucial Conflict: The Case of Simone Weil." *Hibbert Journal* 49 (1950–51): 333–40. Compares the Roman Catholic attacks on Weil's heterodoxy to the witch-hunting of Saint Jeanne; sees her Christianity of "mystical anarchism" as a model for modern faith; considers the issue as one of individual integrity versus the totalitarian security of dogma. This is early evidence of how the fascination with Weil in her first years of notoriety not only set Catholics against one another but furthered the age-old brawling between Catholics and Protestants.

Chiavacci Leonardi, Anna Maria. "Simone Weil et la Grecia." *Letteratura* 7 (1959): 44–46. Rightly observes that Weil went to Greek texts not with scientific (philological) precision yet "with the love and penetrating look of someone seeking the truth for her own life" but makes the fundamental mistake (more than once) of confusing Weil's idea of grace with "salvezza." See Quinzio, below.

Clayre, Alisdair. "A Logician of the Human Spirit." *Observer*, November 4, 1962, p. 27. Takes the Rees selection of her essays as examples of how Weil managed to overcome the academic limits of the French essay, where the mind "in a heavy tank . . . can move only by point-blank assertion." Weil's close conjunction of intelligence and love makes even the most fragmentary essays "illuminating."

Colombel, Jeannette. "Simone Weil et la condition ouvrière," *La nouvelle critique* 8 (February 1956): 46–66. This Stalinist's attack on Weil, focused on *Oppression et liberté*, includes the following charges: that Weil takes oppression as a metaphysical donnée; that she has a fatalistic disregard of worker solidarity and an unconscious contempt for working people; that her praise of initiative and invention as aspects of capitalism goes with the "confucianism" of her refusal to make a scientific analysis of social and economic structures; that her subscription to individual values abandons the working class; that her factory experience smacks of Malraux's adventurism and Gide's *gratuité*. Colombel's real complaint is that Weil, "directeur de conscience à la fois de Camus et des dirigeants C.F.T.C.," refuses to see anything but illusion in revolutionary expectations of the future.

Conche, Marcel. "Existence et culpabilité." *Revue de théologie et de philosophie* (3d ser.) 13 (1963): 213–26. Virtually an indispensable companion to Weil's essay "La personne et le sacré" and a no less severe assault on human egotism. Faults Weil's humility in her saying, "I am not and I consent to not-be" (*Connaissance surnaturelle*, p. 48) as proud. "The 'I' has all the same the last word: I give myself the being I take away by my taking it."

Cook, Bradford. "Simone Weil: Art and the Artist under God." *Yale French Studies* 12 (1953): 73–80. An excellent discussion of Weil's aesthetic and how her spirituality dictated her literary preferences. Shows that her Stoicism implied a rejection of imagination and all artistic activity other than a monotonous contemplation such as chant. She had a stringent sense of the beautiful in art. It had to be a balance of impersonality in the artist and full apprehension of what is universally human. Cook does not indicate how closely this aesthetic puts her in Plato's company.

Cranston, Maurice. "Reactionary Mystic." *Guardian*, October 19, 1962, p. 7. Rees's collection of Weil's essays shows how reactionary Weil was. Mystics are seldom liberals, Cranston adds drily, but her stance is that of "the heart which has been contracted by the disappointment of early socialist hopes." That is, a left-wing "fanaticism," thwarted, turned to a transcendental realm of persuasions to which even moderately progressive politics was intolerable. This is rather too neat a view and much too simple an explanation for Weil's *itinerarium mentis*, but it is one that leftists uncomfortable with Weil's religious inspirations are likely to accept.

D'Aubreuil, Guy. "Les erreurs de Simone Weil." *L'âge nouveau* 67 (1951): 70–73. Bitterly attacks Weil for her moral absolutism in regard to colonial reform, charging that she ignores the complexities of colonial problems, the savagery of natives in revolt, and other issues. Objects to her comparison of French colonial policy with Hitlerism. Without ever having lived in a colony, "this pathetic young woman has accused her country of the most horrible crime there is."

Dambuyant, Marinette. Review of François Heidsieck's *Simone Weil: Une étude avec un choix de textes* (Paris: Seghers, 1965), in *La pensée* 125 (February 1966): 137–38. Makes two points: first, the *normalien* experience in Weil's time was too far from real life and real problems to suffice for anyone who wanted to find "practical truth," and so the supereducated ran the risk of ending in action without doctrine, that is, in irrationalism; and second, that in the failure of the educated "to make known the life of revolutionary men and women" with an absolute generosity, others have too easily had "le privilège de la sainteté et de l'amour autrui." Dambuyant does not ask, however, whether this "privilege" is not the effect of Weil's action without doctrine.

Davy, Marie-Magdalene. "Camus et Simone Weil." *La table ronde*, no. 146 (February 1960), pp. 137–43. Tends to slight Camus in the comparisons but sees a kinship in their refusal of compromise, their strict intellectual probity, and their "accès à une plus grande conscience." But their more important common gift, Davy believes, was not intellectual but that they knew how to elevate the human condition to heroic levels.

Devaux, André A. "Liberté et necessité selon Simone Weil." *Revue de théologie et de philosophie* 1 (1976): 1–11. Excellent summaries of Weil's reflections on these subjects, amply documented with citations from her published work. Underscores her differences with humanists: that truth, good, and beauty cannot come without grace. Submits that her confidence in Alain's Cartesian voluntarism was arrested by her factory experience. That is, *malheur* led her to the Stoic quietism of consent to necessity.

———. "Malheur et compassion chez Simone Weil." *Afrique* 265 (1957): 27–40. Unfortunately not easily accessible, this is a thorough and well-balanced review of two cardinal subjects in Weil's writing. It includes a helpful explication of her famous envy of Christ on the cross: suffering when so extreme, placing one at the intersection of creation and Creator, allows one to traverse time and space and arrive in the divine presence. In that sense it is legitimate to pray for a part in the crucifixion's agony.

Dinnage, Rosemary. "The Sergeant-Major Angel." *Times Literary Supplement*, May 13, 1977, pp. 589–90. Uses Pétrement to make a case against Weil's "sanctity," overscoring Weil's faults, that she was "proud, even frighteningly ambitious," "blind to her own powerful will," and so on. The althoughs and despites do not outweigh for this reader evidence that Weil was "continually ridiculous, and left confusion and exasperation everywhere behind her." Weil's life is a caveat about "the special dangers of the spiritual life, the taking of the thought for the deed, the hair's breadth separating pride and humility." Yet she concedes that Weil's writings show how well she was aware of her faults.

Draghi, Gianfranco. "Simone Weil." *Aut aut* 16 (July 1953): 325–33. A unique reading of Weil's spirituality, implying that Weil believed works save and faith does not, "works" including submission to God's will. (Salvation is not one of Weil's preoccupations.) Draghi says that in the love of beauty we are saints, but Weil does not say so, and reads beauty and renunciation as Anaximandrean complements, the one sought and taken, the other willed or imposed. Weil might well have been intrigued by such a notion, but she does not pose it. The essay is a series of striking and hazardous inferences. Caveat lector.

Dreyfus, Dina. "La transcendance contre l'histoire chez Simone Weil." *Mercure de France*, May 1, 1951, pp. 65–80. Contends that Weil's decreation is not so much a virtuous self-forgetting as the result of an attitude, her relentlessness toward herself. Weil's impersonality leads to the love of neighbors without faces. Dreyfus feels Weil was powerfully attracted to the exteriority of the collective and that her love for vanished cultures like that of Languedoc was ambiguous. She embraced their "spiritual" message but loved their disappearance as such, as part of her desiderated "déréalisation totale de la creation et des créatures." Fascinating hypotheses.

Edwards, Thomas R. "Epic and the Modern Reader: A Note on Simone Weil." In his *Imagination and Power* (London: Chatto & Windus, 1971), pp. 10–16. The mistake in Weil's reading of Homer is that it is too modern; she ignores what was meant in Homer's time—that bitterness and horror necessarily go with the glory of heroic effort but do not cancel it out. Warfare carries with it a dynamism that makes valor superhuman. Homer's epic must be read as more than an exposé of force; otherwise we cripple our capacity to understand it.

Epting, Karl. "Blick in der Richtung zu Gott: Schmerz, Leiden und Unglück im Denken von Simone Weil." *Zeitwende* 43 (1972): 322–31. Weil's importance to many in postwar Germany is hinted here: she is a paradigm that Christ "even today still breaks directly into history to fetch humanity." The limits of voluntarism, the supernatural uses of suffering, the redemptive and releasing effects of *attente* and of obedience so that one ceases to be a creature (*Geschöpf*)—what curious lessons for Germany after Hitler.

———. "Das Lächeln Christi: Die Gedanken der Simone Weil über die Schönheit der Welt." *Zeitwende* 30 (1959): 813–22. Defends Weil's aesthetic assumption that beauty has sacramental power. Her proceeding from Kant and Plato to Christ is legitimate for "eines ineinandergehenden Sich-öffnens neuer Räume ihres Wesens." Attention to the world's beauty is not a heterodoxy but a deepening of our understanding of God.

Feuillade, Lucien. "Simone Weil, anarchiste et chrétienne." *L'âge nouveau* 61 (May 1951): 14–18. First in a series of four contributions, the others by Michel Collinet, Jean Rabaud, and Louis Mercier. Rabaud's is the most interesting. He recalls his acquaintance with Weil dating from 1933, when she already showed "des tendances christianisantes" amid her anarcho-syndicalist activities. Says her "extreme generosity of comportment" came from masochism; her love of others came from their suffering. Noting her propensity for putting herself in morally impossible situations, he concludes that she embodied "un destin révolutionnaire avorté."

Fiedler, Leslie. "Introduction" to *Waiting for God*, trans. Emma Craufurd (New York: Putnam's Sons, 1951). A breezy appraisal of Weil but very important as an indication of why she was a postwar celebrity. No matter what one's religious background, "we have all turned to her with the profound conviction that the meaning of her experience is our meaning, that she is really *ours*." This is in fact a Gidean pitch for the outsider, for all "humanists" insistent upon distance from conventional religion, but for all that it is no less an essential document of Weil's reception in America prior to the publication of her notebooks and essays.

Fleuré, Eugene. "Albert Camus devant Simone Weil." *Cahiers Simone Weil* 1 (September 1978): 10–17. This is a late entry in the chronology, but it concerns an old story, Camus's deep interest in Weil. His letters to Fleuré about her are included as well as his remarks on *L'enracinement* in the *Bulletin de juin 1949 des éditions Gallimard*, where he identifies her "folie de verité" as "grande par un pouvoir honnête, grande sans désespoir." Camus submits that the 1940 defeat and the enforced idleness of the years following were perhaps necessary so that Weil's ideas and "des jugements qui renversent tant d'idées reçues, qui ignorent tant de préjugés" could at last take hold.

Ginzburg, Natalia. "Sul credere e non credere in Dio." In her *Mai devi domandarmi* (Milan: Garzanti, 1971), pp. 213–29. A meditation of exceptional eloquence, insight, and beauty, inspired by Weil's "The God we ought to love is not there." For those who credit Weil with the genius of humility this essay should be compulsory reading.

Gollancz, Victor. "Waiting on God." In his *More for Timothy* (London: Camelot Press, 1953), pp. 84–115. The left-wing publisher finds Weil both attractive and repellent, lovable and perverse, and finally irreligious because she insists on finding a reason behind every mystery and is too confident in her own certainties. Her God, he says, is "a monster of self-love, in the bad not the good sense, and a tyrant of tyrants."

Goulinat, Anne-Marie. "Le message ouvrier de Simone Weil." *Revue d'histoire economique et sociale* 36 (1958): 202–19. Discusses Weil's assessment of Taylorism and her nonpartisanship, specifically where she differed from the *syndicats*: factory work is not to be alleviated but rather enlightened. Weil is, in Zeev Sternhell's phrase, "ni droite, ni gauche."

Greene, Graham. "Simone Weil." In his *Collected Essays* (London: Bodley Head, 1969), pp. 372–75. There are some superb insights here. On her refusal to enter the church: "She could not see it as a being like herself, anxious to share the sufferings not only of the poor but of the imperfect, even the vicious." (What does this mean, though, in the context of French anti-Semitism in the Vichy years?) Her alleged confusions are owing to her pride, that "she claims too much . . . and too stridently." And then there is this unforgettable remark: "She talks of suffering 'atrocious pain' for others, 'those who are indifferent or unknown to me . . . including those of the most remote ages of antiquity' and it is almost as if a comic character from Dickens were speaking."

Grumbach, Doris. "The Vestibule State of Simone Weil." *Catholic World* 175 (June 1952): 166–71. Claims that Weil is guilty of Protestant pride in refusing spiritual direction. "I think there has rarely lived a deeply religious woman with so strong, so individual and so perverse a sense of her own destiny and vocation." Weil ignored the Devil, and her Stoic acceptance of the world precludes any need for the church or for anyone's concern to join it. Grumbach misconceives *attente* as an abandonment of spiritual activity.

Guéhenno, Jean. "En marge de Simone Weil." *Figaro*, December 20, 1973, p. 6. Pardons Pétrement's hagiographic tendencies. Writes of meeting Weil in the 1930s and recalls her "audace éclatante dans les yeux" and "une volonté evidente d'aller toujours au bout de la vérité." Yet talking with her left him with "une sorte de gêne." One wonders if, as he says, Alain taught her to be always "du côte de l'esclave." Contestants of ideas today, he ends, are nothing next to her because she had "a great love of people and a need for sacrifice."

———. "Simone Weil et la condition ouvrière." *Le peuple*, October 25, 1951, p. 6. "Nous passons . . . naïvement quelquefois à côté des héros ou des saints," but he finds in Weil's essay "Condition première d'un travail non servile" more poetry than reason. This is the "ineffectual angel" view against which the late Dorothy Day, herself the victim of amateur canonizers, used to protest. Weil, Guéhenno notes, died of avidity for truth. This, too, is more poetry than reason.

Halda, Bernard. "La conversion de Simone Weil." *Pensée française* 19 (January 1960): 23–30. Many if isolated insights, for example, that Weil's preference for Hindu texts in solving "certain problems" (chastity?) suggest she did not spend contemplative effort on the Pauline letters. Her Orientalism seems to have been aesthetic; she was "seduced by a certain poetry of expression in the *Gita*."

Hannedouche, Simone. Review of *Pensées sans ordre concernant l'amour de Dieu*. *Cahiers d'études Cathares* 15 (Autumn 1964): 49–53. Notes some basic differences between Weil's spirituality and Catharism. For her, the Holy Spirit is divine love in the aspect of fire, but for the Cathars it was (is?) a divine force deposited in the human being, permitting escape from the fall and ascent to the divinity of humanity's origins.

Hautefeuille, François d'. "Simone Weil et l'église." *Revue générale* (formerly *Révue générale belgique*), no. 4 (1970), pp. 47–59. Argues that Weil's approach to Christianity was not so much one of *syncretisme* as of *panchristisme*, that is, she read Christ into all the alien cultures she loved. If this is so, it implies on her part an ideological totalitarianism scarcely less objectionable than the social and political totalitarianism she attacks in the church. It is the old patristic argument for appropriation of "good" paganism and that whatever is true is Christian.

Henriot, Emile. "Simone Weil et l'enracinement." *Le monde*, September 7, 1949, p. 3. Denominates her a granddaughter of Rousseau in her "absolutisme sans merci," finds her criticisms more solid than her conclusions, in part because of her "croyance inflexible en la vertu" and her belief in the regenerative power of Platonic ideals. Henriot contends that Weil compromises the nobility of ends with a totalitarian "dirigisme" and yet finds the religious presuppositions of *L'enracinement* sentimental. A solid essay with many convincing points.

Heppenstall, Rayner. "Fastidious Thoughts." *Listener*, October 25, 1962, p. 674. Takes Rees to task on minor matters in his editing of Weil's essays, judges her "without question the most searching religious inquirer and the most fastidious political thinker of our time." High praise, indeed, from a friend of Orwell.

———. "Unquiet Grave." *New Statesman* 76 (September 13, 1968): 323. Puts up with Weil's "maddening yammer" and mysticism for the sake of her "uniquely valuable" social and historical insights. He feels all political partisans could draw upon her to "purify themselves" of their idolatries.

Hohoff, Curt. "Christin ausserhalb der Kirche." *Merkur* 24 (1970): 234–43. Says that the source of Weil's appeal is in her union of politics, theology, and aesthetics. On her early influence during the Fourth Republic, "it seemed for a long time [*jahrelang*] as though a French Rosa Luxemburg was emerging there." Identifies Weil on her terms as a new religious type, the Christian without a church, but persists in seeing her as a Cathar or Gnostic. Her "Hungertod," for example, was a Catharist attempt at purification.

Hourdin, Georges. "L'expérience ouvrière de Simone Weil." *La vie intellectuelle* 19 (July 1951): 63–72. In her notion of toil, Weil's Platonic concern for justice, good, and purity takes on a human profile. That is, her remedies for workers' problems are at once concrete and "highly spiritual." In her time, stirred up as it was with such chimerical dreams, she had the courage to affirm that there will always be painful tasks to perform and that it would be good for someone to assume them. Hourdin's statement, "Elle était vraiment l'amante du malheur," is silly.

———. "Simone Weil et l'église catholique." *Le monde*, May 9, 1950, p. 5. Although he scolds Weil for the pride of "pretending" she had always been implicitly Christian, he says, with prophetic accuracy, that *Attente de Dieu* will have an audience not only among the church's faithful but also among those seeking God, who, when finding Him, cannot give themselves to the church. He points to Weil's peculiar gift for transforming into "living objects of love or reproach" all the dead things that her immense erudition made known to her.

Hunter, Guy. "The Sabbath Made for Man." *New Statesman and Nation*, April 5, 1952, pp. 410–11. Looks to modern industrialists to learn from Weil's gospel of work as spiritual redemption. Takes the unusual line of deploring her "descent" from prophecy to practicalities—a technique, he observes, that ruined William Morris. *L'enracinement* shows the "burden in handling sociology for an individual with so vivid a personal relationship with God." One wonders, Did that disqualify her from the task?

Kaelin, Jean de la Croix, O.P. "Réponse à Simone Weil." *Nova et vetera* 27 (January–March 1952): 32–46. Admirable discussion of what he sees as Weil's forced marriage of pagan cultures and Christianity. She is sensitive to the poetry of pagan texts rather than to their content; she imports into them her own notion of God. He believes she stayed "hors de l'Eglise" because the church would have forced her to accept Israel. She suppresses the basic fact of Judaism: revelation, or God's entry into history. Kaelin says the church considers the just who remain outside the church its latent or tendentious members, but he denies Weil's spiritual vocabulary any authentic signification.

Kahn, Gilbert. "L'idée d'une beauté diabolique chez Simone Weil." In *Entretiens sur l'homme et le diable* (Paris: N.p., 1965), 115–30. No one can surpass Kahn for developing fine points in Weil's arguments. Here he takes up her consideration that although a love ("admiration pure") of authentic beauty is sacramental, Satan as Prince of this world can corrupt through beauty, that is, when it is falsely perceived. Beauty is God's trap for catching the soul unawares, Weil argues. Kahn concludes that for her "la beauté demoniaque" cannot truly be beauty. Includes a stimulating discussion of this paper, with several shrewd respondents.

Kalow, Gert. "Simone Weil." In his *Christliche Dichter der Gegenwart* (Heidelberg: Rothe, 1955), pp. 160–71. Kalow, one of her foremost German enthusiasts, says Weil achieved a Copernican revolution in morals by her writings on the illusions of self and that her thoughts on *pesanteur* are comparable to relativity theory, "eine einheitliche Feldtheorie des Seelischen im Sinne Einsteins." Rhetoric apart, he defends her "hors de l'église" beliefs fairly and forcefully. She does not deny eschatology; a concern for salvation is meaningless for her. She does not deny immortality; she simply regards preoccupation with it as superfluous and shameful, an attempt to fill the void.

———. "Simone Weil: Die Versuchung der Macht." In his *Zwischen Christentum und Ideologie* (Heidelberg: Rothe, 1956), pp. 61–81. Includes comparison with Musil ("Pathos der 'Eigenschaftslosigkeit' ") and contrasts with Bloy and Péguy. Her view that suffering makes us godlike puts Weil in company with Eckhart. Kalow says that Weil's aphoristic simplicity and penetration entail possible misunderstandings, one of which he may have fallen into in presuming that her statement of Christ's descent and possession of her signifies "ein unio-mystica Erlebnis hier und heute, ganz und gar ohne sektiererhafte Verzückung!" Nothing succeeds like certainty.

Kazin, Alfred. "The Gift." *New Yorker*, July 5, 1952, pp. 54–56. Identifies for the postwar generation what is peculiarly valuable in Weil's life: her complete openness to human experience, including what is dark, ugly, and painful. That accessibility, integral to her desire for reality, is, according to Kazin, her gift for those to whom "the living world has become a machine unresponsive to the human heart."

Kemp, Friedhelm. "Das Werk von Simone Weil." *Merkur* 5 (December 1951): 1194–97. Makes the intriguing argument that Weil's philosophical perspective has more affinity with Plotinus than with Plato. Claims that Weil's dogma of pure attention has a "helping, healing, truly creative power"—an extravagant view that Weil herself does not make, at least in those terms, but which might have been timely in postwar Germany.

Kemp, Robert. "Une martyre de la pensée." In his *La vie des livres* (Paris: Albin Michel, 1955), pp. 257–65. Too often carried away by rhetorical effusions, he nevertheless speaks for all Weil enthusiasts in the remark, "Comme on voudrait la rappeler sur cette terre, pour lui dire qu'on l'aime, et pour lui demander certaines précisions."

King, J. H. "Simone Weil and the Identity of France." *Journal of European Thought* 6 (1976): 125–48. Examines her historiography as an exercise of her moral absolutism and commends her for "the extraordinary mixture of pure idealism and hard-headed realism in her outlook." Her view of the Resistance, however, he finds fuzzy and unrealistic; she did not understand its propagandistic requirements. That may be so, but she spent a great deal of written effort to elevate its sights. King makes some interesting comparisons of Weil and de Gaulle.

Lichtheim, George. "Simone Weil." In his *Collected Essays* (New York: Viking, 1973), pp. 458–76. This is one of the best short discussions of Weil's intellectual affinities. The distinguished historian of Marxism is particularly well-qualified in putting Weil into the ideological milieux of her time, showing the derivative nature of her utopist leanings and yet discerning her uniqueness.

Little, J. P. "Albert Camus, Simone Weil and Modern Tragedy." *French Studies* 31 (January 1977): 42–51. Takes Weil's notion that suffering to be pure must be wholly without consolation and applies it as a criticism of Camus's play *Les justes*. Because Camus gives the revolutionaries consolation (whatever their personal failure, the revolution will go on), he has fallen short of genuine tragedy. But this, as Little admits, is to invoke classical norms such as Weil reverts to in her *Venise sauvée* but which have no hold on modern drama.

———. "Heraclitus and Simone Weil: The Harmony of Opposites." *Forum for Modern Language Studies* 5 (January 1969): 72–79. In both philosophers of contradiction Little sees a monism or divine unity, wherein opposites are not resolved but sustained so that the soul can apprehend their divine harmonizing. Little brings in Weil's Christology of suffering, but that has nothing to do with Heraclitus.

———. "The Symbolism of the Cross in the Writings of Simone Weil." *Religious Studies*

6 (1970): 175–83. Economical but well-documented study of Weil's mathematics of the cross, with references to non-Christian (including Gnostic) myths.

Macdonald, Dwight. "A Formula to Give a War-Torn Society Fresh Roots." *New York Times Book Review*, July 6, 1952, p. 6. Reviewing *L'enracinement*, the veteran anarchist finds Weil "possibly a saint and certainly a genius" but faults her for "pushing abstract logic to absurd, even vicious extremes," in her assumption that God exists and that she knows what God wants. He commends her analysis of uprooting but deplores her remedies. This essay illustrates the heavy ambivalence postwar leftists tended to feel about Weil.

Madaule, Jacques. "Le Christianisme de Simone Weil." *Terre humaine* 9 (September 1951): 83–86. States that we feel ourselves more Christian after reading Weil but does not indicate whether this assertion includes Jews. Her only error, he says, lay not in what she affirmed (Greece) but in what she denied (Judaism).

Mambrino, Jean. "Simone Weil et George Herbert." *Etudes*, no. 340 (February 1974), pp. 247–56. A disappointing essay, with no real effort to probe any reasons for Weil's fascination with Herbert, especially with his "Love, III" or "Love bade me welcome." The writing is marred by hagiographical phrasing at its most unctuous: Weil is the saint of friends of the Unknown God, she is the image of sacrificial innocence, her death was a disappearance into light, and so on.

Marcel, Gabriel. "Simone Weil." *Month* n.s., 2 (July 1949): 9–18. Weil, he says, is particularly representative of a time when philosophy broke out of the hermetic confines of thought and addressed the world. Marcel's Catholic perspective is unique. He does not waste energy enumerating her scandals of heterodoxy but chides her only for lacking self-love, a failure that extends to a hatred of existence. How can it be reconciled with her love of God and with her own awareness of the world's beauty? Her immoderate and impatient writing leaves strange impressions. God loving only himself, for example, becomes a bad joke that confounds the meaning of creation.

Martindale, C. C. "Simone Weil." *Month* n.s., 8, (September 1952): pp. 175–77. Reviewing *Waiting for God* and *The Need for Roots*, he doubts that Weil could have assimilated several ancient languages and cultures and criticizes her for accepting theories without evidence and recasting what she kept for her own convenience. "Her 'Waiting on God' really meant that she waited for God to act in the way *she* wanted." Concludes that her tendency to "an almost Hebraic denunciation" interferes with French clarity of expression.

Mauriac, Claude. "La rubrique du mois." *La table ronde*, no. 29 (May 1950), pp. 111–20. Finds in Weil an erotic mysticism akin to Eckhart's. Notes her self-mutilation of heart, believes it was prompted by her ugliness, "le plus grand malheur pour une femme." Characterizes her as the walking stick for nonbelievers and calls this "the miracle of faith by an interposed person" (*personne*, but not as Weil understood this word), adding that "perhaps we have never felt it in such a convincing fashion" as in Weil's example.

———. "Simone Weil et la connaissance surnaturelle." In his *Hommes et idées d'aujourd'hui* (Paris: Albin Michel, 1953), pp. 299–334. The principal shortcoming in Weil's thinking is that she continually leaves the reader with *petitiones principii*, "the weakness of all believers in respect to nonbelievers." Her personal mysticism is admirable but nontransferable. It is fine to denounce illegitimate uses of intellect but what, then, of its legitimate uses? Just how far does its competence extend? Weil does not trust it enough to say.

Meyerhoff, Hans. "Contra Simone Weil." *Commentary* 24 (September 1957): 240–49. Takes Weil's ontological statements as signs of self-hatred; presumes she was consumed by despair; misreads her idea of indispensability in contradiction; ignores her Platonic belief in the uncreated part of the soul; omits her positive readings of the Old Testament (Job, the prophets, Daniel); and too facilely equates her spirituality with gnosticism.

Moeller, Charles. "Simone Weil et l'incroyance des croyants." In his *Littérature du XXe siècle et christianisme, 1: Silence de Dieu* (Paris: Casterman, 1953), 220–55. The most thorough and consistently negative assessment of Weil by an orthodox Roman Catholic, this essay appeared at a time when Weil was still exerting a strong influence on many Catholics in France and abroad. Moeller catalogs what he calls her "intellectual aberrations," including "l'intellectualisme inhumain" in her demand for reason's perfect rigor, the "ressentiment" of her hostility to Judaism, and an alleged Catharism. Her "ontological void" of *décréation* confounds the biblical view of divine creation. He believes she was totally sincere and argues that her errors came from engaging in religious problems alone and on her own terms. He warns that the enthusiasm of many Christians for her writings shows a disarray and confusion about "the authentic Christian message." "We have a bad conscience, we are ashamed of our faith." Hence Christians fail to see the substantially Stoic and Manichean elements in Weil's thought for what they are, non-Christian. Always open to Hellenic symbols, she was blind to Hebrew typology. "Instead of illuminating Greece through Christ, studied for himself, she illuminates Christ through Greece." Moeller overstates the case for Weil's gnosticism, and he indulges in some gratuitous psychologizing about her sexuality, but this essay is generally too well argued to ignore.

Monseau, Marcelle. "L'humanisme de Simone Weil dans la condition ouvrière." *Revue de l'Université Laval* 12 (January 1958): 454–62. Weil's remedy for the slave labor of modern workers is not higher wages. She saw that wage hikes would be impossible in a bourgeois society with limited resources. Enriching the workers would merely immerse them in materialism. Weil's insistence that money is not the measure of humanity marks "the triumph of a humanism deeply respectful of human values."

Moré, Marcel. "La pensée religieuse de Simone Weil." *Dieu vivant* 17 (October–December 1950): 37–68. The first and one of the most substantial assaults on Weil when she was in vogue among Catholics. An acquaintance, Moré criticizes Weil's unrelenting insistence on "je" and her inability to let grace assist doubt. He accuses her of confusing aesthetics with faith and says a Christian has no need to nourish the mind with non-Christian texts such as *Gita*. He denies the authenticity of her mystical experience—how could Christ have left her intellect so arbitrary and willfully insistent on its autonomy? He sometimes takes as certain in her mind what she states to herself as a question. He presumes that she did not believe in a future life, but actually she refused to conceive of one, fearful of coloring it with illusion. Moré's real concern is that Weil represents a dangerous trend among seeming Christians who prefer, like her, certitude and constraint "to the free disposition of the Christian before the grace of Abraham's

God." He also fears that the church will be invaded by Oriental religions importing such dangers as Platonic dualism and Buddhist yoga.

Mounier, Emmanuel. Review of *L'enracinement. Esprit* 163 (January 1950): 172–74. In one of his last reviews, the founder of *personnalisme* hails Weil as "a spiritual Jew" who gave to Christian conscience "la haute intransigeance du Dieu sémite." Despite some *longueurs*, "there's hardly an indifferent page that an inner fire does not animate and color." He commends the book to those embroiled in "the classic intrigues of power" for a reminder that there are only two criteria of choice: good before utility and spiritual good in all respects. Unlike Weil, he believed that the *conception cornélienne* was very much alive in the Free French, but this is a postwar view.

Muggeridge, Malcolm. "Donna Quixote." *Observer*, June 5, 1977, p. 28. Finds Pétrement's biography a great miscellany for browsing. This friend of Orwell (and a convert to Roman Catholicism late in life) finds several points for comparing Weil to him, but he indulges the view that Weil's life was one of sublime absurdity, and this kind of response implicitly slights her efforts to address and redress real problems in the world she experienced. Pétrement's work documents those efforts amply.

Niel, André. "Simone Weil, pèlerin de l'absolu." *Critique* 114 (November 1956): 968–77. Provides a useful summary of Weil's "free society" of work and argues that an "attente de Dieu" finally failed to satisfy her and that her idea of "travail conscient" enabled her to find a creative exchange between the individual and the world. "The Cross seemed no longer necessary since the earth is divine, once it is considered in all 'lucidity.'"

Nicholl, Donald. "Simone Weil, God's Servant." *Blackfriar's* 31 (August 1950): 364–72. Reviewing *Pesanteur et la grâce, L'enracinement*, and *Attente de Dieu*, he suggests that her writings resist commentary. They are of the sort that one does not, presumably cannot, "excavate" but rather grows into over a lifetime.

Nye, Robert. "Uncanonized Saint of the Uncommitted." *Scotsman*, July 4, 1970, p. 3. Considers Weil "in many respects the most convincing Christian thinker of the twentieth century" because she was beset with doubt and hesitation. He finds particularly attractive her desire to be committed; she saw no virtue in the religious freedom she exercised. But this view underplays her own insistence on intellectual freedom and an integrity that cannot endure if jacketed in any collectivity. Nye suggests that this "miniaturist of metaphysics" will in the future be regarded as "a kind of St. Joan of the intellect."

Oliver, E. J. "Necessity of Affliction." *Tablet*, June 18, 1977, p. 577. Believes Pétrement's biography corrects the impression left by *Pesanteur et la grâce* twenty years before that Weil has affinities with Psichari, Mauriac, and Bernanos. But the "Jansenist streak" to which Oliver refers, the abhorrence of human weakness and particularly of one's own, is much evident in Weil's writing and in her life so that it seems misleading to state that "her life is even more impressive than her work" and thence to conclude that "she was more a saint than a writer." Nonsense.

Ottensmeyer, Hilary, O.S.B. "Simone Weil: perspective chrétienne." *Revue des lettres modernes* 5 (1958): 1–20. Argues that Weil's fundamental Stoicism blinded her to Christian "light." Her echoes of Epictetus and Marcus Aurelius indicate that her thinking was "infected by a prideful sensibility, contaminated by pantheistic error." He overstates Weil's attraction to Spinoza, whom he blames for her disregard of divine transcendence. Even Alain is accused, held accountable for the supposed rationalism in her statement that "God has put into every thinking being the light for controlling the truth of all thought" (*Connaissance surnaturelle*, p. 79). And yet Weil goes on, as Alain never would have, to equate that light with Christ.

Passerin, Ettore. "L'itinerario spirituale di Simone Weil." *Studium* 65 (October 1969): 689–98. Weil's uniqueness is that she was a mystic in a sociological age, a time antipathetic to theology and metaphysics. He credits Alain with helping her to safeguard her autonomy but says she was a prisoner of Platonism and its irreconcilables, viz. necessity and a contemplative drive to the good. He compares Weil with Malebranche and contrasts her with Pascal.

Patri, Aimé. "Carnets de Simone Weil." *Le monde nouveau-paru* 55 (1951): 128–30. Excellent review for its background on Weil's *cahiers* and why *Pesanteur et la grace* is not a representative selection: Thibon kept out of it anything too offensive to orthodoxy. Concerning her many entries on science and mathematics Patri claims "de source certaine" that she regarded her brother's conception of science as "inhumaine."

———. "La personne et la pensée de Simone Weil." *La table ronde* no. 1 (January 1948), pp. 312–21. Concentrates on her cultivation of suffering but defends her from the charge of masochism: she had no taste for being degraded, but her pride kept her from living humanly. For the benefit of leftists Patri stresses that Weil the militant and Weil the theologian are one and the same person, yet he does not attempt to reconcile the passivity implicit in her Stoic *amor fati* to her earlier activism. He claims that she died of despair and *décréation*, but these are not equivalents.

Pétrement, Simone. "Sur la religion d'Alain." *Revue de métaphysique et de morale* 60 (1955): 306–30. Essential reading: it indicates how closely Alain's heterodoxy may have informed Weil's, for example, his view that the images and symbols of Christianity are more important than theology as indexes of Christianity's truth. His humanistic receptivity to all religions, his rejection of political, that is, pseudo-spiritual deity cults which adore force, and his interest in the Hellenic nature of the Christian gospels are only a few of the many points reviewed.

Préau, André. "Simone Weil ou la découverte de la tradition." *Etudes traditionelles* 50 (January–February 1949): 12–17. Observes that Weil is at "l'antithèse même de l'existentialisme" in positing that existence has a sense even though that sense cannot be found in existence itself. Complains of anti-intellectualism in Weil's utterances on love and intellect. One of Préau's remarks has been confounded in the present book: "Rien ne laisse supposer qu'elle ait eu connaissance de l'oeuvre de M. René Guenon."

Przywara, Erich, S.J. "Edith Stein et Simone Weil: essentialisme, existentialisme, analogie." *Les études philosophique* 11 (1956): 458–72. Weil has often been compared, and sometimes confused, with Stein, a Jewish convert to Catholicism who became a Dominican nun and died at Auschwitz in 1942. This is undoubtedly the best attempt to distinguish them. It is a dense and difficult essay. It shows how Weil can be considered existential: whereas Stein is Parmenidean, takes Aristotelian analogy, *allo pros allo*, and stresses resemblance in *pros*, Weil is Heraclitean, isolating each term of the analogy to stress "dissemblance." Przywara notes that the *noche oscura* of San Juan de la Cruz is not a Weilean *décréation* but a union in God. Weil's night is existential, a light manifested as darkness.

Quinzio, Sergio. "La grecia di Simone Weil." *Tempo presente* 12 (September–October 1967): 98–100. Makes three points against Weil: (1) her sundering of Christianity from Judaism is impossible because to reject Judaism is to reject Christ; (2) her Stoic reading of St. Matthew 5:45 ("sun and rain alike") ignores Gehenna and the Last Judgment; 3) her reconstruction of Greek thought is mythic.

Rabi, Wladimir. "La justice selon Simone Weil." *Esprit*, no. 12 (December 1977), pp. 118–27. A lawyer during the 1930s and later a magistrate, Rabi is in an authoritative position to assess Weil's ideas for judicial reform. Finding her far more Platonic than Christian, he identifies how "despite appearances Weil was always impregnated with traditional Jewish thought concerning justice."

Rees, Richard. "Simone Weil's Challenge." *Listener*, December 3, 1964, p. 903. Weil's value lies in her posing "a profound and coherent view of human life and destiny which challenges almost all established modern views, whether of the right, left or centre." He suggests that her religious views seem strange only because they are so simple and make common sense and also because they are morally, not intellectually, demanding.

———. "Two Women Mystics," *Twentieth Century*, August 1958, pp. 101–12. The other is Florence Nightingale. She and Weil had a capacity to *feel* (Rees's emphasis) theocentricity, something which language cannot state and which thought can only "call attention to." Just as Rees's *Brave Men* departs from comparing Weil and D. H. Lawrence into potentially more fertile comparisons of Weil and Orwell, so here Rees's references to Wittgenstein are more fetching than the title's yoking.

Rexroth, Kenneth. "The Dialectic of Agony." *Nation*, January 12, 1957, pp. 42–43. Although attesting sympathy for her, Rexroth passes some very harsh verdicts on her writing and her life. *L'enracinement* he calls "a collection of egregious nonsense surpassed only by the deranged fantasies of the chauvinist Péguy." But then he reveals that it is more than nonsense: "It attempts to enlist on our side the same dark irrational spirits who seemed then to be fighting so successfully on the other side." What these are, he does not say, but he sees in Weil's life "a spastic, moribund, intellectual and spiritual agony" and finds it all the result of her having "made up her revolution out of her own vitals." Unlike Rosa Luxemburg, she had no real capacity for sympathy for others, whom she saw instead as "mere actors in her own spiritual melodrama." He suggests that in her religious crisis she deliberately avoided any cleric who could have helped her. Perrin and Thibon took her too seriously, they lacked "the vulgar but holy common sense of the unsophisticated parish priest," who would have given this "religious adventurer" plain advice.

Roché, Déodat. "Catholicisme ou Catharisme de Simone Weil." *Cahiers d'études Cathares* 19 (1954): 169–82. Unusual in that it presents a neo-Catharist view of Weil. Claims her thought is based on pre-Christian gnosticism—"she didn't seem to realize that Christ by his incarnation acts in time"—but Roché is also honest enough to note where Weil differs from the Cathars and the disciples of Mani.

Rouquette, Robert. "Mystère de Simone Weil." *Etudes* 268 (January 1951): 88–106. Ranks with Moeller and Moré in attacking Weil's heterodoxy. Claims that the dangers of her "gnosticism" are rampant in the church. Faults her for not attending to sin and its destruction on the cross and for ignoring profound differences between Christianity and Stoicism. The paradoxical tragedy in her thought, he says, lay in her presumption of a continuity between them. He misses in her the "danse légère et subtile" he assigns to women writers. He identifies her thought as "so Jewish, it slips between the fingers when you try to seize it," and concludes that her influence is "prophetic and irritating, benign and dangerous at the same time."

Rousseaux, André. "Deux élévations: Edith Stein, Simone Weil." *Figaro littéraire*, April 17, 1954, p. 2. Reviewing an anonymous biography of Stein inspires him to some fulsome remarks on sainthood, Weil's being manqué because she got only "the crown of exceptional heroism." They are alike in passing from the intellectual to the spiritual by means of an extreme mental rigor. Well enough, but why this incredible question: "Et puis pourquoi ne pas penser que par la grâce de l'holocauste d'Auschwitz, le 9 août 1942 [the day of Stein's death], il pouvait bien y avoir un an après à Ashford, le 24 août 1943, au moins une Juive sur cette terre à être sauvée?"

———. "Deux témoignages sur Simone Weil." *Figaro littéraire*, March 1, 1952, p. 2. Views the *cahiers* strictly as mementoes and reference notes, "not to be sought for the least indication of the life of her mind." Rightly says that her thought was "en marche," but that, as he claims, she has bound human distress to divine *salut* better than anyone else in this century is questionable. She could not have guessed at the full scope of *malheur* in her own time.

Rustan, Marie-Josephe. "La notion de limite chez Simone Weil et chez Albert Camus." *Terre humaine* 3 (February 1953): 32–43. A detailed analysis distinguishing Weil's *limite* from Camus's moral voluntarism of *frein*, the perpetual revolt against crime in oneself and others. Weil's mysticism, her conjunction of justice and love, put her opposite Camus's tragic absurdity, that is, reason's inability to maintain a measure between justice and love.

———. "Simone Weil et les moralistes du XVIIe siècle." *Terre humaine* 1 (July 1951): 56–64. Comparisons seem to lie mostly in style, Weil's being one of dogmatic certainty and yet of impersonality as well. She outdoes classical moralists in her *décréation* of *moi*. Also, unlike them, she confronts the Great Beast of collectivity. Rustan dismisses *L'enracinement*, however, as a mélange of utopian socialism, ineffectual corporatism, and "enfantillages genre chantiers de jeunesse."

Salleron, Louis. "Simone Weil et Vatican II." *Itinéraires* 125 (July–August 1968): 271–92. If, as he says, her propositions would make the most liberal of today's theologians jump, why does he ask the dreary question, How could Weil have the authentic mystical life she clearly had and yet not be in accord with Catholic doctrine? At the same time he admits she would be suspicious of the post-Vatican II trends "teilhardisant, bultmannisant, marxisant et maoïsant."

Schlegel, Desmond. "The Spiritual Life." *Tablet*, December 15, 1962, pp. 1225–26. Identifies as Weil's "stumbling block" the "absence of simplicity in all her thinking" and suggests that this deficiency kept her from formally embracing Christianity. He finds in her essays on Hitlerism "an almost crushing weight of historical scholarship," but this point cannot be generalized. Weil is not to be credited with scholarly scruples because she fuels her arguments with *pensées du coeur* that admit no balance.

Schumann, Maurice. "Simone Weil." In his *La mort née de leur propre vie* (Paris: Fayard, 1974), pp. 61–106. Weil's friend in London claims she had no taste for *malheur,* that she was "gaie" as though following Alain's injunction to attain *bonheur.* She wanted danger and suffering only to make sensible to herself the tie between human misery and God's perfection. The neatness of Schumann's view may be a bit suspect, and one wonders how Weil might have felt in being sandwiched between Péguy and Gandhi, Schumann's other subjects.

Sheppard, Lancelot. "Personal Angle." *Tablet,* November 7, 1953, p. 452. Believes that Weil's religious views "involve no rejection of, no infidelity to, the light." Her Catharism is easily exaggerated. Besides, she was not fully informed about Albi. Her greatest fault is her lack of historical objectivity. He feels her charity is more instructive than her writings. Those bothered about her *hors de l'église* position may be suffering a guilty conscience. "Was it Christians who prevented her from recognizing the face of God in the Church?"

Smith, Stevie. "A Decided Girl." *Listener,* November 4, 1965, p. 715. Takes the unusual view that Weil's "cocksureness" is too innocent and energetic to be offensive and finds Weil's religious thought particularly engaging because "the notion that we want truth to come from God, want there to be a God of Love and Power to tell us the truth and pay attention to us, never came to trouble her." This seems an odd misstatement, for what are Weil's dogmas of *attente* and *attention* but various expressions of such wants?

Sproxton, Vernon. "Flaming Soul." *New Statesman,* August 28, 1970, pp. 246–47. Apart from some nonsensical rhetoric (he characterizes some of Weil's work as "pure blooms of almost ravishing chastity"), this review of Rees's translation of *La connaissance surnaturelle* makes some points. One difficulty of the notebooks is that they are often too terse and cryptic to afford meaning—a reminder that she wrote them first for herself. He misses in them "the sense of malicious fun which so endeared her to her friends." Her real value is her absurdity, for "each age needs people of almost insane sensibility to call attention to . . . impossible ethical ideals."

Sulzbach, Maria. "Simone Weil: Primitive Christian." *Theology Today* 8 (October 1951): 345–53. Weil is not a true mystic because she recognizes no human ascent to God, no *unio mystica.* Her stress on human self-effacement and a love of others derived from divine love shows that she is closer to primitive Christianity than to the contemporary church, whose natural theology, allowing people to participate in their own salvation, is wholly foreign to her. The article ends by saying that Weil is basically Protestant in making certitude of faith and a fascination with God's will uppermost.

Thiout, Michel. "Jalons sur la route de Simone Weil." *Archives des lettres modernes* 3 (August–September 1959): 1–35. Submits that Weil's *cahiers* were strictly personal entries for her own use. Like Alain, she never crossed out anything she wrote (the archives tell us differently), but it would be a disservice to her to take all she wrote *au pied de la lettre.* Thiout does not indicate the criterion for deciding which thoughts are Weil's and which are not.

Tomatis, Renzo. Review of *Venise sauvée. Il ponte* 12 (April 1956): 667–69. In her aspiration to absolutes she did not succeed in transcending an earthbound pessimism. The difficulty lies in the ambiguity of her *malheur,* that she arouses suspicion in having suffered so much in her thought ("la propria filosofia") without ever managing to resolve it into a higher vision.

Toynbee, Philip. "The Agony and the Ecstasy." *Observer*, July 5, 1970, p. 29. He commends Weil's "heroic passion" in assaulting the ineffability of spiritual truth. He cites as the two errors of her greatness her "religious melodramatics" and "naive ferocity which led to dryness and sterility." Of the latter he gives as an example her notion that "the creature let itself be created because it was evil." This "painful mumbo-jumbo" comes from her being "too hot for certainties" where none can be found.

Treu, Anna. "Esperienza di fabbrica, teoria della società e ideologia in Simone Weil." *Aut aut* 144 (November–December 1974): 79–101. One of the most lucid and penetrating studies of Weil. Relating Weil's approach to Marxism and the French metaphysical tradition in which she was educated, Treu notes that Weil does not address the issue of how new conceptions of science and new uses of technology presuppose new relations of production. Weil's dualism keeps breaking up the unity of any praxis by which the worker can control the natural world. In keeping society and the factory discrete as two systems, Weil gives way to a radical pessimism; hence her dependence on an enlightened paternalism in management.

Uellenberg, Gisela. "Nihilismus der Gläubigkeit über Simone Weil." *Merkur* 7 (1953): 446–52. Weil's merciless metaphysics evoke awe and horror. The scenario of an absent God and a pitiless world is the atheist's par excellence, yet Weil's aim is to surpass God in suffering. Uellenberg notes that guilt plays no role in Weil's thought because she admits no possibility of innocence, only a conscious assumption of the void. This review, published before most of Weil's other works were available, shows how Thibon's selections from the *cahiers* crystallized Weil's hairshirt image.

Van Rutten, Pierre. "Plaidoyer pour Simone Weil." *Synthèses* 185 (October 1961): 72–81. Rejects Moeller's view of her dangerousness and finds her life of thoughts without system a model for Christians. Defends her against the imputation of heresy ("Can we take for convictions what were only ideas?") on the questionable assumption that her *syncrétisme* will remain predominantly Christian. It is an example of apologetic and appropriative Christian response to Weil.

Vetö, Miklos. "Simone Weil and Suffering." *Thought* 40 (Summer 1965): 275–86. An insightful essay, recommended for those who cannot read the French of Vetö's *La metaphysique religieuse de Simone Weil*. Argues that Weil's forging of philosophical, theological, and mystical elements results not in synthesis but in a "personal" non-Christian theology. Contrasts Weil's view of accepting death as release from the illusion of self with Heidegger's free projection of one's own death as a means of self-authentication.

Viatte, August. "L'itinéraire spirituel de Simone Weil." *Revue de l'Université Laval* 5 (October 1950): 122–29. Criticizes Weil for ignoring the meaning and purpose of Christian sacraments. In her attraction to a demanding asceticism she, like Léon Bloy, did not realize that communion is not intended for the pure and saintly but for sinners. He says that a certain kind of anti-Semitism is more Jewish than Christian, "c'est du judaïsme retourné." But Viatte fails to account for the predominance of a "Christian" culture that prompted this inversion.

Waugh, Evelyn. Review of *Waiting on God*. In *The Essays, Articles, and Reviews of Evelyn Waugh*, ed. Donat Gallagher (Boston: Little, Brown, 1984), pp. 432–35. This convert to Catholicism reads Weil's *attente* as an attempt to secure some order from God "in an unmistakable and personal way." He recasts her apologia in unfriendly terms: "The Church isn't quite good enough for *Me*, but, of course, if God really insists." The review includes notice of Edith Stein and is perhaps the first to make a comparison. Waugh says that those "dismayed by the vogue of Mlle. Weil may find a prompt restorative in Edith Stein."

West, Paul. "Simone Weil." In his *Wine of Absurdity* (University Park, Pa.: Pennsylvania State University Press, 1966), pp. 147–53. West gives many summary judgments, too few of which are close to the mark. The giveaway is his tagging her "an old-fashioned Gnostic," and yet he also writes of her "pantheism." Was Weil "disconsolate at being human" so that "she was reassured only by extra suffering"? Was she "more concerned with perfecting God's geometry than with confronting the human lot"? Was she "really on the side of death"? In isolation from complex facts, West's assertions seem impressionistic at best and flippant at worst, but they have the tone of assurance which helps to perpetuate the caricature Weil has had to sustain for two generations.

Woolger, Roger. "The Importance of Simone Weil." *Theoria to Theory* 4 (October 1970): 27–39. That importance is her perception that aesthetic, philosophical, and scientific awareness must be combined and that only in such a total response to reality can we overcome the disenchantment of our age. He accepts uncritically her injunctions to Christian love and Stoic obedience.

Zolla, Elémire. "Simone Weil." *Questioni* 6 (September–November 1958): 24–32. Makes the intriguing suggestion that "Poème de la force" was composed "secondo gl' insegnamenti del suo maestro Alain." Alain's cold lucidity may be there, but the metaphysics of force is Weil's own. The article closes with an attempt to show how Weil's thought, although lacking system, is coherent and simple. Her *attention*, for example, is at once a dialectic that negates all final determinations and an intuition of being free of all conceptualization.

Index